EPIC FAIL
The Southern Tier

Why Many Aspiring Cross-Country Cyclists FAIL and How to Avoid It!

Sean Hockensmith

EPIC FAIL
The Southern Tier
Why Many Aspiring Cross-Country Cyclists FAIL and How to Avoid It!

by
Sean M. Hockensmith

Copyright © 2024 by Sean M. Hockensmith.

Printed in the United States of America. All rights reserved. No part of this book may be reproduced or transmitted in any form or by any means, electronic or mechanical, including photocopying, recording or by any information storage and retrieval system without written permission from the publisher, except for the inclusion of brief quotations in a review, article, or book.

Published by:
Iron Capital, LLC
PO Box 5472
Johnstown, PA 15904
814-418-5496
tinaraehock@gmail.com

ISBN 979-8-89546-010-8

Table of Contents

Disclaimer 6
Introduction 7

1. Work 9
2. New Life 12
3. 41 Dog Chases 16
4. Warmshowers 19
5. Clipless Pedals 23
6. Road Tires 25
7. Flat Tires 27
8. Clean Bike 29
9. Cross Chaining 31
10. Panic Attacks 32
11. Bike Box 33
12. Paper Route Maps 35
13. Cell Phone Mount 36
14. GPS Phone App Map 37
15. Starting Early 39
16. Heat Exhaustion 41
17. Cold Weather 43
18. Rain 47
19. Wild Camping 50
20. Drinking 52
21. Eating 53
22. Saddle Sores 55
23. Injured Knees 59
24. Sponsorship 61
25. Divine Calling 65
26. AAA 68
27. Chain Repair 69
28. Clean Clothes 70
29. Clean Body 72
30. Costs 73
31. Resting 76
32. Dashboard 80
33. Reading 82
34. Naps 84
35. Second Set of Paper Maps 85
36. Bike Fall 86
37. Support Team 88
38. Sick Loved Ones 91
39. 43 Daily Rides 94
40. Rainsuit 95
41. Head Up 97
42. Tire Air Pressure 98

43. Pouch 99
44. Rear-View Mirror 102
45. Wind 104
46. Headwind 106
47. Plan B 108
48. Bike Lock 109
49. Credit/Debit Cards 110
50. Body Weight 111
51. Helmet Brim Hat 112
52. Sunglasses 113
53. Visibility 114
54. Rubbing Toes 115
55. Ear Buds 116
56. Poop 117
57. Talk Less 119
58. Headlamp 121
59. Sleep 122
60. Preparation 127
61. LIFE 360 129
62. Stand Up 130
63. Walk 131
64. Lost 132
65. Prohibited Gear 134
66. Luggage Help 136
67. Bike Assembly 137
68. Broken Spokes 139
69. Flooded Roads 141
70. Detours 142
71. Boogie Man 144
72. Bonk 145
73. Physical Preparation 148
74. Cleat Stone 151
75. Loneliness 152
76. Second Cup of Coffee 154
77. Lights 155
78. Debris 157
79. Why 158
80. Aching Legs 162
81. Loving Advice 165
82. 86 Traffic Violations 167
83. Nice People 169
84. Prayer 171

3

85. $1.00	174	
86. Directions	175	
87. Bike Seat	179	
88. Bike Weight	181	
89. Power Bauk	184	
90. COVID-19	185	
91. Water	186	
92. Unsupported	189	
93. Overnight Food Storage	193	
94. Maintenance	196	
95. Vehicle Harassment	199	
96. Changing Plans	203	
97. Start Date	205	
98. Bike Marriage	208	
99. Rest, Comfort, Balance	210	
100. Granny Gear	213	
101. Holidays	216	
102. YOUR Ride	219	
103. Training Rides	221	
104. Enjoyment	223	
105. Private Goals	228	
106. Low Expectations	232	
107. Cheating	235	
108. Kickstand	239	
109. Cash	241	
110. Thinking	243	
111. The Southern "Tear"	247	
112. Songs	252	
113. Identification Band	256	
114. Soul	257	
115. Suffering	259	
116. 200 Miles to REAL	262	
117. Cold Desert Nights	264	
118. No Vacancy	267	
119. One-Lane Bridges	270	
120. Mystery Illness	271	
121. Stroke	273	
122. Horn	277	
123. Padded Handlebars	278	
124. Taking a Loss	280	

125. Texas LOVE	285	
126. Cheap	287	
127. Finish Strong	290	
128. Next Goal	292	
129. Eastbound in Louisiana	297	
130. Delayed Goals	300	
131. Vegetarians	303	
132. COVID-19	305	
133. Mosquitoes, Ants, & Pigs	308	
134. Medicine	310	
135. Feelings	312	
136. Oncoming Vehicles	313	
137. Encouragemeut	316	
138. Untied Shoe Laces	319	
139. Annoyed	321	
140. Camera	322	
141. Food	325	
142. Receipts	327	
143. Secret Weapon	329	
144. 300 Hours	330	
145. Adventure	332	
146. Bicycle Route Navigator	334	
147. Morning Transition	336	
148. BAMF	338	
149. Rest Days	343	
150. Dry	346	
151. Aches and Pains	350	
152. Plan B	352	
153. Hamstrings	354	
154. Tent Zipping	356	
155. Personal Transformation	357	
156. Bears, Coons, & Coyotes	360	
157. Journal	364	
158. Time	367	
159. Curbs	369	
160. Intersections	371	
161. Garmin InReach Mini	373	
162. Life Bivy	374	
163. Passing Vehicles	375	

164. Daily Destination Arrival To-Do Checklist	376
165. Airport Containers Checklist	379
166. Bike Box Checklist	381
167. Airport Clothing Checklist	383
168. Pouch Checklist	384
169. Front Left Pannier Bag Checklist	385

170. Front Right Pannier Bag Checklist	387
171. Rear Left Pannier Bag Checklist	388
172. Rear Right Pannier Bag Checklist	390
173. Tower Stack Checklist	391
174. Handlebar Bag Checklist	392
175. Other Possible Items Checklist	393
176. Questions and Answers	394
177. Sean's Daily Destination Listings	398
178. Sean's Journal	403
About the Author	443
Book Sales	445

Disclaimer

Pedaling a bicycle down the street is a risky activity! There are hundreds of potentially tragic scenarios which could result in injury or even death. Riding a bike 7 hours a day for 43 days straight crossing an entire country is an EXTREMELY DANGEROUS and massively difficult endeavor! Reading this book will help you to prepare for an arduous cross-country bike trip, but this book CANNOT fully prepare you for the grueling caliber of experience awaiting you!

Verify everything you read as there are likely errors contained herein and/or important omissions as crucial information tends to change frequently. Do NOT rely on the author's opinion! Ultimately, YOU must decide what level of risk you are willing to accept.

The author and publisher take NO RESPONSIBILITY for the ideas and suggestions made in this book. The strategies in this book are just ideas for you to consider. Do NOT rely on any single concept, strategy, or bit of advice as absolute truth. For most of you, a cross-country bike challenge will be far beyond your capabilities! You might want to reconsider. Long distance biking could cause severe mental health issues, physical injury, and even death.

The author and publisher wish to provide helpful ideas to prepare you for a long and fulfilling bike journey, but neither the author or publisher pose to be experts. All of the information contained in this book should be carefully considered before implementation. The purpose of this book is to reveal many of the challenges and dangers encountered on a long bike ride and how to handle them, but this book is NOT a complete textbook and does NOT list all possible dangers or potential solutions.

Do NOT rely on the information in this book as fact! Use your own common sense and do additional research before you make any decisions pertaining to the subject matter contained within this book. This book is ONLY for ideas. The author and publisher hereby waive all liability associated with any choices the reader may make or choices the reader may NOT make as related in any way to the suggestions contained in this book.

Introduction

On Day 2 of my epic cross-country bike ride as I struggled to pedal my bike out of the greater San Diego vicinity, I couldn't spin my pedals another stroke. The whole cross-country biking experience was too much for me! While hobbling off of my bike with tears in my eyes, I QUIT! Thus, the title of my book, EPIC FAIL!

No, I didn't go back home on Day 2 as I was too STUBBORN to leave the well-respected Southern Tier Bicycle Route. Instead, a failure of a man too PROUD to go back home remained to pedal ONE MORE DAY. An inadequate, ill-prepared cyclist REFUSED to abandon the big-time bike route despite having already QUIT! What an interesting combination of facts! Maybe the pages to follow will help to better explain my apparent dichotomy.

Although EPIC FAIL was written to HELP aspiring cross-country cyclists PREPARE for their upcoming EPIC bike ride across the country, EPIC FAIL is also an entertaining and informative story of how one man struggled and failed repeatedly as he eventually achieved his cross-country cycling dream. A cyclist will find the information contained herein to be CRUCIAL and a regular non-cycling reader will find the following information to be enjoyable. Regardless of whether you are a cyclist or not, get ready to enjoy "the ride" as EVERY significant detail of my cross-country bike ride will be shared; the good, the bad, and the UGLY!

Pedaling a bicycle across the country is REALLY hard! In my opinion, it is even harder than it is to complete an Ironman triathlon! As an amateur triathlete, I have completed 4 Ironman triathlons in my lifetime. An Ironman triathlon consists of swimming 2.4 miles, biking 112 miles, and running 26.2 miles, all of which are completed NON-STOP within one day. My average Ironman finishing time was 17 hours and 30 minutes! The training necessary to complete an Ironman is 90 minutes per day EVERY DAY for at least one year. The Ironman triathlon is a BRUTAL undertaking and ONLY a WORLD-CLASS athlete can finish it! Despite the ruthless demands experienced by an Ironman athlete, I have carefully considered the mental, physical, and spiritual challenges associated with a SOLO, UNSUPPORTED, and CONTINUOUS cross-country bike adventure to be at least three times MORE DIFFICULT than completing an Ironman triathlon!

EPIC FAIL is organized into over one hundred short chapters. Each chapter relates to one particular topic, if not handled well, could END a cross-country bike trip. These chapters are completely RANDOM. There has been no attempt whatsoever to organize the subject matter. The chapters will bounce around covering pre-trip, trip, and post-trip topics. Don't try to figure out why one topic was mentioned before another topic! Part of the random nature of this book involves my own personal health as shortly after the completion of the Southern Tier, I suffered 3 separate life-threatening occurrences including a major stroke involving brain damage.

Near the end of the book are numerous chapters each covering EXACTLY what I packed in each of my bike pannier bags and how I prepared my bike box for airplane travel. Use the lists to create or refine your own packing lists. For some of you aspiring cross-country cyclists, the packing chapters of this book might be most VALUABLE as I am a TEDIOUS packer!

After the packing list chapters is a chapter listing all of my daily destinations for my entire cross-country bicycle journey. The list of daily destinations is broken down day-by-day noting exactly where I started and where I ended on each particular day. My approximate daily mileage is also included as is the exact location where I spent each night. You can use this section for a quick reference to get an overview of my entire bicycle plight across the country!

The last chapter of EPIC FAIL is also the longest. This chapter contains my own personal journal entries day-by-day for my entire cross-country escapade. The comments tend to be rather personal at times, but I believe in sharing EXACTLY what I experienced as to FULLY DISCLOSE my overall state of mind for any particular day of my trip. For many, this chapter might be the most interesting chapter of the entire book. You might even want to read this chapter first.

It is my hope you will read EPIC FAIL while holding a pen. Mark up this book and make it YOURS! If you are reading for pure enjoyment, I hope you enjoy my many factual stories as I believe my biking crusade was very interesting and entertaining. If you are reading as preparation for a possible cross-country journey yourself, then you will find CRUCIAL information to answer many of your questions. EXTREME effort has been exerted to include as much critical information as possible. I want you to succeed! You don't have to FAIL!

Enjoy the book!

Chapter 1: Work

When I was 20 years old, I studied hard, took lots of action, and acquired a few rental houses, thus officially starting my rental real estate business. 28 years later, my wife and I have grown our rental home portfolio to nearly 200 rental homes.

Over the years, we have worked SUPER-HARD leveraging our time, money, and assets to achieve a sizeable rental home company. Our houses and apartments are on our minds every day of our lives. We continue to be the managers of our homegrown enterprise and we know every working detail about our business. Never before had I even considered taking off 45 days of work to pursue a cross-country bicycle adventure!

COVID-19 occurred at the perfect time as to give my wife and I a bit of relief from the massive daily undertakings required to operate our sizeable rental home business. In my heart and mind, I KNEW it was the right time for me to take on my long-time goal of crossing the United States on a bicycle. Nonetheless, I had significant reservations about my wife and other workers being able to handle the day-to-day workings of our demanding business without my actual presence in the office as there were numerous tasks completed ONLY by me.

Prior to my cross-country bicycle adventure, I met with my wife numerous times preparing her to carry more of the business load as it was necessary for her to take over many of my office tasks. Our other contractors and workers also had some new responsibilities as to pick up any slack while I was away. In short, everyone was given as much responsibility as they were capable of handling. And of course, I would still be handling many phone calls, texts, and emails during my bike travels, but intuitively I knew the BULK of my energies over the next MANY DAYS would be dedicated toward spinning my pedals round and round for many hours daily!

No, I was NOT completely abandoning my part in our rental home business, but I was LETTING IT GO into the hands of others while I dedicated my heart and soul into my cross-country cycling pursuit! My wife was now the "CEO" of the company and suddenly she had an enormous amount of responsibility shifted on to her. Prior to my trip, my wife had a BIG part in our business in which she performed excellently, but now she was responsible for a GIANT portion of our business!

As we planned for my departure, we were NOT sure how much cell phone service I would have. We assumed there would be entire days I wouldn't have any cell service, but we discovered this was NOT the case. For about 80% of my bicycle journey across the country, I had active and working Verizon cell phone service. It was particularly surprising how much of the 1,000 miles of desert travel I could continue to make and receive phone calls with my Verizon cell phone. At times, I would have no cell service, but usually within ten miles or so, phone service would return.

As I progressed across the country, I made good use of my wireless Bluetooth ear buds as I handled many calls while pedaling my bicycle. Talking on the phone while pedaling my bike wasn't really much different than the thousands of phone conversations I had for years while sitting in my office chair! My new "mobile office" was actually quite awesome! Handling business matters as I pedaled through the southern portion of the United States was a great fit for me. With the exception of those times when the wind was strongly whistling into my phone, I could handle most of my phone calls without having to pull over to the side of the road.

In addition to handling many phone calls while pedaling my bike, each evening I would also spend about 90 minutes making additional phone calls and responding to texts and emails from my cell phone. Over the years, I've become accustomed to NEVER having a true vacation. No matter where I find myself in the world, EVERY DAY I make time to handle my business affairs. For me, work is an HONOR. I'm truly privileged to be able to work! Someday, I will probably write a book about working as a real estate investor!

Although I handled lots of business on the road while pursuing my bicycle mission, there was an ENORMOUS amount of business responsibilities suddenly shifted to my wife in which she handled VERY WELL! Although I did NOT train my wife as diligently as I should have prior to leaving for my epic bike ride, Tink rose to the occasion and got the job done! Tink is an AMAZING business partner dedicated to excellence! Years prior when she owned her own cleaning and painting business, Tink's company motto was "EXCELLENCE is the ONLY result!"

Upon leaving for my epic cross-country bike journey, my overall office strategy was to LET IT GO! When I left our office, I KNEW there would be some problems, but I trusted my good people to figure out reasonable answers while I was away and they DID! While I was pedaling my bike in a foreign land, I helped with what I could, but many daily decisions were made by different people in the company and everything seemed to be fine.

By removing myself as the micro-managing CEO of the company, I gave those in my inner circle a chance to expand their abilities and develop their talents. It was a great way for EVERYONE to grow! It was a pleasant surprise to come home and find our business stronger than ever.

As for our contracted workers, I did NOT tell them I was leaving. Instead, I just left! After a week or two, many of them began wondering where I was. After about 4 weeks, many wondered if I was ever coming back. In my mind, nothing about our business should ever change regardless of whether I'm sitting in my office or sitting on my bike on some lonely street in the middle of the desert. All contracted jobs should be completed in the same professional way regardless of my particular geographical location on the planet!

Despite requiring HEAVY DUTY cycling efforts on the Southern Tier Bike Route, it was also necessary for me to apply a certain amount of effort EVERY DAY toward my business affairs. My business is what allowed me to have this special opportunity to pursue a cross-country bike quest and I wasn't about to abandon my business endeavors. By personally investing about 60-90 minutes daily on key business issues, my team back home seemed like they could handle the rest!

My role in our real estate home rental company is similar to that of an athletic coach as I'm the guy who assigns jobs to the rest of the team and then they do it. Rarely does a coach ever run on to the field and actually participate in the game! Instead, a coach makes the key decisions as to which players will participate in the game and exactly when they will make their unique contribution to the team. If you carefully analyze our rental real estate company, you would notice I really don't do much! My days mostly consist of telling other people what to do and then they do it! This type of business delegation was a complete contrast to my personal Southern Tier bike outing.

While on my bike journey, I didn't have anybody to assign the pedaling of my bike, the packing of my camp, and the purchasing of my supplies. All of these activities and everything else I did throughout my days on the road were done by me and only me! Other than the booking of a couple overnight accommodations, contacting a few hosts, and buying a train ticket, I handled everything else myself. Unlike back at home, I had no assistants, employees, or subcontractors to assist me on my daily bicycle rides. It was only me maintaining my bike, washing my clothes, planning my upcoming day, finding food to eat, and making arrangements for overnight accommodations. It was a new way of life for me!

DAY 1: The famed Southern Tier Bicycle Route starts HERE at the tip of the Pacific Ocean in San Diego, California! The sand was REALLY deep! I was so SCARED!!!

Chapter 2: New Life

Before you hop on an airplane and fly to a far-away ocean shore to begin an epic cross-country bicycle adventure, you might want to CAREFULLY consider the severity of your decision. Riding your bike across the country is NOT just an activity! Riding your bike across the country is a NEW LIFE! Pedaling a bicycle across the country is much more than just FEELING like a new person. You will be a new person with a new life!

In my case, I had a wonderful life with a loving wife, dear children, supporting parents, precious pets, loyal friends, trusted business associates, and many other caring family members whom loved me. My wife and I had a thriving real estate business and our health was slightly better than decent overall. Tink and I worked hard, long hours in our real estate rental home business, but we also had flexible schedules allowing us to take many 3 or 4-day adventures throughout the year. We lived in a nice home in a safe neighborhood. We prayed daily, attended church periodically, and we felt close to God. In short, my wife and I were blessed! There was really no good reason I needed to get a "NEW LIFE!"

Despite not needing a "new life," I could not resist pursuing my unconventional cross-country biking aspiration. My cross-country bike adventure wasn't just something on my bucket list! I was CALLED to take on the challenge! Pedaling my bicycle across America was something I felt deep in my soul and I intuitively KNEW it would be the SIGNATURE OF MY LIFE!

My cross-country bike ride was not a joy ride nor was it a sight-seeing tour. My pedal adventure was my MISSION! And I knew this mission could NOT be truly served by me unless I DIED to my old life and was BORN into a new life! In my new life, I had a new full-time job as a pedal spinner! For 7 hours a day, 7 days a week, my job would be to rotate my pedals around in circles. That's what I did in my new life....... I PEDALED!

It didn't take me long on Day 1 to FEEL the MAGNITUDE of what I was attempting. This cross-country biking pursuit was REALLY BIG! While sitting at the Pittsburgh, Pennsylvania Airport waiting for my plane, I could already feel myself DYING to my old self and being born into my NEW LIFE! Clearly, I was quickly evolving into a different type of person as my current level of development was NOT enough and I KNEW it as I sat in the airport chair!

Pedaling 3,000 miles across the country on a bicycle WILL change your life! Instead of being surprised with your new life like me, it might be a better idea to expect the massive changes and WELCOME your new life! It is MUCH BETTER if you realize the change before you find yourself pedaling your bike in a faraway land in the middle of nowhere! Accept the CULTURE SHOCK you are about to encounter BEFORE you actually encounter it and you will have a better chance of

WITHSTANDING the PAIN! Welcome the TERROR you are about to face as you HUMBLE yourself to endure the demanding experiences awaiting you.

A cross-country bicycle adventure is NOT Disneyland and it is NOT a sight-seeing tour or some type of luxurious vacation. Crossing the country on a bicycle is an unforgettable mission of self-discovery. Little did I know, but I was about to meet MYSELF! During the next 43 days, I was about to challenge the essence of my being and meet parts of my SOUL that have been asleep for many previous years! Unbeknownst to me at the time, I was about to experience REAL FREEDOM! The intensity of my upcoming bike travels was HIGH and I knew I was NOT coming home the same person as when I left!

Fortunately, I ACCEPTED the death of my former self as I sat in my airport seat waiting to board my plane to San Diego. Although I KNEW this bike trip was big, I didn't realize it was THIS BIG! It took several hours for me to reach a state of equilibrium as the sheer magnitude of my bike expedition was almost TOO MUCH for me to handle! As I contemplated my upcoming days, it was obvious my only chance to sustain my cycling cross-country dream was to DIE to my former life! Early on Day 1, I knew this biking experience was going to be like no other!

To make it across the country pedaling a bicycle, you must RELEASE your previous ties to your "old life" including your business, job, pets, friends, children, and even your spouse. No, it is not necessary to divorce your spouse or abandon your kids or pets, but you MUST let them go while you pedal seemingly endless miles along your solo bicycle journey. This is YOUR special TIME alone with yourself and your only CHANCE to succeed is by RELEASING your ties back home and allowing yourself to grow into a NEW person with a brand-new life!

In my case, accepting my new life was my duty as I <u>KNEW</u> I was CALLED by God to pedal a bicycle across the United States of America. The "calling" came 9 months prior to my epic ride as I was jogging in Mexico during our annual Cancun vacation. As I jogged along the road, a group of cyclists passed me. While the bikes passed by, a strong feeling came over me. There was NO DOUBT in my mind. The time had come for me to take the cross-country bike ride I have dreamed about ever since I was 20 years old!

As the sun broke through the sky on that warm early Cancun morning, my body shivered with electrical impulses giving me goosebumps despite simultaneously sweating profusely from jogging. As I felt the calling process throughout every cell of my body, I recall glancing upward and noticing a billboard containing four words. The billboard read "THE TIME IS NOW." In that moment, I was absolutely CERTAIN it was time for me to pedal a bicycle across the United States of America. In my mind, I had just been drafted by God himself to serve a mission involving the pedaling of my bicycle across the USA! Shortly thereafter, I began seriously planning for my EPIC CALLING, my new life! Southern Tier……. Here I come!

Without the strong calling to this new life, I seriously doubt I would have even completed the exhausting climb out of San Diego on Day 1! Being called and adopting a NEW LIFE is an absolute prerequisite to a solo, unassisted, continuous bike odyssey across the country. Without the total acceptance of a new life, you will NOT have the ESSENTIAL resources needed to complete the journey. Otherwise, the obstacles are too many and too difficult!

When you find yourself in a foreign city at the airport sitting on the floor at the baggage claim area putting your bike together, you will understand what I mean by your "new life." As you are tightening the bolts with your Allen wrench, the trembling sensation of panic will set in. For me, my new life was confirmed as I sat at the Pittsburgh, Pennsylvania Airport waiting to board my airplane for my flight to San Diego, California. While sitting in the airport chair closest to the large glass panels overlooking the airport runway, PANIC set in! In desperation, I grabbed my 2 bags and began pacing back and forth as pacing has been one of my most effective coping mechanisms for several decades. Something REALLY BIG was happening to me and I could clearly sense the only way to make it through was to DIE to my old life and embrace a totally new life. As per the gut-wrenching feelings of dread, it was clear to me the transitional process wasn't going to be pretty!!!

Most of the conveniences I had grown accustomed to over my many previous years were suddenly gone. While sitting at the Pittsburgh Airport, I was all alone and on the brink of facing CULTURE SHOCK! Although I didn't know as of yet what type of specific experiences I was about to encounter, I could sense my biking adventure was going to be very DIFFERENT and very HARD as the completion of this special, God-inspired biking mission was now in the hands of one person.... ME!

Nobody else was going to exert the energy needed to propel my bicycle across the United States of America. Nobody else was going to face the darkness and the howling coyotes in the Yuha Desert in the middle of night. Nor would anyone else endure the blistering 105-degree desert heat in Blythe, California or the unsuspecting frigid, hypothermic 5-degree Fahrenheit wind chills in the blustery desert of Sierra Blanca, Texas. Nobody else was going to face 41 dog attacks or have to find a place to lay their head when they BONK on the ridiculous ascent out of San Diego on Day 1! Intuitively, I knew the only way to even have a chance to finish this EPIC ADVENTURE was to relinquish my old life and EMBRACE a whole new life!

As I struggled to maintain my sanity as I paced the concourse aisles of the Pittsburgh Airport, it was clear to me this bike trip was going to require nothing less than 100% of my effort. My new life required letting go of my old, familiar life and adapting a brand-new, strange type of life. Yes, I still loved my wife, pets, and family. I continued to maintain my financial responsibilities, conduct my business affairs, and pay my taxes, but I could FEEL I was about to become a new person with a NEW LIFE!

Biking across the country is REALLY BIG! Doing the laborious task ALONE, UNSUPPORTED, and CONTINUOUS is a massive task! Your physical body will be stretched to its limit and possibly beyond. Your mind will be tested in ways you could never imagine and during your trip, you might even meet the strangest person you could ever imagine……. YOURSELF!

To my amazement, cross-country bike touring was more SPIRITUAL than it was physical or mental. On my ride, I never felt so close to God in all of my life as the closeness was actually scary at times as the caliber of experience on those lonely, barren roads was almost overwhelming. Every facet of my contorted life seemed to be stretched far out of whack and I was barely hanging on. It took EVERYTHING I had to hold myself together.

Taking on this HUGE cross-country biking undertaking required a death to my former self! Accepting a new life was a requirement. Spinning my pedals round and round for seemingly endless hours a day was my new reality and although it was a fascinating phenomenon at times, it was also a CHILLING undertaking. Get ready for the adventure of your LIFE!!! Welcome to the Southern Tier!

DAY 1: The beginning few miles of the Southern Tier…… Little did I know, but I was embarking on the adventure of a LIFETIME!

Chapter 3: 41 Dog Chases

Only a few miles after entering west Texas, I encountered my first and my most fierce "dog chase" of the entire Southern Tier Bicycle Route. Seemingly out of nowhere while pedaling on the desolate Texas Highway 152, a pack of four dogs emerged from one lonely farmhouse on the right side of the road. One small dog, two medium dogs, and a large Great Dane all came charging after me prominently displaying their sharp canine teeth. The 4-pack of dogs chased me as if I was going to be their next meal!

As every hair on my body stood straight up, I pedaled with a fury and a pace I didn't realize I possessed. Apparently, either myself or my bike brought out a primal instinct in these four dogs as they ferociously pursued me. After about a quarter mile or so of frenzied pedaling, the last of the four dogs gave up its chase and I remained unscathed!

The first question most people ask me when I bring up the topic of dog chases is, "Were they wild dogs?" Each time I hear that particular question, I chuckle as I didn't see a single "wild dog" for the entire 43 days of my bike ride. No, ALL of the over 60 attacking dogs during my 41 dog chases were domestic dogs! The chasing dogs were someone's pet!!! But do not underestimate the severity of some of these "domestic" dog chases. When domestic dogs spot a cyclist on a fully-loaded touring bicycle, it's NOT a laughing matter. On more than one occasion, I would have SHOT the dog(s) if I had a gun. Most of the dogs I encountered looked as vicious as I could ever imagine an attacking animal!

So, what's the secret to successfully dealing with dog chases? Well, it wasn't until about dog chase number 20 in East Texas when a Pitbull suddenly spotted me and with all of his primal energy initiated a full-out, passionate pursuit of his prey...... . ME! After experiencing my usual jolt of pure terror as the dog was about 15 feet away from my shins, I yelled in my loudest and most commanding voice I could muster, "YOU SIT!" To my amazement, the dog's eyes rolled up in his head as if he was just utterly taken back and he suddenly STOPPED! The dog chase was over! My newfound "YOU SIT" dog chasing strategy proved effective or at least somewhat effective about 60% of the time. Quickly, I noticed the LOUDER and more FORCEFUL I used my voice, the more the attacking dogs would obey my firm command and STOP their pursuit!!!!

While riding the Southern Tier Bicycle Route, most of my dog chases occurred in East Texas, Louisiana, and Mississippi as these are the states where 38 of my 41 dog chases occurred. In my case, not one dog chased me in California, Arizona, or New Mexico and only a total of 3 dog chases occurred in Alabama and Florida.

Although some of you reading this book are probably chuckling about me being AFRAID of these pursuing dogs, but I urge you NOT to underestimate the intensity and possible severity dog chases! If somehow a Pitbull dog clamps hold of your shin with its sharp teeth and vice-like jaw power, then you are coming off of your bike and in most cases, you will NOT be finishing your bike journey! If a pack of angry dogs pull you off of your bike, the results might even be worse! In most cases, the dogs chasing you and your bike will NOT be the pleasant, good-natured Golden Retrievers who run and fetch a ball cordially returning the ball gently back to the thrower. Most of the dogs who chased me on the Southern Tier seemed to be more on the ferocious side and definitely were NOT playing around!

Only three times did a dog actually outrun me and get in front of my bike. In one case, I came inches from running over a medium-sized dog who seemed determined to stop me. Despite my love for animals and dogs especially, I would have run the dog over instead of stopping my bicycle! Wherever possible, it was my strategy to pedal hard and avoid letting a dog get in front of my bike as a dog out in front of your bike may pose the greatest risk of a physical encounter. Pedaling hard and using my "YOU SIT!" technique was the best way to decrease the odds of an unfavorable dog encounter.

When dealing with chasing dogs, your first line of defense is to yell "YOU SIT!" If you QUICKLY yell as fiercely as I, then the magical words will work A LOT. During the few times when your fierce command does NOT fully work, then you must pedal as fast as possible hoping to outpace the dog(s). Other authors have published advice to stop your bike, take off your helmet, and show the dog you are a nice human. Some other cyclist authors have even advocated talking nicely to the dog and trying to pet it. In my experience, I wouldn't advise any of these absurd courses of action. Instead, I'd much rather try to outrun the dog than to try to make a new friend! In my experience, I needed to increase my bike speed to about 15 miles per hour to overtake almost all of the chasing dogs. If you are tired, out of shape, or going uphill when a dog chases you, then your particular dog chase could possibly be a more severe problem.

If the chasing dog succeeds in stopping you and your bike, make sure you dismount your bike on the OPPOSITE side of the dashing dog. Always keep your bike between you and the dog. Once your feet are on the ground, it's now "Hand to Paw combat!" Keep your helmet and gloves on and quickly grab the Pepper Spray you have hooked on your handlebar bag, release the trigger lock, and get ready to use it. As the dog(s) get close enough, spray the dog directly in the face. Aim your pepper spray into the dog's eyes if possible. And spray as much of the chemical as needed to subdue the dog. Then, quickly get back on your bike and pedal like HECK!!!

If you don't have mace (pepper spray) and the dog(s) get hold of your leg, then fight like crazy to remain upright. Do NOT let the dog pull you to the ground! Grab your water bottle and smash the dog in the face. Use your fingers and poke them directly into the dog's eyeball. Do whatever it takes! Your bike trip and your good health could be on the line! Kick the dog. Do whatever is necessary. Fortunately, it is VERY rare for a dog encounter to get this involved, but it could and you should rehearse your planned retaliation in advance!

Despite the variable severity of my 41 dog chases, I must admit an interesting fact. After the first 38 dog chases or so, I finally got used to the chasing dogs! Upon entering Alabama and then Florida, I actually ENJOYED my last three dog chases as they broke up the MONOTONY of riding endless miles a day! At the halfway point through the lovely state of Florida, I actually found myself MISSING my chasing dog friends! While pedaling back in West Texas, I never thought I would actually miss the dog chases! Time, experience, and fatigue must have changed me! Welcome to the Southern Tier!

DAY 1. On Night 1 of the Southern Tier, I wild camped underneath this gazebo in Alpine, California! Surprisingly, nobody bothered me!

Chapter 4: Warmshowers

Warmshowers is a CLASSY organization dedicated to hosting cyclists on long-distance, overnight bicycle tours. After becoming a member of the Warmshowers network by paying a small nominal fee and completing a short profile questionnaire, you can perform a simple computer search and find possible "hosts" in any particular city in the WORLD. You can read the profile for each prospective host and decide for yourself which host you would like to contact to request an overnight stay. Sometimes a host will agree to host you and other times the potential host may be unavailable. Hosts are supposed to update their "availability status" on the Warmshowers website so cyclists do not waste their time contacting unavailable hosts, but sometimes hosts forget to do so.

Each night I would review my map, weather forecast, wind predictions, and terrain elevations to predict what town I would set as my daily destination goal for the following day. Once I made a town selection, I would immediately search for a Warmshowers hosts in the particular town or city. In about 40% or so of the larger towns on the Southern Tier, there is at least one host listed on the Warmshowers website.

Since I rode the Southern Tier during the peak of COVID-19, some Warmshowers hosts listed themselves as "UNAVAILABLE" on the website and it was no surprise to me as the COVID virus was an international concern. But to my surprise, many Warmshower hosts continued to list themselves as "AVAILABLE" even during one of the most fatal pandemics ever to plague the WORLD!!! Remaining AVAILABLE during such catastrophic devastation is one of the strong indicators of the high-quality of people involved with Warmshowers hosting!!

Upon locating a potential Warmshowers host, I would contact them first by text message. My phone text message to my potential Warmshowers host would go something like this:

> "Hello Pat. You are listed as an "available" host on the Warmshowers website. My name is Sean Hockensmith. I am a 48-year-old male and I live in Johnstown, Pennsylvania. Currently, I am pedaling my bicycle across the United States. On October 10th, I took an airplane flight from the Pittsburgh, Pennsylvania Airport all the way across the country to San Diego, California. At the San Diego airport, I assembled my bicycle and began the "adventure of a lifetime" pedaling my bike toward my eventual goal of the Atlantic Ocean in Florida! Tomorrow, I plan to spend the night in your town. Would you possibly consider hosting me at your home for only one night? I am traveling alone so it would only be me staying at your home. I'm very clean and organized. I'm also very quiet and respectful. Most likely, I

would arrive at your home sometime near late afternoon or early evening tomorrow and I would leave your home before sunrise the next morning. Please respond promptly to my request so I may plan accordingly. Thank you for your consideration! Sean Hockensmith"

To my pleasant surprise, along my bike ride across America, I discovered something special about cyclists. It is almost as if there is a silent brotherhood. In most cases, Warmshowers hosts are either active cyclists, former cyclists, or simply cycling fans. Many of my hosts could hardly wait to meet me and hear my story! And that's exactly why most of the Warmshowers hosts sign up. It's EXCITING to host a cross-country cyclist as their stories are CAPTIVATING!!!!

Warmshowers hosts want their family to be exposed to determined, dynamic, goal-pursuing cross-country cyclists! They want their children to meet people like me and be INSPIRED to do something great with their life as well! Most hosts were HONORED to have me stay at their home. On many occasions, my heart was touched by the genuine hospitality given to me by pure strangers through the AWESOME Warmshowers cyclist hosting community!

Regardless of whether or not the Warmshowers network lasts the test of time and is still around when you read this book or whether a new and/or additional cyclist networking organization is created, you should DEFINITELY pay the fee and become a member. Being a member with other HIGH-CLASS, bicycle-minded people is POWERFUL, but I must warn you, sometimes you might come across a SCARY Warmshowers host.

One particular Warmshowers host late in my cross-country escapade ALMOST frightened me. It was early evening shortly after entering Florida when I arrived at a VERY run-down house. The house appeared to be in shambles so I double-checked my phone assuming I must have entered the WRONG address into Google Maps, but my phone indicated I was indeed at the CORRECT location! For my previous 7 states, I pulled up in front of my Warmshowers homes and I was IMPRESSED by the beauty and magnificence of the home and neighborhood, but it was NOT the case with this particular Warmshowers house! This specific house in Chattahoochee, Florida was an eye sore! Although I had temptations to pedal past the wretched house and find another accommodation for the night, I decided to remain open-minded and stay at the deplorable home as I was exhausted after my 85-mile biking day.

Surprisingly, my host, Gene Floyd, was VERY friendly and I got a relaxing warm shower. Although the house was in overall bad condition, it really didn't bother me much as my overall life expectations are very LOW anyway. What did bother me was when my host gave me a tour of the property. Gene showed me his chicken coop where many chickens and rabbits lived. Then, he informed me that those cute little chickens and harmless rabbits served as his food for the upcoming year!!!

Despite being slightly taken back by the reality of the food chain and Gene's upcoming food source, I remained calm until two hours later when Gene pulled out his old army assault rifle. When my Warmshowers host started talking about the "silencer" he installed on the gun, I got chills. Was this my last evening alive on planet Earth? Was I about to be quietly executed and possibly added to Gene's menu? But despite these legitimate MAJOR "concerns" including the rough physical condition of the house, the onsite butcher shop, and a collection of very dangerous assault guns, my cordial and gracious Warmshowers host, Gene Floyd, was really AWESOME and I slept well inside his fixer-upper home inside my own bedroom in which I LOCKED the door. Thankfully, none of my fears manifested into reality!

Although Warmshowers is an amazing organization and I WILL continue to use and maintain membership as should YOU, it is important to remember that some of the hosts are VERY different than me and you. From time to time, you WILL feel uncomfortable. Although it is highly unlikely, there is also a slight risk any given host may have BAD intentions. Regardless of the condition of any particular home, always remain alert and be prepared.

If I ever got overly concerned with regard to my safety, my plan was to excuse myself to ride my bike down to the store to get chocolate milk and then NOT to ever come back!!! My other last resort plan is to sleep beside my cell phone and to call 911 immediately if ever the need arises.

On another occasion in Las Cruces, New Mexico, I stayed with Warmshowers host, Dan Phillips. Many years prior to my stay, Dan pedaled his bicycle all the way across the United States leading a group of cyclists on a trip organized by Adventure Cycling Association. Although Dan now has a compromised immune system and doesn't cycle as much as he has in the past, he graciously accepted my hosting request, even during the turbulent COVID-19 times.

Upon accepting my request, Dan asked me exactly what I wanted to eat. Since I have been trying to push beyond my naturally shy and reserve nature, I responded to his text with a complete wish list of my ideal foods. Upon arrival at Dan's beautiful suburban home, I discovered Dan bought EVERYTHING I had asked for!!! Dan knew firsthand the HARSH toll a cross-country journey can take on a human being and he was HONORED to provide me with luxury accommodations including 2 DREAM MEALS!

In almost every case, Warmshowers hosts are AMAZING!!! While passing through Surprise, Arizona, Warmshowers host, Pat Scocuzza, asked me if I like steaks. "Of course!" was my immediate reply. Pat proceeded to grill some of the best steaks and asparagus I ever ate in my life!

In similar fashion, Dave and Carol Konopnicki from Silver City, New Mexico welcomed me into their exquisite home high atop the respectable city and cooked me an amazing meal. The gracious Konopnicki family even let me use their washing machine and dryer to clean my clothes.

For 12 nights of my Southern Tier journey, I enjoyed staying at Warmshowers houses! Each stay was different, but all 12 experiences were amazing and resulted in solid friendships and renewed hope for the next day of my bike journey. In the future, I will continue to use the Warmshowers hosting resource and I recommend you do the same! Even if you are NOT a cyclist, consider joining the Warmshowers community as a potential host. You will not be disappointed by the high-quality people you will meet!

DAY 2. The Yuha Desert is BREATHTAKING! The desert is now permanently an integral part of my SOUL!

Chapter 5: Clipless Pedals

It never made sense to me why the cycling world refers to pedals designed for "clipping" on to your shoes as "clipless pedals." Regardless of the absurdity, I consider "clipless pedals" as a necessity on your cross-country expedition! Without having your shoes clipped into your pedals, your feet will be slipping off of your pedals and you will be torturing your shins and possibly compromising the safety of your ride.

Prior to my extended bike travels, I decided to invest in pedals with two separate sides. On one side, you can clip the pedal into your shoe and on the other side is a full, regular, every-day pedal you can operate with any type of shoe without having to clip your shoe into the pedal. This type of versatile pedal gave me options in case my knees or any other body part began to hurt at any point during my ride causing me a desire to change my feet position on the pedal.

Somewhere along your ride you may discover it becomes comfortable for you to unclip one or maybe even both of your shoes and ride for a while on regular pedals as to trigger a slight change to the exact leg muscles you are using and the specific angle at which you are applying your pedal force. This may provide a welcomed sense of relief to your overall biking experience. Having options with regard to your pedals can be very helpful!

When you buy bike pedals, make sure the bike shop adjusts both of your pedals to your preferred riding style. In my opinion, most clipless pedals clip on the biking shoes are positioned slightly too close to the toes. I prefer a pedal that clips closer to the middle part of my foot and NOT so close to my toes. Before riding the Southern Tier, I adjusted both of my pedals and my shoes ALL THE WAY back as to put my full foot under as much of the actual pedal as possible as this was by far the most comfortable and effective pedal position for me. Maybe your preferred foot position is different than mine?

It is crucial for you to have "the right feel" for your pedals as this basic feel is largely responsible for propelling you from the Pacific Ocean to the Atlantic Ocean or vice versa! If your pedal position is NOT comfortable, then you will begin to feel pressure in various parts of your leg until the pressure turns into pain and finally the pain will STOP YOUR RIDE! As a method of prevention, before you even start your epic journey, make sure you log at least 100 miles on your new pedals to make sure they are properly adjusted for YOU!!! Don't let the bike mechanic tell you what you should do. Speak up and figure out what feels right for you. Despite how much comfort you THINK your pedals are providing you, have the bike shop mechanic show you how to make adjustments to your shoes and your pedals so you can EASILY make adjustments, if necessary, while on your epic cross-country bicycle route!

Riding with your shoes attached to your pedals becomes natural after a few hundred miles, but at first it can be downright dangerous! Although I did NOT fall to the ground at all on my 3,000-mile bicycle odyssey across the United States of America, I ALMOST fell as I was traveling through the Phoenix area. Upon stopping at a traffic light, I forgot about my biking shoe being attached to my pedal. Almost instantaneously, I felt myself falling to the pavement as I barely caught myself and quickly twisted my shoe out of the clip in time to prevent a crash to the asphalt. Only by putting in the miles will you ever get used to riding with your shoes attached to your pedals, but you MUST learn the skill. It is unreasonable for you to attempt a cross-country trek without making good use of the increased pedal power, added safety, and extra comfort of having your shoes attached to your pedals!

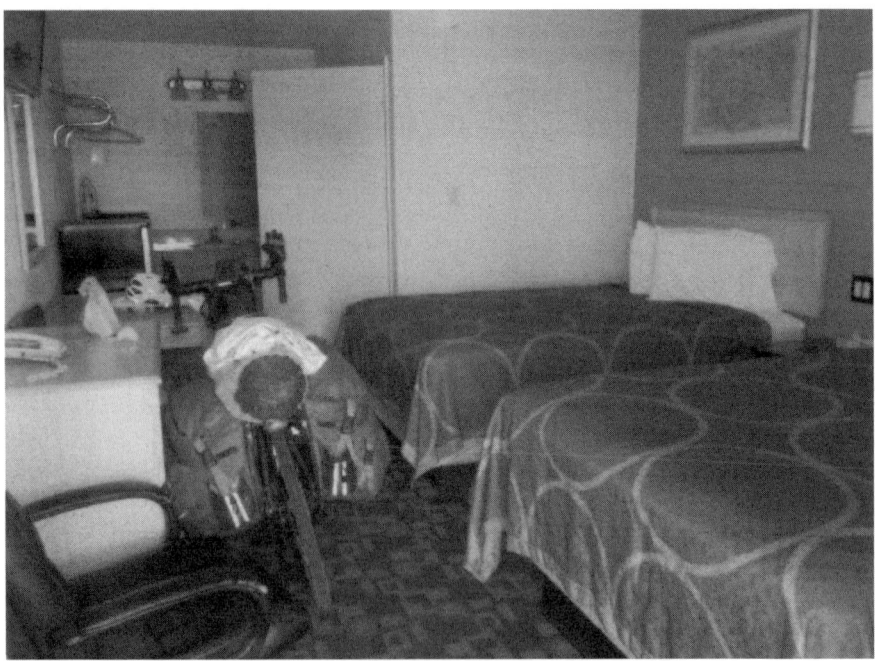

DAY 3: Here is my hotel room at The Desert Inn in Brawley, California. On this day, it was over 100 degrees Fahrenheit in the afternoon. I decided to ride my bike in the middle of the night on DAY 4 to escape the heat!

Chapter 6: Road Tires

Being a "cheapskate," I bought my precious cross-country bicycle from Bikes Direct. Bikes Direct is an internet company known for selling quality new bikes at wholesale prices from their website at www.bikesdirect.com. Although I've been happy with my various bike purchases from Bikes Direct throughout the years, for some strange reason, one of their phone reps recommended me to buy a "gravel bike" for my cross-country ROAD adventure. Taking the advice of the Bikes Direct representative, I purchased a Motobecane Gravel XPRO bicycle.

Overall, I was impressed with my new gravel bike from Bikes Direct, especially the low cost of only $800, but the moment my dad saw my new bike, the first words out of his mouth were, "Are you sure those gravel tires are appropriate? Shouldn't your bike have ROAD tires?" In my typical know-it-all persona, I shrugged off his sage comment by assuring him I knew what I was doing. In my mind, I was SURE the gravel tires would be fine, but early on my epic trip I discovered otherwise.

On Day 4 as I was ATTEMPTING a 96-mile ride through the scorching hot Yuha Desert from Brawley, California to Blythe, California, I experienced my second, third, fourth, and fifth flat tires of my trip. At first, I had no idea what caused the flat tires, but by my 4th flat tire, I figured out the sidewalls of my gravel tires were NOT strong enough to handle the intense 105-degree heat combined with my 85 pounds of gear attached to my fully-loaded touring bicycle! When the sidewalls of my gravel tires would flex, extreme stress would be placed on my tire tube thus eventually causing the inner tube to sustain a hairline fracture which was enough of a leak to cause my tire to go completely FLAT!

Looking back, I wish I would have been smart enough to follow my dad's advice and buy excellent ROAD tires BEFORE I began pedaling across the country, but I wasn't! Buying a "gravel bike" really wasn't a problem as my Motobecane Gravel XPRO bike was overall WORTHY, but the gravel tires were NOT up to the task!!! Had I purchased an actual "road bike" from Bikes Direct, I'm sure the corresponding ROAD tires would have been more than adequate!

My foolishness cost me over 3 hours in 105-degree scorching, unshaded heat in the relentless Yuha Desert changing flat tires while teetering on the brink of heat exhaustion. My stupidity also cost me the ENTIRE following day as I was forced to rent the only U-Haul truck left in Brawley, California and drive 85 miles to Havasu City, Arizona to Cycle Therapy, the closest available bike shop, to have proper road tires installed on my bicycle. Thanks to Brett and Ryan from Cycle Therapy in Havasu City, Arizona, quality, new road tires were installed on my bike! Brett and Ryan made it their mission to get me back on the road pedaling the following day as most bike shops will offer the same IMMEDIATE service to a bona fide CROSS-COUNTRY cyclist!

It is also important to note that most road tires should be inflated to about 70 pounds of air pressure for the front tire and about 80 pounds of air pressure for the rear tire. Proper air pressure is equally important as to having the correct type of road tires. Most days I made a habit of checking my tire pressure to make sure the air pressure was adequate as to avoid any unnecessary maintenance issues.

After having FIVE FLAT TIRES within the first 300 miles of my trip, I am extremely pleased to report I did NOT get another flat tire for the entire remaining 2,700 miles!!!!! The moral of my story is.............Start your trip with the proper gear!!! Make sure you have EXCELLENT, professional-grade ROAD tires for your cross-country bicycle ride! Nothing else will do!

DAY 4: This was my 3rd flat tire of the day. Why am I getting so many flat tires? It's too hot to be changing flat tires!!! It was 105 degrees Fahrenheit today!

Chapter 7: Flat Tires

Although I am NOT very mechanically inclined, I made it my business to KNOW how to change a flat tire PRIOR to taking my first pedal stroke on my cross-country expedition. Knowing how to change a flat tire is a MUST for a cross-country cyclist, but before you can even think about changing a flat tire, you must have one or more spare tire tubes available.

Having at least 3 or 4 spare tire tubes is a very good idea! And buying the BEST quality spare tire tubes as possible is NOT a waste of money, even if they cost a bit more!

While purchasing spare tire tubes, make sure you get a valve slightly longer than a usual tire valve as a longer valve will make changing a flat tire even easier with the extra length. As a way to save money, I foolishly bought cheap eBay tire tubes with short valves which further complicated the process of changing my flat tires.

There are two types of bike tire tube valves on the market today. There is the "standard valve" and the "Presta valve." Always use the same bike tube valve as per the manufacturer. Otherwise, the valve stem will NOT fit properly inside your rims. In my opinion, either valve is adequate and I have no preference. My road bike has a "standard valve" and my mountain bike has a "Presta valve." Either valve seems to be fine!

Consider buying the thickest and most durable tire tubes you can find as they will be less likely to go flat. You might even put some type of "slime" in your tubes as to make a flat tire even more unlikely. And if you are super smart, you will upgrade your overall bike purchase and buy a bike with TUBELESS TIRES! Bikes with tubeless tires seem to have the best chance of avoiding flat tires, but you should still carry 2 or more spare tire tubes in case one of your tubeless tires ever goes flat. When a tubeless tire goes flat, you have to either fix the breached rubber on the tire or install a tube until such time you can make a more permanent repair to the actual tire.

Changing a tire is relatively easy, but there is a lot that can go wrong! Follow the steps below to give yourself the best chance of successfully changing your flat tire……

1. Shift down to the LOWEST gear on your sprocket. Shifting to the lowest gear will put the chain CLOSEST to the end of the sprocket making the chain as LOOSE as possible. A loose chain will make the whole process of removing and re-installing your rear tire as easy as possible as flat tires are most common in the rear!
2. Remove your phone holder, headlight, handlebar bag, and anything else from your handlebars.
3. Remove all four of your pannier bags from their hardware frames.

4. Flip your bike over and let your bike rest on your seat and your handlebars.
5. Take off the entire wheel with the flat tire. You will notice it is much easier to remove your front tire than it is to remove your rear tire as your rear tire is attached to the chain of your bike which slightly complicates the procedure. Maintain IMPECCABLE order as to keep all bolts, nuts, and springs TOGETHER as they are CRUCIAL to the successful operation of your bike and must NOT to be misplaced!
6. Remove your tire from your rim as to gain access to your deflated tire tube. In most cases, you will need the assistance of one, two, or even three little tools called "tire irons." Tire irons will help you to pull the tire out over the end of the rim. It is best to use METAL tire irons as opposed to the more common plastic tire irons as plastic tire irons have a tendency to break!
7. Inspect your tire for any thorns, glass, etc. which may have penetrated the tire and poked a hole in your tube. Run your fingers all the way through your tire, but be careful you don't cut your hand or finger in the process! Make SURE there are no foreign objects lodged into your tire or else you will quickly get ANOTHER flat tire!
8. Put a very small amount of air into your replacement tire tube. Add just enough air to let your new tire tube maintain a proper round shape.
9. Insert the valve stem from your new tire tube through the rim.
10. Install your tire over top of your new tire tube and securely attach it to the rim. Use your FINGERS to get the tire all the way on to the rim, but if you need help, you can use one or more of your metal tire irons to assist.
11. Inflate your new tire to the proper manufacturer recommended air pressure (usually 70 pounds in front and 80 pounds in the rear) with a small manual air pump or a CO2 compressed air cartridge.
12. Reinstall your tire on your bike. Reinstalling the rear tire involves making sure the chain is placed correctly as to facilitate proper function. Also, make sure you re-install the nut, spring, and bolt back in perfect position as to hold your tire exactly in place on your bike.
13. Flip your bike back over and reinstall all of your handlebar gear and pannier bags.
14. Start pedaling EASY as to ensure everything feels RIGHT with your gears and with your newly changed tire tube!

In most cases, it takes the average cyclist about 5 tire tube changes to obtain and RETAIN the mastery skill to change a tire "under pressure" on a major bike route. Of all the possible bike repairs, changing a flat tire should be at the top of the list for repairs you SHOULD be able to handle by yourself. Invest the necessary time AT HOME to make sure you have the skill to handle a flat tire on your special trip. Be ready. You WILL get flat tires!!!

Chapter 8: Clean Bike

Sporadically over the course of many years, I would use a hose and blast my bike from front to back attempting to knock off most of the dirt and crud, but this type of LAZY, cursory "cleaning" was NOT enough! It's no wonder I struggled with gearing issues for decades on my various bicycles. Mounding crud was prohibiting the proper engagement of the various gears of my bikes!

Truly cleaning a bike is more of a DETAIL clean than a hasty clean. It is so easy to get a build-up of grime at various key places on your bike, especially on your chain and your sprocket area. For the FIRST time in my life, two days prior to the start of my epic Southern Tier Bike Route across the country, I DETAIL-CLEANED my bike. While doing so, I discovered an EXTREME amount of filth build-up on my rear sprocket. There was so much hard MUCK in this area, it took using a screwdriver to get it all out. There was so much grime on my bike, I didn't even know it needed clean as the crud appeared to be a mechanical part of my bike!!! The filth on my bike was so thick, it covered over the actual piece of hardware on my bike and fooled me into thinking it was its own piece of hardware! And to think that I was two days away from leaving on the most important bike expedition of my life!

As I cleaned the rear mechanical area of my bike, I noticed big greasy flakes chipping off and eventually revealing a piece of hardware resembling teeth. It was at this point when I knew for sure the importance of detail cleaning my bike. As I continued digging around with a screwdriver, wire brush, and finally an old rag, I reveled in wonder at the sparkling new bike mechanicals I just re-discovered underneath a small mountain of YUCK! Upon riding my bike after this deep clean, I noticed my gears once again shifted like NEW! It was a MIRACLE!

As a child I watched my father meticulously clean his various tools, equipment, and especially his vehicles. For all those years, I wrongly assumed dad invested many HOURS of concentrated effort because he really liked the looks of clean vehicles, but there was more to my father's madness than mere appearance. Dad KNEW the secret to a good-working piece of equipment, a secret I didn't realize for 48 years......... CLEAN is the BEST repair!!!! Meticulously cleaning your bike or any other mechanical piece of equipment is the BEST repair you can possibly do! The time you spend cleaning your bike will save you an equal amount of time making repairs alongside the road or getting a ride to the closest bike shop for maintenance.

Cleaning the chain, sprocket, and all those other little unfamiliar parts of my bike was probably the best ONE HOUR of time I invested prior to departing on my cross-country bicycle ride. Even with VERY LITTLE repair skills, it was EASY for me to use a screwdriver, wire brush, and a rag to clean my bike as good as new! Cleaning my bike was by far the best repair I ever made!

As I progressed across the country on my bicycle, I would regularly inspect my bike mechanicals for crud build-up. While I was checking my tire air pressure, the bolts on my seat and handlebars, and examining the tread left on my tires, I would also look for any grime build-up, especially on or near my rear sprocket. On my bike multi-tool there was some type of little gadget resembling a screwdriver which worked well to remove any detrimental build-up of scum. No, I didn't spend hours taking my tire and chain off to make them perfectly clean, but I meticulously cleaned every last square centimeter I could reach with my hand. And cleaning what I could easily reach proved to be GOOD ENOUGH! When I stopped at the bike shop for the standard 2,000-mile maintenance, the bike mechanic took off my tire and chain and METICULOUSLY cleaned a few of the areas I could not access without disassembly. Removing the tire and chain gave the bicycle mechanic FULL ACCESS to all the little, hard-to-reach parts of my bike.

DAY 4: This was my 4th flat tire of the day. Finally, I figured out that my gravel tires were NOT adequate for the intense 105-degree afternoon heat in the Yuha Desert! The flat tires took as much energy out of my as did the scorching heat!

Chapter 9: Cross Chaining

Despite completing four Ironman triathlons, taking hundreds of daily bike rides, and embarking on dozens of 1 or 2-night overnight bike trips throughout the course of my life prior to the Southern Tier, I still didn't understand cross-chaining until I met one of my "angels" on the Southern Tier, Layne Gneiting from Mesa, Arizona. Layne explained to me how bike chains are affected by wear and tear. He advised me to AVOID using certain bike gears as they apply EXCESSIVE strain on my bike chain thus weakening the chain over time causing the chain to be much too loose or much more susceptible to BREAK apart! Layne referred to these cross-chaining gears as "FORBIDDEN GEARS."

Cross-chaining occurs when your bike chain is in the big sprocket gear up front and the smallest sprocket gear in the back. That's when your chain experiences the MOST tension as it is "crossed" to the MAX! If your bike only has 2 front sprockets like the bike I used on the Southern Tier, then simply remember NOT to use the hardest gear in your front sprocket with the easiest gear in your rear sprocket. Instead, use the second or third easiest gear in the rear as to put LESS STRESS on your bike chain! If your bike has more than 2 gears up front, then pay close attention not to use the gears which require the maximum crossing of your chain!

Prior to meeting my mentor Layne, my favorite gear was the hardest gear in the front and the easiest gear in the rear sprocket. When Layne brought up the topic of cross-chaining, he said, "Let's go look at your bike and I will explain cross-chaining to you." Upon reviewing my current bike gear, Layne discovered I was already cross-chaining! As I pulled into Layne's driveway, I was cross-chaining!

Cross-chaining is not the worst thing in the world, but it does weaken your chain much faster than normal wear and tear. After learning about cross-chaining, I made sure to stop my shifting at least one gear before it became an official cross-chaining gear. The change was easy and I quickly had a new favorite gear. But even with my new adaptation, my chain still stretched out over the course of my long bike ride which required a chain repair a little over 1,500 miles into my bike travels. Maybe if I would have known about cross-chaining prior to my cross-country ride, my chain might have lasted much longer?

Chapter 10: Panic Attack

If you are considering a cross-country bike ride, then you are about to attempt a task which WILL change YOUR LIFE! Making the decision to ride your bicycle from "sea to shining sea" is no small chore! At some point during your preparation for your trip, all of the various mounting pressures will be released into your mind, body, and soul. You will feel the "breaking point" as you ponder whether or not biking across the country is really a good idea or not.

Prepare yourself. The PANIC is coming! Usually, the panic will ATTACK on Day 1, but it is possible it may attack a couple days earlier or a few days later! Regardless of the exact timeframe, panic will confront you and the formidable challenge will occur at one of your weakest moments!

Panic WAITS for you to finish all of your reading, complete all of your training rides, pack all of your bags, buy all of your tickets, and say all of your good-byes, then in a single vulnerable moment when you sit alone, panic will STRIKE! All the culmination of your anxiety and nervous energy gets together and EXPLODES as REALITY sets in. Suddenly, you are consumed by a tidal wave of RAW emotion. This is the moment you say, "What have I gotten myself into?"

It was at the Pittsburgh Airport at 6:45 a.m. on Saturday October 10, 2020 as I was waiting for my plane when my internal "boiler" finally exploded with pressure. All of my pent-up stress from the previous weeks of insane preparation suddenly released and burst throughout my body. As I began to breathe heavy and fast, I tried to regain my sense of calm. Being an experienced meditator of many decades, I assumed my mental stability was strong enough to counteract any type of bout with fear and panic, but I was wrong!

The over-powering flow of nervous energy seized me and I began to feel faint. Instead of falling over into the aisle of the American Airlines airport lobby, I hastily grabbed my 2 bags and began to pace the concourse desperately trying to stabilize my emotional state. It felt like an evil power outside of myself took possession of my insecure mind and I had NO CONTROL over what was happening. At that moment, I knew I was having a full-fledge PANIC ATTACK.

Being no stranger to fear and uncertainty, I knew my best chance to regain internal stability was to KEEP MOVING. So, I continued pacing back and forth until I finally regained my regular breathing rhythm. As I sat down in a private area by myself, I focused on deep nostril breathing while passionately affirming, "I am calm." methodically hundreds of times over. After eating a granola bar and taking a drink of water, my mind and body finally settled down a bit and my body stopped shaking and overheating. During that memorable moment of mounting pressure, I realized I was "dying." My old self was departing and as I took inventory of what remained, I realized the "old Sean Hockensmith" was nowhere to be found. The terror of my massive panic attack marked the official beginning of my NEW LIFE......... Welcome to the Southern Tier!

Chapter 11: Bike Box

If you are flying to your starting destination to begin a cross-country bicycle ride, then you will need to package your bike in a "bike box." After spending many HOURS searching the internet, calling bike box companies, comparing prices, and considering box sizes, I finally stopped at my local bike shop, Fat Jimmies in Johnstown, Pennsylvania. Bike specialists, Mike and Conner, not only gave me a bike box for FREE, they also showed me how to pack my bike PROPERLY in the box as to avoid damage during the transit process.

Instead of wasting hours of time like me, just stop at your local bike shop and ask for a USED bike box to fit your bike. Most likely, whatever size box they give you will be permissible for your airline as bike manufacturers are very aware of box size limitations. Nonetheless, it would be prudent on your part to double-check with your airline to make sure your box fits within the specification size range as determined by your airline. The bike box I used was from an electric bike which gave me a little extra space.

Most airlines have a very reasonable cost for transporting bikes for their ticketed passengers. In my case, American Airlines charged me only $40.00 extra for transporting my bike along with me on my flight. Of course, there are box-size restrictions, but the restrictions are printed on the airline's website. The restrictions are very reasonable and shouldn't cause you a problem.

To prepare your bike for the box, you must take off the pedals, remove the front tire, slide the seat out of the long metal tube, and unbolt the handlebars. That's it! Doing so will allow your bike to fit properly inside the bike box!

The pedals come off with a single Allen wrench. You might also note that one of your pedals will come off "lefty loosey" while the other one will come off backwards, "righty loosey." Not quite sure why, but it is a fact!

The seat is super easy to come off as most bike seats require no tools. Opening the quick-release feature will allow you to pull the seat tube all the way out of the frame of your bike.

Most handlebars come off with the removal of four Allen bolts. After you remove your handlebar, you leave all of your wires attached and you simply twist the handlebar sideways and stabilize them with some electrical tape to your top bar of your bike frame. It is also very important to screw the four Allen bolts back into their places so all the pieces are available when you reassemble your bike at the airport before you start your epic ride.

Most front tires can also be removed without the use of any tools. Just turn the quick-release until the bolt is loose enough for the tire to come off. Make sure you re-insert the long quick-release bolt, nut, and spring back into your tire as not to lose any critical parts.

Most airlines have a maximum weight of 50 pounds for your bike box. Your strategy should be to place as much of your bike stuff into the bike box as possible including lightweight items like your helmet, gloves, and your empty water bottles.

Putting some cardboard around your front tire will also help guard against possible spoke damage during air travel. You should also ask your local bike shop for a FREE plastic cover to slide over the rear cog/sprocket of your bike to help protect these important mechanicals while being shipped in the bike box.

After your bike is all packed and carefully weighed on your home scale, it is time to tape the box shut. But before you tape your bike box shut, practice unpacking your bike and re-assembling your bike. My practice assembly at home was INVALUABLE as it gave me a short boost of mechanical confidence. When you are at the baggage claim area in an unfamiliar airport trying to reassemble your bike, you don't want it to be your first bike assembly!!!!

As you plan to fly to your starting point, you will also want to check-in a second piece of luggage. Stop at Goodwill and buy an old piece of luggage. Use the luggage to store more of your bike gear as per my specific instructions in one of the final chapters of this book. It is likely you will also have to keep this bag under the 50-pound weight limit and it will cost you at least an additional $40.00. In addition, most airlines will allow you to carry 2 of your bike pannier bags along with you on your flight. The airline will most likely refer to one of your bags as your "personal item" and other as your "carry-on bag." Double-check with your airline as to exactly what is permitted and what is not. You don't want any surprises on the day of your flight!

While spending time at the airport, flying in the plane, and claiming your check-in luggage at Baggage Claim, you MUST also closely watch your two carry-on bags. If you lose even one bag during your travels, you will have lost crucial items for your bike journey. Pay attention. Keep good order. You cannot afford to misplace anything!!!

Chapter 12: Paper Route Maps

A total of 8 times throughout the state of Texas, my cell phone broke loose from my handlebar mount and fell to the ground. 7 times I easily turned around and found my phone with minimal effort and only mild stress, but one time as I was riding on a busy road in Montopolis, Texas, I looked down and noticed my phone was GONE! Panic filled me as I frantically pulled off the road and parked my bike as I ran backwards scouring the road looking for my phone amidst semi-heavy traffic! About 100 yards behind me after crossing 2 busy intersections, I found my phone on the edge of the road. Luckily, it was NOT yet run over by the dozens of vehicles that had since driven past it!

Nowadays, you can get almost everything you need on your phone, including excellent GPS bike route maps, but despite the modern advances in technology, it is ESSENTIAL for you to have a paper route map as well! During a cross-country bike trip, a phone could be easily lost. Phones can lose service. Phones can stop working altogether. You CANNOT rely solely on a phone-based map on a cross-country bike quest. You need a paper map as a back-up! A paper map gives you peace of mind and saves the day in the case your phone becomes lost or disabled.

DAY 7: Desert sunrise. Splendid!!!

Chapter 13: Cell Phone Mount

Mounting your cell phone on the "dash" of your handlebars is essential to modern-day bike travel! Your cell phone should be in clear and prominent view as to allow you to easily follow your electronic map directions and to take important phone calls from time to time. You will also use Google Maps periodically when you are trying to locate the nearest McDonalds, find the exact location of your overnight host, or locate a particular store or bike repair shop in town.

Make sure you buy a 100% waterproof cell phone handlebar mount. You will be riding in all types of weather and cell phones don't do well when they get wet! Test out your new handlebar cell phone mount by putting an old piece of cardboard securely into the cell phone holder and then forcefully spraying the entire holder with water from your garden hose. If the cardboard remains dry after a complete dowsing of water, then you have obtained true waterproof equipment!

After the 8th time my cell phone became dislodged from my cell phone holder, I finally stopped in the vicinity of Bogalusa, Mississippi at Dollar General, one of my favorite stores on The Southern Tier, spent one dollar and bought a tiny tube of super glue. Ever since gluing the connection point of my cell phone holder, my cell phone did NOT disengage from the holder for the rest of the trip! Clearly, I bought the WRONG cell phone holder as your phone should not fall out of a good holder or require super glue, but at least I was creative enough to resolve the matter on the road without losing my precious cell phone!

DAY 7: Slowly, I am becoming ONE with the desert!

Chapter 14: GPS Phone App Map

It is hard enough to pedal 3,000 miles or more across the country on a bicycle, but it is pure TORTURE when you add needless miles to your trip by getting LOST! After getting lost a total of 9 times in about 24 days, I finally decided in east Texas to splurge and buy the $55 Adventure Cycling Southern Tier GPS phone app map known as "Bicycle Route Navigator."

Being a VERY cautious spender, I did not want to waste any money buying a non-essential phone app map. Originally, it was my assumption that the paper map series of the Southern Tier bike route were good enough. I didn't think I needed to buy a separate phone app map. But after getting lost the 9th time and acting like a pure LUNATIC, I finally decided to add the fabulous Bicycle Route Navigator GPS phone map system to my arsenal!

At first, the GPS phone map seemed overly simplistic as it only showed the route line and a little dot to indicate where I was in relation to the route line, but as time elapsed, I grew to LOVE the phone app! A GPS signal constantly updated my little dot and as long as my little dot was on the route line, I knew I was moving in the correct direction! Bicycle Route Navigator was such a RELIEF to my worries! It was the TURNING POINT of my cross-country trip!

At times, I would glance down to my dash and notice my dot was off of the route line. During those few moments, I realized I was LOST! Although I felt REALLY STUPID, getting back on track was easy as I could watch the pink dot move as my bike moved. As the pink dot got closer to my blue route line, I knew I was getting back on course. It was AMAZING to watch myself (the dot) get back on route, a feature a paper map could never offer!

For a cheapskate like me, Adventure Cycling should consider it a pure honor for me to HIGHLY recommend their GPS phone maps as I don't buy anything unless it is absolutely essential! It is absolutely mandatory for me to think carefully about all of my purchases as to make sure I am NOT wasting money. After a lot of pondering, I finally bought the Southern Tier GPS map on Bicycle Route Navigator and it proved to be well worth it!

Buying the GPS phone map from Adventure Cycling let me know exactly where I was in relation to the actual route itself. As long as my pink dot was on the blue line, then I knew I was ON ROUTE! With paper route maps, you can see all the roads, but the map does NOT indicate where YOU are in relation to your route! Having a GPS satellite in outer space keep track of your constant location makes it easy to get back on track as you can see your EXACT location and the EXACT location of your route!

Spend the extra money and get the Adventure Cycling GPS phone map known as

Bicycle Route Navigator, but also get the paper maps as well just in case you lose your phone and/or your phone app stops working (which never happened to me!). It is interesting to note that over the course of approximately 1,400 miles of using Bicycle Route Navigator, not once did I lose GPS signal! Even when I passed a lonely Texas ranch with an archway reading "Welcome to the end of the Earth," my GPS phone map remained accurate and current!

In addition to the paper map series from Adventure Cycling and their Bicycle Route Navigator GPS phone app, you should also get a AAA state map of each state on your route. The AAA maps are FREE to AAA members! Doing so gives you another additional layer of "insurance" just in case. The paper state maps will also give you a much better view of where you are currently located within any given state in case you actually care. For me, I just pedaled the miles without much consideration of my exact location as I relied on my father to enlighten me as to my exact current location on a day-to-day basis. My job was simply to PEDAL!!! I didn't really care where I was!

DAY 8: I LOVE riding with my shirt off!

Chapter 15: Starting Early

Most days of my 43-day cross-country biking escapade began with my first pedal stroke occurring while it was dark outside. Usually, I began riding at approximately 5 a.m. with some days as early as 3:30 a.m. Of course, I used my headlight and taillight while riding in the dark.

Being a "morning person," it seemed natural for me to wake up early and start my day. Instead of sleeping in, I'd much rather take an hour nap immediately after lunch. But despite whether or not you classify yourself as a "morning person," it might make good sense for you to consider an early morning start on your cross-country cycling quest for numerous good reasons to follow.

Before you even consider riding before sunrise, you MUST have an excellent headlight and taillight. My amazing BLAZE headlight had a powerful rechargeable battery and lasted me about 2 hours as long as I didn't use it on the most powerful setting. My battery-operated SWERVE taillight also worked wonderfully and only needed the batteries changed out one time during my entire 43 days. Not one time during the approximate 60 hours of riding in the dark did a vehicle honk at me or give me any indication whatsoever they were unpleased with me! It is so important to be VISIBLE while riding in the dark!

By starting your daily bike ride prior to sunrise, you get a chance to feel the "power of the night." There is something special about being outside in the complete dark on a desolate road with only your headlight to guide the way. There is a special energy given off by the night especially as the transition occurs with the oncoming sunrise. The mysterious energetic vibration was extremely powerful and I began to look forward to my early morning rides as I could FEEL something special in the air!

During my cross-country bike travels, I was privileged to witness about 35 sunrises as I traveled eastbound toward the Atlantic Ocean. Some of the marvelous sunrises actually brought tears to my eyes! To say the sunrises were MAGNIFICENT would be understated. Mere words are not suitable to describe some of the exquisite sunrises I experienced while pedaling the Southern Tier. Yes, many I captured on my camera, but a photo (no matter how good) CANNOT compare to the actual experience of these spiritual masterpieces!

Another advantage of early morning riding allows you to increase your "before noon mileage" as one cross-country bike author advises biking AT LEAST half of your daily mileage goal by noon. This particular author believes your total daily mileage will usually be <u>DOUBLE</u> your total mileage tally as of NOON and I agree! Getting up before sunrise and logging in 10 to 15 miles in the dark will give you an incredible start to your day and will likely propel you to a higher mileage total than you may have considered possible for yourself! At least give it a try!

If you take my advice and begin pedaling before sunrise, make sure you have a spare headlight as well. During my travels, I had a spare headlight in which I used about 5 times after the rechargeable batteries in my primary headlight died. Having a second headlight, even though it adds a few ounces to your total weight, is a great idea. You do not want to encounter a headlight problem leaving you stranded alongside the road until the sun finally comes up! It is also a great idea to have a spare taillight in case your primary taillight breaks or becomes dislodged from your bike.

Riding in the dark also gives you a much-needed break from the sun. Despite traveling in October and November along the Southern Tier, I had PLENTY of sunshine. The early morning darkness was welcoming to me and helped to balance my overall health and stability without getting too much sunshine. The special times I experienced in the early morning DARKNESS on the Southern Tier will never be forgotten!

DAY 8: Here is a photo of me and Layne Gneiting. Layne is an international bike tour leader. Layne was one of my ANGELS of the Southern Tier!

Chapter 16: Heat Exhaustion

Everyone knows the desert is hot, but you won't really understand the magnitude of desert heat until you pedal your bike through the desert at 1 p.m. in the afternoon on a blistering hot, sunny day without a bit of shade anywhere! When the temperatures exceed 100 degrees, the heat can be BRUTAL making heat exhaustion a very real danger! Every year, people DIE from the negative effects of the relentless desert heat and I came rather close to being one of those grim statistics......

As I biked through the blistering desert from Brawley, California toward Blythe, California, I started to notice the heat was affecting me. It was more than just feeling hot as I was beginning to sense the intense heat was robbing my core energy reserve and triggering strange thoughts in my mind.

At the 86-mile point of my planned 94-mile day, I was no longer eagerly awaiting my next drink or anticipating my next planned 10-mile rest. Instead, I recognized I was in TROUBLE! Suddenly, I found myself struggling to remain conscious as severe symptoms of heat exhaustion set in VERY QUICKLY. In my mind an active debate was going on between my various thoughts. Would I pass out in the middle of the lonely desert road or would I go unconscious along the barren side of the road? After a brief consideration of the two equally dismal alternatives, I decided it was wiser to go unresponsive in the middle of the road as I might have a better chance of living as a passing car would be forced to stop if my listless body was blocking the center of the roadway. Unfortunately, at the time, cars were only passing me at the rate of about one car every 10 minutes or so!

Upon entertaining such morbid thoughts, I figured it might be time to call 911 as to avoid a potential dire situation, but at that moment I glanced down at my phone to call for help and noticed my phone was SHUT OFF! The sun was so HOT, the sweltering temperature was too much for my phone to withstand and it automatically shut ITSELF off as to protect itself from fatal damage! Without a phone, I was NOW officially stranded in the middle of the desert with no form of communication to save myself as I felt my health plummeting FAST! Had I used more sense, I would have taken my phone off of my handlebar dash and placed it in my handlebar bag to keep it out of the path of the direct unrelenting sunlight. Better planning may have allowed my phone to remain functional during this incredibly HOT day! Instead, I was left WITHOUT a lifeline!

As I contemplated my pending doom, I decided to pedal down the MIDDLE of the "highway" as to FORCE any passing vehicle to STOP and help me! Pedaling another 8 miles to Brawley, California was NOT happening! I needed SAVED! My current state of health needed critical care NOW! As my eyes began to get blurry, I wondered if I was really seeing a large commercial building about a half mile down the road on my left or whether it was a MIRAGE. The closer I got, the more certain it seemed the object of my fantasy was indeed a large block building. Yes, a big block cement commercial building was DEFINITELY up ahead on my left! It was my LAST RESORT and I was stopping no matter what!!!! Maybe I could find a human being? Maybe someone could help me? Upon arrival, I collapsed on one of the few spots of shade on the entire property.

As I relished in the COOL 90-degree shade, I quickly realized the severity of my situation. Dying in the desert was a real possibility! I felt like I was overcome by the heat and I had nothing left. An empty feeling took over my bodily sensations and I felt like it was over. It was like a car chugging as it coasted to a halt on fumes after using up its last ounce of gasoline. My current situation was nothing less than DESPERATE!

Moments later as if I had a guardian angel watching over me, a young man named Rudy walked outside of the block building and noticed me awkwardly spread out on the ground in the shade. Without a moment of hesitation, Rudy hustled over and quickly assessed I was in CRITICAL condition. Being no stranger to the EXTREME HEAT of the desert, Rudy swiftly helped me inside the building, set me down on a full-size couch located directly in front of a huge commercial air conditioner, and he cranked the A/C to the MAX while simultaneously placing two large bags of ice on my neck and wrists. Rudy continued talking with me as to prevent me from nodding off and losing consciousness. After another 10 minutes of time elapsed, I finally felt myself beginning to recover. As soon as I felt semi-stable, Rudy let me use his company phone to call my family to let them know I was still alive!

My new lifesaving friend, Rudy, was the owner of a commercial pest spraying company. Rudy graciously gave me and my bicycle a ride in his fancy truck to the Travelodge hotel 6 miles away in Blythe, California. Along the way, I continued applying ice to my neck and wrists while I continued to recover slowly.

Severe heat is tricky! It will NOT give you a 15-minute warning before you pass out. You must monitor yourself VERY CAREFULLY to make sure you don't "cross the line" like I mistakenly did! As you are pedaling, you might not even know how severe your situation is until it is possibly too late. Riding in conditions over 100-degrees Fahrenheit is extremely DANGEROUS and I do NOT recommend it!!!!! Take major precautions while biking in extreme heat as the consequences could be fatal, especially on a big-mileage day.

In my case, I was NOT dehydrated. I had plenty of water as I planned very well. For me, the EXTREME HEAT was just too much for me. My body just couldn't take anymore exertion in the 105-degree relentless heat. No clouds. No trees. No shade anywhere. Just pure unrelenting, blistering sunshine. The breaking point had been reached and I was done! The added stress of my 4 flat tires on this perilous day also made a HUGE IMPACT on my dire situation as my negative thoughts weakened my overall life energy possibly as much as the sun! When you LOSE your composure, your bodily capabilities will also decrease QUICKLY! I'm lucky I didn't die on this near-tragic, sweltering-hot day in the California Desert!

Chapter 17: Cold Weather

Choosing the Southern Tier as my cross-country bicycle route had a lot to do with nice, warm weather as I am definitely a warm weather kind of guy! But to my dismay, I discovered it is possible for west Texas to have sub-freezing temperatures in October as I found myself faced with a bitterly cold 27-degree Fahrenheit day with consistent 30 mile per hour easterly headwinds plaguing me for most of my 5-hour ride!

The previous day was really tough as the headwind was consistently between 15 to 20 miles per hour ALL DAY. As the day unfolded, I also felt the temperatures beginning to drop in what seemed to be non-typical fashion. Upon finally arriving at my motel in Sierra Blanca, Texas, I was relieved to get out of the wind and the cold. My motel room was nice and warm, but the air outside seemed to be getting MUCH colder. Upon referring to the local weather forecast for tomorrow, I was surprised to discover a projected HIGH of only 30 degrees with possible snow. I couldn't believe it! Surely the weather forecast must be wrong!

My trusted daily weather advisor (my father), strongly advised me to reconsider riding tomorrow. "Just take the day off!" was his final words before we hung up the phone that evening. My wife also agreed with my father stating, "The weather forecast is TERRIBLE. Take a ZERO-MILE-day tomorrow." Despite the cautions expressed by my father and my wife, I went to bed hopeful I could at least travel a mere 34 miles to the next closest city of Van Horn, Texas tomorrow despite the anticipated frigid weather. Instead of waking up before dawn like usual, my plan was to sleep in until daylight and then possible begin biking about two hours after sunrise hoping by then any possible overnight ice on the roads would be melted by the prevailing early morning sun.

As I awoke the next morning and peered outside my hotel window, I noticed the ground was white as it was partially covered with snow! The current temperature was 26 degrees and there was a STRONG easterly HEADWIND ripping through the parking lot of the hotel. As I stepped outside my room to get a real-world taste of the inclement conditions, the hotel manager happened to be walking by and resolutely stated, "I hope you don't plan to ride today!" With a sense of meekness I replied, "Well, I'm considering my options…." To my reply he stated, "If you decide to ride, you would be making a BIG mistake!"

Looking back to reassess this scenario, it appears I may have made a blunder as this hotel manager was probably an angel in disguise whom was trying desperately to keep me from biking in this hideous weather! But in my typical stubborn nature, I refused to take a day off as NOTHING would break my positive momentum, not even a nasty winter storm. As I began getting dressed for my daily bike ride, I decided to put on every bit of clothing in my possession, including my full rain suit over top!

Moments before I began my ride, I text my wife "I'm going for it.... I love you!" Then, I closed the hotel door, dropped off my key in the hotel key drop box, and I was on the road pedaling through the bitter cold desert onward toward Van Horn, Texas!

For the previous 17 days, I wondered if having my winter mittens were "extra weight" in my pannier bag, but today they proved to be an ABSOLUTE NECESSITY! My pair of wool winter socks also paid big dividends today as did my full baklava which covered most of my head and neck.

As I began my route for the day, there was still snow laying on the ground in various places. Much worse than the snow was the bitter cold 20-plus mile per hour easterly headwind making each pedal stroke feel like I was climbing a mountain. With each mile I fantasized the wind suddenly stopping and allow me to pass through without issue, but it seemed with each dreadful mile the wind velocity actually increased until I found myself biking through CONSISTENT 30 mile per hour HEADWINDS! The wind chill on this frigid day was 5 degrees Fahrenheit making it the COLDEST day I ever rode a bicycle IN MY LIFE!

Mile after mile I congratulated myself for being so "brave" despite knowing deep within my heart, I was an IDIOT for willfully exposing myself to this EXTREME life-threatening danger! Within only a few miles, I noticed I was expending a VERY HIGH degree of effort to maintain my paltry 6 mile per hour pace. All the while, I knew I was beginning to sweat BIG-TIME underneath all of my clothes due to my high level of physical exertion being applied to each of my pedal strokes. With all the build-up of sweat underneath my many layers of clothes, I suddenly realized I could possibly die of HYPOTHERMIA if anything at all went wrong with myself or my bike over the next 5 hours as I COULD NOT stop pedaling or else my sweat would turn to ICE and I would risk freezing to death!

Pedal stroke by pedal stroke I struggled through the pure TORTURE of west Texas. No other human being was outside and there certainly wasn't another biker on the roads. As I fought through the agony of the strong 30 mile per hour headwind, I adopted a mantra which I estimate I repeated over 1,000 times on this frigid day. "I AM MOVING. I AM WARM." were the words I repeated silently under my frozen lips over and over for hours. As long as I kept spinning my pedals around, the bike would keep moving even though I was convinced my speedometer must have been broken. Nonetheless, as long as my pedals continued to revolve, I knew I was still alive!

At mile 10, I called my mom and told her to find a phone number for an UBER driver in case I succumb to the cold and needed rescued. After panicking a bit, she agreed and I pressed on.

At mile 13, I seriously thought about turning around and riding an amazing 30 mile per hour tailwind back to the exact same hotel in which I stayed the previous night, but with monumental stupidity and pathetic perseverance, I kept pedaling eastbound toward my unreasonable daily destination goal of Van Horn, Texas.

At mile 17, I remember taking a drink and then missing my water bottle cage for the first and only time during my entire Southern Tier journey as my water bottle fell to the ground. "Oh my God, I'm going to die!" were my immediate desperate words as I stopped my bike to retrieve my tumbling water bottle from the street below. No longer was I moving and I could feel my wet sweat on my skin underneath all my layers of clothes. Within seconds of stopping my pedal cadence, I could feel the NASTY chill of the air affect my core. What have I gotten myself into? After frantically grabbing my dropped water bottle and feeling the severity of my evolving winter scenario, I continued my mantra "I am moving. I am warm." over and over until the words eventually reached my soul.

At mile 20, I reached down to get a drink of water and discovered one of my water bottles were now FROZEN SOLID! My other water bottle was still almost full and I managed to suck a few ounces of water through the icy wintry mix.

At mile 21 as I SLOWLY moved across the freezing land, another dominant thought slipped into my mind as a result of the DIRE weather conditions. "I am a man." was now my new dominant thought. Yes, I may freeze to death today, but I felt like after 48 years of existence, I had finally become "a MAN!"

Throughout my life, I looked up to my father, Thomas Hockensmith, and his brother, my uncle, Larry Hockensmith, as being "real men." To me, a real man was someone who didn't make excuses, someone who never quit, someone who was reliable, and someone who was loyal to their calling. For all of my previous years, I considered myself to be mostly "a kid," but today as I struggled through the harsh weather elements as I propelled my bicycle to Van Horn, Texas, I finally felt like I was an official MAN!

Clearly, I was now a MAN as no "boy" could have pedaled a bicycle through the punishing elements I faced on this miserably ARCTIC day. ONLY a real man could pedal for 4 hours into a fierce, relentless 30 mile per hour headwind with a wind chill of only 5 degrees Fahrenheit! In my mind on this unforgettable day, I finally became "a man" much like my father and my Uncle Larry!

As a child, I had the wonderful firsthand opportunity of seeing my father leave our cozy, warm suburban home and venture off into the harsh Pennsylvania wintry conditions to work as an electrical lineman OUTSIDE all day, sometimes in weather conditions much worse than what I found myself in west Texas. In similar fashion, my Uncle Larry was known for chopping down trees and working outside in the most brutal weather conditions imaginable. These two real men worked through

ALL weather conditions and got the job done! They were loyal MEN who did whatever it took to PROVIDE for their families! Although I don't dare claim to have the same level of esteem as my father or uncle, at least I can say with absolute certainty, "I am now a man!" Yes, I finally became a MAN on this memorable frozen day of senseless bike travel as I struggled ever so slowly to my daily destination of Van Horn, Texas!

As I fought, affirmed, and prayed, only progressing one mere mile about every 10 minutes, I finally reached the 24-mile point of my tour of Hell only to be greeted by Satan himself! To my dismay, I was PULLED OVER by a uniformed man driving a white Chevy Suburban SUV with a green horizontal stripe across the vehicle highlighting the words "UNITED STATES BORDER PATROL." There I was, 1,200 miles into what was supposed to be a nice, warm bike ride across the pleasant southern portion of the United States, being pulled over by a federal authority at a time when I could lose about one degree of body warmth in as little as two minutes of inactivity. This was NOT the right time for a conversation with a governmental officer! Unbelievable!

Without wasting a moment of small talk, the border patrol officer quickly approached me and sharply exclaimed, "What the hell are you doing outside riding a bicycle on a miserable day like this?" Through my frozen lips I muttered, "Riding to Florida!" Being quite pleasant and mostly feeling sorry for me, the respectable officer offered me some non-frozen water to drink! In my typical insane, self-torturing, completely illogical self, I declined his gracious offer for a "rescue" and I continued riding. Pedal by pedal I resumed, all the while affirming, "I am moving. I am warm."

At mile 25, amidst the last possible moment of which my body and mind could withstand any more abuse, the forceful wind gusts abruptly decreased to a much-welcomed and more manageable 15 mile per hour mild pace. To my great pleasure, I enjoyed a bit of RELIEF for the last 10 miles of my bicycle journey on this unforgetting abusive day as I traveled on the breakdown lane of the mammoth Interstate 10 highway all the way to the PROMISED LAND, Van Horn, Texas!

At mile 34, in what seemed like an eternity, I finally reached Motel 6 in Van Horn, Texas. Luckily, three hours prior, my mom, Mary Jo Hockensmith, lovingly and diligently called ahead and booked the third to last hotel room in this lovely motel as all the other hotels in Van Horn, Texas were FULL on this wintry day as nobody was outside working in these EXTREME conditions and few were even traveling by vehicle on the treacherously slippery roads!

Chapter 18: Rain

If you ask most cyclists what they think about rain, they would express their strong dislike. As a cross-country cyclist, you are free to make your own opinions and beliefs about rain and about anything else for that matter, but I would urge you to reconsider your choices. To me, rain inherently is neither good nor bad. Rain is just rain, a natural phenomenon. It happens every day, somewhere. Rain is needed and is essential for life to continue. It's just water coming out of the sky, nothing more!

Yes, there are those few times when you are riding your bike and you are super-hot and a nice, little, gentle rain shower comes through at just the right time to cool you off, but in most cases, rain is very cold and unpleasant, especially if you are unprepared! But if you have the right rain gear and you properly transition into your rain gear before you get hammered by the storm, then you can withstand a significant rain shower like a champ!

Some cross- country cyclists claim only a rain jacket is needed, but I would disagree. My philosophy is ALWAYS to prepare for the WORST! Yes, you can make it through the perfect, little storm with no rain gear or maybe just a raincoat, but you CANNOT make it through a nasty, COLD rain without having a truly waterproof rainsuit.

A full rainsuit, in my opinion, consists of bib pants with adjustable straps extending up over your shoulders along with an excellent rain jacket. You should also have either a hooded rain jacket allowing you to wear the hood either inside your helmet or outside your helmet depending on your preference. You may also use a helmet rain cover to prevent water from entering the top of your helmet. It is also advised to waterproof your shoes by zipping a waterproof shoe cover over top of your cycling shoes. Also, remember to use one or two strong Velcro straps around your lower leg to keep your rain pants from getting caught in your bike chain or other mechanicals.

Having a really good rainsuit means it might be slightly on the heavy side and may cause you to sweat causing you to be about as wet from the sweat as you would be from the rain if you were not wearing a rainsuit, but in my opinion, I'd MUCH rather be warm and sweating than freezing cold with goose bumps and chattering teeth. As the rain subsides, you can slowly take off layers of clothes. Gradually, you can let more and more of your damp, sweaty inner layer of clothes dry as you continue your bike ride.

As I was preparing for my cross-country ride, I took an overnight 83-mile training ride in my home state of Pennsylvania. In most cases, I refuse to let the weather dictate my plans. It is my foundational belief that there is no such thing as "BAD WEATHER!" There is only improper gear for any particular weather condition!

Anyways, this particular overnight bike ride taught me about rain as I rode through 9 separate rainstorms and one hailstorm over the course of 2 days with a few of the storms being SEVERE.

During this particular buffet of rain, I tested all of my pannier bags as well as my rainsuit for true waterproofing, but most of all, I tested my mind! Quickly, I realized my MIND was the key factor to my success or failure. It seemed like the more I actually EMBRACED the troublesome rain with my thoughts, the better chance I had to complete my planned mileage. As I hung on mentally and experienced the reality of the rain, I realized the rain was here to stay! It was folly for me to EXPECT every biking day to have ideal conditions with partly sunny skies and 72 degrees Fahrenheit! Expecting perfect mild weather would make me "dumber than a box of rocks" as my garrulous son, Curtis Hockensmith, would say!

Only once during this particularly rainy training ride did I actually stop and seek cover as one specific rain storm was torrential and severely compromised my safety on the road. At the onset of this particularly heavy rainstorm, I stopped at the first house with a reasonable front porch to shelter me from the barrage of water coming from the sky. Although I did NOT know these people nor did I have any type of prior permission, I took it upon myself to take cover under their large, beautiful covered front porch. Shelter is what I needed and shelter is what I found! When the homeowner pulled her mini-van into her driveway about 20 minutes later, she was surprised to see me on her front porch, but after I shared my story with her, she was totally understanding and she was fine with my liberties.

With regard to rain, about 90 percent of the time or more, I ride IN THE RAIN and LOVE IT! During the 10% of times when the rain and wind is too FIERCE, I find shelter! Never ride when the rain is so strong the overtaking cars CANNOT see you!!!! Never ride when the winds are strong enough to blow your bike out into the vehicle lane. Never ride when the fog is so severe, you can barely see approaching cars! During these times of truly adverse weather, you are well-advised to take a nice long break under cover and WAIT it out! In most cases, you can find some type of short-term shelter, but be forewarned, there are many roads in our vast country which do not offer much respite for a cyclist who encounters a terrible rainstorm. Sometimes, you just have to pull off the road and hunker down until the rain lets up. How tough are you mentally? What level of storm does it take to break you?

In the case of a lightning storm, it is best to find a covered porch, store, or some type of temporary shelter and wait for the lightning to pass. If there is no such cover available, just keep pedaling because you have no reasonable alternative. It is possible you could be struck by lightning, but it is extremely unlikely. You are riding a bike with a metal frame known for conducting electricity making you more likely to be hit by lightning, but you also have rubber tires that repel electrical surges making you slightly less likely to be hit by lightning. There seems to be an ongoing debate as to the exact scientific degree of danger associated with cycling during a lightning storm, but sometimes you simply have NO CHOICE!

Outlasting extreme weather has a way of building confidence like NOTHING ELSE! The first time you OUTLAST a severe rainstorm will leave you feeling AMAZING! If you ever find yourself in extreme weather, thank God as this might be your opportunity to take your mental game to the next level! Rain can be very uncomfortable at times, but it also possesses the power to transform YOU if you can hold on!

DAY 8: Here is a photo of the Layne Gneiting family. I will NEVER forget eating supper with this AMAZING family and the impressive 3 visiting Mormon missionaries whom joined us!

Chapter 19: Wild Camping

Both of my alarm clocks sounded at 3 a.m. It was time for my wife and I to get out of bed and prepare to be picked up by my parents for a 2-hour car ride to the Pittsburgh Airport. Today is Day 1 and I'm scheduled to fly to San Diego to begin my epic bike journey. In typical fashion, my prompt parents arrived exactly on time for our 3:45 a.m. planned departure from our home. My bike box, check-in luggage bag, and 2 carry-on bike pannier bags were all meticulously prepared the day before and it was no trouble loading them into the bed of my dad's truck.

The good-bye at the airport was gut-wrenching. Tears abounded as I walked toward the airport doors. My knees buckled as the last word I hollered back to my family as I approached the airport doors was "St. Augustine" which was my intended destination for the completion of my epic Southern Tier bike journey. Never in my life did I ever feel so PHONY as when I yelled back "St. Augustine" as to imply I might actually make it there!

My Southwest Airlines airplane departed at 8 a.m. and we had a layover in Dallas, Texas. Finally, my plane landed in San Diego, California at 12:15 p.m. My luggage was on the carousel at Baggage Claim area and an airport representative pointed me toward the special conveyer belt containing my large bike box. By 1:30 p.m., I had my bike assembled and my pannier bags were attached to my bike. My three 25-ounce water bottles were filled from the public water inside the restroom. My handlebar dash was in good order and my helmet and gloves were on. It was time to begin the "adventure of my life!"

After getting lost riding my bike in San Diego for 45 minutes or so, I finally found my starting point at Ocean Beach. It was a gorgeous, sunny day and the first guy I approached on the beach agreed to take several photos of me with my bike tires touching the salty waters of the Pacific Ocean. After struggling to push my bike back out of the deep sand, I began my 3,000-mile bike trip at about 3 p.m. on the local San Diego bike trail leading out of Ocean Beach and through the GORGEOUS city of San Diego.

By the time I pedaled out of the city limits of San Diego and struggled through the MAJOR inclines of the small communities of Santee, Lakeside, and Alpine, I was physically exhausted! After having rode my bike 45 minutes in the dark, I was still about 12 miles away from my intended campground destination for the day! Combining my physical exhaustion with a severe case of culture shock, mental fatigue, and lack of sleep, I was DONE for the day! But there was one minor problem   I had nowhere to stay!!!

Several months prior, I added a new goal to my list of personal life goals. The goal was to "wild camp" at least once in my life. Never did I imagine the achievement of my goal of wild camping was about to occur on my first night while riding the magnificent Southern Tier Bicycle Route!

As I glanced to my left while feeling on the brink of exhaustion, I saw a community building where some type of craft fair had taken place and the vendors were packing up their booths into various trucks and trailers as the festival had obviously concluded. Being a "carny" myself with my previous extensive job experience working at various fairs and festivals selling cups of gourmet coffee, I decided to talk to some of the vendors and ask if they had any ideas where I could spend the night. After getting nowhere with the first several vendors, I approached a lady who casually said, "Why don't you just sleep under the pavilion in the back part of the property?"

As I walked out back, I saw the perfect little pavilion, but there was one MAJOR problem...... I didn't have permission! My female vendor friend said, "If it was me, I'd just stay there. What's the worst thing that could happen?" Having liked her zesty attitude, I decided to give wild camping a try!

Wow, this was going to be my first WILD CAMP of my life! My decision was made. As soon as the last vendor left the parking lot, I quietly erected my tent, blew up my air mattress, set up my sleeping bag, took a "man shower" with my bath wipes, brushed my teeth, and went to bed in my first-ever wild camp location.

Not once during the night did anyone bother me. Of course, I was careful NOT to draw unnecessary attention to myself by doing something stupid like making a bunch of noise, building a fire, or even using my flashlight more than needed.

Before the sun even began to rise, I had my camp packed up and loaded on to my bicycle. The area was left EXACTLY as I found it the night before! It was like I wasn't even there! If someone didn't see me there, there would be NO TRACE of my stay!

Wild camping is when you camp somewhere WITHOUT permission! As long as you do NOT have permission, then you are wild camping! Wild camping can occur in a wooded area, a public area, a town park, a baseball dugout, a soccer field, behind a fire department, or anywhere else you can imagine. Normally, it is best to look for an open area where you can get as far away as possible from any conceivable intruders. But sometimes it is best to wild camp in the OPEN as it has been said, "Sometimes, the best 'hiding place' is out in the open for all to see." Even if someone challenges your wild camping, in most cases, your smile, positive attitude, and kind words will facilitate a favorable outcome with regard to your contested overnight accommodations!

In most cases, if you are polite, then most people will do whatever they can to help you! But if you act like a disrespecting nimrod, then you will be treated as such and you might find yourself having to relocate in the middle of night! Yes, wild camping takes some "balls," but so does cross-country cycling! Do you have what it takes to make BOLD decisions? Do you have what it takes to handle UNCERTAIN outcomes? Do you have the nerve to beg for forgiveness instead of asking for permission? Welcome to the Southern Tier!

Chapter 20: Drinking

Regardless of whether or not I was thirsty, I was told by one of my original bike mentors, cross-country cyclist, Dan Shearer, "Drink before you are thirsty and eat before you are hungry!" Dan warned, "If you find yourself getting thirsty or hungry, then it is TOO LATE and you have already damaged your body and decreased your chances of completing your scheduled mileage!" During the first few days of my epic bike ride, I was taking a drink every two miles, but after several days of doing so, I felt like I was drinking TOO MUCH and I changed my drinking pattern and began consuming liquid every 3 miles instead.

One of the fastest ways to end your special cross-country bike trip is to dehydrate yourself! And there is no good reason to do so! Regardless of whether it is hot or cold, ALWAYS take a drink every 3 miles. Drink every 2 miles if you wish, but at least take a good solid 3-ounce drink every 3 miles. Think of the drinking requirements as consuming AT LEAST one ounce of liquid for every one mile pedaled. Drink more if you are able! On a really hot, sunny day, you might need to drink 2 ounces of water for every mile you pedal, but for a general gauge, the one ounce for one mile recipe will be a good foundational formula for you to use. Establishing the habit of drinking every 3 miles will keep you regimented as it is easy to FORGET to drink and then after many miles of NOT consuming any liquids, you might wonder why you have no energy. Remember what Dan Shearer recommends, "Drink BEFORE you are thirsty and eat BEFORE you are hungry!"

On various occasions in the past, my wife, Tina Hockensmith (Tink), explained to me how water helps to keep muscles loose and reduces muscle pain significantly, especially for the following day! For these reasons alone and many dozens of other positive reasons not mentioned herein, I followed my wife's sage advice! Every 3 miles I kept the water going down my throat, no matter what!

On my bike, I had three water bottle cage mounts. Each of my water bottles held approximately 25 ounces of water. In addition, I also carried two 32-ounce bottles of Gatorade or Powerade in my pannier bag. If all of my drinks were weighed, it would transfer to an additional 10 pounds of weight, but the extra liquid weight was well worth it! As I gained additional daily cycling experience, I cut back slightly on the total amount of drinks I brought along with me daily, but as I passed through the 1,000 miles of wicked HOT desert expanse, I ALWAYS had an OVERABUNDANCE of drinks as described above to ensure I kept myself HYDRATED! In addition to water and sports drinks, I also discovered CHOCOLATE MILK as my AMAZING secret potion of the Southern Tier! There will be more comments regarding the magic of chocolate milk in an upcoming chapter!

Chapter 21: Eating

Cross-country biker, author, and kindred soul, Patrick McGinty, advises cross-country cyclists to stop every 10 miles and take a short walk. Brief walking stints every 10 miles breaks up your ride, gives you something to anticipate, and provides your sore legs a chance to reboot!

As long as I was stopping every 10 miles, I figured it made good sense to eat something as I paced back and forth along the roadway. Eating at every 10-mile stop helped to establish the crucial habit of refueling my body with enough energy to rise to the demands of my big 70-mile daily bike rides.

Over the course of my long, cross-country bike ride, I ate many different foods. Below is a listing of the foods I regularly ate while pacing along the berm of the hundreds of different roads across the southern portion of the United States:

Power bars
Brownies
Pound cake
Donuts
Pizza
Grapes
Fig newton cookies
Cinnamon rolls
Crackers
Raisins

Cereal
Granola bars
Apples
Spinach
Cereal bars
Pie
Candy bars
Bananas
Peanut butter
Anything else that looks good!

By reviewing my dietary listing above, you might notice many of the foods on the list would NOT be highly acclaimed by a health food expert, but my diet gave me a huge number of calories and I NEEDED those calories to pull off my cross-country escapade! In my estimation on a normal non-biking day, I would eat about 2,000 calories per day, but during my cross-country excursion, I estimate I ate 5,000 calories per day which is 2 ½ times my regular caloric consumption! In short, I ate 2.5 times more than usual while struggling through a FULL Southern Tier biking day!

When I pushed down my first pedal stroke in San Diego, California, I weighed 182 pounds and I was NOT over weight. 43 days later when my front tire touched the Atlantic Ocean in Jacksonville Beach, Florida, I weighed 162 pounds. It was quite the luxury to literally eat EVERYTHING I wanted and still LOSE 20 pounds while doing so!!!

Some of you may laugh at me dedicating a small section of my book to reminding you to eat, but on Day 4 of my trip, I could FEEL myself losing weight much TOO FAST. Within the first four days, I dropped about 10 pounds!!! Had I not FORCED myself to eat, I would have been on an airplane flying back home within the first two weeks due to my fast and severe bodily weight loss. It would have been IMPOSSIBLE for me to continue to sustain this type of mammoth weight loss without horrible consequences! I had to eat A LOT!

As a result of the sheer CULTURE SHOCK of my circumstances, I didn't feel hungry for the first week of my cross-country tour despite the enormous number of calories I was burning daily. Only through pure discipline did I eat during the first week. It wasn't until about Day 9 when I actually got "hungry" like normal. Up to Day 9, I ate only because I knew I biologically NEEDED to eat in order to continue my quest for another biking day.

Some aspiring cross-country cyclists plan to "DIET" as they pursue a crossing of the country. To those foolish dreamers, I advise them to WAKE UP as a dieting cross-country cyclist is unrealistic unless the plan is to pedal only about 20 miles per day! Dieting and bike touring do NOT go together! It is like trying to force a square object into a round hole. You can push all day and it won't work! A HEALTHY cross-country cyclist NEEDS to eat about 5,000 calories a day to produce the 70 miles of travel repeatedly mentioned throughout this book. Traveling longer mileage will require even MORE FOOD! If you travel lower miles per day, then you would require less food as will be dictated by the specific number of pedaled miles.

A car's engine won't even start without gasoline. So, don't think for a moment your body's engine is any different. Without eating food regularly every ten miles, you will be depleting your "gas tank" and you will put yourself at risk of BONKING which occurs when a cyclist is suddenly DONE for day, wiped out, and CANNOT pedal one more mile!

While pedaling a major bike route, regardless of whether it's the Southern Tier, Northern Tier, or the Transatlantic Bicycle Route, it does NOT really matter what type of food you eat! Just eat something! Eat anything that looks good to you! Cross-country cyclists do NOT need to be reading labels and counting calories. EAT WHATEVER YOU WANT! Grab a bag of donuts, carton of chocolate milk, a pizza, a snickers candy bar, and some raisins and then hop back on your bike and continue pedaling! It's not so much what you eat, it's HOW MANY CALORIES you eat! You need lots of calories to keep your pedals spinning!

While I paced alongside the road, I probably only ate a few hundred calories of food at a time, but when I saw those golden McDonalds arches in the horizon, I could easily eat 1,000 calories or more of food at one sitting! Like me, most cross-country cyclists eat 2.5 times the amount of a normal adult while on tour!

Despite eating much more than usual and eating huge amounts of food at one time, I did not experience any cramps or stomach issues while I was touring the United States on my bicycle. As long as I resumed riding with a nice and SLOW transition as to gently and easily re-acclimate my body with the pedaling chore, it seemed like all of my bodily functions cooperated, especially my DIGESTIVE system!

Chapter 22: Saddle Sores

Every year, saddle sores send many aspiring cross-country cyclists back home early! Do NOT underestimate the severity of saddle sores! This might be one of the MOST IMPORTANT chapters of this entire book!

Saddle sores are a skin irritation in your saddle area. No, I didn't research the medical definition or the scientific molecular make-up of saddle sores, but I can inform you quite accurately from vivid firsthand experience. Saddle sores HURT and they can form ANYWHERE underneath your bike shorts!

During one of my training rides prior to my cross-country effort, I developed saddle sores on Day 2 of a 176-mile ride. During my 88 miles pedaled on this memorable Day 2, my tail was ON FIRE! Upon arriving home and getting into the shower after my long cycling outing, my saddle area was scorching in searing pain as the warm shower water contacted my heavily agitated skin. The heavy-duty PAIN brought TEARS to my eyes!

After torturing myself in the shower, I looked down at my saddle area in the mirror at my BRIGHT RED rump which was STILL pulsating in pure agony! For the rest of the evening, I walked stiff-legged as any movement of my injured saddle skin would prompt high-level impulses of pure pain! There was NO POSSIBLE WAY I could have ridden my bike the following day! It was absolute agony to walk!

Some of you probably assume I was NOT wearing padded bike shorts when I got my SEVERE case of saddle sores, but that was not the case. On Day 1 of my long training ride, I wore bib bike shorts with straps extending up over my shoulders with a second pair of padded regular bike shorts over top of my bib bike shorts. After Day 1, I had no saddle sores, but on Day 2, I only wore one pair of regular padded bike shorts as I decided NOT to wear my bib biking shorts underneath. As a result, I got BIG-TIME saddle sores on the returning 88-mile ride home which gave me a vivid warning about the prevailing DANGER of saddle sores!

Beginning on Day 3 of the Southern Tier through Day 8, I developed saddle sores which increased in severity each progressing day despite wearing TWO PAIRS of good padded bike shorts! Fortunately, on Day 8 I stayed with Warmshowers host, Layne Gneiting, in Mesa, Arizona. Layne is a WORLD-CLASS bike touring guide. He has lead groups of touring cyclists throughout many countries! After asking a few questions and analyzing my situation, Layne discovered my bike shorts were TOO LOOSE! My shorts were moving and rubbing creating consistent friction on my skin which created a bad rash on the head of my penis and several other saddle areas. Luckily for me, none of my saddle sores were yet broken open or deemed to be at the SEVERE stage!

To remedy my serious saddle sores dilemma, Layne and I hustled over to the local

Mesa, Arizona bike shop, Paragon Cycling, minutes before closing on a gorgeous, sunny Arizona Saturday afternoon and I purchased the tightest, the highest quality, and the most expensive bib bike shorts available. The bike store owner told me he provides the EXACT SAME bib biking shorts to his sponsored cycling team! For once in my life, I bought THE BEST!

The top-quality, TIGHT, bib bike shorts combined with Layne's expert knowledge SAVED my bike trip! Otherwise, it would have only been a matter of days before the saddle agitations would have broken my skin and I would no longer have been able to tolerate the pain! Instead, thanks to my new friend Layne, with each new day, I could feel my saddle area being relieved of pain and returning back to stability! By the start of Day 14, my saddle area had finally healed despite my ongoing constant daily demand of big biking mileage.

As an important side note, I feel compelled to make a confession to you. International bike touring expert and Arizona State University professor, Layne Gneiting, firmly told me I was "CRAZY" for riding the Southern Tier solo, unsupported, and continuous. He also warned me I was doing TOO MANY miles per day. With due respect to Layne and in the spirit of FULL DISCLOSURE, I wanted to share those bits of information with you considering the source of this sage advice came from a bona-fide biking LEGEND! But despite Layne's high status in the biking community, I decided FOR MYSELF as I believe I AM MY OWN MAN and NO ONE (not even a biking legend) will dictate my future! My lifelong philosophy is to "Listen to EVERYONE and then decide for MYSELF!" Therefore, I continued my daily high-mileage quotas ALONE despite Layne's advice to the contrary!

Anyways, saddle sores are probably in the top five most common reasons many cyclists FAIL to complete their cross-country biking goal. When saddle sores exacerbate and actually break the skin, there is a HUGE problem! Broken skin means much more pain, much greater chance of infection, and much longer time to heal. Most of the time, when your skin breaks, your cross-country biking dream is almost OVER! Most cyclists abandon their dreams and fly back home about 2 days after their first saddle sore breaks the skin as the pain becomes almost UNBEARABLE! Under no circumstance, do NOT allow your skin to break!

To avoid saddle sores altogether, I highly recommend you follow my lead. Wear TIGHT, padded bib biking short against your sensitive skin. There should be NOTHING underneath your bib biking shorts. For years, I didn't know any better and I wore various types of underwear underneath my biking shorts only to suffer through many saddle sores until my Ironman coach and great friend, Bill Riggs, finally advised me to remove my underwear and ONLY wear padded biking shorts against my fragile skin!

Buy TIGHT bib biking shorts, but be careful your bib biking shorts are not too tight.

If you are a man, your balls should NOT be smashed into your stomach! Underneath your bib biking shorts should be NOTHING but bare skin. Underwear is NOT worn under biking shorts! Over top of your bibs should be worn a good pair of padded biking shorts SLIGHTLY bigger than normal, but snug. This combination of snug bib shorts against my skin with regular padded bike shorts over top got me across the country in 43 days without the potentially fatal consequence of saddle sores! Heed my advice or you WILL PAY dearly! You don't know pain until you get a BAD CASE of saddle sores!!!

Although having the properly-sized bib shorts and regular cycling shorts are crucial, it is also very important to prepare the skin around your saddle area for your ride EVERY DAY! During my 43 days of riding my bike along the Southern Tier, I experimented with various cremes, powder, gels, and balms. Although everything seemed to work pretty well, I must recommend using BAG BALM.

Bag Balm is the fine product Vermont farmers use on the udders of their cows to prevent chaffing from the constant daily milking. If Bag Balm is good enough for the Vermont farmers, then Bag Balm is good enough for me! Look for it on eBay, Amazon, or at your local bike shop. Buy it in a tube or in a jar. Make sure you buy it in a 3-ounce or less containers if you plan to transport it with you on an airplane to your starting point as airline security does not permit the transport of containers carrying more than 3 ounces of liquid, balm, or crème.

Every morning on the Southern Tier prior to beginning my daily ride, I would rub Bag Balm all over my saddle area and then I would put on my bib shorts followed by my regular biking shorts. About halfway through my daily ride I would reach down into my sweaty pants and lube up my saddle area again with another healthy dose of Bag Balm. Keeping your downtown area healthy is PARAMOUNT to your cross-country success. Do NOT underestimate or make light of the IMPORTANCE of maintaining a healthy saddle area!

In the shower each day, I would meticulously scrub my saddle area with soap and a wash cloth. One particular cross-country biking book I read described saddle sores as being similar to face acne in which a thorough cleansing each day prevents an outbreak. With that thought in mind, I was extremely diligent to get my saddle area sparkling clean every day! Clean, clean, clean! Of course, I was careful NOT to rub so hard as to irritate the skin on my saddle area.

It is also important for you to get your shower as soon as you possibly can each day. Every minute you delay causes your body to endure another minute in your sweaty, tight cycling shorts and exposes you to a greater risk of developing saddle sores! Get your bib shorts and biking shorts off as soon as possible, get into the shower, and get yourself clean and DRY as soon as possible! Do not delay!

After showering, I made sure my saddle area was SUPER DRY! Then, I used a special crème commonly regarded as the epitome of crème for cyclists. It is called "Chamois Butt'r" (pronounced "Shammy Butter"). Chamois Butt'r is a thick crème with a distinctive sweet-smelling odor. You can buy it at most bike stores or on eBay or Amazon. The crème is rather expensive, but is worth every penny!!! Do NOT get cheap on me here. Buy Chamois Butt'r and do NOT buy an imitation. This effective specialty cycling crème is THE BOMB! No, I do NOT own the manufacturing company for Chamois Butt'r nor am I a paid sponsor. The product simply works and you need to use it daily on your bike tour! Immediately after your shower, spread Chamois Butt'r all over your saddle area. Even consider laying around naked for a little bit to let the crème soak in and give your saddle area some additional "breathing" time.

Before going to bed, I had a nightly ritual. A towel would be laid on the floor and I would take my shorts off and lay naked on the towel. Then, I would grab my little bottle of "Anti-Monkey Butt" powder and coat my penis, balls, butt, and the rest of my saddle area front and back. Then, I would gently dress myself with boxer shorts and gym shorts and go to bed. The Anti-Monkey Butt powder gave me such a cooling effect! By morning, my saddle area felt fresh and alive! The time I dedicated to the middle section of my body was not time wasted!!!!

DAY 9: I could FEEL the POWER of the incredible desert landscapes!

Chapter 23: Injured Knees

About half the way through the 1,000-mile-long, seemingly endless state of Texas, my bike seat came loose and slightly moved on me. Not thinking much about it, I stopped pedaling, pulled over to the side of the road, grabbed the appropriate-sized Allen wrench, and tightened my bike seat back in place.

About 75 miles later, during the following day of biking, I noticed an unusual twinge on the outside of my right knee. Without giving much attention to the twinge, I pedaled through the pain as I typically ignore most bodily aggravations until they go away. But after pedaling through another 40 miles or so, the twinge of pain on my right knee escalated to a level of pain demanding a significant portion of my ongoing attention. After another 25 miles or so, I realized I was now dealing with a real disabling problem. Why is my knee hurting? What can I do about it?

How can I ride over 1,500 miles with absolutely no knee issues and then suddenly have knee pain strong enough to end my plight? As I continued along my route hurting more and more with each stroke of my pedal, I overcompensated the pedal force on my left leg as to try to minimize the force applied involving my right knee. As I struggled along thinking about a solution to my troubled knee dilemma, I remembered a book I read preceding my epic adventure in which the author indicated knee injuries are often a direct result of the positioning of your bike seat!

That's it! My seat! Instantly, I recalled two days earlier when my seat broke loose from its original position and I fixed it in a cursory manner, not really giving any thought to exactly how the seat was angled up and down or how far my seat was positioned toward the front or the back of my bike. Immediately, I got my Allen wrench out and re-adjusted my bike seat. Unfortunately, I couldn't quite remember exactly where the seat was originally positioned during my initial 1,500 miles of pain-free riding.

Over the course of the next three days, I kept making adjustments to my seat forward and backward, up and down, and to various angles. During this time of experimentation, my right knee worsened as I developed a noticeable limp when I got off of my bike and began to walk. To make matters even worse, my left knee also began to mirror the exact same symptoms as my right knee. The pain also began to extend down the shins of both of my legs making me MISERABLE as I pedaled my bicycle!

While staying at the Bastrop Inn in Bastrop, Texas, I walked over to Walmart and bought $40 worth of knee compression sleeves, knee braces, ace bandages, Icy Hot, and medical tape. The next day and the two following days, I used Bag Balm and lubed my knee area and then applied a base compression sleeve with a tight Velcro knee pad over top. For my shins, I wrapped an Ace bandage around both of them, taped them with medical tape, and then pulled my socks up as high as they would go as to cover part of the Ace bandage. Although I looked like a clown, the compression seemed to give me the relief I needed.

Here I am, a man in the middle of nowhere with 2 injured knees and 2 sore shins on a bicycle trying to figure out where the heck my stupid bike seat needs to be positioned in order for me to obtain the relief I so desperately needed! For many days, I KNEW the answer to my lower leg problems would be found in my bike seat, but I couldn't seem to figure out the EXACT correct positioning of my seat! For some reason, I kept thinking my seat needed to go backwards, but after two days of minimal results, I finally decided to move my seat forward as much as possible. Then, all of a sudden, I felt some RELIEF! The answer to my pain wasn't so much in the angle or height of my seat as much as it had to do with my seat being positioned closer toward the front of my bike! My discovery was paramount to my continued daily biking efforts. Without figuring out this simple seat adjustment, I definitely would NOT have been able to finish!

Once again, GOD was on my side as I needed a prompt seat solution. On the third day of wearing all the knee sleeves, knee pads, and ace bandages, I committed a MORTAL SIN. The skin on the back side of my right knee broke OPEN in two places. As a cyclist, you NEVER want your skin to break open!!!! Broken skin is like getting a ticket back to the nearest airport for a flight back home. Broken skin is often the END of a trip for a cyclist! Once again, the continuance of my mission was very questionable. At the very least, I KNEW I could no longer wear my lower leg supports as my broken skin would not allow it!

Luckily for me, the timing was perfect as the pain-relieving forward adjustment on my bike seat could not have come at a better time. With each passing day thereafter, my knees began to heal. And after four days, I could walk normal again without limping.

By moving my seat forward, it allowed me to use more of my LARGER leg muscles to exert each pedal stroke instead of relying on and OVER-USING my smaller leg muscles to make my pedal revolutions! Primarily using my quads and hamstrings to propel my bicycle down the road instead of stressing my smaller muscles and tendons on my lower legs was the key to my ongoing pursuit of my eventual finish at the Atlantic Ocean!

What a joy it was to solve this HUGE knee injury dilemma and figure out the solution on my own with the help of God through prayer. When my knees started to heal, I found myself riding in East Texas thinking, "Maybe...... Just maybe..... I MIGHT be able to finish?" This was the first time during my bike ride in which I briefly allowed myself to contemplate the real possible completion of the AMAZING Southern Tier Bike Route!

Chapter 24: Sponsorship

If I had my "Bike Across America" travels to do over, I would contact the United Way or another worthy organization and arrange some type of charitable affiliation. Maybe I could have raised some money for a good cause? Although I have little idea about exactly how raise money with charities, I do know for a fact that many people were really interested in my bike trip across the country and certainly a few people and several businesses would have gladly donated money toward a well-intentioned cause.

Maybe you could find some friends or family to make a sizable pledge on your behalf? Maybe you could make an arrangement where the donor agrees to pledge a certain amount of money IF you finish your bike journey? Making the pledge contingent on whether or not you finish might even give you a greater chance of completion. Maybe other donors would make a monetary contribution regardless of whether you finish or not?

When you mention to the average person about pedaling a bicycle across the nation, most people will give you a dumb stare. For most, riding a bicycle to the next town is incomprehensible, lead alone riding a bicycle across a state, or especially the unimaginable task of biking across a COUNTRY! When these aghast people realize you are not joking about your grand cycling plans, most will be interested in making at least a modest donation and maybe A LOT more.

The average person YEARNS to be a part of something really BIG and powerful! We all want to be a part of something great and SHARE in the glory! Maybe you could allocate half of the donations to go directly toward the charity of your choice and the other half to help you cover the various costs of your bike trip? As long as you fully disclose your plan and explain EXACTLY how the raised money will be allocated, many people and a lot of companies would be very interested in your respectable proposal!

You might even consider printing a short letter explaining your cross-country bike adventure. In your letter, explain about the opportunity for making donations toward your worthy cause. With a small amount of effort on your part, I'm sure your labors would bear fruit and result in significant monetary donations.

On Day 3 when I arrived in Brawley, California at the lone, local gas station at the edge of town, some man in an old beat-up car drove up beside me. Without saying a word, this guy dressed in grungy clothing looked at me and my bicycle and then handed me a one-dollar bill. After looking each other squarely in the eye, this old man drove away without saying a word. For the next week or so, I could not get this guy out of my mind! Several times EVERY DAY I would think about this mysterious guy and I would wonder why he gave me a dollar! Maybe the old man thought I was homeless or maybe I looked poor, but neither explanation really convinced me of the man's true intentions.

It wasn't until Day 8 in Mesa, Arizona while staying the night at Layne Gneiting's family home when Layne figured it all out for me. The old guy who gave me a dollar KNEW I was on the Southern Tier Bike Route and he admired what I was doing! In fact, the old man wanted desperately to somehow be a part of my adventure. So, to cement his relationship with me, he decided to GIVE me one dollar.

My guess is the old guy probably prayed and blessed the dollar before handing it off to me as this guy may have been one of the many angels sent to protect me and deliver me through my very dangerous and very scary cross-country excursion. Maybe this guy who handed the dollar bill over to me somehow knew more than I could ever imagine? Whatever the case, this strange, old man succeeded in making a connection with me and DEFINITELY became an IMPORTANT part of my journey! And it only took one dollar!!!

All throughout my bike crusade across the country, various strangers dropped their jaws in awe after asking me "Where are you going?" and me responding "Florida!" When I said, "Florida" while I was still biking in Arizona, people looked at me as if I was lying or just delusional. They would say, "Do you know how far away Florida is?" In California, I was so embarrassed about my cross-country undertaking, I actually LIED when people asked me where I was going! Instead of telling them "Florida," I would tell them I was riding my bike to whatever town was my projected daily destination for the day. It wasn't until Arizona when I hesitantly answered the question HONESTLY for the first time telling the particular stranger the TRUTH about my intentions of biking to Florida! Even when I told strangers I was pedaling to Florida, I still felt like a PHONY as I really didn't believe I would ever arrive at the salty waters of the Atlantic Ocean!

When strangers in New Mexico and Texas would inquire about my bike travels, I could see them doing mental calculations as they were sincerely intrigued as to how someone could actually travel 1,000 plus miles on a bicycle alone through the desert. Even with their great admiration of my sincere efforts, they would remind me "Florida is a LONG way away!"

When I got into Louisiana, Mississippi, and Alabama, inquiring people were AMAZED. Most people I met never before heard of someone pedaling a bicycle across the HUGE 1,000-mile-long state of Texas lead alone someone starting a bike trip at the Pacific Ocean in San Diego, California.

By the time I finally arrived in Florida, my bike journey was considered INCOMPREHENSIBLE by most people I met. In Florida, I literally felt like a ROCK STAR as strangers would hail me as some type of FAMOUS PERSON while they shook their heads in utter disbelief as most considered my bike travels to be IMPOSSIBLE.

One man outside of McDonalds in Quincy, Florida became so excited about my cross-country bike journey, he appeared to be close to having a convulsion. Upon hearing how many thousands of miles I had already pedaled my bicycle, he started NERVOUSLY reaching in his pockets frantically searching for his cell phone as if he only had seconds to capture this special moment. As he anxiously pulled out his phone, he began recording an impromptu interview with me on the sidewalk outside of McDonalds. This bizarre, hyper guy clearly had intentions of posting the interview with me all over social media as he clearly assumed I was some type of celebrity!

No matter what state I found myself, people were VERY INTERESTED in what I was doing. Upon seeing me and my "rig" pull into town, pure strangers wanted to know where I started biking and where I was going. Most of the people I met along the way were touched by my journey and I was touched by their truly caring remarks. The connections I made across this great country solidified my belief with regard to the United States and the many kind people residing in the great country! If I had some type of charity associated to my ride, I suspect many people I met along the way would have happily made a donation. Maybe I could have handed out letters or business cards to my new friends? Nonetheless, people were VERY interested in me and what I was doing!!!

Another possible idea I might consider if I had my trip to do over, would be a blog. Instead of sending out lots of separate texts and photos every day, it would have been much easier to create some type of internet blog for my loved ones to monitor and keep updated on my bicycle adventure. Posting daily photos, miles pedaled, and giving a brief caption of the day's events would have been be VERY INTERESTING for most.

My mother's close friend, Marie Jarabak, called my mom almost every day to get an update on me as she SHARED the excitement of my bike travels through daily conversations with my mom. Getting daily progress reports from my mom was exciting as Marie could sense the mounting anticipation as I inched closer to closing the gap on my epic accomplishment! My biking updates were often the HIGHLIGHT of Marie's day!

Most people have an adventurous side to them, but most people don't ever get off their couch and PURSUE a life-changing adventure! Almost EVERYONE loves adventure, but few are willing to chase after it! So, when someone like myself steps outside of the comfort zone and takes on a HUGE endeavor like pedaling a bicycle across the country, people pay attention! Your neighbors and family will YEARN to feel a part of your special adventure. Most of your loved ones would relish in the fact that they even know you and it would be an HONOR for them to track your progress across the country!

There is something special in the daily uncertainties of one man and his bike crossing the nation. My family still teases my mom as she spent nearly as much time following me on the LIFE 360 GPS phone app as I spent pedaling the epic

Southern Tier!!!! Every morning, my mom would open her eyes and within two minutes of becoming conscious to the new day, she would check her phone to see where I was and if my bicycle was moving. It was an adrenalin rush for her! To say she was interested in my trip would be an understatement! And on my last day, Day 43, the mounting anticipation of a possible cross-country finish gave most of my followers CHILLS!

Despite not having a blog or website for the public to share in my trials and tribulations of the Southern Tier, every day I would record a daily journal entry as a "DRAFT" on my email through my cell phone. After my epic cross-country journey, I transferred all of my emails to my computer journal and later to this book! You can read my 45 days of journal entries in the last chapter of this book!

DAY 9: Here is a popular Arizona biker bar in the middle of nowhere. The bikers were VERY impressed with me riding my bicycle all the way up the mountain pass on this 102-degree Fahrenheit afternoon!

Chapter 25: Divine Calling

Nine months prior to my epic, cross-country bike ride across America, I was jogging in Cancun, Mexico. It was late in January and a group of racing cyclists passed by me. Shortly after seeing the twenty or so cyclists pass me by, I was PASSIONATELY moved by a seemingly higher power to pursue my 28-year-old goal of pedaling a bicycle across the United States of America.

No, I didn't hear a voice from the Heavens, but I FELT the "calling" from head to toe. The emotion was PURE and SEVERE! There was NO QUESTION as to my upcoming MISSION. Although the MASSIVE rush of raw emotion was definitely enough to cement my divine calling, my upcoming mission was even further established as I glanced upward and saw a giant BILLBOARD with huge block letters that read "THE TIME IS NOW!" There was absolutely NO DOUBT in my heart, mind and soul! This was the year for me to pursue my longstanding cross-country biking dream! It was 100% solid! My time had come!

The inspiration came to me out of "nowhere." It was CLEARLY a power outside of myself. No, my "calling" was not an earthshaking movement that brought me to my knees nor did it involve blinding lights, but it was POWERFUL! There was no doubt! Although the nudge was gentle, the commanding feeling took over my thoughts as I KNEW my life was about to change. My calling was polite and cooperative, but it had a quiet sense of SUPREME power. The chills rushing through every hair follicle on my body commanded my attention. It was obvious I was being drawn toward something beyond myself, something BIG, something EPIC! It was during this particular early morning jog in Cancun, Mexico as the sun was rising up into the sky, I was clearly inspired and instructed to begin planning for my soon-to-be life-altering bike journey across America only 9 months later in the year.

Each day, my wife and I pray TOGETHER in the morning. Most of our prayers are not so much about what we want to happen or how to meet our own needs. We mostly pray for "God's will be done!" Tink and I believe God knows better than we do. We believe God has a special plan for our marriage as well as for each of us individually and for our beloved family members. During our prayers we frequently remind ourselves about how little we know as we RELEASE our upcoming days and weeks to the almighty. My wife and I live humble, simple lives. We believe we owe our next breath of air to our Lord God and we try to live well spending our time on worthwhile tasks as to expand God's glory.

Considering our frequent daily connection with God, for me to claim I was "moved" is NOT really an oddity. On many times prior, I had been "moved" or "called" to do various tasks. Although I have been MOVED to take on some very odd undertakings throughout my past, ALL of my divinely-prompted projects have proved to be nothing less than AMAZING!

A FEW of my various life callings include attending college in Tampa, Florida which was 1,000 miles away from my Pennsylvania home, quitting college after two successful years and opening a coffee stand despite having no prior business experience, writing my first book, Smashing the Wall of Fear, without having a traditional publisher, acquiring a large rental house portfolio starting with NO money, adopting 3 wonderful and precious children despite having no prior parenting experience, and completing 4 Ironman triathlons without initially knowing how to swim, being a poor runner, and being a weak cyclist.

All of these "callings" and many more unmentioned callings have turned out for the better for me! Each inspiration point in my life has been super-exciting and FULFILLING as I have never regretted doing any inspired task throughout my varied past!!! And I was not about to ignore my current calling to take on "The Southern Tier!" Being CALLED or being MOVED is like taking a drink of warm hot chocolate when you are freezing cold. It feels right!

Only a few days after my moment of inspiration while jogging in Cancun, I bought 10 cross-country cycling books. Over the next few months, I dedicated the necessary time to reading eight of those ten original books. As I read, I used a pen and made my notes. When I read a book, I CAPTURE the book by using every bit of useful information to take my life to the next level. With each paragraph I was carefully designing my own "adventure of a lifetime!"

After developing a basic knowledge base from the various books, I did a Google Search on the Internet and found several cross-country maps for sale. When my packet of Adventure Cycling Association maps of "The Southern Tier" arrived in the mail, my cross-country biking dream felt REAL as I now had in my possession an actual bicycle route to follow! No longer was it my "dream" to ride from coast to coast. Now, it is was an actual goal in which I was taking consistent daily ACTION toward achieving!

The old adage goes, "For everything, there is a season." and I knew my "season" was NOW! Significant life experiences cannot be forced. My inspiration was NATURALLY felt in my heart as I was "moved" to take on the challenge. After my spiritual connection with my newest divine calling on that early Cancun morning, riding my bicycle across the country became my new OBSESSION. There wasn't a single passing day I didn't think about my upcoming bike trip. Most days I thought about my upcoming adventure OFTEN! Biking across America was now MY PASSION! Despite being unqualified for a cross-country bike attempt, I felt like somewhere deep within my soul I had the resources necessary to pull off the mammoth undertaking! And as it turned out, I was right!!!

My story is not much different than the popular Biblical story of David and Goliath. David was a frail youngster who challenged the "unbeatable" and powerful giant, Goliath. Nobody thought David could win, except David himself. In unlikely fashion, David defeated the mighty Goliath. David's triumphant story proves if you truly have God's strong "calling" backing you, then you have ENOUGH! You don't need any additional support!

Being truly moved to do something significant is one of life's great honors! Feeling captivated to take on a task is an indication of God's grand expectations for your life. When you are called, you become an EXAMPLE of what is possible to others. Just take one step at a time while you pray daily and consistently correct your course of ACTION and you might surprise yourself, like I did! You can do it, but it won't be easy! Welcome to the Southern Tier!

DAY 10: As I was riding along, I met a kindred soul, Matthew Wentzell, whom was mountain biking with his friend all the way from the Canadian border to the Mexican border. Matt was scheduled to conclude his incredible 2,000-mile cycling journey in a few days!

Chapter 26: AAA

AAA members traveling on a bicycle can call AAA in an emergency 24 hours a day and AAA will send an affiliate out to your exact location to either make a quick repair to your bike or to pick up you and your bike and take you to the nearest repair shop. For a very reasonable annual fee, anyone can be a AAA member. With consideration to this one benefit alone, I highly advise you to take advantage of this valuable membership as it offers HUGE consolation, especially to a touring cyclist!

Although I did not use the valuable services of AAA on my cross-country bicycle travels, there was a time or two in which I came awful close to making the privileged call for help! AAA can literally be a lifesaver in some circumstances, but membership in AAA is mostly for your peace of mind. Simply Knowing I COULD call AAA in a bind, gave me a little bit of extra reassurance helping me to HANG IN THERE one more day at various points during my extensive bicycle travels. It was very comforting for me knowing a AAA representative was sitting at a desk 24 hours a day WAITING for my emergency call!

Another great advantage to AAA membership is the FREE state maps and FREE "Trip Tik" route maps which are available to all members. Having a traditional state map in addition to your paper Adventure Cycling route maps and Adventure Cycling's Bicycle Route Navigator phone app GPS map is probably a good idea as you never know what surprises you may encounter causing you to alter your plans. In all likelihood, there is a GOOD CHANCE you will experience one or more significant, unexpected detours along the way.

Although AAA maps are great, it is important for you as a touring cyclist to BUY your specific route maps from Adventure Cycling as their maps are MUCH BETTER and will guide you along the SAFEST bike route possible! In the case you are traveling by bicycle on a route NOT published by Adventure Cycling, then getting a AAA route map or "Trip Tik" is a good idea. In general, it is a good idea to have a state map with you for every state you plan to pass through during your bicycle tour. It is a great reference tool and you might really have a need for greater clarification on any possible changes you may need to make along your epic cycling route.

AAA maps are also great for your at-home support network. Each night, my father carefully mapped and noted on a AAA national map each of my daily destinations for every day of my bike trip across the country. Reviewing his notes on the national AAA map continues to bring back amazing cycling memories of a very special time in my life. It is exciting to follow dad's s marker lines all the way across the United States while relishing all the various daily destinations I called "home" for a particular night of my unforgettable cycling journey! Even to this day, I look at dad's map and shake my head in disbelief wondering how the heck I ever made it through!

Chapter 27: Chain Repair

If your bicycle chain breaks, it might end your travels for the day unless you have a small, spare 2-link connector piece to adapt to your bike chain. The tiny chain piece I'm referring to weighs less than 1 ounce, but can be the MVP of the day if you snap your chain! Make sure you get one of these 2-link chain connecting adapters even if you are like me and have never broken a bike chain in your life!

During my cross-country bike odyssey, the bicycle repair technician in Austin, Texas at Pedal Pushers advised me to replace my worn chain while he was repairing my broken wheel spoke. 3,000 miles is a long way. Lots of wear-and-tear will occur to your bike. It is a good idea to anticipate certain repairs, especially your chain. Being reasonably prepared decreases your chances of being stranded along the side of the desolate road!

While we are on the topic of chains, I'd like to recommend you to use a product called White Lightning to lubricate your chain. There are several good bike chain lubricants on the market, but there are also many products you should NOT apply to your precious chain. Make life easy on yourself and spend a few dollars more to buy the high-quality, name-brand White Lightning and you will be sure you are using a GOOD chain lubricant.

Lubricating your bike chain every 200 miles or so is probably a good idea. It's also a good idea to use a cloth and wipe off any excess lubricant from the outside of the chain as the excess will be a magnet for dust and general road crud. Lubricant is needed to keep your gears shifting smoothly and accurately. This crucial benefit alone is good reason for you to put proper attention on your bike chain!

DAY 10: What an awesome overnight camping location in the far corner of the Apache Grand Casino!

Chapter 28: Clean Clothes

Wearing foul-smelling, sweaty, nasty-dirty clothes day after day WILL negatively affect your attitude and may eventually end your trip. Dirty, yucky clothing could also trigger a nasty skin reaction and manifest into some type of skin infection like jock itch, MRSA, Impetigo, or some other bacterial infection! As you make daily progress on your bike, carefully consider your hygiene. Your hygiene choices could make or break your cross-country biking dream!

Several days on my cross-country expedition, I did not have a reasonable opportunity to clean my clothes properly. As a result, I was left wearing revolting, stinky clothes the next day. Wearing your previous day's clothes won't hurt you as long as you only do it on rare occasions, but don't make a habit of it! And NEVER wear the same clothes on a third day in a row no matter what! Each day, I made a diligent effort to clean my clothes THOROUGHLY! One way or another, I found a way to at least rinse out my sweaty clothes before wearing them the following day. Wash your clothes in a McDonalds sink if you have to! If nothing else, you will give the other bathroom users at McDonald's a story to tell their family at home!

Many days my biking clothes did NOT dry completely overnight before I had to put them back on again the next morning. There are few experiences less desirable than putting on wet clothes early on a chilly 45-degree Fahrenheit morning, but despite the unpleasantry, it is much better to wear wet, CLEAN clothes than it is to wear dry, foul, dirty clothes from the previous day!

If you can get a shower, then you should have clean clothes. All across the country I took my dirty clothes into the shower with me. As a part of my regular shower routine, I would jam my socks partially down the drain of the tub in a manner causing the tub to fill up with water. As the water level rose above the level of my clothes, I would add shampoo or whatever type of soap I could find and then I would wash my clothes with my bare hands. The water would turn dirty brown as a testament to my quality washing job!

As I completed the washing of ALL of my sweaty clothing items, I would drain the muddy, dirty water from the tub and begin "the rinse cycle." With nice, clean water I rinsed all of my clothes squeezing each piece of clothing making sure all the soap and shampoo was removed. Afterward, I twisted each piece of my clothing as tight as possible until at least 80% of the excess water was removed from the fabric. Then, it was just a matter of drying my clothes.

Sometimes, I would hang my clothes from a tree to dry. Many times, I hung my clothes from my bike or on a fence or anywhere the sun could work its magic! In the cases where the sun was blocked by the clouds or it was dark, I would use the heater or fan in my motel room or simply hang the wet clothes on the inside of my tent. If I was in a motel with a hair dryer, I used it! Drying your clothes is NOT essential, but putting on dry clothes the following morning is much more pleasant than the WET alternative!

Only four times during my 43 days on the Southern Tier did I use an actual washing machine and dryer to clean my clothes. Despite lacking the modern conveniences of home, I enjoyed clean clothes for about 37 of my 43 days on the road. If you are ever left having to prioritize what clothes you will clean, then I suggest you ALWAYS clean your bib shorts as your bib shorts actually contact your PRECIOUS saddle-skin area. While on a cross-country bicycle ride, there exists no other portion of skin on your body even half as important as your saddle-skin area! If your saddle-skin area becomes irritated, you could become MISERABLE very easily and your special pedal adventure could end ABRUPTLY!

DAY 11: Another POWERFUL sunrise!

Chapter 29: Clean Body

Some nights on the Southern Tier, I took what I call a "Gatorade bottle shower." A Gatorade bottle shower is when you fill up your empty Gatorade bottle with water, dump the water over your head, lather up with soap and shampoo from top to bottom, and then dump an additional Gatorade bottle of water over your head and body until you are adequately rinsed. In most cases, the water I used was COLD as finding hot water at times was impossible.

Only five nights out of my 42 overnight stays did I have to resort to a "Man Shower." A "Man Shower" is a big wipe designed to clean your entire body. When using a "Man Shower" or "bathing wipe," you might want to consider the order in which you clean your body parts! I always used the bathing wipe on my face first and then my saddle area second as I regarded my saddle-area skin to be the most important skin area on my body. Next, I would use the "man wipe" to clean my upper body, lower body, my feet, my butt cheeks, and then finally, my BUTT CRACK!

When possible, I always opted for a nice warm shower, but some days you have to take what you can get. With the exception of Day 1 when I experienced undue duress, I did NOT skip cleaning my body on a DAILY BASIS, even if it meant using only "man wipes!" Keeping yourself clean is PARAMOUNT to a healthy mind and body which translates down to a potentially successful bicycle journey!

DAY 12: The Southern Tier landscape is more than INCREDIBLE!

Chapter 30: Costs

Riding your bicycle across America or any other country on our amazing planet Earth will cost you money! For 43 days from October 10, 2020 to November 21, 2020, I spent a lot more money than I would have spent had I not embarked on my crazy cross-country bicycle adventure. Below is a breakdown of my expenses:

$100	One-way flight to San Diego to start of my journey.
$100	Cost to transport my bike and one checked-in piece of luggage on the airplane
$70	Paper Route Maps (Adventure Cycling – Southern Tier)
$60	GPS Phone App Route Map (Adventure Cycling – Southern Tier)
$200	Amtrak Train ride home (Jacksonville, FL to Johnstown, PA)
$50	Amtrak costs to transport my bike and pannier bags
$900	15 Cheap hotels (an average of $55 per night)
$300	15 Cheap campgrounds (an average of $20 per night)
$100	Bike Repairs (2 general "tune-ups")
$150	Two new road-bike tires (road tires only last 2,000 miles)
$50	A new bike chain
$430	Extra food ($10 per day more than normal to sustain my high caloric requirements)
$301	Extra drinks ($7 per day more than normal to sustain my high caloric requirements)

$2,811 TOTAL

Most of my food was purchased at McDonalds, Burger King, Subway, Walmart, Dollar General, and Family Dollar. Some days I would splurge and eat at a moderately priced restaurant for lunch or supper, but most days saving money was at the top of my mind. My mission was to eat much like our son, Sean Thomas, as his eating plan while he lived in the high cost-of-living area in downtown San Diego was to get his stomach full for as little cost as possible. Sean Thomas' eating philosophy was an inspiration to me!

Even if you were NOT on a bike tour, you would still have to eat and your food would undoubtedly cost money. So, it is NOT fair to attach your entire food bill to your cross-country bike adventure. In my case, it seemed appropriate for me to allocate an extra $10 per day to my above Southern Tier expenses for "extra food" and $7 per day for "extra drinks." When not on a bike tour, I could probably feed myself for $10 per day, but while riding the Southern Tier, it cost me about $27 per day to maintain the excessive calories needed to sustain my 70 mile a day habit. It takes a massive amount of food and drink to sustain enough energy to replenish the 5,000 plus calories you will burn daily as you pedal seven hours a day. While pedaling the Southern Tier, your food and drink costs will probably be slightly more than double your normal at-home food costs.

Certain expenses were intentionally omitted from the above list as I felt they were not actual specific costs of my particular Southern Tier journey. The costs of my bike and my necessary bike touring accessories were NOT included as an expense for my cross-country adventure as I have used my bike and gear before and after my Southern Tier adventure! In short, they were NOT Southern Tier specific! Nonetheless, here are the costs of my bike and accessories as they were back in 2020:

$800   Bike (I purchased a new bike from www.BikesDirect.com) Buy a heavy-duty road touring bike!!! Don't buy a "gravel bike." Buying your bike from your local bike shop is probably the BEST idea!!!
$200   Pedals and Shoes (Buy from your local bike shop.)
$50   Bike assembly (Hire your local bike shop.)
$400   4 Arkel Pannier bags (2 front and 2 rear)
$50   Handlebar bag (I bought a cheap non-waterproof handlebar bag from eBay, but you might want to check with Arkel and get something better and something waterproof.)
$100   Brooks Flyer seat (eBay)
$250   Biking padded bib shorts, biking padded shorts, biking shirts, and a lightweight rain coat
$100   Anker battery power bank (to recharge your phone, lights, watch, etc.)
$200   Raingear (tops and bottoms, medium-weight)
$100   Helmet with attaching brim hat (bright yellow)
$200   Bike accessories (headlight, taillight, phone handlebar mount, bike repair tools, spare tubes, chain lube, etc.)

$2,450   TOTAL (Bike and necessary touring equipment)

If you add up the TOTAL costs listed above, you come up with a grand total cost of $5,161.00. This is exactly what I spent for everything I needed for my special bike ride back in 2020. By the time you read this book, the costs will be significantly HIGHER. By 2025, it will cost you about $8,000.00 or more. Even if you are CHEAPER than me, a cross-country bike trip poses a significant cost. Doing a major bike tour by yourself without signing up for an expensive group ride with a cycling company will save you lots of money, but the trip will be MUCH MORE DIFFICULT and possibly less enjoyable!

There is nothing wrong with taking a cross-country bike adventure with an experienced bicycle touring company!!!! You don't have to be as extreme as me and try to do a cross-country bike tour all alone! Group cycling can be AMAZING, but there is <u>NOTHING</u> like a SOLO ride!

Taking an epic journey with a legitimate national organization like Adventure

Cycling would cost you about $14,000.00 or more to participate in their 60-day Southern Tier cross-country tour. Other groups have similar tours across the country with varying prices and varying optional perks. Most of these organizations provide an opportunity for a LIFE-CHANGING experience!!! The cost is SMALL compared to the life-changing benefits you will receive from the adventure of a LIEFTIME!!!

Another idea is to include all or a portion of the costs of your trip into the money raised for your trip. It makes perfect sense to fund your expenses from the money you raise for whatever charity(s) you partner with. If you really put in the effort and get sponsors and donors, you might be able to make your cross-country cycling dream come true with ZERO dollars out of your pocket!

Although I am NOT an expert on fundraising, common sense coupled with FULL disclosure should help you to raise significant money for your expenses and have plenty of funds left over to make a healthy contribution to a worthy cause or charity!

DAY 12: The desert is NOT all flat!

Chapter 31: Resting

On Day 2, I struggled pedaling up what seemed like an endless uphill coming out of the San Diego, California vicinity and heading into the desert expanse. Looking ahead as far as I could see, I wondered if the next turn might mark the end of this crushing ascent! To my disappointment, the next turn merely provided another view of more uphill and a new turn far off in the distance with no downhill in sight! It was Day 2 when my mind was at its WEAKEST point of my entire trip. Day 2 was when the devil made his best attempt to prompt me to turn my bicycle around and ride a HUGE downhill directly back into San Diego and take an airplane back home to Pittsburgh.

As I stopped to take one of my regular breaks, I considered the mere 50 to 60 total miles I had accumulated so far and how bad I was feeling. Being a "math guy," my mind instantly started doing calculations regarding distance, time, and effort exerted. It wasn't long until I realized my scheduled 3,000-mile cross-country bike trip was a BAD IDEA! As I pounded some Gatorade alongside the lonely road, tears formulated in my eyes and dripped down my cheeks as I considered another major LOSS in my life.

In that moment of utter despair, it was clear to me only a few miles outside of San Diego that I was NOT completing my special bike journey! I QUIT!!!! The terrain was TOO TOUGH and I was TOO WEAK mentally. Considering all the effort and time exerted planning this once-in-lifetime excursion, it was gut-wrenching to feel my dream slip away so easily! As I sulked in my misery, I couldn't help but think, "Wasn't the southern part of the United States supposed to be FLAT?"

As I processed my pending EPIC FAILURE, I contemplated turning around and immediately going back to the airport, but instead I decided to ride as far as I could on this disappointing final day and then find my way back to the airport tomorrow. Dejected, I got back on my bike and went slower than ever as I sulked in my most recent life FAILURE. No longer did I even have a fleeting thought about arriving at my planned destination at the sunny shores of the Atlantic Ocean on the Florida coast. My new goal was simply to make it to tonight's destination point in the Yuha Desert in Ocotillo, California.

Seemingly endless hills can quickly contaminate your thoughts and promptly send you back home feeling embarrassed you even considered such a RIDICULOUS cross-country cycling pursuit! Pedaling your bicycle across America............ Who are you kidding? Hills, mountains, upgrades, ascents, elevation gains, or whatever you call them, play a huge part in your biking journey as they seem to affect your mind and quickly trigger harsh negative decisions. If the ascent is long enough, you could be surrendering your special biking dream before you even reach the first significant summit.

Many cyclists consider uphill travel as a necessary evil of the cycling sport. Ascending an incline can be very challenging. Your quads can burn. You may feel out of breath. You could be overheating or even feeling faint. Therefore, it is no surprise pedaling up a long ascending grade can be burdensome, but it doesn't have to be that way!

By the end of my Southern Tier bike travels, I developed some significant overall success with regard to processing elevation gains. No, I'm NOT a champion cyclist capable of competing in the Tour de France, but upon completing the Southern Tier, I was able to OUTLAST almost any upgrade and keep a pleasing attitude while doing so! Instead of worrying about the upcoming climb, I have actually trained myself to LOOK FORWARD to it! As I write these pages, I can actually say with complete certainty that uphill is now my favorite aspect of cycling!

Having this newfound love for ascending hills and pedal-climbing mountains has the most to do with an unlikely strategy I developed on the Southern Tier involving REST. Unlike most cyclists who are "killing" themselves with EXTREME uphill efforts, I am focused on RESTING while pedaling uphill. My goal is contrary to most as I aim to arrive at the summit in BETTER condition and with more energy than I had at the base of the mountain!

Resting on the hills is not as difficult as it sounds. Resting involves mostly your thoughts and breathing much more than the actual physical act! Having the proper mindset coupled with a calm, consistent breathing rhythm during the climb can be INVIRGORATING with some diligent implementation!

Resting during a climb involves monitoring your exertion level as to make sure you can still maintain regular breathing. If you are performing this resting technique properly, then you should be able to maintain a conversation as you ascend the uphill. If you have no riding partner to converse, then you should be able to breathe in and out through your NOSE without using your mouth.

Many years ago, I briefly studied the Eastern tradition of Ayurveda which has also been used by many successful high-level athletes worldwide throughout many previous decades. During my Ayurvedic training, I learned that the human body can sustain itself for extremely long distances when the mind and body are in the CORRECT RHYTHM with each other.

One of the Ayurvedic techniques I learned during my studies had to do with REST, COMFORT, and BALANCE. Using the Rest-Comfort-Balance strategy during my athletic endeavors has allowed me to maintain my strength and overall energy permitting me to perform much longer and more effectively than another comparable athlete who overexerts himself and is "out of breath." With Ayurveda, the plan is to fuel yourself AS YOU CLIMB the mountain. You are to feel your BEST when you reach the top of the mountain!

As I pedaled the 14.1-mile eastbound climb through the Black Mountain Range in New Mexico toward the 8,228-foot summit at Emory's Pass, I kept reviewing each of the three Ayurvedic indicators of REST, COMFORT, and BALANCE. As I was pedaling, I would concentrate on the word "REST" while analyzing my entire body and mind to make sure that I was indeed resting despite the fact I was pedaling uphill tackling a formidable mountain ascent!

After I made sure I was indeed resting, I would then concentrate on the word "COMFORT" as I examined my body to make sure all of my body parts were relaxed and feeling good. It was important not to overexert myself in any way as to feel PAIN! If I started to feel pain, I would go even SLOWER!

Finally, I would focus on the word "BALANCE" as I made sure I was in good physical biking position and my mind was centered and at ease without any stressful expectations or hasty inclinations. Everything physically and mentally had to be SOLID and STABLE as per my governing strategy of REST, COMFORT, and BALANCE. Nothing in my mind or body were permitted to operate outside of my locus of control as to pose any type of imbalance risk.

After analyzing my thoughts and my form, I would repeat my key trigger word "CALM" over and over as a mantra. For over 25 years I have used the word "CALM" repeatedly in my morning meditation as a way to maintain my self-composure throughout my very stressful work career buying, renovating, and leasing houses and apartments. Repeating "CALM" over and over directed my body and mind to maintain a constant state of equilibrium which translated into the LEAST possible expenditure of effort needed to summit New Mexico's Emory's Pass!

With the addition of ample food and drink, the revolutionary REST, COMFORT, and BALANCE principle will provide rather astounding results as you refine this transforming technique over time! Applying a genuine effort with this special Ayurvedic method will help you to excel at times when your previous unstable mind and past imbalanced body may have let you down. Repeating "Rest, Comfort, Balance" over and over will train your body and mind to be CALM and conserve your energies during difficult times when it is easy to lose your composure and WASTE your precious energy!

Although the Rest, Comfort, Balance technique is beneficial, it is NOT magical. Hills and mountains will still seem wicked tough at times, but there is a HUGE difference in your overall energy supply and your positive mindset when you are calmly resting all the way to the summit! Even as I write these words, I admit my advice sounds suspect, but I urge you to give it a whole-hearted try and you might be surprised as I have been! Maybe you'll be like me and discover the human mind and body is capable of much more than we currently realize! Much of our success and failure in life have more to do with our mental perspective than the actual physical challenge at hand. Focusing on REST-COMFORT-BALANCE might be the missing piece to your uphill puzzle!

As you are pedaling, it is important to keep your speed SLOW. The only way to really make the REST – COMFORT – BALANCE technique your own is to go SUPER SLOW, especially at first! Remember, you must be able to talk regularly and breathe normally through your nose while pedaling in order to gain mastery of this profound procedure. As you are pedaling uphill, alternate between the seated position and the standing position at reasonable intervals. With every pedal stroke, use as little effort as possible to maintain your cadence while monitoring yourself to make sure you are still resting. There should be no stress or hurry in your cadence. It's not about the time it takes. It's all about the FEELING of bodily control that really matters!

What truly matters is how you FEEL while ascending the mountain. If you maintain a feeling of REST for the entire ascent, then you have just mastered a HUGE problem which has plagued cyclists for decades! As you gain more cycling experience and greater discipline into the Ayurvedic tradition of Rest, Comfort, and Balance, you will GAIN speed on hills without any additional conscious effort. For now, just maintain your overall calm balance and keep resting with every pedal stroke uphill! Remember, you want to feel your BEST at the crest of the mountain top!

After about 21 days on my epic bike trip, I discovered my mind was stabilizing and my legs were like iron! Hills that once troubled me were now easy. Approaching an incline became an anticipated pleasure as my 3 weeks of "training" were now paying BIG benefits in my overall mental and physical performance thanks to the very old REST-COMFORT-BALANCE principle!

Overly exerting yourself during long-distance endurance activities like riding your bike across the country is COUNTERPRODUCTIVE! Stressing your mind and over-taxing your body parts will result in instability, illness, and injury. Only with a calm and stable mind and body will you position yourself to have the best chance of overcoming the odds and completing a very challenging cross-country bike ride.

If you want to greatly increase your chances of completing a cross-country bicycle ride, then you might want to reconsider exactly how you view uphill climbs. Are those hills in the distance a chance for you to rest and increase your energy reserve or do you already DREAD the thought of your upcoming, exhausting climb? The relevance of this particular chapter is so mysterious and profound, I have included an ADDITIONAL chapter later in this book also dedicated to the phenomenal REST–COMFORT–BALANCE biking strategy!

Chapter 32: Dashboard

The dashboard or "dash" is the area on a bicycle spanning across the handlebars. It is the prime area for attaching very important touring bike equipment. On my dash was a waterproof phone holder, a BLAZE rechargeable headlight, and my handlebar bag. A horn or some other type of loud sounding device SHOULD have also been a part of my dash, but I foolishly neglected to do so! There will be more about the importance of having a proper sounding device in an upcoming chapter.

For the first 3 weeks of my cross-country ride, I also had a Garmin GPS odometer mounted on my dash until I finally decided to remove it. For the most part, it just got in the way. Instead, I used my Garmin Fenix wrist watch as it had a much longer battery life and it didn't unnecessarily clutter my dash.

My waterproof phone holder was great as long as the holder wasn't disconnecting itself and falling to the road below! No less than 8 times did my phone and holder detach from its mounting piece and take impact with the ground during my many biking miles. It wasn't until over halfway through my bike travels when I finally got smart and super-glued the phone holder to the mounting band! From that point on, my phone stayed put inside the waterproof casing and never detached itself again! Super-glueing my phone case to the mounting strap in no way caused me any type of inconvenience or disruption as I remained able to easily take my phone out of the holder whenever necessary, but having to use glue speaks volumes about the inadequacy of the original piece of equipment!

My BLAZE rechargeable headlight got LOTS of use as I estimate I traveled about 60 hours of my bicycle adventure in complete darkness! The most I traveled in the dark during any one given day was about 3 hours. While using the recommended middle setting, my BLAZE headlight provided me with ample light for about 2 hours. Using the splendid headlight on the highest, most-bright setting would only last me about 1 hour or so.

My biggest complaint with the BLAZE headlight was its inability to operate while I was actively recharging it with my Anker power bank, which I stored in my small handlebar bag. Although it was annoying having to un-attach my BLAZE headlight and put it into my handlebar bag to recharge, it was not a big deal as I simply and quickly attached my back-up BLAZE headlight to light the way while my primary BLAZE headlight was recharging! Having a spare headlight was MANDATORY considering the extensive time I spent pedaling in the DARK!

After experimenting with several different handlebar bags prior to my epic journey, I settled on a generic handlebar bag with three simple Velcro straps used to anchor it to my dash. The cheap $10 handlebar bag sagged just enough as to barely give my BLAZE headlight enough space to illuminate the road ahead without any interference. My handlebar bag was small and only fit my Anker Power Bank and my camera.

It would have been nice to have a bigger handlebar bag, but I traveled so much in the dark, it was vital for me to give the proper operation of my headlight preference over a larger handlebar bag! In the future, I might consider getting a bigger, waterproof handlebar bag and adjusting my headlight in a way as to continue to provide proper lighting. Surely, there must be a reasonable way to get a much better handlebar bag than mine while still having plenty of room to mount a nice bright headlight, even if I must install some type of extension piece to allow my headlight to shine over the top of my handlebar bag!

On the top of my handlebar bag is a clear plastic map holder. If you are anything like me, you will reference your paper map OFTEN during the day as you are relying on this piece of paper to get you to your daily destination! The only problem is when it is raining. In preparation for upcoming rain, you will have to store your paper map into a Ziploc bag as my map holder was not waterproof. If you buy a better-quality handlebar bag, then you will likely have an adequately-sized WATERPROOF map holder securely attached to the top. Depending on the quality of your handlebar bag, you might also have to use a chip clip or some type of paper clip to attach your paper map as to prevent a potential loss.

DAY 12: I stayed in this exquisite courtyard at the Simpson Hotel in Duncan, Arizona.

Chapter 33: Reading

Your willingness to read about 8 books prior to the commencement of your epic bike travels is a crucial early determinant as to whether or not you are even worthy of taking the first pedal stroke of your special cross-country bicycle feat. Without a prior knowledge base of at least 8 good cross-country cycling books, you are starting your adventure with a HUGE handicap!

When you read a book, you are acquiring the mind of the author. Even a small book, unlike the one you are reading now, takes hundreds of hours of work by the author. In most cases, it takes more time to write the book than it does to pedal across the country as was definitely the case with me! Caring authors like myself try to share as much useful knowledge as possible with you, the reader. For me, it is my CALLING to share with you the maximum critical biking information as possible as to give you the BEST chance at success. Even at the risk of some of the enclosed information being embarrassing or too personal, I still included it if I felt you could benefit from reading it!

Reading 8 books was one of the key components which allowed me to prepare my mind for the challenges ahead. Without reading these books, my already low chances of finishing would have been much lower yet. Carefully choosing the books you read is also very important. Is the book a bestseller? Who recommends the book? Who is the author? What do the reviews say? Does Adventure Cycling Association sell the book? Buying about 12 books is probably a good idea as a few of the books you buy will NOT spark your interest. If a book does not pique your interest within the first chapter, then discard it! Life is too short spending time reading BORING books! Start reading the most interesting books and then continue down the line from there. Never read a bad book!

As you read the first chapter, you will KNOW if a particular book is meant for you or not. If you don't even like chapter one, then you won't like the book! In this case, put the book aside and grab your next choice. Do NOT waste your time reading a book in which chapter one didn't even grab your attention! There are too many truly awesome books on the market for you to waste your time reading something that doesn't align with your particular rhythm!

As I read a book, I ALWAYS have a pen in my hand. While I'm reading a book, I mark especially powerful sentences and ideas. Marking the book as I read it allows me to quickly review the key points of the book at a later time and date. And every time I review key information, the closer the information becomes to being my own! After a certain number of reviews, I OWN the information as it is now firmly established in my mind and my thought pattern. Every bit of knowledge you cram into your mind is another bit of wealth NO ONE could ever take from you. Once you own a piece of knowledge, it is yours forever! Especially during challenging times on the Southern Tier, you will draw on specific knowledge as your particular scenario calls for it!

During my epic bike travels, I recalled one author whom advised starting early each morning as to get at least half of the planned daily biking mileage completed by noon or else it would be unlikely to meet the daily mileage goal. As it turned out, the author was correct! Another author advised cross-country cyclists to stop every 10 miles and walk. This bit of simple and profound advice also gave me huge benefits and saved me on more than one day!

Focusing on your daily destination instead of your ultimate trip destination may have been the most valuable piece of advice I read from other cross-country cyclist authors. Without this tidbit of advice, I would have certainly failed! Only by concentrating on my DAILY destination was I able to hang in the "game" long enough to finish the grueling Southern Tier!

Find a quiet, well-lit place in a comfortable chair and put your full attention on your book. Reading is a LEVEL A use of your time. If you had to choose between an extra ten hours of cycling time or the reading of one additional book, then you might want to choose the book, especially if you have not already read at least 8 books! Reading is CRUCIAL to your cross-country cycling success!!!!

Believe me, as you are riding your bike countless miles across the country, you will recall many passages from the books you read. Just at the right time, you will remember how the author handled a particular problem when his spoke broke or what the author did to get back on course after being lost! It is startling how just the right book memories seem to appear during your most appropriate biking struggles. Reading is MANDATORY!

Review the books in Adventure Cycling's CYCLOSOURCE magazine and search eBay or Amazon for "cross-country bicycle books." Ask your local bike store for recommendations. Buy a bunch of books and then make the BIG INVESTMENT to actually read them! This level of mental preparation will do more for your possible future cross-country finish than physically training an extra half hour a day!

Chapter 34: Naps

Ever since I was 14 years old in 9th grade at Richland High School in Johnstown, Pennsylvania, I took regular naps in the afternoon. All through high school, I would lay my head down on my desk during my afternoon study hall and actually fall asleep. For me, naps were a big part of my days as they left me feeling refreshed and well-prepared to face the second half of my days. Even today, more than 30 years later, I take a regular nap shortly after lunch almost every day.

Even with an established long-term napping habit, I couldn't find a reasonable way to incorporate regular naps into my Southern Tier excursion. Prior to my epic trip, I imagined taking a nice nap at lunch in the shade next to my bike, but only once did I take a nap at any rest stop during my daily 7 hours of pedaling time on the Southern Tier. And only a few times did I manage to nap upon arrival at my various daily destinations early in the afternoon.

If you are an even more committed napper than me, then you can probably find a good spot each afternoon to get a quick nap, but for most of you reading this chapter, don't expect to get too many naps. Traveling unfamiliar roads in unaccustomed areas of the country alone and unsupported didn't quite breed a prime napping atmosphere for me. Maybe if I had someone riding with me or if I had a support van following me, then I might have been relaxed enough to consider a nap, but I had none of those luxuries and therefore, regular naps were NOT happening for me!

Changing some of your regular day-to-day habits is something you will have to get used to as you pursue your cross-country cycling dream. For me, operating without my daily naps was NOT easy! At noon my body was yearning for a nap, but it wasn't happening! After a couple weeks, my body and mind adjusted and a new life pattern emerged which extended throughout the terminus of the Southern Tier until such time I got back home and resumed my regular nap regime.

Waking up early each morning is paramount to my success in life. Those first few early morning hours of my day allow me get a great start before anybody else is around me and before my phone starts ringing. Early morning is probably the most productive time of my day. As a "morning person," it makes perfect sense for me to take an hour nap around lunch time to break up my day and recharge my battery! Others, like my wife, would rather sleep an extra hour in the morning and skip the afternoon nap, but my bodily rhythms do much better with an hour nap after lunch! Listening to your own body rhythms is probably my best advice to you.

Chapter 35: 2nd Set of Paper Maps

Having a full set of paper maps along with your GPS phone app map are essential as you navigate across the country on your bicycle. Without a good map, I don't know how you would do it! Maps guide you across the country! There are no signs on the roads reading "Southern Tier Bike Route...... Turn Here." Although a good primary set of paper maps combined with an amazing GPS phone app map like Bicycle Route Navigator is necessary, I would also recommend you buy a second set of paper maps to leave with someone back home.

Being a cheapskate, I was NOT willing to spend the extra money and buy two sets of paper maps. Instead, I foolishly WASTED many hours of my valuable time taking cell phone photos of the entire 118 Southern Tier individual map pages and then printing each of the maps, elevation charts, accommodation listings, etc. for my dad to use while I was away on my bike trip. After spending about 10 hours of my valuable time tediously compiling my own homemade cheesy set of paper maps for my dad, it suddenly occurred to me....... I just accepted a $5 per hour job!!! For about $50 or so, I could have bought a much higher quality second set of paper maps without all the wasted time and effort! How stupid of me!!!

Although I wasted lots of time giving my father a set of very tacky, unprofessional paper maps which were cut off at various places, hard to read, and illogically organized, I still managed to receive a significant benefit from my newly found low-paying "job." Having a phone photo of each page of my Southern Tier map gave me additional peace of mind in the case my paper maps were somehow lost, stolen, damaged, or destroyed during my biking efforts. In the worst-case scenario, I still had a photo of each of the 118 little Southern Tier maps stored on my phone for easy potential reference. When it comes to maps, having a plan A, plan B, plan C, and plan D is smart!

When a key loved one back home has a paper copy of your biking route maps, it makes the whole cross-country biking process easier on you, the cyclist. Each day my father would give me a preview of the challenges awaiting me the next day. My dad informed me of the elevation, the weather, the type of roads, the wind direction, and possible overnight accommodations. My dad was like my own private logistical travel consultant! Many days he pointed out dangers and ideas which often proved to be very valuable during my bike travels. Benefitting from dad's FREE travel service was a nice fringe benefit on my bike adventure! Having a full set of paper maps, even if they were CHEESY, allowed my father to work on my behalf in a way he otherwise would have had great difficulty.

In addition to using my copied Adventure Cycling Southern Tier maps, my father also acquired a free AAA map of the USA in which he charted each day of my trip. By using a marker, he noted my route and with a pen he scribed exactly where I stayed each night. Looking back at his maps after the completion of my bike adventure was quite gratifying. Remembering the many small towns and desolate roads traveled made my special achievement that much sweeter!

Chapter 36: Bike Fall

As an extremely conservative person, I am VERY careful NOT to exaggerate. When you read my words "ALWAYS" and "NEVER," I mean always or never! If an event happened even one time, then I would NOT say the word "never." So, with that disclaimer out of the way, I hereby make the following statement. Throughout my entire 43-day demanding bicycle adventure along the Southern Tier, my bicycle NEVER fell to the ground! Even amidst the harsh desert winds of the southwest, not once did my bike crash to the ground! If my kickstand wasn't sturdy enough to properly stabilize my bike, then I would make good use of the guardrail, fencing, or the side of a building to ensure my bike remained UPRIGHT at all times!

Attempting a solo, unsupported, and continuous cross-country bicycle adventure may be one of the hardest tasks you ever face. There isn't anybody else in your immediate vicinity. It's just YOU and YOUR BIKE! All of your belongings are either attached to you or attached to your bike. As your taxing journey evolves day by day, your bicycle becomes more and more a part of YOU! As the days go by, your bike becomes more and more alive. By fostering the proper healthy thoughts, you might even be able to FEEL the energy of your bike! After the first 1,000 miles or so of my bicycle travels, I seemed to have developed a great sense of LOVE for my bike as we continued to overcome dozens of regular setbacks to arrive at our various daily destination points TOGETHER!

Just like anything you truly LOVE, your bond with your bicycle is VERY fragile and can be broken easily if you are not careful. Perhaps the easiest way to sever your connection with you bike is to allow your bike to fall to the ground! Falling to the ground is symbolic of FAILURE and might affect your mental state more than you might initially realize! As you read and chuckle at my "ridiculous" claims, you will remember my words the first time your bike falls over during an epic ride! It will AFFECT you!

It wasn't until the wind suddenly picked up as I was pacing the berm of the road near the eastern end of New Mexico when I first realized I was FALLING IN LOVE with my bicycle! Feeling the swift gust of the powerful easterly wind blowing into my face instantly alerted me to the pending risk of my bike being blown over. Frantically, I SPRINTED over to my bike parked alongside the road with only a kickstand keeping it upright. In utter desperation I aggressively grabbed hold of my bike and carefully moved it to a more secure location leaning it securely on the guardrails before it was blown over by the fierce winds.

In most cases, bikes fall to the ground because they were parked using their kickstands on unstable ground. Wobbly ground usually causes your kickstand to slowly sink further and further into the dirt until the angle of your bike becomes too severe and results in your bike collapsing to the ground. With a fully loaded touring bike, the chances of this type of crash happening are much greater than usual by considering the heavy added weight of the pannier bags, extra water, etc.

If your precious bike crashes to the ground, it WILL disturb you! A physical collapsing of your bike may trigger a simultaneous mental "crash" within your mind. And when you crash mentally, the completion of your trip is suddenly at risk! Although your bike can be damaged by falling to the ground, the worst damage from a fallen bicycle occurs within your own mind and within your own spirit. To my surprise, I discovered there was something sacred about taking excellent care of my bike at every moment of my extended trip. Keeping my bike upright was a mandatory commitment of mine! If my bike had fallen to the ground even once, it would have been a MORTAL SIN!!!!

Each time I would stop alongside the road or at a store, I would carefully locate a solid level area where my kickstand would easily support the weight of my bike. Sometimes I would even place a rock, piece of wood, or any other roadside object under my kickstand as to give it the perfect solid balance. Other times when I was not alongside the berm of the road, I would carefully lean my bike against a building or structure in a way as to prevent any strong wind from potentially blowing my bike to the ground.

Each time I stopped alongside the road, I found a solid area of ground firm enough NOT to sink my kickstand. Even after finding this ideal solid piece of ground, I made sure the angle at which my bike was tilting as it rested on the kickstand was PERFECT! Finally, I would turn my handlebars one direction or the other as to displace the exact remaining amount of weight exactly where needed as to counterbalance the overall weight and ensure my bike had the BEST chance of remaining upright. During this whole process, I retained a really good hold on my bike making sure there was NOT any mishaps!

One of the biggest potential "mishaps" you will encounter along any major bike route are the abundant 18-wheel tractor trailers buzzing past you on the various 2-lane state highways. Any large box truck or tractor trailer produces a passing wind strong enough to cause you to stumble. This same manufactured wind from these big trucks is definitely strong enough to easily knock your bike to the ground! And the next tractor trailer is never far behind you! When possible, I parked my bike as far from the edge of the road as possible to slightly minimize the potentially damaging effects of the powerful crosswinds generated by these massive passing trucks!

Chapter 37: Support Team

Your solo, unsupported, continuous bike expedition across the country is NOT all about you! Yes, you are making each of the pedal revolutions, but it is usually a TEAM effort!

Thinking way back to my early childhood as I was first learning to ride a bike, my father wore out a pair of his shoes chasing me down the street holding on to my bicycle as I was learning to ride on two wheels. Relentlessly, for MANY weeks, my dad worked with me through dozens of scary crashes, significant drops of blood left on the asphalt, and countless band-aids. Much of his spare time, my dad would apply heavy-duty efforts to teaching me how to ride a bike, but the truth could not be denied as I was a HORRIBLE cyclist with almost ZERO natural ability!

Naturally, Dad assumed there was something wrong with his teaching method. Certainly, any reasonably healthy 5-year-old could learn to ride a bike! So, as a way to test his hypothesis, he grabbed my 3-year-old sister, Kelli, and put her on a bike and with the EXACT SAME teaching method and within 15 minutes sister Kelli was riding her bicycle up and down Salmon Avenue all by herself! Clearly, there was nothing wrong with dad's teaching method! The problem was with me! My sister was a cycling PHENOM and I was a pitiful LOSER!

Although it appeared as though I was a LOST CAUSE, dad maintained his dogged belief in my eventual triumph until he could take no more! One day in pure frustration, dad burst into the house and forcefully exclaimed to my mother, "Our son is NEVER going to ride a bike!!!" It wasn't long after dad bought a new pair of shoes when it finally clicked and I began to ride a 2-wheeled bike! Dad was elated! It was one of the HAPPIEST days of dad's life!!! On that momentous evening, more than one beer was toasted by my dad to our long-fought biking victory! And thanks to dad's relentless efforts and his never-ending SUPPORT, my father passed along a lifetime of biking joy to me!

Back home during my Southern Tier journey, my mom seemingly watched my every move for 43 days on her LIFE 360 phone app which through the technology of satellites gave her my exact location, speed, and direction of travel during my entire bike travels with very little loss of service, even throughout the remote desert regions! Upon opening her eyelids in the morning, my mom would refer to her phone to locate my whereabouts.

At one point in Louisiana, mom actually recognized I made a wrong turn and she called me within 2 minutes of my blunder and said, "Do you know you are heading westbound?" My mother also made a critical hotel booking for me on the most dangerous day of my bicycle outing and possibly saved me from freezing to death as I pedaled 34 miles from Sierra Blanca, Texas over to Van Horn, Texas on a 26-degree Fahrenheit day with 30 mile per hour headwinds!

My father reviewed the Southern Tier paper maps back home and advised me of upcoming dangers and gave me an overall daily preview of what was to come. My dad is highly skilled at travel planning and map reading. He kept me on track and made critical suggestions greatly helping me with my daily cycling decisions.

My wife, Tink, gave me the emotional support I needed to keep pressing on despite my endless doubts. My wife and I have an incredibly close relationship in which we both missed each other GREATLY while I was away on my pedaling rendezvous! Speaking with her every day and receiving her encouragement definitely spurred me to continue. Talking to her also gave me something to look forward to each day as the monotony of cycling for many hours daily can be emotionally and physically PAINFUL.

Tink also took over my CEO position in our home rental company while I was away biking. During my absence, she worked 10-hour days earnestly managing the tedious operation of our long-standing rental home company. Although Tink handled much of my stress-ladened work load while I was away, it quickly became apparent we did NOT invest in enough training prior to my departure. Tink got the job done, but the whole process could have been much smoother without so much unnecessary stress had I spent more time training Tink to carry out my job functions. Nonetheless, in typical "Git er Done" Tink fashion, my wife found a way to produce the quality results our company needed to continue to thrive. For Tink, excellence is the ONLY result!

My sister, Kelli, also charted my biking course daily and consistently expressed her pride in me, her only sibling. Kelli's daily interest in my cycling trip was inspiring to me and gave me another key person whom BELIEVED in me. Several times during my trip, she gave me very effective MOTIVATIONAL SPEECHES. Her most effective "speeches" encouraged me to take my cross-country trip <u>one day at a time</u>.

Kelli could sense I was "over-chunking" my cross-country goal in my mind causing unnecessary stress for myself. Kelli believed my bike travels could be much more manageable if I would focus on TODAY without any thought of the day after! Her overall positive vibration was felt in my soul and it gave me additional strength. Every night, Kelli wanted to know exactly where I was staying. She also wanted to know my daily destination goal for the following day. Each day, Kelli looked forward to getting my group text letting everyone know when I arrived SAFELY at my daily destination.

After finding out about my heat exhaustion on day 4 of my trip, my brother-in-law, Steve, sent me an angelic text which might have saved my ENTIRE trip. His monumental, yet simple text read "Out of ALL the people I know, YOU are the ONE person who might actually be capable of finishing a solo, cross-country bicycle ride!" Upon receipt of his famed text, I was seriously debating about my future plans as my parents and myself unanimously sensed this cross-country biking fantasy was well beyond my current limited capabilities.

My mom told me, "You are already SUCCESS for flying to California and starting this trip. You have nothing more to prove." My dad said, "You got some REALLY BIG MOUNTAINS in front of you. Maybe you can get a flight home in Phoenix and do another section of the route next year." My wife said, "You can come home anytime. You have nothing to prove to me. You are my one-and-only. I love you no matter whether you finish or not!" And of course, by this time, I had already QUIT back on Day 2, but nobody knew it as I kept that "minor detail" to myself as I REFUSED to come back home, at least for one more day......

It was at this moment while I was considering all of the loving, but terminal input from my loved ones when brother Steve's text came through to my phone. As I considered Steve's sage text, a helpful thought popped into my mind, "Steve is one of the smartest guys I know and Steve knows A LOT of people! If Steve thinks I am THE ONE PERSON with a realistic chance to finish the Southern Tier, then maybe I should at least pedal one more day!?" In my closest estimation, I probably referred to Steve's encouraging text more than 100 times during my 43-day challenge. Every time a demon backed me into a corner, I would remind myself about Steve's text and how Steve genuinely BELIEVES in me! Steve's text and his overall positive energy and support may have been the last little push responsible for my finishing the Southern Tier!

A support team is NOT mandatory, but it sure helps!!!!! It irritates my wife anytime I make claim of finishing the Southern Tier "solo and unsupported." In quick fashion, Tink reminds me I had A LOT of help along the way! And my sage wife is right! Without all the help back home, it is unlikely I had enough personal resources and self-development to finish such an incredulous biking adventure!

DAY 13: I never got tired of the majestic sunrises!

Chapter 38: Sick Loved Ones

In 2018, two years prior to my epic across-the-country bike ride, my wife, Tink, was diagnosed with a rare blood disease. Her blood disease is part of the Lupus family known as Myeloproliferative Disorder in which her body makes too many platelets and puts her at high risk of a fatal blood clot. Since 2018, Tink has had several episodes resulting in overnight hospital stays and even surgery. Tink is also especially prone to highly emotional situations as they quickly prompt the appearance of severe symptoms.

While I was on the Southern Tier, my wife was taken to the hospital three times. One of those times were by ambulance. The stresses of Tink's new work responsibilities were more than what her health could bare. And instead of doing less, she exerted herself much too hard and found herself in the hospital 3 different times for health issues in which were all stress-induced. Being thousands of miles away, it was impossible for me to get home quickly. Instead, I relied on my parents to assist my wife in which they gladly did.

Tink stay overnight with my parents at their home from the middle of my trip until the conclusion of my trip. My mom and dad kept Tink grounded and calm as she continued to manage our company in my absence. Regrouping with my mom and dad daily was enough to keep Tink semi-stable until I got back home. For Tink, my parents were a rock of stability for her. Without them, we are unsure what could have transpired with regard to Tink's health and well-being!

As my wife was taken to the hospital by ambulance on Day 30, I was pedaling my bike toward Shepherd, Texas. Pedal after pedal I was thinking about her and praying for her. It was a battle in my mind as to what to do. Should I stay on the inspired Southern Tier route or should I figure out how to get back home? Of course, when I spoke with my wife, in her normal UNSELFISH way, Tink encouraged me to remain on my bike route as she KNEW I was CALLED to ride my bicycle across the country. Tink understood how my cross-country bike ambition was NOT a sightseeing tour, it was a MISSION from God!

With great reservation, pedal stroke after pedal stroke I remained on the lonely streets of the Southern Tier as my tears rolled down my cheeks deflecting off of my bike and landing on the hard asphalt road. My wife really needs me. What kind of husband would abandon his wife when she needs him the MOST? How could I be so COLD? What if my wife doesn't make it? As a wide variety of thoughts made their way through my mind, I considered my options, but in the end, I held fast and hard to the notion I was CALLED to do the Southern Tier. My bike ride must continue…....

Being away for many weeks at a time makes it inevitable for a family member or close friend to suffer a severe health issue or even die! During the second week of my epic ride, Debbie Trotz, a dear friend of mine and a best-friend of my wife, died a cancer-related death. Debbie was struggling for over a year with lung cancer and finally passed on despite much hope to the contrary. Finding out about her untimely death while pedaling through New Mexico on October 25th shook my soul as I was unavailable to pay my respects to Debbie, her loyal husband Bob, her devoted and super-talented granddaughter, Jordan Feliciano, nor to comfort my grieving wife.

To make it across the country pedaling a bicycle, it is likely you might have to be somewhat SELFISH. On more than one occasion, I had to make MAJOR decisions as to how I would handle adversity, illness, and even death as my pedals kept spinning 7 hours a day over a thousand miles away from home.

For most of you, you might be pondering about taking a REALLY LONG bike trip, but for me, it wasn't a "really long bike ride," it was the "MISSION OF A LIFETIME!" My "bike ride" was the SIGNATURE OF MY LIFE!!!! As far as I was concerned, I was NOT touring the country on my bicycle, I was discovering MYSELF! I was not seeing the sights; I was finding the MAN hidden behind my many insecurities. I was not exploring unseen land; I was discovering the depth of my own SPIRIT!

My cross-country bike ride was the MOST SPIRITUAL experience I've ever had! It had very little to do with cactus, mountains, deserts, rivers, and oceans. It had everything to do with my own DEVELOPMENT as a child of God! My Southern Tier bike trip was about fulfilling God's plan and I KNEW I was meant to do it! I could FEEL it! Even though I didn't believe I would ever finish, I knew I was meant to ride another day! Despite the hardship back home, my pedals continued to spin! There was no turning back!

If you ask my wife about her sickness and how it related to my cross-country bicycle ride, Tink would swear on a stack of Bibles that I would NOT have returned home even if she would have DIED! In Tink's own words, "My husband would have put my body on ice until he FINISHED the Southern Tier." No, I'm not proud my wife feels this way nor do I necessarily agree with her overly harsh statement, but her pointed words do convey my extreme level of utmost dedication to my bike endeavor as my high-level of stubbornness and willingness to endure suffering cannot be denied! If you ask my wife, I might be one of the most stubborn people in the world! Maybe the Southern Tier was too much for me, but I was NOT coming home! As far as I was concerned, I'd rather DIE on those barren streets than to come back home!

Hearing these punitive words of callous detachment from my wife might prompt many of you to assume our marriage relationship was "on the rocks" and we were heading toward a divorce, but nothing could have been further from the truth! We were and are TOTALLY in love with each other and our marriage keeps getting stronger every day! Nonetheless, the fact remained......... I was CALLED to pedal the Southern Tier and pedal was what I did!

My calling was no different than Moses whom was called to climb the mountain and receive the Ten Commandments from God. To me, my bike trip was sacred! To this day, I'm really not sure what it would have taken for me to abandon my hallowed cross-country pursuit and I'm glad I didn't find out!

If you ask my daughter, Stacey Hockensmith, she would swear on her soul, "If necessary, my dad would have CRAWLED to the finish! My dad is STUBBORN! Nothing could stop him!" Stacey KNEW I would finish. She NEVER had a doubt, but I had many doubts as I truly did NOT expect to finish. Each day I opened my eyes, I thanked God for another day as I assumed I would DIE on the Southern Tier. Never did I EXPECT To finish. All I knew is I was called, even if it meant the end of my life while crossing the southern part of the United States on my bicycle. At times, I would DREAM about finishing, but even on my last day, Day 43, I doubted my eventual finish!!!

As this short chapter comes to a close, consider having a heart-to-heart talk with your near and dear family members about your long, upcoming bicycle journey. Let them know what the trip means to you. Communicate clearly your level of commitment. Put it all on the line as your cross-country decision WILL be SEVERELY tested while you are away! Sickness and various other MAJOR problems at home are another reason why the odds of completing a continuous bicycle trip alone across the country is staggeringly LOW!

If a MAJOR devastating situation like a death of your spouse, parent, or child DEMANDS your return home, your "continuous" bike ride can still be "continuous" as long as you return to your exact point of exit and resume riding your route AS SOON AS YOU ARE ABLE!!! Sometimes, even a divine calling from God can be sidetracked for scenarios outside of your control. All you can do is consider your options and live your BEST LIFE! It will be you, and only YOU, who will face your creator and be judged according to your decisions on one great day after you pass on from life on Earth. Make sure you FEEL good about every decision you make!

Chapter 39: 43 Daily Rides

One of the biggest mistakes a cross-country cyclist could make is trying "TO RIDE ACROSS THE COUNTRY!!!!" If your goal is to ride your bike across the country, then you better adjust your BIG GOAL down to a daily goal. Starting in San Diego while thinking about Jacksonville, St. Augustine, or whatever eastern seaboard destination city, is only going to bring down your morale. You must RESIST the temptation to think about Florida while you are still in California! Think ONLY about TODAY! Think only about California when you are in California! Almost nothing is more discouraging than thinking about finishing during the first week when you are struggling to adjust to your new life!

After deciding to ride your bike across the country, you need to stop thinking about "RIDING YOUR BIKE ACROSS THE COUNTRY." The truth is...... You are NOT riding your bike across the country. You are merely riding your bike TODAY to your NEXT DESTINATION! A cross-country bike adventure on the Southern Tier is really 43 INDIVIDUAL DAY TRIPS! After the commencement of your bike travels, your daily destination should be the ONLY terminus on your mind! Thinking about Florida while you are in California can decimate your thinking pattern to the point of possibly tapping out!

Attempting to plan out your entire trip in advance is also nothing less than ludicrous! The only reasonable way to manage the mammoth endeavor of pedaling a bicycle across the country is by managing your adventure ONE DAY AT A TIME! The night before, you should establish a REASONABLE goal for the following day. Consider the upcoming weather, the terrain, the wind, how you feel, etc. and then set a goal for yourself for the following day. It is also reasonable and advised to plan overnight accommodations for the following night, but do NOT plan out multiple days in advance! Strategize only 24 hours in advance as there are too many variables to plan any further into the future.

Most of the time, your 24-hour itinerary will NOT work out exactly as you have designed anyways. That's why you are on an "adventure!" Surprises are SUPPOSED to happen while you are on an "adventure." Only plot out 24 hours into the future and then be open to making changes. Forecasting out any further than 24 hours is counterproductive in a variety of ways! Your mindset needs to be focused on producing 7 hours of pedaling per day and letting all the other details fall in place NATURALLY in due time!!!!

Chapter 40: Rainsuit

As you are standing outside on a beautiful, sunny 80-degree Fahrenheit day, you might be tempted to leave your rainsuit at HOME! While enjoying the comforts of the warm sun, you might be tempted to forget about the nasty weather around the corner, but don't fall prey to such shortcomings with your thinking. Don't leave your rainsuit at home! When I'm asked if it is going to rain today, I always answer, "Yes!" Regardless of what time of the year you are cycling or no matter what the particular weather projections are forecasted for your trip, you MUST have an excellent rainsuit top with excellent rainsuit pants!

My initial rainsuit purchases prior to the Southern Tier were complete failures! Despite claiming to be "waterproof," I quickly discovered they were NOT! To me, "waterproof" means "no water gets in no matter what," but to these clothing companies, "waterproof" means "waterproof up to a certain amount of water." Thus, all waterproof clothing is DIFFERENT! Some rainsuits will keep you dry in a drizzle and others can keep you dry in a monsoon! For me, I was determined to find TRULY WATERPROOF gear to keep me COMPLETELY dry in the WORST IMAGINABLE rain!

Choosing the lightest rainsuit on the market is not always the best choice! Light rainsuits might be nice for a day ride in the summer with a brief passing rain shower or to wear as a windbreaker on an early morning ride, but extremely light rainsuits are NOT appropriate for a cross-country expedition. Neither is a heavy rainsuit appropriate as these are made for people whom are mostly standing outside in the rain, not pedaling their bike. Cyclists need a medium-weight, FULLY waterproof rainsuit! If you can find a rainsuit with some ventilation WITHOUT giving up any of its waterproofing function, then it would be a fine choice!

Bib rain pants were a key feature of my Pioneer-brand rainsuit used on my Southern Tier journey as my bib rainsuit pants extended up to the nipples on my chest. Straps extended over my shoulders and buckles were used to ensure a snug fit. By having my rain pants extend up to my chest, it prevented any gapping between my pants and my rainsuit top as is the case with most other types of rainsuits.

Some cyclists argue about a medium-weight rainsuit with bib pants being too heavy for biking and causing excessive sweating. Yes, sweating will definitely occur under your rainsuit, but I would MUCH RATHER be warm and sweating instead of shivering and FREEZING! If you are wearing a wicking base tight "skin" layer of pants and shirt as I advise, then your sweat will be quickly absorbed and shouldn't cause you too much of a problem.

My recommendation is to buy a qualified rain jacket and rain pants from Adventure Cycling's CYCLOSOURCE catalog. Even if you don't buy bib pants, research the best possible rain gear for long-term touring and consider your options. Adventure Cycling knows the gear needed to OUTLAST the cold rain! Spend the extra money and get truly WATERPROOF gear as you cannot risk having inadequate gear amidst EXTREME weather conditions while you are captive to the various elements on your epic bicycle ride!

Before departing on your cross-country journey, make sure you take AT LEAST one long ride in the pouring rain while wearing your new rainsuit. The harder the rain, the better! Make sure your rainsuit keeps you dry! You don't want to find out the answer to the dryness question on your third day on the Southern Tier!

In addition to your rainsuit, you should also have a pair of rain shoe covers to go OVER TOP of your cycling shoes. Buy a shoe cover made exclusively for cyclists as the shoe cover will have the bottom cut out properly as to allow you to continue to clip your shoe into the bracket on your pedals. Rain shoe covers are NOT perfect at keeping your shoes completely dry, but in my opinion, they help a lot! Plus, rain shoe covers also help to keep your feet a bit warmer on very cold days as your FEET are most susceptible to the cold!!! Therefore, use every reasonable method available to keep your feet from turning into ice!

Since my rainsuit pants were a bit baggy near my shins and ankles, I wrapped 2 Velcro straps over the shin-area of my rain pants as to keep my rain pants from getting caught on my bike chain, sprocket, pedal, etc. You must be able to pedal freely without the risk of any piece of your clothing causing unnecessary complications by getting tangled somewhere in your bike's mechanicals. Any loose-fitting pant worn on a bicycle is a bad idea and could result in torn clothing, damaged mechanicals, or even a possible crash!

Another option is to buy a one-piece rainsuit which makes water entry even more unlikely. The only issue I have with a full one-piece rainsuit is you no longer have the option to wear the top rain jacket alone in certain cases and conditions. When Tink and I go canoeing in cold weather, we often wear full dry suits to make sure we stay completely dry! In a similar fashion, when I ride my gas-powered scooter in the cold rain while making shuttle runs on our various adventures, I also wear my canoeing dry suit or a full piece motorcycle rainsuit as it is important to be WELL-PREPARED when you encounter inclement conditions on a motorcycle, but a one-piece rainsuit is probably NOT the best choice for a cyclist!

Whatever you do, don't be like my gullible wife and try to fool yourself into thinking a nice, little summer rain will "cool you off." After extended thought-processing on the subject matter, I've come to the firm conclusion……. ALL rain is cold and miserable!!! There is RARELY a rain which will "cool you off" or "feel good." Even if I was riding my bike through the desert in the summer, I'd still bring a qualified 2-piece medium-weight rain suit with me! NEVER underestimate the PAIN of rain! There are few conditions more capable of destroying a cyclist's positive attitude more quickly than a cold rain shower combined with unqualified gear! So, the next time someone asks you, "Is it going to rain today?", answer your friend with a resounding "Yes!"

Chapter 41: Head Up

As time goes by and the hours sitting on your bike seat amount to days and weeks and possibly months, your neck will get sore and you will be tempted to put your head down to feel some temporary relief. Big mistake! DANGER is closer than you realize!!! Putting your head down even for a few seconds is all it takes to END your special journey!

Putting your head down obviously means you are no longer looking at the road in front of you. When you take your eyes off of the road ahead, you are setting yourself up for a CRASH! And a crash not only damages your bike and body. Most importantly, a crash could cause FATAL damage to your thinking!!!

When your mind is weakened, every other part of your body will follow suit! Weak thoughts will decrease your pedal cadence, affect your level of concentration, and decrease your endurance. You will get cold much quicker and thoughts of ending your epic trip may metastasize. It is IMPERATIVE to pay close attention AT ALL TIMES and avoid crashing at all costs!

While in the perfect-little town of Poplarville, Mississippi as I approached my lush, single-family rental home paid for by my generous and loving parents, I looked down to adjust my music. That fast my bike veered to the right and nearly dropped into a very deep, open drainage area alongside the road! All it took was about 2 seconds and I almost sustained a MAJOR TRIP-ENDING CRASH despite my bike only moving at about 6 miles per hour in a "harmless" residential neighborhood less than one mile from my daily destination!

Another time while I was waiting at a traffic light at a busy intersection in El Paso, Texas, I noticed the light turned green so I put my head down and I began to hook the bottom of my shoes into my shoe clips as I pedaled forward. Unbeknownst to me, the car in front of me suddenly stopped and I pedaled into the bumper of the vehicle making an undeniable THUMP! The good-natured driver in the car didn't even get out of his car or make a big deal of my blunder, but I felt like an idiot! Although I didn't even come close to getting injured on this particular mishap, I realized how close I was to danger and how fast I could get SERIOUSLY injured! After pedaling into the car in El Paso, I paid much closer attention to keeping my HEAD UP! It only takes a moment to find yourself in a bad situation!

Chapter 42: Tire Air Pressure

Prior to starting my bike ride each day, I quickly inspected my tires to make sure they had an adequate inflation of air. In most cases, I casually used my finger and pressed on my tires to make sure they felt as solid as a rock! If my finger felt any sense of give, I would take my tiny air pump out of my pannier bag and pump the tire back to its proper air pressure.

Having too little pressure in your tires will SLOW you down and make a flat tire more prevalent. Having too much air in your tires will make for a slightly uncomfortable, rough ride and also increase the chances of a flat tire. Your tires should be nice and hard, but NOT too hard.

Mechanic Jacob from Tri Hard Sports in Ocean Springs, Mississippi advised me to keep the front tire on my touring bicycle inflated to 70 pounds per square inch (70 psi) and my back tire inflated to 80 pounds per square inch (80 psi). Prior to Jacob's advice, I rode two thirds of the way across the country with both my front and back tires inflated to 60 pounds of air pressure which also proved to be adequate. Every manufactured tire should have the recommended psi listed on the sidewall of the tire in clear print.

My 41 dog chases were nothing compared to this cyclist's bear chase!

Chapter 43: Pouch

If you are a close adventure friend of mine, then you know I don't go on many adventures without my trusty POUCH! A pouch is a small sack designed in most cases to strap around your waist. Oftentimes, I am teased by others as they humorously refer to my pouch as my "purse" or my "man purse." Even though I am 100% straight and heterosexual, my pouch still feels right for me and I don't really feel like less of a man.

My pouch gives me the extra space I need to access important items quickly. It doesn't matter whether I'm flying to a winter Cancun, Mexico vacation, camping at Lake Raystown in Huntingdon, PA, taking a canoe trip down a beautiful Pennsylvania river, hiking the Appalachian Trail, or taking a bike trip, my pouch is an integral part of my adventure attire! If you ask me, a pouch is ESSENTIAL!

During my bicycle travels across the country, I kept my pouch on top in my left front pannier bag. Upon arrival at McDonalds, Dollar General, or wherever else, I would quickly and easily get my pouch out of my left front pannier bag and strap it around my waist. After transferring my cell phone from my bike handlebar to my pouch, I knew I had everything I needed in my pouch. It didn't take me any extra thinking to know I was fully prepared to go into the store and get what I needed since my pouch was already carefully stocked with money, credit cards, ID, a pen, reading glasses, and numerous other necessary items as will be listed below.

To me, it is an absolute REQUIREMENT of mine to be organized. My wife and others who accompany me on various adventures know I am VERY SLOW prior to the beginning of any expedition as I think, double-think, and triple-think to make sure everything is perfectly organized. In my case, it is absolutely unacceptable for anything to be out of place! When I go looking for something, it better be EXACTLY where I put it, or I won't be able to find it! If you ever want to hide something from me, all you would have to do is move the item a few inches away from the exact spot where I set it and I won't be able to find it! Most people who know me quickly realize I have A SEVERE ORGANZING PROBLEM and I quickly add unnecessary stress to most outings!

My "man purse" gives me a chance to store everything in one place. When I grab my pouch, I am also grabbing everything that RESIDES inside my pouch! No longer do I have to THINK about what I need and where the item is located. Upon arrival at any particular destination, I simply open my pannier bag and click my pouch strap around my waist and I'm READY! Although it takes me much longer packing before starting any trip than it does for my peers, my tight organization pays BIG DIVIDENDS during the process, thus saving me A LOT of time!

It is my belief everybody should wear a pouch! Pouches make life EASY, especially on adventures! You don't need the extra drama of trying to find the stuff you need!

Believe me, the Southern Tier will provide more EXCITEMENT than you will likely be able to handle! You don't need any extra thrills! A pouch allows you to keep everything in one place without unnecessary tensions. Below is a list of exactly what I keep in my pouch:

    Cell phone
    Reading glasses
    Ear buds
    To Do list
    Several pens
    Checklist for trip
    Whistle (with a small string to wear around my neck)
    Coins
    Facial Mask (for COVID-19 times)
    Wallet
    Receipts from trip purchases
        *** Every week or so, I would transfer all of my receipts from my wallet to the zippered compartment inside my pannier bag.
    Cash
    AAA card
    Debit/ATM card (for cash access)
    Credit card (for purchases)
    Health insurance card
    Health Savings Account card
    Driver's license
    Mission Card (a card to remind me WHY I am on this crazy bike adventure)
    Note from my wife (No matter what happens, my wife still LOVES me!)

Having my phone, money, and credit card with me inside of my pouch and strapped around my waist while inside the store or restaurant seemed A LOT safer than leaving these valuable items stored outside with my bike. Despite NEVER ONCE in 3,000 miles having anyone even try to mess with my bike or belongings, I didn't want to take any chances as I am ultra-conservative and a bit paranoid with regard to theft! Losing my wallet or having it stolen would have caused a great inconvenience for me even though I did keep a second credit card and emergency cash stored inside a "decoy-labeled envelope" zipped securely inside the small interior compartment of my front, left pannier bag!

Although losing my wallet would have been very tough for me to take, losing my phone or having my phone stolen would have been a much greater potential loss as I relied on my phone many times throughout every day. My phone contained the Adventure Cycling Bicycle Route Navigator GPS phone app which kept me on my route. My phone also was used to contact Warmshowers hosts, campgrounds, motels, bike shops, and my support team back home. Today, more than ever, our cell phones are our lives! With regard to your special possessions, don't take unnecessary chances. Have a pouch to safely and securely store your wallet and phone while you are in the store buying Powerade, donuts, pizza, raisins, or fig bars.

For those of you who do NOT use a pouch, I ask, "How do you do it?" Seriously, I don't understand how the rest of you stay organized. The fifteen items or so listed above which rest inside of my pouch would probably take me an extra five minutes or so to locate all of these loose items in my various pannier bags before I entered a store. Once located, I'd probably lose at least one item per day as I don't have any idea how I would securely carry all these tiny, necessary items with me into the store.

In my opinion, I'd much rather be called a "Fairy" than to be without my trusty pouch. For me, my pouch is an extension of me. It is the quick container responsible for holding my "important stuff." Taking away my pouch would be like taking away one of my organs. My pouch goes where I go! Even when I go jogging, my pouch is what holds my cell phone as my cell phone is necessary to play the sound through my ear buds.

Throughout the years, I've purchased pouches at Walmart, TJ Maxx, eBay, and Amazon. Pouches come in many different sizes. My standard pouch is probably considered by most to be mid-size. Today, there are even shoulder pouches you can buy if you are NOT secure enough in your manhood to wear the pouch around your waist like me. Other manufacturers call their pouch an "athletic pack" or "sports pack" as to make it sound less feminine and increase sales among men in particular. Regardless of what you call it, make sure you get yourself a POUCH!

DAY 14: I LOVE New Mexico!

Chapter 44: Rear-View Mirror

Throughout this book, I've made many mentions about my stupidity. It is important for me to let you know that it is NOT necessary for you to be "smart" to ride your bike across the country. There are many other mental, physical, and spiritual traits much more important than intelligence to determine whether or not you succeed in your cross-country bicycle crossing!

For many years, while riding my bicycle, I would turn my neck and survey any potential rear-approaching traffic. It was no wonder why I frequently had neck problems! It wasn't until recent years I found out it was possible to install a rear-view mirror on my bicycle. Immediately upon my valuable discovery, my local bike shop, Fat Jimmy's, installed a convenient rear-view mirror on my bike. On my first long training ride after the installation of the rear-view mirror, I was HOOKED! I LOVED my rear-view mirror!

Countless times throughout any given biking day, I found myself using my mirror. If nothing else, it saved a lot of strain on my neck!!! Consistently twisting my neck to look behind me has caused neck cramps which have lasted for as long as six days! Six days in pain not being able to twist my neck was NOT fun! Nor was level 7 neck pain conducive to enjoying a bike ride!

In addition, when I would turn my neck to look behind me, it also would cause my body to twist. Twisting my body naturally veered my bike to the left directly INTO TRAFFIC!!! Obviously, it is VERY dangerous veering into traffic as a bicycle is NO MATCH for a multi-thousand-pound hunk of metal quickly approaching from the rear! A rear-view mirror avoids the twisting of your body and the faulty positioning of your bicycle! Installing and using a rear-view mirror is an important safety feature for long-term bicycle touring and for anyone who plans to ride a bicycle on the public roads or trails for any amount of time!

At a quick glance, a rear-view mirror gives you valuable information regarding approaching rear vehicles. In most cases, you wouldn't do anything different with regard to your bike position on the road regardless of whether or not you see the vehicle approaching in your rear-view mirror, but the mirror is still a GOOD IDEA! It is wise to know what is going on all around your bicycle as you are by far the most vulnerable person on the road as you are most susceptible to serious injury or even death. No longer would I even consider riding my bike on the public roads without a rear-view mirror!

During the summer prior to my October 10th departure on the Southern Tier, Fat Jimmy's installed the rear-view mirror at the bottom of my handlebar on the far-left side which is the only side of a bicycle in which a rear-view mirror is really needed in most cases. The newly-installed mirror was such a game-changer! Now, I could easily glance into the mirror and see the approaching vehicles from behind me.

As amazing as the rear-view mirror was, I had a slight issue with it. When I installed my pannier bags and my "stack" on the back on my bicycle with my gear piled up behind my seat, I only had about 50% visibility out of my rear-view mirror. Looking into my rear-view mirror would show me about 50% of my pannier bags and stack and 50% of the traffic behind me. Basically, 50% of my vision in the rear was BLOCKED by my biking storage bags!

All through the Southern Tier, I dreamed about someday buying a new rear-view mirror, a mirror to extend out an extra 2 inches as I only needed about another 2 inches and I would be able to easily gain full vision in the rear. It would be so amazing to get a 50% visibility improvement of the traffic approaching me!

For all 43 days on the Southern Tier, I dealt with my semi-inadequate rear-view mirror while making the best of a marginal scenario. For over 3,000 miles, I traveled across the country rather safely with no major "scares" or wrecks despite having a handicapped rear-view mirror. Every time I glanced in the mirror, I wondered why the manufacturer didn't make the mirror another 2 inches longer as to provide me with a better rear view around my pannier bags.

Upon arriving back home, I asked one of my housing repair contractors, Matthew Sever, to install a new rear-view mirror on my bike as to provide me with the increased rear visibility I so desired. Matt took one look at my Southern Tier rear-view mirror which was currently attached to my bike and he said, "Why don't you just pull your rear-view mirror out like this?" To my amazement, contractor Matt pulled on my mirror and within seconds the mirror was extended exactly two inches out to the side of my handlebars providing me with PERFECT rear vision! It was exactly what I had dreamed of for 3,000 miles while crossing the United States. Thanks Matt!

On any one of my 43 long days biking the Southern Tier, I could have simply pulled on my rear-view mirror and I could have extended the mirror outward gaining FULL rear visibility, but I was too STUPID to figure it out on my own and I was too STUPID to ask someone for help as I was convinced my mirror was immovable! All the while I struggled to see beyond my pannier bags in the rear, the answer to my rear vision issue was close at hand, but I could not see it! All I needed to do was to pull on the mirror and I could have enjoyed greatly increased rear vision!

Hopefully by now, you are figuring out a very important revelation. I am NOT anybody special! I'm probably even more senseless than you are! I'm just a guy who gets crazy ideas and takes great pride in being a positive example for others. I don't know much and I'm definitely not a cycling expert!

Regardless of my lack of cycling credentials and certifications, get a rear-view mirror installed on your bike and get out on the roads. Get familiar with using your rear-view mirror and you'll soon LOVE it! Best of all, your rear-view mirror will help keep you safer!

Chapter 45: Wind

Ask any experienced cyclist about wind and they will admit it is a MAJOR factor during any bike ride, especially going long distance across the country! Wind can definitely slow you down, but wind can also blow you and your bike into traffic or even knock you completely off of your bike causing a severe crash! For some strange reason, wind is especially notorious for terrible bicycle crashes as you approach or while you are crossing a bridge!

As I was traveling across the Gordon Persons Bridge, just south of Alabama Port on Route 183 in Alabama, the wind gusts spiked at about 60 miles per hour! While I was pedaling along this very high 3-mile-long bridge on this EXTREMELY windy day as I approached Dauphin Island, I pedaled my bike as if I was in a race as I kept my body and head as LOW as possible as to create as little wind resistance as possible. By pedaling hard, I kept my momentum propelling forward trying my best to avoid the VERY DANGEROUS wind blowing across my body pushing my bike sideways toward the guardrail at the edge of the estimated 100-foot-high bridge! As I quickly glanced over the bridge railings to the choppy waters 100 or more feet below, my entire body got stiff as I feared my pending fate in this relentlessly fierce wind! Without a doubt, my bicycle and I were in acute danger of being blown completely OFF OF THE BRIDGE and into the threatening waters of Mobile Bay below!

As I neared the peak of the bridge, a forceful gust of wind trembled my bike thrusting me inches closer to the edge of the guardrail. This particular bridge had standard guardrails of reasonable height, but I promise you, with just the right gust of wind, my biking adventure could have easily transformed into a swim-for-your-life survival test with only a moment's notice. Only a few times in my life could I recall my body, mind, and spirit being so ALERT!

During these pivotal several minutes in which I crossed the Gordon Persons Bridge, I felt the MOST ALIVE in my entire life! My ATTENTION was absolute and complete making sure my body stayed as low as possible as I battled the fierce blowing winds. My only thought was to get off of this treacherous bridge as soon as possible! At one point, a gust of wind hit me so hard I seriously contemplated abandoning my bicycle and lying flat on the bridge to protect myself from the mighty gusts as I felt my life was in grave danger. It felt like another wind gust, even five miles per hour stronger, could have been enough to thrust me and my bike over the metal guardrail and into the cold, choppy waters of Mobile Bay!

Wind can be severe anytime during a bike ride, but there is something extra special about forceful gusts of wind on a bridge! Panic is the only word I can use to describe the feeling when a truly powerful gust of wind impacts your body while traveling across a bridge. While reading the narrative about San Diego on one of my Adventure Cycling paper maps of the Southern Tier, I read about wind warnings near certain bridges. The map mentioned how heavy gusts of winds in certain predictable locations, mostly near bridges, have toppled more than one cyclist to the ground as a result of the over-powering gusts!

Regardless of whatever windy conditions you find yourself, keep a TIGHT GRIP on your handlebars as you are crossing a bridge of any size. Even in a scenario with no wind, hold on tight and stay to the right as even a small car could produce a gust a wind affecting your trajectory and pushing you outward toward the perilous guardrails! A big tractor-trailer truck or box truck could definitely generate enough wind force to tragically end your trip if you are not paying close attention with a nice, tight grip on your handlebars!

While traveling through the western states of California and Arizona on the Southern Tier, I was amazed to discover MANY bridges with extremely LOW guardrails. When I encountered my first bridge in California with one of these low guardrails, I was scared passing over the bridge even with NO WIND and no cars! In my home state of Pennsylvania, the guardrails on most bridges are much higher! As I passed over these California bridges, I couldn't help but to think about what would happen if a strong gust of wind came and pushed my bike toward the guardrails or if my attention drifted for a second or two and my bike shifted a few feet to the right and contacted one of these low guardrails. Regardless of whatever scenario I reviewed in my mind, the common end-result was a fatality!

As you pass over bridges with low guardrails or even bridges with guardrails of more reasonable height, put your FULL ATTENTION in the present moment! For some reason, bridges are natural wind tunnels. Hold your handlebars tight and remember, DANGER is never far away! Get ready for the next big gust of wind! Welcome to the Southern Tier!

DAY 14: Here I am high atop the Black Mountains in New Mexico getting ready to summit the highest point of the Southern Tier, Emory's Pass (8,228-foot elevation).

Chapter 46: Headwind

As I pedaled from Sierra Blanca, Texas to Van Horn, Texas, I encountered the toughest headwind of my entire 3,000-mile biking journey. For almost 4 hours of this relatively short 34-mile daily bike ride, I struggled as I faced a consistent 30 Mile per hour HEADWIND blowing directly into my face causing full resistance to my pedaling efforts! Prior to this unforsaken windy day, my average daily biking speed was a respectable 11 miles per hour, but on this memorable day, my average speed quickly dropped in half to about 5.5 miles per hour as I pedaled HARD into the relentless headwind using about 85% of my FULL STRENGTH.

This particular day was the shortest mileage day of my entire 43-day biking adventure, but it was also by far the toughest day! As I pedaled, the incessant headwind was unyielding. There was a steady stream of wind with intermittent, sudden wind bursts topping 50 miles per hour which would almost completely stop my momentum. If given the choice, I would have graciously opted to climb a 20-mile mountain pass with no wind than to deal with the WICKED headwinds of this unforsaken day!

Most of my biking efforts eastbound from California to Florida involved a regular headwind to various degrees and this predominant wind tendency was no surprise to me. Before I even took my first pedal stroke, my research indicated prevailing EASTERLY winds along the Southern Tier throughout the Fall, which meant I would be facing a predominant headwind on most days.

Easterly winds blow from the east to the west. So, for a cyclist heading eastbound, this dominant easterly wind pattern presents a significantly more difficult challenge. To the contrary, a WESTERLY wind blows from the west to the east. This is the type of wind capable of putting a giant smile on a cyclist's face whom is traveling from the west to the east as the wind blowing into the back of the cyclist gives the cyclist an extra boost. This glorious wind pattern is known as a tailwind.

Despite being fully aware of the predominate wind patterns of the Southern Tier, I felt like I was called to ride my bike from the west to the east contrary to favorable cycling winds. So, I did! And I'm glad I did! Riding east to west would have been a wonderful bike ride also, but for some unknown reason, I KNEW I was called to ride west to east. If you are considering riding the Southern Tier or any other major bike route, I recommend taking full advantage of the predominant seasonal wind patterns by planning your cross-country escapade accordingly!

Riding the Southern Tier in the Fall only makes good sense to travel east to west as to take full advantage of the natural wind tendencies thus regularly enjoying frequent tailwinds! In the Spring, the prevailing winds on the Southern Tier are WESTERLY as the wind offers a predominant tailwind to those cyclists starting in San Diego heading eastbound toward Florida.

Despite my dealing with mostly headwinds and crosswinds with very few tailwinds during my 43 days of bike travel, the winds didn't bother me much. Most days the wind was only blowing about 10 miles per hour or less and it didn't make a significant difference to me. To me, I really didn't care if I was going 12 miles per hour, 11 miles per hour, or even 10 miles per hour! Although the wind DEFINITELY slowed me down most of the time, I wasn't trying to break any speed records anyways! The slower, the better for me!

Most days upon arrival at my daily destination, I would check my phone for the weather forecast for the next day. As part of my preparations for the following day, I would also check the projected wind velocity as well. Knowing a likely projection of the upcoming weather helped me to more accurately plan my total number of miles for the following day. On days with significant headwinds, I might decrease my anticipated mileage down by 25-50% depending on the severity of the projected headwinds. In a wicked headwind like the one I had coming out of Sierra Blanca, Texas, my estimated mileage was cut down by more than 50%! On the contrary, in a strong tailwind, you might pedal 25-50% more miles than on a regular, non-windy biking day.

For two consecutive days in Louisiana, I enjoyed a nice 17 mile per hour tailwind for about 3 hours in each of the two afternoons from 1 p.m. to 4 p.m. Both of those days, I covered 108 miles on my bicycle. These two days were the longest mileage days of my bike journey and the only two days in which I surpassed the magical 100-mile mark!

DAY 14: The Gila National Forest is massive and BEAUTIFUL!!!

Chapter 47: Plan B

Regardless of how much time and effort you invest planning your epic bicycle tour, there WILL be days when you don't achieve your daily destination goal. For any one of hundreds of possible setbacks, you will NOT arrive at your planned location. On these days and EVERY other day, it is wise to have a "Plan B." Plan B is your second plan in case Plan A doesn't work out. Plan B allows you to take proper care of yourself despite missing your daily mileage target.

Look at your map. Consider the towns and cities you will be passing through. Be prepared to stay the night in any one of those towns along the way if you are not able to continue to your original destination. One of the worst scenarios is to find yourself BONKED in the middle of nowhere with nowhere to sleep. Bonking is a cyclist term describing a rather common cycling phenomenon occurring when your legs and body are DONE biking for the day. Bonking is when you CANNOT go any further. When you BONK, you are FINISHED for the day!

In preparation for a possible BONK, I kept a tent and sleeping bag with me at all times. In an emergency, my plan was to set up my tent in the first semi-reasonable location off to the side of the road! And despite my obsessive planning, this semi-unpleasant "Plan B" scenario happened a few times during my bike travels resulting in "wild camping" which is defined as "camping somewhere without permission."

Fortunately, I had a tent and sleeping gear with me at all times throughout my bike travels. Without a tent, you would most likely have to use your cell phone to call for help if you cannot pedal anymore. But keep in mind, you might not have cell reception on various parts of a remote bike route. If you BONK and you find yourself in a bad cell phone reception area, then you might have to flag down a passing vehicle and beg for help.

No matter what happens to you, keep in mind what my brother-in-law, Steve, often reminds me, "Be ready for anything when you are on an ADVENTURE!" The actual definition of an "adventure" according to Google is "an unusual and exciting, typically hazardous, experience or activity." Regardless of which particular definition you choose, adventures inherently revolve around a sizeable amount of uncertainty! Some days, I had to change my plans several times to accommodate the evolving circumstances in which I found myself.

Expect the unexpected! Assume changes and surprises will fill your day. Cultivating an attitude of such broad non-specific anticipation will better prepare you for the inevitable adversity awaiting you! Only by preparing your mind with a Plan B and maybe even a Plan C will you truly have a chance at crossing the country on a bicycle! When you finally become comfortable being uncomfortable, then you will receive a glimpse of REAL freedom! Welcome to the Southern Tier!

Chapter 48: Bike Lock

A bike lock might weigh one pound, but it is weight I don't mind carrying! For the first couple weeks while pedaling the Southern Tier Bicycle Route, I locked my bike every time I went into a store or restaurant. I guarded my bike as if it was my last possession on Earth! While on tour, my bike was MY LIFE and I couldn't afford to have it stolen.

My bike lock was about 3 feet long and it had a combination keypad attached to the end of the locking cord. By using four rotating cylinders made up of letters, I choose an easy-to-remember combination code to open my bike lock. Of course, I chose my wife's nickname, "TINK" as my bike lock combination code!

When I stopped at the convenience store, I would loop my bike lock cable around a heavy picnic table, propane gas cylinder rack, awning post, fence, or whatever else seemed most suitable. After making sure my bike was positioned perfectly as to avoid falling to the ground, I would lock my bike and scramble the combination code. After attaching my trusty pouch around my waist and inserting my cell phone into my pouch, I would enter the store.

Almost any bike lock will work, but the best type of bike lock in my opinion is the all-in-one bike lock like mine because all of the pieces are hooked together. There was NO KEY needed for me to open my lock. Nor was there a separate lock to attach to the cable. Not having a separate key or lock meant two less things I could possibly lose or misplace!

When locking your bike, situate the locking cord around part of the frame. Locking your bike only around the tires is also fine, but most tires nowadays can be quickly and easily removed as they are equipped with quick-release levers which make them slightly more susceptible to theft. Regardless of where you place your lock, try to keep your visit inside the store as brief as possible as it does not take long for a thief to cut your lock with a pair of bolt cutters.

When possible, keep your bike within your sight. Always monitor your bike! If your bike and gear were to be stolen while you were on an epic trip, it would be quite a loss, maybe enough to send you home! Of course, there is always the choice to buy a new bike and gear. Although your new bike and gear would be expensive, you should be able to salvage your trip if you have "deep pockets!"

As your biking trip unfolds and you gain confidence in yourself, your bike, and your fellow citizens, you will find yourself leaving your bike UNLOCKED from time to time in certain circumstances as you will intuitively feel when and where it is safe to do so. I'm not sure if you become more attune to danger as your voyage unfolds or if you become less WORRISOME as it is natural to become LESS UPTIGHT with each passing week. Becoming less worrisome is a sure-sign of emerging as a new person as you become MOLDED by the Southern Tier!

Chapter 49: Credit/Debit Cards

For a cross-country bicycle adventure, you better have at least 2 credit cards and maybe 3! One credit card should be in your wallet which is inside your waist pouch. The other credit card should be placed inside an envelope and zipped into one of the very small compartments inside one of your bike pannier bags.

As a BIG-TIME adventurer, you must PLAN FOR THE WORST! Imagine paying for your donuts at a gas station and the clerk forgets to return your credit card to you. What happens the next day when you are at the next store 70 miles away and you need to make a purchase? You better have one or more spare credit cards on hand!

Having two credit cards in two totally DIFFERENT locations inside of your bike pannier bags is the proper way to overcome common mistakes and make sure you don't find yourself dealing with unnecessary hassles. Remember, pedaling your bike 7 hours a day for MANY WEEKS is already asking a lot from you. Don't add additional pointless stress to your life by poor planning and careless actions!

In addition to two credit cards, make sure you have at least $500.00 in cash in your possession and available for use. Again, put a small amount of cash in your wallet and then carefully zip the rest of your cash into an envelope and zip it into another small location inside one of your pannier bags.

As you progress across the country on your bicycle, you will encounter numerous establishments unwilling to take your credit card as a form of payment. You will also encounter other places willing to give you a lower price if you pay with CASH instead of a credit card! Having a debit card in your possession is another wise strategy which allows you to pull cash out of an ATM machine if you run out of your initial cash reserve. Always plan for the worst in advance!

Although I have heard stories about cross-country cyclists whom despite having VERY LITTLE money and no credit cards, still made it across the country, I don't recommend this strategy for you. One cross-country cyclist I read about made it a habit of stopping at dumpsters looking for scraps of food instead of buying food. But with the exception of these VERY RARE and UNUSUAL cyclists, you should plan on spending a bare minimum of at least $3,000.00 in 2020 currency value to fund your cross-country efforts, even if you are a CHEAPSKATE like me!!! And that $3,000.00 does NOT include the cost of your bike and your gear. $3,000.00 only covers bare minimum food, drink, travel, and lodging for 45 days!

Save yourself the hassle and come prepared for your bike journey of a lifetime! Have 2-3 credit cards, 1 debit card, and at least $500.00 cash to start your epic bike travels!

Chapter 50: Body Weight

Here's the good news... If you ride your bike for 7 hours a day for 43 days, you WILL lose weight. Not only will you lose weight, you will be able to EAT ANYTHING AND EVERYTHING YOU WANT!!! At the beginning of my epic journey, I weighed 182 pounds. After my first seven days of riding, I weighed about 175 pounds.

Due to the CULTURE SHOCK combined with my MENTAL INSTABILITY, I had a hard time eating for the first week of my bike trip. As a result, I was losing one pound per day. Losing one pound per day is fine if you have the weight to lose, but I did NOT! I weighed 182 pounds when I started my epic bike ride and my IDEAL WEIGHT was only a mere two pounds lighter at 180 pounds!!!

It didn't take me long to calculate how my body would be in DANGER if I kept losing weight at this hasty pace. So, I FORCED myself to eat at EVERY 10-mile break. It didn't matter whether I ate at a local restaurant or whether I ate straight out of my pannier bags. Food was food! I needed CALORIES!!!

After the first week of long and lonely bike travels, I finally began to accept my NEW LIFE. With my acceptance of my new birthright, sometime during the second week of my bike travels, I regained my hunger and I finally got my weight under control. For the remainder of my bike journey, I maintained an acceptable weight of 162-167 pounds on my 6-foot one-inch body frame. Despite being slightly underweight, I greatly enjoyed my new body weight which was 15-20 pounds under my "regular weight" of 182 pounds.

During my third week of biking, I glanced in the full-length mirror at my hotel and I was surprised to see muscles on my body I had never seen before! To my pleasant amazement, from the top of my body to the bottom, I resembled a poster-body for a health and fitness magazine! In my own humble opinion, I must admit, I looked REALLY GOOD! It was a delight to view such a strong and flexible physical physique.

The human body/mind/spirit is more amazing than we realize. Your body will SETTLE IN at whatever weight you need in order to continue to produce 7 hours of pedaling output per day. All you have to do is follow the daily basics of kindergarten cycling. Drink every 3 miles. Eat every 10 miles. Sleep well. Think pleasant thoughts. Pray a lot. Keep yourself CLEAN! And pedal A LOT!!!

Always eat something BEFORE you start your ride in the morning, even if it is only a granola bar and a box of raisins or a doughnut and a banana. Remember to mix in some sports drink as to replenish your electrolytes and other important nutrients required for you to maintain the ridiculous daily biking demands! Oh, and remember my biking secret weapon, chocolate milk! Upon finishing your bike ride for the day, eat everything you possibly can and flush it down with a half-gallon of chocolate milk. You will NEED those calories tomorrow!!!

Chapter 51: Helmet Brim Hat

Two months before departing on my epic bicycle ride, I discovered a "brim hat." A brim hat is a 3-inch sombrero-type, circular-brim which attaches to your bike helmet with Velcro. The brim hat goes all the way around your helmet and does a GREAT JOB keeping excess sun and rain off of your face, neck, and shoulders.

Adventure Cycling sells the brim hat for about $50.00, but since I am EXTREMELY cheap, I found a similar bright yellow brim hat on eBay for only $15.00. The generic brim hat I used worked great, but I had to use some extra Velcro and a few plastic cable ties to properly anchor the flashy brim hat tight to my helmet. With some slight modifications, you should be able to fit your brim hat to your helmet in a way it can withstand at least 30 mile per hour winds. Even if your brim hat flips up a bit when you exceed 30 miles per hour, in most cases, it will easily adjust back into place.

In addition to the practical benefits of my useful brim hat, I LOVED the FASHION of my brim hat. Wearing my bright yellow sombrero hat made me feel SPECIAL! Over time, my brim hat became an ESSENTIAL part of my bicycle attire!!! Several times daily, random people would comment to me about my AMAZING yellow brim helmet hat!!! It was common daily for numerous strangers to yell out to me, "Hey man, nice hat!"

Over time, my bright yellow brim hat became a significant part of my new identity. I loved the look of my stylish brim and MANY others commented on my unusual distinct helmet hat. Most likely, strangers referred to me as "the biker guy with the bright yellow hat" and I was completely fine with such a distinct reputation!

Male or female, get yourself a big, bright, audacious brim hat! Buy the brightest color you can. With safety foremost in my mind, I purchased lots of BRIGHT YELLOW cycling gear as to give the vehicles around me the best chance of seeing me and my bicycle. Trust me. You will LOVE your new brim hat! Plus, it folds up small enough to fit into a sandwich Ziploc bag, but I NEVER take my brim hat off of my helmet since it is somewhat permanently attached as I wear my brim hat in ALL conditions!

As soon as I put my bold brim hat on my head, my entire psyche transforms and I immediately harness all the confidence I had gained from the Southern Tier. My brim hat is no different than the bright red, magical cape used by Clark Kent to transform himself into Superman!

Chapter 52: Sunglasses

God blessed me on my 43-day bicycle excursion across the southern United States with an ABUNDANCE of sunny, warm during most of my days. With the exception of 3 cold days and one ridiculously BITTER COLD day, I mostly rode my bike through relatively sunny, warm weather.

Despite being sunny, I only wore my sunglasses on a few occasions. In fact, I almost shipped my sunglasses back home when I mailed my second and final return package back home, but at the last moment I decided to keep my sunglasses with me. In my case, my bright yellow brim hat seemed to keep most of the sun out of my eyes. Most of the time, I really didn't need sunglasses.

When I did wear sunglasses, they would often get blurry as my sweat would run off of my head and quickly smear my sunglasses. It wasn't a huge problem, but it was a bit annoying as my sunglasses needed wiped clean regularly and I spent lots of time looking through unclear lenses!

Decide for yourself about sunglasses. For me, I'll probably continue to bring sunglasses along with me on my upcoming bike tours, but I would NEVER leave my gaudy, bright-yellow brim hat at home!

DAY 14: I stayed for FREE in this 1947 camper in Hillsboro, New Mexico thanks to the gracious owner of the park, Kristin. The makeshift building in the back of the camper was my bathroom!!!

Chapter 53: Visibility

If you get run over by a vehicle and die while pedaling your bicycle, then you will NOT finish your epic, cross-country biking goal! Therefore, safety is of utmost concern in your cross-country planning. For me, bright yellow was the theme. Start with your bike. If you can order a bright yellow or bright orange bike, then do it. In my case, I was stuck with a boring blue bike as I couldn't locate an adequate fluorescent-colored or reflective bicycle. Maybe one of the really smart bike manufactures will read this book and understand the need to produce more brightly-colored reflective road bicycles!!!

Next is your clothing. Wear bright, reflective clothing. For some reason, bike shorts seem to be boring black, but if you can find something more colorful, then buy it. In most cases, you should easily locate a bright shirt to buy. Your rain gear should DEFINITELY be super bright with built-in reflectors as visibility is often highly compromised when it is raining.

Rigged to the back of my helmet and attached to the back of my rear pannier bag frame was a bright blinking SWERVE taillight. As it approached darkness, I would turn on BOTH of my awesome taillights. Having a bright yellow helmet is also a good idea as is having the brightest and most reflective pannier bags you can find.

Also consider buying reflective stickers to add to your pannier bags, bike, and helmet to further increase your visibility. For my spokes, I even bought some bright-orange reflective covers as to add to my overall visibility. My stack on the back of my rear rack was also bright pink for a very good reason! Your governing philosophy should be to be as VISIBLE AS POSSIBLE. Don't worry if your random bright colors don't match. One qualified cross-country cycling author advises being as bright as a Christmas tree. Your job is to be visible and STAY ALIVE!

Chapter 54: Rubbing Toes

For some unknown reason, after an extended amount of time in my biking shoes, my 4th little toe (the one next to my smallest toe) got irritated, swelled up, and began to cause me rather severe pain on several instances while making my cross-country attempt. Although I never had my left foot checked by a foot doctor, I knew I had a severe fallen arch and it appeared as though my toes might be slightly wider than the area provided by my bicycle shoes.

Prior to my cross-country trip, I never had problems with my 4th toe on any of my other much shorter bike rides, but while pedaling the Southern Tier, sometime during the 3rd week, my 4th toe on my left foot began to hurt. And once my toe began to hurt, it hurt more and more until I was forced to stop pedaling, take my shoe and sock off, massage my toes, and apply BAG BALM to relieve the throbbing pain.

Bag Balm is a product that resembles jelly. It either comes in a tube like a crème or it is packaged in a small metal container. Bag Balm was first used by farmers in Vermont to prevent chaffing with their dairy cows. The product worked so well on the cow's udders, it was finally marketed and manufactured for human use as well. Cows or not, I give my stamp of approval for Bag Balm. This fine product is effective to relieve chaffing skin caused from consistent rubbing on any area of your body.

Without Bag Balm and the consistent STRETCHING of my toes, it is possible the SEVERE pain in my left foot could have been enough to send me back home!!! The pain stemming from toe number 4 on my left foot was almost unbearable at times. The pain would consume my every thought until such time as I pulled over, took off my shoe and sock, and stretched my toes apart!

Another solution to toe pain has to do with wearing 5-toe socks. 5-toe socks are socks manufactured to give each of your 5 toes their own dedicated sock compartment. No longer do all 5 of your toes have to share the same single sock compartment. Now, each toe has its OWN toe compartment! Although rather expensive, my favorite pair of 5 toe socks are made by Injinji and can be purchased on eBay or on the Injinji website.

It is also a great idea to buy WIDE biking shoes whenever possible as your feet will SWELL during your ride. When buying bike shoes, always buy shoes at least a half shoe size to a full shoe size larger than your "regular" everyday shoes! Having slightly more space than necessary is much better than experiencing the potentially excruciating pain of crowding your toes in your narrow biking shoes!

Chapter 55: Ear Buds

Riding your bicycle seven hours a day, 49 hours per week, gets a little monotonous at times! Although it is paramount to your safety to keep your attention focused on the repetitive, but critical task at hand and upon the unfolding of your immediate surroundings, there are many times you can enjoy some music, listen to a podcast or educational recording, take a few phone calls, or most importantly, get turn-by-turn directions from Google Maps.

Although I used my ear buds to handle many business calls as I rode my bike across the country, at times it was slightly tough for the other person to hear me with the interfering sounds of the wind and the road. Maybe if I got better ear buds, the speaker feature would be better? Nonetheless, for the most part, I had many successful phone conversations while using my ear buds as I pedaled my bicycle along the southern portion of the United States of America.

Wireless Bluetooth ear buds will easily pair with your cell phone and provide you with an excellent audio experience and you won't have to worry about wires getting snagged on your clothing and/or bike. Purchasing an ear bud designed to loop over the top of your ear will make it very unlikely they will ever fall out of your ear while you are pedaling.

Of course, it goes without saying to pay extra careful attention while using your ear buds. You are traveling on a road with vehicles and it is important to know what is occurring in your immediate vicinity. That's why some cyclists are vehemently opposed to the use of sound while biking as they feel it impairs their hearing and compromises their safety. Despite the reasonable safety concerns expressed by other cyclists, I continue to recommend the prudent use of ear buds as an acceptable risk to take while cycling on certain roads with either big berms and/or very little traffic. Make sure your gear list includes wireless ear buds!

Chapter 56: Poop

If you expect to have a CHANCE at completing an epic, cross-country bicycle ride, then you better learn how to poop alongside the road! As you pedal for many hours at a time, the call of nature WILL occur. Maybe you can "hold it" for a few miles causing a slight delay to nature's process until you come to a store or gas station, but oftentimes you will find yourself on desolate roads either surrounded by trees or engulfed in desert cacti and there won't be any reasonable facility to relieve yourself of the budding half-pound of waste product. Admittingly, it would be ideal f it was possible to pre-plan this important bodily function to occur seamlessly at the next McDonalds, but it doesn't usually work that way! The urge to poop will come when the urge to poop decides to come! Sometimes you will find yourself pooping alongside your bike route in the middle of nowhere.

Holding your poop inside of your body for more than a couple minutes is a VERY POOR choice as the possible ramifications for doing so could cost you DEARLY! Poop is made up of POISON and you must release this putrid chunk of toxin from your body within minutes of getting the URGE! Holding back the poop could potentially release part of the contaminant back into your body and create discomfort and illness lasting for one or more days. When you get the urge to defecate, you need to release the pressure and drop your load QUICKLY!

Pull off to the side of the road and securely park your bicycle. Go to the "easy access" zippered compartment on the outside of your rear left pannier bag and grab your quarter roll of toilet paper which should be securely placed inside a Ziploc bag. Then, carefully walk about 20 feet or so into the woods being very careful with every step not to step on or near a snake, etc. Find a location away from any type of creek, spring, or any other type of water source as you want to avoid contaminating the fresh water with your excrement!

Clear a spot on the ground with your feet. Use your 1-ounce backpacking shovel to dig a small hole about 6 inches deep with about a 4-inch circumference. Fold 1 or 2 pieces of toilet paper and lay them in front of you on the ground for easy access. Pull down your pants to your ankles and squat nice and low with your heels straddling your newly dug hole. Make sure your heels are placed just barely in front of the hole and then give a strong push and LET IT OUT! As you squat, make sure you pull your pants/shorts all the way down close to your ankles as to avoid the possibility of pooping on your clothes!

Bill Ladika, Sr, a dear friend of mine, was hunting in the woods during winter. Early in the morning, Big Bill got "the urge" and he struggled to get his one-piece winter hunting outfit down below his waist as to provide enough room to relieve himself. As Bill took a nice, healthy crap in the woods, he smiled in delight and didn't think much more about it, but to his dismay, off and on throughout the day, Bill caught a nasty whiff of poop as he walked through the woods. The nasty feces odor perplexed him all day until early evening when he returned to his truck, took off his jacket, and discovered he accidentally pooped into the hood of his one-piece hunting outfit! All day, Bill carried his load of feces with him inside his hood as he walked through the woods!!!

As you are pooping, spread your butt cheeks nice and wide. Doing so will expand your skin apart and create a slightly larger opening for your dung to leave your body without creating any sticky, leftover butt-crust residue on your pristine tail cheeks. After your stinky deposit has been made into the hole, then you MUST clean your butthole COMPLETELY and THOROUGHLY! There are few things so irritating to a cyclist as trying to ride a bike with "Crust-a-Butt!"

If you have a bit of hand sanitizer or liquid soap, it is a GREAT IDEA to apply a few drops to your last piece of toilet paper as to make absolute sure your tail end is CYCLING CLEAN!!! Clean is the theme!!! If you have poor hygiene in any way, your meager habits will eventually cause you to pay BIG-TIME during your cross-country event! CLEAN, CLEAN, CLEAN should be your operative philosophy!!! Clean is your theme!

As you finish your necessary deed, use the loose dirt to cover over your feces and then place a nice heavy rock over your newly buried treasure as to memorialize the event and to prevent any animal from unearthing your gem. The general pooping premise is for your poop to be never again seen or detected by man or by animal. After the proper burial, your crap should decompose into the ground and become important fertilizer for the benefit of future generations!

As disgusting as this all sounds, effective pooping is a CRUCIAL part of long-distance bike travel. If I was to omit this critical section, I would be doing a major disservice to any aspiring cross-country cyclist! Despite being a tad silly at times with regard to this delicate subject matter, I am DEAD SERIOUS about the necessity of having the proper "pooping mindset." Successful cross-country cyclists are SAVAGES with the capability of pooping in any halfway reasonable location! Don't be too picky. Just pull over and let your intuition guide you! If you can't find an "appropriate place" to crap alongside the road, then you do NOT have what it takes to complete a cross-country biking crusade! Welcome to the Southern Tier!

Chapter 57: Talk Less

In January 2020, 9 months prior to my cross-country bike ride, I was "moved" to pedal my bicycle across the United States of America! As per my divine prompting, 2020 was the year for my epic cross-country bicycle adventure! From March 2020 to August 2020, ONLY my wife knew about my "crazy" biking plans. Not another human being on planet Earth knew about my cross-country intentions. During this secretive time, I read 8 books, gathered necessary equipment, made my checklists, and planned for my upcoming mission to cross America on a bicycle. My children did not even know about my intents. My parents were clueless about my newest absurd pursuit and my sister never found out about my trip until I was already in flight to my starting destination in San Diego, California!

Only out of pure necessity in September, one month before my epic departing, did I share my surprising cross-country biking plans with my parents as I had particular questions only my father was qualified to advise me. After numerous trips to my local bike shop throughout the summer in preparation for my big cross-country outing, two of the workers finally asked me what I was doing as they could sense it was something immense. Reluctantly, I disclosed my true intents to each of them! But for the most part, my October 10th cross-country bicycle undertaking was a SECRET!

Throughout my life, I've noticed most people do A LOT of talking without much ACTION to back it up! To me, it is important to keep my mouth shut and let my actions do the talking for me! If you really want to find out about a person, don't ask him, WATCH him! What a person does is who they are. What a person says is just a bunch of meaningless words! Talk is NOTHING! Action is EVERYTHING! Talk is a dream. Action is life! What you do is what counts!

When you talk too much about something, you actually weaken yourself making your desired outcome much less likely to occur. Excessive speech wastes your critical life energy on words instead of deeds! For me, it was hard enough to get myself to take on the challenge of pedaling a bicycle across the United States of America. The last thing I needed was other people reminding me about the massive difficultly of my upcoming, rigorous bicycle travels!

If you are an outgoing type of person who enjoys talking about your life, your plans, and your goals, then I guess it is fine to share your "bike across America" plans with others, but be careful! Too much talk is DANGEROUS! The more you talk, the less likely you are to FINISH! For me, my undertaking was PERSONAL. My cross-country bicycle venture was NOT a public matter! My cross-country biking adventure had to do with what it would make of me as a person and not so much about anything else.

If you are a very social person and you enjoy talking about your upcoming travels, then make sure you spend at least ten times more energy PLANNING your special bicycle tour than you do talking about it! Otherwise, you may not even take the first pedal stroke!

DAY 17: The desert can be very LONELY!

DAY 18: The bike riding day from HELL! Here I am FREEZING as I pedaled through a 30 mile per hour headwind for 4 hours in the desert on my way to Van Horn, Texas. This photo is NOT indicative of my WORST condition on this UNFORGETTABLE day! Today, I became a MAN!

Chapter 58: Headlamp

Almost every single day of my 43-day bike ride across the USA, I made use of my headlamp. A headlamp is an essential piece of gear for a cross-country cyclist. A headlamp should be stored in the "easy access" compartment inside your rear left pannier bag. When it is 4:00 a.m. and you are broken down in the middle of the desert with a flat tire, you will be thankful you have a headlamp to strap to your forehead as to free your hands to quickly change your flat tire.

Headlamps usually operate by a button. Pressing the button on the headlamp will activate various levels of brightness. It's always a good idea to use as little light as possible to get the job done as to preserve your precious battery power. Most headlamps use 3 AAA batteries and will probably last for your entire trip. Having 3 brand new spare AAA batteries on stand-by as potential replacements for your original batteries is also an excellent idea.

During my many nights sleeping inside my tent, my headlamp was placed directly beside my head as to provide easy-access throughout the night. When I awoke 1,2, 3, or 4 times during the night to pee, I would grab my headlamp as I exited my tent to relieve myself. As my bike travels extended, I learned about the glorious "whiz bottle" in which case I would grab my headlamp and illuminate my tiny, sleepy penis as I CAREFULLY whizzed inside my "whiz bottle" while remaining mostly tucked away inside of my cozy sleeping bag. Either way, my headlamp proved to be MAJORLY convenient! Upon waking in the morning, I also used my headlamp to get dressed as I began riding most days in complete darkness.

Shop around a bit and look for a lightweight, powerful, long-lasting headlamp. Make sure the battery compartment is very secure as to decrease the chances of losing your batteries or dealing with poorly constructed equipment. You should also be certain to buy a headlamp with an AMAZING head strap as there are many headlamps on the market with chintzy head straps. Each piece of your gear should be personally tested for proper quality prior to your epic bicycle adventure! There are a lot of "cheesy" headlamps in the marketplace. Again, you might be best advised to buy whatever headlamp is being sold by Adventure Cycling in their annual CYCLOSOURCE magazine as you can rest assured, if Adventure Cycling Association sells it, the product will be GREAT quality!

Chapter 59: Sleep

If you don't get adequate sleep, you will NOT be able to finish your cross-country bicycle quest! Sleep is your body's chance to recover (or semi-recover) from the previous day's activities. If you do NOT sleep well, your body will only be partially recovered and you will start less than 100% or possibly a lot less than 100%.

Riding your bicycle 3,000 miles might be the biggest challenge you ever partake! Even if you are 100% rested every night, you will push your body, mind, and spirit well beyond any former boundary. In short, you really can't afford to sleep poorly. The many various impacts of poor sleep will also flow over into your attitude which is the absolute WORST place for you to be affected. When aspiring cross-country cyclists suffer any dip whatsoever in their governing attitude, giving up and going home becomes a VERY CLOSE reality!

Poor sleep will make you:
1. Physically weak
2. Mentally weak
3. Spiritually weak

The good news about sleep and aspiring to be a bona-fide cross-country finisher is......... With the right daily habits, sleep will NOT be a problem for you! EVERY single night of my 43-day biking journey was a GOOD NIGHT'S SLEEP! Not one night did I have a poor night's sleep! EVERY single night I slept well! And if you follow my advice, you will be SOUTHERN TIER TIRED at the end of the day and you will also sleep well EVERY night, just like me! Here's my formula:

1. Wake up and get out of bed before sunrise. I woke up at 4:30 a.m. most days on the Southern Tier.
2. Praise God for the gift of another day!
3. Meditate for one minute or more while you are still inside your tent.
4. Start pedaling before sunrise.
5. Pray on the phone with your spouse as you ride.
6. Ride <u>really</u> SLOW at first. Continue to pedal SLOWLY throughout the day. 11 miles per hour is slightly too FAST!
7. Drink every 3 miles.
8. Eat every 10 miles.
9. Walk every 10 miles.
10. Arrive at your daily destination.
11. Set up your tent and arrange your sleeping gear.
12. Get a shower.
13. Wash your clothes in the shower.
14. Squeeze-dry your clothes as best you can and then hang them to dry overnight.
15. Take meticulous care of your "saddle area" applying chamois buttr and

anti-monkey butt powder.
16. Eat and drink everything you can in the evening. Your stomach should be FULL!!!
17. Plan your destination for tomorrow. Contact the motel, campground, Warmshowers host, etc.
18. Make a few SIMPLE entries in your daily journal.
19. Study a foreign language or spend 10-20 minutes doing something educational.
20. Process texts, emails, and phone messages. Take care of any business or personal matters back home.
21. Call your spouse and your loved ones.
22. Go to bed EARLY!!!! 9 p.m. was my bed time on the Southern Tier!

Prior to going to bed, you MUST make sure ALL of your belongings are in excellent order.

1. Lock your bike.
2. Hang your washed, wet clothes somewhere to dry.
3. Hang your food bag in a tree or place it at an appropriate inside overnight location.
4. Open your paper route map to the correct page for tomorrow's big cycling journey.
5. Review the first 10 miles of your bike route for tomorrow.
6. Recharge your GPS watch, headlight, cell phone, battery bank, etc.
7. Set out the exact clothes you anticipate you will wear cycling tomorrow.
8. Make sure all of the various nuts and bolts on your bike are tight.
9. Check the air pressure in your tires. 70 pounds of pressure in front. 80 pounds in back.
10. Put a few drops of lubricant on your bike chain.

My goal was to have my belongings in excellent order the night before. Saving precious time in the morning was important to me! Plus, having your personal and business affairs in good order helps you to sleep better! Remember, your "new life" requires a lot of pedaling. Spinning your pedals is YOUR JOB! Close your eyes early and keep them closed all night. You have "work" early in the next morning!

Keeping your eyes <u>closed</u> is the SECRET to getting a good night's sleep! Yes, this bit of advice might seem overly simplistic, but I PROMISE you, MANY people sleep poorly because they open their eyes, even for one second, for various reasons before they fall to sleep. When you make the choice to fall asleep, you should NOT open your eyes at all for any reason! Keep your eyes COMPLETELY closed NO MATTER WHAT! Follow my advice and you will sleep well. Open your eyes and you will have sleeping problems!

Another key to good sleeping is to use your sleeping pad for SLEEPING ONLY!

Don't lay down on your sleeping pad and browse the Internet on your phone. Don't lay down on your sleeping pad and read your book. Don't lay down on your sleeping pad and talk on the phone. Don't lay on your sleeping pad gazing at the stars for 30 minutes. Your sleeping pad and sleeping bag should be used for one thing and one thing only...... TO SLEEP! Nothing else should be done on your sleeping gear other than sleeping! SLEEP should be the one and only association you have to your sleeping pad and sleeping bag. Using your sleeping pad and sleeping bag for any other purposes is counter-effective to your goal of sleeping well.

The ONLY exemption to this golden rule concerning the proper use of your sleeping gear for only sleep would be in the case you were laying on your sleeping gear HUMPING your wife! As my long-time loyal friend, Shawn Hollis, would say, "If you are getting some "work," then it's OK!"

The human body operates according to the thought patterns dictated by the human mind. It is crucial to make sure your mind sends your body a clear message about your sleep pattern. When you snuggle inside your nice warm sleeping bag, it is NOW time for sleep. Nothing else! Your only thought should be of sleep. Your cell phone should be turned OFF and all other thoughts should be RELEASED from your mind. It is now time to SLEEP! By taking this type of concerted sleep approach, you are *training* your mind and body to FALL ASLEEP when you lay down. When you couple this simple advice with keeping your eyes completely closed and being "Southern Tier tired," you will sleep WELL! Trust me!

It also doesn't hurt to say a quick prayer moments before closing your eyes. My regular night time prayer goes something like this, "God, grant me a peaceful, restful, and safe sleep tonight. May I wake up in the morning feeling energetic and healthy. Amen." Drifting off into sleep with these simple and powerful words will also serve to make the final important transition as you attain proper rest.

In the unlikely case you don't sleep well on any given night, don't panic. Your body can easily handle one bad night's sleep, but don't experience a second night of poor sleep in a row or else your performance WILL suffer!

Simply close your eyes and keep them closed. As long as your eyes are closed, you are sleeping! Don't try to judge your quality of sleep. Just lay down and close your eyes and RELAX! If you close your eyes and keep them closed as of 9 p.m., then as per my decree, you are officially SLEEPING as of 9 p.m. regardless of whether or not you consciously toss and turn a bit.

When you pedal a bicycle for 7 hours a day, it is unlikely you will have any problems sleeping. Even if you suffer from a sleep disorder, you may find long-distance bicycle touring curative of your sleeping impediments! Cross-country cycling is capable of CHANGING your life in MANY ways!

You might notice from my preceding listing; I did NOT include drinking excessive alcohol or hanging out at the local bar late into the night as part of your daily ritual to ensure quality sleep. There is absolutely no way I could have logged the miles I did if I drank alcohol, hung out at bars and night clubs, or stayed up late. A dedicated cross-country cyclist has their priorities in order by keeping their habits healthy and strong as to produce the required energy needed to complete the scheduled mileage for the following day!

Each of us have our own life rhythms. Some of us are "morning people" and some of us are "night owls." Others thrive during the middle of the day. For me, my most precious time of the day is EARLY MORNING. On normal, non-bike touring days, I like to stay awake until about 11:00 p.m. and wake up at 6 a.m. with an hour nap around noon. While on the Southern Tier, I woke up most mornings at about 4:30 a.m. and was pedaling no later than 5:30 a.m. Since my bike ride across the country was more like a MISSION than a TOUR, I would go to bed at approximately 9 p.m. every night. Sleeping from 9 p.m. to 4:30 a.m. WITHOUT an afternoon nap gave me about 7.5 hours of sleep per day which seemed to be adequate for me.

On more than one occasion, I fell asleep during an evening phone call with my loving wife. After many days pedaling 7 hours a day, I never felt so tired in all of my life. My common terminology for my deep level of fatigue was "Southern Tier tired!" When I mentioned "Southern Tier tired" to my supportive wife, she knew exactly what I meant! My sudden nodding off while speaking with Tink on the phone was an obvious testament to my high-level of daily exertion.

Being on a mission, I had NO DESIRE to hang out at the local bar, night club, etc. The primary thought in my mind was planning for and arriving at my next day's destination. Tv shows, books, and even my Duolingo Spanish course was NOT enough to take my attention away from preparing for my big biking adventure the following day! My bicycle quest was not about sight-seeing, studying foreign languages, watching tv shows, drinking beer, or mingling with the public. Instead, my biking travels were a mission to FIND MYSELF! I was pedaling across the United States of America to figure out what I was made of and to DEVELOP myself into a better person. My cross-country biking adventure was all about PERSONAL DEVELOPMENT! I took on the cross-country challenge for WHAT IT WOULD MAKE OF ME and I was NOT distracted for long by anything unrelated!

If you are NOT on a "mission" and you want to take in all the sights, mingle with the locals, study foreign languages, read books, and watch tv, then it is also very possible for you to complete your "sea to shining sea" quest, but your experience will be vastly different from the approach I share in this book! Instead of partaking in extracurricular activities, I used any spare time for rest and to ensure I got at least 7 hours of sleep per night as to properly prepare my body for an onslaught of biking mileage the following day.

Although I keep mentioning "7 hours of sleep," don't worry about calculating your exact sleeping time. Simply lay your head down on your pillow and close your eyes. The moment you close your eyes and keep them closed; you are officially "sleeping!" Discipline yourself to keep your eyes closed, stay in bed, and either silently say prayers or think healthy thoughts. Whatever you do, don't try to add up the hours of your sleep for any given night. Don't worry about specific times while falling asleep as your body, mind, and spirit will naturally make sure you are well rested as to recover from your deep level of bodily fatigue!

As for naps, it is DIFFICULT, but not impossible, to get a nap from time to time along the Southern Tier. In my opinion, you are better off sleeping an extra hour through the night than trying to take a nap during the day. Nonetheless, if you are a dedicated napper, like me, then it is POSSIBLE to get a nap from time to time. Just find a shaded place out of the way of vehicles where you can close your eyes for a while. Anything is possible on the Southern Tier if you want it bad enough!

DAY 20: Only by pedaling the Southern Tier Bicycle Route can you EXPERIENCE the true beauty of the precious landscape!

Chapter 60: Preparation

Hurray! You have arrived at your daily biking destination for the day! It's time to celebrate! As for me, it was always a huge RELIEF and a JOY when I finally arrived at my planned daily destination!

Upon arrival at your daily destination, it is now time to pull out your map and determine a new destination for tomorrow. Start by locating a destination approximately the same number of miles away as is your average daily distance of bike travel. If you are like me, then you would advance about 70 miles ahead on your map and choose a proposed ending destination for tomorrow.

Most days, I did NOT travel exactly 70 miles! Some days were less mileage and some days involved more mileage. 70 was my average daily mileage total over my 43-day cycling escapade. If you remove my 2.5 days of rest from the equation, then I traveled an average of 74 miles per day.

After you figure out how far along the route 70 miles or so would get you, then refer to your elevation chart to determine what type of terrain you will be traversing. Is it rolling hills, flat, or mountainous? The higher the elevation gains, the less mileage you will cover.

It is also VERY important to consider the wind forecast for tomorrow as you are deciding upon your proposed overnight destination. If you are traveling east and there are 20 mile per hour EASTERLY winds forecasted, then you will be dealing with one heck of a headwind and you should probably scale back your planned mileage. On the other hand, if the forecast calls for a 20 mile per hour WESTERLY wind, then you might want to increase your planned mileage since you will be getting a HUGE assist from a significant tailwind! Remember, westerly winds blow from the west to the east. Easterly winds blow from the east to the west. Northerly winds blow from the north to the south. And southerly winds blow from the south to the north.

Another factor you might want to consider are the cities you will be traveling through. Big cities will definitely slow down your progress as there are many more turns to make. Big cities also have lots of traffic lights. Oftentimes, there is construction, delays, and other possible detours. Add about an extra one hour to your estimated travel time if you will be passing through any major cities along your way. Along the Southern Tier, you will pass through numerous big cities including: San Diego, Tempe, Phoenix, El Paso, Del Rio, Austin, Mobile, Tallahassee, and Jacksonville. You will also pass through many smaller cities like Mesa, Silver City, Navasota, New Rhoads, Poplarville, Lake City, etc. It is important to note that Jacksonville is NOT an official Southern Tier city, but I chose to finish in Jacksonville instead of St. Augustine which is the official end point of the Southern Tier Bicycle Route.

Once I got a general idea of where I expected to finish the next day, I would open my Warmshowers app on my phone and search for a Warmshowers host in the general area where I wished to arrive. While searching a particular city or town, a buffet of potential hosts would populate my screen. Sometimes there were ZERO hosts in a particular town and sometimes larger cities had dozens of hosts! Some hosts were marked "available" and others were marked "unavailable."

Review the potential Warmshowers hosts and read their blog. Decide which host seems like the best fit and then call or text the person and directly ASK them to host you tomorrow night. Some Warmshowers hosts ask for 2-3 days advance notice, but on a cross-country bike trip, this is an unreasonable request as it is usually too difficult to try to plan more than one day in advance. In most cases, Warmshowers hosts are more than happy to accommodate you with a standard 1-day advance notice regardless of the specific wording on their particular profile!

As you are considering your options for the upcoming day, it is important to check in with yourself as well as the spiritual POWER pulsating within you. There is DEFINITELY a major spiritual and intuitive aspect to solo cross-country cycling!!! Tap into your intuition, subconscious, God-power and make sure your destination choice has a positive, healthy VIBRATION within your body, mind, and spirit! Make sure your final targeted choice FEELS GOOD!

As you are making your decisions for tomorrow, also consider your current physical condition. Do you have any developing injuries? Are you strong and healthy? Plan accordingly!

DAY 20: Nice big berm! Also notice the rumble strips to help keep the vehicular drivers off of the berm!

Chapter 61: LIFE 360

LIFE 360 is a GPS phone app. LIFE 360 can be downloaded on your cell phone for FREE! The superb LIFE 360 phone app allows you to track the specific location of any particular person in your established group. All you do is form a group, all members of which agree to disclose their phone's location to each of the other members of the particular group. After downloading the app, each member of the group completes a brief confirmation process after receiving an "invitation" from the creator of the group. Even being somewhat non-technical, I found the whole group-forming process on LIFE 360 to be rather easy!

After you complete the simple confirmation steps, you will be added to the group. Your photo will show up as a small round circle on the map. Next to the name of each member of the group is a short phrase revealing their current location such as "near 123 Main Street in San Diego, CA."

Using the LIFE 360 phone app will let everyone included in your group know EXACTLY where you are at all times, providing you do not turn off your phone, turn off your location setting, or lose your phone. In my case, while traveling 1,000 miles through the harsh southwest desert, my LIFE 360 presence was only out of service for very brief durations of time! It was surprising how well LIFE 360 maintained my whereabouts despite my being at "the ends of the Earth!"

Through the use of complex satellites orbiting our superlative planet Earth, LIFE 360 keeps everyone in your group informed as to where you are located and the current speed in which you are moving. My mom would watch me for hours as I traveled on average about 11 miles per hour across the southern portion of the United States of America on my bicycle. LIFE 360 saved my mom from many hours of unnecessary worry as she could stare at her phone and see me progressing along the revered roads of the Southern Tier.

Depending on the particular area and other variables outside of my knowledge, my mom was also often able to zoom in on LIFE 360 and see my specific-traveled road and in some cases, the actual house of my particular host. Myself and my family were VERY impressed with LIFE 360 and I HIGHLY recommend the stellar phone app to you! Much thanks to the creator of this useful mobile application! My LIFE 360 family group consisting of myself, my wife, my mother, my father, and my sister used the FREE version of LIFE 360 app, but there is also a paid version which is probably even more AMAZING and can likely provide much better service, but for all intents and purposes, the free app was more than adequate for our limited purpose.

Chapter 62: Stand Up

Most cyclists get annoyed as they approach a hill, but NOT me! As I approach hills, I get happy! Hills are a chance for me to get out of my sitting position and STAND UP on my pedals for a while! Standing up on your pedals creates an ENTIRELY different pattern of movement with your bodily mechanics. Standing not only allows the use of different muscles, but it also relieves many aches and pains created from excessive time spent in the standard seated position.

Standing up rejuvenates your body by stretching your muscles, ligaments, tendons, and blood vessels as you are riding your bicycle. It is also a wonderful way to promote a more comfortable sense of longevity on your bike ride! Making regular changes to your body positioning by standing up wherever and whenever possible is exactly what every cross-country cyclist needs to break up the monotony of the long-distance ride and to maintain loose key bodily components.

Long distance bike rides create a natural tendency to fall into a TRANCE as you ride in one position for an extended amount of time. As you go deeper and deeper into your trance, you become less and less aware of your surroundings. And as you know by now, DANGER is all around you ALL THE TIME! You cannot afford to be lulled into a semi-conscious mindset while cycling. It is important to battle this dangerous haphazard tendency by standing up at EVERY opportunity you get and renewing your overall sense of awareness. Get happy when you see a hill approaching. That approaching hill is your chance to keep yourself SAFE, ALERT, and HEALTHY!

As you grind out mile after mile on your new "job," remember, this cross-country cycling journey is NOT a race. Moving slowly is to be expected. Traveling between 9 to 11 miles an hour is going to be your average overall speed if you are similar to me and many other successful cross-country finishers. While climbing hills, your speed will decrease to about 5 miles per hour and your downhill can be as fast as 40 miles per hour at times, but I highly suggest to keep your maximum touring speed no more than 30 miles per hour as per reasonable safety concerns.

Stand up and enjoy your new slower speed as you tackle the ascent facing you. Plow ahead as you keep your pedals revolving around in a circular motion at a steady cadence and you will be doing GREAT. As long as your pedals are spinning, you are moving, even if there are times when it doesn't really feel like it!

Chapter 63: Walk

If you think you can put your head down and crank out 70 miles per day at one sitting on your bike, then maybe you should be reading a book about participating in the Tour de France or some other radical 2,000-mile bicycle race.? When you are traveling across the country with a heavy touring bike containing 70 pounds or more of gear, you will NEED to get off of your bike REGULARLY throughout each day and WALK!!! Do NOT try to be "Superman" and ride your bike NON-STOP daily! Every 10 miles you should pull off to the side of the road, carefully park you bike as to make certain your bike does NOT fall over, and then pace back and forth alongside the road for about 5 minutes while you eat a snack.

Pacing back and forth alongside the road will relieve your bodily muscles of the constant strain of staying in the same compromised cycling position for extended periods of time. Spending too much time in any one position is a recipe for cramps, very sore muscles, pinched nerves, and a variety of other ill health effects! Instead, get off of your bike seat and put some walking steps on your legs! This type of interval change will activate unused muscles and "reset" your entire body from head to toes quickly causing you to feel rejuvenated.

God blessed each of us with an amazing human body capable of producing more than we realize, but we must take good care of our magnificent specimens! Yes, our bodies can withstand and even possibly thrive during a cross-country bike excursion, but you MUST give your body regular RELIEF! Walking every 10 miles is the exact type of relief your body is yearning! Invest the necessary time to pace back and forth every 10 miles and your body will thank you with greatly improved overall performance!

Walking back and forth every 10 miles will slow down your progress in the short-term, but it will actually INCREASE the speed of your overall trip! By giving your body frequent daily walking breaks, you will be allowing your body to BUILD strength which will translate into more mileage during the second half of your bike journey. If you push and tear your body without any walking reprieve, then you will damage your muscles, wear down your mind, and create a scenario where your overall health is DECLINING!!! Take a break EVERY 10 miles and walk out the kinks! You will FEEL BETTER and you will build a stronger, healthier body more capable of enduring your entire cross-country biking endeavor!

After several days of sustaining my new walking habit, I began to look forward to my 10-mile walking breaks. I would actually count down the miles until my next break! Pedaling a bicycle non-stop for days and weeks without regular stops is pure abuse! In my opinion, stopping every 10 miles for a walk-break is MANDATORY!

Chapter 64: Lost

When I glanced down at my newly acquired Bicycle Route Navigator phone application while biking through East Texas just outside of Shepherd, Texas and realized I was 3 miles off-course, I began an outright verbal assault on MYSELF. My immature and harsh words sounded something like this....

"How could you be so _____ stupid? You are such a _____ idiot! Can't you follow a simple _____ road sign? People like you shouldn't be allowed to pedal a _____ bicycle on the _____ public roads! You can't even follow the _____ route. How do you expect to finish the _____ Southern Tier?"

When you are 60 miles into your daily ride and you are dreaming of a warm shower, the LAST THING you want to do is climb an unnecessary hill on your bike, reach the top of the hill, and discover you are LOST. When I got to the top of that hill outside of Shepherd, Texas and realized I was LOST, I went ballistic! My actions were no different than a 2-year-old throwing a temper tantrum! Getting lost sent me into an immediate RAGE! If you met me in person atop this particular hill outside of Shepherd, Texas and heard the intensity of my barrage of words, you would lose all respect for me and you would certainly NOT be reading this book right now!

For some cyclists, getting lost could be the DEATH NAIL in their Southern Tier coffin!!! Few other obstacles deplete a cyclist's spirit more than pedaling miles in the WRONG DIRECTION, especially uphill! Getting lost is also extremely dangerous to your continued efforts as it can easily disrupt your delicate mental balance. Without stable mental balance, a CRUCIAL piece of the cross-country puzzle has been lost! Even me, possibly the calmest guy you will ever meet, went BONKERS after only being lost for slightly less than 3 miles.

There is something INFURIATING about getting lost on a cross-country biking expedition. Not only me, but other cross-country cyclists similarly report losing their composure and going "crazy" as a result of getting lost. Other lost cyclists report using horrible swear words with loud verbal screaming as a quick way to dispel their frustrations! No matter how you look at it, getting lost on a cross-country bike ride sparks unusually HIGH emotion and can result in mental devastation if you are not ready for it! Maybe EXPECTING to get lost is a better mindset, but best of all is probably to stay committed to tracking your little pink dot and making sure your pink dot stays on the blue line as per your Bicycle Route Navigator phone app from Adventure Cycling!

During my 43-day bike ride, I got lost approximately 10 times. My 3-mile mistake mentioned above was the second longest amount of time I was lost. My longest stretch of being lost occurred BEFORE I even started the Southern Tier. After departing from the San Diego Airport on my bicycle, I was lost for approximately 8 miles as I searched for the starting point of my cross-country route as I mistakenly assumed the famed starting point of the Southern Tier was at Mission Beach, but the beginning of the highly touted route as per my map was actually at Ocean Beach! For 45 minutes, I frantically searched for the proper place to begin my long bike ride as I almost got run over three times in heavy San Diego traffic as my mental composure vanished and I panicked over my ineptitude! For me, there was emotional carnage each time I got lost, especially in San Diego!

Despite all my efforts to stay on course, I continued to get lost! It is so EASY to get lost! Plan the best you can and pay attention to your maps, but accept the simple fact....... You WILL get lost! Despite your best efforts to remain on track, you will get off route from time to time! Expecting to get lost a few times per week will soften the actual blow when you find yourself a mile or two off course and lost. Maybe expecting to get lost from time to time will actually prevent you from having a completely IMMATURE, childish outburst similar to mine!

Getting lost is all the more dramatic the smarter you think you are and the more skilled you think you are. Thinking you have it all together is a BIG MISTAKE! It is far better to realize ahead of time how dumb you really are. Accept your incompetence and expect to get lost in advance. Then, when you get lost, try to keep your composure as you turn around and get back on route! It is easier than you think to get lost. EXPECT to spend some time being lost and you will likely handle these frustrating situations much better and with less of a mental breakdown than me!

DAY 20: Here is the official entrance to the La Loma Del Chivo Hostel in Marathon, Texas.

Chapter 65: Prohibited Gear

Airline companies and government security are very strict about what is permitted on airplanes. You must pass through security before you will be permitted access to the airport gates to board your plane. High-tech computers are used to analyze EVERY piece of your luggage. Leave the following items at home. Do NOT bring these items with you as they will be confiscated by the airline personnel:

- CO2 air cartridges (to inflate your bike tires)
- Isobutane fuel cannisters (for a camp stove or Jetboil)
- Mace or Pepper Spray (of any size)
- Any bottle over 3.4 ounces in size containing any type of liquid, crème, gel, etc.
- Medium-sized or larger lighters (A very small lighter might be permitted.)
- Medium-sized or larger knives (A very small knife might be permitted.)
- Etc… (Check with your airline and airport for a full list of prohibited items.)

Even worse than bringing the prohibited items mentioned above is trying to "hide" any prohibited items as you will only make your travel experience worse. Airport security WILL find whatever it is you are trying to hide as the airport personnel are trained to keep air travel safe for all of us. When I arrived at San Diego Airport to begin my cross-country bike trip, I was surprised to find clear evidence the airport staff had cut open my bike box to inspect the contents inside. Fortunately for me, they did re-tape my bike box after their thorough inspection.

My advice is to consolidate ALL of your small personal items like deodorant, soap, toothpaste, etc. into one large dry bag near the top zipper of your "carry-on" pannier bag, the bag you plan to carry on the airplane with you. Having a single dry bag near the top of your "carry-on" pannier bag will give you easy access in the case there are any questions from the airport security team or in the unlikely case airport security decides to take a closer inspection of the contents as these toiletry items are usually the items most likely to trigger an actual inspection.

Put only 100% completely permissible items into your bike box and your checked-in luggage. Avoid any unnecessary problems with these very important travel containers, especially since these containers will be transported to your final destination by airport personnel without any of your personal handling. Any questionable items should be carried through security personally by you. To my surprise, I was PERMITTED to take a super-small folding knife and a tiny lighter on board the airplane with me as each of these items were packed in my toiletry bag. Airport security also did NOT hassle me about taking numerous small 3-ounce bottles of Chamois Crème, shampoo, and sunscreen along with me in my toiletry bag.

Once you book your plane flight, take time to read the airline's most updated literature regarding what items are permitted and what items are NOT permitted on the airplane! Making a phone call to the airline is also a great way to make important clarifications as to avoid additional hassles, delays, and unnecessary stressors on the day of your flight. Keep in mind, airline restrictions do change from time to time.

During my bike travels, the only airline prohibited item I ended up buying at a local store was a small bottle of mace. The mace gave me one more potential weapon in my arsenal to use on my many dog chases. Fortunately, I never used the mace as my AMAZING "You Sit!" strategy worked extremely well with my furry, little friends.

Instead of using the airline-prohibited CO_2 cartridges to refill the air in my bicycle tires, I simply used a small manual air pump. Although my small manual air pump was VERY slow, it did an adequate job filling my tires on the few rare occasions I needed to do so.

As for fuel canisters, I quickly determined they were not really needed as I considered my Jetboil mini-stove as an unnecessary item on my bike adventure. My food requirements were easily met thanks to the many great food stores located along the Southern Tier Bicycle Route. Therefore, there wasn't much need for me to carry a boiling device to boil or cook anything for myself, but you should consider your own circumstances before blindly obeying my advice.

DAY 20: I spent the night at "The Beehive" at the Marathon, Texas hostel named La Loma Del Chivo. My overnight accommodation only had a total of 42 square feet inside, but I slept WELL!

Chapter 66: Luggage Help

When you arrive at the airport, you will have in your possession a big cardboard bike box, one big piece of regular check-in luggage, one "carry-on" bike pannier bags, and one "personal item" bike pannier. These four containers are much more than one person can carry! If you are trying to transport all of this stuff to the baggage check-in area of your particular airline, then I recommend getting dropped off at the exact location where your airline handles checking in bags and boxes. Lugging a big bike box, a piece of check-in luggage, and 2 bike pannier bags to the check-in counter at the airport will be an adventure in itself! It might be wise to use some type of airport dolly cart or have some temporary assistance from a loved one to help you get your bike box and check-in luggage checked-in with your particular airline.

When I got dropped off at the Pittsburgh International Airport to check-in for my flight to San Diego to begin my epic bike travels, my wife, Tink, helped carry my four containers inside the terminal. Tink stayed with me at the Pittsburgh Airport until my bike box and my check-in luggage bag was processed by my airline. My parents waited inside their Dodge truck at the "Departing Flights" drop-off location for about 15 minutes until my luggage check-in was complete and Tink returned to their pristine vehicle to ride back home.

Regardless of the particular scenario, keep reminding yourself you are on an ADVENTURE! Even the airport check-in is part of your adventure! If you dream of becoming a cross-country cyclist, then you MUST find a way to get all of your stuff where it needs to be!!! Without this adventurous type of "can do" attitude, your cross-country biking hopes are soon to be SHATTERED!

DAY 21: The Southern Tier will CHANGE you!

Chapter 66: Bike Assembly

One of the truly unique undertakings you may ever have the distinct privilege to experience in your life might come at the Baggage Claim area in your starting destination airport as you remove your bike from your bike box and attempt to assemble it! Airports are busy places with lots of people swiftly moving all around you. It is SUPER-EASY to misplace your check-in luggage bag, carry-on bag, or personal item. It is also too easy to lose your essential bike parts. Losing even one bolt to your bike could pose a MAJOR setback for the onset of your Day 1 of your biking adventures!

Successfully assembling your bike in the Baggage Claim area of a foreign airport actually begins long before you even arrive at the airport. At least TWO TIMES prior to arriving at the unfamiliar airport, you should have assembled and reassembled your bike as to create "muscle memory." When the pressure was on at the Baggage Claim area of the airport, I was grateful to have had some prior muscle memory of the critical task at hand as the stress is more than you think! Having prior bike-assembly experience will pay HUGE DIVIDENDS on "game day!" As my plane landed in San Diego, I kept replaying the assembly of my bike over and over in my mind as to be fully prepared for my pending bike installation. In my case, a bike installation was a MAJOR accomplishment as I am NOT a "repair guy" nor am I a mechanic!

If you are anything like me or even if you happen to be a professional mechanic, you will feel some "nerves" when you start to assemble your bike at the airport. People will be looking at you and they will be making funny faces. People will be talking about you and some people will talk to you and ask you questions. Someone might even try to help you. Worse yet, someone might yell at you or tell you to get out of the way! All the while, you MUST remain focused on the critical task at hand as you cannot afford to lose even one bolt as you NEED every last little piece of hardware as your beginning pedal stroke is only about a half hour away!

My advice is to keep ALL 4 pieces of luggage with you at ALL TIMES. Scan the entire Baggage Claim area and find the LEAST OCCUPIED area you can locate. Ideally, you will locate a vacant corner of the large room to place your four containers as you attempt to put-together your bicycle, the bicycle that will hopefully take you across the country!

While assembling your bicycle, try not to talk to anyone and whatever you do, do NOT ask for permission!!! Act like you OWN the airport and quickly and methodically start your bike assembly. If someone comes over and talks to you, answer the person kindly and briefly, but KEEP WORKING as you speak. Don't take too long and don't get the attention of an airport supervisor who might not take well to your mechanic work at their airport!

Most lower and middle tier airport employees will smile at you. Smile back and be super-friendly and polite, but KEEP WORKING and don't let anyone interfere with your concentration. You cannot miss one washer or lose one part. Your attention MUST be fully on the bike assembly task at hand. Be organized and methodical. Remember, you are on a MISSION!

"If it's going to be, it's up to ME!"

If you have assembled your bicycle at least two times prior at home, then you should have your handlebars, pedals, and front tire installed in about 30 minutes or so. Then, you only have your handlebar bag, pannier bags, phone carrier, water bottles, headlight, and taillight to install which might take another 15 minutes. The last 5 minutes should be spent double-checking your work and thinking carefully. Your total assembly time should be under one hour.

Upon completion of your top-quality bike assembly, you might wonder what to do with your bike box and your empty check-in luggage bag. The answer to this reasonable question is   Neatly package any scraps or garbage into your bike box as to avoid placing any waste on the airport floor and then LEAVE IT THERE!!! Place you bike box and luggage neatly against a wall and LEAVE IT THERE! Do NOT ask for permission! Just leave it there and walk away!

As I pushed my fully-loaded bicycle away from my bike box and my abandoned check-in luggage bag, I made a quick pit-stop at the restroom to relieve myself. After I filled my 3 water bottles with some public water from the airport water faucet, I glanced at my "rig" and I felt VERY proud of myself! Despite NOT being mechanically inclined, I just pulled off the BIGGEST and ONLY airport bike assembly of my life! The bike assembly was a HUGE win for me!!! It felt like I conquered the world!

DAY 22: God is an amazing architect!

Chapter 68: Broken Spokes

After my regularly scheduled 10-mile walking break, I was about to resume pedaling the final 25 miles or so toward my daily destination of Hyde Park Campground in Easleyville, Louisiana along the majestic, but lonely Louisianna State Route 422. As I glanced down at my rear tire, I noticed one of my spokes was broken in half, completely severed. Immediately, I felt a sinking feeling of pain descend to my stomach area. Although one broken spoke was not the worst possible conceivable damage to my bicycle, the impairment represented a rather serious malfunction to me!

In the tube of my bike seat, I had some spare spokes. Also, in my possession tucked away in my pannier bag with the rest of my spare bike parts was a product called Fiberfix. Fiberfix is a rope-like product which serves as a temporary replacement for a broken spoke. Although it seemed like I had the necessary parts to make the spoke repair, I had never installed a new spoke nor had I ever used the Fiberfix product! Anxiety was mounting on this sunny November afternoon alongside this very lightly-traveled Louisiana country road!

After taking off all of my pannier bags, removing my phone from the handlebar case, and unhooking my headlight, I flipped my bike upside down which seemed to give me the best chance to replace my broken spoke. After about ten minutes, I managed to remove the broken spoke, but after an hour, I was still UNABLE to install a new spoke as the large rear mechanical near the rear tire possibly officially known as either the fly wheel, cassette, or sprocket was in my way and there was NO WAY I was attempting to remove such a major mechanical component from my bike while alone alongside the road! Even if I had the proper tools to remove the major cog mechanical, I lacked the experience necessary to get involved at that particular high-level of repair!

Had my broken spoke been located on the front tire, I think I could have easily installed a new spoke as there would have been much less interference with other extraneous parts, but my broken spoke was on the rear tire and I was in a bind. After about another 45 minutes of fumbling around trying to make the repair, I finally succumbed and gave up on my repair efforts as I was UNABLE to install the Fiberfix product as I couldn't get the little Fiberfix rope through the little spoke hole as the Fiberfix material began fraying apart at the end. As my total repair time approached the two-hour mark and I felt sheer frustration, I decided to GIVE UP on my repair efforts and ride my bike with 31 spokes instead of 32 spokes!

Riding the next 25 miles to my daily campground destination at Camp Journey's End in Easleyville, Louisiana was VERY stressful, but my bike performed perfectly fine and nothing seemed any different than usual. The next day I pedaled into Ocean Springs, Mississippi and bike repair expert, Jacob, easily repaired my rear spoke. Jacob didn't really think it was a big deal riding on one less spoke. In fact, Jacob believed I could have actually ridden the last 500 miles or so of my epic cross-country trip WITHOUT the missing spoke and not have had any additional issues!

Although I did NOT succeed in repairing or replacing my broken spoke alongside the road, taking the time to remove the broken spoke from my wheel was very IMPORTANT as my broken spoke put my other spokes and nearby mechanicals in danger of collateral damage. At least, I improved the situation and prevented additional and more severe damage to my bicycle! Bike mechanic Jacob also informed me about the possibility of taping any future broken spokes to a neighboring "healthy" spoke as another creative and effective way to prevent additional damage in the short-term until I got the broken spoke replaced properly at a qualified bicycle repair facility.

Jacob agreed my broken spoke did weaken the overall strength and balance of my rear wheel. He also agreed it was a good idea to get my broken spoke fixed at the first available bike shop, but he didn't think the repair was quite as urgent as I originally assumed. Jacob seemed to think I could have successfully ridden my bicycle for possibly hundreds of miles on one or two broken spokes as long as the spokes were properly secured or removed, but he seemed to think a third broken spoke on any given wheel is much closer to an emergency requiring a proper professional repair as soon as possible. On that sunny Sunday morning in November, I paid close attention to Jacob and learned a lot about bike repairs from a true bike repair master!

DAY 22: The open road……

Chapter 69: Flooded Roads

As I traveled through Texas, I noticed MANY unfamiliar measurement signs alongside the roads. These uncommon signs seemed to measure the distance from the ground upward, but at first, I had no idea why the signs were designated in certain areas. Most of the signs seemed to be maxed out at about 6-8 feet in height. After witnessing many of these signs, I finally figured out the mysterious signs were actually water level signs. The footage designations on the various signs are used to alert traffic (especially bikers) as to the current height of any standing water at each particular sign location.

As you travel through Texas or any state for that matter, you might be tempted to discard the threat of "flash flooding," but I urge you to reconsider. Each year, flash floods KILL people and you don't want to be one of the statistics! Water level signs are strategically placed in low-elevation locations which are prone to flooding. The purpose of the signs is to give accurate information as to the depth of the water in the exact location of the sign. These locations are also likely to attract brisk moving water which could also potentially take out a car, person, and definitely a bike. Please don't underestimate the sheer power of water and the danger moving water presents to you and your epic adventure!

If you are traveling in severe rain and you encounter a water level sign, at least consider the information on the sign. It's probably not advisable for you to ride your bike, chain, sprocket, and pannier bags submerged through the deep water. Whatever you do, make sure you are cautious enough to keep your equipment safe and yourself alive. If the water is too swift, turn around and go back. Don't dare try to cross certain underwater locations as the force of the water is more than you realize! Plus, the added heavy-duty water force exerted directly on the side of your pannier bags could easily strip your bike away from you and take your bike for an unplanned off-road ride!

Even if the roads are not flooded, water poses a MAJOR problem for bikers. Every water puddle looks the same from the surface, but you really have no way to determine how DEEP the "puddle" actually is! In some cases, the depth of a seemingly harmless puddle could be a foot or more deep! Riding over top of an undetermined puddle could easily result in a NASTY wreck and severely damage your body and your bicycle! Always ride AROUND puddles, not through them!

Chapter 70: Detours

For the first 2,000 miles or so while riding the Southern Tier Bicycle Route, I viewed "DETOUR" signs more like SUGGESTIONS than laws! It wasn't until Chiswick State Park in Louisiana when my overly-confident "detour" attitude got crushed. Repeatedly throughout my trip, I would encounter detour signs and I would continue along my route completely IGNORING the detour sign! Not one single construction worker, boss, or authority ever made a mention to me about my blatant disregard of clearly-posted detour signs. With complete confidence, I traveled through every FORBIDDEN detour area on my bike as if I was the President of the United States!

My detour strategy seemed INVINCIBLE until I arrived at the Chiswick State Park in Louisiana where one particular State Ranger in Chiswick State Park didn't take well to my ignoring a GIGANTIC 6-foot by 8-foot neon-flashing sign clearly reading "ROAD CLOSED." As I biked passed the ranger sitting in his truck alongside the road, I assumed my normal strategy of disregard had worked once again, but about 15 seconds after I passed the ranger truck, I heard the sound of a familiar police siren and I knew my luck had run out and I was about to have an UNPLEASANT encounter.

The stern Louisiana ranger got out of his truck and with an extremely annoyed expression said to me, "What are you doing?" Immediately, I could sense the ranger's discontent so I figured I would use my "bike across America" story and earn his respect as I proudly declared, "Several weeks ago I started at the shores of the Pacific Ocean and I have been pedaling this bicycle every day as my goal is to cycle all the way across the United States to the eastern shores of the Atlantic Ocean in Florida. I'm trying to stay on my route without getting lost on unfamiliar roads. In no way did I intend to disrespect you."

Without any indication of sympathy from the ranger, he asked me, "Are you aware you blatantly disobeyed a federal ROAD-CLOSED sign?" Immediately, I acknowledged I had indeed disregarded the massive neon federal sign and I apologized as I ultra-politely asked, "Could I PLEASE continue biking through the closed area?"

In one of the most serious tones coupled with the strongest body language I ever experienced in my entire life, the strict ranger exclaimed, "You just violated federal law. I could take you to JAIL right now!" Certainly, I didn't expect to find myself in jail during my "adventure of a lifetime." In pure fright, I expressed my apologies once again while I graciously and quickly offered to turn around and get off of this forbidden road. Fortunately, the ranger permitted me to do so. Wasting no time, I abandoned my primary route as I gladly pedaled the long 12-mile detour around the stunning Louisianna State Park. As far as I was concerned, any detoured road or any amount of extra biking mileage was better than JAIL!

During my bike travels, I encountered 5 "Road Closed" signs and I ignored all of them. With the exception of the Louisiana ranger, nobody else cared one lick about me passing through any posted areas while riding my bike. One of the "Road Closed" signs I ignored took me over a sizeable bridge under major construction. The dozen workers or so were on lunch break and they all looked at me as I passed along. With a brief head nod, I quickly acknowledged them, but I did not slow down nor did I speak to them as my goal was to pass through as quickly as possible while they were still confused as to who I was and what I was doing. Most likely, the workers could care less what I was doing as they were much more concerned with enjoying their hearty lunch!

The other 3 "Road Closed" signs didn't have any rangers or workers at all present. The "road closed" signs simply indicated a closed section of road and the reason for the closure was unknown to me. Nothing was different about these closed roads and there was no construction occurring. On these barren roads, I pedaled along similarly as I did on any other "open" road as I stayed on my published route. Nobody bothered me at all!

My official cycling advice is to always BE SAFE and pay attention to possible dangers, but don't be too quick to adjust your route because of a posted detour sign. If you decide to pass through the closed road in similar fashion like me, then make sure you do so like you are the BIG BOSS, maybe even like you were the guy who ordered the placement of the detour sign in the first place! Whatever you do, don't stop to talk to anyone, just keep pedaling and mind your own business! Definitely don't ASK anyone for permission before passing through. Pedal slow and be careful like always! In the unlikely case someone in uniform stops you, in your most humble, respectful, and polite voice say, "Oh, I'm sorry. I thought the "road closed" sign was for cars, not for bikes. I'll be extra careful as I pass through." In most cases, you will be permitted to continue along your route!

It is ALWAYS very important to be 100% respectful and apologetic if you do get stopped while passing through a posted road. As a result of your respectful interaction, 99 out of 100 public officials will NOT fine you or take you to jail, especially when you mention you are a cross-country cyclist as is also clearly obvious as per the load attached to your bike!

On the other hand, if you act like an arrogant idiot with no self-control, then you should expect to get a fine and possible worse! Most of the time, the boss, police officer, ranger, or other public official will allow you to pass through the closed road IF the uniformed official LIKES you. As you pedal across the country, you will be hard-pressed to find someone who doesn't like a cross-country cyclist! Most of the strangers you meet along the way will go to great lengths to be supportive of your adventurous cross-country biking dream, even uniformed city, county, and state employees!

Chapter 71: Boogie Man

Day after day exerting big forces of energy piling up 70-mile biking efforts eventually took a toll on my mind as I began to see and hear things that were NOT really there! As darkness set in at my camp, my mind would wander as I heard a variety of questionable night noises and saw many unconfirmed images lurking in the trees and bushes. Like fellow cross-country author, Patrick McGinty, at times I feared those noises and images off in the distance might indeed be my worst nightmare……. THE BOOGIE MAN!

Along my journey, I did NOT carry a gun. All I had was a tiny 1-ounce can of mace spray in which I purchased at Walmart about 1,500 miles into my bike journey in the glorious state of Texas. Could something terrible have happened to me? Yes, but most likely it wouldn't! With the help of lots of prayer and some soothing words from my loved ones back home, and one of the most stubborn mindsets you would ever wish to meet, I managed to face the Boogie Man and manage to fall asleep soundly within the confines of my tent.

In the vast majority of cases, whatever you THINK you hear or see is just your imagination playing tricks on you. When human beings reach exhaustion levels, it is NOT uncommon to see and hear things that are not really there. The Southern Tier and other major bicycle routes specialize in developing your mind, especially when you have used every last drop of personal effort to arrive at your daily destination. Then, when you cannot take anymore, you will be forced to deal with troubling images and bothersome noises until you feel like you are about to break.

Even as I write this suspect chapter, I imagine many of you consider the Boogie Man to be an exaggeration, but I urge you to put your doubts aside as I PROMISE you there will be times when you are alone on the majestic bicycle route when you will be scared out of your mind! When you "see" or "hear" the Boogie Man, your hairs will stand up straight on your forearms and your heart will beat like a drum! When this happens, remember how special you are! You are riding your bicycle across the country! You can HANDLE this! When I got scared, I PRAYED. It worked for me! The Boogie Man never got me, but I think he might have claimed a permanent place in my mind! Welcome to the Southern Tier!!!

Chapter 72: Bonk

Although the BONKING phenomenon has been briefly mentioned in prior pages, bonking is so important it deserves its own chapter! Bonking is a MAJOR problem with all types of cyclists. Demanding hours upon hours of physical performance from your body eventually results in a stalemate. At a certain point, there is simply NOTHING left to give. Your body has worked enough and it is DONE! Bonking is the cycling term for "Your ride is over today!" Once bonked, you are finished for the day. It is time to call the cab or hitchhike your way to the nearest town. You are NOT pedaling one more mile. A true bonk is an END to your pedal revolutions for the day!

One clue you are near bonking is when you are pedaling on level terrain and it seems like you are pedaling up a steep mountain pass. Your legs will feel heavy and slow like they are ready to give out and you will sense your mind is ready to shut down. Bonking is when you reach the conclusion of your body's cooperation with your desired mileage goal.

While in the Yuha Desert on a scorching hot 105-degree afternoon making my way to Blythe, California, strange thoughts began entering my mind as to whether I would COLLAPSE on the berm of the road or if I would succumb to the heat and fall over in the middle of the road. It was during these troubling moments I KNEW I was about to BONK or worse. Hopefully, you don't let yourself get as far gone as me!

Pay attention to how you are feeling and act accordingly, especially when you are riding in severe conditions like hot conditions above 90 degrees Fahrenheit. But don't underestimate mild riding conditions as a bonk can easily occur at ANY temperature. All bicycle riding conditions should be respected as there is grave danger in pushing yourself too far without the proper food, drink, rest, and proper prior physical endurance training, especially in whatever extreme weather elements you may find yourself!

As I struggled through the unrelenting Yuha Desert on this particularly hot 105-degree day at 3 p.m. amidst the pure uninhibited sun, I could sense myself on the verge of bonking. In pure desperation, I pathetically collapsed in the shade of the ONLY building in sight for miles as a nice man named Rudy assisted my dilapidated body into his pesticide spraying business and helped me. After placing several bags of ice on my wrists, neck, and legs, the nice man loaded my bike and bags into the back of his truck and gave me a ride 8 miles over to Brawley, California where I got a cheap motel, regained my strength, and had a serious talk with MYSELF about whether or not I should attempt to continue my quest to finish the Southern Tier!

There are many legitimate strategies I used along the Southern Tier to prevent bonking. Drink before feeling thirsty. Eat before feeling hungry. Ride in the early morning to avoid MAJOR heat. Ride at a SLOW pace. Take regular 10-mile walking breaks. Remain calm! Take a day off biking every ten days or so. Pray a lot. And many more….. Adopting these types of behaviors into your cross-country ride will help keep you healthy, but even with all the right habits and daily actions, you may still find yourself on the brink of bonking if you reach a certain high level of exertion output on any given day!

The human body is capable of INCREDIBLE physical exertion and endurance, but there are limits. Practicing good habits is the best way to increase your bodily threshold to bonking and increase your outer bonking limitation. Skimping on water is the FASTEST way to bonk! The second fastest way to bonk is skimp on food! Another prime bonking cause is exposing yourself to excessive heat. The fourth major culprit of bonking is getting too little sleep.

As I toured the Southern Tier, attached to my bike were three 25-ounce water bottles. Two water bottles were attached in the standard places on my bike frame below my top bar. The third water bottle was mounted underneath my bottom bar, not too far from the ground. Each morning, I made sure each of these water bottles were full of either water or sports drink. FORCING myself to take a 3-ounce drink every 3 miles kept me properly hydrated. On super-hot days, it is even more important to drink MORE THAN one ounce of water or sports drink (Gatorade, Powerade, Propel, etc.) for every mile you pedal. On cooler days you can probably get away with drinking about 1 ounce for every mile you ride. Either way, you should be taking a REASONABLE drink EVERY 3 miles as to habituate yourself into the process of providing your body with ESSENTIAL liquid fuel!

Eating is another CRITICAL component necessary for endurance cyclists to avoid bonking. Even at times when you don't feel like eating, you NEED to eat anyways. On long bike rides, you MUST eat BEFORE you are hungry and drink BEFORE you are thirsty. If you find yourself hungry on your bike, then you waited TOO LONG! At least every ten miles you should be eating a granola bar, small box of raisins, 3 fig cookies, a handful of cereal, a big spoon-full of peanut butter, a doughnut, or some type of food with lots of calories.

Long bike rides require sustained CALORIES! If you provide your body with adequate calories, then you might be surprised how LONG you can travel on your bicycle! Since I'm NOT a nutritionist, I'm not going to get into the science of foods, but I will give you some simple advice from a guy who went the distance. EAT SOMETHING! Get a lot of calories into your body. Eat whatever you want! As long as the food has lots of calories and it tastes good to you, then EAT IT! After your long daily bike ride while you are at the local diner getting supper, you might want to consider some vegetables, but while on your daily ride, eat whatever you WANT!

Sleeping is also essential to avoid bonking as it is CRITICAL for your body to

RECOVER each night after the huge mileage from earlier in the day. Without adequate sleep, your body will bonk much sooner than it would otherwise. For me, sleeping was no problem as I slept in some of the strangest places I could ever imagine while biking the Southern Tier. Only half-jokingly, I advise people who claim to have sleep problems to bike across the country and their sleep problems will be CURED!

Regularly along my bike journey, I would mention to my dedicated wife about being "Southern Tier tired" and she knew exactly what I meant as I fell asleep on her during several different phone conversations! As long as you give yourself 6-8 hours to sleep per night, you will be fine. If you try to party until 2 a.m. and then squeeze in 3 hours of sleep before tomorrow's ride, then you will be setting yourself up for a pending BONK! Don't underestimate the necessity of SLEEP!

As we consider the fourth BONKING factor of HEAT, I'd like to remind each of you; MANY regular people DIE of heat exhaustion EVERY year. Heat is a VERY dangerous factor and should be carefully considered as you plan your bicycle excursion. Throughout my life I have found myself VERY vulnerable to excessive heat. If you are anything like me, you might want to ride through the middle of the night and deal with slightly cooler temperatures as to avoid the hot sun than to face the full power of the mighty sun in the middle portion of the day.

As I approached Surprise, Arizona eagerly anticipating the meeting of my outstanding Warmshowers host, Pat Scocuzza, on Day 7, the heat got to me and I pulled over into the shade in the parking lot at a Dollar General. As I considered my options, I looked up and noticed the manager of the Dollar General store suddenly dumping a half bag of ICE on to the landscaping out front of the store. It was a GOD SEND! Without a second thought, I quickly grabbed three of my small Walmart bags from my rear pannier bag pouch and I scooped up the discarded ice. For the next 20 minutes I packed myself in ice. The three bags of ice were rotated from my neck to my wrists to my elbows to my legs and to my back. On this warm 103-degree day, those little bags of ice saved me from bonking!

Throughout my bike trip across the United States, I discovered an interesting fact. If you CARE for your body, your body will output like you may have never imagined. Systematically providing your body with the proper amount of water, food, and sleep while limiting extreme heat exposure is the proper recipe to take you across the country on your bicycle without any BONKS!

Chapter 73: Physical Preparation

For 8 months leading up to my epic bike journey, I dedicated myself to REMAINING in good physical shape! Throughout my entire adult life, I maintained a rather high-level of physical fitness and vibrant health. For me, it was pretty easy to habituate myself to doing the following physical activities to prepare for my cross-country bike adventure:

1. Stretch for 15 or more minutes EVERY day. Stretching is a MAJOR key to long-term good health!
2. Do push-ups, planks, crunches, toes-raises, and various leg lifts every day.
3. Lift weights twice per week. The older you are, the more important it is to lift weights!
4. Jog twice a week. Cross-training is important!
5. Bike at least 50 miles per week. Indoor biking is fine, but outdoor biking is better.
6. Take 3 or more overnight biking trips. Rehearsal outings will fine-tune your gear selection, packing precision, and sharpen your mental faculties.
7. Drink 64 ounces of water EVERY DAY! Water does not include Gatorade or other sports drinks, milk, tea, coffee, or alcohol. Water is WATER! Drink 64 ounces of pure room-temperature WATER every day for the 6 months prior to your epic ride!

Although it is possible to show up for your cross-country bicycle expedition without any prior physical training, your chances of completing your prized cycling route solo, unassisted, and continuous will only be about 3% unless you happen to be a former professional cyclist or some type of experienced adventure guide. Taking your biking adventure seriously by habituating yourself to performing the proper DAILY physical training actions every day for the six months leading up to your cross-country quest will greatly increase your statistical odds of completion.

If you ever complete a cross-country bicycle ride, you will certainly be asked about your physical conditioning. For me, I kept myself in rather good athletic shape all of my life. My cross-country journey occurred when I was 48 years old and I was in excellent physical shape. No, I wasn't in exceptionally good "biking shape," at the time, but overall, I was healthy, strong, and flexible at the onset of my mammoth bike adventure across the southern portion of the United States.

Even considering my above-average level of fitness, it would have been a HUGE mistake for me to push the limits of my daily mileage during the first CRITICAL week of my extended bicycle ride. 80 miles per day was my original mileage goal at the onset of my biking adventure, but as you know, I only averaged 70 miles per day. During the first 3 weeks or so of my bike ride, I only averaged about 60 miles per day and I did so ON PURPOSE. Yes, I could have done more mileage on some of those early days, but I'm glad I didn't! Pushing my mileage limit too early in my trip could have BACKFIRED in a massive way and sent me back home early! Build a strong base at the beginning!!! Excessive mileage too early in your bicycle travels can be FATAL to achieving your cross-country dream!

Take it from me, start off with at least one week or more of 60% days. A "60% day" is a bike riding day where you only complete about 60% of your total possible miles. For me, if I really pushed hard, I could do a 100-mile ride even with 85 pounds of gear on my bike. 60% of 100 miles is 60 miles and that is why I aimed for 60 miles during my first three weeks of the Southern Tier. No, your daily mileage doesn't have to be exactly 60% of your potential miles, but my point is to ride A LOT less miles than you are capable of riding during the first two weeks of your trip. If you want to ride BIG MILEAGE, then wait until you have at least two weeks of limited miles. Only then will your body and especially your butt be ready for the bigger mileage numbers!

As I was researching long-distance bike touring, I read about two women who signed up for a group bike ride across the country. Both of the women were in BAD physical shape, but their plan was to "get in shape during the ride." After only a few days participating in an expensive group cross-country cycling tour, both of the women quit and went back home with their heads hanging between their legs! Although it is possible, to "get in shape" during a cross-country bike trip, you owe it to yourself to arrive at the starting line with at least a semi-decent basic physical condition. It is completely unreasonable to expect to cross a country on a bicycle if you are in BAD physical shape at the onset!

Even pedaling 40 or 50 miles a day, which is a common mileage figure for commercial group rides among many bike-touring companies, is a HUGE amount of mileage to do day after day if you start with an inadequate physical foundation. It is completely unreasonable to expect to "get into shape" by doing a cross-country bike tour. The only possible scenario for someone completely out of shape is to start with very low mileage days of 20 miles per day or less and slowly work upwards to more miles per day over the course of 8 weeks or so. Going only 20 miles a day would take you about 5 months to complete the Southern Tier, but it is still possible and might even be more life-changing when you eventually finish!

My recommendation is to start your cross-country journey with a good base-layer of fitness. You should be able to easily handle 40-mile biking days when you show up to begin your cross-country ride. To do so, you need to follow my brief fitness plan as outlined above. Doing so should put you at least at a baseline to begin your incredible cycling journey!

Remember, error on the side of doing TOO LITTLE mileage, especially on the first few days. Many cyclists with big dreams QUIT their potentially life-changing cross-country ride because they were OVERZEALOUS and pushed too hard during the first 3 days! Do LESS miles early on. Think long term!

After you cross the midterm of your destination, you can ramp up your mileage. If you still feel strong, you can even MAX OUT a few days here and there and grab some 100-plus-mile days, especially if you get a nice tailwind like I did in Louisiana where I produced back-to-back 108-mile biking days on Day 33 and Day 34!

DAY 22: Vehicles travel VERY FAST throughout most of the Southern Tier and especially on this 2-lane highway!

Chapter 74: Cleat Stone

At times, I actually get mad at myself for being so DUMB! If you ever meet me, you might wonder how someone like myself ever made it across the United States pedaling a bicycle. My niece, Jordyn, considers me to be one of the most senseless people she ever met and she will openly advise anyone of her deduction. In a similar manner, all throughout my childhood upbringing, my father reminded me to use my head for "more than a hat rack!" Do you get the idea? Can you sense that I have some glaring weaknesses in my overall mental development and common-sense ratio? Now that my sensitive, non-complimentary self-disclosure has been made, I think it is only fair to share this particular episode of stupidity with you.

For 850 miles and almost 2 weeks of bike riding, I battled my right biking clip-in shoe as it repeatedly dislodged from my pedal clip. Hundreds of times I would try to get my right biking shoe to snap in just right, but it NEVER would! So, instead of stopping and examining my shoe and pedal looking for a simple remedy, I repeatedly struggled with the irritating and debilitating shoe function involving my bottom cleat. Finally, after 850 miles of annoyance, in utter frustration I stopped my bike abruptly in anger, carefully parked it alongside the road, ripped off my right shoe, and carefully analyzed the bottom of my cleat.

Within seconds of glancing at my cleat, I diagnosed the problem. A small rock was jammed tightly between the two cleats on my biking shoes which prevented me from obtaining a complete lock between my shoe and my pedal! After calling myself every derogatory name imaginable, I easily used my hand and ripped the tiny rock out of my biking cleat. From that moment on, I enjoyed riding my bike with my right shoe PROPERLY and securely clipped in to my pedal.

Despite being the type of person who does NOT complain much, the mounting frustration over many days caused by my loose right shoe finally triggered me enough hindrance to pull over and solve the riddle. Why did I have to wait 850 miles until I resolved my cleat issue? Sometimes I find myself being SO DETERMINED to accomplish a particular goal that I don't take the time to STOP and find a quick solution to my minor problems. For 850 miles I suffered the effects of my improper shoe cleat connection, but I never took the time nor did I have the BELIEF I could figure out the solution to my problem. Therefore, I continued riding for HUNDREDS of miles with a mild shoe problem!!!

It took my level of anger to cross the threshold of tolerance for me to finally say "Enough is enough!" Only then did I pull off to the side of the road to investigate a possible solution. On my next bike trip, I'm going to try to be smarter! When something goes wrong, I'm going to look at the problem and think for at least 30 seconds before I continue to ride in disabled fashion! If I can incorporate this type of reasonable problem-solving repertoire into other areas of my life, maybe my loving and brazen niece, Jordyn, will finally acknowledge some improvement in my developing common-sense ratio?

Chapter 75: Loneliness

If you know someone who is contemplating suicide, then encourage your friend to ride the Southern Tier before possibly committing the terrible act! Taking a cross-country bike ride ALONE is a more effective therapy than a lifetime of counseling or reading any number of self-help books!

When I left on my epic bike trip, I wasn't involved in counseling or taking medicine for any of my various psychological deficiencies and I definitely was NOT suicidal, but I still came back a different and more SOLID man. Considering the adversity involved in completing a solo, unsupported, and continuous cross-country bike ride, it would be IMPOSSIBLE to return the same person as when you left! You WILL be a different person upon arriving back home! You might even HEAL many of your mental deficiencies along the way!

Becoming a different person is guaranteed upon the completion of an epic bike route, but completing an arduous bike tour is NOT easy. Along the way, there are many WICKED obstacles to be faced which can be borderline terrifying! Facing these formidable challenges ALONE can be enough for many aspiring cyclists to QUIT!

Being mostly a "loner," I take part in many activities by myself. In my case, I don't feel the need to surround myself with lots of people, but unlike some loners, I do like people. Nonetheless, I find myself doing many activities ALONE. Why would biking across the country be any different for me?

Even though I am a solitary man, I must admit the Southern Tier presented a whole new level of solitude! For 1,000 miles through the secluded southwest desert, it was one lonely pedal stroke after another as I biked through the vast wilderness. Every once in a while, a car would pass, but for the most part it was just me and the road! As I rode mile after mile, I would yearn for a familiar voice. Sometimes I would stop and call my wife or talk with my mother just to hear another person's voice. The loneliness was DEEPER than I had ever anticipated prior to my life-changing cycling journey!

My first multi-day overnight bike adventure occurred in my mid 20's with my fiancé at the time, Gina Leis, whom later the following year became my first wife. With great excitement and vigor, Gina and I pedaled our bicycles on a 3-day, 2-night 100-plus-mile bike excursion from Johnstown, Pennsylvania over Pleasantville Mountain into Bedford County and down through many country roads eventually summiting the great 2,800-foot Mount Savage in Garrett County, Maryland. We rode our bikes through Somerset, PA and returned back to our respective homes in Johnstown on Day 3. Having Gina accompany me on my first-ever long-distance bike tour was huge as looking back, I'm sure I could NOT have accomplished the feat alone as I was not mentally or physically prepared for all the various demands of a long bicycle ride.

Having Gina alongside me made the critical difference as to ease my many mental instabilities. Eating mostly pop tarts and barely drinking anything combined with high levels of general anxiety also made my finish very UNLIKELY. To the contrary, Gina was a much STRONGER cyclist than me and our strange diet didn't seem to affect her nearly as much as it did me. With Gina's great patience and positive example combined with my grim sense of determination, I made it back home on Day 3 despite having a quite severe stomach sickness. Without Gina to share in my emotional pain and my other follies, my long bike ride would have ended in a similar "EPIC FAIL" fashion as did many of my other overly-zealous bike rides in which I pathetically phoned my dad to come pick me up!

If you are a very social person, you might want to seriously consider if you have what it takes to pedal 3,000 or more miles across the country including 1,000 barren miles through the secluded southwestern desert. Feeling "Southern Tier lonely" is a whole new depth of lonely! Many days I questioned my motives as I pressed on, not feeling inclined to do so, but oftentimes only continuing my pedal strokes because I said I would!

Accepting your pain and pushing on eventually releases a HUGE reward. The CONFIDENCE you gain from OUTLASTING the pain of loneliness and pushing through the hundreds of solemn challenges knowing you did it BY YOURSELF is something you take with you for the rest of your life. It is a level of self-belief capable of extinguishing many of your past psychological issues and self-doubts! Many times, throughout the year following my Southern Tier finish, I drew upon the CONFIDENCE I <u>unlocked</u> while pedaling those desolate streets in the southern part of the United States! Many times, I have since used my newfound self-confidence from the Southern Tier to overcome BIG life issues which would have certainly squashed my previous self!

If you can withstand the loneliness, you will reap BIG! Something extremely positive happened to me when I finally realized I didn't REQUIRE anyone but myself. An unfamiliar type of strength slowly gained breath inside of me as I methodically went the Southern Tier distance all by myself!

No, I wasn't really all alone as I felt the presence of God frequently during my trials as I pedaled my bike across the country, but when I looked to my right and to my left, there was no other person for me to share my woes. Despite the lack of human companionship, it seemed as though the lonelier I got, the closer I felt to God as the Bible clearly refers to God's great power as being "closer than breathing and nearer than hands and feet." As I pedaled and prayed, I maintained my connection in spirit as I could sense the pulsation of God in the terrain and inside my heart! Although no other human was in my physical proximity, I promise you, I was NOT alone!

Chapter 76: Second Cup of Coffee

Talented author and amazing cross-country cyclist, Patrick McGinty, in his quality book, "A Bike Ride Across America" mentioned the "2nd cup of coffee" numerous times. Patrick warns touring cyclists of the dangers of drinking a 2nd cup of coffee in the morning as a precursor usually resulting in a "zero day" (zero miles). According to Patrick, it is far better to get on your bike and start spinning those pedals around instead of drinking a second cup of coffee! The second cup of coffee has a way of relaxing you to the point where your biking motivation is GONE for the day! My advice is also to skip the early morning indulging and get on your bike before you even drink your FIRST cup of coffee!!! Start pedaling as you bite down on a nasty power bar or some other revolting bit of food containing lots of calories. Don't risk any type of fancy breakfast before you establish yourself on your bicycle for the day. In most cases, I would require myself to travel at least 10-20 miles on my bike before I would even consider any type of "luxury" breakfast at McDonald's or Burger King.

If coffee is your thing, then there is nothing wrong with drinking it as I recognize the ongoing coffee craze in our nation. Drinking coffee in moderation is fine. Drinking excessive coffee breeds too much comfort which could stale your daily biking progress!

For me, caffeine is my ENEMY as my body is VERY SENSITIVE to caffeine, alcohol, and medicine. It is in my best interest to be very CONSERVATIVE with my caffeine intake and in most cases, I won't drink caffeine AT ALL! During my cross-country travels, I did not drink a drop of coffee.

In most cases, it is best to listen to your own bodily needs. If you are craving some coffee, then drink it, but don't over-due it. One cup of coffee is ok, but two cups might be dangerous! Consider following my lead and eating a quick initial breakfast consisting of bars and raisins as you start pedaling early in the dark morning. Wait to stop at the hallowed golden arches for BREAKFAST #2 and have a cup of coffee only after you have at least 10 miles tallied on your daily bike odometer!

Chapter 77: Lights

Although many cross-country cyclists initially expect to ride only during daylight hours, usually this type of ideal expectation does not prove to be the case as the days and weeks unfold! For various reasons, there will be days you will be forced to ride in the dark or in the almost-dark even if you didn't originally plan on doing so. On an epic bike route like the Southern Tier, known for TREMENDOUSLY hot temperatures, you might even find yourself like me, riding through the middle of the night to help combat the extreme heat of mid-day. On any bike route, you may also find yourself in heavy fog at any point throughout the day in which case may require the use of lighting. At other times, the sky will get dark at the prelude of a pending rainstorm or you could find yourself struggling to complete your daily mileage as the sun is setting in the sky. For these situations and a myriad of other circumstances not mentioned herein, cross-country cyclists find themselves needing headlights and taillights much more than they may have originally suspected!

Having a bright front headlight and a bright rear flashing taillight is MANDATORY, even for a cross-country cyclist determined not to ride in the dark. Both front and back bike lights should have secure mounts as to minimize the chance of ever becoming dislodged. Adventure Cycling Association sells a front headlight called BLAZE. You can either get a rechargeable BLAZE headlight or a battery-operated BLAZE headlight. For my cross-country trip, I used a rechargeable BLAZE headlight which served me well as my primary headlight, but it would only last about two or three hours on the middle setting. Having a spare, battery-operated BLAZE headlight which shares the SAME handlebar mount was convenient as I quickly interchanged it when my primary BLAZE headlight ran out of battery power and needed to be re-charged.

In my handlebar bag, I kept a heavy 1.3-pound Anker battery bank. Although my Anker battery bank weighed over one pound, it was vital to keep my phone and headlight charged while I was riding. While riding very early in the pure darkness of the morning on California Interstate 8, my primary BLAZE headlight went dull. As I pulled to the side of the road, I attached a charging cord from my battery bank to the BLAZE headlight, but the BLAZE headlight would NOT work while being charged. For some reason, my BLAZE headlight would only work when it was NOT being charged. Fortunately, I had my back-up battery-operated BLAZE headlight to easily exchange as both headlights shared the same common mount.

Over the years, I fooled around with various inferior taillights until I finally came to my senses and bought the awesome SWERVE taillight from Adventure Cycling. SWERVE is high-quality taillight with a super-easy switch to turn off and on. It also flashes as bright as any taillight on the market. Everything about SWERVE is first-class and I highly recommend you learn from my foolishness and buy a SWERVE taillight from the onset from Adventure Cycling instead of experimenting with lesser quality products as your visibility on the roads is vital to your ongoing existence! SWERVE not only flashes brightly, it also has a distinctive flashing pattern which commands EXTRA attention from passing vehicles as a means to increase your overall safety. This quality taillight also has one of the BEST mounts in the industry as mine was easily mounted securely on the back of my rear rack.

In addition to my front headlight and my rear taillight, I also used a flashing red SWERVE taillight mounted directly on the back of my helmet with the help of a couple simple plastic zip ties. The extra flashing light on my helmet was one additional light I used to help ensure my ongoing safety as it was imperative to be SEEN by all approaching vehicles. My helmet light also provided me with a backup plan in case my rear taillight suddenly stopped working for some unplanned reason. In the unlikely case of a malfunction in any one of my two rear lights, at least I would maintain one working taillight at all times! Plus, in my opinion, it is better to have two working taillights instead of only one! Safety was a supreme concern of mine as I progressed across the country on my bicycle. If my life was to end on my epic bike trip, at least I wanted to make sure I was completely VISIBLE to the driver responsible for my demise!

During most of the days of my epic bike escapade, I used all of my bike lights as I usually started pedaling in absolute darkness about an hour before sunrise. In most cases, there was very little traffic at this pre-dawn time and it was VERY PEACEFUL, but I used all of my bike lights anyways! As the sun rose in the sky, I felt the POWER of the new day and I knew it was about time to turn off my lights. Numerous times, I also used my biking lights in the evening as there were times I finished my biking miles for the day close to or beyond sunset. Other times, I rode in the dark upon returning to my campsite from a quick visit to the local store or restaurant down the street. Whether it was early in the morning or late in the evening, almost every day of my bike outing, I used my bike lights and I was very thankful to have good, reliable lights to help keep me SAFE!

Chapter 78: Debris

As I pedaled across the southern portion of the United States, I encountered plenty of debris on the berm and along the side of the road. Some roads were mostly clear of debris and other roads were loaded with debris. Debris can be rocks, blown-out semi-truck tire remains, soda bottles, candy wrappers, sticks, dead animals, broken glass, etc. Regardless of the specific type of road debris, my plan was to avoid ALL debris! Debris of any kind posed a big risk to the positive FLOW of my bike travels. Debris of any kind, no matter how tiny it might be, translated into a possible flat tire, bike damage, or even a wreck!

The implementation of my "zero debris" strategy paid huge dividends as I had ZERO flat tires during my 3,000 miles of bicycle travel! Yes, late on Day 3 I had a flat tire and early on Day 4 I had a flat tire followed by 3 more flat tires during the same challenging day, but ALL of those five flat tires were caused by my inadequate gravel bike tires and NOT because of road debris! Ever since I replaced my inadequate, faulty gravel tires with excellent road tires, I had ZERO flats for the entire remaining 2,700 miles of my biking adventure as I passionately avoided any and all road debris!

Although it was important for me to avoid all road debris, it was much more important to keep myself alive. Safety was my top concern as I would CAREFULLY avoid debris, but I would NEVER swerve away from debris at the risk of getting struck by a vehicle! My safety trumped the ongoing care of my bike tires! At all times, I remained alert to the vehicles in my vicinity as I also tried my best to avoid every single piece of road debris.

If you ride the Southern Tier Bicycle Route as published by the iconic Adventure Cycling Association, you will encounter many dead animals on and alongside the road. Dead animal carcasses were especially prevalent in west and central Texas for whatever reason. When my dad asked me if I saw any armadillos on my southern USA bike travels, I answered "Yes" as I saw about ten dead armadillos on the road, but to my surprise, I did not see a single, live armadillo. It is also interesting to note, the largest animal I saw dead along my bike route was a HUGE wild pig alongside the road. The giant pig clearly weighed well over 200 pounds!

Along portions of the Southern Tier, the smell of death was familiar, especially throughout much of Texas as I wondered if the great state of Texas had a dedicated public official or game commission officer assigned to the clean-up of road kill. Although the smell was unpleasant, it did not pose any danger to me. The danger of road kill lies in the sharp and jagged bones of the dead corpses which pose a major threat to bicycle tires. Dead animals have spear-like broken bones which can easily puncture a bike tire and cause unnecessary aggravation and delay. For these reasons and many more, I steered clear of all animal remains alongside the road!

Chapter 79: Why

"What the HECK am I doing out here?" was the resounding question reverberating back and forth in my mind throughout the first week of biking the Southern Tier. At times, I felt PANIC as my body, mind, and spirit tried to acclimate itself to my new life as the unfamiliar settings were almost too much for me to handle initially. As I was pedaling along, my mind would suddenly demand answers as to WHY I was out here spinning my pedals around in this vast expanse of desert. Questions would abound in my mind. "Where am I?" "Why am I not getting paid to do this?" "Where am I going?" "Where am I at?" "Where am I going to stay?" "What if I get hurt or sick?" "Is it safe out here?" "Who is going to help me when my bike breaks down?" "How could I be so stupid to get myself into this situation?"

As an amateur philosopher of life and a regular guy who has read hundreds of personal development books, listened to hundreds of audio programs, and attended more seminars than I can remember, it gives me great joy to analyze challenging situations as I try to uncover THE TRUTH of any given occurrence. As these seemingly spontaneous futile questions popped into my consciousness, I was intrigued as to the source of my potentially trip-ending litany of questions. After some consideration, I came to the conclusion that most of my negative questions were aimed toward discovering the answer to one primary question............"WHY AM I RIDING MY BIKE ACROSS THE COUNTRY?" As far as I could determine, my mind DEMANDED to know WHY! Why am I out here in the middle of the desert riding my bike?

The German philosopher Friedrich Nietzsche was quoted as saying, "When the WHY is big enough, you will find a HOW." Throughout much of my adult life, my interpretation of the famous Nietzsche quotation revolved around uncovering enough legitimate, self-inspiring REASONS to do something. Upon gathering a critical mass of compelling reasons "why," the "how" would always seem to take care of itself and I would find a way to accomplish my goal!

As I contemplated taking on the Southern Tier challenge, I finally decided to go for it as a result of one primary reason, what it would make of me as a person! Clearly, I did not ride the Southern Tier for the money as completing the task did not create any revenue for me and actually cost me thousands of dollars. Biking the Southern Tier for pleasure DEFINITELY was not my compelling reason as the Southern Tier was not really my idea of pleasure! There wasn't even a special cause or charity associated with my cross-country cycling efforts! My family certainly didn't gain any benefits from me leaving home to ride my bike for 43 days. My very long cross-country bike ride was merely for my own personal development! As I pedaled my bike throughout the south, I had NO INTENTIONS of ever writing a book! The calling for this book came near the end of my cross-country bike ride when God finally placed this purposeful task on my heart.

For me, self-development was enough of a reason to hang in there on my bike ride when most others would have quit. Many times, I found myself "sweating my balls off" as my mind and body would be agitated by the pain and suffering until I refocused my thoughts and reminded myself WHY I was doing it. Developing myself into a "real man" was enough of a reason for me. The cross-country ride was my calling to take my life to the next level despite many random thoughts urging me to go back home. In strange fashion, I believed by spinning my wheels around for 7 hours a day, eventually I would be transformed! And I was RIGHT!!!!

For some of you, a single goal of SELF-DEVELOPMENT is probably NOT going to be enough of a reason for you to CONVINCE your mind to pedal 3,000 miles or more across the country! Don't use my WHY! Get your OWN why! Figure out exactly what is motivating you to consider such a HUGE challenge. What is driving you? Why are you CALLED to take on such a grand task? Find the core of your calling NOW. Don't wait until you find yourself in the middle of the desert wondering WHY you are there! Don't wait until you are actually on the Southern Tier to figure out why you are pedaling your bike across the country as it might be too late! The emotions I felt during the first week of the Southern Tier posed a struggle similar to being dropped in the middle of an ocean without knowing how to swim very well. Many times, I could not see my way out, but I could at least keep my pedals spinning for one more day as I reminded myself about my powerful WHY!

Even with my BIG WHY, I must admit by Day 2 of my grueling bike travels, my doubts had already caused me to write off the continuous completion of my cross-country biking goal. On Day 2, I assumed I would pedal as many days as I could withstand and then go back home. The following year I could return to do another section of the magnificent Southern Tier route and then again for several more sections until I finally complete the entire Southern Tier. But deep inside of me, I feared I might never come back and complete the Southern Tier. This might be the last chance in my life to face the formidable route. Maybe I can go ONE MORE DAY!? Knowing how BIG this bike journey was for my soul; I couldn't let this opportunity of PERSONAL GROWTH go without a fight!

When I felt like quitting, I urged myself to pedal ONE MORE DAY. Every single day on the Southern Tier provided me with an incredible amount of personal growth! Each day, I would spin my pedals while focusing on my BIG WHY. Despite the physical pain, mental discomfort, and spiritual torture, I pushed my pedals around intuitively realizing that NOTHING ELSE in this world would EVER give me this kind of opportunity to DEVELOP myself. Nothing in my past 48 years on planet Earth even came close to the power-packed growth potential involved in riding the glorious and untamed Southern Tier Bicycle Route! So, despite all the hardship involved in my bicycle endeavor, I continued spinning my bicycle pedals, knowing I was in the midst of uncovering something really SPECIAL deep within MYSELF!

As you are pedaling along early in your cross-country adventure, it is VERY LIKELY you will face-off with your own mind! Your mind will want some answers as to what exactly is going on? WHY are you doing this? And the only way you can remain on the grand route is if you can CONVINCE your mind of a BIG ENOUGH reason WHY.

Only YOU can convince your mind to ACCEPT the hardship you are placing on yourself! All of your body, mind, and spirit were designed to PROTECT you and keep you alive. When you do something "stupid," like taking on a new life on deserted streets in the middle of nowhere, your mind will naturally try to DETER you from getting too close to danger. Even when you are NOT in pressing physical danger, you will experience this type of radical response from your mind as your current activity is so foreign to anything else you have ever done and your mind considers it "dangerous" and will send you signals to STOP.

Prior to taking on such a daunting challenge like the Southern Tier, you are advised to spend time every morning in silence considering exactly why you are making the decision to pedal a bicycle across the country. Put your answers on paper or type your responses on the computer screen. Don't leave your answers within the vast open spaces of your mind. Put your soul-searching answers "on paper" and then question your answers to make sure they are REAL and motivating. Lukewarm answers to your big question of WHY will NOT be enough to pull you through the heightened emotions of the Southern Tier when you find yourself on the isolated desert road alone in the dark with howling coyotes all around you!

It will be during challenging times when you are SCARED or times when you are physically exhausted when your mind will question your reasons most severely. It's almost like we have a DEVIL inside us lurking around waiting for us to reach the absolute lowest point of weakness and vulnerability to make its evil move! Waiting until you are sick, tired, and scared, it is at these moments your mind will TEST your reasons of why as only during times of emotional and physical severity can it be determined if your WHY is worthy or not!

Most of you reading this book will fail on your initial attempt at a solo, unsupported, continuous cross-country bike ride across the country, but don't let your seeming failure stop you from trying again at another future time. Riding an epic bike route for any amount of time is quite an accomplishment! Most aspiring cross-country cyclists quit before they even take their first pedal stroke on the actual route as most don't even make it to the starting line! So, if you make it to the starting line and you push your pedal around even one time, you are much further ahead of many other wishful cyclists who only dreamed about taking a cross-country ride, but for a myriad of reasons never made it to Ocean Beach to start on Day 1!

Keep your WHY close at hand as you start your epic bike journey. Maybe even keep a pre-printed card in your wallet like I did! Remind yourself why you are pedaling seven hours a day. Having a small card in your wallet will be valuable when your mind goes haywire and begins to demand a logical answer to the prevailing question "What the heck am I doing out here?" Your written mission card inside your wallet might be enough to get you past a serious, potentially trip-ending test from deep within the confines of your own head!

Remember, reasons come first and answers come second. Don't expect to know what to do until you know WHY you are doing it! If you want to complete the Southern Tier, then you better know WHY you are doing it!

DAY 23: I had an enjoyable stay at the Fort Clark Army Campground in Brackettville, Texas.

Chapter 80: Aching Legs

Sore legs are NOTHING! All athletes get sore legs from time to time. Sometimes my legs are sore for a day or two after I jog or take a long one-day bike ride. It's really no big deal! Soreness is simply a part of being an athlete.

It wasn't until the Southern Tier when I discovered ACHING legs!!! By Day 4, my legs were much beyond sore; they were ACHING!!!! As soon as I applied any amount of pedal force to my bike, my legs felt like they were on FIRE! The BURNING pain was most intense early in the morning as I began to spin my pedals around, but the pain remained for most of my beginning days on the Southern Tier. At times, it felt like TORTURE!

Most long-haul cyclists get sore legs on Day 2 and Day 3. By Day 4 the leg pain can escalate and reach the "ACHING" status. Aching cycling legs could last for a week or possibly even as long as two weeks depending on numerous factors, especially current fitness level. After about a week or two, the human body will finally get used to the constant daily demand of pedal rotations and most of the leg pain will subside, but in the meantime don't underestimate aching cycling leg pain! While riding the Southern Tier, my legs got brutally aching sore. My legs were so uncomfortable it was hard to walk when I got off of my bicycle! More than one bystander cringed as they watched me dismount my bike and take my first few dreadfully painful steps.

During the first week or two of my cross-country travels as I dismounted my bicycle approximately 10 times a day, there were occassions when I came very close to collapsing to the ground in sheer agony. The devastating pain could only be described as BRUTAL, but worse yet was the wrenching agony I felt as I lie in bed at night as my leg muscles cramped and seized STIFF like they were being crushed in a vise! Severe aching leg pain is NOT pretty and it has sent many cyclists back home in tears! Do NOT underestimate the importance of proper leg health!

Although sore, aching legs can be DEVASTATING, the cramping tightness in my hip areas was even worse! My hips got so tight, at times, it was almost UNBEARABLE!!! After several days of repetitive pedaling motion, my hips seemed to LOCK. As long as I was pedaling, I was OK, but when I went to bed at night, several times, I was awoken out of a deep sleep with hip cramping so TIGHT I could barely move as I desperately waited helplessly in my bed for the cramping to subside and to experience some RELIEF as the tightness left me unable to get out of bed. During this late-night struggle I remember one time gasping for air as I could barely breathe as the muscles in my hip were SEIZED so tight!

Severe pain and cramping may also occur in your quads or in your calves. The pain could easily escalate to the point in which you lower back may also have muscle spasms, cramping, or severe piercing pain. As you ride day after day, you will UNDERSTAND how all the muscles in your body are TIED together for better or for worse! After experiencing crushing, cramping pain, you will gladly trade regular standard pain as your preferred alternative!

To lessen the effects of sore legs, the consumption of lots of water is needed. Water is key to keeping your body flexible and healthy. Walking every ten miles is also a crucial habit necessary to keep cramping at bay. The transition from riding your bicycle to walking will give your legs a chance to recover from the relentless cycling exertion of spinning your pedals round and round and allow your muscles, tendons, and arteries to find reprieve. After your walk, do a few simple stretches for a minute or two. The water, walk, and stretch will rejuvenate your legs and make the pain somewhat bearable. If the pain becomes too intense, you might try swallowing a couple Ibuprofen or my miracle drug, Naproxen, but don't make it a habit! Excessive ibuprofen can be damaging on your liver and other precious bodily organs!

If you are imprudent like most long-distance cyclists and you keep cranking out the miles without adequate water, walking rest, and regular stretching, then you will encounter a level of ACHING leg pain capable of curtailing your entire biking dream! Take your time. Your bike journey is NOT a race. Think SLOW, SLOW, and SLOWER! Give your legs some rest through the day. Get off of your saddle seat and walk thirty yards down the road and back. Do 3 different basic stretches at each of your walking breaks. Interrupt the monotony of your ride. Your body and especially your legs will thank you!

If you can make it through the first week of your lengthy bike tour, your body will begin to adapt to your "new life" and your legs will begin to feel better during your second week. If you can make it to your third week, your legs might even start feeling good. By the beginning of your fourth week, you might even discover what I did, your legs will feel like they are made of IRON! IRON LEGS are one of the truly special rewards you will reap as you hang on and delve deeper and deeper into the Southern Tier!

The critical part of your bicycle journey is in the first week. Take it slow. Establish positive patterns of drinking, walking, and stretching. Take care of your legs. Stretch OFTEN and stretch as long as you can force yourself to do so. Every minute invested with STRETCHING will pay you back with HUGE rewards!!!!! Trust me!!!

Resist the urge to jump on your bike early in the morning and start hammering out the miles. EASE into your miles with SLOW pedal revolutions until you warm up all of your little muscles. It is EASY to injure your cold, early-morning muscles. In most cases, injuries occur as a result of improper WARM UP!

The first five miles of your bike ride each day should be EXTREMELY SLOW as your only objective in the first five miles is to reacclimate your muscles to cycling as you SLOWLY set the tone for the day. When you think you are going slow enough, FORCE yourself to go even SLOWER! Your early morning mantra should be "SLOW!"

Show ultra-respect to your on-call muscles during the first week of your bike ride and the first five miles of biking every day and your responsive muscles will answer with increased performance as your cycling journey unfolds across the country! Maintain high levels of respect for proper leg health as well as good health with all the various parts of your body. Aching legs are a BIG PROBLEM. If you are not careful, aching legs can <u>EASILY</u> take you out! Welcome to the Southern Tier!

DAY 24: Kings Restaurant is for COWBOYS or wannabe cowboys like me! You gotta stop here to eat!!!

DAY 25: Magnificent sunrise!

Chapter 81: Loving Advice

On Day 4 when I was super-close to coming back home, my mom called and LOVINGLY proclaimed, "Anyone who attempts a cross-country biking goal should be VERY PROUD of themselves. You actually flew to San Diego, California, assembled your bicycle in the airport, dipped your tire into the Pacific Ocean at Ocean Beach, and road over 200 hundred miles. You are a CHAMPION!!! You can come back home and be proud of your accomplishment!" As I considered my mom's kind words, I completely agreed with her! It really took some sincere effort for me to get to the starting line of the Southern Tier at Ocean Beach in San Diego! Truly, I was one of the few cyclists who ever actually made it to the sparkling sands of the Pacific Ocean to start such an unusual quest! Only a very small percentage of aspiring cross-country cyclists ever board an airplane to fly to their starting location. Clearly, I was SPECIAL. With my head held high, it was completely acceptable for me to take the next plane back home!

There probably isn't a mother alive whom loves her son more than my mother loves me! When mom shared her supportive and congratulatory remarks with me, it was tempting to take her good, loving, and accurate advice, turn around, and board the next flight back home to Pittsburgh. At the time, I didn't realize it, but her words might have been the most <u>dangerous,</u> potentially trip-ending comments I encountered on my entire cross-country cycling pursuit. Fortunately for me, I LISTENED carefully to mom's advice, thought about it diligently, and then I OBEYED my own HEART and REMAINED on the Southern Tier!!!

For my entire adulthood, I've been well-known for being "my own man." Ignoring my mom's loving advice was not surprising to her or to any of my other family members as I've established a lifelong pattern of taking my own direction! My bike adventure would be no different as I decided to carry on, at least for another day.

It would have been very easy to turn around in San Diego or anywhere along the way to Phoenix, Arizona and take the next flight back to Pittsburgh as I was tempted DOZENS of times. Listening to a loved one is enticing at times, but great triumphs take something more. Achieving significance has to do with holding on to your dream even when there are times you can't even remember why you are doing it. Sometimes, you just have to do it because you SAID you would do it! Sometimes, getting ANGRY and being STUBBORN is all you got!

Despite the truth and sincerity of my mother's words and her great wisdom, I wanted MORE! Flying to San Diego and riding a few hundred miles was not enough for me! I had to GO FOR IT! The Southern Tier was calling me! And even though I KNEW within the first two days I could NOT pedal my bicycle all the way across the country and I was DESTINED to FAIL, I also KNEW I was NOT going back home! This was my time to shine and I was prepared to <u>DIE</u> along the Southern Tier if it so be my divine fate!

Taking my mom's advice and getting back on an airplane to Pittsburgh might have been acceptable to my immediate family as a "champion's effort," but it wasn't acceptable to me and I wasn't going down that easy! Despite the rather intense experience at hand, I decided to hang on for ONE MORE DAY. More firmly than ever, the magnitude of my adventure was confirmed as this bike trip was no longer a "bicycle ride across America," it was now a God-ordained MISSION into the depth of my own SOUL! Onward I pedaled alone, unsupported, and continuous as I spun my pedals around for what seemed like an eternity! My cross-country cycling quest endured!

DAY 25: As an avid cyclist, I love to see "SHARE THE ROAD" signs!

DAY 25: My bicycle also served as a drying rack!

Chapter 82: 86 Traffic Violations

According to federal law, a cyclist must follow the rules of the road in the same manner as the driver of a motorized vehicle. As far as I know, there are no special exemptions regarding vehicular laws and/or traffic lights as they pertain to cyclists! Therefore, cyclists are required by law to stop at all red traffic lights and wait for the red light to turn green before crossing. Crossing through a red light is a driving violation and poses a risk of the issuance of a traffic citation fine which would certainly apply negative marks against a cyclist's personal driving record.

As I approached BUSY or moderately-busy intersections on my bicycle in various towns and cities throughout the southern United States, I would claim my spot in traffic behind the car in front of me and obey all traffic lights as not to put myself or anybody else in danger nor to subject myself to any unnecessary fines or unpleasant interactions with the police. But when I approached a traffic light in the wee hours of the morning with only one or two cars on the road or when I encountered a traffic light on a near-desolate country road, I would VIOLATE federal law by slowing down at the desolate red light, hugging to the right of the lane in the same area a pedestrian would use as a crosswalk, and pedaling onward through the RED traffic light.

During my 43 days of bicycle travel, I estimate I illegally pedaled through about two red traffic lights every day for a grand total of about 86 traffic violations. Despite breaking the law no less than 86 times, not once did I get pulled over nor did I receive a single traffic violation ticket. Although I'm not bragging about committing an illegal act, I was 100% safety-conscious as I rode my bike through the dozens of red traffic lights and I did not feel as though I put myself or anybody else in danger. No, I'm NOT proud of my irresponsible actions, but I felt they were REASONABLE as it didn't make sense for me to wait all by myself for a red light to turn green when there were one, two, or often ZERO other vehicles in sight!

During times of heavy, slow traffic, I took my place amidst the cars and waited patiently like a good boy behind the vehicle in front of me. Amidst traffic I did NOT pull to the side of the road nor did I ride on a sidewalk! My bicycle was out in traffic with the cars and trucks as to claim my OWN spot on the road amidst the vehicles surrounding me!!!! Cowering to the vehicles and riding on sidewalks or riding too tight to the curb is an invitation to an accident as many cars quickly make right hand turns without looking to see if a cyclist might be directly to their right. You must BOLDLY (and carefully) claim your spot in the MIDDLE of the right lane in heavy, slow traffic.

While you are stopped waiting for traffic lights, you should remain in the MIDDLE of the lane directly behind the vehicle in front of you. Trust me, you will be MUCH SAFER and the vehicles WILL respect you and your bicycle if you treat yourself the same as any other motorized vehicle and take over the FULL lane of travel.

Once you pass through the traffic light and the traffic becomes less congested and vehicles regain greater speed, you should RETURN to the side of the road or the berm of the road as not to unnecessarily slow up traffic in your lane.

DAY 26: A "cattle guard" keeps the cows from wandering off of the ranch property. Apparently, a cow is NOT capable of passing through a cattle guard without entrapping their hoof.

DAY 26: Here is a close-up of my homemade padded handlebars. My hillbilly handlebars helped to diminish the numbness in my hands and forearms.

Chapter 83: Nice People

While riding my fully-loaded touring bicycle across the country, I did NOT notice one person whom I perceived to be a threat to me! In fact, the complete opposite was true. Pulling my "rig" into any parking lot often prompted complete strangers to speak with me. Without fail, most of the strangers I encountered along my long bike route were VERY interested in me and wanted to know MY STORY.

Complete strangers wanted to know where I started and where I was headed. Unfamiliar people wanted to know how many miles I pedal in one day and how many total miles I have traveled. Others were curious about what I eat, where I go to the bathroom, where I sleep at night, or if I ever get lost. Many others asked me about flat tires and some were intrigued as to whether I was some type of "professional" cyclist. And the questions went on and on. These good-hearted "strangers" and their OBSESSION with me and my bike were a big part of why I decided to write this book as their high-level curiosity was clearly apparent.

Throughout my entire bike escapade across the United States of America, I cannot recall more than a few semi-ignorant strangers. In all 8 states traveled, NICE PEOPLE was the common theme! It was such a pleasing relief for me to find out first-hand about the many genuinely NICE people living in the great country of the United States of America! If I was more of an outgoing type of person, I could have probably made many more friends along the way, but I tend to keep to myself and do my own thing without paying much attention to others.

Even with my tendency of being a bit of a recluse, many unfamiliar people couldn't resist the urge to speak with me and I was HAPPY to converse with them and answer their questions. Over all, the citizens of the USA couldn't have been any more pleasant! Many strangers encouraged me and congratulated me while making comments like, "I could never do that!" or "You're crazy!" On more than one occasion during my solo bike travels, it felt like I was a celebrity!

After encountering hundreds of short interactions with various people along my extensive bike travels, I definitely found Americans overall to be VERY kind. The positive, friendly trend I experienced during my bicycle adventure proved to me beyond a shadow of a doubt about how pleasant most people are, which was contrary to my original expectations prior to my epic ride! Maybe the amiability of the American citizens stemmed from my vulnerability riding a bicycle with all my belongings attached to it? Or maybe people from the USA are just kinder than I thought? Regardless of the reason for their friendliness, I can attest to a SOLID FACT, America has a strong base of truly kind-hearted citizens!

On one occasion, I was wild camping in a vacant lot adjacent to a church in Kirbyville, Texas. Two elderly female members of the adjacent church approached my unofficial campsite and asked me what I would like to eat for supper. Without being shy, I shared my dream supper wish list with the forthcoming women, but I didn't count on ever seeing them again.

To my surprise, about 30 minutes later, the two generous women delivered me the dinner of my dreams directly to the "doorstep" of my tent! These two caring women were somewhat cautious with me as they wouldn't even share their first names with me, but they were DETERMINED to make sure I had PLENTY of food to eat! At many other times during my bike travels, strangers unexpectedly gave me water, directions, or advice as they obviously gained as much giving to me as I gained from their generous gifts! All in all, the people I met along my biking adventure were extremely kind and CARING!

Despite the many good people I encountered while crossing America, I kept reminding myself to be on guard for evil people as I knew our society has some BAD people as well! Although I didn't directly experience any such malicious individuals along my way, I was alert to their possible presence! Being prepared for the worst is always a good strategy to live by!

Even as nice as the citizens of the USA were to me, I was careful not to expect favors from them. My overall philosophy was to mind my own business and let everything else fall into place. Not once did I EXPECT strangers to help me, but many times I received unsuspecting assistance! Not once did I expect people to be nice to me, but almost without fail, the public was extremely cordial. My governing strategy was to rely on MYSELF as I knew I would become WEAK if I expected others to do nice gestures for me! When I was lucky enough to get help, I expressed my thanks, but I never expected anyone to help me!

The success and failure of my journey across the country had to deal with <u>only</u> ONE PERSON...... ME!!! By fostering my mindset of personal independence and NOT relying on the generosity and pure altruistic compassion of my fellow brothers and sisters, I set myself up for a big WIN! By NOT expecting help, kindness, and encouragement, I ended up GETTING help, kindness, and encouragement!!!!! The twisted reality of my biking experience was a bit strange, but TRUE!!! Welcome to the Southern Tier!

Chapter 84: Prayer

Without a doubt in my mind, God inspired me to ride my bicycle across the country! My cross-country journey had very little to do with my own PERSONAL planning. I was CALLED to take on the incredible feat!

Despite my privileged calling, I hugely UNDERESTIMATED the SPIRITUAL dimension of my upcoming bike trip. Naturally, I assumed the bike ride would test my physical and mental capacity to the limits, but I did NOT expect the physical outing to be such a spiritual revelation! My spiritual experience was INTENSE!!! If I spent 7 hours a day for 43 consecutive days inside a church, I would NOT have had the same level of spiritual growth and connection with God as I did riding my bicycle across the southern portion of the United States for 43 days in a row!

If you want to FIND God and KNOW God, go out and get yourself a bicycle and start pedaling across the country by yourself. You WILL find God there!!!! In a very mysterious manner, it seems taking a solo bicycle journey across the country UNLOCKS some mysterious GATEWAY to the divine. It must have something to do with the RELINQUISHING of many of your personal possessions and taking only what you need on your bike to survive as you pedal completely ALONE and VULNERABLE through some of the most magnificent landscapes in the world!

By Day 4 on the Southern Tier, I realized my cross-country pursuit was going to be a VERY LONELY tour. Feeling exposed and defenseless was an everyday occurrence for me. As I glanced around me, the pure VASTNESS of the desert encapsulated me. At times, I yearned for a friend, and a "friend" is indeed what I found!

As I pedaled day after day, I would spend HOURS reciting the "Our Father" and "Hail Mary" prayers from my Catholic upbringing in the Christian faith. Doing so caused me to feel closer to God than ever before in my life. Pedaling further and deeper along the Southern Tier Bicycle Route, the words of these 2 common Catholic prayers revealed their DEEPER meanings to me. Although I have recited these prayers THOUSANDS of times prior to my epic bike travels, I never FELT the magnitude of the individual words until I recited them on the Southern Tier! Every word from these two common prayers became SACRED to me as I contemplated the words and KNEW the prayers in an innovative and marvelous manner. These two standard prayers will be forever etched upon my heart.

HAIL MARY

Hail Mary, full of grace, the Lord is with thee. Blessed art thou among women and blessed is the fruit of thy womb Jesus. Holy Mary, mother of God, pray for our sinners, now and at the hour of our death. Amen.

OUR FATHER

Our father, who art in Heaven, hallowed be thy name. They kingdom come, thy will be done on Earth as it is in Heaven. Give us this day our daily bread and forgive us our trespasses and we forgive those who trespass against us. Lead us not into temptation, but deliver us from evil for thine is the Kingdom, power, and glory for ever and ever. Amen.

As I write this brief chapter, I am tempted to scribe a passage about EVERY SINGLE WORD used in these two commanding prayers as there is HUGE untapped power enclosed in these two HEAVYWEIGHT prayers, but I have declined to do so as your own personal experience will be more powerful than any words I could possibly use as an interpretation of the two short, but elite prayers listed above.

Even today as I habitually continue to recite these lifechanging prayers, I often get CHILLS all over my body as my Southern Tier memories are FOREVER tattooed on my soul as the transcending power of these common, but power-packed prayers continue to spark my own personal spiritual journey. Although I signed up for an amazing cross-country bike ride full of physical and mental challenges, I got an unsuspecting HEAVY DOSE of spirituality bringing me closer to God than ever before!

Deep in the desert of the Southern Tier, my prayers AWOKE a sleeping spiritual power inside of me. On a daily basis, chills of enthrallment showered my body from head to toes. The Southern Tier route was similar to an ancient Egyptian pyramid as I have read it is possible to tap into and AWAKEN the sleeping, but ever-present power of the pyramids through prayer, meditation, and fasting. The Southern Tier was no different as I PROMISE you there is ACTIVE spiritual power contained in the sacred route! Many times, I FELT glimpses of the transcending power of good as I sat on the seat of my bike. With very little exception, my very lengthy bike trip was NOT what I had originally expected it to be!

Prior to taking my first pedal revolution of each day as I was about to mount my bicycle and begin my daily journey, I would speak out loud a humble prayer. My simple prayer would usually go something like this:

"God bless this biker. God bless this bike. God bless my equipment. God bless all of these vehicles. God bless these drivers. God bless these roads. God bless these animals living near these roads. If it be your will dear Lord, deliver me, my bike, and my gear safely to the special overnight accommodation you have reserved for me. Amen!"

After a few days, this homemade prayer of mine, was used not only at the beginning of each day, but also after each of my regular ten-mile walking breaks. After a few weeks of habitually using my special prayer of divine protection, the prayer became an ESSENTIAL part of my bike ride. If I would resume my bike ride after one of my ten-mile breaks without saying my newly adopted prayer, I would immediately cease pedaling, stop alongside the road, and recite my heartfelt prayer. Prayer became MORE IMPORTANT than eating as I progressed along my bike journey across the country. Without prayer, I GUARANTEE I would have FAILED and returned home early!!!!!!

Within the first week of my epic struggle, I discovered the 3,000-mile bike ride was much BIGGER than me! With my limited personal development, I had NO CHANCE of completing the Southern Tier on my own accord. Something more than just physical prowess and mental strength was required to get the job done and it was apparent I was still lacking in one imperative additional category. Although I had previously conquered a lot of the physical and mental thresholds involved in high-level athletics, I was still missing a crucial piece of the Southern Tier puzzle and the missing piece was GOD! Without prayer on the Southern Tier, I'm CERTAIN I would have come back home early!

By far, the biggest surprise of my bike ride across America involved spirituality. Wrongly, I assumed my cross-country bike ride would be primarily a physical and mental task, but to my surprise my daily exertions were the most spiritual activity I ever experienced! As I began riding the Southern Tier, I felt like I had a good, solid relationship with God, but being alone in the desert, I met God in a whole new and powerful way! Taking on the Southern Tier opened up a spiritual chapter in my life triggering tears of joy dripping down my cheek, splashing on my bike bar, and dispersing to the scorching-hot asphalt below. In all my life, I don't think I cried as much as I did while pedaling the Southern Tier!

Regularly, I felt overwhelmed with the pulsating spiritual power surge surrounding me and bubbling INSIDE of me. On a few occasions, I even felt SCARED as I would experience a mere sampling of God's pure almighty power! The spiritual presence of God was alive and REAL along the Southern Tier!!!!

About two-thirds of the way through my odyssey across America, I KNEW I had to write a book about my thrilling experience. No longer was my bike trip all about me as I felt an OBLIGATION to share my uncommon biking experience with others and to encourage others to FIND themselves in the same way I found covered-over parts of MYSELF! Little did I know as I took my first pedal stroke at Ocean Beach in San Diego, California, the Southern Tier was about to be THE SIGNATURE OF MY LIFE!!!! Tapping into the PURE POWER of God through prayer mixed in with the natural WONDERS of the majestic Southern Tier Bike Route gave rise to a spiritual experience much more INTENSE than my mere words can convey on this page! Welcome to the Southern Tier!

Chapter 85: $1.00

As I pulled into the sole gas station at the edge of town in Brawley, California, an older, rough-looking, scruffy-bearded man in a really outdated, big, beat-up, rusted, four-door car stopped alongside my bike, gave me a dollar, and then left without saying a word. For days, I struggled to find meaning in this odd occurrence. It wasn't until my Mesa, Arizona Warmshowers host, Layne Gneiting, suggested the odd act of kindness might have been the man's way of becoming part of my epic bicycle journey!

Maybe this rough, old guy always dreamed of doing something "crazy" like riding his bike across the country? Or maybe this bizarre man did ride his bike across the country and he now appreciates the effort involved in such a task? Despite the eccentric man's exact motivations, I'm sure he had good intentions regarding his small contribution to my cause! And even though the man was obviously of VERY POOR means, the dollar he gave to me was as valuable as a ONE HUNDRED DOLLARS as I immediately sensed the undeniable connection with my elder brother!

Almost every day of my long biking excursion involved similar strange, serendipitous occurrences as are listed throughout this book. After a few weeks of cycling, I was no longer surprised by these "chance" encounters as each unfolding day made me realize more and more that I was indeed on a DIVINE MISSION. But as common as these unforeseen acts of goodwill became, each unexpected occurrence continued to intrigue me!

Maybe it was my pure vulnerability and innocence which attracted me to these chance happenings? Maybe by spending so much time outside my comfort zone, I gravitated to nice people with pure intentions? It was eerie how my 'luck" would unfold and always keep me safe and well. By stretching my comfort zone well beyond my current limits, I seemingly ATTRACTED these startling occurrences as naturally as the north end of a magnet attracts the south end.

Although many would consider it a BORING task to spin your pedals around for 7 hours a day for 43 days straight, my experience of the Southern Tier proved to be the MOST EXCITING experience of my life! It was an AMAZING feeling to be completely FREE in a brand-new life without a riding partner in my near vicinity to offer protection and or comfort! Having no human being at my side for much of my epic ride seemed to cancel out frequent mortal interference and make room for the divine as it is difficult writing about a phenomenon so mysterious. From my best account, it just seemed as though outlandish happenings were "normal" on the Southern Tier!

Chapter 86: Directions

Pedaling on hundreds of different roads, traveling through countless small towns, and riding on many well-established biking trails required myself to make A LOT of turns! And prior to every turn is the dubious chance of getting lost! Although my father is a walking, talking, real-life version of Google Maps, I did NOT get the "map gene" from my father. At best, I was BELOW AVERAGE reading maps as of Day 1 of my Southern Tier crossing. Fortunately for me, I did improve my map-reading skills as my biking days progressed along the southern portion of the United States of America.

While planning my epic bicycle journey, I carefully studied the map of my intended direction of travel. Although I was of low-skill level reading maps, I did understand my proposed route involved traveling eastbound. In my case, it meant gazing at a beautiful sunrise EVERY morning as the sun ALWAYS rises in the east and ALWAYS sets in the west. Traveling east also meant north would be to my left and south would be to my right. West would be behind me. By the time I arrived in Florida, it seemed like I had finally mastered my basic directions!

While traveling eastbound, numerous times early in my trip, I quickly discovered riding a bike and simultaneously looking at my physical map was a recipe for disaster! By Day 3, I discovered it only takes about half a second to either drift into traffic or to drift off the side of the road. After a few potentially trip-ending scares resulting from my careless map reading, I finally decided to pull over and stop my bicycle before looking at my physical map. The same level of danger was also evident about halfway through Texas when I finally acquired my first non-paper Bicycle Route Navigator GPS phone application map.

With consideration for my below-average map reading skills, it was especially vital for me to dedicate time each evening toward planning my destination for the following day. With the generous help of my dad, I would carefully consider the elevation gain, the forecasted wind direction, the wind velocity, and the road terrain as I would decide about how many total miles I planned to travel for my upcoming day. After having an idea about my anticipated mileage total, I would look for the nearest town or city closest to my desired mileage and then I would make plans to spend the night in that general vicinity.

Before going to bed, it was my habit to spend a few minutes reviewing tomorrow's map. While glancing at my map, I would acclimate myself to the direction in which I was traveling and I would become familiar with at least my first turn of the day as I deemed it CRUCIAL for me to at least make my first turn correct! Knowing the street name or state route number was also a habit of mine as one of my bigger fears was getting lost!

Spending this quality time at night with my map also gave me greater confidence in the morning when I re-visited my map for final clarification. There are few other challenges more frustrating than making a wrong turn on a cross-country bike route. When you have 3,000 or more miles to pedal, you cannot afford to pedal even one mile in the WRONG DIRECTION!

For the most part, I am a VERY CALM guy. Some of the friends and family in my inner circle have even stated on various occasions, "You have ICE in your veins!" Whether or not their uncommon compliment had any validity of truth or not is certainly debatable, but if any of these close family friends saw how I reacted on the Southern Tier upon making a wrong turn, they would instantly retract their complementary statement regarding my calm state of mind.

Each time I made a wrong turn and got lost, I went insane! I literally went BONKERS!!! If any of you would have seen my IMMATURE actions resulting from a simple wrong turn on my bicycle, immediately you would drop this book and NOT read another page as you would NOT invest your precious time trying to learn something from such an emotionally unstable person like me! For some reason, getting LOST sent me into RAGE prompting me to curse myself out with words I haven't ever used before! It was like I was possessed by the devil! For someone who RARELY swears, I was NOT at a loss for expletives directed at my pitiful self when I made a wrong turn and got LOST on the Southern Tier!

After eventually realizing my unsuspecting tendency to act irrationally when getting lost, I made it my business to be VERY CAREFUL with every turn I made. My map became my best friend as I could not risk making any additional wrong turns as in a moment of lost self-control, I feared I might actually harm my woeful self! My simple goal was to STAY ON ROUTE. Getting lost for more than a minute was out of the question! To risk expressing my pent-up rage was too much.

In most cases, I knew approximately how many miles I was to travel on each road before making the next scheduled turn. Plus, my GPS phone app (Bicycle Route Navigator from Adventure Cycling Association) was open and available for easy access inside my waterproof phone holder which was mounted on my handlebars. If my little pink dot wasn't directly on the blue highlighted Southern Tier Route, then I knew I was LOST and it was time to QUICKLY get back on route!

It was my habit to pay close attention to my GPS phone app at least every 3 miles, but usually much more often. If you were watching me, you would probably determine I was OBSESSED with my Bicycle Route Navigator GPS phone app! And when I arrived at big cities like Austin, New Roads, Mobile, Pensacola, Tallahassee, or Jacksonville, my attention was glued to my phone app as I would use my fingers to ZOOM closer to each street as to easily determine the proper street in which to turn in order to remain on route.

It was MUCH MORE DIFFICULT navigating through the other big cities on the

Southern Tier route like San Diego, Tempe, Phoenix, El Paso, and Del Rio prior to my purchase of Bicycle Route Navigator as I was relegated to using a paper map which was much more challenging and much more dangerous to try to follow as I was pedaling. Although I spent TOO MUCH TIME glancing at my GPS phone app and physical maps, I was DEDICATED to keeping myself and those around me safe. At all times, SAFETY was foremost on my mind.

One of the most annoying aspects of using the GPS phone app was how my phone went dark after a few seconds of inactivity requiring me to "wake it up." Being a below-average tech guy, I never did figure out how to keep my phone "awake" during those critical times when it would have been much more convenient for my phone to stay BRIGHT without having to scramble to hit various buttons to wake my phone back up! I'm sure there is probably a simple way to keep your phone "awake" while you are traveling through a big city as I found it to be DIFFICULT maneuvering through a city relying solely on a physical map.

It amazes me how cyclists of the past actually used physical maps as their primary guide while traveling through the big cities! It confounds me as to how quickly they referenced the physical map and still pedaled their bike. To be safe, a cyclist using a physical map should STOP each time a reference is made to the map as to maintain proper safety.

When it was time daily for me to locate my Warmshowers host, special restaurant, bike shop, or campground, I enjoyed using the Google Maps phone application instead of the Adventure Cycling Bicycle Route Navigator. Bicycle Route Navigator kept me on the Southern Tier Route with AMAZING accuracy, but Google Maps gave me detailed visual and AUDIO directions through my ear buds which allowed me to keep my eyes on the road while locating my many different food, lodging, and other necessary places of interest which were usually only a short distance off of the actual Southern Tier route.

Using my ear buds made the perfect integration for the turn-by-turn directions from the very precise and well-spoken Google Maps lady. Although this method of direction is very convenient, I found it BEST to continue to glance down at my phone periodically to ensure I remained on Google route as I am VERY CONSERVATIVE and I habitually double and triple-check myself as I have a tendency to make a lot of MISTAKES!

Many cyclists have used the Google Maps "bike" feature as their PRIMARY guide to travel to far-off destinations, but I have found some of the Google Map biking routes to be slightly more dangerous than those offered by Adventure Cycling on their Bicycle Route Navigator GPS phone app. It would be great to use Bicycle Route Navigator EVERY time I ride, but Bicycle Route Navigator ONLY sells their route guidance for specific major bike routes. So, the plan is simple. Buy and use Bicycle Route Navigator whenever you can and use Google Maps or some other

GPS phone app program for the rest of your non-Bicycle Route Navigator bike route guidance.

In those cases in which Adventure Cycling Association does not have an established route to my desired destination, I have no problem using Google Maps for directions to get me there. All you do is click on the bicycle icon to alert Google Maps to give you BICYCLE directions and NOT vehicle directions!!! Regardless of whatever source of direction I was using at any particular time, my TOP priority was always to pay close attention to exactly where I was as well as the cars and people surrounding me. Making a mistake and causing an accident could have been done very easily if my attention was to wander. In most cases, I would consider myself a responsible cyclist user of our public roads!

Using the powerful Google Maps function to choose your directions based on whether you are walking, riding a bike, or driving a car is an important feature. Based on your travel-type, Google Maps supposedly directs you on the most appropriate roads as per your means of travel. Although Google Maps is great, I've personally had a time or two in the distant past while using the vehicle function when Google Maps directed me to a dirt road leading to nowhere. In frustration I would turn around and reverse my direction, but this type of mishap is a rather rare occurrence and has not happened recently.

My final word on directions is to make good use of current technology and use your phone app, but also make sure you have a paper map with you as well for additional reference. BOTH are needed!!!! Adventure Cycling Association makes AMAZING paper maps as well as their INCREDIBLE Bicycle Route Navigator phone GPS phone maps. On an EPIC ADVENTURE, you should be using BOTH!!!!

Although at times throughout this book, it might appear as though I am an owner, employee, stock holder, or some other person of interest with regards to Adventure Cycling, I assure you, I am NOT!!!! I have no gain whatsoever if you buy their products or not. I'm just a guy who benefited greatly from their AWESOME maps, advise, and gear. With my highest recommendation, I urge YOU and all other cyclists to become familiar with Adventure Cycling as to gain the information, gear, and maps needed to complete a major bicycle route!

Chapter 87: Bike Seat

While considering the 300-plus hours I was about to spend sitting on my bicycle seat, I did myself a favor and bought the BEST bike seat I could find. My research indicated the average factory bicycle seat was NOT going to be adequate for my upcoming cross-country task. Adventure Cycling Association produces a small catalog each year called "CYCLOSOURCE" which lists some of the best cycling products in the world. If I could go back in time, I would have made my life much simpler by reading the Adventure Cycling magazine and then buying their suggested products without trying to save money buying inferior, cheaper products elsewhere. By trying to save money, I actually LOST money and time spending countless hours tabbing through eBay and Amazon looking for discounted biking equipment instead of spending a few dollars more and buying exactly what I needed directly from Adventure Cycling Association.

In all fairness to myself, I did locate some excellent bike equipment on eBay and Amazon, but I could have saved so much time by doing my shopping solely on the Adventure Cycling Association website or through their excellent CYCLOSOURCE catalog! If you are not a member of Adventure Cycling Association, then you need to become a member. Annual membership is cheap, even for someone super-thrifty like myself! The splendid monthly magazine alone is worth the cost of membership! The benefits of Adventure Cycling membership are too extensive to be listed here. Trust me on this particular recommendation!

My research into bike seats kept pointing toward the English brand named "Brooks" which was repeatedly touted as "one of the best bike seats in the world." After much deliberation, I finally decided to order the Brooks Flyer as my bike seat to be used to cross the USA. And I'm glad I did! The Brooks Flyer is a hard leather seat with some springs in the back designed to help to absorb the shocks of the road and the hailed seat turned out to be fabulous!

At first upon delivery of my new Brooks Flyer seat, I was NOT impressed, but after I applied the special leather crème which was included in the purchase, I noticed my new Brooks Flyer seat was conforming to my exact riding position while molding itself into the exact curvature of my butt as I logged more and more miles on my bike. Eventually, the Brooks Flyer became a perfect custom seat for my own uniquely-designed butt! After riding all the way across the United States on my Brooks Flyer, I can fully recommend this top-notch bike seat. Spending the extra money on a world-class bike seat was one of my best decisions!

For years, I struggled with a sore lower back. My back troubles started during junior high school football and never got much better. Although I have achieved some significant athletic accomplishments in my life, my back has always been a sore point in all of my various athletic and non-athletic activities. For the most part, my back has hurt me almost every day of my life. But by the second week of my EPIC

Southern Tier journey, my back pain VANISHED and did NOT return for the rest of my bike trip! It was a miracle! I'm not sure exactly why my back pain ceased, but I believe a small part of my good fortune involving my back remedy might have had something to do with my top-quality Brooks Flyer bike seat!

DAY 27: Keep this seat bolt tight! Once you find the perfect position for your bike seat, you don't want to ever lose it!

DAY 27: My brothers and sisters!

Chapter 88: Bike Weight

Prior to leaving my home to take on the mighty Southern Tier, I spent more than 20 hours carefully considering the EXACT gear I would bring along with me on my epic bike adventure. My goal was to have EVERYTHING I needed regardless of the weight. It wasn't until I arrived in Mesa, Arizona when I met an ANGEL in human flesh whom taught me differently. My angel's name was Layne Gneiting. Layne quickly determined I had TOO MUCH WEIGHT on my bike!

Layne and his lovely family were my Warmshowers host for the night I spent in Mesa, Arizona on Day 8 of my cycling odyssey. Prior to my memorable and pleasant stay at the Gneiting homestead, I did not know Layne Gneiting was an INTERNATIONAL bicycle touring leader and coach! To my complete surprise, I found myself staying at the home of a cycling LEGEND! With similar Southern Tier magical fashion, it just so happened I came across Angel Layne at the PERFECT TIME!!!!

As I pulled into the driveway of Layne's attractive suburban home, Layne met me in person, immediately posed with me, and took a selfie photo of him and I while I remained on my bicycle. Layne proceeded to help me park my bike in his garage. While removing my pannier bags, Layne growled in disbelief stating, "Whoa, this is heavy!" as he shared some priceless words of wisdom with me, "Ounces make pounds and pounds make PAIN!" Layne believed lighter was better! He urged me to consider unloading some of my weight and only keeping CRUCIAL items in my pannier bags.

As I finished my nice, warm shower and got dressed in my assigned bedroom, Layne knocked at my door and said, "Dump your bags." As a respectful guest in Layne's house, I complied with his simple request and I dumped my pannier bags all over the bed. For the next 60 minutes, Layne performed a "shakedown." A shakedown is when EVERY item is carefully evaluated and a decision is made whether or not the particular item is CRUCIAL or not. If the item was NOT critical, it would be disposed of or mailed back home! After the 60-minute shakedown, I LOST 13 pounds of gear!!!

Looking back, I'm lucky I lost 13 pounds, because the following day involved an INCREDIBLY difficult climb into the Arizona mountains amidst temperatures surpassing 100 degrees Fahrenheit! As I struggled up the mountain pass battling the extreme heat and relentless sunshine, there wasn't a single cloud in the sky. The sun's heat was pure and fierce. The only bit of shade I encountered was a sliver of shade stemming from a single overpass bridge and the shade only lasted for about 3 seconds as I biked underneath the short-lived shaded bridge.

While struggling to climb the mountain, I passed a man with a long, grey beard whom appeared to be about 10 years older than me on this dangerously, scorching hot day as the older cyclist was STOPPED along the side of the road amidst the blazing hot sun, only about halfway up the HUGE uphill mountain climb. As I stopped to help the trodden man, I asked him if he wanted some of my water, but he declined as he had plenty liquids to drink. Although my peer claimed he had enough water, the scorching heat was obviously getting to him. Despite affirming to me he could make it; I had my doubts to the contrary as it seemed as though the man was already teetering on verge of heat exhaustion.

When I asked if I could call for help, this stubborn, bearded man once again declined as he had his own cell phone in the case of an emergency. My new, elder friend promised me he would be ok so I passed over him and continued on my route amidst this ruthlessly HOT afternoon as it is not my preference to force help upon anybody! Although I would venture to guess my depleted friend did NOT make it up the relentless mountain ascent, I hope he called for help in time and didn't get too sick or worse on this super-hot, scorching sunny day!

Pedal by pedal I OUTLASTED the heat on this blistering hot day and I made it to Tonto Basin Inn in the desolate area of Tonto Basin, Arizona! Without losing the 13 pounds on the previous day thanks to Layne's shakedown, I might have had a different ending to my story on this intensely HOT day! Surmounting the incredible Arizona mountain pass took almost everything I had to give on this BLAZING hot afternoon!

About a week after meeting my very special bike coach, mentor, and friend, Layne Gneiting, I stopped in west Texas at a local post office in Leakey, Texas and mailed another big package home losing another 9 pounds! If you add up the 13 pounds I lost with Layne at his home, the 9 pounds I lost in Leakey, Texas at the United States Post Office, and the 20 pounds I lost on my own physical body, my total biking weight was reduced by a whopping 42 pounds since the beginning of my bike travels!

Losing 42 pounds made an ENORMOUS difference! My bike was much easier to propel forward. It was like a baseball player who weights his bat with a heavy metal "doughnut" and then takes off the extra weight moments before coming to bat in the official game. The bat feels so much lighter!

Instead of waiting until you are on tour with your bike, carefully analyze every piece of equipment while you are still at home. Try your best to take only what you truly need. Refer to my packing lists near the end of this book and then make your own informed decisions as to what to take and what to leave at home. Ask yourself regarding EACH one of your items, "Is this absolutely necessary?" If you need it, take it! If you can do without it, leave it at home!

One of the heaviest single items on any bicycle is usually WATER! Water weighs 8 pounds per gallon (128 ounces) or 1 pound per 16 ounces. Carrying three full water bottles each with a 25-ounce capacity meant I was carrying 75 ounces of water which weighed almost 5 pounds. Often, I would also have another 4 pounds (64 ounces) or so of sports drink in the outside compartment of my right pannier bag. At my heaviest, I carried 12 pounds of liquid weight on my bicycle! While I was crossing the desert, I made sure my 3 water bottles and my two 32-ounce sports drink containers were FULL at the start of each day as to prevent any potentially fatal emergencies on the road! At other times during my trip in non-desert areas, I was much more relaxed with my liquid storage, but regardless of the weather or the particular terrain, not once during my bike travels was I ever completely out of drink as I meticulously managed my liquid reserves! From the start, I was dedicated to staying well stocked with adequate drink at ALL TIMES because I knew without water, I could possibly suffer SEVERE consequences!

Riding a bicycle across the country is HARD! Riding a fully loaded touring bicycle across the country is REALLY HARD!! Riding a loaded touring bike is completely different than riding a regular bike. Yes, after a few days, I got used to my HEAVY "rig," but at first, I had some significant challenges with the weight and the balance. Thankfully, the several overnight bike trips I took prior to the Southern Tier were VERY HELPFUL as they gave me some idea about the excessive weight of my bike and what it would take to propel the monstrosity up MOUNTAINS! It would have been CRAZY on my part to take on the mighty challenge of riding my bike across America without embarking on 2 or 3 smaller overnight bike trips FIRST! Handling a heavy touring bike alongside significant traffic is also quite a chore, but it is a skill I learned quickly.

After learning much about the importance of losing weight from my unofficial cycling coach, Layne Gneiting, I discovered my IDEAL gear weight was about 70 pounds. The 70 pounds included all of my gear and all of my storage bags including my two front pannier bags, my two rear pannier bags, my pink dry bag "tower", my handlebar bag, and my phone carrier case. In addition to my 70 pounds of gear, I also carried an average of about 8 pounds of drink and about 7 pounds of food. If you add 70 pounds of gear, 15 pounds of food and drink, a 35-pound bike, and a 180-pound person, you get a total whopping weight of 300 pounds rolling down the road! It sounds like a lot and it felt like a lot pedaling across the country, but I got used to the weight and eventually, it became second-nature to me!

Prior to my trip, my 6-foot 1-inch-tall body weighed 182 pounds. Even though I lost about 20 pounds or so on my bike tour, my beginning weight wasn't a major problem for me as I felt like 182 pounds was a HEALTHY weight for me. During my bicycle travels I tried to maintain my weight, but I couldn't help losing 20 pounds even though I piled tons of calories into my mouth! My plan was to eat everything I could as to build up my caloric reserve because I knew I would need it! Upon arriving back home after the amazing 43-day bike tour of America, I knew I had to stop overeating or else I would suffer negative consequences. Unfortunately, changing my Southern Tier eating pattern upon arriving back home was much more difficult than I had originally planned.

Chapter 89: Power Bank

Although my Anker power bank weighed a monstrous 1.3 pounds, it was worth every ounce! Every day of my trip, I used my Anker power bank. My Anker power bank recharged my cell phone, my headlight, and my Garmin GPS watch every night. My particular Anker power bank was rectangular and extended about 8 inches or so in length. It stayed in my handlebar bag to keep my phone charged throughout the day as my phone would die in about 4 hours without a connection to the power bank, especially when I was using the Bicycle Route Navigator GPS phone app.

Although the Anker power bank cost me about $100.00 to buy new, it was worth every penny as it supplied me with consistent power when I needed it! No wonder Anker is considered one of the best power banks in the world. While fully charged, my Anker power bank was capable of recharging my Samsung Android phone 7 times! When the opportunity presented itself, I would make good use of an electrical outlet and recharge my Anker power bank back to 100% strength. Never once on my trip was I without adequate battery life with my phone, headlight, or GPS watch thanks to my delightful Anker power bank and all of the proper attaching USB charging cords!

DAY 27: Here is my WORLD-CLASS Brooks Flyer seat! Notice, I keep my seat slightly tilted back as to keep a bit more pressure off of my hands and forearms as to help prevent numbness.

Chapter 90: COVID-19

My cross-country biking journey began on October 10, 2020 which was during the height of COVID-19 when the United States government was closing "everything." When I began my long bike tour, there was enormous uncertainty involving all that was once considered to be normal. It was completely uncertain as to whether or not Warmshowers hosts would host me or if campgrounds or motels would be closed. It was also questionable if certain roads would be closed or actual cities would be shut down. There was speculation as to whether or not the railroad staple of the United States, Amtrak, would still be in operation or if all the airline flights would be cancelled. There was even a question as to whether or not I would be permitted to re-enter my home state of Pennsylvania after exiting the border.

COVID-19 had the whole state of the world in question at the time of my epic bicycle departure. Morbid questions arose in my mind. What if I get really sick? Where will I go? What will I do? How will I take care of myself? Leaving for my special bike trip was a very scary time for all of humanity and especially for me! COVID was a very mysterious virus sweeping across the world leaving remnants of catastrophic death behind.

Despite the millions of deaths and the eminent prognosis of a bleak future, I made the decision to pedal my bike across the United States of America! My uncommon decision to cross the country during COVID times was based primarily on my notion of being CALLED to take on the bold challenge. In my mind, biking across America trumped the current conditions of the health of the world. Eventually in my restless mind, I came to terms with my grim prognosis and the severe dangers associated with COVID-19 and whatever other viruses were contaminating our darkened society at the time. Basically, I accepted the risk of pending death. If I die on my bike, so be it!

Chapter 91: Water

Although I am NOT a doctor, nurse, or nutritionist, I KNOW water is IMPORTANT! Water is life! The human body is comprised of at least 75% water and probably much more. Therefore, it seems to be common sense to drink a lot of water!

During my first few days of pedaling on the Southern Tier, I had no specific plan for my water consumption. Water was consumed basically as I felt the urge to do so. It wasn't until Day 4 as I battled intense desert heat when I decided to pay very close attention to my water intake. Avoiding dehydration and remaining healthy enough to continue my bike travels was foremost on my mind.

My initial plan was to drink water every 3 miles. As I glanced down to my GPS watch, I would notice each three-mile advancement which prompted me to grab my water bottle and take a healthy drink of approximately 3 ounces of water. This strategy worked well for me because of its simplicity. One ounce of water for every mile traveled. Since I pride myself on being a simple man, this convenient approach was acceptable and kept me hydrated even in the most severe conditions!

In addition to straight water, I also drank LOTS of sports drinks including Gatorade and Powerade as BOTH water and sports drinks are essential on an EPIC bike ride. Sports drinks have electrolytes which are critical to an ultra-marathon bike ride across the country.

During my epic bike travels, I had three 25-ounce water bottles mounted on the frame of my bicycle. Two of the water bottles were easy access and the third bottle could only be accessed when my bike was completely stopped as it was mounted on the bottom side of my bike frame. It is interesting to note that my third water bottle on the underside of my bike frame facing the ground was 1/16th of an inch away from contacting my front tire. Although it was an extremely tight fit, the water bottle NEVER contacted my tire nor did it ever cause any difficulty at all for me! In addition to my three water bottles, I also kept two 32-ounce bottles of sports drink in the outside compartment of my rear right pannier bag for easy access when I would stop my bike for a walking and eating break every 10th mile of my bike tour.

Having a plan to drink water every 3 miles caused me to look down at my Garmin wrist watch frequently and sometimes even obsessively to see if it had been three miles yet. At each 3-mile point, I would take a large mouthful of water in which I would estimate to be about 3 ounces.

Looking back on my epic ride, it is possible I may have mistakenly drunk a bit TOO MUCH water at times which was indicative of having to urgently pee almost EVERY 10 miles. But even if I drank too much water at times, it was still much better than NOT drinking enough liquids, drying up my body, and possibly putting myself at risk of dehydration.

By keeping my body full of fluids, I maintained my energy on a daily basis, remained alert, and kept my muscles LOOSE, all of which were VERY important considerations. Tight muscles are prone to cramping and cramping is big trouble for a long-haul cyclist! Consistent water consumption combined with some light stretching from time to time seemed to keep my body flexible, well-hydrated, and healthy. The water also seemed to keep my mind quick and alert as to promote more emotional stability.

In all likelihood, I probably drank TOO MUCH water as was indicative at most of my 10-mile walking breaks. Upon dismounting my bike, I would have to pee so badly I could hardly pull my bike shorts and bib shorts down before my urine would squirt all over the place. Sometimes, I didn't even dismount my bike as I quickly pulled down my biking bibs in an urgent manner as I would often accidentally pee all over my pants, shoes, bike, and front right pannier bag. It was a common ridiculous scene! Taking a pee often felt like handling a gusher! The combination of a sudden deluge of excessive water into my body mixed with an unusually increased amount of SUGAR in my diet seemed to create this wild urination scenario. My aging kidneys and bladder probably factored in as well as they were not as strong as in my younger years. Regardless of the particular cause, my urination issues were quite annoying!

As I look back and consider my own problematic urination issues, I suggest an aspiring cross-country cyclist to begin drinking 64 ounces or more of water daily for at least 6 months in advance of their epic ride. Doing so will acclimate the human body to a major increase in water intake and should result in a less urgent peeing issues while on route. Our bodies need TIME to establish the pattern of processing large amounts of liquid. Do not follow my example of drinking small amounts of liquids leading up to my epic bike ride and then suddenly flushing GALLONS of daily liquids into my body as I began my bike tour. Bad idea!!! You might also want to try to slightly limit the amount of sugar entering your body as excessive sugar seems to trigger frequent and urgent urination as well, but it is better to sustain your caloric intake than to try to count your sugar grams!

After the completion of your bike tour, I recommend continuing your positive habit of drinking 64 ounces of water daily. You might notice as I did, the extra water makes a positive contribution to overall good daily health. At least try it and see if it works for you. Maybe 32 ounces of daily water is enough for you? Maybe a gallon of water a day works best for you? Regardless of your own particular personal water consumption quota, make sure you drink plenty of pure, unaltered water as part of daily regimen.

Another important idea to keep in mind about water consumption is to fill ALL of your water bottles each time you stop for a refill. Do NOT run out of water!!! NEVER run out of water!!! For marathon cyclists, running out of water is a MORTAL SIN! Water is LIFE! Water is more important than your spare tire!

Regardless of the terrain or temperature, you must ALWAYS have adequate water and/or sports drink available for your frequent consumption!

During the 1,000 miles of desert expanse on the Southern Tier, there were times I didn't have a chance to refill my water for 40 miles or more. If you run out of water in the desert, you could put your LIFE at risk!!!!! Yes, there are passing vehicles from time to time and I've heard stories of sympathetic vehicle drivers pulling alongside the road giving a cross-country cyclist a bottle of water or some sports drink, but don't count on this fortuitous act of generosity occurring during your bike travels. Be prepared! Have more than enough water and sports drink on your bike and IN your body!

Stories have been told about unprepared cyclists battling the desert heat with an inadequate amount of water. Some of these poor-planning cyclists made a handwritten sign and hung it off the back of their shirt or on the rear of their bike rack. The homemade sign usually reads "HELP, WATER!" Well, if you are that ill-prepared, you have no business trying to pull off a SOLO, UNSUPPORTED cross-country bicycle ride. Instead, you might want to sign up for the van-supported group ride!

In rare instances, there have also been cyclists in the desert who ran out of water and found themselves in a semi-delirious state of mind on the brink of heat exhaustion. In a last-ditch act of pure desperation, these unprepared cyclists parked their bikes perpendicular in the middle of the desert highway and put both of their hands high up in the air as to FORCE the next vehicle to stop and help them. Let's hope this form of utter desperation does not ever describe you!

Keep in mind while you are filling your water bottles, always fill the MOST IMPORTANT water bottle FIRST! The most important water bottle on EVERY bike excursion is YOUR OWN BODY! Your body is the biggest and the most important water bottle on any bike ride you will ever take! FILL up yourself first. Drink as much water as you possibly can and THEN fill up your plastic water bottles!!!

My internal water bottle seems to hold about a maximum of 40 ounces of water in one intake session! One young cross-country cyclist, Isaiah Rain Maynard, author of the excellent book entitled "You Can Bike Across America" referred to this particular water consumption strategy as his "Camel Technique" in which I agree. Camels are known for storing water inside of themselves for many long miles and you should follow their lead! Drink as much water as your own physical body can withstand and then fill up all of your water bottles!

Chapter 92: Unsupported

Whenever my wife, Tink, hears me describing my cross-country bike trip as "unsupported," she immediately and firmly corrects me as she is convinced my trip was SUPPORTED!!! Tink believes I had HUGE support during my cross-country bike excursion even though NOBODY physically accompanied me. Tink argues, and I agree, I had FOUR people back home who kept in DAILY communication with me and would do ANYTHING for me as I pedaled my bicycle across America. Despite Tink's support argument being 100% correct, I continue to claim I completed the Southern Tier unsupported as nobody was physically riding with me nor was there a van following me providing me with food, drink, supplies, bike maintenance, shelter, or transportation!

Although there were no other cyclists on the road pedaling their bicycle next to me providing me support as I traveled across the United States of America, there were four people back home providing me with AMAZING SUPPORT. My daily support team from back home included my wife (Tink), my mother (Mary Jo), my father (Tom), and my sister (Kelli). There were also MANY wonderful, seemingly angelic supporters whom I met along my way across the outstanding country of the United States. My "angel team" in which I met one-by-one while pedaling along the famed Southern Tier Bike Route were dressed as human beings, but seemed to be sent by God to help me! In reality, I had A LOT of help!

My mother would sit for hours watching me on her I-phone on the LIFE 360 phone application as I traveled along the country at a pace of about 11 miles per hour. One time, my mom actually called me while I was on my bike riding through Louisiana and questioned me as to why I was suddenly riding westbound instead of eastward! She actually knew I made a WRONG TURN before I did!!!! What an AWESOME mom!

My dad would trace my route each day on a paper map he acquired from AAA. Each day he would use a pen to indicate the specific route I took and exactly where I would spend the night. He would also advise me about the upcoming terrain and the weather forecast for the next day. Dad was also a bit confused as it seemed to him the Adventure Cycling map made LOTS of unnecessary turns on their cross-country route which seemed to add unnecessary mileage to the trip, but I'm SURE the Adventure Cycling Southern Tier Bike Route was created with SAFETY foremost in mind even at the cost of adding a bit of extra mileage to the trip as Adventure Cycling uses backroads as much as possible as to limit the exposure to unnecessary vehicular traffic!

As for my sister, Kelli, she wanted to know how many miles I completed each day and in her typical CONTROLLING personality, she demanded I text her IMMEDIATELY upon arriving at my daily destination. Kelli worried about me and wanted DESPERATELY to help me in any way possible. Her sheer, unwavering, positive belief in me exceeded my own limited self-concept. Kelli KNEW I could finish the arduous Southern Tier Bicycle Route even though I DOUBTED myself and knew I was unable to finish. Kelli was also my problem solver as she would diagnose each of my issues and then she would tell me exactly what to do to SOLVE my dilemma. Kelli should have been a medical doctor or a psychiatrist! She is also much more intelligent and talented than I!

Sister Kelli has a way of breaking down MAJOR problems into manageable segments. For some mysterious reason, after speaking with my sister, my personal issues didn't appear all that bad! As long as I followed her sage advice, it seemed like I could see a light where there was only darkness prior! Kelli also kept me focused on ONE DAY AT A TIME and consistently told me "You can do it!" even though internally I called her a liar many times! Obviously, she must have known me better than I knew myself as I did eventually finish the demanding and mysterious Southern Tier Bike Route just as she repeatedly proclaimed! I guess my sister really does know me well!

As for my wife, Tink, it felt like she was on my actual biking adventure with me. We spoke so much on the phone during my bike travels, there were times I expected to turn around and actually see her pedaling behind me, but that was obviously not the case. Although I was very much ALONE for my special bike journey, it was reassuring to have such a close SOUL connection with my dear wife despite being thousands of miles away from each other.

Tink was my rock as she NEVER doubted my finishing of the Southern Tier! In fact, her UNWAVERING belief in my ability to finish the seemingly endless route actually ANGERED me at times as I felt like she didn't understand the utter difficulty of my cross-country undertaking! Tink referred to the Southern Tier more like a leisure trip over to the local grocery store and back than the arduous, soul-searching, intensely emotional, gut-wrenching, mentally wrecking, physically exhausting, bodily-breaking, life-endangering crusade it really was!!!! And no matter how many crippling facts I shared with her trying to convince her of the SHEER MAGNITUDE of my Southern Tier endeavor, she still thought I would finish as she considered me to be INVINCIBLE!

After several weeks of arguing with my wife about the difficulty involved with my cross-country bike outing and all the problems I faced daily, I decided to drop the subject matter and let her think whatever she wanted as it didn't matter what I said, she maintained had her own beliefs about me and about my epic bike ride and she was NOT changing her beliefs NO MATTER WHAT!!!! She told me EVERY DAY, "You will make it!" I remember trying to tell her "NO, I'm NOT going to make it. I've already LOST. I just cannot seem to get myself to come home yet!" My paltry words meant nothing to her as she knew my SOUL and my soul was not going to stop pedaling until my front tire contacted the pristine saltwater of the Atlantic Ocean on the shores of the distant Florida beach!

In my mind, I had already QUIT and I was merely taking ONE MORE bike ride before coming back home, but Tink recognized my determined tendencies and she knew I was "called" to COMPLETE the Southern Tier no matter what! She was certain I was NOT coming back home early. The ONLY way I was coming back home was if an emergency medical technician (EMT) had to scrape me off the Southern Tier pavement and the county coroner had to ship my dead body back to Pennsylvania!!!

One day while on the phone with Tink, my daughter, Stacey, chimed in and said, "Yeah, Dad aint comin home until he FINISHES. If he has to, he will CRAWL to the finish line!" Although Tink and Stacey's overly-confident, biased, and distorted belief in me was ANNOYING at times, their passionate energy directed at my overall well-being helped me to keep my pedals spinning! Their annoyance prompted by their unrealistic words and obvious miscalculations of my abilities also helped me to FORGET about my other many daily difficulties as I kept my pedals revolving around in circles. Despite their annoying and overly encouraging words, Tink and Stacey's love for me was UNDENIABLE!!!!

During the first few weeks away from home, it was much more relieving to speak with my mom and dad whom both encouraged me and believed in me, but clearly did NOT expect me to finish. My parents were VERY PROUD of me for ATTEMPTING a cross-country bike ride, but they both seemed to KNOW the cross-country task was too much for me!

During the first week of my trip, my dad would advise me daily about how many miles I was away from the Phoenix Airport without directly telling me to resign my efforts. It wasn't until I crossed the halfway point of my epic bike ride when I finally got out of the desert in mid-Texas that I felt like my mom and dad considered my finishing as a legitimate possibility. Regardless of what they believed personally about my chances to finish the complicated bike ride, all along they were amazing supporters of my uncommon endeavor and loved me 100% regardless of whether I finished or not!

Having an amazing group of support persons at home greatly increased my measly odds of finishing my epic bicycle adventure! Although I won't go as far as to say I would NOT have finished without my four key support group members, I must give credit where credit is due. My support team at home was VALUABLE!!! Each day I looked forward to talking with my homebound supporters and reflecting on my incredible day! The closeness I developed with each member of my support group while on the Southern Tier was AMAZING and everlasting!

It is CRUCIAL to note there was one day early in my bike journey where I was FIGHTING some major demons inside my head and I considered abandoning my bike ride while sitting in my hotel room in the California Yuha Desert, but my brother-in-law, Steve, sent me the following text: "Out of ALL the people I know, YOU are the ONE person who might actually be capable of finishing a solo, cross-country bicycle ride!"

All through the night, Steve's words resounded in my mind and spirit. As I estimated the number of people Steve actually knows, I figured he had to be friends with over 1,000 people and for Steve to EMPHATICALLY proclaim I was the special ONE IN A THOUSAND person, I felt like I didn't want to let my brother-in-law down! After all, I consider Steve to be one of the most intelligent, talented, and gifted people I ever met! If Steve thinks I can finish this insane bike ride, then I can at least pedal ONE MORE DAY! So, the next morning, I put on my biking attire and I spun my pedals around one more day as an acting tribute to my BROTHER!

Although it is nice to have support from home, be very careful NOT to tell too many people about your special goal. Only tell about 2 or 3 people what you plan to do or else you may succumb to a mysterious power-sucking phenomenon which can occur when too many people know about your grand plans. Confiding in too many people will WEAKEN you and possibly DESTROY your cross-country cycling dream!

In my case, only 6 people knew about my bike trip prior to me flying to my starting destination in San Diego, California. Telling too many people saps away your essential internal energy and power. For every person you tell, you remove a certain percentage of RAW personal power inside yourself. The more you TALK about something, the less critical personal resources you have to draw upon as you prepare to take the BIG STEP. Remember, talk less, do more! Save the talking for after you FINISH!!!!

If you are lucky like me to have a handful of people back home as a SUPPORT TEAM, then make good use of them. While you are away, have them take care of your pet. Have them check on your house. Have them get your mail or pay your bills. Have them book a motel or campground for you or have them contact a potential host on your behalf. If nothing else, have someone you can call on the phone as the LONELINESS of a long-term biking tour is heavy at times.

Although there is nothing wrong with having consistent daily contact with support people back home, take the actual bike trip ALONE if you can. Being physically ALONE on your bicycle ride will DEVELOP you faster and more thoroughly than probably anything else you could possibly do. Nothing else I've ever done in my ENTIRE life has made such a transformational difference in my own personal development as biking the Southern Tier ALONE, UNSUPPORTED, and CONTINUOUS!

Chapter 93: Overnight Food Storage

It is with great reservation I use the words "ALWAYS" and "NEVER," but in this case, I advise you, "NEVER store food inside your tent!" There are many different species of nocturnal animals (animals active at night) throughout the world whom would be VERY interested in eating a late-night snack at YOUR expense. Biking seven hours a day leaves you feeling more than a bit tired at night and you cannot afford to have your sleep interrupted by some animal or pack of animals trying to bite or claw through the side of your micro-thin tent wall to get your food stash!

Part of your touring bike gear should include 50-feet of paracord (small, strong rope used in parachuting) which should be used to hang your overnight food pannier bag from a tree branch. Simply tie a one-pound rock to the end of you paracord and then toss it up and over a horizontal tree branch which is at least 17 feet high. Make sure your paracord is also at least 4 or more feet out from the trunk of the tree. Then, tie your food pannier bag to the end of the paracord and pull the other end of the rope hoisting your food up into the air. Stop your food bag about 4 feet below the overhead branch as to place your food bag at least 13 feet up from ground level. Once your food bag is situated, you should keep the rope tight and wrap it around the trunk of the same tree or a different tree while tying a knot as to firmly stabilize your food pannier bag in the air as to secure your precious food throughout the night.

If you are camping in bear country, then you MUST follow the previous overnight food storage directions precisely for your own safety and the preservation of your food. While camping amidst bear population, your food bag should be at 13 feet high, 4 feet or more away from the trunk of the tree, and at least 4 feet below the supporting branch. When choosing your overnight food storage tree, pick a tree that is AT LEAST 50 feet away from your tent, but preferably 100 feet or more away. If you are in grizzly bear territory, then you might want to pick a tree location 200 or more feet away from your tent. Though nothing is ever a GUARANTEE on an ADVENTURE, my outlined overnight food storage recommendations should keep your food safe throughout the night and prevent any unwanted visitors from prowling around the outside walls of your tent or worse.

Even if you are NOT in bear country, your precious sleep could be heavily interrupted by all sorts of animals. Once while my wife and I were bike camping on the incredible 184.5-mile C&O Towpath in Maryland, we were sitting around our campfire enjoying the lovely evening while having some pleasant conversation. As we were talking and watching the sun set in the sky, a meddlesome raccoon climbed up on my wife's bike and tried to open her pannier bag! The raccoon was so BOLD and confident, he refused to move despite my yelling at him. To my dismay, I actually had to CHARGE at the raccoon with a long stick to scare him off.

About one hour after going to bed, the same intrusive raccoon whom we fondly named "Curtis" in honor of our meddling son, returned and actually OPENED my wife's pannier bag and tossed out over half of her storage items as my wife's bike came CRASHING to the ground. Quickly, I grabbed my can of mace, strapped my headlamp to my forehead, and ran out of the tent as I saw raccoon Curtis quickly scurry away. Clearly, Curtis was an experienced late-night thief and our bike pannier bags were NOT the first pannier bags our new raccoon friend had ever opened! Curtis used his THUMBS much like a human and with great dexterity opened Tink's SEALED pannier bag and got at our supplies in which he rudely threw all over the ground! Fortunately, our food bag was SAFE and SECURE as it was hung in a nearby tree EXACTLY as I described above! Curtis did NOT get any extra food from us on this eventful night on the C&O, but he sure caused quite a commotion!

Another time I was hiking with two friends, Scott Bassett and Brandon Pileski, in the deep mountains of northern Pennsylvania on the pristine 43-mile Black Forest Trail near Ansonia, PA. After a long, hard day of hiking the rugged mountain trails, I tied up our food bag as described previously with one tiny exception. The tree I used to secure our overnight food was only about 25 feet away from my hammock! Shortly after falling asleep, I was awoken in my hammock by the sounds of a frustrated bear who smelled our food bag, but couldn't figure out how to get it. As I laid still with my rain cover tightly pulled down over my hammock not allowing me to see outside, the hairs on my arms stood straight up as I clutched on to my BIG 9-ounce bottle of bear spray mace. Hearing the unsatisfied bear snorting and growling VERY CLOSE to my hammock was TERRIFYING!

As I laid motionless in my hammock awaiting the hungry bear to nudge my hammock with his nose, I was FULLY ready to douse the bear with a full dose of bear spray, but the close encounter never materialized. Eventually, the frustrated bear left our campsite. In all my life, I never felt my heart beat so strongly as it did while the bear was roaming around my IMMEDIATE sleeping vicinity. At one point during the encounter, I thought my heart was going to actually beat out of my chest as the thumping was ridiculously loud and strong! At the height of my terror, I was concerned my LOUD heart beats might actually draw the bear even closer to me as to investigate the mysterious rhythmic sounds. On that chilling night on the Black Forest Trail, I learned 2 lessons. Lesson number one was to hang the food bag FURTHER from camp. Lesson two was...... SEEING a bear can be a VERY SCARY experience, but HEARING a bear up close and personal is TERRIFYING!!!!!

Riding a bicycle across the country is hard enough without adding stupidity to the mix and causing yourself UNNECESSARY stress from irresponsible overnight food storage. Keep your food safe through the night without any unnecessary eventful occurrences! Follow my overnight food storage recommendations and you will have a much more pleasant night's sleep!

As I traveled across the intriguing Southern Tier, there were many times I did NOT have a tree to hang my food and I was forced to forgo my own advice. Each of those nights I would CAREFULLY consider the most reasonable alternative place to store my food which was usually INSIDE a building, if possible. Some nights, I just left my food in my pannier bag on my bike, but in no case would I EVER leave one bit of food inside my tent!

All food should be stored as safely as possible OUTSIDE and as FAR AWAY from your sleeping quarters as is reasonably possible! Your tent is your SAFE HAVEN. Unwanted visitors are not allowed near your sacred space!

DAY 28: I was in the "middle of nowhere" almost every day of the Southern Tier!

Chapter 94: Maintenance

After struggling through heat exhaustion in the Yuha Dessert and finding myself stuck in Blythe, California with a bike poorly equipped with INADEQUATE gravel tires, I searched for the nearest bike shop to purchase two quality ROAD bike tires! To my surprise, there were NO bike shops anywhere close to Blythe, California! After spending much of the morning making phone calls from my hotel, I finally found a bike shop, Cycle Therapy, in Havasu City, Arizona whom agreed to put me at the TOP OF THE LIST and replace my bike tires immediately as to allow me to resume my cross-country bike travels the following day.

The only problem with the repair plan involved Havasu City, Arizona being situated 80 miles away from my hotel location in Blythe, California! Since my gravel bike tires were in no condition to pedal 80 miles to the bike shop, I was forced to find vehicular transportation. After calling many car rental places and considering Uber services, I finally found a small truck at the local U-Haul dealership in which I rented for the day.

After making the beautiful, scenic 80-minute drive to Havasu City with my bike in the bed of my leased U-Haul truck, I pulled into Cycle Therapy and the owner, Ryan, immediately gave me top-notch respect as a cross-country cyclist. Ryan re-arranged his schedule and within a few hours had my bike fully repaired. For the FIRST TIME on my epic bicycle adventure, I NOW had a fully repaired and truly ROADWORTHY bicycle!

Although I had ZERO miles on Day 5 of my bike adventure, I did ride my bike a few hundred feet as I took a very brief TEST DRIVE to ensure everything worked properly with my bicycle after the fantastic maintenance efforts from my friends at Cycle Therapy. It literally took me ALL DAY to find a bike shop, lease a rental truck, drive 80 miles to the bike shop in Havasu City, wait for the completion of the repairs, drive 80 miles back to Blythe, and return the rental truck. This was also the day in which I came closest to driving my U-Haul rental truck to the Phoenix Airport and flying back home. As I battled my negative thoughts in Blythe, California, with significant mixed emotions, I decided I would take ONE MORE bike ride the following day and then decide if I would go back home at the conclusion of my daily ride.

As you undertake an epic bike journey, you will find yourself in "the middle of nowhere" more often than you might originally expect. Adventure Cycling and other excellent bicycle route mapping services intentionally try to keep cyclists on less traveled roads as to minimize the amount of vehicular traffic and lessen the chances of an accident. For good reason, you will often find yourself pedaling on desolate roads with very little vehicular and commercial activity in your vicinity! Considering the limited commercial districts, you will not be passing bike shops on a daily basis!

During my cross-country bike ride, I made use of three bike shops along the way. The first bike shop, Cycle Therapy, was in Havasu City, Arizona in which the polite workers replaced my junky GRAVEL tires with top-quality ROAD tires. The next bike shop, Pedal Pushers, was in Austin, Texas where two broken spokes on my rear tire were replaced and my chain was shortened by a single link piece. The final bike shop, Tri Hard Sports, was in Ocean Springs, Mississippi where I had my third broken spoke replaced and I got my second pair of excellent quality ROAD bike tires as my last pair of road tires from Havasu City, Arizona was completely worn-out as even supreme road bike tires only last about 2,000 miles.

While in Bastrop, Texas, I arrived at a kayak shop named Rising Phoenix Adventures and waited for over an hour for the AWESOME company to open as my map listed the reputable business as a bike repair facility. To my disappointment, a young female employee informed me that Rising Phoenix Adventures stopped repairing bikes about 10 years ago. Her disappointing words proved to me that even the best maps, whether paper or phone apps, will provide a partially INACCURATE listing of bike shops and other services along the way! Despite NOT handling bike repairs, the owner of Rising Phoenix Adventures, Jamie, made some phone calls on my behalf looking for a bike repair shop, but couldn't find a bike repair shop in the close vicinity. The nearest bike repair shop was "Pedal Pushers" which was 35 miles away in Austin, Texas.

Instead of leaving me to my own solution, Jamie put my bike in the back of her truck and personally drove me to the bike repair shop in Austin, Texas, waited two hours for my bike to get serviced, and then drove me back to Bastrop, Texas to resume my epic travels. Jamie's act of LOVE will always remain very special to me as she went SO FAR above and beyond a general level of human kindness. Jamie touched my heart with her KINDNESS! With 100% sincerity, I can truly say, "I LOVE her!" Jamie is proof there are still GOOD PEOPLE in our communities as Jamie didn't want a single dime from me! She didn't know me and she didn't want my money. Jamie ONLY wanted to help me!!! Jamie sacrificed half of her work day simply to HELP me, a stranger, as she was impressed with me riding my bicycle all the way from San Diego, California to Bastrop, Texas.

During my bike travels, I encountered numerous "strangers" whom I felt sincere LOVE as I met many fine, angelic people during my bike trip. It was so pleasing to discover there remain A LOT of really NICE people in our beautiful country!!! In fact, almost all of the people I met during my extensive bike travels were KIND and HELPFUL!

The third and final bike shop I visited was Tri Hard Sports in Ocean Springs, Mississippi. When I called the shop late on a Saturday afternoon, the fine business was closing in TWO MINUTES as I spoke with mechanic Jacob. Being so impressed with the mention of my cross-country bike ride, Jacob agreed to open the bike shop the following day on Sunday and meet me at 9 a.m. to repair my bike despite the business being officially CLOSED on Sundays!!!

Regardless of only being a 19-years old kid and Tri Hard Sports being closed on Sunday, Jacob opened the bike shop and not only repaired my bike, but gave me SUPREME service as well as a tutorial on exactly how he repaired my bicycle. Jacob gave me the best service possible which prompted a new-sense of HOPE deep inside of me. For a few brief seconds, I wondered if I might actually be able to complete my cross-country quest! Once again, I felt TRUE LOVE in my heart for this fine, young man, Jacob, my teenage angel dressed in shorts!!!

In most cases, if you are SUPER-NICE, RESPECTFUL, and extremely PLEASANT, most bike shops will stop what they are doing and give you SUPERIOR SERVICE as a cross-country cyclist. As a cross-country cyclist, it seemed like I had an ALL-ACCESS pass. Almost instantly upon mentioning my cross-country efforts, I would gain an automatic HIGH-LEVEL of respect from almost everyone I met.

It's easy for others to love a cross-country cyclist as a cross-country cyclist has their entire life packed in their pannier bags. Cross-country cyclists pose a VERY LOW level of threat to others! The vast majority of people you meet will INSTANTLY like you because you are NOT scary as you have NOTHING but your bicycle and a few belongings! Some special people will even do whatever it takes to meet your needs and HELP you to quickly resume your cross-country venture as they want to be a part of your SUCCESS! The supreme level of sincere help and sheer love expressed by pure strangers is almost uncanny!

As you gain cycling experience, you will get to know your bike better and better. You might even get to the point where you can anticipate necessary maintenance before you break down. Scheduling bike repairs while you are in the vicinity of a bike shop is MUCH BETTER than waiting until your bicycle actually breaks down. Trying to figure out how to get yourself and your bike to the nearest bike shop can be stressful at times. If you get REALLY SMART, then you will take your bike into your local bike shop BEFORE you even leave for your epic journey and get a FULL tune-up!!

Watching YouTube and getting slightly familiar with your bike prior to your trip is also a great way to build a bit more confidence as it is highly unlikely you will pedal 3,000 miles without needing to perform at least a few minor repairs to your bicycle. Buy a book and read about bike repairs. Watch videos on your phone or computer about how to perform certain bicycle repairs. Ask your local bike shop if you could WATCH them repair your bike or other bikes for a few hours. Tell them you will help them for FREE. You can learn so much by watching a PRO!!! And if you ask nice enough and you are NOT a pain in the butt, then most bicycle repair guys are honored to have you watch them fix your bike. Think of it as paying for your bike repair, but getting a FREE bike repair seminar!! Remember, the more you learn about bike repairs, the less you will have to interrupt your epic ride looking for a bike repair service. More pedaling and less waiting at bike stores is what we all want!

Chapter 95: Vehicle Harassment

All it takes is ONE vehicle to contact your bike and you will find yourself skidding across the unforgiving, hard asphalt road ripping the skin open on your body as you prepare to collide with the first stationary object in your path. As a cross-country cyclist, it is wise to periodically remind yourself about your VULNERABILITY!! You are pedaling a bicycle without any type of containment around you for protection. You are sitting on a little seat out in the wide open completely unprotected with many 4,000-pound-plus chunks of metal passing you by at speeds ranging from 30 to 80 miles per hour. Cycling is an EXTRMELEY DANGEROUS task easily capable of killing you! The good news is 99.9% of the drivers are very careful, especially when they recognize someone on a FULLY LOADED bicycle. The bad news is it ONLY takes one careless driver to end your life! Bottom line... …. BE CAREFUL!!!!

Throughout the 43 days and 3,000 miles it took me to cross the United States on a pedal bicycle, I only had THREE drivers honk their horn at me in a DISGRUNTLED fashion while approximately 200 drivers honked their horn at me in an ENCOURAGING manner! For the most part, it seemed like almost ALL of the thousands of passing vehicles were super-respectful of me and my bicycle. The vast majority of cars and trucks would pass me as far to the left as possible making sure not to "squeeze" me.

In addition to the 200 or so encouraging horn honks I received, dozens of other drivers would waive or flash their lights at me as to convey their admiration for my biking efforts! And for those of you whom might be wondering the difference between a polite honking of the horn and a disgruntled honking of the horn, I assure you, it is OBVIOUS as you are pedaling your bike on the open road. On more than one occasion, a single encouraging honk from an unsuspecting vehicle invigorated me and gave me a second wind exactly when I needed it most!

Despite all my prayers and all the WONDERFUL passing drivers on the road, my good fortune was SEVERELY tested in TALLAHASSEE, FLORIDA! While traveling through the beautiful college city less than one mile past the prestigious Florida State University, I noticed a sign on the side of the road: "BIKERS MAY USE THE FULL LANE." My first thought was "Wow, this city is super-supportive of cyclists!" as I imagined there are probably hundreds of students who make good use of their bikes as they attend their various classes! But only a few minutes after reading the encouraging street sign, I was startled by a completely OBNOXIOUS horn beep from a driver who was obviously VERY UPSET about sharing the road with me and my bicycle even though I was over far enough on the right side of the road for the vehicle to easily pass me!

Instead of easily passing me like the THOUSANDS of previous vehicles during my pedal crusade across the country, this ignorant guy honked harshly a second time at me and triggered a MAJOR shot of adrenaline pumping throughout my entire body. All of a sudden, I was ANGRY!!!! Despite usually being an EXTREMELY CALM man, I suddenly became an ENRAGED LUNATIC! No longer was I one man crossing the country on a bicycle. After this non-deserving, disrespectful horn honk from this low-life, vehicle-driving scumbag, I was NOW the self-proclaimed official REPRESENTATIVE for cyclists all over the world!!!!

Not in a million years was I about to permit this PUNK DRIVER behind me to get away with his DISGRACEFUL antics!! Immediately, I decided I would NOT stand for such an incredulous act of disrespect to the biking community!!! So, without any prior thought or plan, but with great care, I veered my bicycle from the far-right side of the road into the CENTER of the road COMPLETELY blocking any chance of the subject vehicle over-taking me as the disgruntled driver directly behind me was now COMPLETELY BLOCKED from going around me! If this rude and uncaring guy wanted to pass me, he would have had to RUN ME OVER!!!

As I took up the ENTIRE LANE, I changed my speed from 10 miles per hour down to a trifling 5 miles per hour as I leisurely eased my pedal-pace downward to the point where I was barely pedaling. The speed of my bike was so slow, I wondered if the passenger in the undeserving car behind me would actually jump out of the vehicle, chase me down on foot, and try to knock me off of my bike. As I slowly pedaled along the prestigious city of Tallahassee, Florida, the impatient, cyclist-hating driver in the car behind me honked again and again as I shook my head in disgust as I reveled in providing the maximum level of FRUSTRATION for the hyperactive, impulsive driver following VERY close behind me.

As several additional seconds of time elapsed, I now noticed numerous cars in traffic behind me. All of a sudden, instead of having only one disgruntled driver, there were now several cars backed up whom also seemed to take offense at my deliberate attempt to slow down traffic. As the numbskull driver directly behind me rolled down his window and began yelling obscenities at me, I released one hand from my bicycle handlebar grip and gave him the second BIGGEST middle finger of my life which in turn prompted the whole procession of cars to begin honking their horns and yelling obscenities at ME! Clearly, I had created quite a raucous in downtown Tallahassee! It felt like some-type of wild parade and I was the MAIN ATTRACTION!

As the single lane road expanded to a two-lane road, I could no longer effectively back up traffic so I reverted to riding near the berm on the right side of the road. As the callous, indignant driver behind me finally passed me, he revved his car engine extremely loud as he came way too close to striking me as to seemingly remind me about how easily it would be for him to dismantle my bike and end my biking efforts for the day. Another car or two from the rear also revved their engines at me and yelled an obscenity or two as they passed, but it was all worth it because I had now accessed the biggest SECOND WIND of my life! After my experience with the senseless, idiotic college-town drivers in Tallahassee, I pedaled the next 20 miles or so without even feeling remotely tired or fatigued! Thank you, Tallahassee!!!

Another time prior to my adventures on the Southern Tier, I was taking a nice 35-mile day bike ride on a Sunday morning in my hometown in Johnstown, Pennsylvania. This particular weekend, Johnstown was the venue for the well-known annual "Thunder in the Valley" motorcycle rally. Thousands of motorcycle riders come from hundreds of miles away to attend this super-nice annual biker festival in downtown Johnstown, Pennsylvania and surrounding areas. Thunder in the Valley is a MAJOR national biker event!

As I was pedaling my bicycle along Somerset Pike in Conemaugh Township, just outside of Johnstown, I noticed a bunch of large barrels neatly placed out in the middle of the road with some formal-looking guy standing in the middle of the street with both of his hands held high up in the air as to STOP all traffic. It was obvious he was halting traffic as to allow a LARGE motorcycle GANG to enter the roadway as there was a HUGE line of motorcycles waiting in the parking lot of a fabulous local biker bar and grill named "Jim and Jimmies." As I approached the stoic, commander-type guy standing in the middle of the barricaded road motioning for me to stop, I could see about 50 motorcycles, all waiting in line to pull out of the parking lot in unison as they were certainly heading back to the festival grounds in downtown Johnstown.

Instead of being compliant and stopping as the authoritative man and his barrels clearly conveyed, I decided NOT to stop! In an instant of non-logical, childish disobedience, I decided I was going to RUN THROUGH THE BARRELS and blow up the entire road blockade! At the moment, it just seemed to me like the right thing to do! After all, I deduced that gas-powered motorcycles were no more important than my pedal-powered bicycle!!!! The decision was made...... I was NOT stopping!!!!!

Instead of stopping or even slowing down my bicycle, I sped up to about 15 miles per hour and DISRUPTED the entire motorcycle parade by whizzing past the traffic controller man and his blocking barrels as the confounded man watched in disbelief as he pressed his two hands high up into the air trying desperately to get me to STOP! All the while, about 50 rough and tough, hardcore bikers watched my inconsiderate, arrogant actions while they were eagerly waiting to exit the congested parking lot as a group.

Immediately upon witnessing my outright disobedience, I heard about 50 motorcycles revving their engines EXTREMELY loud, clearly in a derogatory manner directed specifically toward me. Uh-oh……….. It was on!!! Within 30 seconds of my impromptu shenanigans, the enraged bikers came roaring out of the parking lot headed straight for me! As I hugged the right side of the road, the first motorcycle came about 3 feet from contacting my bike as he intentionally directed me and my bicycle further off to the side of the road as if to send a firm message of protest on behalf of his perplexed motorcycle gang.

The next motorcycle gangster came even closer to contacting my bicycle as he was within 12 inches of impacting my rear tire, clearly delivering a similar message of disapproval for my immature and disrespectful antics. As my heart pounded hard in my chest and my throat felt so tight I was unable to swallow my own spit, the rest of the motorcycle gang passed by me as I feverishly pulled my bicycle completely off the road, stood up tall and gave the biker-bullies the BIGGEST MIDDLE-FINGER of my life as I yelled with all of my might hoping one or two of the biker gang members would turn around and come back so I could knock some sense into them! To my disappoint, ALL of the gas-powered gangsters maintained their progress back to the festival grounds and none of them returned to go a few rounds with me!

As the dust settled and my heart regained a much less fervent beating, I smiled and relished in my simple act of DISRESPECFUL assertiveness! At times, cycling can be a bit boring. Sometimes you need to spice it up a bit! A little bit of ZEST is not a bad thing!

Although I was VERY upset with the motorcycle gang and their diminished view of me and my bicycle, I've found bikers of all types to be very respectful of cyclists unless you intentionally disrespect them as was the case in my previous story! In most cases, motorcycle riders have HUGE respect for cyclists as they know how challenging it is on the roads on a motorcycle lead alone a bicycle! Most of the motorcycle groups I encountered along the Southern Tier seemed to view me as ONE OF THEIR OWN! In fact, most of my biker friends from the Southern Tier viewed me as a "BAMF!" There will be much more on this hardcore acronym in a later chapter!

As you pedal along your bike journey, keep glancing in your side view mirror where possible and be aware of traffic around you. Always be super alert and keep yourself far to the right, but not too far to the right. Always give yourself about 2-3 feet of good solid riding surface to your right, just in case a dangerous situation unfolds and you need the extra 2-3 feet to keep yourself safe, especially if you encounter an ignorant driver determined to scare or harass you.

To all those 200 or more drivers who honked encouragingly to me while pedaling the Southern Tier, I thank you! The pleasant honks, thumbs up, and flashing lights really helped to keep my pedals going around. There is NOTHING like encountering a kindred soul along your bike journey, someone whom without words conveys an unspoken message of respect, admiration, and even LOVE!

Chapter 96: Changing Plans

A long-distance cycling adventure will require many changes in your plans! Reviewing your maps in the comforts of your home on your familiar recliner chair can be VERY misleading and tempt you OVERESTIMATE your abilities and UNDERESTIMATE the plethora of challenges involved in your particular bike route. Lines on a map are only lines, but the actual roads will be much different. Once you begin pedaling on your specific epic route, you may quickly realize your initial plan is NOT going to work exactly as you have prearranged!

Prior to my start at Ocean Beach on the water's edge of the Pacific Ocean, I heard stories about MANY hopeful cross-country cyclists QUITTING on the FIRST DAY as they encountered the GRUELING 4,000 foot upward climb out of San Diego! Even being a semi-experienced cyclist myself, I UNDERESTIMATED the difficulty of the first 50 miles of the Southern Tier! Riding through San Diego was PURE BLISS, but as soon as I got to the city limits, the increasingly difficult uphill felt like it would never end!

On Day 1, I didn't start pedaling my bike until 2 p.m. on Saturday afternoon. By the time I got lost in San Diego and finally found the correct starting point of the Southern Tier at Ocean Beach, it was almost 4 p.m. and I was already fatigued, anxious, and jet-lagged from my flight. Nonetheless, I had a goal of reaching Ma-tar-awa RV Camper Park in Alpine, California which was located about 50 miles or so eastbound from the Pacific Ocean. The sun began to set and I turned on my bike lights even though my original plan was to arrive at the Ma-tar-awa campground prior to dark! For another 45 minutes or so I continued pedaling through the dismal darkness one pedal stroke at a time SLOWLY making my way up the HUGE ascent out of the San Diego region!

As I entered the outskirts of Alpine, California I began to feel anxious as I sensed with every pedal stroke I was entering a more remote wilderness area. My legs were tired and my mind was breaking down as my pre-planned camp destination remained about 12 miles away. While glancing over to my left during the height of my frustration, I noticed some type of small flea market or craft fair closing and the vendors were packing their supplies into their vehicles. Since I owned three gourmet coffee concession trailers myself and I have worked at many similar types of events for decades prior, it only seemed fitting to stop and ask some of the vendors if they had any ideas where I could spend the night as it quickly became apparent, I was at the brink of my physical and emotional limits.

One vendor lady casually stated as she was leaving the venue, "If I was you, I would sleep under the cute gazebo in the back of Town Hall." After walking around Town Hall and checking out the small gazebo, it seemed like the ideal place to stay on NIGHT 1 of my epic bike odyssey! There was only one minor problem. NOBODY was around to give me official permission to stay overnight under the perfect-little gazebo! So, in typical Sean Hockensmith bold fashion, I gave MYSELF permission to "wild camp" in the quaint location as one of my overall life mottos is "Don't ask for PERMISSION. Beg for FORGIVENESS." Quietly and unobtrusively, I quickly set up my tent on the hard concrete under the gazebo roof and enjoyed an EXCELLENT, uninterrupted night's sleep. Wild camping on the first night of my bike journey set the proper tone for the entire remainder of my bike trip on the Southern Tier!

Thinking back, I'm not really sure what would have occurred had the police or some other local authority tried to remove me from the gazebo. Like I mentioned early, I was DONE biking for the day as I was as close as a cyclist could get to BONKING when I finally stopped for the night! There was no more bike riding coming out of my legs on that relentless first day! If some overzealous community authority REALLY wanted to remove me from underneath the gazebo, then they would have had to transport me and my bike somewhere in their vehicle!

Being NICE is a primary and overall effective general strategy and a regular way of life I have maintained throughout all of my existence on planet Earth. No matter what situation I find myself in, I usually try to be extra nice! It really takes a lot for someone to push me over the edge into anger. Over many decades, I've found being kind is usually enough to get the police, a local government employee, or ANYONE else for that matter to be reasonable with me. In my case on Day 1 in Alpine, California, all I wanted was a small piece of ground to put up my tent as I wasn't making loud noise or doing anything disruptive at all. After eating a few pieces of food, all I wanted was to go to SLEEP! As my good luck would have it, NOBODY bothered me on my EPIC Night 1 of the Southern Tier!

With regards to full-disclosure, I must mention my map did indicate a possible motel in the small town of Alpine, California, but I am very CHEAP and I was DETERMINED not to pay big money for a hotel on my first night! Although I am not poor and I could easily afford a motel, I hold on tight to my money, especially on my adventure excursions!!!

My point in this chapter involves being prepared to CHANGE plans. Be prepared for "longer and harder" instead of "shorter and easier." Overestimate the difficulty of the climb and underestimate the downhills. Having a TOUGH mindset is NECESSARY on an epic bike ride. The best mindset is probably to expect to pedal UPHILL all day while you learn to LOVE it!

OUTLASTING every hill and mountain you face will TRANSFORM you over time. If you have to make adaptations to your daily planning, then roll with it! Within the actual definition for "adventure" involves the concept of CHANGE! It is IMPOSSIBLE to plan your trip perfectly as the UNKNOWN frequently requires change! Even the best planning will often FAIL! There are too many variables including temperature, weather, terrain, and incline which are only a few of the formidable variables capable of drastically changing your biking plans. Instead of being rigidly set in your ways, EMBRACE change and accept the unknown as your daily NORMAL! Get ready to make some changes while pedaling the Southern Tier!

Chapter 97: Start Date

If you plan to pedal the Southern Tier, then it is easier to ride eastward starting in San Diego, California around March 1st as the winds are primarily blowing westerly during this time of the year. Westerly winds blow from the west to the east, thus giving an eastbound cyclist an amazing TAILWIND! If you start at the Atlantic Ocean in St. Augustine, Jacksonville, or any other eastern Florida shoreline city, then you should start around October 1st to benefit from a prevailing easterly wind, thus providing a nice tailwind for the westbound cyclist. Easterly winds blow from the east to the west.

For some unknown reason, I was clearly and unmistakably CALLED to ride my bike from San Diego, California eastward to Jacksonville, Florida into a prevailing HEADWIND! This nonsensical direction of travel was completely contrary to the official advice I offered in the preceding paragraph. Instead of benefitting from a tailwind for most of my bike trip, mysteriously and contrarily, I CHOSE to battle a consistent headwind day-after-day for 43 days!

For most of my life, it seems like I have intentionally chosen more difficult alternatives instead of taking much easier options. At times, my wife wonders if I like to SUFFER! Back in high school wrestling under the unprecedented leadership of our highly-esteemed, Hall of Fame coach, Ed Zimmerman, my wrestling team at Richland High School operated under the precepts of "No Pain. No Gain." Maybe that's why I am the way I am today! Sometimes it just feels like I am unconsciously seeking pain and difficulty, but it is more likely I seek tough situations as I believe tough situations make me tougher and I YEARN to be TOUGH! Despite my conflicting sources of unusual motivations, I made the unorthodox decision to start my epic bike trip in San Diego in the Fall instead of beginning my bicycle odyssey more logically in the Spring. With loads of supported data, I knew I would be riding into a headwind about 75% of the time.

Riding into a headwind for 75% of your bike travels can be VERY discouraging! Each day I found myself hoping the wind pattern would suddenly reverse its course and start blowing the opposite direction, but rarely did the atypical weather pattern occur. Just as my research indicated, my Fall bike ride involved a prevailing EASTERLY wind! It wasn't until two consecutive glorious afternoons in Louisiana when the wind suddenly stopped blowing easterly and made a complete reversal and began blowing westerly which caused me to enjoy a strong TAILWIND assisting my bike travels upwards to about 16 miles per hour propelling me forward with an extra burst of unsuspecting speed. During these two memorable days filled with glorious westerly tailwinds, I took full advantage of the conditions and tallied two consecutive 108-mile days with the wind at my back! These were the only 2 days of my bike trip in which I exceeded the magical 100-mile daily mileage mark!

Using my own common sense with only a very small amount of prior research, I decided to depart from San Diego on October 10th. With the very little common sense I possessed at the time, I figured the desert would be MUCH cooler in October than it would be in July or August! It also seemed to me that an October starting date would also provide myself with warmer temperatures throughout the southern USA as my Vata body type generally responds well to lots of sun! For me, cold weather is usually tougher than hot weather, but little did I know what type of HARSH, sweltering weather was in store for me as I approached the Arizona border in California's Yuha Desert! There will be more on the topic of extreme heat in later chapters………

Upon initially sharing my "CRAZY" cross-country bicycle plan with my very wise father, Thomas Hockensmith, he warned me about the Black Mountains in New Mexico as the summit at Emory's Pass has an elevation over 8,200 feet. As part of his extensive motorcycle touring all over the United States including his epic 30-day 9,000-mile-plus cross-country-and-back motorcycle adventure with my mother, Mary Jo Hockensmith, he was VERY familiar with the effects of high altitude on weather conditions.

Dad warned me to pay very close attention to the weather as I approached the Black Mountains of New Mexico. He warned me about how fast the weather changes and how severe the conditions can be with increased elevation! Feeling a bit discouraged and slightly feeble, I decided to do a weather search for Emory's Pass on Google. To my SURPRISE, I learned about Emory's Pass having FREEZING temperatures in September! UNBELIEVABLE!!!!! If the weather atop the Black Mountains of New Mexico is frigid in September, then what the heck kind of weather was I going to encounter when I pedal through Emory's Pass a month later in mid-October?

Despite the many weather-related obstacles infringing upon my choice of start date, the overall weather conditions during my actual biking adventure were WONDERFUL! The weather was FLAWLESS most of the days! Yes, I had 4 miserably hot days and 2 wicked cold days, but the other 37 days were IDEAL biking days with temperatures in the 70's and 80's! Many of my Southern Tier days I rode without a shirt for at least part of the day! By the end of my epic journey upon arrival at the hallowed Jacksonville Beach, I had one of the best sun tans imaginable! Many of the afternoons were warm with highs around 75 degrees or so. Despite most mornings being chilly or even downright cold, I quickly warmed up as I began to pedal.

During my epic travels, I only had 2 days of minor rain and only one day with snow and hail! It was also apparent to me I was riding through a drought as the great Rio Grande River was completely dry in some areas! There wasn't even as much as a puddle of water in some stretches of the Rio Grande River! Being a Pennsylvania native, it was strange to witness completely dry creeks and rivers as Pennsylvania always seems to have ADEQUATE and even plentiful water resources all throughout the year.

In other chapters of this book, I have included a checklist of clothing and gear I brought with me on my epic bike ride. When preparing for any adventure, it is wise to pack for the WORST-CASE scenario! Always expect the weather to be rainy and cold and then pack appropriately, even if the current weather is hot and sunny! To my surprise, there were FRIGID days on the Southern Tier in which I wore every piece of clothing in my possession! Under no circumstance should you ever suffer through wet and cold without the proper gear! Later in this book, I will share with you the story of my COLDEST DAY on the Southern Tier as I feared for my life while pedaling in snow and obscene freezing temperatures from Sierra Blanca, Texas to Van Horn, Texas.

DAY 28: Here are all the products I used to help resolve my very serious knee injuries!

Chapter 98: Bike Marriage

Having the proper mindset is crucial as to whether or not you will have a CHANCE to complete a solo, unassisted, continuous cross-country bicycle ride. As I write these pages, my goal is to share with you some MANDATORY thoughts you will need in order to complete the laborious task of a multi-thousand miles bicycle crossing!

Most aspiring cyclists view their bicycle as a hunk of metal with some rubber and a few other materials mixed in, but if you wish for that hunk of indiscriminate metal to take you across the country, then you need to make some upscale adjustments to your thinking! Your bike is NOT just a hunk of metal. Your bike is YOUR new WIFE! Your bike is your new HUSBAND! After all, you are going to be attached to your bicycle for about 7 hours a day for the next many weeks. Even when you are not riding your bike, your bike will be in your IMMEDIATE vicinity awaiting your beck and call! No matter how you look at it, you will be MARRIED to your bicycle as you attempt to cross the country!

Your bicycle is your SOLE means of transportation on your particular epic cycling journey. Your bike is all you got! Your bike is your LIFE! Therefore, treat your bike gently and hold it in high esteem. Bless your bike. Pray for your bike. Honor your bike with your thoughts and with your actions. Remember, while on this cross-country cycling mission, your bike is your SPOUSE!

Marrying your bicycle involves a COMMITMENT to taking excellent care of your bike and treating it with the utmost consideration. If your bike gets a little muddy or dirty during the day, then take a few minutes at your daily destination to wipe off the dirt and grime. Putting a few drops of chain lubricant on your bike chain every few days is another sign of deep love. Adding 10 or 15 pounds of air pressure to your tires and removing any crud from your rear sprocket is also a loving act which is mandatory for a successful marriage.

Taking a few minutes each evening to EXAMINE your bike spouse from top to bottom and front to back is also necessary to maintain a great relationship. Become FAMILIAR with your bike. Know the exact position of your seat and make sure all the nuts are tightened regularly as to prevent the loss of your perfect seat position. Recognize which nuts hold your handlebars together and which nuts are responsible for attaching your pannier bags and keep everything taut. Check to ensure your tires are nice and hard like a good road bike tire should be! Identify each of your spokes to make sure there are no breaks and touch them to make sure each one feels strong and secure. Glance over your frame to make sure everything is solid without any damage. Make sure your water bottle cages are fastened securely without any loose Allen bolts. Inspect your pedals to make sure everything is proper and there are no rocks or dirt trapped inside the connecting cleat framework. Confirm your handlebar bag is still fastened snug as well as the proper operation of your front and rear lights.

Treating your bike as your WIFE should ensure you take proper care of her! Your bike is IMMENSELY important to the success or failure of your cross-country aspiration! Giving your bike proper daily attention is important to avoid unnecessary mechanical problems and/or bodily injuries.

One of the prime causes of bike malfunction and injury is road debris. As you are riding your bike along many miles of roadways, avoid EVERYTHING laying on the road. Do not ride over a stick, piece of garbage, dead animal, or any type of broken glass or rock. Don't even ride over a smashed paper cup and be sure to swerve safely as to miss even a tiny piece of road debris like a candy bar wrapper! Dedicate yourself to keeping your rubber bike tires on pure asphalt. Trash of any kind should be avoided as to dodge potentially doomful contact with your precious bike tires! When you get careless and you suddenly get over-confident, you WILL get a flat tire or worse. Stay alert and carefully AVOID all road debris!

As you take your standard 10-mile breaks to eat a piece of food and to take a short walk, park your bike CAREFULLY alongside the road. Make sure your bike is completely STABLE and strong as to be capable of withstanding even the forceful wind of a passing tractor trailer! Your bike is your LOVE and it must NEVER fall to the ground. Tears should come to your eyes if your bike ever crashes to the asphalt! True love also involves taking the extra 2 minutes to LOCK your bike upon stopping at Dollar General to buy some Powerade. If your bike ever goes missing, then you have just delayed your trip by at least 3 days and probably cost yourself $2,000.00 or more. In most cases, a stolen bike ENDS a cyclist's dream of completing their epic cross-country ride!

LOVE your bike in all these ways and more. Name your bike if you feel compelled. For years I thought it was ridiculous and childish how my wife named her car "Suzie," but the more I reflected on my wife and the special relationship she has with her prized car, the more I realized how well Suzie is taken care of by my wife and the utmost level of reliability exhibited by Suzie in return.

Maybe you could attach a special sticker to your bike or make a special label to adhere to your bike. Some cyclists even adhere a religious symbol to their bike as to make the bike their own! Bless your bike with Holy Water. Gather your special friends around you bike and offer prayers for yourself, your bike, and your upcoming adventure. Actively involve your bike with special endeavors and you might be surprised how well it performs!

One of the worst mistakes you can make is to disregard your bike as "just a bike." Your bike is your love! Gently maneuver your bike up the cement steps at your motel as you take careful efforts to make sure you don't harm any part of your bike. Take off your pannier bags carefully before you park your bike for the night as not to stress or damage any of your bike components. Most of all, make sure no amount of wind or no intruding animal critter is going to knock your bike to the ground. Fostering a strong marriage involves taking all reasonable precautions to keep your bike safe and secure no matter what!

Chapter 99: Rest, Comfort, Balance

On Day 1 and Day 2 it is EXTREMELY important to go SLOW! Keep affirming to yourself, "Slower. Slower. Slower." The ONLY purpose of your first two days of bike travel is to establish yourself on the coveted cross-country route. Covering a particular number of miles means NOTHING on Day 1 or Day 2! All that matters is making a bit of progress as you SLOWLY acclimate yourself to biking. Don't be concerned at all with the number of miles you travel or your average rate of speed during your initial days.

Day 1 and Day 2 are transition days. Under no circumstance should you push your heart rate to the point where you are gasping for air. As you are making the massive 4,000-foot climb out of San Diego, you should be able to speak regularly and feel like you are getting stronger with every pedal stroke! If you find yourself breathing heavy and fast, then back off of your pedal cadence. SLOW DOWN! Train your body and mind to be methodical. Racing out of San Diego has prematurely ENDED more cross-country attempts than you may ever realize!

Years ago, I researched the eastern discipline of Ayurveda, especially as it relates to endurance athletes. In the esteemed Ayurvedic tradition, endurance athletes are trained to focus on three primary words: REST, COMFORT, and BALANCE. Each of these words are cultivated as to maintain a CALM mindset throughout the ENTIRE athletic activity. Ayurvedic athletes consistently monitor their overall well-being. Am I RESTING? Am I COMFORTABLE? Am I BALANCED?

In no way am I an authority on Eastern disciplines and I am certainly not pretending to be an expert on Ayurveda, but I can relate to the importance of maintaining a sense of restful calm throughout your physical biking activity. Resting as you ride your bike may seem completely foreign, but I PROMISE you it is possible! While I ride my bicycle, I try not to consider the terrain, my mileage, my speed, or even the current weather conditions. My primary focus is RESTING! My goal is to feel like I am "taking a break" while I am pedaling, especially as I climb hills and mountains! Learning to REST while you ride allows your body to perform in an amazing fashion day after day for as long as you desire.

COMFORT is the second Ayurvedic word in the magical eastern potion for endurance. Comfort is basically another component used to make sure you are RESTING. Do I feel comfortable? Am I relaxed? Does my activity seem EASY? If you DON'T feel comfortable, then you are NOT resting. You must get comfortable and remain comfortable to facilitate a resting response from your body and mind. Only by truly developing a level of comfort on your bike will you be able to maintain a sense of relaxation.

Physical comfort involves riding a bike that is PROPERLY fit for your physical stature. Mental comfort has to do with thinking the right thoughts. For now, realize your mind and body must feel an overall sense of comfort if you are to maintain high daily mileage quotas!

BALANCE is the third and final word in the magical eastern Ayurvedic mantra. Balance reminds you to keep everything FLOWING. There should be NO heavy physical exertion of any kind at any time. Your cross-country cycling venture is NOT a race, but even if it was a race, a good argument could be made to retain your valuable sense of balance. Balance has to do with remaining in CONTROL of your physical and mental expenditure of energies. If your balance is proper, you should feel steady and strong as you easily rotate your pedals while simultaneously gathering greater storage levels of strength and vitality.

If you ever find yourself unable to speak while you are pedaling, then you are exerting too much effort. At all times, you should be able to speak and think clearly while you are physically propelling the pedals of your bike round and round. For hours while pedaling the great Southern Tier, I would silently repeat over and over to myself inside my own head and sometimes out loud with my own physical voice the seemingly enchanted words "Rest, Comfort, Balance."

Over and over, I would repeat this mantra as it slowly, but surely, PROGRAMMED my mind, body, and spirit for optimal performancacke day after day. Instead of panicking when the rain started, I would default to a calm demeanor in which I methodically continued to gently push my pedal cadence and GET THE JOB DONE! Rain, winds, hail, or traffic could not affect my calm as I obsessively focused on REST, COMFORT, and BALANCE as I let my comfortable pedal zce take care of the ridiculous number of miles as my primary job was merely to "REMAIN CALM" as my highly-athletic "little brother," Caden McCully, so often advises me. Remaining calm and in control has been a focal point of my life, but never before did I ever use my posture and poise to such a high degree as was evident and necessary on the Southern Tier!

The earlier you can PROGRAM your mind/body/spirit to accept a calm and methodical approach to your cross-country aspirations, the quicker you will notice a HUGE improvement in your cycling efforts. Prior to my 43 DAY trek of the Southern Tier, I NEVER completed a road bike trip lasting longer than THREE DAYS! In ALL of my previous multi-day bike excursions, I over-exerted myself resulting in trip-ending injuries, but by practicing a more calm and methodical approach, I finished the Southern Tier in great shape after pedaling my bicycle for 43 consecutive days.

Upon completion of over 6 weeks of daily biking, I felt THE BEST I have EVER felt in my entire life. My level of good health was so strong, turning around and riding the Southern Tier westward back to San Diego would have been no problem at all for me! By the time I had arrived at the Jacksonville Beach on my 43rd and final day, I was in the BEST shape of my life! NOTHING hurt on my body and I was a prime and elite athlete!

The most important aspect of the Rest, Comfort, Balance strategy is the underlying principle to TAKE IT SLOW! Start slow and then go slower. How SLOW can you go? For my entire Day 1, I kept telling myself, "Slow" and "Slower." Join the vibrational frequency of REST, COMFORT, BALANCE with a slow and steady pace. Unless you are a professional cyclist with huge recent biking experience, the first week or two of your cross-country bike efforts should be SLOW as not to injure yourself or put too much stress on your heart or other organs. Go slow and in due time, you will notice your speed and mileage increasing NATURALLY. Overdo it on Day 1 and Day 2 and you will be injured on Day 3 as you try to figure out how the heck you are going to get yourself, your bike, and your gear back home!

If you can hold on through the first three or four punishing days of the Southern Tier, then you will GREATLY increase your chances of finishing as MANY aspiring cross-country cyclists QUIT early in their cross-country attempts as they quickly realize they do NOT have what it takes to take on a major bicycle route! But if you hang in there clinging to my proposed SLOW STRATEGY using the Ayurvedic REST, COMFORT, BALANCE principle, then your body will begin to CHANGE and adapt to your newly placed cycling demands.

One of the many changes invoked by the REST, COMFORT, BALANCE principle involves your heart rate. After a couple weeks, your resting heart rate will DECREASE. If you are one of the few who actually complete an epic bicycle ride, then you will likely have a resting heart rate in the forties! On Day 1, my resting heart rate was 58. On Day 43, after pedaling 7 hours a day for 43 days, my resting heart rate was 46! How SLOW can you go? Welcome to the Southern Tier!

DAY 28: Here is angel Jamie from Rising Phoenix Adventures in Bastrop, Texas. Without any pay from me, Jamie graciously transported me and my bicycle 30 miles to Austin, Texas to get my bike fixed!

Chapter 100: Granny Gear

A "granny gear" is the LOWEST and easiest bicycle gear. The granny gear is so easy to pedal, even a Granny theoretically could do it! Prior to attempting a cross-country bicycle trek, you might want to make sure your bike has a granny gear as there are plenty of hills and MOUNTAINS on every cross-county bike ride! You will NEED a granny gear unless you are a professional cyclist! Otherwise, you will probably be WALKING your bicycle up the mountains!

As you consider which ROAD BIKE you wish to purchase, inquire carefully as to ensure your road bike has a granny gear as all bikes do NOT have a granny gear! To my surprise after receiving my bicycle by mail order from Bikes Direct, I quickly realized my new bike did NOT have a granny gear! My bike had two big sprockets in the front and each of the sprockets had ten separate gears in the back on a smaller sprocket. There were 20 total gears on my bike, but not one of them was a granny gear!!!!

While pedaling the epic Southern Tier bike route, there were OVER 100 times in which I pressed my right gear shifter to give me one more gear lower only to be DENIED as my desired granny gear did not exist! My downshifting range had fully concluded and there were no more available gears! If only I had one more downshift gear. If only I had a granny gear!

Professional cyclists and other very well-developed cyclists don't need a granny gear as they have developed their muscles much more extensively than you and I. Therefore, some bikes do NOT have a granny gear. In my case, I wanted a "Granny" and she was nowhere to be found! What a crucial mistake I made...... or so I thought!

The human body is so amazing. When something is missing or lacking, your body will COMPENSATE. So, without a granny gear, my legs eventually got used to it and after about three weeks of daily cycling, my lacking a granny gear was not much of an issue. By Day 22, I didn't need a granny gear at all as I learned to do without it! By the time I arrived in Florida at the conclusion of my adventure, I actually preferred NOT having a granny gear!

My official advice is for you to buy a ROAD BIKE with a granny gear. It is MUCH HARDER ascending the hills and mountains without the help of Granny! A granny gear allows you to "walk" your bike while you are actually riding it! A granny gear allows you to catch your breath and REST without actually stopping your bike which is a key element of my predominant REST, COMFORT, BALANCE strategy, my MAJOR Southern Tier biking concept and a governing operating principle for my entire life!

Professionals and other advanced cyclists don't need a granny gear because they do not "walk" their bike up elevated terrains! For a high-level cyclist, a granny gear is a waste of a gear, not to mention an embarrassment to their EGO! But most of us are not professional cyclists and when we get tired, it is helpful to have one last downshift before the shifting lever gets HARD and refuses to engage into a lower gear.

As my cross-country ride lengthened and my body began to develop into better shape, I found myself climbing very steep hills in my second or third gear, not even my lowest non-granny first gear!!!! After several weeks of cycling, I actually PREFERRED to climb the hills in my second or third lowest gear which was definitely a testament to my body evolving into better and better shape each day as my pedaling efforts progressed!

Most bicycles with THREE big sprockets in the front generally seem to have a granny gear while those bikes with only TWO big sprockets in the front (like mine) generally do not have a granny gear. Bikes with three sprockets in front usually have about 7 or 8 separate gears on the rear sprocket which gives the bike a total of either 21 or 24 gears. My bike had 2 sprockets in front and 10 separate gears on the rear sprocket thus giving me a total of 20 gears.

In all fairness, I must admit the first 100 or so times I pulled down on my shifting lever for one last downshift, only to be declined, was very DISCOURAGING. The precipitous mountains in the western portion of the United States were very demanding and I could have really used one last gear, the granny gear, but it wasn't there. During my first two weeks of biking, I struggled to maintain my pedal cadence in a gear too tough for my current level of physical conditioning. What I really needed at the time was one more gear lower! How could I buy a bike without a GRANNY GEAR? What was I thinking? The Southern Tier bike route is hard enough WITH a granny gear. Without a granny gear, the Southern Tier was BRUTAL!

Although my legs were forced to work MUCH HARDER than I had originally planned, after several weeks of continuous biking, my leg strength was no longer a problem. By the beginning of the 4th week, my legs felt like they were made of iron! It is unfortunate how many aspiring cross-country cyclists QUIT long before their legs transform into IRON!

As glorious as my story about overcoming the granny gear deficit might sound, it is only appropriate for me to mention an injury to both of my knees around Week 3 on the Southern Tier. Although there were several contributing factors possibly responsible for my knee injuries including a change in my seat position, I believe I pedaled TOO HARD for TOO LONG in gears too high for my current physical capabilities. If I had a granny gear, I might not have injured my knees!

When I first decided to ride the Southern Tier, I chose the particular route because it was "mostly flat" or so I thought! Little did I know, the Southern Tier has approximately 100,000 feet of elevation gain from coast to coast and is rated as an "ADVANCED" bike route by Adventure Cycling Association! The Southern Tier is appropriate only for very experienced cyclists, not a cyclist like me and especially not for someone like myself pedaling it ALONE! By combining the extreme elevation gains with the consistent easterly desert headwinds, you have a recipe for disaster! Take my advice and get a granny gear. You will need it!

DAY 28: There are some bridges with very LOW guardrails like these on the Southern Tier. Hold on tight when you are anywhere close to a bridge as a strong wind could give you the scare of your life!

DAY 29: Another brilliant sunrise! I LOVE riding in the dark anticipating the marvelous breakthrough of the mighty sun!

Chapter 101: Holidays

Part of the reason I am writing this book as a SUCCESSFUL cross-country cyclist is because I was naive! When I began my biking adventure, I didn't know how long my bike-across-America outing would take to complete. My best guess was 30 days which proved to be a sizable miscalculation as I drastically overestimated my cycling abilities!

On Day 2 of my bike journey, no longer did I even expect to finish the coveted route. Day 3 and beyond merely consisted of single bike riding days, any of which could have been my LAST! As I write this paragraph, I wish I could tell you I had a CHAMPION mindset all the way, but the truth is……… I was a BIG MESS! If you accompanied me and my bike across the country, you wouldn't even buy this book because you wouldn't waste your time reading even one chapter from someone as pitiful, pathetic, and unstable as I!

October seemed like a good time for me to start my epic cycling crusade even though I had very little clue about what type of weather New Mexico, Texas, Louisiana, Mississippi, or Alabama had during the late Fall, but I heard that California and Arizona were warm. Of course, I knew Florida was warm in the Fall as I attended the University of Tampa before dropping out prior to my junior year. While making my decision on a starting date, not once did I ever consider starting my bike ride in October meant I would miss the Halloween holiday!

Putting on a frightening mask and scaring the young local Trick-or-Treaters is a lot of fun to me! It also gives me great joy to frighten our own adult children in a similar and unsuspecting manner! Visiting Haunted Houses and creepy cornfields during the Halloween holiday season are also activities in which I relish, but during the year of the Southern Tier, none of these anticipated holiday activities were happening for me!

As I exceeded my meager expectations and somehow made my way on my bicycle through the HUGE stated of Texas into Louisiana while missing my anticipated Halloween holiday, I began to wonder if I would also miss the prized holiday of Thanksgiving. Missing Halloween was BIG, but missing Thanksgiving with my family would be almost UNIMAGINABLE! What have I gotten myself into? How could I possibly continue my bike trip through the major Thanksgiving holiday? The unpleasant thought of missing Thanksgiving actually prompted me to pedal FASTER!

Imaging myself absent from my family on Thanksgiving was very difficult for me to process! After many years of habitual holiday celebrations, Thanksgiving became a tradition with great intrinsic meaning to me. Despite my gorgeous niece, Jordyn, being a bit annoying at times, I longed to be a part of my family's Thanksgiving holiday and I had NO IDEA whether or not I would attend the celebration on this particular year. My old life was over and my new Southern Tier life was my new normal. Included as part of my "new life" was a whole lot of UNKNOWNS, including attendance at holiday functions!

During my lonely evenings on the Southern Tier, I didn't even take the time to calculate my distances and probability of making it home for Thanksgiving as I doubted my overall chances of completing the iconic Southern Tier Bike Route anyways! All I did was pedal, day after lonely day. My job was simply spinning my pedals around for 7 hours every day. Pedaling was my life! Eating alone on Thanksgiving was my assumption as my primary focus was keeping my pedals revolving as I was on a MISSION bigger than myself and much more superior than any holiday! Missing a holiday or two was a disappointment, but it wasn't enough of a setback to remove me from the Southern Tier Bike Route and cause me to come back home!

In an attempt to console myself, I would deduct my reasoning much like the loving wisdom of my gram, Hilda Cemo, whom regularly declared, "Holidays are just another day on the calendar, nothing more special than any other day." But despite my best efforts of self-consolation through the application of my Gram Cemo's profound advice, I was deeply saddened at times as I expected my bike ride would cause me to miss a major holiday with my family.

Missing a holiday is definitely something worthy to consider when planning to pedal a long bike route. For some, missing a holiday, wedding, or other once-in-lifetime event could be the last push to halt a cyclist's pedal cadence, send them "over the edge," and curtail their entire bike trip!

For me, missing Thanksgiving or even being absent on my favorite holiday of Christmas was something I was more than willing to do, if necessary. My bike trip was a MISSION, not a "sight-seeing tour!" I was on a God-ordained JOURNEY of self-discovery through the intriguing deserts and tall mountains as I desperately sought to discover the MAN INSIDE OF MYSELF! Even as pitiful as I seemed at times, my longstanding determination to "do what I said I would do" seemed to pull me through the most challenging times when I felt like I couldn't withstand anymore! Yes, the thought of missing a holiday or two affected me deeply, but it was not enough to put an end to my bicycle mission!

Without a doubt, the Southern Tier was the most SPIRITUAL experience I ever had. It was me and God throughout a VERY DESOLATE bike route. It was a very long date with MYSELF as God kept revealing more and more of MYSELF to MYSELF. It wasn't about the days or the upcoming holidays as much as it was about the development of my spirit and emergence of THE MAN within! At times, I wandered about the deeper meaning of my Southern Tier travels, but never once did I ever doubt my divine calling to remain on the hallowed route!

Although holidays are important and even critical to a family's heritage, holidays can be forsaken, but only for a BIG reason. Only if your biking REASONS are BIG enough will you have the fortitude to OUTLAST the pain of missing a major holiday as you spin the pedals on your bicycle! Make sure you know exactly WHY you are riding your bike across the country and you will stand a better chance to overcome the trip-ending pain of missed holidays!

DAY 29: Here is my trusty tent at the Navasota Fire Department in Navasota, Texas. Instead of sleeping inside, I decided to sleep outside in my cozy tent. I PREFER sleeping in my tent!

DAY 30: You will get all kinds of weather conditions on the Southern Tier. Make sure you have ALL of your lights turned on during foggy conditions!

Chapter 102: YOUR Ride

As much as I want you to read my book and follow my exact instruction, I must advise you to MAKE YOUR OWN DECISIONS! As for me, I'm just another author with a bunch of semi-conflicting ideas. Many of my concepts, strategies, and recommendations enclosed in the pages of this book might be useless to you as you contemplate your own cross-country bike ride! In my prejudiced view, I don't believe the prior statement to be the case as I suspect we are made of a similar mold and we are kindred souls, but I do realize your needs and objectives might be very different than mine! It is impossible for me to know all of your own personal preferences and all the intricate needs you have as a unique human being. Your personal situation might be strikingly similar to mine or it might be completely different!

Only YOU can design your own cross-country bike travel itinerary. Only you can fulfill your spiritual dharma and embark on your own meaningful bicycle journey! In no way is this book the final authoritative word on bike touring! Your cross-country ride is YOUR cross-country ride! Just because it took me 43 days to complete the 3,000-mile Southern Tier Bicycle Route averaging 70 miles per day does NOT mean anything for YOU! You might be slower or faster than me. You might take a different route. You might go with a group. You might ride the route in spaced-apart sections. Whatever you do, move at your own pace! Design your own special adventure. It's YOUR ride!

While you are making decisions with regard to a possible cross-country trek of your own, don't believe a single word you read in this book! Read this book carefully, but ultimately decide for YOURSELF! Feel for yourself which recommendations of mine resonate deep within you and then discard the rest. YOUR plan must be in alignment with your particular life rhythm.

Maybe you'll be like me and feel called to ride your bike in the Fall eastbound into a prevailing headwind? Or maybe you would rather take advantage of the natural easterly winds and ride your bike westward in the Fall as to take full advantage of Mother Nature's prevailing tailwind? Maybe you want to spend every night in a hotel? Maybe you want to split your time between campgrounds, cheap motels, and various Warmshowers hosts like I did? Like my great friend, Mike Wolf, often says, "It's YOUR world!"

While you are considering your many options, remember, you are considering an epic trip of a LIFETIME. Carefully listen to your own intuition and follow it! Saving money was VERY important for me as I ate the majority of my daily calories from the most INEXPENSIVE food sources I could find. In most cases, I looked for a McDonalds, Burger King, or some other inexpensive restaurant and ordered the CHEAPEST food with the MOST CALORIES from the value menu. Dollar General was another primary source of CHEAP CALORIES for me. For supper each night, I would generally try to eat some higher quality calories by going to a nice, reasonably-priced hometown restaurant offering a well-balanced home-cooked meal with some vegetables on my plate! Maybe you want to eat all of your meals at nice restaurants? Whatever you decide is what you decide! It's YOUR trip!

This is your special once-in-lifetime bike ride, an epic adventure only for YOU! Hopefully this book HELPS you to make key decisions to support your enjoyment, spiritual growth, and personal unfolding as you partake in a life-changing bicycle experience. You, the aspiring cross-country cyclist is whom I'm thinking about as I write these pages. My arduous efforts exerted on these seemingly endless pages are aimed at helping you as much as I possibly can to help make your cycling dream come true. My inspiration to write this book was for YOUR benefit!!!

DAY 30: I feel like I am finally out of the desert.

Chapter 103: Training Rides

From the moment you accept your calling and make the firm decision to take on the Southern Tier or whatever other particular epic cross-country bike route, you must be VERY careful with the choices you make leading up to the departure of your big adventure. What I'm mostly referring to are your bicycle training rides as they are MUCH MORE IMPORTANT than you may initially realize!

EVERY training ride following your firm decision to pedal your bicycle across the country is a CRUCIAL part of your upcoming, epic cycling journey. The importance of your training bike rides cannot be over-stated as it is vital for you to SUCCEED in ALL of your training pursuits! The GOLDEN RULE with regards to training rides is DO NOT QUIT! Quitting during a training ride leaves a lasting impression in your heart, mind, and soul providing "quitting" as an OPTION while you are actually out on the streets pedaling toward your cross-country goal. At all costs, design your training rides carefully as to make sure you SUCCEED on every one of them!!!

When you train, you need to take the training session very SERIOUSLY! If you plan to ride 93 miles from Johnstown, PA to the Sorrel Ridge Campground at mile marker 154 on the C&O Canal Towpath Bike Trail like I did, then you better not let heavy winds or 7 different rain storms deter your decision! In most cases, you are better advised to set SHORTER training goals and to EXCEED your goals as it is much more beneficial to achieve your goals than to create an initial pattern of failure!

At mile 35 of my particular training ride mentioned above, I encountered a level 4 rainstorm with a 20 mile per hour HEADWIND which lasted for 60 minutes. During the wind and the rain, my mind began drifting until I finally found myself contemplating the possibility of QUITTING. Little by little, I got more and more discouraged until I almost QUIT!

As I stopped alongside the rural road on PA Route 96 in Manns Choice, PA, I had perhaps the most crucial "bike talk" of my life with myself. While pulled over to the side of the road, I contemplated calling my cousin, Scott Bassett, for a ride back home as he was on his way to meet me in Cumberland, Maryland to ride the final 30 miles with me on the C&O Towpath. As I contemplated my options to continue or to QUIT, I finally decided to accept the wind and tolerate the rain and to keep pedaling through the agony of the inclement weather!

At this point in my long training ride, my speed no longer mattered. My mileage was of no concern. My only care was to keep my pedals spinning around! As long as my pedals were spinning, then I was content no matter what the weather dumped on me! After many miles of using this newfound mental focusing strategy, I found myself ACCEPTING the weather conditions instead of JUDGING the weather! What a HUGE distinction!!! No longer did rain or wind affect me as I pedaled through all of it! My new acceptance approach with regard to the inclement weather conditions combined with my natural-born STUBBORN tendencies NOT to quit ended up being one of the primary reasons which allowed me to complete the Southern Tier!

Only by ACCEPTING the current weather conditions can you OUTLAST the current weather conditions! When you get upset over weather conditions you CANNOT control and you begin to curse the rain, cold, or wind, you are only empowering those conditions over you. Instead of cursing God's amazing choice of weather, just accept them for what they are and simply "DO RAIN" or "DO COLD" or "DO WIND."

Rain, cold, and wind are NOT inherently bad! They are only a particular weather pattern unfolding in the present moment. Rain is just rain and NOTHING MORE! The weather elements cannot hurt you as long as you have proper gear which is covered elsewhere in this book. Don't make rain, cold, or wind anything more than it is. Hang in there and OUTLAST the elements and you will set yourself up for possible success on your upcoming epic cross-country bicycle ride.

Training is important as it sets the pattern for your big upcoming cross-country ride. While on the Southern Tier, I had frequent FLASHBACKS of my training days. The wind and rain in my face….. The chilling temperatures….. The doubts penetrating my mind as I summit another mountain….. But the BIGGEST flashback from my big training day was FINISHING every one of my training rides! Instead of quitting and calling my dad for a ride back home like I had done MANY TIMES previously, I OUTLASTED the wind and the rain and I FINISHED my Southern Tier training rides!

Having even one special training ride VICTORY prior to your epic cycling expedition will help keep your pedals revolving when conditions are less than ideal. Never discount your training rides as unimportant because FLASHBACKS will occur during your epic "bike across America" ride and you will either draw on the successes of your training rides or you will sink closer to quitting as you recall your previous failures. In most cases, you will ultimately make the SAME DECISIONS on your epic cross-country ride as you did on your training rides!!! So, even if you have to go through Hell like I did for a few hours during a particular training ride, then DO IT! It is much less painful overall to withstand the wet and cold for a while during a training session than it is to live with the failure of quitting on the "ride of your life!"

Believe me, you don't want to find yourself in the middle of the desert lacking the mental fortitude necessary to continue! Struggle BIG in training while you are in the "comforts" of your own home area as it is VERY DIFFICULT to develop yourself to a proficient level while you are on a major bicycle route stuck out in the middle of the desert or at the base of a huge 14-mile ascending mountain pass! Pay the price early before you even take your first pedal stroke on the ultra-demanding Southern Tier Bicycle Route!

Chapter 104: Enjoyment

Throughout this book, I've hammered home the critical point about your cross-country bike ride being a MISSION and NOT a sightseeing joy ride! Although I will NOT take back a single word, I must admit it is also important to ENJOY your ride! Although enjoyment is not really possible on the first few days or maybe even unlikely during the first two weeks of a major bike tour, at some point in the first half of your bike ride, you NEED to foster a sense of enjoyment in order to SUSTAIN your cross-country efforts. Enjoying your epic bike ride is NOT as important as your MISSION-DRIVEN mindset, but enjoyment is nonetheless a vital ingredient in your ultimate success! In a very convoluted manner, you MUST figure out how to enjoy yourself on your epic bike ride while still maintaining your overall TOUGHNESS or else you will FAIL!!!

At first, I was ALL-BUSINESS as I began the Southern Tier, but little by little I began to take in more and more of the natural beauty surrounding me! As my bike ride evolved, I allowed my mission to be enjoyable WITHOUT taking anything away from my committed daily cycling efforts. Somewhere during the late part of the second week of my bike adventure, I was surprised to notice myself actually ENJOYING brief portions of my bike ride!

Interestingly enough, I found by consciously ENJOYING myself more, I became more mentally and emotionally STABLE! Suddenly, I felt a part of the landscape which surrounded me. It felt like I was at ONE with the darkness and the spectacular sunrises. As I released more and more of my stresses, I began to relax a bit and feel more enjoyment as I experienced more of God's daily beauty while pedaling the Southern Tier. And the more I enjoyed myself, the closer I felt to my surroundings and the more INTENSE the chilling experience.

At times, my experience on the Southern Tier was so riveting, I would feel TINGLES all the way down my body. When you feel these vivid physical sensations, you KNOW you are living right! You know you have found the somewhat elusive balance between enjoyment and mission and you will know your life is ON PURPOSE!

Becoming too mechanical can lead to boredom which can then prompt thoughts of doubt which combined with other negative variables could be enough to end your special ONCE-IN-A-LIFETIME cycling excursion. Only by RELEASING your stresses and permitting yourself to experience some enjoyment will you have enough energy to complete the arduous cross-country journey. Although you might be like me and consider enjoying yourself as a difficult task, it is nonetheless absolutely necessary for you to figure out how to do it.

Finding enjoyment didn't come easy for me. Along the way, random people would ask me, "Are you enjoying your ride?" and I would stammer for an answer as I really never thought about my bike journey as being "enjoyable." The more I was asked about my personal enjoyment with regard to my special cycling travels and the more I considered the intriguing question, the more I began to TRY to enjoy myself. Despite being a "Git er Done" kind of man, I was determined to find enjoyment in the Southern Tier even though it was much more difficult than you might think! It took dedicated and concentrated efforts for me to RELEASE my internal tightness and succumb to the RELAXATION and ENJOYMENT of the Southern Tier Bike Route! But the deeper my release, the more enjoyment I experienced, and the better my overall bike travels!

Habitually, I would look all around myself while negotiating the Southern Tier. As I looked up, down, and off into the distance, I was surrounded by natural beauty! Even in the complete dark, I felt the power of the night encapsulating myself as the sunrise approached. Sacred landscapes ENCIRCLED me on every side! Over time, I DEVELOPED the ability to ENJOY this special privilege as I was slowly and methodically experiencing a true milestone in my life!

For a hard-driven, Type A personality guy like myself who always needs to be THE BOSS, it can be very difficult to take time off work and simply ENJOY the activity at hand. People like me ALWAYS need to be doing something PRODUCTIVE or achieving something worthwhile. Guys like me don't enjoy small talk and we don't do well at cocktail parties. Results-driven people like myself like to make business deals and achieve MAJOR accomplishments. We consider life as short and we want to pack every day with as much effort as possible as to create favorable results as quickly as humanly possible. Enjoyment is rarely a goal for results-driven people WIRED like myself!

For all the goal-oriented cyclists like me, it's even more important to CHILL OUT a bit and ENJOY more of the day. Surprisingly, I've found by enjoying more of my day, I actually become MORE PRODUCTIVE! During the last few years of my life, I have been more pleasant and less stressful than my previous years and I even like myself better now! Plus, I get MORE done in a shorter amount of time!!! So, my advice for you is to develop and retain your "DO IT NOW, NO MATTER WHAT attitude," but as you maintain your hard-driven, "Git er Done" attitude, also sprinkle in some ENJOYMENT into your recipe!!! You might really like the new person you become!

My wife, Tink, is another example of a DOER! When her feet hit the floor in the morning, she goes hard all through her day. Don't get in her way or she might run you over as she suddenly becomes "TANK" instead of "TINK.". When Tink tells me she is going to do something, SHE DOES IT! Nothing seems to ever stop her. She is a FINISHER!!!! One of her many nicknames is "Git er Done Tink." Often, I ask my overly-efficient wife, "Did you enjoy your day?" Tink's common answer is often, "I have too much to do to enjoy my day."

Despite my wife's continued tunnel vision, lately Tink and I have both acknowledged the IMPORTANCE of enjoying more of our daily activities. Although we both have a long way to go with regard to tapping into our own personal enjoyment factors, we are showing progress as we are trying to slow down a bit and ENJOY more of "the ride."

Pedaling a bicycle 3,000 miles or more across challenging terrain is a monumental task reserved ONLY for the very courageous, fiercely-dedicated, hard-driven person. Trying to ENJOY yourself early in your sacred journey is NOT realistic as your ONLY GOAL should be to SURVIVE the first week of your bike travels! Don't even try to enjoy yourself until you begin your second week of biking!

Only after having a week or so of biking success will you be strong enough to begin to process a small amount of enjoyment. Otherwise, too much enjoyment too early in the ride could mark disaster as it may take away from the other MORE essential gritty qualities needed to keep you on your bicycle and not in an airplane flying back home!

For the first week or so of your epic bike ride, your sole intention is to REMAIN. The first week of your NEW LIFE will be filled with very powerful emotions easily disrupting your positive thought process making it almost possible to enjoy yourself. Maintain your tough business attitude for the first week before you even think about trying to enjoy yourself. But if you surpass the odds and you are pedaling on Day 8, then you MUST start working on the "enjoyment factor" as your enjoyment now becomes HUGELY IMPORTANT and could be enough to END your ride if you don't CONSCIOUSLY find a way to ENJOY your ride! Without feeling any enjoyment on your epic bicycle outing, your mind and spirit will eventually CRACK and you might find yourself boarding an airplane heading back home wondering why you QUIT!

DAY 30: I stayed at "The Love Shack" inside the Shepherd Sanctuary Campground in Shepherd, Texas. Owner Peach and her friends were very generous to me!

Chapter 105: Health Issues

Around the age of 25, for some unknown reason, I began to experience a heart condition known as Supraventricular Tachycardia (SVT). Approximately on a monthly basis, my heart would suddenly and unexpectedly beat EXTREMELY fast. At times my heart would beat 180 beats or more per minute which caused me great concern.

When this strange heart-related phenomenon would occur, I would usually stop what I was doing and sit down for about a half hour and my heart would gradually resume its regular 60 beats per minute. Although the SVT episodes were very scary, I learned to deal with them as I tried my best to avoid triggering an SVT episode as it seemed like potential SVT triggers included intense exercise, certain medications, caffeine, stress, highly emotional events, and eating spicy foods.

As I was bringing my pedaling day to a close about 3 miles from the Fort Clark Army Campground in Brackettville, Texas on Day 23 of my epic bike journey, I had my first and only SVT attack on the Southern Tier. This particular SVT required me to stop for about 10 minutes along the side of the road to settle down and regain my regular heartbeat. It was a very mild SVT attack, but the episode was SUPER SCARY as is the case with ALL of my SVT events! Although many other people are frequently taken by ambulance to the hospital during an SVT attack, I've always handled my SVT attacks on my own without professional healthcare intervention.

Although an SVT is a very serious health condition, there are many other health conditions much more serious. If you happen to have a serious health condition, you will want to have a solid PLAN in place as to how you will handle your own particular health episode if an "attack" would occur while riding your bike in a distant land. For many, special daily medicine is required and for others a shot, crème, or some other type of application might be necessary to ward off a particular health issue. In my case, all I needed was ten minutes of rest and a few Tums to move past my SVT episode.

As you read, you might notice a continuous theme of PLANNING mentioned throughout this book. That's because planning your trip is MORE IMPORTANT than your actual trip! And I'm NOT just talking about planning what you are going to take inside your pannier bags. I'm talking about having a PLAN for ALL of the potential problems you WILL experience while you are away on your monumental bike journey, especially health-related proceedings.

As a side note to my SVT condition, two years after the completion of the Southern Tier, I chose to get a heart ablation surgery to rid me of my SVT episodes. During my major heart ablation surgery, my incredibly talented and extremely caring heart doctor, Dr Genevieve Everett from Altoona, PA, used electrodes to burn away the particular nerve endings in my heart responsible for causing the SVTs to occur.

Although I still get the ominous "trigger beat" preluding my former SVT attacks, I no longer get the actual SVT attack as Dr. Everett successfully ablated the former SVT pathway and I have been feeling much better as a result of her diligent efforts and precise care.

DAY 31: Wild camping in a vacant lot out in the open view of dozens of houses and a huge church. Nobody bothered me, but 2 generous senior ladies from the church brought me supper to my tent!

DAY 32: Camping on the front porch of the Allen Parrish Tourist Commission in Oberlin, Louisiana.

Chapter 105: Private Goals

My official advice is to keep your really big dreams and goals to yourself until you HAVE TO tell someone! Why? Because the people with whom you want the most to encourage you, won't! Almost without fail throughout my life, my parents whom LOVE me to the absolute highest degree humanly possible and would literally give their own lives for me, have OFTEN discouraged me when I shared with them the next REALLY BIG THING I planned to do with my life.

Back in high school when I was seriously considering attending the University of Tampa, Florida for college, my parents reminded me that I would be 1,000 miles away from home and I didn't know anybody in Tampa. While writing my first book "Smashing the Wall of Fear" at only 21 years of age, they reminded me about how I got poor grades in English class while making insinuations I was unqualified for the task. When my first wife, Gina Leis, and I adopted 3 biracial children in a 99% white Caucasian neighborhood, mom and dad reminded me about the racism still existing in the small town of Windber, Pennsylvania and did not originally approve of our adoption decision. When I was training the for the Ironman triathlon, my parents reminded me of the heavy toll the grueling training would take on my family life and my personal endeavors. When I told my parents I was learning to speak Spanish, my mom said, "You live in America. You should speak English only! Why are you wasting your time learning Spanish?" And when I disclosed my plans to ride the Southern Tier, my mom was so startled by my proclamation, she said, "Is that even possible? Has anyone ever done it?" Even as I pedaled the entire first week on the Southern Tier, my dad reminded me daily about the next major airport in Phoenix as he suggested "You could always do your bike trip in sections."

Despite having 100% PURE and TRUE love for me, my parents naturally discouraged me in the same manner as any other loving parent would do for their precious child! My parent's discouragement was NOT a display of a lack of love, but rather a PROCLAMATION for the love they have for me. In their minds, they thought I was setting myself up for pain and failure and they only wanted to help me to avoid the devastation. Any parent or loved one who truly LOVES you will probably be less than supportive when you tell them about your big plan to ride your bicycle across the country. Thus, you must be ready for a natural lack of support from your loved ones, especially your parents!

In order for your cross-country biking dream to come true, it must be YOU generating the necessary PASSION to SUSTAIN your dream. Your inner drive must be GREATER than the negative drain around you. Mustering up the necessary gusto needed to overpower the insidious doubts all around you, whether outright stated or silently expressed, can be extremely grim and add a layer of unnecessary difficulty to your cycling ambition.

Recognizing the discouragement tendency in advance allowed me to keep my plans to myself as long as possible. The ONLY people whom I revealed my cross-country biking plans prior to me taking my first pedal stroke were my wife, my two parents, my daughter, and two of the workers at my local bicycle shop. Keeping my cross-country cycling ambition personal allowed me keep my dream alive without too many others contaminating my thoughts with negativity and doubt.

Pedaling a bicycle across the country had to do with my own personal calling and not for any other reason. My special adventure had NOTHING to do with others as I was pedaling my bike from the Pacific Ocean to the Atlantic Ocean for ONE REASON...... what it would make of me as a person! Personal development was my STRONGEST motivating force responsible for me propelling my bicycle along the mighty Southern Tier! The Southern Tier provided me with an excellent opportunity to develop myself into the best ME possible! And the Southern Tier did NOT disappoint!

While anticipating the Southern Tier, my attention maintained constant and my energy remained high. As the departure date grew nearer and nearer, my thoughts about the Southern Tier began to increase until the Southern Tier DOMINATED my thinking for the FULL two weeks prior to my departure. During my final week prior to departure, there were NO OTHER DOMINANT THOUGHTS in my mind, as my complete attention was on my upcoming bike ride. It was a date with destiny! On the final day when I was dropped off at the Pittsburgh Airport with about 130 pounds of bike and gear, my mind became OVERLOADED with emotion as I was TOPPLED into a SEVERE panic attack in the terminal of the Pittsburgh Internation Airport.

Always try to generate your OWN inner motivations. Don't let other people dictate what is important in your life. Follow your callings in your own life and let other people think whatever they want. Never let another person determine your future! Keep your goals private and let your ACTIONS do the talking in your life! Be your own person and live or die by your own choices!

Earlier in the year when I was first "called" to do the Southern Tier, I kept the mysterious and compelling urge to myself. For about 3 months, I didn't tell a single human, not even my wife, about my plans to ride the Southern Tier only 8 months later. It wasn't until April before my October departure when I finally told my wife about my plans to pedal my bicycle across the United States of America. And it wasn't until September (one month prior to departure) when I finally told my parents and my daughter about my new and strange cross-country cycling undertaking. The two workers at my AWESOME local bike shop, Fat Jimmies, also found out about my cross-country trip about 2 months before my departure as they KNEW I was planning something really big as per my regular line of questioning over the course of several months prior to my cross-country effort.

It is interesting to note, my wife still claims TO THIS VERY DAY, I did NOT tell her about my plans to ride the Southern Tier back in April as I absolutely KNOW I did! I would even bet my life on the fact I told my wife about my upcoming cross-country ambition in April! Apparently, my cross-country biking idea was so foreign to my wife, she clearly couldn't process the critical information even as I CLEARLY disclosed my intentions to her.

In some strange way, Tink's mind refused to accept my decision to leave her for many weeks to pursue my bizarre biking agenda. Tink really didn't truly believe I was "leaving her" until the day I actually got dropped off at the airport! "How could the love of my life just get up and leave me like this?" were Tink's befuddled words as she re-entered my parent's truck after dropping me off at the Pittsburgh International Airport.

It wasn't until July prior to my October departure when I finally took the ENORMOUS STEP and purchased my ONE-WAY airplane flight from Pittsburgh, PA to San Diego, CA. As I was using the Internet to purchase my ONE-WAY flight, I could NOT get myself to push the PURCHASE NOW button on my computer to complete the acquisition of my airline ticket. It was like someone was restraining my hands in a manner I was NOT able to complete the transaction. Only with a pounding heart and a sweaty brow did I eventually complete the flight transaction and push the final button to consummate my travel itinerary!

While purchasing the airline ticket, my anxiety was mounting and I could FEEL my former self already starting to die! After the completion of my airline booking, I walked out to the kitchen and I tried to tell my wife about my very significant purchase, but I couldn't do it! Each time I attempted to speak; no words came out of my mouth. Even when I regained my conversation piece, I tried to make a segway into the airline ticket conversation, but I couldn't do so. The thought of leaving my precious, loving wife for an extended amount of time was almost unbearable! On this convoluted day, it was crystal clear; my bike trip was going to be more than HARD for BOTH of us!

After four days of numerous nervous false rehearsals and pitiful failed communications with regard to my newly purchased one-way airline ticket to San Diego, I finally blurted out "In October of this year, I am going to ride my bicycle across the country!" as I showed my wife my airline booking confirmation. With my plane ticket in hand and the completion of my second full cross-country cycling disclosure to my wife, my epic bike trip immediately became a whole lot more REAL! "What have I gotten myself into now?" was my dominant thought. At this moment, it seemed like there was no turning back!

Even my very supportive and sympathetic wife, as close as she is to me, could not understand why I would want to pedal a bicycle across the United States. She was baffled as to what nonsense was going on in my mind as she secretly wished I would come to my senses and CANCEL my crazy biking agenda and stay at home like a good husband, but it wasn't the case! The cross-country cycling urge inside of me did not cower and I was about to thrust myself into an unfamiliar reality involving thousands of daily pedal revolutions regardless of whether my wife liked the idea or not!

DAY 32: I'm definitely out of the desert now, but the route is still LONELY!

DAY 33: Here is the HUGE sign and barricade at Chiswick State Park in Louisiana clearly indicating the road being CLOSED! In my typical fashion, I did NOT obey this obvious sign and pedaled 3 miles past the giant sign when I was finally pulled over by a stern ranger who threatened to put me in JAIL!!!

Chapter 106: Low Expectations

As I prepared for Day 1 of my epic bike ride, I EXPECTED the weather to be what MOST people would label as "HORRIBLE." In my mind, I imagined beginning my trip on a cold, rainy, and windy day. And I was READY for it! Not once did I look at the weather forecast for San Diego prior to my arrival as the weather did NOT matter to me! As far as I was concerned, the weather conditions were going to be cold, rainy, and windy! To my dismay, the weather conditions at the onset of my cross-country adventure were warm and sunny with a gentle breeze.

Being a VERY SERIOUS and DEDICATED student of life, I studied the power of expectations and how expectations can DESTROY a relationship, BANKRUPT a business, and even TERMINATE a special biking trip! Although expectations are simply a group of beliefs about something, your beliefs GOVERN your life. Everything you do or don't do is determined by your beliefs!

It has been said by many masters throughout the ages, "Whether you believe it is or you believe it isn't, you're right!" Considering the wisdom of previous generations, it seemed logical for me to set my overall beliefs and expectations really LOW thus making it much EASIER for me to be remain STABLE on my bike journey without becoming ADDICTED to idealistic conditions! As I sat in the airplane approaching the San Diego International Airport, my expectations of cold, rain, and wind guarded me against being DISAPPOINTED!

If I was EXPECTING cold, rain, and wind, then how could I be disappointed? Expecting "nasty weather" also created the NECESSARY mental toughness needed to take on a formidable challenge like the Southern Tier! Hoping for ideal conditions is one of the most common recipes for FAILURE. After all, if you EXPECT favorable conditions and you get "nasty" conditions, then you will be UPSET and when a cross-country cyclist loses their composure and gets upset, the end of the epic trip might be much sooner than originally planned!

A truly wise cross-country cyclist will take my advice on expectations one step further by actually becoming ACCUSTOMED to the rain, cold, and wind instead of becoming ACCUSTOMED to sunny, warm, and calm conditions. Being FAMILIAR with heavy rain, bitter cold, and harsh wind will make it EASY to handle ALL of the other non-severe weather conditions you will encounter on your esteemed route. Starting with "beautiful weather" with lots of sun, warmth, and calm winds could mark the beginning of the end of your epic bike ride if you get TOO COMFORTABLE with these pleasing weather elements and EXPECT to bike in these same desirable elements every day of your adventure.

Setting your expectations too high by EXPECTING warm, dry, and calm biking conditions will likely cause you SEVERE difficulty when the cold, windy rains occur. But if you set your expectations on cold, rain, and wind, and you are already

FAMILIAR with cold, rain, and wind, then every other weather condition is an UPGRADE in which you can EASILY and happily endure without losing your crucial, hardcore positive mindset!

To master this principal involving LOW EXPECTATIONS, you must begin with your TRAINING RIDES! When the windy, cold rains come, you need to get out there on your bike and become FAMILIAR with these challenging conditions. You need to COMPLETE your training sessions as planned regardless of whatever weather condition you encounter! During the Southern Tier, there were MANY times my thoughts drifted back to one particular rainy day during a training ride in Manns Choice, PA when severe wind and rain pounded on me for hours, but I did NOT give up! Instead of calling for a ride home, I centered my thoughts on keeping my pedals going round and round until finally, I OUTLASTED the challenging weather elements!

One side note to consider....... I do NOT believe in "nasty conditions." Over the years, I have grown to LOVE rain, cold, and wind!!!! As long as I am wearing the proper clothes and have the proper gear, I actually PREFER to ride in these "nasty" conditions!!!!!! To me, there are no "nasty conditions"! In my mind, there is only different types of conditions in which each particular condition is interesting and ENJOYABLE! Be prepared with your expectations, clothes, and gear and there will be NO nasty conditions, only DIFFERENT conditions, all of which can be EXHILARATING!

Looking back on my pivotal training ride through the rain, cold, and wind in Manns Choice, PA, had I called for a ride home on that particular day, it may have been enough to set a very DANGEROUS pattern in place for my future biking endeavors. Instead of drawing upon my inner strength during the challenges of cold, rain, and wind, I may have established a pattern to rely on others to pick me up and remove me from these "foul" weather elements.

Make certain you COMPLETE your training rides! Your training rides are setting your expectations for your big once-in-a-lifetime bike outing as well as for the rest of your life. Set VERY LOW expectations and make sure you exceed them! Your expectation level might determine whether or not you are a cross-country bicycle CHAMPION or just another Southern Tier FATALITY!

If the weather conditions are severe, it is reasonable to set a goal to ride less miles than normal, but once you get started, make sure you complete your ride. As you are crossing the country on your bicycle, there will be MANY TIMES you will recall your toughest training rides!!! You will be wise to have some VERY STRONG reference points to draw strength from because you will NEED those positive memories to get you through!

When you find yourself in challenging circumstances and you begin to DOUBT your ability to SUSTAIN your cross-country journey, your brain will search your past experiences looking for a SIMILAR EXPERIENCE to draw from. If you have one or more SOLID and SUCCESSFUL training rides in which you pedaled through HELL, then your mind and body will SETTLE DOWN and follow your PRE-PROGRAMMED guide to SUCCESS! After all, if you made it through the cold, rain, and winds during training, then it you can do the same while riding the Southern Tier! But if your past includes INCOMPLETE training rides and cancelations due to "bad weather," then you might be in BIG TROUBLE when you are facing the brink of termination on the Southern Tier!

Start small while training. Set small mileage goals and make sure you achieve ALL of your goals. If you have a 10-mile training goal for a particular day and you achieve your goal, then it is totally fine to pedal a few more miles, but do NOT pedal any number of miles less than 10. It is much better to EXCEED your goals than to fall short, especially while training! The whole purpose of "training" is to acclimate your mind and body to ACHIEVE certain results. Be careful not to program FAILURE into your habit patterns!

Once you depart on your cross-country bike journey, goals become a little different. There were many days on the Southern Tier, especially in the second half of the trip when I only had a slight idea where I would stop for the night. Other days, especially during my final week of my cross-country odyssey, I had absolutely NO IDEA where I was going to stop and spend the night. Having no idea where you will lay your head at night, but still EXPECTING to be OK is a POWERFUL mental state of mind as this is a clear indication you have taken BIG STEPS in your personal development. When you are OK with major uncertainty and you can REMAIN CALM, then you are advancing forward in your maturity! You are growing into a person with confidence. And once you OUTLAST enough storms, you will have found your true POWER!

Chapter 107: Cheating

While growing up in Johnstown, Pennsylvania, my mother taught me to TELL THE TRUTH, no matter what! Pure Christian honesty is what mom's parents DEMANDED of her decades previously and it was not different as mom and dad raised my sister, Kelli, and I. Never cheat! Never lie! Mom considered a cheater and a liar as one and the same. All cheaters are liars and all liars are cheaters! "You can never fool the person in the mirror!" was my mom's foundational words for a well-lived life. A cheater looks in the mirror and a cheater look back! Mom was honest to a fault!

For most of the Southern Tier, you will be ALL BY YOURSELF! It is a LONELY journey of self-discovery! Nobody is around watching you and it would be EASY to cheat, but I never even considered the possibility of dishonesty. If I was to succeed in my cross-country cycling escapade, then I would succeed by pedaling EVERY SINGE MILE of the Southern Tier Bicycle Route! It's NOT a cross-country ride if you put your bike in someone's truck and skip a mountain range or two!!!! For me, I was UNABLE to cheat even if I wanted to. Thanks to my mom's raising, I would instantly have a terrible gnawing pain of personal disappointment if I even considered the possibility of cheating! The irritating pain of dishonesty would eat away at me and never go away. The pain of deceit would be too much for me to handle! Cheating was out of the question for me!

In order to properly proclaim yourself as an authentic cross-country cyclist, you MUST pedal EVERY SINGLE MILE of your particular route! Don't take rides from passing cars. Don't jump on buses or trains and skip portions of the route. Don't even let another person pedal one mile in your place! Never succumb to temptation to settle for anything less than PEDALING across the ENTIRE country!

Even when I nearly collapsed from heat exhaustion and was saved by one of my many Southern Tier angels named Rudy, two days later when I recommenced my bike travels, I pedaled back to the EXACT PLACE of my heat-stricken demise and resumed my arduous trip from the exact point where Rudy transported my collapsed self. Every mile of my Southern Tier bike outing was pedaled by ME even if it meant back-tracing my route westward to redo eight miles of my trip!

Never cheating also includes your fidelity to your mate for those of you in a committed relationship or marriage. You are undertaking a VERY LONELY journey and it is possible a temptation could arise at some point. In my case, I had no temptations whatsoever. Seven hours of biking per day left me desiring only sleep at night. For me, I had no desire to meet new people, take sightseeing tours, or hang out in bars or clubs. My mission was to cross the country on a bicycle, nothing extra! Cheating or doing anything even remotely dishonest was NOT going to happen on my watch!

Riding your bicycle across the country is a MAJOR FEAT! It is a feat you can include on your resume for the rest of your life! When future employers, partners, investors, etc. read your biography, they WILL remember YOU! Anybody who pedals a bicycle across America is going to STAND OUT!

Biking across the country is an absurd achievement! Clearly you will be different and set far apart from your peers! For the rest of your life, you can tell anyone you ever meet about how you PEDALED a bicycle across the United States of America. Tingles just came down my head as I wrote this paragraph as I still shake my head in disbelief as it is hard for me to believe I actually pedaled a bicycle across the country ALONE, UNSUPPORTED, and CONTINUOUS! As far as I can decipher, the cross-country cycling thrill never leaves!!! The Southern Tier has become part of my SOUL!

When you make mention of your special cross-country biking achievement, you will be well received by others. People will gasp in utter disbelief. Others will be bewildered as they never considered such a feat to be possible. Without fail, you will get a lot of attention when you share your special accomplishment. There is just one caveat……. Make sure you actually did it! You cannot skip a single mile of your cross-country route!

Somewhere on the northern part of the iconic 2,200-mile Appalachian Trail walking path, there is a body of water where thru-hikers can either abandon the official trail-blaze and paddle a boat across the water and shorten the trail's walking distance by a few miles or they remain on the official walking path and forgo the dishonest shortcut. To my understanding, this particular lake is NOT part of the OFFICIAL Appalachian Trail and therefore I do NOT agree with a thru-hiker taking a boat and saving a few miles of walking! If the lake was part of the official A.T., then I would have no problem with the decision to cross the lake on boat, but to my knowledge, crossing the waterway in a boat is NOT the official trail and therefore indicates DISHONESTY!

While I was suffering from heat exhaustion on Day 4 in the Yuha Desert, I LUCKILY arrived at a commercial pesticide building in the middle of desert about eight miles from the closest town of Blythe, California. Rudy, the owner of the commercial pesticide business, packed me in ice, threw my bike in the back of his truck, and delivered me to a hotel in Blythe for the night.

When I resumed my trip two days later after taking the next day off, I did NOT start pedaling eastbound toward the Arizona border from my motel in Blythe. Instead, I pedaled backwards (westbound) on my bicycle at 4 a.m. in the morning to the EXACT PLACE where 36 hours previously Rudy saved me from dying from heat exhaustion. Upon arrival at the exact location at Rudy's pesticide company, I said a VERY SPECIAL prayer of thanks to God for keeping me alive and for all the nice people like Rudy whom helped me through my tribulations as I turned my bicycle around and resumed my eastbound pedal cadence as planned.

There was no person on Earth whom could have convinced me to CHEAT the Southern Tier! It was my destiny to pedal EVERY MILE of the official Southern Tier Bicycle Route NO MATTER WHAT! Even if I had to travel 8 miles backwards, I was doing all of it. Not a single mile was being left undone. Yes, Rudy DROVE me and my bicycle 8 miles in his fancy red truck to Blythe and maybe some other people would be ok continuing their trip eastbound from Blythe, but not me! For me, it was MANDATORY for me to travel 8 miles westerly backwards to resume my trip HONESTLY, just like my mom would do! And I'm glad I did! Otherwise, how could I live with myself? How could I be a cheater and call myself a bona-fide cross-country cyclist?

Freelancing your route by taking different roads than what is listed on your official route map is completely OK, but it is CHEATING if you get a ride and skip an entire portion of your route! If you PEDAL across the country, then you don't even get a ride for one mile! "Pedaling a bike across the country" is PEDALING a bike across the country. Vehicular transportation is UNACCEPTABLE!

As I approached Mobile, Alabama on my bicycle, I noticed on my Southern Tier map a large waterway spanning several miles. To my AMAZEMENT, I discovered the Southern Tier route actually guided me to board a ferry to cross Mobile Bay. Up to that point, I have followed the Southern Tier map exactly, but as I approached Mobile, Alabama, I considered taking the 40-mile longer detour route to go out around the bay as to NOT interrupt my continuous pedaling with an unsuspecting ferry boat ride. After much deliberation, I decided to stick to the official Southern Tier route as my map RECOMMENDED and take the ferry across Mobile Bay. Of course, my mom advised me to take the 40-mile detour as her father, George Cemo, certainly would have done, but I chose differently as I boarded the ferry and crossed Mobile Bay on boat as I felt in my heart that my choice was completely honest and proper as per the OFFICIAL map of the Southern Tier.

Technically, someone could claim I did NOT ride my bike across the country as per the 3-mile ferry ride, but the 3-mile ferry ride was part of the official Southern Tier route and I am GLAD I did it. The whole ferry experience and the bike ride crossing the 3-mile Gordon Persons Bridge on the way to the ferry was AMAZING! It was an experience I'll never forget! Later in this book, I'll tell you my story about my harrowing adventure with SEVERE WINDS while biking on the Gordon Persons Bridge as I approached the ferry at Mobile Bay!

When you are confronted with difficult choices, carefully consider your options. For me, nobody on Earth could have persuaded me to skip the 8 miles westward of Blythe, California, but for me to ride the ferry across Mobile Bay in Mobile, Alabama was completely OK as it was part of the officially sanctioned Southern Tier Bike Route. Both of my decisions were SOLID decisions and I do NOT have any regrets. Make certain you don't regret any decisions you make while on your special bicycle journey. If you find yourself torn about a particular decision, then consider the advice from the legendary poet, Jack Frost, and "Take the high road!"

Remember, one location you will NEVER find on a map is HONESTY. Only in your own mind and with your own CHARACTER will you arrive at the hallowed destination of HONESTY!

DAY 34: Crossing over the Mississippi River was a HUGE win for me as I felt my confidence increase!

DAY 34: Check out the HUGE berm and rumble strips. A cyclists DREAM!

Chapter 108: Kickstand

Believe it or not, not all bikes come with a kickstand! As far as I know, most road bikes, like the kind of bike used by cross-country cyclists will include a factory kickstand, but if a kickstand is NOT included, it is wise to have a kickstand installed!

A good kickstand is an essential part of a cross-country excursion. It is POSSIBLE to complete the lengthy trip without one, but I HIGHLY recommend having a kickstand! Otherwise, you will be forced to find something to lean your bike on as it is a MORTAL SIN to let your bike fall to the ground under any circumstance or for any reason!

My kickstand had some type of junky, tiny, plastic extension piece on it which eventually broke off and slightly shortened the overall length of my kickstand causing my bike to lean a bit too far toward the kickstand side on the left thus putting my bike at frequent risk of falling over. This particular manufacturing shortcoming caused me to find a slightly humped up area with a slightly higher elevation every time I parked my bike. Had I been smarter, I would have had another slightly longer kickstand installed in place of my problematic kickstand, but I made my handicapped kickstand work with a little extra exertion on my part each time I parked my bicycle.

Despite having a mildly inadequate kickstand, my bicycle NEVER fell over. For 45 days, including my 2 travel days home, my bike did NOT fall to the ground! One time I was having trouble parking my bike securely alongside a very lonely desert highway when a huge 18-wheel tractor trailer came out of nowhere as I was finishing taking a whiz. With a dash like an Olympian sprinter, I sprinted toward my bicycle as I KNEW the strong air force from the large truck would be enough to possibly crash my precious bike to the ground. Luckily, I got to my bike a moment before the truck passed and MY BABY was ok!

A proper kickstand should feel STRONG and HEAVY DUTY. It should not feel flimsy at all. Your kickstand should also be long enough as to lean only slightly to the left when you are on level ground. Your bike should NEVER be at risk of crashing to the ground. Also, make sure your kickstand isn't so long it keeps your bike too vertical as your bike would then be at risk of crashing to the other non-kickstand side on the right.

Despite the particulars of your kickstand, make sure to pay CLOSE ATTENTION when parking your bike. For me, I would CAREFULLY park my bike against road guardrails, trees, picnic tables, or the sides of buildings before I would even use my kickstand. Only when I absolutely had to use my kickstand without the additional support of a solid object to lean against would I use it! Sometimes I would even engage my kickstand when I leaned my bike against a solid structure as to provide even greater assurance my bike would remain upright as I was FANATICAL about keeping my bicycle in PRISTINE upright condition!

While parking a bicycle, it is rare to find a completely level surfaces. In most cases, it took me a minute or so to find the PERFECT spot where I felt like my bike was SOLID and my kickstand was situated in the most secure position as possible. Not once did I park my bike in a haphazard fashion. Even when the big tractor trailer truck was coming as I was finishing my whiz, it is most likely my bike would have remained upright, but I was a bit paranoid as I felt like if my bike crashed to the ground my epic cycling trip would be over! My bike and I were truly ONE and the same! To say we were married to each other would not be an exaggeration!

It wasn't until late in the evening on Day 45 as I was departing from the Amtrak Train Station in my hometown of Johnstown, Pennsylvania when my bike almost fell to the ground as my wife was pushing it down the exit ramp! As I noticed the first sign of my bicycle becoming unsteady, without a moment's hesitation, I caught my bike BEFORE it fell to the ground. It was like I suddenly tapped into some type of supernatural power connecting my mind to my bike. My bike was SAVED!!!

Of course, after my bike's near-fall I reminded Tink in a good-natured way about how I traveled over 3,000 miles without a single bike fall incident. We both laughed as we agreed the close-call incident was an ironic occurrence. Never let your bike fall to the ground!

DAY 34: I had a stone wedged in my shoe cleat for HUNDREDS of miles before I realized it! If your shoe does not click securely into your pedal, then check your shoe for a possible wedged stone! Don't wait for hundreds of miles like me!

Chapter 109: Cash

At 19 years old with very little experience and almost zero guidance, I opened my own gourmet coffee business. For 30 years I maintained my little business which consisted of several gourmet coffee trailer concession stands. Using my own van or motorhome, I would tow my commercial coffee stand trailers to big fairs and festivals along the eastern coast of the United States and sell cups of delicious specialty coffees to the general public.

On an interesting note, I opened my gourmet coffee business BEFORE the coffee giant, Starbucks, was even born! If I was smarter and more daring, I would have gone BIG like Starbucks, but I didn't! Even though my coffee concession business didn't rise to be a superstar in the corporate coffee world, I did make a good living selling cups of specialty coffee like cappuccino and espresso! "The Killer" was the most popular drink as my great friend, Eric Bowser, created the epic drink while helping me out at the South Florida Fair in West Palm Beach, Florida long ago.

Anyways, selling coffee at fairs and festivals was a "cash business" which regularly involved me walking out of the fair late at night with thousands of dollars jammed in my pockets as I headed for my van to go to sleep. My dad being a rather wise man often warned me to "Keep your money in more than one place." Dad figured if somebody ever robbed my van, maybe they would only take the cash in the one location and not realize there was a second cash location. Dad's cash theory made good sense to me!

The same is true on your bike trip. Use my dad's wisdom and store your cash in more than one place. For your cross-country travels, you should probably start with about $500.00 or more in cash and you should keep your cash in two different locations. One cash location should be located deep within the inside zippered compartment of your pannier bag inside a plain envelope possibly with some type of misleading label on the outside like the printed word "Directions" or "Packing List." Your other cash location should be located inside your wallet which should be stored inside of your waist pouch. Don't worry, there will be an entire chapter in this book dedicated to the importance of having a waist pouch.

In addition to your two different locations of cash, you should also have a debit card stashed away inside a remote location inside your pannier bags inside your same spare cash envelope. A debit card will allow you to access any one of the hundreds of ATM money machines located on or within a short distance of your cross-country route. With each successive year, it seems our economy is moving closer and closer to a non-cash system, but for now I still advise to carry about $500.00 in cash and to have a debit card to get more cash if needed. On my cross-country travels, I encountered MANY vendors who accepted ONLY cash.

Lastly, make sure you have 2 credit cards. One credit card goes in your wallet and the other credit card is stashed away safe and securely inside the same envelope responsible for containing your spare cash and debit card. Most of my purchases were made with my credit card, but I did encounter many stores where cash was needed or seemed to be most appropriate.

In summary, carry about $200.00 in cash inside your wallet and pack away about $300.00 cash inside one of your pannier bags. Also, have a debit card and credit card inside your pannier bags and have 1 credit card inside your wallet. The overall plan is to keep your cash and credit cards in separate locations as to minimize your chances of suffering a trip-ending loss or a devastating theft of all of your financial resources all at once. As long as you have your wallet with cash and cards and a separate location with your spare cash and cards, you will be about as safe as you could expect to be.

Throughout my entire trip, NOT ONCE did somebody get into my stuff or even give me a hint of suspicion. As far as I'm aware, my bicycle and gear were completely undisturbed for the duration of my entire adventure! Of course, people get robbed every day in America, but my experience was not so! For the most part, I did not feel at risk of theft. As my bike travels progressed and I gained some confidence, there were times I didn't even lock my bike when I went inside a store, but I do not recommend you being so careless!

DAY 35: Crossing into the MAGNIFICENT state of Mississippi marked a SUPREME win for me as my ALIAS is "Johnny Flick-a-Terd Humdinger" and I live in MISSISSIPPI with all of my family. Every name in our family begins with the letter J - Jasmine, Jeremiah, Jacob, Jezabel, Jessie, and Jethro. We ALL have the SAME "Flick-a-Terd" middle name and "Humdinger" last names! JFH rules!

Chapter 110: Thinking

The MOST DANGEROUS and most likely obstacle to END your dream of a successful cross-country bike traverse will NOT be found on your physical bike route! Your greatest nemesis will certainly be your OWN THOUGHTS!

By now, we all have heard about the many benefits of positive thinking and we are well aware of the many drawbacks of negative thinking. So, instead of me rehashing the importance of positive thinking and the potential destructive results of negative thinking, I will simply share some of my own strategies I used during my bike travels to help keep my own thoughts POSITIVE enough to maintain my pedal stroke day after day without abandoning my dedicated route!

As I traveled the isolated roads of the Southern Tier all by myself with no support, continuously day after day, I had a lot of time to think. Like most people, my thoughts seemed to be drawn to the negative and I found myself asking myself NEGATIVE "what if" questions like, "What if I get too tired and I cannot pedal anymore? What if heavy rains come and flood my route? What if a hurricane strikes? What if I get lost? What if my bike gets stolen? What if my bike breaks down in the middle of the desert at night? What if there is no cell service? What if I get bit by a rattlesnake? What if I get run over by a vehicle? What if the motel or campground is full? What if I get sick with COVID-19 or worse? What if I lose my maps? What if I get injured and cannot continue?"

As these negative thoughts and many others like them jetted through my brain on a consistent basis, I chose to PRAY as I pedaled along the roadway. Being raised a devout Catholic and having a great devotion and love for Christianity, I decided to pray the "Our Father", "Hail Mary", and "Glory Be." In another chapter of this book, I dedicated the whole chapter to the importance of prayer so I will only briefly mention it here as it relates to overcoming negative thinking and tapping into the many benefits of positive thinking.

As I repeated these prayers over and over for hours at a time day after day, my mind would settle and I would feel stable. Without my prayers, negative thoughts would have filled my intellectual void VERY quickly. So, anytime I felt my mind drifting, I would consistently return to my stable place of prayer and in a short amount of time, everything would be fine. When prayer occupied my mind, I had NO ROOM for negativity. It was a simple and AMAZINGLY effective cross-country cycling strategy!!!

As I write this book trying my best to share with you the strategies and techniques most responsible for me finishing the Southern Tier, I would list prayer at the TOP of my list! Without my daily and ongoing prayer, I would NOT have finished! The Southern Tier was much TOO TOUGH for me to handle without prayer.

Although I was raised a Catholic and I LOVE Catholicism, I have GREAT RESPECT for all of the particular sectors of Christianity as well as ALL world religions! Although religion is very important to me, I would consider myself to be more of a SPIRITUAL guy than a RELIGIOUS type. To me, spirituality CANNOT be condensed into any one religion as I believe the same God works through ALL of us. God is not any more or less amazing despite the particular name attached to a certain religion. Having great respect for the differences in each religion, I feel we are all praising the SAME wonderful creator whom I can guarantee you is very much ALIVE and well all throughout the Southern Tier!

While riding the Southern Tier, I felt closer to God than at any other time in my life. Despite looking around and not seeing anyone, I sensed I was NOT alone! It was like my prayers ACTIVATED the DORMANT powers of the Southern Tier Bicycle Route. As I pedaled along, I could feel the spiritual power in the changing landscapes unfolding as I passed by. Regularly, my skin would tingle and I'd feel chills on my sweated body as I traveled through the intricate, awe-inspiring lands. And this same spiritual energy was magnified to an even greater degree when I rode through the darkness as I did most early mornings as it seemed as though the darkness AMPLIFIED the vibrations of the land as it yearned for the rising sun. There was clearly spiritual POWER present along the Southern Tier route!

Riding ALONE seemed to give me a special spiritual access, reserved ONLY for solo riders! If I was accompanied by even one other person, I'm SURE my spiritual experience would have been diminished greatly! Only in the silence of ONE would the POWER of the landscape share the greatest glimpse of its mysterious POWER! Something pure and pristine was emitted from the land throughout the day as I invoked its presence through my prayers. A sense of peace would settle in my mind calming my negativity. It was this feeling of PEACE that prompted me to continue to ride through the early morning darkness even after I had passed through the scorching hot desert and no longer had a weather-related reason to continue to ride in the much cooler early morning hours. It was the special spiritual FEELINGS prompted by the very early morning riding time which caused me to continue to spin my pedals through the darkness as to gain access to these special spiritual feelings.

As I continue to write about a spiritual phenomenon that CANNOT be described with words, it is my hope you will get on your bike and see for yourself what I mean. It was during those very early mornings on the Southern Tier when I first discovered I was NOT really on a bike trip! The Southern Tier was my spiritual journey, a special process in which my thoughts were purified and made SIMPLE while slowly revealing more of my hidden manhood. I wasn't really traveling on a bicycle as much as I was traveling in my spirit. And as I incorporated prayer into the natural beauty and power of the land, there was an amazing sense of peace and well-being surrounding me and delivering me as I pedaled mile after mile completely vulnerable while riding my bike through the desert and beyond.

In between my many prayers, I also spent MANY HOURS speaking homemade AFFIRMATIONS as to assist the programming of my mind and to trigger my default thoughts to be MORE POSITIVE. Some of my homemade affirmations included the following...

> I am strong and healthy.
> I am one with God and God is everything.
> God is delivering me.
> I am calm.
> May God's will be done.
> Rest, Comfort, Balance.

Affirmations should be short and they should be present tense as NOW is the only time and NOW is the only place change can occur. Affirmations should be spoken out loud verbally where appropriate and high energy should be infused into your words. "Speaking" your affirmations inside your head is also very effective and was my primary method used on my bike journey. Most of all, your affirmations should be MEANINGFUL to you!!!! Finding the perfect short phrase containing your own words or borrowing one or more of my affirmations will create a RHYTHM in your thinking allowing you to press on through a difficult bicycle route.

Affirmations are interesting as they don't seem to do much at first, but eventually after hundreds or thousands of repetitions as was the case for me, the words eventually became MEANINGFUL! After a certain number of repetitions, my words crossed over a critical mass and formulated a strong mental pattern in my ailing mind. The words seemingly came to life and created a VERY STRONG thought pattern keeping me healthy and strong amidst a world of doubt! Repeating the affirmations listed above and many other affirmations just like them settled my mind and allowed POSITIVE THOUGHTS to rule my conscious mind during pivotal moments on the unforgiving Southern Tier!

Prayer and affirmations gave me the necessary peace to OVERCOME the CULTURE SHOCK of the Southern Tier Bicycle Route and remain on route. As I pedaled up into the mountains ascending out of San Diego and then down into the desert, there were times I felt engulfed with fear. My prayers and affirmations reminded me about who I was and how BIG was my God! Through consistent repetition, my mind settled enough to keep me pedaling. Without a passionate commitment to prayer and affirmation, it's really no wonder why SO MANY aspiring cross-country cyclists quit before their third day! Don't underestimate your thoughts! A mind filled with NEGATIVITY can EASILY be enough to end your epic bike crusade. You can either program your own thoughts with prayer and affirmations or you can let DOUBT fill your mind and weaken your soul as you look for the next flight home!

Be ready with some special affirmation language of your own. Develop a meaningful phrase or two and write the phrases on a card. Put the card in your handlebar bag so you can glance down and see the words in print. Have your affirmations READY on Days 1, 2, and 3 as these first few days will be your highest probability of quitting!

As I pedaled out of San Diego, I kept thinking about my mom's words, "It's OK if you come home now. You did enough!" Mom was right, I was a champion for flying to San Diego with my bike in a box, assembling my bike all by myself at the airport, and then pedaling over to the Pacific Ocean for my start. Although I was a champion for making it to the starting line, I felt like I was called to do more. Instead of quitting, I pushed forward, pedal stroke by pedal stroke, repeating my prayers and affirmations in DESPERATE fashion as to maintain reasonable progress. My prayers mixed with positive affirming words SAVED me from going home early and eventually introduced me to one of the most intriguing persons I ever met...... MYSELF!!!!

As you are preparing your lists and packing your gear, don't neglect to invest considerable time into your THOUGHT PLANNING! Make a list of special affirmations. Carry along distinct Bible verses, poems, or quotes. Fill your mind with meaningful passages capable of inspiring your core spirit. You might even decide to make your own HOMEMADE audio recording! Whatever you do, be ready because you are going to need these positive reminders! Don't underestimate the heavy-duty emotions you will feel during the first week of your bike travels on the Southern Tier!

On Day 2, I ALMOST turned around and pedaled back to the San Diego Airport. With tears in my eyes, I felt like I couldn't go on. The hills were too long and the culture shock, lack of sleep, lack of food consumption, homesickness, sore body parts, and a wondering mind almost resulted in another "Southern Tier Fatality." But as I leaned on my bike crying as I cursed myself for another life failure, one more time I felt the divine calling. The unnerving spiritual presence of God on the Southern Tier was calling me to press on! And even though I did not consider myself capable, it was clear God knew otherwise. With tears in my eyes, I got back on my bicycle and continued to plow ahead for ONE MORE DAY.....

Chapter 111: The Southern "Tear"

The AMAZING bicycle route spanning the southern portion of the United States has been appropriately named "The Southern Tier," but the official name is really a play on words as the REAL NAME of the route should be "The Southern Tear" as this route WILL make you cry! More than a few times, tears rolled down my cheeks ultimately splashing on the hard Southern Tier pavement below. To say the Southern Tier cross-country ride is INTENSE doesn't even come close to defining the level of power stored in this legendary bicycle route!

If you are making your first cross-country bicycle attempt, then you CANNOT be completely ready for what awaits you. Reading this book and every other book of its kind will still NOT leave you prepared for the tribulations ahead! There are countless dangers and real problems along the way in which no single author could ever completely reveal. One or more issues are bound to BREAK you, thus the title of this book, EPIC FAIL! The "bike across America" journey is REALLY hard! Statistically, your SOLO attempt is destined to fail, but there exists a chance for success if you can handle some VERY INTENSE emotions along the way!

Many would-be cross-country cyclists make the COMMON mistake of classifying their cross-country bike ride as a physical and mental event when it is actually more of an emotional and spiritual event! As you prepare for the adventure of your lifetime, don't make this crucial mistake! Preparing only for a physical and mental event while neglecting the CRUCIAL emotional and spiritual preparations will likely END your trip QUICKLY! Only by giving the necessary emotional and spiritual aspects of your bike trip due attention will you have a chance of completing your cross-country pursuit.

As I pedaled out of San Diego into the mountains on Day 2, I ALMOST turned around and headed westbound back to the San Diego Airport as it felt like my body and mind were being CRUSHED, not so much physically by the seemingly endless ascent, but rather by the RAW emotions flooding my nervous system. At one point on Day 2, I recall a moment when my emotions hit a high threshold of OVERLOAD prompting me to suddenly STOP my bicycle in the middle of the barren asphalt road at a non-scheduled rest break as I seemingly lost the power to pedal. My legs REFUSED to apply anymore force as my body and mind seemingly LOCKED itself as I KNEW I had FAILED! My trip was OVER!

My ONLY saving grace was the MELTDOWN I experienced in the middle of the solitary road as I contemplated all the AGGRAVATION involved in having to re-package my bike in a box, book a new flight home, and make arrangements for someone to pick me up at the Pittsburgh Airport. Only after considering all the hassles involved in going back home did my legs finally seem to unlock and allow me to mount my bike and continue my monotonous pedal strokes.

Throughout this book I give various ideas about how I handled my many untamed thoughts and raw emotions as the Southern "Tear" is VERY emotional! The emotional intensity packed within the esteemed route is MORE THAN ENOUGH to take you out! Don't neglect to prepare for the emotional and spiritual components of this magnanimous bicycle adventure.

Emotions are triggered directly from thoughts and therefore your THOUGHTS are the MOST DANGEROUS obstacle you will face on the Southern Tear! The thoughts inside your own head will cause you to "tap out" faster than any other hindrance along the way!

Surprisingly, even more severe than my thought-driven emotions were the spiritual power saturated in the glorious Southern Tier Route. Within the first two days, I had already been overwhelmed with mini-doses of spiritual experiences causing goose bumps and tingles all over my body. The whole Southern Tier spiritual experience was so much more than I was prepared to encounter!

For now, accept the FACT that SIGNIFICANT emotional and spiritual forces will be present on any epic bicycle route. Be ready to face these forces as they CANNOT be disregarded! In other chapters in this book, I will ATTEMPT to offer more ideas to handle these overpowering spiritual forces, but for now, realize tears are part of the heartfelt Southern Tier process! It might take MORE THAN everything you have to complete the biking journey across America!

If you happen to be one of the lucky SOLO cyclists who somehow overcome the HUNDREDS of potentially trip-ending obstacles as outlined in this book, then you might find yourself heading eastbound ten miles from the Atlantic Ocean at Jacksonville Beach, Florida on the verge of completion. Riding the last 10 miles of my 3,000-mile bike journey was the most incredible HIGH I ever experienced. A whole new set of tears was discovered as I completed the most fulfilling adventure of my life!

Chapter 112: Example or Warning

Pedaling a bicycle across the country is an activity most people will never even consider! Most people would proclaim the demanding cycling endeavor to be an IMPOSSIBLE pursuit! Congratulations are in order to anyone who even considers taking on such a grueling and uncommon mission of self-discovery! As for each person with a fully-loaded bicycle whom arrives at the start of a major bike route, you deserve a parade in your honor! And for those few individuals who go ALL THE WAY, you are truly INCREDIBLE!

During the dozens of times when I severely doubted myself on the Southern Tier, I would ask, "What am I doing out here?" With little hesitation, my mind would reply, "Because you are STUPID!" It was in those moments when I needed to regroup and refocus my mind as to exactly why I was pedaling my bicycle in this vast wilderness expanse. My two primary reasons for taking on the Southern Tier were……

>#1 What it would make of me as a person.
>#2 To be a positive EXAMPLE for others.

As a human being, it was very important to me to provide a positive example of possibility to others. Being a regular, non-celebrity guy easily allows other people to relate to me. If I can do it, then so can the others who are watching me! By taking the same actions and thinking the same thoughts as I did, anyone of reasonable physical and mental ability could attain my same results!

Throughout my dozens of years studying and paying very close attention to human behavior, success, goal attainment, and personal development, I have classified people in one of two ways. People are either an EXAMPLE for others to follow or they are a WARNING for others to avoid!

At a very young age, I felt inspired to live my BEST life! As I developed throughout the years, I have followed many different paths of success and some have resulted in great achievements and most others resulted in FAILURE, but I am still excited about improving myself and stretching myself into a better person and as long as I am still alive, I believe God still has something special for me to do!

As I follow my various callings in life, it is of the utmost importance for me to be a positive EXAMPLE for others to emulate! Regularly reminding myself of this important personal value pulled me through many challenging moments on the Southern Tier when I was at HIGH risk of abandoning the difficult journey at those down times when I slipped back into a grim negative pattern of thinking.

When you are on your bike ALL ALONE with nobody else in your immediate vicinity to encourage you, there will be more than a few times when you will begin to question yourself. You might even wonder like me, "What the HECK am I doing out here?" Riding your bicycle day after day in the middle of nowhere will certainly provoke some DEEP questions in which you must be prepared to answer.

Most days, I had to remind myself of my two primary reasons why I exchanged my old, comfortable life for a new PAINFUL life consisting of relentless pedaling. And even though it felt ABSURD at times to be pedaling a bicycle across the country, I would continue as my REASONS for taking on the grueling cross-country challenge were inspiring to me. Reason #1 involved my own personal self-development and reason #2 involved my serving as a positive example to others. Both of my primary reasons at various times during my bike travels compelled me to continue my pedal strokes when I was severely tempted to do otherwise.

A goal of pedaling a bicycle across the country sounds really exciting when you are at home resting in your relaxing evening chair surrounded by many of your daily comforts, but riding your bike across the country is totally different when you are faced with a headwind in the middle of the desert and it doesn't even seem like you are moving! Times like these are when you must remind yourself about WHY you are pursuing such a strange objective. Frederick Nietzsche, the German scholar and philosopher once said, "If you have a big enough WHY, you will find the HOW." Nietzsche seemed to be reminding us about the importance of having one or more compelling reasons as to WHY we are doing a task, then in most cases, we will figure out the means to accomplish the task IF our "WHY is big enough."

Even though I did not feel like pedaling on many days, I continued to spin my pedals around as I knew my disciplined efforts would eventually result in a level of personal development second to none and my efforts would also serve as a positive EXAMPLE to my loved ones and maybe even to YOU. Without finishing my bike ride, I would NOT have had the credibility to write this book or to proclaim myself as a bona-fide "cross-country cyclist."

Talking about riding a bicycle across the country really doesn't mean anything unless you actually spin your pedals around and DO IT! Doing the task is what makes the MAN! TALKING the task is NOTHING at all! What really counts in life is what you DO, not what you SAY!

The Southern Tier or any other long-distance biking event is achieved or failed in the GRIND of each day. Most days I could probably think of about 20 other things I'd rather be doing than spinning the pedals of my bicycle round and round, but I REPLACED my useless thinking patterns with more positive thinking patterns as I imagined the many people my long bike ride would eventually impact!

Most of the time, pedaling the famed Southern Tier was NOT fun, but it was certainly WORTH IT! Pedaling an epic bike route can be the MOST FULFILLING experience of your life if you can make it through the daily grind by maintaining your mental focus on what really matters to you! Keep your personal goals close in mind as to keep yourself motivated daily to complete the quest! Remind yourself about setting a positive example for your children, grandchildren, and great-grandchildren for generations to come. Who knows, maybe you will be the SPARK for someone in your sphere of influence or even possibly someone in your own family tree to do something significant with their life?

DAY 35: After 35 days of biking, I was lean and muscular! In all of my life, I never looked so GOOD and felt so GOOD!!!

Chapter 112: Songs

Each of us has specific types of music and particular songs that inspire and motivate us. Certain songs and familiar beats or rhythms have the power to quickly alter our states of mind. As I rode the Southern Tier, specific songs would replay in my mind. Throughout the 1,000 miles of desert, there were two Jon Bon Jovi songs that seemed to capture the essence of the magnificent Southern Tier desert and gel DEEP within my soul. "Wanted Dead or Alive" and "Blaze of Glory" replayed in my mind at regular intervals as it felt like the two Bon Jovi songs were somehow indicative of my solo, desert wilderness bicycle travels. To this day, I'm still brought back to the Southern Tier in my mind each time I hear one of these brilliant inspiring songs.

Although songs have an undeniable influence on our precious states of mind, songs can be DANGEROUS as well! In my opinion, it is a GRAVE mistake to rely on songs to set your state of mind for the day. The precious morning hours of your ride are better left to silence as the landscape around you will be speaking to you and you don't want to miss a word! Listening to music during this sacred pre-dawn and early post-dawn morning time can be uplifting, but it should NOT be a consistent daily habit!

My music rule while grinding out miles on the Southern Tier was simple. No music until I had AT LEAST 50% or more of my targeted daily mileage completed. For me, music was a REWARD for a hard day's work! Remember, you DIED as you started your cross-country bike adventure and in this NEW LIFE you have a NEW JOB. Your job title is "A PEDALER!" Your daily purpose is to spin your bike pedals round and round stopping every ten miles for scheduled breaks. Your job is NOT to listen to music!

One particular day I broke my music rule and listened to my favorite music playlist on Spotify in the morning and although I greatly enjoyed the music, doing so seemed to CONTAMINATE my overall mindset for the day causing me to be very GRUMPY! It was almost as if enjoying the music too early in the day caused me to forget about my prayers, affirmations, and the power-packed landscapes surrounding me resulting in a distorted and convoluted negative mindset.

Considering the negative ramifications experienced by me seemingly caused by my excessive early morning music enjoyment, I quickly decided it was better for me to WAIT for my music gratification until AFTER my mind and spirit had been first-filled with prayers, affirmations, and the proper attentiveness to the gorgeous physical landscapes encapsulating me. Late afternoon music after obtaining at least half of my daily miles DEFINITELY worked best for me! Consistently listening to music in the morning could have been a MAJOR disruption had I continued the negative habit!

As you prepare for your cross-country pursuit, take special care to create an appropriate music playlist. Include a variety of songs to uplift your soul. Just the right DOSE of inspiring music has a way of FINE TUNING your mindset and clearing out problematic thinking. Having your playlist accessible on your cell phone through the Spotify, Pandora, Apple, or any other musical phone app will give you a powerful and automatic way to get yourself back into a powerful state of mind. My late afternoon music gave me a "second wind" on numerous occasions, but be careful as TOO MUCH music any time of the day will have a NEGATIVE effect on YOU!!!!! BALANCE your music time! Make sure your prayers and affirmations take precedent over your music!

Using music as a reward is another way to motivate yourself to grind out those necessary miles in the morning hours as you look forward to listening to your prearranged playlist in the late afternoon. Most afternoons I would glance at my Garmin GPS watch and say to myself, "Only 15 more miles and I get to listen to some music!" Having daily short-term goals as such helps to make the miles go by faster as you slowly make your way across the country on your bicycle.

DAY 36: A splendid Mississippi sunrise on a lightly-traveled road with no berm.

"Wanted Dead or Alive"
Jon Bon Jovi

It's all the same
Only the names will change
Everyday
It seems we're wasting away

Another place
Where the faces are so cold
I drive all night
Just to get back home

I'm a cowboy
On a steel horse I ride
I'm wanted
Dead or alive
Wanted
Dead or alive

Sometimes I sleep
Sometimes it's not for days
The people I meet
Always go their separate ways

Sometimes you tell the day
By the bottle that you drink
And times when you're alone
All you do is think

I'm a cowboy
On a steel horse I ride
I'm wanted
(Wanted)
Dead or alive
Wanted
(Wanted)
Dead or alive

Ohh alright
Ohh

Oh, I'm a cowboy
On a steel horse I ride
I'm wanted
(Wanted)
Dead or alive

When I walk these streets
A loaded six string on my back
I play for keeps
Cause I might not make it back

I've been everywhere
(Ohh, yea)
Still I'm standin' tall
I've seen a million faces
And I've rocked them all

Cause I'm a cowboy
On a steel horse I ride
I'm wanted
(Wanted)
Dead or alive

I'm a cowboy
I got the night on my side
And I'm wanted
(Wanted)
Dead or alive
And I'm right
(And I'm right)
Dead or alive
I still drive
(I still drive)
Dead or alive

Dead or alive
Dead or alive
Dead or alive
Dead or alive

"Blaze of Glory"
Jon Bon Jovi

I wake up in the morning
And I raise my weary head
I've got an old coat for a pillow
And the earth was last night's bed
I don't know where I'm going
Only God knows where I've been
I'm a devil on the run
A six-gun lover
A candle in the wind
Yeah!

When you're brought into this world
They say you're born in sin
Well at least they gave me something
I didn't have to steal to have to win
Well, they tell me that I'm wanted
Yeah, I'm a wanted man
I'm colt in your stable
I'm what Cain was to Abel
Mr. catch me if you can

I'm going down in a blaze of glory
Take me now but know the truth
I'm going out in a blaze of glory
Lord, I never drew first
But I drew first blood
I'm no one son
Call me young gun

You ask about my conscience
And I offer you my soul
You ask if I'll grow to be a wise man
Well, I ask if I'll grow old
You ask me if I know love
And what it's like to sing songs in the rain

Well, I've seen love come
And I've seen it shot down
I've seen it die in vain

Shot down in a blaze of glory
Take me now but know the truth
Cause I'm going down in a blaze of glory
Lord, I never drew first
But I drew first blood
I'm the devil's son
Call me young gun
Yeah!

Last night I go to bed
I pray the Lord my soul to keep
No I ain't looking for forgiveness
But before I'm six foot deep
Lord, I got to ask a favor
And I'll hope you'll understand
Cause I've lived life to the fullest
Let this boy die like a man
Starring down the bullet
Let me make my final stand

Shot down in a blaze of glory
Take me now but know the truth
I'm going out in a blaze of glory
Lord, I never drew first
But I drew first blood
And I'm no one's son
Call me a young gun
I'm a young gun
Young gun, yeah, yeah, yeah
Young gun

Chapter 113: Identification Band

Being very frugal and even downright parsimonious at times, I almost skipped spending $20 on an identification band, but my wife did NOT! Without my prior approval, Tink took it upon herself to buy me an amazing identification band which fit perfectly on my wrist. The ID band included my name and home address as well as two other emergency contact phone numbers, my wife's phone number and my dad's phone number. If worst came to worst, Tink made sure emergency personnel would at least have an address to ship my dead body back home!

An emergency identification band probably won't cause you to pedal any faster nor will it help to prevent any accidents, but it WILL give you and your loved ones back home some peace of mind in the case something terrible was to happen to you. At least the emergency first-responders would know who you are and whom to call as to notify of your specific condition and whereabouts.

EVERY time you take a bike ride, even if the trip is only 3 miles down the road, you SHOULD wear your identification band! Your ID band should be AUTOMATIC, just like your helmet! You never know when something could happen and it is important to be prepared! An ID band takes only seconds to attach as most ID bands hook back through a small loop and then Velcro securely around the wrist to secure a comfortable and non-intrusive fit.

Each day when I arrived at my destination, I would take off my wrist band and Velcro the band to the handlebars of my bicycle. By doing so, it made it very difficult for me to forget to attach the ID band back to my wrist prior to starting the next day's ride. Plus, it was nearly impossible for me to lose my ID band as the only way it could be lost would be if the Velcro somehow gave loose which was NOT going to happen!

In addition to attaching my identification to my bike, I would also secure my biking gloves to the outside of my handlebars in an open way as to allow the sweat to dry overnight. I'd also attach my helmet to the frame of my bike as to keep all of my biking accessories at the POINT OF USE! At all times, I was thinking ahead of myself as to keep all of my gear and belongings in perfect placement.

As a cross-country cyclist, you will either NEED to be an organized person or you will have to develop yourself into an organized person. It is super easy to forget necessary items as you pack and leave on any particular morning. Without a thought, you could easily forget your biking gloves, helmet, or ID band.

During the first week of my odyssey, I had a flat tire at 4:30 a.m. in the middle of the Yuha Desert in California amidst complete darkness with no one around except the sound of howling coyotes on both sides of the road seemingly closing in on me. This particular harrowing moment was one of the FEW TIMES on my trip when I got frazzled as I haphazardly gathered my belongings after fixing my flat tire in the dark and I LOST one set of my biking gloves and my sunscreen!

Chapter 114: Soul

My beautiful and charismatic daughter, Stacey Hockensmith, often comments on her "soul" while referring to REALLY DEEP topics. When Stacey mentions her soul, something MONUMENTAL is about to come out of her mouth!

There is a HUGE difference between taking an epic bike ride with a group of people and taking an epic bike ride ALONE! Nothing is wrong with taking an epic ride with another rider or even a group of riders as I HIGHLY recommend it, but there is something VERY SPECIAL about taking an epic SOLO bike ride!

When I started my solo bike excursion, I assumed the journey across the country would be mostly about biking, but I was wrong! To my dismay, the Southern Tier was the MOST SPIRITUAL event of MY LIFE! In my wildest dreams, I never imagined such a deep connection to my SOUL! In similar fashion to my semi-dramatic daughter, Stacey, I quickly discovered a glimpse into the magnanimous depth of my own soul!

As I pedaled mile after mile through mostly lonely roads, I met many interesting people, but the most interesting person I met by far was MYSELF! All the years prior to the Southern Tier, I thought I knew myself, but for 43 days while pedaling my bicycle along the southern portion of the United States, I finally met a small portion of my SOUL, my real AUTHENTIC self!

Maybe it was the consistent rigorous daily physical exertion? Or maybe it was the uncontaminated, pure, raw power of the pre-dawn mornings as I rode through the darkness sensing the world coming alive? Or maybe it was the feeling of God and his angels protecting me as I pedaled across this beautiful country praying incessantly? Or maybe it was "dying" and leaving my "former life" behind as I began my "NEW LIFE?" Or maybe it was simply all those sausage, egg, and cheese breakfast sandwiches from McDonalds? I don't know exactly what was responsible for the introduction to my soul, but it was nothing less than MIRACULOUS! NEVER before had I ever gone so DEEP within myself as to seemingly catch a faint glimpse of my soul!

Riding your bike across the United States or across any other massive body of land can be life transforming! As I was pedaling along, I thought numerous times about how this bike journey would be perfect for someone whom was considering suicide.

Suicide is basically killing your PHYSICAL body like many desperate, mentally ill human beings wish to do, but to die FULLY, there must also be a spiritual and emotional death in addition to the basic physical demise! And I don't know any better way to DIE fully than to face the pure terror of the Southern Tier alone for 43 days. Along the Southern Tier, there WILL be a partial death of your past self, but there will also be an emergence of a new self, more capable than you ever imagined!

For me, the Southern Tier was the best therapy I ever received. My personal transformation while pedaling the Southern Tier was so INTENSE I am STILL processing many of my jagged emotions and revealing flashbacks released during my epic bike ride, emotions stored deep within my most guarded locker of my soul. It was in my soul where it felt like a wick on a stick of dynamite was lit causing a great explosion completely dismantling my most secretive and vulnerable lockbox of insecurities. During the Southern Tier, I literally EXAMINED a portion of my soul!

Most aspiring cross-country cyclists are seeking an amazing experience and the Southern Tier will not disappoint, but this book is not about acquiring an amazing experience. EPIC FAIL is more about attaining a TRANSFORMATIONAL EXPERIENCE as you will NOT be the same person when you return! Even if you don't finish the demanding cross-country adventure in one attempt, the personal transformation will remain significant! You will be CHANGED!

When I use the word "Soul," I am referring to the most BASIC part of you, the REAL you! It is everything about you, especially all the emotions and experiences you have been hiding. Your soul is your perfect reflection back to God. It is all the qualities, good and bad, that make you who you are! Your soul is your uninhibited self! It is your completely naked and true self. Your soul is the REAL YOU! Analyzing your real uncontaminated self is quite a privilege! It might even be our purpose for living!?

Riding your bicycle alone and unsupported across the great country of the United States of America could give you much more than you bargained for! Taking inventory of your soul and figuring out what kind of person you really are is quite a bonus! Seeing yourself as you really are as per your SOUL can enlighten your thoughts and trigger newfound motivations and life goals, all of which you can take with you when you return back home! Prepare yourself for the most AWAKENING spiritual experience of your life! Prepare to meet your soul!!! Welcome to the Southern Tier!

Chapter 115: Suffering

After listening to several of my Southern Tier stories upon the conclusion of my epic bike tour, my great lifetime friend, Michael T. Wolf, asked me, "Do you enjoy suffering?" upon which I was stunned. As I tried to answer his intriguing question, words would not come out of my mouth. After stammering around searching for a semi-intelligent answer, I finally replied with some lame type of generic response, but I knew there was a deeper, much more accurate answer inside of me with regard to Mike's sincere and ingenious question! There was clearly something special and significant about suffering, but I wasn't exactly sure what it was!

Taking a continuous, daily cross-country bicycle ride involves plenty of suffering! Your hands and fingers will go numb at times. Your neck will get stiff and sore. Your back will likely hurt. Your legs will ACHE. Your knees could develop sharp pains. Your hips might get super-tight. You will get cramps in your calves. And at times, your whole body will feel like you were run over by one of the THOUSANDS of tractor trailer trucks prevalent along the Southern Tier Bicycle Route!

Although the physical pains of long-term cycling can be severe as is evidenced in the previous paragraph, much worse suffering is the emotional pain. Certainly, by Day 2, you will find yourself pedaling along and suddenly a VERY POWERFUL thought will enter your mind, "What the HECK am I doing out here?" You will feel homesick. You will miss your spouse, kids, parents, pets, and friends. Surprisingly, you might even miss your JOB!!! All of these thoughts and many more will team up together and try to convince you to ABANDON your "crazy" bike expedition!

Any truly GREAT achievement in life, like riding your bike for thousands of miles continuously across the country, will require very high PAIN TOLERATION! One of the BIGGEST mistakes you could possibly make is to EXPECT your bicycle ride to be comfortable and EASY! The cross-country ride you have your sights set on will be one of the TOUGHEST tasks you will ever attempt in your entire life! A cross-country bicycle trip is NOT easy and you will feel much more than a little bit of pain.

Most days, you will feel similar to a martyr back in biblical days as my amateur biblical understanding of a martyr is a person who CHOOSES to suffer for their cause. Although most martyrs suffered to the point of death in biblical times as they championed their cause along their pathway to purity and fulfillment, you would be wise to expect a similar type of emotional pain as you endure your trials and tribulations along the Southern Tier! To make matters worse, you will SUFFER without being paid one cent and without any publicity! It might be most appropriate to refer to yourself as a "VOLUNTEER SUFFERER!"

In no way am I some freakish type of person who seeks out suffering, although

Mike Wolf and several other loved ones would possibly disagree, I do BELIEVE in the power of suffering! Suffering constitutes HOLDING POWER. Holding on when times are difficult is a quality capable of taking your overall life character to a whole new level! Today, it seems like less and less people have a strong sense of holding power, determination, perseverance, or whatever other synonym you wish to use. Today, most people want to take the "quick and easy" route instead of the "long and hard" route. Most people want to AVOID suffering and pain at all costs, but I'm "old school" as I believe a reasonable amount of suffering and pain is necessary for positive growth.

If you have lived a sheltered life shielded from pain while having your needs met instantly, then you better stop and consider what you are getting yourself into by attempting a grueling cross-country bicycle expedition. Riding a bicycle cross-country is PAINFUL! You will SUFFER! It is hard. A cross-country bike ride is NOT pleasurable! Much of the time, you will NOT be enjoying yourself! If you have expectations of ENJOYMENT, then you might want to consider a group ride or some other type of catered cycling journey. Riding solo, unsupported, and continuous is a journey involving lots of pain, but on the other side of the notorious pain is ENLIGHTENMENT!

Like I have said and will say many times over, riding your bike solo and unsupported across the country is NOT about taking a sightseeing tour. Yes, you will see an AMAZING country and the sights are STUNNING at times, but the heart and soul of the ride is the inherent MISSION, the basic fabric of the trip. It's the mission to DEVELOP yourself into a person who can withstand PAIN, a person who is deeply familiar with INCONVENIENCE, a person capable of doing HARD! If you are not ready for this type of SUFFERING, then you are not ready for the Southern Tier! Don't take on the Southern Tier expecting easy or else you will be shocked very early in your bike travels! Thinking a cross-country bicycle journey is easy is a crucial mistake!

For the average person to complete an ultra-marathon cross-country biking crusade alone, unsupported, and continuous is a statistical improbability. Even if you expect to have lots of pain and suffering, it is unlikely you will complete your extensive biking goal.

As I have carefully analyzed my own bicycle journey step-by-step beginning from the moment I first made the decision to ride my bicycle across the country to the moment when I concluded my trip as I pedaled on to the beach of Jacksonville, Florida, my careful statistical estimation of my probable success was only a mere 8% chance of completion. After having completed the Southern Tier alone, unsupported, and continuous, I estimate only 8 people out of every 100 would actually complete the arduous solo, unassisted thru-ride on their first attempt. Clearly, I overcame the heavily discouraging odds and earned the distinct privilege to write this necessary book!

The more familiar you become with pain and suffering; the BETTER are your odds of possibly completing the formidable cross-country cycling task. The more you can tolerate unpleasant weather, damage to your bike, health problems, and closed campgrounds, the quicker you will develop your character and the more progress you will make along your targeted route. As you advance across the country, there will be times you will enjoy the ride, but the enjoyment is reserved ONLY for those RUGGED cyclists whom meet the initial demands of suffering.

It's like a freshman college student who is required to take the boring "prerequisite core classes" before they can take all the intriguing, specialty classes relating to their particular major. Universities arrange their curriculum in a way as to force each student first to get through the general classes before they are permitted to take the more enjoyable specialized classes. You are no different on the Southern Tier as there are prerequisite core "classes" you MUST pass before you can feel the true JOYS of the Southern Tier.

The old adage, "You get what you give." is very true on a major bicycle route. The more effort you apply to withstanding the pain and suffering, the greater the joy on the other side! And believe me, when you discover the JOY of the Southern Tier, you have truly made an amazing discovery as the JOY is saved only for those special cyclists with enough holding power to withstand A LOT of initial suffering!

As you process this information, it is important to understand "joy" is NOT the same emotion as "fun" or "enjoyment." JOY is a deep, genuine feeling which stems from your soul. Joy is a feeling you get ONLY when you expand your character in a POSITIVE manner. Joy has to do with <u>lasting</u> PERSONAL GROWTH! It is a SACRED emotion, not even remotely similar to fleeting fun, pleasure, or enjoyment.

Joy is a long-standing emotion which can be drawn upon as needed throughout your life and joy never subsides unlike the fleeting sensations of pleasure. Joy is the LIFE-LONG feeling of sincere satisfaction of accomplishment you will earn as you go deeper and deeper into the Southern Tier, but you must first SUFFER enough to be WORTHY of the prize! Welcome to the Southern Tier!

Chapter 116: 200 miles to REAL

For the first 200 miles of any epic cross-country bike outing, the excursion will NOT seem real. During my first four days or so, the whole new biking life felt extremely unfamiliar as I felt like a fish out of water. Repeatedly, I found myself asking the MOST COMMON question of the Southern Tier, "What the heck am I doing out here?"

During your first several days on any epic cycling route, it is natural to feel like you made a mistake as there are times when you are bombarded all at once with excessive new stimuli and you will feel overwhelmed to the point in which you question your reality! Feeling out of place is completely normal and should be expected as you begin your epic bike adventure.

As I began my bike cross-country pursuit in San Diego, I referred to my feelings as "culture shock," but they could have easily been labeled "anxiety" or "panic" or a slew of other similar words. If you are lucky, your seemingly false sense of reality will eventually move past your culture shock and begin to gel with some sense of normalcy within the first week, but it might take 2 full weeks or more until you actually feel SEMI-STABLE in your new life.

In most cases, it is around the magical 200-mile landmark when your mind will slowly begin to accept your "new life" and allow you to feel "semi-normal." Maybe around Day 4 or Day 5, you might feel an inkling of familiarity in your new life, but prior to reaching the critical 200-mile point, EXPECT to be a MESS! Unless you are extremely focused on your mission, your thoughts will be all over the place. It is common to feel panicked or worse on your initial days. Your heart will beat much faster and harder than you may have ever experienced prior to your life-changing bicycle excursion. You might even discover a level of alertness or "aliveness" rarely experienced during your former life. Prior to reaching 200 miles, you will probably MISTAKENLY breathe too hard, pedal with too much exertion, and try to maintain too high of a speed, all of which will contribute to your distorted sense of reality.

If there were two words I would INSTILL upon your heart and brain before you take your first pedal stroke, the two words would be "CALM" and "SLOW!" Focusing on calm and slow will do wonders to battle the instability of non-reality inherent during your first 200 miles of cycling an epic bike route!

Upon reaching the magical 200-mile mark, something special seems to happen internally. It's as if your mind, body, and spirit finally give up the fight-or-flight struggle and settle down. The 200-mile point seems to be SIGNIFICANT as your chances of completing the FULL route increase significantly! Think of the first 200 miles of an epic cross-country bike ride as the application for the rest of the route. The "application" process during the first 200 miles is a pretty accurate indicator as to whether or not you are truly WORTHY of spinning your pedals on the glorious Southern Tier asphalt! Most aspiring solo cross-country cyclists do NOT make it through the first 200 miles! Will your application read "APPROVED" or will it read "DENIED?"

During my first 200 miles in California, random strangers would approach me alongside my fully-loaded touring bicycle and ask, "Where are you headed?" To each of these people, I found myself UNABLE to truthfully answer. Instead of saying, "I'm riding to the Atlantic Ocean on the eastern coast of Florida," I found myself stammering for words and saying something much less epic like, "I'm riding over to Pine Valley." or "I'm pedaling to Ocotillo." or "I'm traveling to Brawley." or "I'm biking to Blythe." It wasn't until I finally crossed over the Colorado River at the border of California and Arizona when someone asked, "Where are you riding?" and I replied "Florida!" for the first time!

All through California, I was uncapable of admitting my epic cross-country intentions to anybody. After all, who was I to think I could pedal a bicycle all the way across the United States? My mouth would open to answer the golden question concerning my eventual destination, but I was too embarrassed to speak the truth! But after crossing by the "Welcome to Arizona" sign on the other side of the Colorado River after about 200 miles or so of biking, my cycling trip began to feel more REAL. After all, I just pedaled my bicycle across the entire state of California! Wow!!!! Prior to exiting California, my cross-country biking was just a dream, but after pedaling through an entire state, my cross-country pursuit felt much more substantial.

Completing my first state of California was HUGE! Even if I would have quit in Arizona and flew back home from the Phoenix Airport, no one could ever take away from me the FACT that I pedaled a bicycle across the entire state of California! What an accomplishment! The feeling was truly JOYOUS! All by myself I pedaled through California. Crossing into Arizona was VERY GOOD for my waning self-confidence! Welcome to the Southern Tier!!!!

Chapter 117: Cold Desert Nights

If you ask most people for the first word they think of when "desert" is mentioned, the vast majority of people would say "HOT." And I would agree! It gets VERY hot in the desert and the Southern Tier Bike Route includes approximately 1,000 miles of pure desert! There are times during the summer months on the Southern Tier when the desert temperature reaches as high as 125 degrees Fahrenheit with regular high readings around 110 degrees! During my ride in October and November, there were five days of 100-plus degree Fahrenheit temperatures with 105 degrees being the highest temperature I endured.

Although the desert is usually very hot, it is also very COLD at times, especially at nights! The temperature can drop DRASTICALLY, especially as the sun sets in the sky. All of a sudden, you could go from being very hot and sweating to having shivers and reaching for a sweatshirt.

The coldest part of the night is usually the hour or two before dawn which coincides with the exact time, I chose to start pedaling most of my Southern Tier days. Riding at this quiet time of the day meant getting myself out of my cozy sleeping bag and instantly feeling the brisk early morning air. Many of my pre-dawn rides had chilly temperatures in the low 40's, but after the initial shock, the cool temperature wasn't too bad as I started to spin my pedals. After about five minutes of pedaling, the chilly weather actually felt great!

The TOUGHEST part of the early mornings on the Southern Tier was getting dressed for my daily ride. Since I was OBSESSIVE about washing my clothes the night before, most mornings my clothes were still mildly WET. Even with my best drying efforts the preceding afternoon, my clothes usually remained damp as I put them on early the next morning. Through the night I would hope for my clothes to dry, but in most cases, they were about as wet as they were last afternoon after I finished washing them. Putting on wet clothes in 43-degree weather was NOT a pleasant undertaking, but the more I did it, the more I got used to doing it. After a while, I LOOKED FORWARD to putting on my moist, cool clothes as the routine became my very own special passageway into another AMAZING day of pedaling on the magnificent Southern Tier!

Bringing extra dry clothes as to try to avoid this early morning unpleasantry seems reasonable, but the extra clothing weight makes it a BAD IDEA as ounces make pounds and pounds make pain! Plus, fearing your own wet clothes is a sign of weakness which could easily spread to other layers of your precious thinking process. If you can't even put some wet clothes on your body on a chilly early morning, then you have no business attempting the Southern Tier! Getting dressed with damp clothes is a PREREQUISITE of the Southern Tier!

If you are lucky enough to get to your daily destination while the sun is still shining, then you could strategically lay your newly-cleaned wet clothes out for the sun's rays to dry, but unless you get some direct sunlight on your wet clothes, they won't dry much! With regard to wet clothes, your best chance for your clothes to dry has to do with how well YOU fold and squeeze every last drop of water out of your clothes after washing them!

Wearing damp clothes first thing in the morning actually helped me to adopt the right HARD CORE mental attitude necessary for each day of my bike travels. Having nice, warm, cozy clothes actually seemed to WEAKEN my RUGGED mindset by creating a deteriorating forthcoming EXPECTATION of warm, dry clothes every day! In short, you could say the Southern Tier taught me to LOVE pain! At one point I remember being slightly irritated when my biking clothes were completely dry in the morning as I had become accustomed to wearing moist cycling clothing! When you get to this strange and illogical thinking pattern, you will know the transforming spirit of the Southern Tier is truly getting inside of you!

Sometimes while staying at Warmshowers homes, my host would offer me to use their washing machine and clothes dryer, and every time the offer was made, I accepted! In most cases, it was a TREAT to wash and dry my clothes with modern equipment and it usually felt GREAT to put on nice, warm, fresh clothes to begin my ride the next day even though doing so did not necessarily support my ongoing mental toughness!

No matter what situation you find yourself, ALWAYS wash your clothes on a daily basis NO MATTER WHAT. Wearing dirty, stinking clothes from the day before will eventually result in a rash or some type of undesirable medical condition which may ultimately cause a break-down of your skin or maybe even a partial collapse of your fragile positive attitude. Riding your bike for many hours a day results in LOTS of sweat, dirt, and grime on your clothes, especially the clothing contacting your fragile saddle skin.

Take every effort to THOROUGHLY wash your clothes EVERY DAY. Do a GREAT job washing your vitally important cycling clothes! My hand-washed clothes were as clean as any machine-washed clothes as I made it my duty to match or exceed the quality of an electric washing machine!

Having a nice, CLEAN body and having fresh camp clothes is also highly advised as it is counterproductive to disperse your sweat and grime all throughout your sleeping bag. Keeping your sleeping bag fresh and clean can be an important contributing factor to your crucial rejuvenation throughout the night as your body, mind, and spirit try to recover for another long day of biking tomorrow!

While on the topic of sleeping bags, you would be wise to have a sleeping bag rated at 0 degrees Fahrenheit as the nights on any epic bike route can be FRIGID! One particular night while I was pedaling the Southern Tier, the temperature dropped down to 25 degrees Fahrenheit. Although I slept in a motel on that frigid night, there have been many other non-Southern Tier nights in which I have slept outside all night in temperatures below 32 degrees with 5 degrees being the coldest night I ever slept outside. There are few things in life worse than being cold throughout most of the night! Sleep recovery is VERY IMPORTANT toward achieving your lofty cross-country cycling goal and you will not sleep well if you are cold! Get a GOOD, warm sleeping bag and make sure you keep it dry!

Keeping your sleeping bag and camp clothes COMPLETELY DRY is a key component to warding off the cold nights. It's one thing to start your day with damp clothes, but you should NEVER go to bed in wet clothes! Packing your camp clothes and your sleeping bag in an extra waterproof storage bag and then storing them inside your waterproof pannier bags is the best plan to ensure dryness. Under NO CIRCUMSTANCE can your camp clothes or sleeping bag get even one drop of wetness on them. Wetness is the FASTEST WAY to decrease your body temperature! You NEED dry camp clothes and a dry sleeping bag in order to remain warm and to experience a GOOD night's sleep!

For my 43 nights on the Southern Tier, I slept well EVERY NIGHT! Not one night on the Southern Tier was I too cold or too uncomfortable. Each night of my epic adventure I went to bed wearing DRY clothes as I snuggled inside a highly-rated, DRY sleeping bag. Sleeping well on the Southern Tier is not hard thanks to the very challenging terrain, long miles, and breathtaking vistas, but sleep could go bad if you are cold. Regardless of the particular season, be prepared for cold nights!

DAY 36: After applying super glue to the base connection of my waterproof cell phone holder, I never again had I to deal with a detached cell phone holder! Losing my phone was one of my WORST nightmares!!!

Chapter 118: No Vacancy

Immediately upon arriving at my daily destination, I would be thinking about my destination for THE NEXT DAY! After considering the projected temperature, wind direction, wind speed, elevation ascent, and my current physical and mental condition, I would make an estimated mileage goal and then look for a small town or city close to my estimated mileage range. Once I located a city or town, I'd open my Warmshowers phone app and attempt to locate a Warmshowers host somewhere in the vicinity of my projected destination town.

Upon locating a Warmshowers host near my desired destination, I would text the potential host a request to stay at their home the following night. If I could not locate a Warmshowers host in my desired vicinity, then I would scan my map for the nearest campground, hostel, or biker accommodation to my desired ending location as my goal was to get FREE housing with Warmshowers if possible and then to seek FREE or CHEAP overnight accommodations as my next option. My third option was locating a CHEAP motel to spend the night as it was important to me to SAVE as much money as possible during my extensive bicycle travels.

Before I would count on a particular motel for my lodging, I would call the motel to confirm they were still in business as it is VERY COMMON for even the best maps to have ERRORS and omissions. If you get lazy and decide NOT to call the motel ahead of time, you might be in for a big surprise. Several times during my quest across the country, I rode for many hours eagerly anticipating the arrival at my desired motel only to find it was closed or booked full. During these unsuspecting scenarios, you might feel some heavy-duty anxiety as it can be very scary not knowing where you will be resting your head for the night, especially during possible SEVERE weather!

As I gained confidence crossing the country on my bicycle, I became more and more fascinated with WILD CAMPING even though I only did it three times on my entire trip. Wild camping is when you camp in an UNAUTHORIZED location. Wild camping could occur at a city park, baseball field dug out, corner of a soccer field, woods area, church grounds, athletic field, vacant lot, open field, picnic grounds, state park, etc. Basically, wild camping could occur anywhere there is a tiny 64 square feet of ground space available for you to erect your tent!

Despite lacking the proper formal permission to camp in a particular location, as long as you don't cause a disturbance, you will probably be ok. Wild camping fits well with one of my overall life mottos...... "Ask for FORGIVENESS instead of asking for PERMISSION!" Getting FORMAL prior authorization can often be very time consuming, frustrating, and draining of your precious energy. Instead, I found it much easier and healthier for me to give MYSELF permission and hope for the best!

After I made the decision to wild camp in a particular location, I would keep to myself and be REALLY nice if I was approached by a uniformed official asking, "What are you doing?" As long as you are respectful and pleasant, you should be ok. Just think of the THOUSANDS of homeless people living on the streets of America. Are you and I really any different than any of them?

On EVERY DAY of your bike crusade across the country, it is vital to remind yourself you are on an ADVENTURE! All adventures have some degree of UNCERTAINTY. If you were to define the word "adventure", you would have to use the word "uncertainty" as part of your definition. In many cases, your days will NOT unfold as you have planned! Thanks to many unexpected obstacles, there were times I did NOT make it to my desired daily destination.

One time the heat got to me and I couldn't do the mileage. Another time it got dark and I got scared which curtailed my day. Two other times I decided to pedal 30 miles longer than I originally planned thanks to an unexpected tailwind! Late in my bike trip, there were also several days I PURPOSELY chose no ending destination as I wanted to experience what it would be like to be more of a WILD CARD as I played out my newly cognized "pedal eastbound and hope for the best" strategy! It is a certain sign of growth and emerging internal power when you can pedal onward with confidence WITHOUT any prior overnight accommodation plan in place!

While riding your bicycle across the country, you MUST maintain an adventurous attitude. You must be PREPARED for your desired motel to be booked solid despite your calling the day before. You must EXPECT to encounter bike maintenance issues thus cutting your estimated daily mileage in half or worse forcing you to change your itinerary. You must adjust your plans when a harsh 4-hour headwind cuts your speed down to 6 miles per hour. Expecting problems and adjusting your agenda is a daily MUST on the Southern Tier!

While riding from Sierra Blanca, Texas to Van Horn, Texas I encountered the most inclement weather I have ever experienced while pedaling a bicycle. The temperature never reached 30 degrees Fahrenheit ALL DAY. For 4 hours I pedaled into a 30 mile an hour headwind. The wind was fierce and direct! There was also a brief hailstorm with hard ice pellets bombarding my helmet creating pounding harsh crackling sounds. Overall, it was the bike riding day from HELL!

On this notoriously frigid day as my jaw tightened from the freezing temperatures, I made one last phone call to my mom before my phone FROZE and shut itself off, begging her to book me a room at ANY available Van Horn motel. The riding conditions were miserable and I felt like I NEEDED a hotel on this arctic night.

As I pulled into Motel 6 on my bicycle amidst snow flurries, I collapsed my head on to the counter at the front desk. Without even speaking a single word, the nice lady worker gently put her soft hand on my frigid head and said, "You must be Sean." As I shook my frosty head in confirmation, the sweet lady informed me, "The hotel is BOOKED FULL, but thanks to your mother's determination, she reserved you the third-to-last available room. If your mom had waited another thirty minutes, this hotel would have been SOLD OUT!" On this unseasonably ice-cold night, I was 29 minutes from sleeping outside somewhere in my tent!

With the horrid, cold conditions in West Texas on that memorable October day, many truck drivers and other highway travelers chose to get a hotel instead of risking the potentially dangerous icy road conditions thus filling up EVERY available overnight room QUICKLY. All it takes is one good burst of inclement weather or one big event in town to fill up all the overnight accommodations. Planning is IMPORTANT, but it also pays to maintain your adventurous attitude as your attitude will be TESTED more than once on your bike ride when your first plan fails and you discover there is NO VACANCY! Welcome to the Southern Tier!

DAY 37: Jacob from Tri-Hard Sports in Ocean Springs, Mississippi was FANTASTIC! He fixed my bicycle on SUNDAY when his bike shop was officially CLOSED!!!! I tipped Jacob $40!

Chapter 119: One-Lane Bridges

On the Southern Tier and other published bicycle routes, there are many bridges with only one operative lane of travel. In some cases, these one-lane bridge are intentionally designed as such and in other cases, one or more lanes are under construction thus making the particular bridge a "one-lane bridge" by default.

As you are approaching a one-lane bridge, it is best to take over the FULL LANE of travel as most of these bridges are TIGHT and there is <u>barely</u> enough room for a vehicle to get past a bicycle. Riding in the middle of the lane is often your SAFEST option! Riding in the middle of the lane clearly alerts any rear-approaching vehicle there is NO POSSIBILITY to pass you! Otherwise, by riding tight to the curb, you could send a mixed message to a rear-approaching driver causing the driver to try to pass you despite lacking adequate space to do so safely!

Remain calm as you lay claim to the FULL LANE of travel as you cross over the bridge! Don't get all worked up as most drivers understand and will be more than patient with a cyclist as it is obvious you cannot travel at the same high speed as a motorized vehicle. Even at the risk of upsetting a rare, grumpy vehicular driver, maintain your position in the MIDDLE of the road until you safely cross the entire bridge and then politely succumb your dominancy of the road back to the vehicle(s) behind you.

If you are pedaling on a one-lane bridge and you suddenly notice an oncoming vehicle approaching you, it is best to quickly pull off to the right side of the road, dismount your bike, and STOP until the vehicle(s) pass. It is TOO DANGEROUS to ride your bike into oncoming traffic with only one open lane and no berm. After the vehicle passes by, only then can you resume riding your bike across the bridge.

SAFETY at all costs is your ongoing PLAN! Sometimes you will have to wait longer than you would like, but your safety is well worth it! Even if you have to walk your bike across the bridge, it sure beats putting your health at risk by a car contacting your bicycle! The rule is simple. Anytime you are in doubt, STOP and WAIT! NEVER make hasty decisions!

Chapter 120: Mystery Illness

Upon finishing the Southern Tier, I felt so GOOD, maybe the best I've ever felt in all my life. But on January 29th, only 67 days after completing the Southern Tier, my wife and I were taking a familiar airplane flight to Cancun, Mexico. As the airplane began to gain altitude, my chest suddenly felt heavy and my heart started beating very rapidly. Instantly, I found myself with a very high fever, shortness of breath, light-headedness, and a debilitating overall weakness. For the next five minutes I battled to remain conscious. At any moment, I could have easily passed out into the aisle of the plane! In a desperate attempt to avoid going unresponsive at 30,000 feet in the air, I ripped off my sweatshirt and began rubbing ice all over my face, neck, wrists, and arms as the ice seemed to lessen the severity of my debilitating symptoms. For the next several hours, I struggled to remain stable as I eagerly counted down the time until landing.

Upon finally arriving in Mexico, I rejoiced as I was so happy to be back on ground, but I was very confused as to what happened to me on the plane! For more than 20 years, I've had SVT episodes which involved my heart beating REALLY fast for a few minutes and then the situation would cease, but never in my entire life had I ever felt all of these other disabling intense symptoms all at once! Although I'm not a doctor, it felt like I had a heart attack!

After getting a taxi ride to our resort, I seemed to be feeling better so my wife and I decided to take a short walk on the beach. During our short walk, I felt a DEBILITATING WEAKNESS take over me. It took me every last bit of effort I could muster just to make it back to our hotel! At that moment, I knew I was dealing with a significant health issue! Never in my life had I ever felt such an overall drain of energy and overcoming weakness. Not even my worst day on the Southern Tier was this catastrophic level of prevailing WEAKNESS triggered!

Throughout our ten-day Cancun vacation, I struggled with EXTREME weakness and EXTREME shortness of breath. My condition was so severe I could NOT even sit in direct sunlight for more than five minutes and I was unable to walk up more than 20 steps at a time. It was like I was handicapped! Nothing made sense. Only two months after the completion of my epic 3,000-mile cross-country bike trip, I was not able to walk up a flight of stairs. What happened to me?

Upon returning to the United States, I visited numerous doctors and had many heart tests performed. All of my test results were NORMAL despite my continued severe weakness and terrible shortness of breath, both of which ravaged me for many additional months! Nobody in the health field could give me any answers! Some doctors actually thought I got some form of COVID-19 despite testing NEGATIVE for it in Mexico. Other doctors thought I had a major panic attack. And others in the medical field thought I just had a really bad SVT attack. To me, none of these "guesses" were accurate as I KNEW there was something bigger going on. Despite the various professional opinions, I believe I had a heart attack. After all, what else could have incapacitated me to such a high degree?

After struggling for 3 months with debilitating weakness, I finally regained enough strength to begin exercising again. Little by little I worked to get myself healthy again. For the next 13 months, I continued to struggle with shortness of breath, but I eventually got myself back into excellent physical shape once again. Finally, I felt like I moved past this unknown health episode that plagued my life for 16 months!

Looking back and learning from my mysterious health scenario, I advise you to take more time off during your cross-country bicycle trip. REST a little bit more than you think you should!!!! For me, I only took two and a half days of rest during my entire 43-day excursion. I PUSHED myself HARD every day. Maybe I should have taken more time off.? Maybe I should have scaled my mileage back a bit? Maybe I should have taken longer 10-mile breaks?

It is also completely possible my mystery illness didn't have anything at all to do with the Southern Tier.? After all, I felt AMAZING upon completion of the Southern Tier!!!!! Could it be all the mounting psychological and physical pressures of the Southern Tier finally caught up with me two months afterward.? Did I finally break 67 days later after my successful completion of the Sothern Tier? I might never know, but if any of you reading this book has any ideas, please let me know. You may email me at seanhockensmith@verizon.net.

My final thought on the mysterious illness is to advise each of you to adopt a "cool down" process into your cross-country biking plan. Instead of completely halting your bike riding habit upon completion of your cross-country tour, continue to ride your bike daily as to give your body and mind a sense of TRANSITION back into regular life. Slowly decrease your mileage daily and then begin to skip entire biking days as you SLOWLY resume back to "normal" living. In my case, I stopped riding my bike abruptly which may have contributed to my mystery illness.? Maybe my transition back to normal life was too drastic for my body, mind, and spirit to process? Maybe my abrupt re-entry to regular life BROKE my overall being?

Chapter 121: Stroke

After completing the Southern Tier, it was 19 months before I took my next EPIC bike trip as I battled the mysterious illness as mentioned in the previous chapter for 16 months. Only after what I assumed was a full recovery did I resume the pursuit of my newfound passion for LONG-DISTANCE bike travel. My first quest was to pedal my bicycle from my home in Johnstown, Pennsylvania to Myrtle Beach, South Carolina. The trip would be roughly 600 miles and I was planning to take 8 days to complete the long journey. I was so excited!!!!

After completing a strong 93 miles on Day 1, I felt pretty good! It was great to be back on my bike going long distance! As I began the second day, initially I felt pretty good, but as the morning progressed, I didn't feel quite right. The feeling wasn't anything major, but I definitely didn't feel GOOD! As I crossed over the 40-mile point, I suddenly started seeing very strange metallic images in front of me much like you would see if you stared at the sun too long. Then suddenly, without much warning I almost passed out while riding my bike on the very busy Highway Route 522 in Winchester, Virginia. What the heck is going on? Had I actually passed out, I could have been easily killed amidst the heavy vehicle traffic!

Immediately, I pulled over to the side of the road and took a drink even though I had been drinking regularly every 3 miles exactly as I advise other cyclists to do. My current state of health was like NOTHING I had ever felt as I was not exhausted nor were I sick in a traditional sort of way! What could be going on with me? As I got back on my bike, I noticed a Sheetz gas station in the distance. My plan was to eat a good lunch and move past whatever strange occurrence just happened as it is not my style to complain much!

After eating my lunch, I continued not feeling quite right. For many minutes, I tried to walk off my strange overall feelings of mildly ill health, but the walking did not seem to help. Something was wrong with me and it had NOTHING to do with fatigue, nutrition, or hydration! Something else was going on and I couldn't figure out what it was! Suddenly, thoughts entered my mind, "Just call for a ride home." As I was pacing back and forth at Sheetz trying to figure out how I was feeling and what was going on with me, suddenly I felt my entire left hand and wrist go COMPLETELY NUMB. Moments later my teeth went COMPLETELY NUMB and then my tongue, lips, and left eye went COMPLETELY NUMB. "Oh my God, I'm having a STROKE!"

Although I didn't really know anything about strokes, I KNEW whatever just happened to me was MAJOR. It had to be a stroke! As I struggled to get over the initial shock of the experience, I recall a VIVID thought entering my mind, "My bike trip is OVER!" Clearly, I needed to get to a hospital FAST!

As I peered out to the Sheetz gas pumps searching for someone to help me, I noticed a guy pumping gas into his truck. The truck would be PERFECT to transport me and my bike to the hospital. As I approached the guy, I begged, "Please help me. I think I just had a stroke. Please take me and my bike to the nearest hospital." The guy seemed uncomfortable with my request and reluctantly said, "Ok. Go get your bike and I'll take you." As I began walking my bike over to the guy's truck, unexpectedly the truck sped away as the guy obviously didn't feel comfortable giving me a ride two miles down the road to the hospital.

Having failed on my first attempt to secure vital assistance, I quickly approached another man with a truck and I pleaded with him to take me to the hospital. In an unconcerned and rather aloof manner, this second guy flat out told me he didn't have enough room for me and my bike even though I could clearly see there was ample space in his truck bed! As I was struggling for my life, I thought, "How could someone deny a ride to a guy who is having a stroke? Did this man not have one morsel of human compassion?" Maybe the guy was just stupid? Or maybe he was scared of me? What has become of mankind?

Finally, in utter desperation I looked around and saw one more truck, but there was a MAJOR problem! The owner of the truck was the kind of guy your mother warned you to NEVER approach. This guy had lots of tattoos and he was big, muscular, tough, and mean. He walked around with a semi-permanent frown expression and he had TROUBLE written all over his face! Any sane human being could take one look at this THUG of a guy and KNOW immediately he was NOT the right guy to approach to provide my transportation needs This big, rugged, man dressed in dirty blue jeans was the epitome of the drug-dealing, gang-banging, BAD dude we all had nightmares about during our childhood, but I was out of options and I felt like my life was on the line. In that moment of utter despair, my level of personal discretion was at the lowest level in all of my life!

Without hesitation, I approached this VERY scary man and asked him for a ride to the hospital. Without a second of hesitation, this unsuspecting brute of a man agreed! With one hand this POWERHOUSE man picked up my bike and gear and placed it in his truck bed. As I was thanking him, he interrupted my speech and FORCEFULLY said "GET IN!" in which I promptly complied with his stern demand. As we drove over to the hospital, I asked my new friend's name and he said, "You can call me Q!" "Q" was the one gracious human being whom stepped up and gave me a ride to the hospital during my time of urgent need! Forever, I will be grateful of the lifesaving actions of my fellow brother, Q!

After having some tests performed at the hospital, it was indeed confirmed I had a MAJOR stroke! But how could a recent cross-country cyclist only 19 months prior have a stroke at only 50 years old? The CT scan of my neck revealed a 100% occluded right carotid artery. "Occluded" means my right carotid artery was 100% CLOSED! No blood was getting through to my brain from this MAJOR artery! The hospital tests revealed a dissection in my right carotid artery. A dissection is a tear of the artery wall usually resulting from a severe past injury. The tear of the artery wall created a flap which eventually blocked off my entire artery with a blood clot thus causing the stroke as my brain did NOT get enough blood flow to warrant proper functioning which resulted in damage to the right frontal lobe of my brain.

For many YEARS previous, I felt mildly dizzy and "cloudy" in my head, but I never got checked out as it isn't my style to complain much or to visit with doctors. In my estimation, my right carotid artery was probably closed for at least five years prior my stroke although my neurologist does NOT agree. Nonetheless, I never even considered my regular dizziness was being caused by a blocked artery in my neck. It is possible I may have ridden the entire 3,000-mile Southern Tier with a completely occluded right carotid artery and I didn't even know it!

If you are smart, you will learn from my inattentiveness and ignorance. When you feel dizzy or strange, go get checked out by a doctor. Don't ignore your chronic symptoms! Had I gotten a CT scan of my neck sometime during the five or so years when I regularly felt dizzy and cloudy on a DAILY basis, I could have likely avoided having a major stroke and setting back years of my life!

Most likely, my artery tear probably resulted from one of my MANY severe wakeboard or intense mountain bike crashes as it is my style to PLAY HARD! If you watched me ride a mountain bike or ride a wakeboard without knowing my age, you would guess I was between the ages of 14 and 20, certainly not in my late forties!!! My riding style was high-flying and overly aggressive, especially for my "older" age!

If I could rewind my life, I would show more respect to my body. At most times, I was more aggressive and wilder than my WILD crew of teenage PEERS including Zack, Caden, Jordyn, Sydney, and Curtis. We spent lots of time having CRAZY fun taking part in VERY aggressive speed boat tubing, cliff-jumping, wakeboarding, mountain bike riding and other physically engaging activities while partaking in UNFORGETTABLE camping trips at Raystown Lake over the course of many years!

NOBODY could keep up with me on the mountain bike trails as I rode wild and free as if I was INVINCIBLE regularly taking full-speed crashes over top of my handlebars! Not even the animals of the woods would get in my way as I was clearly the KING of the mountain trails!

As for wakeboarding at Raystown Lake, even at 48 years old, I would hit the crest of the wake behind my parent's 200 horsepower 1995 Four Winns 5-liter V-8 speed boat at FULL APPROACHING SPEED and fly 20 feet or more through the air clearing the ENTIRE wake of the boat. Some of my crashes were so severe I was knocked literally SENSELESS! Upon regaining some sense of my mental faculties as I floated in the disturbed water of Raystown Lake, I would intuitively feel for my head as to make sure it was still attached to my neck. Only my great true-friend, Jamie Weis, has taken high-speed, open water crashes on his kneeboard more severe than I!

Looking back, it might have been a better idea for me to treat my body with greater care. Doing so would have avoided the dissection in my carotid artery and I would not have had a stroke! Consider myself as living proof; even the healthiest guy you know could have a MAJOR health setback by being too rough with the human body! Learn from me and take good care of your body from a young age! Be <u>GENTLE</u> with your body!!!! Being too rough with my body cost me YEARS of inactivity trying to recover from my prior abuse!

DAY 37: What a glorious biking lane!

Chapter 122: Horn

Only once on my entire 43-day cross-country bicycle tour did a car pull out directly in front of me. The driver of the car was stopped at a stop sign on a desolate Louisiana country road. As I was about to pass in front of the stopped car and make my left turn, the distracted driver surprisingly pressed the gas pedal and the car suddenly pulled out directly in front of me causing me to SLAM on my brakes to avoid a collision!

Although it appeared the preoccupied driver did not purposely pull out in front of me, the driver's careless actions could have cost me a serious injury or even the loss of my life! Clearly, the driver had something else on his mind other than safe driving. The inattentive driver didn't even seem to be in an excessive hurry as he was stopped at the stop sign for about 5 seconds prior to my passing. This numbskull driver actually looked directly at me and STILL proceeded to pull out in front of me! He was clearly thinking much more about his most recently sent text than he was about driving safety!

Although making eye contact with vehicular drivers is a REALLY GOOD IDEA, it also makes good sense to make a sound as you are about to cross in front of a single car or especially a moment or two prior to passing in front of several cars at a busy intersection. Having a horn or some other type of loud, sounding device engages two senses of sight and sound instead of just the one most common sense of sight. All it takes is one respectful toot of your horn to let a vehicular driver(s) know you are crossing in front of him.

A horn serves as a PATTERN INTERRUPT as many vehicular drivers are so concentrated on their current thoughts or their current phone conversation, they could look directly at you and still NOT see you as was the case with me. Interrupting the driver's current thought pattern and bringing him back to the situation at hand will keep you and your bike a lot safer. It will also give you a much better likelihood of finishing your special cycling mission! It's hard to finish your cross-country quest when you are in the hospital and your bike is at the metal recycling factory!

While pedaling the Southern Tier, I did NOT have a horn or sounding device, but I wish I had one! A bike horn used properly could have saved me from a potentially harmful experience, an experience which could have ENDED my adventure! Today there are many bicycle sounding devices on the market. Install some type of horn or sounding device on your handlebars and use it when you approach and cross-over vehicular traffic! Be seen! Be heard! Be SAFE!

Chapter 123: Padded Handlebars

Ask most long-distance cyclists about their hands, fingers, and forearms and they will admit to some level of numbness from time to time. As I was preparing for the Southern Tier, I battled pain and numbness in my hands and arms on many previous bike rides. The painful tingles would work itself all the way up from my fingers to my "funny bone" in my elbow area causing me rather SEVERE discomfort at times!

For years, I fantasized about having a PADDED handlebar to grasp instead of the standard hard metal factory-made handlebars. Padding seemed like it would alleviate some of the numbness in my limbs, but for years I had no solution to my dilemma. Wearing two biking gloves helped a tiny bit, but I fantasized about a much better solution to my numbing extremities!

One day as I was throwing away some plastic packing padding after opening my package from a recent eBay delivery, I had the idea of taking the plastic padding material and wrapping it around my bike handlebars. With the help of some common black electrical tape, I fabricated a nice, THICK, padded handlebar. Although my handlebar looked a bit "ghetto," the BRILLIANT padding idea worked well for me throughout my entire Southern Tier adventure and continues to work well today!

After thousands of miles of biking with my homemade handlebar pads, my hands, wrists, and arms have had VERY LITTLE numbness! Despite having all the extra padding, I still wear my biking gloves as to give me an additional level of padding and to avoid unnecessary wear and tear to the exterior skin on my hands. Maybe it's not even necessary for me to wear the gloves, but I do anyways as to keep the tender skin on my hands free of common cycling abrasions.

As an adventurer, you MUST have some personal ingenuity. Whether it's your handlebars or some other part of your bike, you need to THINK about the solution to your problem. Be creative. The answer is probably right in front of your eyes! For me, the answer to my numbing hands was available for years as I threw away countless plastic padding from my many eBay and Amazon mail orders throughout the years.

Looking back on the value of my creative handlebar padding remedy which cost me NOTHING in padding and about 20 cents in electrical tape, I would have paid THOUSANDS of dollars to relieve my hands and arms of their previous numbness. In my best estimation, I figure I would have paid AT LEAST $3,000.00 and probably much more for a legitimate solution to my numbing hands and arms. Solving my numbness riddle for almost FREE was super-pleasing to my naturally parsimonious nature!

For years, I dealt with nerve pain wreaking havoc from the palm of my hand all the way to my funny bone at my elbow. My simple homemade handlebar solution was a GAME CHANGER as I could now ride my bike mostly pain free! My simple "hillbilly" solution was HUGE! This particular remedy alone is probably one of the TOP FIVE reasons I finished the Southern Tier!

It is now years later and my ghetto handlebars of the Southern Tier are still in tack. No, I don't ride my bike every day, but the electrical tape is still holding and the padding is as good as ever. Maybe I'll never have to replace my padding.? But even if I do, it would be TOO EASY! I LOVE finding effective creative solutions! Every time I put my hands on my Sean Hockensmith-crafted handlebar cushions, I feel a sense of ACHIEVEMENT and JOY!

DAY 37: "Sweet Home Alabama" never meant so much to me as it did when I crossed over its privileged barrier!

Chapter 124: Taking a Loss

If you are one of the relentless few cyclists who happen to make it to Day 2 or Day 3 on your epic bike adventure, you will soon realize the Southern Tier is NOT about winning. On the contrary, the Southern Tier and other major bike routes are more about taking a LOSS well! "Winning" is not an accurate depiction of what occurs on a major bike route. Truthfully, most days riding a bike across the country feels more like a LOSS as it is a daily STRUGGLE to keep your pedals spinning.

During the first couple weeks of my incredible cross-country escapade, I KNEW I was LOSING. In fact, my confirmed FAILURE on Day 2 was the impetus for the title of this book, EPIC FAIL! Riding across the country has a lot more to do with handling failure than it does with achieving success!

It was a humbling experience to feel the reality of putting my entire life into a few bike pannier bags, pedaling 7 hours a day, and getting nowhere fast! To make matters even worse, I wasn't even getting paid for my new "job" in this strange new life! After "losing" my wife, children, parents, friends, business, house, and my pets, the overall sense of loss was now a major part of my overall attitude. With each passing day, my losses mounted on top of each other and at times I felt SAD and even LONELY. My old life was LOST and it now felt like a distant memory as the new world in which I found myself was STRANGER than I could have ever imagined! To say I was "messed up" mentally by the Southern Tier would be a HUGE understatement!!!

Many aspiring cross-country cyclists suffer SEVERE mental ramifications resulting from their inability to ACCEPT the loss and to KEEP PEDALING!!!! The humbling admission of defeat is too much for most to adapt. As panic sets in, the chances of an early Day 1 or Day 2 termination is very HIGH!

On Day 2, my panic hit a threshold and I could NOT pedal anymore. This was the ONLY time on my entire trip when my body STOPPED while I still had plenty of energy! As I dismounted my bike, I asked myself, "What am I doing out here?" Upon grasping my bike while standing in the middle of the road, it was abundantly clear I had LOST. My cross-country efforts were an EPIC FAILURE!!!! And there wasn't any mental gymnastics or creative strategy I could implement to counteract this high-level LOSS! It was over! The Southern Tier defeated me just like it did to thousands of other cyclists who came before me!

The whole culture-shocking cycling experience was almost too much for me to handle. My ONLY consolation was to mourn the loss of my former self as I knew in the moment, I would NEVER again be the same. The old "Sean Hockensmith" officially DIED and he was not coming back. In this strange land, I was left with a lost self and a seemingly endless number of miles left to pedal.

Although my "cross-country" bike ride was over, I REFUSED to go home! Instead, I accepted the loss, accepted my new life, and resumed pedaling as a completely downtrodden, hopeless, pitiful display of a man! One pedal stroke after another I sulked in my loss and FORCED myself to pedal as if it was my PUNISHMENT for being so stupid as to think I could actually pedal my bicycle across the country! So pedal is what I did. Pedaling was my penance. Pedaling was MY NEW LIFE!

Instinctively, I KNEW months before leaving for my cross-country bike ride, the harsh experience was going to be BIGGER THAN BIG. My anticipated cross-country bike adventure was going to be HUGE! It was not going to be one of my traditional overnight bike rides. This cross-country bicycle escapade was going to be EPIC, but I still didn't and couldn't imagine just how GIGANTIC it was going to be!

The culture shock offered by the unfamiliar climate and diverse landscapes blasted me off balance. The Southern Tier rattled me. It made me cry. It shook the foundation of my thought process causing me to question EVERYTHING! What was real? What was true? Where am I? Where am I going? I was LOST! Everything about me seemed like a LOSS!

Had it not been for my many previous years of intense high-level athletic competition, passionate personal development, fierce business dealings, and a STRONG Catholic upbringing, I don't think I would have been durable enough to hang on. The intensity of the Southern Tier biking experience was more than I can describe on paper. The sheer HOPELESSNESS I felt as I dismounted my bicycle on Day 2 prompted feelings of DREAD only rivaled by the most intense prior experiences of my entire 48 years on Planet Earth. The Southern Tier assaulted me and it took MORE THAN everything I had to remain pedaling for ONE MORE DAY. My loss was certain. My cross-country ride was OVER and the only remaining question was "How long could I hold on?"

If you ask most people about my personal athletic abilities, they would classify me as a GOOD athlete, but NOT as a great athlete. Despite my athletic shortcomings, I still dreamed of being the champion, defeating all of the opponents in my class, but rarely did that ever happen in my sports history. Instead, I would win a few and then lose a few.

My winning and losing pattern was probably most exemplified in my youth wrestling career as I would regularly win two or three matches in a wrestling tournament only to fall to a "stud" wrestler in a later round. In most of my wrestling competitions, I would compete for third place instead of pushing for first place. Regardless of how hard I worked or which wrestling camps I attended, I remained only a slightly better-than-average wrestler with big unmaterialized dreams! Throughout my life, LOSING was all too familiar to me.

In a similar fashion, as a baseball player, I was good, but not great. Most games I played well, but when I faced top-notch pitchers, my batting skills couldn't contend with the high-level pitching. Baseball was my love and I dreamed of being a PRO, but as I traveled 1,000 miles from home to play college baseball at a division 2 school at the University of Tampa in Tampa, Florida, my dream didn't work out. My baseball dreams were crushed as it is not possible to play in the big leagues when you aren't even talented enough to play division 2 college baseball.

LOSING was also common to me in other athletic sports like tennis and volleyball. In both of these sports I showed solid talent and I worked REALLY hard to be one of the better players, but I never really attained the type of success I envisioned. With so many other sport "failures" in my long-standing past, another failure on the Southern Tier wasn't really that uncommon!

As I stood alongside my bicycle on that very memorable Day 2, I felt many of my mounting losses of the past as they related to my newest Southern Tier loss. Standing alongside the road contemplating whether or not I was crazy left me to experience those similar feelings of loss as I failed to achieve most of my previous athletic pursuits. Not a single loved one in my life would have thought less of me had I decided to terminate my cross-country cycling efforts on that momentous Day 2 and come back home early!

As I stood idle beside my bike sulking in my most recent loss, I suddenly remembered I was CALLED to take on this strange biking adventure. This crazy and unsuspecting cycling adventure really had very little to do with ME! My cross-country bike ride was God's plan! The LEAST I could do was to pedal ONE MORE DAY. "Tomorrow I can find a way back home, but today I will continue to pedal" were my words of wisdom meekly spoken to myself amidst my apparent roadside FAILURE. Despite feeling heavy loss, I pushed my pedals around as my tears deflected off of the frame of my bike and found their permanent resting place on the hot asphalt of the Southern Tier.

My many athletic losses gave me enough familiarity with those desperate feelings of dreadful pain as to keep pedaling for one more day. Had I been a big-time athletic winner throughout my life, I'm not sure I would have been able to handle the INTENSE emotions of LOSS as I felt on Day 2 of the Southern Tier. Winning is great and we all want to do it, but the Southern Tier taught me one of the GREATEST lessons of my life. LOSING holds the real power!

Losing is a SACRED experience. Anybody can win, but only a few can take a BIG loss without breaking. What you choose to do NEXT after a big loss is what determines your FUTURE! In that downtrodden moment on Day 2 of the Southern Tier when my dreams were shattered, I could have turned around and pedaled back to the San Diego Airport and I was VERY CLOSE to doing just that, but instead I ACCEPTED my LOSS and decided to pedal one more day. It might have been nearly impossible for me to re-dedicate myself to completing the Southern Tier while sulking in my sorrow, but I could at least finish my daily ride! Tomorrow I could decide whether or not I would go back home, but as for today, I will pedal on even though my trip was already OVER in my mind!

As I mentioned in previous chapters, my LOSS was really the loss of my former life. My previous, accustomed life was DISCARDED in exchange for this outlandish NEW LIFE involving pedaling for hours daily with all of my belongings attached to the frame of my bike. My LOSS was deep and SEVERE, but I wasn't totally surprised by the feelings although I was NOT prepared for the sheer intensity of the overall experience! Losing my familiar comforts in exchange for a COMPLETE nonsensical existence in the open desert seemed absurd to me many times daily for at least the first week of my trip. To say I struggled with my new life and all the various losses encapsulating me would be a blatant understatement. In reality, it felt like I was DESTROYED!

Meeting your most insecure self is a humbling experience as I previously considered myself strong and able. But with only a bike, a few small bags of belongings, and a seemingly never-ending desert, I was a MESS! In these same moments, you will also realize you are WEAK and AFRAID! You are not as strong as you thought. You are not as able as you imagined. It's you and the desert and the desert won't blink! You will NOT defeat the desert! At best, you might be able to struggle through!

While standing in awe of the desert vastness and giving witness to the overpowering transcendence of its powerful presence, you will feel SMALL too, just like me! 1,000 miles of exposed desert expanse WILL affect you. Your knees will tremble with weakness and you'll feel like your body is close to succumbing to the relentless grip of the raw land. In the many moments like this, you will see YOURSELF clearly and if you are anything like me, you won't be impressed! The Southern Tier desert will alert you to the many missing pieces to your full personal development puzzle! All of your previous "walls" will come down and the only thing left behind will be a very insecure human being obviously needing a lot of additional work!

As you pedal across the barren desert and across our vast and scenic country on the Southern Tier, most of the time you will be doing nothing more than pushing your pedals around enough as not to quit. On Day 2, my long-time dream of finishing a "cross-country bike tour" was discarded as I quickly discovered I was NOT developed enough to withstand such a HEAVYWEIGHT pursuit. For me, I was pedaling for daily goals with NO CARE WHATSOEVER where I was or how long this fruitless bike trip was going to take. As far as I was concerned, my life had already been lost and I was mechanically going through the motions as I endured the emotionally painful process while I fumbled around spinning my pedals for ONE MORE DAY before I actually went back home.

For all intents and purposes, my cross-country bike trip ENDED on Day 2, thus the title of this book, EPIC FAIL! From Day 2 and thereafter, I merely took DAILY bike rides to different destinations. Finishing the Southern Teir was no longer even a possibility in my mind as of the end of Day 2! It wasn't until I crossed over into Texas when I got a fleeting thought, "What if I actually make it to the Atlantic Ocean?", but quickly my fleeting thought was discarded as being classified as RIDICULOUS by my conscious mind! At times I would get mad at myself for even taking a moment to consider the possibility of finishing the Southern Tier as I KNEW I had already FAILED!

My overall bike ride across America was the story of LOSS. It was about an average guy who dreamed of pedaling a bicycle across America, but quickly found out he was too WEAK to do so. Emotionally, he BROKE on Day 2, but instead of going home, he decided to pedal one more day and then quit tomorrow.

At the end of each biking day, he remembered his CALLING and decided to pedal one more day KNOWING he would NOT finish the revered route! Even on his LAST DAY of pedaling, he still didn't think he would finish. It wasn't until 10 miles from the Atlantic Ocean in Jacksonville, Florida as he was ESCORTED by a group of ANGELS to the purest victory of his life, did he realize he had finally OUTLASTED the Southern Tier!

To say the Southern Tier was a victorious ride would be a blatant LIE! Only the finish hailed glory. The rest of the bike ride was a LOSS. Every day I would lose and lose and lose. Doubts filled my mind and after SEVERAL mental breakdowns, only a pitiful make of a man was left to stumble through each day as the bike ride was a mission locked deep within me and I was too STUBBORN to let it go. Not until I finally executed enough pedal strokes, did I even have the boldness to tell another person where I was actually going. When I told the first person, "I'm riding to Florida.", immediately my inner self proclaimed, "LIAR!"

As you consider whether an EPIC cross-country excursion of this magnitude is right for you, remain humble and don't get your hopes up. The emotions on this journey are OVERPOWERING! It will take MUCH MORE mental fortitude than you have! You will LOSE DEEPER than you ever thought possible. The Southern Tier will rip out your soul and place it on the hard road surface and then LAUGH when you bend over to pick it up!

Be prepared to lose. Expect to lose. Get ready to be DEFEATED! Prepare to meet failure at a depth you never before imagined! You are embarking on a class 5 journey to your soul. And along the way, you will lose big as your very core self will be damaged BEYOND REPAIR! You'll be left standing beside the road looking down at the broken pieces of your life. You will cry. You will PANIC.

Get ready for a severe helping of DEVASTATION! And worst of all, there won't be anybody around to console you on your solo adventure. As you experience the dismantling of every bit of confidence you ever had, you will experience TERROR as you consider how the heck you are going to get back home. Get ready to experience a level of LOSS deeper than you can currently imagine! Welcome to the Southern Tier!

Chapter 126: Texas LOVE

When you pedal a bicycle all the way through a state from one end to the other, you will fall in LOVE with that particular state! And when I say "love," I LITERALLY mean LOVE!!! For me, California, Arizona, New Mexico, Texas, Louisiana, Mississippi, Alabama, and Florida are revered states for me and I truly proclaim my most sincere LOVE for each of those 8 special and dear Southern Tier states! Anytime there is a mention of any one of these 8 admired states of the Southern Tier, I feel a very distinct bond of PURE LOVE!

My greatest love affair was undoubtedly with Texas! Prior to the Southern Tier, I thought Texas would be a boring state, but I was completely WRONG. Texas is an AMAZING state offering a WIDE VARIETY of weather, terrain, and population. There were days exceeding 80 degrees Fahrenheit and other days that did not exceed 30 degrees. Much of the terrain was flat, but there were some rather severe climbs and hills. Many areas were desolate, but there were also many highly populated areas. Some parts of Texas get lots of rain and other areas of the state have a tendency to experience lots of draughts. Part of the reason Texas is so diverse is because Texas is so BIG! It is almost exactly 1,000 miles from the western end to the eastern end which easily makes it the longest state on the Southern Tier! Crossing Texas is one third of the ENTIRE Southern Tier route!

When I crossed through my first state of California and saw the official "Welcome to Arizona" state welcome sign, I felt immediate JOY. It was my FIRST major accomplishment on the Southern Tier. Even if I didn't eventually finish the Southern Tier, I pedaled my bicycle across the entire state of California! What an accomplishment!

Considering my special accomplishment, I can say without any doubt that I truly EXPERIENCED California! There is NO BETTER WAY to capture the genuine essence of a state than to pedal a bicycle through it! Riding in a car through a state is great and you will see the various sights the state has to offer, but car travel does NOT allow you to EXPERIENCE the state with your five senses. Yes, you can SEE the state in a car, but on a bicycle, you can also smell, taste, hear, and FEEL the state which provides a truly sacred experience!

Internally feeling the core attributes of a particular state is very spiritual and personal. After pedaling your bike every mile up, down, and through a state, you will KNOW the state and you will be able to easily answer various questions about the state. After all, you will feel every ascent and every descent. You will feel the power of the sun and the force of the winds. You will hear the early morning animals as they welcome the day. You will see the sun rise and set as you feel the temperature drop. You will taste the dust of the roads and you will sense the hot asphalt reflecting its unyielding heat up into your shins. Your body will feel the change of altitude as you climb the mountains. You will breathe the dry desert air.

Cycling through an entire state is completely foreign to passing through a state in the comforts of your vehicle's air conditioning system. While biking, you will EXPERIENCE the state with all five of your senses. Making an INTIMATE connection is what happens when your sweat drips down on the berm of the road as your own bodily resources propel your bike pedals round and round as you OWN every mile of your travel. Dozens of gallons of gasoline didn't thrust you through the state. It was your own muscles governed by your various thinking patterns serving as your fuel.

Pedaling a bicycle through an entire state forms a BOND never to be broken. To me, the 8 states of the Southern Tier are like HOME. We truly know and LOVE each other in a very special way. As I return to visit these amazing 8 states in my upcoming days, it will forever feel like my own special homecoming! So, for me to proclaim LOVE for these dear states is completely appropriate and is not exaggerated in any way. Truly deep within my being, I LOVE Texas and I LOVE each of the other seven Southern Tier states as I earned this special devoted relationship by pedaling my bicycle through each state in its entirety!

DAY 38: There is NOTHING like an Alabama sunrise!

Chapter 126: Cheap

Truly bonding with the SOUL of the Southern Tier involves being somewhat CHEAP! Yes, you can still spend a night at a motel from time to time or even eat at a few fancy restaurants, but your overall mindset must be one of frugality! Remember, your bicycle adventure is NOT a vacation. It is not a glamorous, high class, catered event. The Southern Tier is a down-and-dirty, no nonsense, "meet your soul," sacred journey! Regardless of your particular financial capabilities, your most pristine experience of the Southern Tier will only be accessed through a sense of thrift and basic accommodations. The Southern Tier is NOT a highfalutin affair!

The Southern Tier and other major bicycle routes can be LIFE-CHANGING, but you have to let these routes work their MAGIC on you! You NEED to spend some nights down on Mother Earth in your tent to feel the vibrations of the land! Pedaling your bike to the nearest restaurant after your daily shower instead of calling for an Uber taxi ride is also recommended even if it means eating supper at the local gas station! It's you and your bike. Don't contaminate your SACRED trip with too much luxury! Having limited finances actually puts you at an ADVANTAGE over a wealthier cyclist as the LESS money you spend on your cross-country travels, the MORE benefits you will reap!

When you book your cheap motel room for the night, EXPECT to see a few bugs here or there. Most of my motel rooms were VERY low end and most of them did NOT have bugs until I got to Monticello, Florida. My hotel in Monticello had a few cockroaches, but I accepted them, did not complain, and got another great night's sleep!

When you go to a restaurant, don't judge the food, just eat for caloric intake. If the food is edible, then be HAPPY! Look at the menu and figure out how you can buy the most calories for the LEAST amount of money. Most of the restaurants like McDonalds and Burger King display huge banners offering daily deals as a means to try to get your business. Order carefully from the big signs and you should be able to SAVE money and fill your belly with lots of calories!

Too much expense and excessive luxury will weaken you! Luxury and expense take your mind off of the basics of the land and the overall glorious feel of nature around you and transfers your focus to more of a pretentious catered mindset. The closer you are to the ground at night, the more the trip will IMPACT you. The more time you spend with you bike and away from anything with a motor, the more your biking experience will pierce your soul! Trying to PAMPER yourself is usually the WRONG idea! Providing yourself with slightly above minimum comfort standards is where you want to operate as to gain the greatest benefits from your EPIC ride!

Adopt a mindset of frugality. Being frugal makes you TOUGH. And toughness is something you will need in order to sustain the long duration of an epic bike route. At times you will have to "dig deep" to keep your pedals spinning. If you don't have enough inherent toughness, you will not have the grit to make it to the finish. Without a certain basic level of TOUGHNESS, you WILL definitely fail! Excessive suffering is NOT necessary, but if you cannot eat your lunch out of a bag along the side of the road, then this type of extensive cross-country cycling excursion is NOT for you!

Luxury and high class trick your mind into wanting the best foods, the best motels, and the best transportation. Extravagance is nice and throughout the year my wife and I take several luxurious vacations and will continue to do so, but the Southern Tier is not one of those deluxe experiences! The Southern Tier is more like how the Israelites from biblical times wandered through the desert for many years searching for the Promised Land. In similar fashion, you will also be "wandering" through the vast, open expanse of the Southern Tier seemingly pedaling non-stop without much progress to show. As you pass through the esteemed bike route, the Southern Tier will STRIP you of your family, your possessions, your confidence, your energy, your weight, and your pride leaving only a NEWFOUND MAN; more humble and more CAPABLE than ever before, but you must HOLD ON long enough for the transformation to occur!

There is nothing extravagant about the long bicycle journey awaiting you. Don't confuse yourself or contaminate your holy bicycle journey by being fancy. The most life transforming cross-country bicycle experience is an eat-out-of-the-bag, poop-on-the-side-of-the-road, sleep-on-the-ground rudimentary kind of adventure. If you need a flush toilet to relieve your human needs, then you probably signed up for the wrong outing!

What's needed on the Southern Tier and other soul-seeking biking expeditions cannot be bought. The more you try to buy your way across the country, the further you push yourself away from the inherent powers of the hallowed routes. Only with a sense of frugality will you have a chance to unite with the true prize of the Southern Tier. Only by being as basic as possible will you feel the PULSE of the vast terrain while it affects your basic character and CHANGES you FOREVER.

Character is WHO you are. It's your level of personal growth considering ALL major components of your being. Character cannot be bought and no one can ever take it away from you! Character is the ONLY thing we take with us as we depart from this planet. Character development achieved by personal growth has always been one of my highest motivations for my life. Along with providing a POSITIVE EXAMPLE for others to follow, CHARACTER ENHANCEMENT was one of the two top reasons responsible for my choosing to bike the entire formidable Southern Tier Bicycle Route.

Prior to my long-distance bicycle experience, I hoped the Southern Tier would allow me to grow my character. After biking the iconic route, I can say with 100% certainty, the Southern Tier did NOT disappoint me! The southern bike route across the United States of America provides an opportunity LIKE NO OTHER to develop your character as there is literally no way to avoid character enhancement when you are left to fend for yourself on this grueling quest. Just shut up and keep pedaling! Mile after LONG mile, the magic of the Southern Tier will slowly have its life-changing affect upon you, just like it did for me!

As you ride along the seemingly endless miles, feel the power in the air. Release the need for indulgence and live as SIMPLY as possible. Don't complicate your bike travels with unnecessary fluff as every additional impediment adds another heavy layer of crud you must remove before EXPERIENCING the GLORY of the glorious route!

Take good care of your basic needs and keep yourself healthy and strong, but don't PAMPER yourself as you need to be TOUGHER than ever before. You are about to encounter challenges taking you to the BRINK of sustainability. Hitting these seemingly dominant walls located on the outside edge of your comfort zone as mentioned throughout these pages will test you like nothing you could imagine. At many times, you will be tempted to "tap out," but if you have enough grit and you are cheap enough, tough enough, and stubborn enough, then you might have a chance to be one of the few SOLO riders who make it through the FIRE of your NEW LIFE. Welcome to the Southern Tier!

DAY 38: Check out this AMAZING Alabama biking lane!

Chapter 127: Finish Strong

Whether you finish or not, your cross-country bicycle trek will likely be one of the most grueling physical, mental, and spiritual tests of your entire LIFE! From time to time as I spun my pedals round and round, I fantasized about finishing the Southern Tier. In my dreams, I saw myself completely exhausted with absolutely NOTHING left as I forced myself to make one last pedal stroke to propel my bicycle to the water's edge of the Atlantic Ocean as I collapsed on to the sandy beach in utter annihilation. Tears filled my eyes as I let the cool salt water rush upon me. Loved ones and other spectators were standing around clapping and cheering for me and then.............. I WOKE UP! It was all a dream and I was still a LONG WAY from finishing the rugged bike route!

Little did I know, I would eventually arrive at the sands of Jacksonville Beach and dip my front tire into the Atlantic Ocean at 1:03 p.m. on Saturday November 21, 2020. As the feelings of JOY brought me to my knees, I felt absolutely INVINCIBLE! On Day 43 at my finish as I pedaled my 82nd mile on that glorious day, I felt like I could easily turn around and continue my bicycle marathon back to the Pacific Ocean!!! I felt SO GOOD!!!!!

Upon completion of the Southern Tier, my body was lean and strong. My physique was carved as to see muscles hidden for decades under former mild layers of flab. All of my injuries were HEALED and I was in the BEST SHAPE of my life, even better shape than a decade previous when I completed 4 Ironman triathlons over the course of a two-year span. At the waters of the Atlantic Ocean stood a supremely HEALTHY man, a magnificent SPECIMEN of vigor and fitness!

My splendid finish of the Southern Tier exemplified my entire journey. It was the typical heroic ending to a quest filled with undue trials and tribulations. Not once between Day 2 and Day 42 did I really expect to finish. The tests contained as an inherent part of the Southern Tier were too arduous and I lacked many of the necessary qualities to finish, but I was too STUBBORN to go back home! By riding for "ONE MORE DAY," I eventually outlasted the Southern Tier and united with the Atlantic Ocean as the UNYIELDING underdog winner!

Finishing stronger than you started is an incredible way to complete one of the HARDEST journeys of your life, but finishing strong is only possible by making wise daily decisions as described throughout this book. A haphazard plan will NOT bring you to the beautiful Florida sands with an abundance of energy and vivacious health like it did for me! Consider the following PARTIAL list as these habitual actions are some of my most advised daily behaviors. Taking these daily steps along your cross-country bicycle crusade should help you to finish strong:

1. Pray OFTEN
2. 10-mile breaks (eat food, take a short walk, and do some light stretching)
3. 3-mile drinks (drink water and sports drink as you are pedaling)

4. Sleep at least 7 hours per night
5. Eat LOTS of food (eat 5,000 calories per day)
6. Recite positive affirmations OFTEN
7. Pedal SLOW (especially at first)

When you finish the Southern Tier, you should feel GREAT. Without a doubt, you should feel vibrant enough as to continue biking the following day if you so desired!

DAY 38: Alabama had a HURRICANE shortly before my arrival. Clean-up can take weeks after the massive storm takes its toll!

Chapter 128: Next Goal

While growing up in the eighties, I heard news reports of astronauts getting depressed upon returning home after achieving their goal of walking on the moon. Depression seemed like a bit of an exaggeration to me, but as I conducted further research into the phenomenon of post-goal achievement, I realized it is our goals themselves which create PASSION for life. It is NOT so much the attainment of the goals which creates JOY. Instead, it is the pursuit of worthy goals responsible for the ongoing experience of pure joy! Wow! What a distinction!

Approximately 99% of the people walking on planet Earth wrongly believe it is the ATTAINMENT of their goals which creates JOY, but I assure you it is NOT!!!! The secret involved in discovering true JOY can ONLY be found in the PROCESS itself! Only by pursuing a meaningful and worthwhile goal can you feel real joy! As you spin your pedals around, you might be like me and wonder how true joy could possibly come from such a mundane act of pedaling, but I assure you it does. If you can hang on long enough, you will experience joy from this unsuspecting source!

When you are passionate about doing something significant, you feel most ALIVE. While I was riding my bike through the desert in the middle of the night as to avoid the 105-degree afternoon temperatures, I never felt so alive in all my life. At times the ALIVENESS was actually more than I could handle and I found myself wiping tears from my cheeks as the power in the darkened desert air was almost debilitating. It was incredible to recognize myself pursuing a 30-year goal in such a brilliant landscape full of mystery and brimming with aliveness!

Climbing the Black Mountains in New Mexico on my way to reaching the 8,228-foot summit at Emory's Pass was another vivid experience which brought shivers to my skin as I sensed myself getting closer and closer to the splendid summit. With each switchback of the boundless mountain the turns got tighter and tighter and more and more severe. As I pedaled each bend in the road, resting from time to time, but never walking my bike even one inch, I'd get more and more excited as tingles rushed over me as I was approaching the brilliant peak of a MAJOR mountain pass.

At every turn I expected to be at the top of the mountain and each time my eager anticipation was denied. The crest was seemingly an allusion as the climb felt like it was ENDLESS. My sense of ALIVENESS was on full tilt with my body, mind, and spirit all at one as my bike and I dredged onward with maximal anticipation of the eventual 8,228-foot summit.

Riding across the long 3-mile Gordon Persons Bridge as I approached Mobile Bay in Alabama as crushing cross winds pummeled me forcing me to crouch down low to avoid being thrust over the 100-foot-plus guardrail into the cold waters of Mobile Bay was another bright experience prompting a whole new level of ALIVENESS within my being. Feeling truly alive is a sacred gift as most people usually only feel a basic sense of EXISTENCE from day to day. When you feel truly ALIVE, you are

FREE and your soul is soaring! It is only in those moments of most intense goal pursuit when you feel the real power of life. Attaining a special goal is nice, but its "The Climb" as magnificent musician, Miley Cyrus, claims is the real deal!

The journey itself is the prize! All throughout the Southern Tier, I wrongly assumed only a finish of the lengthy bike route would claim the hallowed award, but little did I realize with each additional daily ride I completed, I was becoming more and more ALIVE! The chains which held me captive for decades were being unlocked and I was SLOWLY set FREE without even being aware of it! No longer would I be contained within my little comfort zone as I was now experiencing a whole new dimension of life! My personal level of confidence was growing and I didn't even know it! It was my unlikely and monotonous DAILY pedaling efforts which enlightened my yearning spirit and gave me true JOY!

If you are anything like me, then you have heard about the many clinical studies PROVING the positive life benefits with regards to setting GOALS! No longer does any reasonable person even question whether or not goal setting is effective as we now know beyond a shadow of doubt all about the wonderful effects of goal-setting! So, instead of repeating the good works of other capable authors concerning goal setting, I will only remind you to keep a list of goals on your computer, in your wallet, or on your phone. Keep adding new goals as you feel inspired to do so. But most importantly, CHOOSE 3 or 4 goals as your PREMIERE GOALS. These goals should be at the top of your goal list as these are the goals you should be PURSUING now! As you accomplish your goals, keep adding new goals as the thrill of life can only be found in the CHASE!

Although setting goals is VERY IMPORTANT, you must remember....... JOY is NOT about achieving goals! JOY is about PURSUING your goals. Whether or not I ever finished the Southern Tier, the JOY I experienced each individual day during my special bicycle crusade made the critical difference no matter whether it was battling heat exhaustion in the Yuha Desert, riding the lonely desert highway in Arizona, climbing the mighty Black Mountains summiting Emory's Pass, outlasting a frigid hailstorm in Sierra Blanca, Texas, enduring the challenging terrain of the Texas Hill Country, feeling the power of the great Mississippi River, daringly crossing the Gordon Persons Bridge high above Mobile Bay during a MASSIVE windstorm, or pedaling without legal permission on the gigantic Interstate 95 in Florida as I approached the shores of the Atlantic Ocean. The joy I felt as I PURSUED my various daily destinations was quietly and unassumingly AMAZING! Finishing the Southern Tier was great, but it was the DAILY dose of joy largely responsible for me mounting my bike for yet another ride the following day.

Having a long list of WILD goals is great, but you must also have a small handful of REASONABLE goals in which you can IMMEDIATELY begin to pursue upon the completion of your current goal. One of my hundreds of lifetime goals is to die while pursuing my goals. My overall attitude is to keep PURSUING my goals every day as to keep myself ALIVE and passionate until the day in which my life is over. My plan seems to be viable and is working out pretty well so far!

As I got closer and closer to Jacksonville Beach, sporadically I would fantasize about a possible finish. I imagined police and fire trucks escorting me the last 3 miles to the gorgeous beach as a small group of people including my family waited patiently for me on the sparkling sands as I conclude my seemingly IMPOSSIBLE cross-country bicycle journey!

As I would allow myself to fantasize about my special Southern Tier calling, sometimes I pondered as to whether or not "my" calling was really all about me.? Maybe I was called to ride the Southern Tier as a necessary component for writing this book? Maybe I would be the vessel to which other aspiring cyclists and would-be cyclists turn to for guidance, support, and real-life advice regarding the completion of such a drastic undertaking? Maybe my initial calling wasn't all about me? Maybe my calling was BIGGER than I had originally envisioned!?

The more I considered my own special calling, the more I realized my expedition across the country on my bicycle wasn't even MY trip. My cycling crusade was becoming BIGGER than I ever originally expected. As I was preparing for the Southern Tier, not once did I consider writing a book about my adventure. In fact, I was determined NOT to write a book about my bike trip. Prior to my marathon bike travels, my mom queried me regarding my motivations for my proposed "insane" bike tour and I assured her my intentions were NOT to write a book, even though I have authored two books over 20 years prior.

It wasn't until I was about 100 miles into my very special sunshine state of Florida and about 300 miles from completion when I heavily felt "THE URGE!" It was the all-too-familiar CALLING I have become accustomed to feeling many other times throughout my life. In that moment of clear inspiration, there was NO DENYING one of my next goals was to write EPIC FAIL!

Considering the plethora of incredible life-altering experiences along my very long bike ride across America, there was NO WAY I could avoid writing this book. This book was DESTINED to come to print as my Southern Tier experience was so INTENSE, it would be ignorant and greedy for me NOT to share my story with you. The Southern Tier showed me her HEART and now it is my ASSIGNMENT to share my vivid experience with YOU!

Thousands of cyclists cross the United States and pedal through other countries on a bicycle, but most of them do so in organized groups or at least along with one other rider. These cross-country cyclists are VERY SPECIAL and deserve a HUGE congratulations as the miles are TOUGH no matter what the size of the group! Many of the setbacks and challenges mentioned in this book also exist for groups of cross-country riders.

Each year there are also numerous riders who initially take on the cross-country biking challenge ALONE and end up meeting up with another rider or two forming a group of their own. Sometimes the meet-up is planned and many other times the joined partnership is purely serendipitous. Of course, there are also cyclists like me who start ALONE and whom are dedicated to remaining ALONE for the duration of the trip!

Despite a brief 15-mile segment of my bicycle travels when I met and pedaled alongside my "brother," Matthew Wentzell, just outside of Globe, Arizona in the Arizona desert as he was traveling southbound to the Mexico border. Matthew and his friend, Michael, whom I did not meet, started at the Canadian border 60 days previous as they were riding their mountain bikes through the wilderness expanse of the United States. Little by little, they were approaching their final destination at the Mexican border. Matthew and I pedaled and talked for about 15 miles as we both quickly KNEW we were kindred souls! With the exception of sharing 15 miles of bike travel alongside angel Matt, I traveled the entire Southern Tier ALONE.

While biking through Florida, the inspirational feelings to write this book were unavoidable. No matter how much I tried to deflect the persistent, provoking thoughts, the stimulation remained! It was like my mind and spirit were POSSESSED until finally two days before completing the Southern Tier, I admitted to my wife, "I'm going to have to write a book." It was interesting as even though I knew I was being CALLED to write a book; I still didn't believe I would actually finish the Southern Tier! Each day my goal was simply to arrive at a particular destination. Some days I would make it and some days I would FAIL, but every day I would pedal my bike the best I could and arrive somewhere.

Writing this book served as my transition from finishing the Southern Tier to resuming "regular life." Yes, the feelings I felt as I approached Jacksonville Beach were the most concentrated feelings of pure joy I ever felt in my life, but after a few hours of near bliss, the feelings subsided and it was now time to adjust my thoughts toward one or more new goals, like hiking the ENTIRE 2,200-mile Appalachian Trail!

Regularly remind yourself about what ignites passion within you. Consider what activities stimulate the most excitement in your life and focus your attention there. At first, all I knew was my UNDOUBTABLE calling to ride the Southern Tier. Other than my quest to GROW my character and serve as a positive EXAMPLE to others, I had no other reason to take on the EPIC bike challenge. Sometimes LIFE doesn't share all the details with you at first. Oftentimes you have to travel down the road to a certain point and only upon arriving at a particular waypoint will LIFE reveal to you the next big step!

Keep taking ACTION toward your calling even if you don't have all the answers up front. The next step will be revealed to you when the time is right. Just keep pedaling and something GREAT will happen to you when you least expect it. Oftentimes, while my wife and I are paddling our canoe down a river, we will glance off to the distance and the river will appear to end, but only with continued paddling are we eventually permitted to realize which direction the water actually flows. The key is to keep moving toward your goal and the next step will be REVEALED to you when the time is right! When you make enough progress forward, the next big step will then become visible!

Don't be like most people who give up long BEFORE the monumental personal transcendence occurs. Hold on to your daily discipline of pedaling as it takes great staying power to keep your pedals spinning. Oftentimes, you won't feel like spinning your pedals and your mind will play tricks on you as you lose your focus. Sometimes you have to pedal merely because you said you would pedal! Remain dedicated to your harsh route and be open to ADDITIONAL CALLINGS as you pedal your bike across our great country!

Cross-country biking is also one of the BEST ways to obtain clear guidance from God as to how you should spend the REST OF YOUR LIFE! Don't go home too early and miss the big PAYDAY from the Southern Tier as your NEXT BIG THING is not far from being revealed to you! Keep pedaling!

As you are in the flow of your current activity, keep an OPEN mind because your next "assignment" is closer than you realize! After being informed of the successful completion of my epic bike ride across America, in utter disbelief my long-time friend, Keith Moors, declared in exasperation at our annual paintball Christmas party, "What are you going to do next? Climb Mt. Everest?" Hmmmm......

DAY 38: SHHHHH! I never told my wife about getting MARRIED to my bike!

Chapter 129: Eastbound in Louisiana

If you ever find yourself driving a vehicle through Louisiana, Mississippi, Alabama, or Florida and you see a cyclist pedaling a fully-loaded touring bicycle headed eastbound on the Southern Tier Bicycle Route, then you have just witnessed a VERY SPECIAL person! The worthy cyclist you passed has most likely completed over 2,000 miles of the Southern Tier and has OUTLASTED dozens of potentially trip-ending challenges while slowly pedaling eastbound toward the Atlantic Ocean. The solo rider you just saw is a statistical improbability and MIGHT actually make it! At least consider giving an encouraging honk of your horn or a "thumbs up" to the valiant cyclist!

As I traveled eastbound through the beautiful state of Louisiana, I came upon some road construction in one of the many gorgeous small towns. Although my progress was slowed down a bit by the road work, I was still moving. As I glanced forward and to the left, I noticed a small group of city workers wearing their bright reflective construction uniforms as they were obviously repairing the road as each of them were holding a shovel and they looked very tired.

One of the diligent workers alongside the road noticed me and my fully-loaded bicycle approaching and by the look on this young man's face, he CLEARLY knew I was an aspiring cross-country cyclist with over 2,000 miles logged into my epic cross-country bicycle journey. Immediately and distinctly, this respectful young man put down his large digging tool and quickly stood up straight never taking his eyes off of me and he clearly and proudly gave me a slow and steady STANDING OVATION for all to see! This man did NOT hold back in any way, shape, or form as he clearly wanted the entire community to see his blatant applause for my seemingly heroic cycling efforts.

As I passed the one-man standing ovation, our eyes met and I swear our spirits joined as my entire body felt chills just as my forearms and legs feel right now as I relive this supreme moment of connection with my young brother! After a brief wave of thanks, our encounter was OVER and I was gone, but the MOMENT will never be forgotten by me! It was the UTMOST act of kindness and support from my fellow man.

This dashing young man, more than 20 years younger my junior and of a different race, gave me a second wind that LASTED FOR DAYS. No matter what I did or tried to think, I couldn't get this unique, outstanding human being out of my mind! Although we only caught a quick glimpse of each other in passing, it was LOVE at first sight as we KNEW each other at some deeper level.

For hundreds of miles, it felt like my new friend was a part of my ride! Even right now, I feel invigorated as I share my story with you. My friend, my brother, made a FOREVER connection with me without speaking a single word. His clear act of respect and admiration will FOREVER remain with me. The whole town could have lined up and gave me a rousing standing ovation, but it would not have exceeded the IMPACT of this one ultra-respectful uniformed township street worker whom gave me the GREATEST standing ovation EVER!

For hundreds of miles after passing my admirer, I was brimming with renewed energy as I rode my 2 STRONGEST days through Louisiana. It was like I whizzed right through the entire stunning state! Even the winds were in my favor as my bicycle dominated the roads of Louisiana. It was in the state of Louisiana when I first SERIOUSLY had a thought I MIGHT finish the Southern Tier. Thanks to the fine young street employee in some unknown small town in Louisiana, I acquired a renewed sense of energy. This young man impacted my soul! I was truly MOVED by his forthright actions.

Another young man also with a different skin color than mine stopped me outside of McDonalds in Quincy, Florida. This reputable man was visibly EXCITED to meet me as he could not wait to find out where I came from and where I was headed. When I told the eager man I began pedaling over five weeks ago in San Diego, California at the Pacific Ocean, he was literally AGHAST. Instantly, this vivacious person seemingly started choking on his food as he began spitting chunks of his breakfast all over the parking lot. Suddenly, he became very nervous and couldn't stop fiddling with his hat as he seemed OVERLY stimulated. All indicators appeared as though this symptomatic guy was about to go into a full-blown convulsion!

As this fine, young, overly-stimulated man stammered and stuttered in his speech, he nervously and desperately searched for his cell phone through every pocket of his clothes as he refused to take his eyes off of me as he feared I would pedal away from him. As he finally grabbed hold of his cell phone, he was so EXCITED he almost dropped his phone to the pavement below. In pure desperation and shortness of breath, my new ADORING fan begged me to do a quick INTERVIEW with him.

Although I'm not 100% certain, I do NOT believe this frantic guy was connected to the local news or regional media. My new friend from Quincy, Florida simply wanted to MEET me and he was DETERMINED to capture this special moment on video as proof to his family and friends. Without even disclosing his own name, my admirer was clearly AWESTRUCK of my accomplishment and pleaded, "Please, just 3 minutes. I have to interview you. Nobody is ever going to believe I met you! Please! Please! Please!"

Considering the unusually high level of admiration exhibited by this high-energy man, I complied with his request and we did a phone video interview on the sidewalk of the Quincy, Florida McDonalds parking lot! It literally felt like I was a CELEBRITY and this was one of my crazed fans! As the interview concluded, the man fervently shook my hand as he stared at me so deeply as to never forget my face while exclaiming, "I never met anybody who pedaled a bicycle across the country. I didn't even think something like that was possible! You are amazing! I will NEVER forget you!"

This overzealous, passionate man clearly suffering from Attention Deficit Hyperactive Disorder (ADHD) brought a tear to my eye as his words of heartfelt sincerity connected with me at the DEEPEST level. As we parted ways, I'm sure he was frantically posting my video on every social media website known to mankind although I never looked for his posting nor did I ever hear any more about it, but it was truly my honor to pose as such a POWERFUL and INSPRIING example for another human being! Maybe someday my interviewing buddy will take on the Southern Tier Bicycle Route himself?

My Quincy, Florida admirer also prompted a sense of excitement and possibility within me. Maybe I could actually complete this ride? For the next 40 miles or so on that sunny Florida day, I didn't even need to pedal!!! My rekindled sense of confidence stemming from the extremely kind words from my adoring fan did all the pedaling work for me!

If you ever pass a cyclist pedaling westbound in New Mexico, Arizona, or California with a fully-loaded bike along the Southern Tier or a biker pedaling eastbound in Louisiana, Mississippi, Alabama, or Florida on the Southern Tier, then you have just witnessed somebody very special. You might want to offer the cyclist a bottle of Gatorade, a nice supportive honk, or a few words of encouragement as you just met a guy or gal who OVERCAME the odds. You just met a very special rider who OUTLASTED Hell and came out on the other side!

DAY 38: It was super-special arriving in Florida! Florida is like my second-home!!!

Chapter 130: Delayed Goals

For the 5 years prior to my cross-country jaunt, I was DEDICATED to learning the Spanish language! EVERY day I studied Spanish inching closer and closer to becoming fluent. Most days, I would use a popular mobile phone application known as "Duolingo" for my daily Spanish lessons.

As I began the Southern Tier, I quickly discovered there was NOT much extra time left daily for my Spanish goal. By the time I completed my daily ride, showered, did my laundry, ate supper, made plans for the next day, replied to my business texts, phone calls, and emails, and spoke with my family on the phone, there wasn't much time at all left in the day. As a result of my tight schedule, my Spanish language progress suffered. Prior to beginning the Southern Tier, I imagined having an extra hour each day to dedicate exclusively to my goal of Spanish fluency, but I was WRONG! By 8:30 p.m. in the evening on most nights, I was so tired I couldn't even think about completing a Spanish lesson!

While riding the Southern Tier, I did not totally abandon my Spanish practice, but I was hardly diligent. From time to time, I would complete a 15-minute lesson, but not often. Spanish is actually a very common language on the Southern Tier Bicycle Route as many inhabitants of the area have Mexican heritage and you will encounter many native Spanish speakers, but sadly to say, even when I came across a native Mexican with a primary Spanish dialect, I did NOT even try to communicate with the person in their native Spanish tongue. Instead of exerting the necessary extra effort trying to have a Spanish conversation with my new friend, I saved my exertion as it seemed like I needed every last OUNCE of my energy, drive, and concentration to pedal my bicycle the necessary miles to arrive at my daily destination.

Although I did NOT need to exert unnecessary energy anywhere else, I do REGRET not investing a bit more energy and using some Spanish communications along the way! Had I not been so obsessively locked into my daily mission; I could have enjoyed talking to a few more Mexican people and enjoying the amazing Spanish language as I normally would on a non-touring day. But like I said hundreds of times prior, my bike trip was NOT a vacation for me. I did NOT ride the Southern Tier as I way to expand my language fluency. My cross-country bike escapade across the southern United States was a divine MISSION from God!

Another ironclad daily habit of mine for the 25 YEARS prior to the Southern Tier was meditation. Each morning for about 20 minutes, I would sit still and quiet in a deep meditation. Meditation is my time of the day to align my mind and to unite with God through the great gift of SILENCE! As I give my mediation time to God, my only goal is to be STILL. I simply WITNESS the silence and acknowledge God as the ALMIGHTY! Without my long-term 25-year-plus daily practice of meditation, I'm SURE I would NOT have even BEGUN the Southern Tier, lead alone FINISHED it! Meditation has been a HUGE part of my life and I give high credit to my daily discipline of meditation for much of my lifetime success.

Despite my long-standing commitment to meditation, with a bit of shame, I must admit as I began the Southern Tier, my meditation practice quickly went from a good solid 20 minutes or more daily down to about 1 or 2 minutes daily. There were even days when I did not meditate at all, but in all fairness to myself and my epic bike journey, the entire Southern Tier Bike Route was a sort of meditation of itself! Instead of sitting with my eyes closed, quiet and alone in the morning, I would sit with my eyes wide open in the dark pre-dawn morning alone and at ONE with my surroundings. The Southern Tier actually provided the HIGHEST state of connection I've ever had with God, but I still slightly regret not meditating for at least 5 minutes EVERY day!

My point with this chapter is to prepare you for some rather major life changes. Trying to bike 70 miles a day will take a toll on your body, mind, and spirit. You will be affected by the daily mileage demands! Many of your regular daily habits and goals will be delayed as your "new life" won't have a lot of extra free time!

Not once during my trip, did I watch television for more than about 10 minutes at a sitting. At most, I glanced at a tv while I was eating supper or standing in line at a convenience store. There was NO TIME to watch tv. Watching TV wasn't even a thought in my mind!

One habit I did manage to maintain and even expand on the Southern Tier was PRAYING. As you know from my previous chapters, I prayed A LOT while riding the Southern Tier! In my case, prayer was an ABSOLUTE NECESSITY to sustain me on the wicked-hard course! Without prayer I GUARANTEE I would NOT have finished the epic Southern Tier Bicycle Route!

My wife and I pray out loud and together EVERY day of our lives. No matter where we are in the world or what we are doing, we PRAY TOGETHER!!! It does not matter if we are in the same room with each other or if we are thousands of miles apart on the phone. We ALWAYS pray together!

On most days, we pray in the morning after my wife wakes up. My wife likes to wake up around 9 a.m. while I like to wake up around 6 a.m. Tink will pray for about 2 minutes and then I will pray for about 2 minutes. We simply talk to God like he is our friend. We are not formal in any way. We calmly ask God to protect and guide us. Most of our prayers have to do with "may God's will be done." We pray for peace in our world and we mention our pets and family members by name. We ask for healing for those who are sick and blessings for our tenants, contractors, and suppliers. We give thanks for our lives and our health and we give praise to God for this beautiful day! We also ask for healing for our personal ailments as well as the necessary strength and energy to pursue our various personal and united divine CALLINGS!

In most cases along the Southern Tier, I would get in touch and pray with my wife while I was on one of my 10-mile breaks in which I paced back and forth alongside the road eating and drinking as I walked. Other times, I would answer Tink's call while I was pedaling my bike and we would pray as I spun my pedals around! We are NOT obsessive over any particular location or position in which to pray. As long as we pray, we are pleased and we believe God is pleased as well!

As you are preparing for your life's quest on a bicycle, get ready to let go of some of your habitual daily habits. You are about to die to your past life and be born to a NEW LIFE, a life filled with pedal rotations, sore muscles, and an army of untamed thoughts! When you are on your solo bike mission, you probably won't be hanging out at night clubs, taking tours of landmarks, or even watching tv. Almost everything you do will be to support your 70-mile daily biking habit! Welcome to the Southern Tier!

DAY 38: Wild camping behind the Pensacola Fire Station #3 on Summit Road was PERFECT! Nobody bothered me at all!

Chapter 131: Vegetarians

Ask anyone who spends significant time with me, "Is Sean Hockensmith an EXTREMIST?" and they would likely reply with a resounding "YES!" Even ask me the exact same question about myself, I would also agree! For me, "regular" is NOT good enough. Very short bicycle rides actually IRRITATE me as they seem like a waste of time!!! LONG DISTANCE cycling was made for me! Going far and going hard is what appeals to me! My spiritual dharma seems to involve GOING BIG! Extreme is what I prefer to do!!!!

As a fellow extremist, you will probably also find it necessary to eat A LOT of food to sustain your high-duration physical activity level. Consuming the ridiculous quota of 5,000 calories a day for me was an absolute requirement as I was burning about 6,000 calories a day, thus losing about a half pound daily. As I sat at the super-cute Majors Diner in Pine Valley, California along Highway 80 on Day 2, I FORCED myself to eat a HUGE breakfast even though I was not hungry at all. The food was GREAT, but I had other things on my mind and it was HARD to get the food down my throat, but fortunately I DID! Forcing myself to eat was absolutely necessary as I KNEW the end result of low caloric consumption could be disastrous to my long-term prospects!

During "regular life" at home, I am careful to eat a well-balanced diet as to minimize my consumption of sugar and red meat, but on the Southern Tier, I was a savage! On Day 7 when I finally got my appetite back, it seemed like I would eat anything. My two favorite stops along the Southern Tier were probably McDonalds and Dollar General. At these "restaurants," I would study the menu and order whatever food was the CHEAPEST with the MOST calories!!! To me, it really didn't matter if the food was considered "healthy" or not or even if I really liked the food! If the food had a lot of calories and it was CHEAP, then it was perfect for me!

Most days, I ate enough food for two and a half regular, non-biking adults. If an average adult human being eats about 2,000 calories per day, then I estimate I ate about 5,000 calories per day. Included in my diet was anything with A LOT of calories including plenty of meat!

At one point in my bike travels, I contemplated vegetarians and wondered how a vegetarian could possibly ride the Southern Tier without eating meat. After much deliberation while pedaling the Southern Tier, I couldn't come up with a reasonable answer and I STILL do NOT have the good answer today! With great apologies to all the AWESOME vegetarians walking around our intriguing planet whom I have GREAT respect, I don't know how you are going to cross the country on a bicycle without eating meat!

Although I am not saying it is impossible to ride a bicycle across the country without consuming meat, I am stating the already super-tough cycling task would suddenly becoming an even TOUGHER chore without eating meat! Only with a very strong calling combined with much more careful food planning than I, would a vegetarian be able to complete the Southern Tier, but I am absolutely CERTAIN it has been done and can be done!

Although I am NOT a vegetarian, I can only imagine the DEDICATION it would take to maintain true to your healthy lifestyle as you pedal a bicycle for 7 hours a day for over a month of your life. Anything is possible, but some pursuits are very difficult! Practicing a vegetarian lifestyle on the Southern Tier would be a TRUE TEST of your dedication to your food choices! Can it be done? YES!!! Will it be hard? ABSOLUTELY!!!!

DAY 39: Florida isn't all orange groves!

Chapter 132: COVID-19

During my cross-country biking expedition, COVID-19 infestations throughout the United States and worldwide were at the PEAK and millions of people around the globe lost their lives to this mysterious virus. Despite the massive loss of life from this powerhouse pandemic, I found myself CALLED to take on my outlandish cross-country bike ride and pedal is what I did!

As I progressed slowly across the country, my family back home warned me about a possible CLOSURE of my home state of Pennsylvania due to COVID-19. The rumor was Pennsylvania would SHUT DOWN its borders, not allowing anybody to return back inside its boundaries. Leaving the state of my lifelong residency was quite scary as I considered the possible repercussions!

COVID-19 only amplified my already-challenging bicycle journey into an even tougher venture! The nasty COVID-19 virus at least doubled my original anxiety and fear as the enigmatic virus literally shut down world economies and canceled holidays. "Regular life" was a distant memory as per the pandemic of 2020. Life as we knew it was different thanks to COVID-19!

Masks and symptom-testing were now the new norm. The ONLY thing I knew for sure with regard to my Southern Tier dedication was the CERTAINTY of my calling. It seemed weird for me to be "called" during the middle of one of the worst pandemics in modern history, but the calling was outside of my control. The Southern Tier was my DESTINY and I took my bizarre cross-country biking ASSIGNMENT very seriously!!!

One section of my Southern Tier Bicycle Route in Chiswick State Park in Louisiana was actually closed due to COVID concerns. There was a HUGE flashing billboard blocking the entire road with an undeniable neon sign reading "CLOSED" in bold flashing letters. Although the sign was undeniable, I IGNORED the giant NEON sign and stayed on route as I was over 2,000 miles into my laborious journey and NOT even the United States government could stop me! Or so I thought……..

It wasn't until about three miles further beyond the closed road sign when a stern Louisiana State Ranger PULLED ME OVER when I first realized the potential negative impact of my brazen decision to forgo the massive road closure sign. My casual ignoring of the giant federal road closed sign almost ended my consecutive bicycle travels as the strict Louisiana Ranger harshly threatened to PUT ME IN JAIL! Even after giving the officer a FULL-DOSE of my most-engaging personality and my most passionate "biking-across-America plea," the stoic police officer placed his tablet on the top of his police truck, took off his dark sunglass, peered deep into my eyes without any hint of emotion, and slowly enunciated each word as he said, "Turn around and get out of here RIGHT NOW. If you say ONE MORE WORD to me, I am taking you to jail!"

Without even a PEEP, I carefully turned my bike around and graciously retraced my route back to the giant road-closure sign and I followed the LONG DETOUR around Chiswick State Park which delayed my bike trip by at least an additional two hours! Despite adding a very long two hours to my already marathon bike travels, I figured the increased distance was MUCH shorter than the time I would have lost had I spent the night in the Louisiana jail! As I followed the detour signage, I also used my newly acquired Adventure Cycling phone app map, Bicycle Route Navigator, to confirm the detour directions. After about 120 minutes of biking ambiguity, I was finally back on route!

During this time of uncertainty amidst COVID-19, there was also talk of the buses, trains, and airlines shutting down indefinitely as many have already canceled thousands of scheduled transports. Many motels and campgrounds were also closed throughout parts of the Southern Tier Bike Route. Restaurants, stores, and visitor centers were either closed or had very limited hours. Life as I knew it was over. Each day was a complete GUESS as to what services would be available. Despite the worldwide hype, I focused on completing my daily mileage. COVID-19 was NOT sending me back home prematurely!!!

No matter whether COVID-19, COVID 20, or some other deadly numbered virus is still a threat or not when you attempt your bicycle crossing, there will undoubtedly be something else of a similar magnitude causing you to rethink your cycling plans! Some illness, war, hurricane, forest fire, or other natural disaster WILL surely challenge your most tedious cross-country cycling plans. The question is not whether or not you will have a big national obstacle to contend with, the only question is, "What exactly will it be?"

Part of partaking in such an extreme adventure like biking across the country involves ACCEPTING and MANAGING the significant national, regional, and local trials and tribulations confronting you. If it's not COVID-19, then it will be COVID-18 or something else, maybe even something completely different. No, I'm not advising you to be stupid and put your life in danger in the name of your bizarre biking adventure, but I am advising you to THINK FOR YOURSELF and resist canceling the experience of a lifetime because of media sensation!

In addition to COVID-19 concerns, there were also MAJOR forest fires within a few miles of my bike route outside of San Diego. Numerous times as I was struggling to climb out of the San Diego outskirts, I witnessed major charred areas of forest devastated by the recent wild fires. Hundreds of miles of forest were completely BURNED! The reality of the devastation was scary!

In all fairness, I must admit I was OBLIVIOUS to most of what was happening around me as I pedaled across the United States. Most days, I didn't follow the news or weather reports. If something REALLY IMPORTANT was going on in the world, then I figured I would hear about it when I checked in with my family at night or some stranger at the convenience store would mention it to me. As for weather, I consider almost all weather as "GOOD" as I believe if you have proper quality gear, then 98% of the weather is "good weather." It is unusual for a cold and dreary local weather forecast or even an international pandemic to change my plans! Maybe that's why it's so hard for me to find others willing to accompany me on my adventures?

DAY 39: No berm, but no big deal!

Chapter 133: Mosquitoes, Ants, and Pigs

To my surprise, mosquitoes were NOT a factor on my bicycles travels across the southern portion of the USA. Not once can I recall being bit by a mosquito or by any type of flying insect and I didn't even wear mosquito repellent, but don't count on being so lucky as mosquitoes can cause a significant disruption to your bike travels! Your best strategy might be to stop at Dollar General or Walmart and buy some mosquito repellent if you encounter mosquitoes. As I have discovered on numerous occasions, itchiness can often be worse than PAIN!

Years prior to my crossing of the Southern Tier, I was removing a row of bushes at our Oak Street rental property in the Hornerstown section of the City of Johnstown with my wife, and two of our children, Stacey and Curtis. While removing the bushes on an extremely hot summer day, we all got a SEVERE case of poison ivy in which the itchiness almost drove us mad! For weeks we battled our outbreaks while on the brink of insanity!

The Southern Tier is hard enough without contending with itchiness as it is possible for a bunch of irritated mosquito bites to drive a person crazy! A few years back in the summer on a multi-day canoe paddling adventure through Wilkes Barre, Pennsylvania on the ageless Susquehanna River, my wife and I were bit over 40 times each by pesty mosquitoes causing us SEVERE agitation. Another time while camping in Florida, I was bit over 100 times THROUGH MY MOIST SOCKS by a mosquito-type insect commonly known in Florida as no-see-um. The itchiness CONSUMED my thoughts for 2 days!!!!

In all sections of the Southern Tier and most other major bicycle routes, ants will also be PLENTIFUL! Ants are known for making little piles of dirt to house THOUSANDS of their family members! These "ant hills" are about the size of your fist and to the untrained eye look innocent and harmless, but they can END your special bike trip if you are not careful! Ants bite and when there are thousands of ants, there is a significant risk to your overall well-being as you could be "eaten alive!"

Before you place your chair on the ground and especially before you set up your tent, scan the ground around you with special emphasis on locating ant hills. If you set your tent on or very near an ant hill, you could possibly find your tent, your equipment, and yourself covered with THOUSANDS of hungry little ants, each one with the potential to make you MISERABLE!

While staying in the quaint little town of Duncan, Arizona in the gorgeous, little, courtyard adjacent to the Simpson Hotel, my Warmshowers host, Deborah Clayton, reminded me THREE TIMES to shut the fencing gate at night. When I asked my gracious host why, she replied, "If you leave the gate open, your tent will be surrounded with wild pigs throughout the night." She went on to explain how the feral swine roam the Arizona night looking for food.

My courteous host informed me that the pigs CANNOT climb very well nor can they jump, but they can walk well and they have no problem strolling through a gate opening and causing me a memorable late-night disturbance. Surprisingly, the pigs are capable of running up to 30 miles per hour and they have a strong muscular build with sharp teeth and hard cloven hooves. No, the pigs are NOT ferocious nor are they known to attack, but they do like to eat and they do travel in packs which was enough facts for me to try to keep my distance from them! Long before I went to bed inside the Duncan, Arizona courtyard, I double-checked to make certain the sturdy fence gate was completely CLOSED! And like every other night on the Southern Tier, I slept like a baby despite knowing the mysterious wild pigs were lurking close by.

One other time I was warned of the "night-time pigs." It was during my stay at Hyde Park Campground in Easleyville, Louisianna. The campground manager permitted me to set up my tent in a large, open picnic area in the far back of the park in a remote location bordering a wooded forest. Under a large pavilion with a cement floor is where I slept.

The good-natured manager advised me to put my food bags on top of the picnic table or even in the rafters of the pavilion as to avoid a late-night encounter with the wild swine! Considering the remoteness of this particular camping location, I was compliant with the manager's advice. Although my camp location was a bit scary as I was all alone in the back of the darkened park, it did not thwart me from getting another AMAZING night's sleep! And to my knowledge, there was no pig activity throughout the night in the vicinity of my tent.

Chapter 134: Medicine

My overall adult medicinal strategy has been to AVOID using medicine as much as possible. Throughout my college years, I even studied Religious Science and Christian Science and attended their services outside of my own already-full collegiate curriculum. With great passion, I believed as a young adult and even now as an older adult in the power of THOUGHT and how it relates to healing while using little or no medicine. Although I definitely believe in the IMPORTANCE of medicine, I also BELIEVE in the under-developed power of thought as it impacts health much more than we currently realize.

Much of my life has been an adventure in discovery as I want to know the FULL STORY about the many different facets of life, especially religion and spirituality. Learning only about Christianity or Catholicism as a child was NOT enough for me. I wanted to know about other religions and others spiritual practices. I wanted to learn about EVERYTHING and then CHOOSE for myself my own beliefs and practices, but with my brimming diversity came opposition as my OWN family wrongly accused me of being in a "cult" during my college years. Despite the harsh criticism, I couldn't resist my own pursuit of THE TRUTH! And I'm glad I did as I discovered the other religions and spiritual practices were all GOOD and were loaded with tons of life-changing principles! Thanks to my OPEN-MINDEDNESS, I learned about many life truths taught by various organizations, disciplines, and spiritual resources despite being less than encouraged to do so.

Despite being semi-opposed to modern medicine, I must admit several medicinal drugs have IMPROVED the quality of my life and one or two drugs had a part in saving my life on various occasions! Therefore, within reason and with good balance, I actually endorse the careful use of medicinal drugs when necessary.

From time to time on the Southern Tier, I would take an Ibuprofen or Tylenol (acetaminophen) to deal with some muscle soreness. While in the vicinity of Austin, Texas I was battling a rather severe knee injury and I took Ibuprofen and Tylenol regularly to deal with the pain and swelling. Both medicines were VERY helpful with my eventual recovery!

Since the Southern Tier, I have also discovered another "miracle" medicine called Naproxen Sodium which has helped me to overcome a VERY SEVERE lower back injury. For years my lower back tortured me with pain at various times. Neither ibuprofen nor Tylenol provided much relief at all! In utter desperation, I scanned our medicine reserves and I found a bottle of Naproxen Sodium in the generic "Equate" label. After reading the bottle, I discovered the medicine was FIVE YEARS expired! Despite my wife urging me to throw the bottle away, I took the recommended dosage and the Naproxen Sodium alleviated MOST of my back pain within 2 days. The effects were MIRACULOUS!

On ALL future bike rides, hikes, canoe trips, and other adventure expeditions, I will be taking my bottle of expired Naproxen Sodium with me! Upon sharing the good healing news with my family doctor, Dr. Travis Rearick of Johnstown, PA, Doc informed me that Naproxen is just a slightly stronger form of ibuprofen. But for some unknown reason, Naproxen Sodium works like a miracle for me regardless of whether the medicine is expired or not! Sometimes there is no medical explanation why a particular drug works so well for one person and hardly works at all for another person. Pay close attention to any medicine you take as YOU are the most significant health provider in your own life. YOU are much more valuable to your healthy future than any doctor you will ever visit!

Another semi-miraculous drug for me is Mucinex DM (1,200 milligrams). If I get a bad cold or flu, the first medicine I grab is Mucinex DM. Mucinex DM dries up my congestion like no other medicine I ever took. Combined with regular Tylenol use, in most cases, I can quickly minimize the effects of a cold or flu!

During my recent 30-day, 373-mile Appalachian Trail hiking adventure, I took ONE ibuprofen every day prior to the start of my daily hike. Prior to my 30-day hiking trip on the A.T., I had NEVER finished a hike longer than 3 nights in my LIFETIME without being injured. Using ibuprofen and many other strategies I'll explain in a possible upcoming book about hiking the Appalachian Trail, I finished the grueling 373-mile section hike of the southern portion of the Appalachian trail from the southern terminus of Amicalola Falls, Georgia to the northbound location at Iron Mountain, Tennessee!

If you have a proven drug that works for you, then make sure you take it along on your epic bike ride. Another effective "drug" for me is TUMS or the generic knock-off. Tums tablets seem to instantly help me with indigestion, heart palpitations, and even seems to minimize any shortness of breath. Taking 3 tablets when needed seems to work fine for me as my family doctor, Dr Rearick, believes antacid tablets are even safe enough for pregnant women to take!

No matter how holistic you are or how holistic you aspire to be, medicine is IMPORTANT and should be considered carefully as you plan your epic bicycle quest across the country!

Chapter 135: Feelings

Since my goal in writing this book is to hold NOTHING back, I feel compelled to share every last potentially-significant piece of relevant information concerning a cross-country bike excursion……. no matter what. Even though I'm not 100% comfortable mentioning this particular semi-sensitive topic, I am dedicated to FULL DISCLOSURE! So, here goes….

Being away from your spouse or significant other for an extended amount of time will create a potential gap in your "sex life" which may create a significant issue with regard to special genital FEELINGS which may arise during your trip. In my case, the culture shock combined with the excessive daily physical exertion demands seemed to drain me of MOST my sex drive. During my 45 days away from home (43 riding days and 2 travel days), only twice did I masturbate and only once was it successful. If you are a teenager reading this book, then your physical urges will be MUCH more severe and much more frequent than mine as I was in my late forties during my cross-country travels!

If there was anything I truly yearned for on my bike trip, it was SLEEP at night. By 8:30 p.m. each night, I was EAGER to go to sleep as I called forth and used every last drop of my daily energy reserves throughout the day on my bicycle. Several times I fell asleep while speaking to my wife on the phone during the evening hours. Most nights I slept from approximately 9 p.m. until approximately 4:30 a.m. It seemed like my body REQUIRED about 7.5 hours of sleep per night in order to maintain the heavy demand of 70 miles of daily pedaling which completely DRAINED me every day. During each day and certainly by the end of the day, I had very little interest in anything other than REST!

Even though cross-country cycling is very tiring, 45 days is a LONG TIME to be away from your spouse, family, and comforts of home. You will experience all kinds of different FEELINGS and URGES during your travels and for the most part, it will be up to you to meet your own needs whether they be emotional or physical. Once again, I remind you, a cross-country cycling crusade is TOUGH in every way you can imagine! Don't underestimate your physical urges and feelings as they could potentially be significant at times! Welcome to the Southern Tier!

Chapter 136: Oncoming Vehicles

For those of you who might be completely new to road biking, the laws of the road require bikes to travel in the SAME direction as vehicular traffic. When possible, it is best to travel on the berm of the road which is the section of road to the right of the white painted line. When the berm of the road is either too thin or non-existent, cyclists are then forced to ride in the SAME lane as vehicular traffic, generally on or very close to the exterior white-painted line along the right side of the road.

Although it is proper to ride on the right side of the road, you must be careful NOT to ride too far and too tight to the right! My unofficial bike coach and official friend, Layne Gneiting, warned me to always give myself at least 18 inches to the right of my bike in case I ever need it! You never know exactly what scenario may unfold on any given roadway, so it is smart planning to give yourself some EXTRA SPACE to move further right, if necessary to avoid an incident!

Anytime the berm on the road is too small or even non-existent, it is important to establish your bike in the vehicular travel lane. Taking up a small and respectful portion of the outer right-side portion of the vehicular travel lane communicates your intent to the vehicles over-taking you from the rear. Your solid presence in the travel lane lets over-taking vehicles know exactly how much room they have to pass by you. The worst thing you can do is to weave in and out of the vehicle travel lane. It is much better to HOLD on to your solid position as not to confuse any vehicular drivers approaching you from the rear. Give the vehicles on the road as much room as you can, but don't short yourself in the process!

My cycling goal is ALWAYS safety first. Establishing myself on the actual ROAD is much safer than riding on the SIDEWALKS! Often, I witness bikers pedaling on sidewalks as to avoid the "dangerous" roads, but I can't help but to pity those ignorant riders as they are multiplying the dangers of their bicycle travels. Sidewalks are very DANGEROUS places to ride! In most cases, you will be much safer riding directly on the road as described above. Road riding puts your bicycle closer to the vehicles, but it also makes you and your bicycle much more VISIBLE than sidewalk cycling!

VISIBILITY is a major KEY to bicycle safety. If the other cars around you can see you, then your risk of an accident is much lower! The most dangerous part of sidewalk riding is when a cyclist approaches a crossroad. Many sidewalk cyclists do NOT stop as they cross over intersecting roads. Without even a glance to their left for any possible right-turning cars, they proceed across the road making for a very dangerous situation for themselves. All it takes for a terrible accident to occur is for one unsuspecting 4,000-pound car to turn at the exact same time as the cyclist is crossing the road!

Instead of sidewalk cycling, establish your bicycle firmly ON THE ROAD and make good use of your rear-view mirror. Remain steady and strong as you take only the portion of road you need to maintain adequate safety. Most of the time there will be a nice, little berm for you to travel, but always be prepared when there is no berm. In most cases, the road is safer than the sidewalk, but in a small number of cases, a sidewalk might be a better choice. If you ever find yourself riding on a sidewalk, then you must be EXTRA ALERT and STOP at every road intersection. You must also be extra alert for cars coming in or out of driveways as well as kids or pets playing on or near the sidewalk.

Prior to the Southern Tier, I was on an overnight training ride pedaling back home on Day 2. As I was traveling along PA Route 96 northbound on a two-lane highway with vehicle traffic traveling both directions in excess of 55 miles per hour, I suddenly looked up and noticed a car from the opposite direction speeding directly toward me IN MY LANE!!! Clearly, the speeding car never saw me as the driver of the car decided to pass the car in front of him which made a VERY DANGEROUS situation for me and my bicycle! Fortunately, I looked up just in time and noticed the speeding car approaching me head-on in my lane. Abruptly, I veered off to my right across the small gravel berm on the side of the road and into the grassy yard of some random homeowner as I saved my own life!

Prior to this HUGE SCARE, never once did I ever stop to consider the possibility of this not-so-strange scenario unfolding as I was taking a bike ride, but now I EXPECT it! Legally and technically, the passing vehicle should NOT have made a pass attempt as my bike was clearly occupying a portion of the opposing vehicular lane needed for the passing vehicle to overtake the car in front of him, but road laws and legalities mean NOTHING if the end result is a DEAD cyclist! Now, I PAY ATTENTION to vehicles on BOTH sides of the road coming from either direction as I now know ALL vehicles pose a considerable risk to my biking safety, especially oncoming PASSING vehicles approaching me from the other side and opposite direction on the street!!!

Road biking is a DANGEROUS activity, but you can GREATLY reduce the risks by practicing the many suggestions offered herein and always being open to learning more with regard to safe biking practices. Having a constant awareness of your surroundings and always being on the lookout for potential dangers will also serve you well and help to keep you SAFE!

During another training ride prior to the Southern Tier, I was riding along and I noticed a man in his driveway waiting to make a left turn on to the road in which I was traveling on my bike. As I approached the man in the vehicle, it seemed like he was about to pull out at any moment. I applied some brake and finally made a solid eye contact with him before I passed by his paused vehicle.

Had I not made a SOLID eye contact with the driver, my plan was to STOP before crossing in front of the turning car as it is foolish to HOPE a vehicle driver won't pull out in front of you! Always EXPECT the worst and then take the SAFE route! Sounding a loud bell or other horn-like device would have been another wise move on my part as I approached the suspicious vehicle. When in doubt, slow down or even stop. Get off the road. Do whatever is necessary to avoid any possible chance of a collision! Be aware at ALL TIMES as it only takes ONE mistake to end your special outing or to conclude your life!

DAY 39: I love to see posted signs for bike lanes!

DAY 39: The Southern Tier includes portions of numerous bike TRAILS. Here is an awesome Florida bicycle trail!

Chapter 137: Encouragement

One of the most IRRITATING comments I heard while attempting the Southern Tier was "You got this!" Almost daily my wife would tell me, "You got this!" What my lovely and sweet wife meant by regularly repeating "You got this!" was simply "You can complete the Southern Tier!" Although Tink meant well and her intent was merely to encourage me, her words actually angered me! How could she tell me "You got this!" when I have ALREADY failed and I'm just hanging around for one more day? Doesn't Tink realize the massive difficulty involved with this ridiculous bike ride?

Each time Tink would make mention about me finishing the Southern Tier, I would argue with her. To me, her words were absurd. Doesn't she understand what I am going through? How could she be so convinced of my eventual completion of this grueling task? Doesn't she have any idea about the PUNISHMENT I am putting myself through on a daily basis to complete these rugged miles? Doesn't she realize the emotional and physical exhaustion I am experiencing? Can't she sense my ongoing struggle with my own thoughts? Doesn't she know I am teetering on the brink of exhaustion?

Although COMPLETING the Southern Tier was my original goal, I quickly learned I had largely overestimated my physical abilities and completely disregarded my current level of mental and emotional development. By Day 2, my cross-country ride was OVER! From Day 2 on, my goals were MUCH SMALLER as I was simply taking DAILY RIDES as I had already relegated my thoughts of completing the Southern Tier as being IMPOSSIBLE! Having felt the pain of failure and having already accepted my defeat, my wife's loving words of encouragement were like an ongoing TORTURE to me!

No matter what I said or how intense I would argue the point, my wife's opinion was NOT to be swayed. In her rigid estimation, I was COMPLETING the Southern Tier and NOTHING LESS! Looking back on the frustrating experience, my wife obviously had A LOT more faith in me than I had in myself. She clearly KNEW something about me I had yet to discover about myself! Tink KNEW my destiny was to be a cross-country cyclist, but her encouragement remained difficult for me to endure!

Had I been more mature, maybe I could have handled myself and my wife's loving words with more patience and calm, but I wasn't yet developed to that level! Finding myself in the MIDDLE OF NOWHERE on a bike with all of my belongings hanging over top of my tires challenged every last bit of my composure and self-control! The Southern Tier EXPOSED all of the weaknesses I tried so hard to COVER UP for all the previous years of my life. As I pedaled alone through the vast desert expanse, ALL of my past INSECURITIES stared back at me! For possibly the first time in my life, MYSELF was revealed to MYSELF! Now, what do I do?

The Southern Tier and all other great bicycle routes will tear open and EXPOSE most of your hidden issues and deficiencies! This is what I mean when I say "You will meet your SOUL!" While riding the Southern Tier, you WILL meet the parts of you that have been carefully covered over for years, the parts of you disguised with a myriad of defense mechanisms. For the first time in your life, the true YOU might be EXPOSED to yourself!

As a teenager, I took a 65-mile bike ride over Tussey Mountain in western Pennsylvania to the Seven Points Campground in Hesston, PA with one of my classmates and lifelong friends, Ryan Imler, whom was commonly known as "Tweeter" back in high school. Tweeter and I were UNPREPARED in every way for the grueling terrain involved in our subject bike ride. Our bikes were average at best. We had limited food and not nearly enough water. And neither of us had any substantial cycling experience. The only thing we really had was each other!

At the 17-mile point of our unforgettable bike adventure while still in Portage, PA, Tweeter declared, "I can't go any further!" to which I replied, "Come on. You can do it!" Reluctantly, Tweeter bought into my short motivational speech, resumed pedaling, and outlasted his initial fears and self-doubt as he seemingly got stronger with each successive mile.

As for me, summiting Tussey Mountain was extremely tough! It took EVERYTHING I had to get over the 2,700-foot crest. After coasting down about 3.5 miles of pure bliss from the mountaintop, I reached mile 45 near the Saxton, PA vicinity and I couldn't seem to pedal anymore. Even on the level roads, I had no more gusto left in my legs, my mind, and my heart. The gap between Tweeter and I kept getting further apart as I finally stopped pedaling as I assumed my biking adventure had come to an end. Moments later, Tweeter appeared and encouraged me in a similar manner by repeating my own previous words of encouragement, "Come on. You can do it!"

Although it was UGLY, I got back on my bike and bought into Tweeter's brilliant motivational speech as Tweeter and I managed to finish our 65-mile EPIC bike ride to Seven Points Campground. Looking back, neither one of us would have completed the rigorous bike ride on that particular day had it not been for each other's positive presence and ENCOURAGEMENT. When Tweeter got down, I picked him up and when I got down, Tweeter picked me up! We were a true team of loyal, determined, teenage dummies!

On the Southern Tier, there were many times I looked over my shoulders hoping to see my buddy, Tweeter, but Tweeter was not there! Only through my memory of Tweeter and my recollection of Tweeter's encouragement could I access his brilliant words sounding off in my mind as I battled the fierce elements of the Southern Tier while pushing onward and eventually completing a formidable cross-country bike quest!

Riding the Southern Tier will likely be the MOST INTENSE psychotherapy you will ever experience! Get ready for some UGLY growth, especially when you take on a crushing cross-country bike route all by yourself! Riding all alone without having any helping encouragement at certain key moments of tribulation is often the departing reason for cyclists whom allow their negative thoughts to take too strong of a position in their fledgling mind! It's strange, but a lack of encouragement or too much encouragement are BOTH especially dangerous to a solo cyclist with a FRAGILE, developing mind and a debatable level of poise.

Blaming your wife or your other loved ones for their well-meant comments won't help your overall cause! YOU got yourself into this mess and YOU are the ONLY one capable of getting yourself out! It does no good to transfer your iniquities over to your loved ones, especially your devoted spouse!

Quitting is an option, but the long-term pain of quitting might be worse than the pain to remain on the route. Quitting has a way of grinding away your spirit. In most cases, it is EASIER to face your fears and reconcile your pressing inner issues than to live with the never-ending gnawing pain of FAILURE!

Taking on a "new life" with RAW emotions left me struggling for some sense of continuity. It felt like my emotions were tearing me apart as I desperately forged on hoping to establish some type of sound emotional foundation, some type of base support! My vulnerability on the Southern Tier was obvious as I was so weak, even compliments and words of encouragement triggered feelings of anger and betrayal deep within me. To my surprise, the Southern Tier provoked me to discover I was a MESS of a human being with many glaring weaknesses! The Southern Tier tested me in more ways than I ever could have previously imagined! Welcome to the Southern Tier!

DAY 39: Florida Route 90 is a great biking road!

Chapter 138: Untied Shoe Laces

As I was pedaling through the vicinity of Wickenburg, Arizona, my right shoelace came untied as it quickly wrapped around my pedal tightly causing me instant concern as I could feel severe pressure on my right foot. It felt like the pressure was enough to cause an accident on my bike or possibly damage my foot before the shoelace would eventually break! Without hesitation, I immediately stopped my bike and unwrapped the shoelace from my pedal before it became a much more serious issue. It was one of the many "close calls" I experienced traveling the solitary roads of the Southern Tier.

Ever since having this particular shoelace scare, I made it my business to tie my shoestrings TWICE and then carefully tuck them firmly under the manufacturer Velcro strap on my cycling shoes. Taking the necessary time to tie my shoes properly is the correct choice as the epic Southern Tier Bike Route is hard enough without adding STUPIDITY to the mix! Under no circumstance should your shoes EVER come untied while you are pedaling! Untied shoes are purely a CARELESS act which can and should be avoided in ALL cases. Like my insightful and cordial son, Curtis Hockensmith, would say, "Don't be a JACKWAGON!"

The same preventative course of action is necessary with rain pants. Sometimes rain pants can be slightly bulky and could possibly cause a potential issue if they were to contact the bike chain or get caught on a bike mechanical. While wearing my rain pants on the Southern Tier, I wrapped 2 Velcro bands around the lower portion of my rain pants near my shins as to prevent any type of possible entanglement in my chain or possible collateral damage to my rain pants.

Since finishing the Southern Tier, instead of using my very-adequate $30 Pioneer rain pant bibs purchased from Amazon, I bought $100 rain pants from Adventure Cycling which were constructed with 2 factory-made Velcro straps at each ankle to keep the pant legs away from the bike chain! Sometimes it pays to get really GOOD EQUIPMENT!

Save yourself dozens of hours of time and hassle and get your equipment directly from Adventure Cycling. Had I done so, I could have avoided the necessity of wrapping hillbilly Velcro straps around my pant legs as proper cycling rain pants already have attached everything you need! Order your gear on the Adventure Cycling website, call them on the phone, or browse through their excellent CYCLOSOURCE catalog! You will thank me later!!!!

Another area of possible safety concern is your "stack" which is located on the frame directly above your rear tire. In order to fasten your heavy-duty waterproof dry bag stack to your frame, you should use ROK straps. ROK straps are basically adjustable Bunji cord straps with loops on each side and a removable buckle in the middle. These extra features allow you to EASILY and EFFECTIVELY tighten the ROK straps as to make your stack completely SECURE! Buying ROK straps are mandatory! Don't even consider trying to use anything else!!! ROK straps are PERFECT for traveling cyclists! There are several sizes of ROK straps available and you should probably get the small or medium size. Of course, ROK straps are also sold in the remarkable Adventure Cycling's CYCLOSOURCE catalog.

After attaching two astounding ROK straps over top of your stack, you will have a leftover portion of the ROK straps that must somehow be secured to your bike stack as to prevent the surplus ROK straps from getting caught in your rear bike tire spokes and causing unnecessary issues. Carefully secure the excess pieces of ROK strap by twisting them around the already tight pieces of ROK straps as to make sure the unused pieces of ROK straps are secured with no chance of coming loose and causing you a potential safety problem.

One night after my stack was already removed from my bike, I rode my bike about a quarter mile down the street without realizing my ROK straps were still attached to my rear pannier frame. Within the short quarter mile distance of travel, one of my ROK straps got caught in my tire spoke and RIPPED IN HALF!!! How could I be so STUPID??? Why didn't I inspect my bike before taking the very short ride? How careless!

Completing all of these "little" tasks involving shoestrings, rain pants, and ROK straps require time before you take your first pedal stroke as these dutiful tasks are a mandatory part of your 30 to 60-minute morning preparation as you prepare for your morning ride. Never hop on your bike in a haphazard way without paying close attention to the various DETAILS needed to ensure as SMOOTH a bike outing as possible. Not thinking enough in the evening before bed and not re-thinking early in the morning before departing on your daily travels will cause you tons of PROBLEMS! Avoid unnecessary problems by investing the necessary preparation time before you leave in the morning. Skipping on your pre-ride preparation will cost you at least 10 times more time and 50 times more frustration while you are broken down alongside the road than it would have cost you to invest a few extra minutes to prepare well in advance!

Chapter 139: Annoyed

On Day 2 of my epic bike journey, I found myself climbing a steep incline going much slower than I had hoped. It felt like I was pedaling and not going anywhere. It was super-hot and I was tired. As I stopped to rest, I wondered if I might have overestimated my abilities. Who was I to think I could pedal a bicycle across the country? I'm barely out of San Diego and I'm tired and my legs are starting to hurt. How long is this trip going to take? Do I really have what it takes?

By the time I entertained all the various thoughts going through my mind, I was left feeling very LOW. In that moment, it was HIGHLY IMPROBABLE for me to finish the cross-country trip. Yes, I overestimated my abilities and now I just have to figure out how to get back home. But getting back home wasn't going to be an easy task! There was A LOT of planning involved in getting myself and all of my equipment off of the popular Southern Tier Bicycle Route and surely there would be a lot of planning and hassles getting all of my belongings back home!

Feeling the sheer ANNOYANCE involved with thinking about all the logistical ways to get my stuff and myself back home, I decided to finish my ride for the day. Then, after my day's ride, I would consider abandoning the devastating course. At the time, the painful miles of pedaling combined with the high anxiety of culture shock ultimately seemed LESS painful than the anticipated hassle and ANNOYANCE of trying to find a way back home. So, mile after mile I kept pushing my pedals around. Eventually, I arrived at my destination for the day, but I was TOO TIRED to even think about going back home as the logistics would take too much effort. Naturally, I decided to postpone my terminal decision until the following day.

The next day arrived and I just kept pedaling eastbound as my map directed me. Why not enjoy the scenery on my LAST DAY? In a manner similar to the previous day, I completed my planned mileage and made it to my destination. Wow, I just finished Day 3!!! Maybe riding across the country was too big for me, but I was definitely capable of riding my bike ONE MORE DAY!

Doubts WILL creep in. Suddenly, you will be riding along and menacing thoughts will take over your battled mind. What am I doing out here? Nobody is paying me to ride my bicycle across the country. Do I really need all this pain? I could be at home watching football right now! What was I thinking?

Prepare yourself for the doubts. If you EXPECT the doubt before it sneaks in, then you will be ready to "ride" it out. If the doubt manifests and you haven't already considered it, then your doubt might be enough to take you to the nearest airport, bus, or train station to go back home! If nothing else works and you are about to abandon your route, take a moment to think about how ANNOYING it would be to change your plans, go home, and answer all the soul-piercing questions regarding your recent DEMISE! Maybe after a careful deliberation, you will be like me and realize it is <u>easier</u> overall to REMAIN on the epic bike route!?

Chapter 140: Camera

As an AMATEUR photographer, I experience great joy taking photos of my various adventures and capturing many of the special times with family and friends. Hopefully, you are enjoying some of my special photos I've enclosed on the pages of this book! If you are like my wife and I, then you too will love looking back through photos remembering distinct times!

As part of my photography hobby, I go to GREAT LENGTHS to make sure ALL of my photos are perfectly organized by event and by year on our long-term photo storage devices. Our photo collection is also backed up and stored in an off-site location as we consider our photo collection to be invaluable. Photos are VERY important to me!!!

While traveling the Southern Tier, I kept a mid-quality waterproof digital camera in my handlebar bag for easy access while spinning my pedals. With relative ease and without the need to stop my bike, I could retrieve my camera and take photos as I was actually riding my bike. Although my Samsung Galaxy cell phone took slightly better photos than my digital camera, I used my digital camera while I was pedaling since my cell phone was much more difficult to access inside the tight waterproof cell phone case which was mounted on my handlebars. Accessing my digital camera only involved a careful and quick unzipping of my handlebar bag which seemed to be a reasonable struggle. Doing so did not seem to compromise my safety in any way.

Each morning, I would marvel at the rising sun in the eastern sky as it would break through the skyline in its majestic manner shedding light on God's world! Not once did I get tired of the majestic sunrises. Most mornings, I was CAPTIVATED with the POWER and BEAUTY of the rising sun as I would try to capture the best of the early morning revelation with my trusty camera. And I must say, some of my photos were AMAZING!

As I entered new towns or noticed brilliant landscapes, I would slow down, carefully get my camera out of my handlebar bag, and take a photo. Although the various landscapes and terrain photos were amazing, my most-prized photos were of the people I met along the way. As you are traveling across the country, remember to ask your new friends if you can take a photo of them. With the proper humble request, most people will comply with your reasonable request and some will even be honored! The photos of the brilliant landscapes will be VALUABLE, but your photos of your new friends will be PRICELESS!

With a significant level of sadness, I must admit I FAILED to take photos of most of the wonderful friends I made along the way pedaling my bike across the country. Only a few of the almost 1,500 photos I took included those special friends whom meant so much to me and my journey. Don't be like me. Take the photo opportunity EARLY and get at least one photo of each person you meet!

With each day I amassed a nice collection of maybe 30 or so photos. As the days piled on top of each other and I got further and further into my cross-county quest, I began to WORRY about my camera and my photo collection. "What if I lose my camera? What if someone steals my camera?" were my passing thoughts. It was hard for me to imagine losing such a VALUABLE part of my sacred journey! At one point near the halfway point, I even considered mailing a memory card back home and starting a second blank memory card as to lessen my chances of a potential total loss, but I did not do so.

During the first few weeks of my bike trip, I worried about my bike being stolen, but as more time elapsed, I worried more about my camera being lost or stolen! Suddenly, my camera was MORE IMPORTANT than my bicycle!!!! My photos were irreplaceable and it hurt deeply even to think they could ever be lost or stolen. On the way back home while riding the Amtrak train, I kept my camera in my possession AT ALL TIMES as I felt like I was transporting a BILLION DOLLARS in my waist pouch!!!

At various times when I was not riding my bike, I used my cell phone to take photos. As a way to minimize my overall risk of losing all of my photos, I would text a couple photos at a time back home to my family. By doing so, someone other than myself had a copy of my prized photos which would help ensure the preservation of my special memories. With each passing day, my photos became more and more valuable!

It was photos like the ones taken by some stranger at Ocean Beach in San Diego moments before I took my first pedal stroke on my 3,000-mile bike quest which were literally PRICELESS! These photos could NEVER be taken again. The same is true of the photos when I finally arrived at the soft sands of the Atlantic Ocean in Jacksonville, Florida. Photos like these would be IMPOSSIBLE to ever recapture! Even now as I write about my prized photos, I feel the positive, pulsating energy in my body riveting up through my torso as I contemplate the tremendous VALUE of the photos of my bike excursion. Losing those priceless photos would have CRUSHED me!

Under no circumstance should you "waste" as much time as me taking 30-plus photos per day, but you should get at least a handful of photos EVERY DAY to document your trip. When you get home, you WILL appreciate the extra effort as you share the photos of your special trip with family and friends. Your local newspaper will also request one or more photos to include with the article they will surely want to publish regarding your cross-country bike ride!

The newspaper article about my cross-country bike trip was published in the Johnstown Tribune Democrat on December 21, 2020 and was titled, "I Never Felt So Alive!" written by the highly-talented journalist, Patrick Buchnowski. Included in the article was a marvelous finish photo of me and my bike at Jacksonville Beach with the ocean waters approaching my bike tires.

The photos you take on your cross-country bike journey will become more and more precious with EACH DAY! Even if you don't finish your cross-country route, your photos will remind you of your bravery taking on such a formidable challenge! Don't let your memories fade away. Preserve your special memories with all of your required effort.

Months and years later, your photos will take you back to some of the MOST SPECIAL times of your life, but be prepared as some of your photos will also TRIGGER heavy-duty emotions. Some very special photos might even bring a tear to your eye. Most of your photos will be "regular," but certain photos will "special" as to signify particular milestones marking your evolution into a REAL MAN or REAL WOMAN!

Don't discount your photos! Buy a QUALITY digital camera and use your camera daily along with your cell phone to document your incredible, transforming JOURNEY OF A LIFETIME! Maybe you will discover as I did, your digital photo memories might indeed prove to be worth more than the combined cost of all of your bike travel expenses!

DAY 41: Am I dreaming? Jacksonville less than 200 miles away???

Chapter 141: Food

Even if you are currently overweight, there is NO SUCH THING as a DIET on the Southern Tier! Pedaling a bicycle for 7 hours a day allows you to eat ANYTHING you want!!! If you like donuts, then eat donuts! If you prefer pizza, then eat pizza every day! Drink soda. Eat ice cream. Chow on a candy bar and drink whole chocolate milk! It doesn't matter what you eat!!!!

While on a MAJOR bike route like the Southern Tier, you can and SHOULD eat whatever you want! As I mounted my bike early in the morning, I would quickly eat some type of basic power bar, granola bar, or cereal bar. It was important for me to get a small early dose of CALORIES into my body as to begin the ESSENTAL caloric storage needed to propel me to my destination for the day!

At your first scheduled ten-mile break of the day, you should eat a SIZABLE breakfast. Open your bag of generic Raisin Bran and chow down on some cereal straight out of the bag. Wash it down with some Gatorade or possibly with some leftover chocolate milk from the night before as you pace alongside the road letting your muscles get a break from the monotony of pedaling. While walking off the first ten miles of your biking day, continue to eat until you are SEMI-FULL!

Included in my pannier bag was usually a small jar of peanut butter, leftover pizza from last night, powdered donuts, cinnamon rolls, brownies, trail mix, fig newton cookies, and whatever else looked good to me. There were NOT many fruits and vegetables in my pannier bags, but on occasion I did eat an apple or a banana. On a major bike tour, CALORIES are needed! Fruits and vegetables are still important, but calories keep the pedals spinning around! And it really doesn't matter where the calories come from! Why not indulge in some of the foods you rarely eat back at home like those I mentioned above! Just get the calories inside your body. Otherwise, you will BONK if your caloric consumption is too low!!!

Bonking is NOT fun. Numerous times prior to the Southern Tier, I have bonked while taking long bike rides, but I only bonked once on the Southern Tier as I greatly feared bonking on such a desolate route! When you BONK, you are FINISHED riding for the day. You are DONE! There is NOTHING left in you! You cannot pedal another mile. As far as the current day is concerned with regard to bonking, your bike travel is OVER!

Eating BEFORE you are hungry is a great strategy to avoid bonking. Keep the calories coming! Although you will still get fatigued from biking, if you eat enough food, it is unlikely your body will SHUT DOWN and leave you alongside the road in utter bonking shambles! As long as you have more calories to burn, your pedals will USUALLY find a way to keep spinning!

My experience of a long-term bicycle tour left me with a total weight loss around 20 pounds. Each day I lost an average of about a half-pound despite my consuming approximately 5,000 calories daily. To me, it seemed strange to eat the equivalent of 2-3 grown adult men and still lose a half pound per day! Wow!!!

At times I got carried away and I purchased TOO MUCH food which added unnecessary weight to my bike. Remember, my bike coach, Layne Gneiting, says, "Ounces make pounds and pounds make PAIN!" Be mindful to keep only a reasonable amount of food in your pannier bags as there is ample opportunity to buy additional food EVERY DAY on the Southern Tier. Don't carry around unnecessary food weight!

All throughout the day, you should be eating. Get used to eating during your ride as the calories are important. Don't convince yourself to wait until after the ride to eat or else you will miss important opportunities to resupply yourself with critical calories when the calories are needed most! No, don't GORGE yourself during your riding hours, but keep your stomach semi-full and you will have the energy reserves needed to propel you to your daily destination.

Most early evenings, I would walk or ride my bike to a NEARBY restaurant to eat a HUGE meal! After concluding my daily ride, I would pack as much food into my face as possible until I was completely FULL! Throughout the night, this food would be stored and processed and then the corresponding energy would be available for my continued use EARLY the following morning.

While we are on the topic of food, it is important to mention, I would try to eat some healthy foods in the evening while dining at a respectable local restaurant. Vegetables and salad are a VERY GOOD IDEA as you should eat them when you can! Try to keep a healthy variety of food entering your body whenever possible, but don't fret over it.

One of my favorite techniques is to buy a whole bag of spinach. Then, like a pure savage, I eat the spinach directly out of the bag forcing thick piles of spinach leaves into the side cheek portions of my mouth maximizing the content of spinach in my mouth. If the cartoon character Popeye could eat a handful of spinach to activate his powerful bodily muscles, then why not me? Every last morsel of spinach from the bag would make its way into my mouth as it is extremely important for me to eat ALL of my food and waste NONE of it! Wasting food hurts me emotionally as I am a true conservationist at heart! On my cross-country bike ride, I ate A LOT of food, but I wasted <u>NONE</u>!

One potential problem with this type of massive food intake occurs when the epic bike trip is over. Creating this type of a colossal food-eating pattern is DIFFICULT to correct! For several weeks AFTER completing the Southern Tier, I continued eating enough daily calories for several adults despite biking zero miles on most days upon my return back home. It took me about three weeks to correct my RIDICULOUS excessive eating frenzy and adjust my food consumption behavior back into alignment with the sensible caloric intake of a single human being!

Chapter 142: Receipts

To become a responsible, financially independent individual in a modern-day capitalistic country in our world, I'm convinced you MUST account for and document EVERY expenditure you make! Keeping true to my beliefs regarding vibrant financial health while traveling by bicycle on the Southern Tier, I kept EVERY receipt no matter how small. After opening my trusty pouch and paying for my purchase with either cash or credit card, I would neatly place each receipt inside the front part of my wallet as to store it for future processing upon returning back home.

In those rare instances where the vendor did not or would not supply me with a receipt, I would use my pen and write my own receipt using the back of another receipt or a small scrap piece of paper. Regardless of the particulars of any given financial transaction, I had a receipt stored away in the front part of my wallet. When my receipts accumulated in the front part of my wallet, I would transfer the small bundle of receipts to a tiny zippered section inside my pannier bags for long-term storage until I got back home and processed the receipts into our "Purchases Notebook."

In my case, I was inspired to write this book as I got a little over two thirds of the way across the country. Prior to my epic travels, I had NO IDEA I would ever write a book about my bike journey! About 2,600 miles into my EPIC ride, I suddenly found myself on a "business trip." Unexpectedly, all of my accumulated receipts had even more significance. They were now legitimate TAX DEDUCTIONS! After all, how could I ever write a book about pedaling a bicycle across the country without actually pedaling a bicycle across the country!? Suddenly, my cross-country cycling expenses were now legitimate BUSINESS expenses as per the United States Internal Revenue Service (IRS) published expense criteria!

No matter whether the particular activity is a business expense or a pleasure expense, my wife and I agreed to save EVERY receipt. When we get back home after making any type of purchase, we have an old-time paper notebook on top of a filing cabinet inside our home office in which we enter each and every item or service we bought. This way we have FULL DISCLOURE to each other about ALL of our individual purchases and we have a chronological listing of all the money spent by our family unit.

At any time, either one of us can look in the notebook and see EXACTLY what the other bought, what date it was bought, how much was spent, and where the purchase was made. This particular discipline has saved many arguments between my wife and I! In most cases, we have little reason to review the notebook, but numerous times we have had good reason to make reference to it. Our purchase notebook also makes us take responsibility for every purchase as not to waste money or appear foolish to each other as our goal is to spend our finances WISELY as to achieve financial independence. We have a common goal to create enough PASSIVE INCOME to exceed our financial requirements as to allow us to "retire." Keeping track of our financial activities give us power to continue to make advances toward our FINANCIAL FREEDOM!

For our business purchases, we enter every purchase into the computer accounting program known as Quickbooks. Quickbooks is a REMARKABLE computer accounting program used to log all income and expense creating a natural segway for our outstanding CPA accountants, Brian Riffle and Tommy Riffle from CFO Strategies, LLC, to prepare our annual income taxes each year.

Precise financial planning leads to healthy monetary results. Being successful in today's hustle and bustle society requires specific economic planning and then it requires dedication to carry out the plan! Carrying out a fiscal plan involves doing LITTLE THINGS like getting and keeping a receipt for every purchase. Keeping your receipts not only will save you money and prevent many arguments with your spouse, it will also create the DISCIPLINE needed to reach your financial goals. There is no better place to begin this positive life-long habit of receipt collecting than on the Southern Tier. Keep every receipt!

Day 41: I'm ALWAYS looking for great deals!!!

Chapter 143: Secret Weapon

Earlier in this book, I wrote a chapter about the importance of eating before you are hungry and drinking before you are thirsty. As you probably recall, my overall thoughts on food and drink are to eat whatever you want and as much as you can. Include a few veggies in your diet when convenient and make sure you drink LOTS of water while you mix in some electrolyte-filled sports drinks.

Despite being mostly indiscriminate about what I ate and drank on the Southern Tier, I must admit there was one particularly POWERFUL drink which seemed to MAGICALLY and INSTANTLY reinvigorate myself. After repeated success with this product, I began to refer to it as my SECRET WEAPON! My unlikely secret weapon of the Southern Tier was none other than CHOCOLATE MILK!

On most days, a nice cold HALF GALLON container of chocolate milk was perfect for me. In most cases, I would prefer to buy chocolate milk at night after supper. When I stayed in a cheap motel, I would put the chocolate milk either in the mini-fridge in my room or I would put it in an ice bucket to stay cold throughout the night.

Drinking chocolate milk before going to bed and then first thing in the morning was a real treat! The chocolate milk was MIRACULOUS for me! No, I don't have any type of scientific reason to support my high acclaim for chocolate milk, but I SWEAR on my pannier bags, chocolate milk provided me with REJUVENATING powers! It was indeed my SECRET WEAPON of the Southern Tier!

Maybe you have a special drink, candy, fruit, cookie, or bar. If so, REWARD yourself with a simple pleasure from time to time. Sometimes a few chugs of chocolate milk may satisfy your craving and be a HIGHLIGHT of your day. Pedaling is long and hard. It will push you to your outer limits. Finding anything to take your mind off of all the pedaling is probably a good thing. Maybe you could even prolong and enhance your pedaling days by making wise use of your new secret weapon?

Chapter 144: 300 Hours

As I contemplated a possible cross-country bike-riding undertaking, I did the math. If the Southern Tier Bike Route was approximately 3,000 miles in total distance and I would likely average a 10-mile per hour pace which seemed to be the average pace for most successful cross-country touring cyclists, then according to my calculator, I would have to pedal my bicycle for 300 hours in order to complete the entire arduous course! Although 300 hours was an intimidating number, at least the absurd number gave me a beginning TARGET!

Prior to leaving behind my former life and going face-to-face with the mighty Southern Tier Bicycle Route, I printed a tiny label. The small label read "300 hours." After peeling off the backing, I affixed the newly-printed label on my bike helmet as a constant reminder of how many hours I had to pedal to FINISH the Southern Tier. Each time I would glance at my helmet, I would be reminded that I "ONLY" had to pedal for 300 hours! In my mind, 300 hours of pedaling seemed much more doable than thinking in terms of 3,000 total biking miles.

Looking back on Day 2 when I first discovered my epic bike ride was going to fail, I'm actually surprised I didn't rip off my irritating "300 hours" sticker from my helmet. In the midst of my anger over another disappointing life failure, I'm pretty sure I would have torn off the frustrating label and tossed it to the ground, but I am HEAVILY against littering. My strong stand against littering is probably the only reason the label is still attached to my bright yellow biking helmet today!

Breaking a task down into manageable pieces is one of the SUMMARY lessons of the Southern Tier. Nobody can ride the Southern Tier all at once, but it is possible for someone to take 43 individual daily bike rides and complete the Southern Tier in predictable segments! All it takes is enough discipline to focus on the CURRENT day and NOT the month or even the week! Your job is to bike ONE good day. Then, after biking ONE GOOD DAY, you can prepare for the next day.

When you get ahead of yourself and try to focus beyond your current day of biking, you WILL have problems either mentally, physically, or even mechanically with your bike! By far, the best cross-country cycling strategy is to FOCUS ON TODAY ONLY! Have no concern or expectation for tomorrow until you arrive at your daily destination, then you can plan for tomorrow. As far as the Southern Tier is concerned, tomorrow is NOT real UNTIL you have completed your daily shower!!!

When I was first "called" to ride a bicycle across the country, I was NOT inspired to ride single day rides. My calling was to pedal across the ENTIRE country and nothing short of it! Although my goal of going the full distance did NOT change, my doubts were TOO POWERFUL for me to concentrate on my original gigantic cross-country cycling goal. The ONLY way I remained on the epic Southern Tier Bike Route was to convince myself to ride <u>ONE</u> MORE DAY.

Only AFTER my shower each day would I consider the next day. Had I thought too much about "completing the entire Southern Tier," I promise you would NOT be reading this book right now because I would have gone back home like the thousands of other shortcoming cyclists who predated me and this massive book would have NEVER been written!

Achieving my BIG goal of pedaling the entire Southern Tier is really the story of achieving 43 DAILY goals. Pedaling the entire Southern Tier route was much too big for me, but taking one long daily bike ride was manageable. Riding single days for 43 days straight engraved upon my mind the power of TODAY!

Tomorrow is just a dream; it is not real. The Southern Tier taught me to work hard TODAY and only consider tomorrow after my daily shower! Looking more than one day ahead might be the single most dangerous thought for a cross-country cyclist as focusing beyond today is one of the FASTEST ways to end your magnanimous cycling adventure!

DAY 41: I ate A LOT of Hunt Brothers Pizzas!

Chapter 145: Adventure

The ONLY way to complete a solo, unassisted, and continuous bike ride across an entire country is to have a STRONG sense of adventure! Being ok with heavy-duty uncertainties is a must! Even with all the planning in the world, riding the Southern Tier or any other epic bike route requires something DEEPER than just prior arrangements. Completing an epic bike route demands something you cannot buy, something you cannot plan for, and something you cannot find in this book. Without a strong sense of adventure, you will FAIL!

A strong spirit of adventure MUST be pulling at your heart strings. Otherwise, you won't even make it a few hundred miles on the epic bike quest. My brother-in-law, motivational speaker, and dedicated high school coach, Steve Travis, reminded me during a critical point of my epic crossing about the importance of maintaining an adventurous attitude. Steve said, "You are on an ADVENTURE. You should EXPECT THE UNEXPECTED!" And Steve was right! Despite being thoroughly prepared for my bike excursion; the Southern Tier Bicycle Route repeatedly thwarted me off course.

No one likes when their bike breaks down. No one enjoys suffering through an injury. And most people don't prefer to ride through inclement weather. But if you EXPECT these inconvenient occurrences to occur, you will stand a much better chance of OUTLASTING the pain and remaining on your route. By EMBRACING your journey with a sense of adventure, you will give yourself a chance to absorb the many uncertainties inherently contained in a cross-country biking outing. Along the epic route, there are too many variables for anyone of sound mind to plan every last detail, nor would anyone of sound mind want to. During any significant adventure, rarely will everything fall perfectly into place!

Several months ago, I was hiking on the 2,200-mile Appalachian Trail in the gorgeous southern terminus state of Georgia. On this particular night, I had slept in the back of my van at the trailhead parking lot. As I awoke early in the morning as I usually do, I discovered a POUNDING cold rain outside. It was tempting to remain inside my nice, warm sleeping bag and wait for the storm to conclude, but I knew my available hiking days on the iconic A. T. were numbered. Considering my limited available time, I decided to hike as much as I could without wasting any of the great opportunity I was afforded.

After putting on my rain jacket and rain pants, I grabbed my 38-pound backpack and stepped out into the "foul" elements. For 6 long hours, I ENDURED pounding rain, fierce winds, and 50-degree temperatures until I finally OUTLASTED the cold, rainy weather. By 11 a.m., the clouds started to break up and I finally saw my FIRST fellow hiker of the day on the glorious trail. Prior to witnessing my first hiker of the day, there was NOT a single other hiker on my portion of the Appalachian Trail! It was a powerful feeling to know I was the ONLY hiker who braved the fierce elements and made it through! For me, walking 6 hours in level 8 rain was INCREDIBLE as my personal level of confidence made a PERMANENT increase on that memorable stormy day!

On this particular hiking occasion and on several of my daily bike rides on the Southern Tier, I could have easily gone back to bed and waited for more favorable conditions to materialize, but instead I FACED the day! And by making it through those challenging days, I now have ACTUAL EXPERIENCES I draw from whenever I need an extra shot of confidence in whatever pursuit I find myself. After all, if I can walk through the Georgia mountain wilderness on the Appalachian Trail in 50-degree, cold, rainy, windy weather, then what else am I capable of doing!?

No matter whether you stay in bed or you get up and face the elements, you are still a WINNER for being on any epic adventure route! You don't have to be EXTREME like me and SEEK OUT "nasty" weather, but you MUST embrace a sense of adventure if you are to have hopes of finishing! Frequently remind yourself you are on an ADVENTURE! If you are ready for just about ANYTHING, then you have the proper mindset! Don't make the mistake of EXPECTING your days to go smoothly. A lot can and will go wrong while you are on your epic route. Listen to the advice of my very wise brother-in-law, Steve Travis, and cultivate your SENSE OF ADVENTURE!

DAY 42: There were LOTS of interesting signs for me to read along the Southern Tier!

Chapter 146: Bicycle Route Navigator

Adventure Cycling Association has a mobile phone application (app) named "Bicycle Route Navigator." On this brilliant app, you can purchase GPS route guidance for most of the published paper bicycle route maps sold by Adventure Cycling. In a convenient manner on your phone, you pay for GPS route guidance for the particular route you are riding. Within moments, you will have instant GPS guidance on your phone. The route is usually in blue and it has little bubbles on and near the route indicating various "places of interest" such as a campground, motel, restaurant, service station, bike repair shop, etc.

Tapping on any one of the bubbles will provide immediate additional helpful information to you. On the fabulous phone app, YOU will be represented by a bright pink dot and you will be able to see yourself progress along the blue route as you pedal along the actual road. Unlike paper maps, GPS mapping allows you to see exactly where YOU are on the map. If your pink dot is on the blue route line, then you are "on route." If your pink dot is off of the blue route line, then you are LOST!

If you are using a paper map and you don't know where YOU are in relation to the paper map, then the paper map is of little use! Without knowing EXACTLY where you are, it is very difficult to make much sense out of paper maps! On the contrary, the Adventure Cycling phone app GPS maps let you know EXACTLY where you are in relation to the route. In most cases, you will be depicted by a colorful pink dot, but the color doesn't really matter. What matters is that you can see yourself in real time actually progressing along your route. Seeing your indicative little pink dot on the bright blue route line can be VERY reassuring at times!

After installing the Bicycle Route Navigator app on my phone and buying the entire Southern Tier GPS map set, I was hooked! Rarely did I make any additional references to my paper maps as the GPS phone map was much more useful than anything I've ever used on paper! As long as I could glance down at my phone and see a pink dot on a blue line, then I knew I was ON COURSE! Numerous times I peeked down at my phone map and noticed my pink dot was NOT on the all-powerful blue route line. During those several startling cases, I immediately made the necessary turns to quickly get myself back on route as I developed a bad habit of getting lost from time to time.

Another great feature of the Adventure Cycling phone app maps is zooming in and out. When I was in a big city making MANY turns quickly as was the case in Austin, Texas, I zoomed very close on the GPS map so I could easily see EXACTLY what street I was to be turning. When I was out in the country on lonely desolate roads, I zoomed out much further as there was no good reason to see details as I knew I would be pedaling on the same street for many dozens of miles.

The only slight inconvenience with zooming all the way in is having to keep expanding and moving your screen with your finger as you progress along the route since only a very small portion of the route can be shown on your phone screen at any one time when you use the zoom feature to the max, but the extra attention and work to make small adjustments to the zoom feature is not a big deal at all in relation to the HUGE payoff provided by Bicycle Route Navigator!

Although Adventure Cycling GPS phone maps do NOT speak to you, they are EXTREMELY helpful and I highly recommend them! I wouldn't even consider riding an epic Adventure Cycling route without using these amazing GPS maps! As long as I kept my phone battery charged, my phone maps performed PERFECTLY. The phone app will drain your battery much faster than if you were not using the GPS guidance, but the additional battery drain is well worth it!

Since these phone application maps are GPS based, they don't rely on your particular phone service. At various times during my bike travels, I did not have cell service at a particular location, but my GPS phone map continued to perform fine. Not once can I remember a single occurrence on the Southern Tier during my 1,500 miles of using Bicycle Route Navigator when the slick phone app map failed me! Remember, I only used Bicycle Route Navigator for the second half of my epic bike travels due to my FOOLISH and parsimonious nature as I was too cheap to buy the fabulous product from the onset!

While we are on the topic of cell service, it is important to note that my cell service throughout the Southern Tier was overall VERY GOOD. With my Verizon cell phone service, I had clear cell service most of the times. The few times when I did lose my cell phone signal, it wasn't gone for long. Even while pedaling through the remote stretches of desolate desert, my Verizon cell phone seemed to maintain cell service most of the time. If I had to estimate the percentage of clear Verizon cell service along the Southern Tier, I'd guess the in-service percentage was at about 85% reliability. Never did I go for a long period of time without cell service!

As my cell phone battery depleted throughout the day, I would reach into my handlebar bag and connect a cable from my Anker battery bank to my cell phone which was located inside my waterproof handlebar-mounted phone holder. Within a short amount of time, my cell phone would be fully charged and I could disconnect the cable as not to waste valuable battery resources. As long as my phone was charged, my GPS phone map app worked PERFECTLY!

Chapter 147: Morning Transition

One of the most frustrating aspects of the Southern Tier for me was the amount of time it took me to transition from waking up in the morning to taking my first pedal stroke of the day. When I stayed at a hotel, it only took me about 45 minutes until I took my first pedal stroke, but on those days when I slept outside in a tent, no matter how hard I tried to decrease the preparation time, it took me about 60 minutes before I began pedaling. By the end of my journey, I had a few days I pushed really hard and began pedaling in about 50 minutes, but the slight time improvement was not worth the extra stressful push. With great frustration I am forced to admit it takes about an hour in the morning to PROPERLY transition from waking into riding! Below is a listing of my daily morning transition tasks:

1. Alarm goes off at 4:30 a.m.
2. Say a quick prayer. Thank God for making it through the night.
3. Meditate for <u>at least</u> one minute. God's voice is SILENCE!
4. Attach headlamp to my head. It is still dark outside!
5. Take a whiz into the dedicated whiz bottle inside of my tent. Make sure there are no spills! Put the cap on tight!
6. Text my wife "Good Morning." Always text the wife BEFORE she texts you!
7. Deflate Therm-a-Rest X-Therm sleeping pad. Laying on the pad helps with the deflation.
8. Roll up Therm-a-Rest X-Therm sleeping pad and put it into the factory compression sack.
9. Roll up Hyke and Byke Eolus mummy sleeping bag and pack it into the factory compression sack. Put an extra waterproof dry bag over the compression bag to ensure DRYNESS.
10. Deflate Sea to Summit Aeros air pillow and put it into the factory compression sack.
11. Do a few morning stretches. Stretch inside the tent.
12. Take off the nice warm sleeping clothes and pack them into a dry bag.
13. Apply Bag Balm to saddle area, lips, toes, and any other applicable areas.
14. Put on wet/moist biking clothes. How tough are you?
15. Put all individual dry bags into their appropriate bike pannier bag
16. Pack tent
    a. Remove all tent stakes and put them into the small tent stake bag.
    b. Remove the rain cover from my tent. Place the small tent stake bag on top of the folded rain cover, and then roll it tightly. Place the folded rain cover in tent storage bag. Folding the rain cover over the tent stake bag helps to avoid any cuts or damage resulting from your sharp tent stakes.
    c. Carefully remove and fold the tent poles as to avoid damage. Put the tent poles back into the factory tent pole bag.
    d. Fold the tent quickly (doesn't have to be neat) and then place the tent

pole bag on top of it. Roll the tent tightly over the tent pole bag and place in tent storage bag.
    e. Fold the ground tent footprint and then roll tightly as to fit into the tent storage bag. The ground footprint helps prevents moisture from entering the tent!
    f. Don't worry if tent or footprint is wet as they will dry quickly later today when you set the tent up in the late afternoon after you complete your daily mileage.
17. Put all miscellaneous items back into the proper bike pannier bag.
18. Eat a quick breakfast bar while packing.
19. Take one ibuprofen.
20. Activate Garmin Fenix GPS wrist watch to "cycling" as to acquire a GPS signal to track the upcoming mileage.
21. Activate Bicycle Route Navigator as to easily follow the mapped GPS phone app route.
22. Put phone into waterproof handlebar case
23. Put on biking gloves.
24. Pack headlamp back into the outside easy-access pocket of the pannier bag.
25. Put on helmet.
26. Turn on bike headlight.
27. Turn on both bike taillights. One taillight should be mounted on the back of your helmet. The second taillight should be mounted on the back of your rear storage rack.
28. ALWAYS say a quick prayer before taking the first pedal stroke. Bless yourself, your bike, your gear, other drivers, the many animals around you, and the roads ahead. End your prayer with "May thy will be done!"
29. Take a BIG drink.
30. Start your GPS watch. Keep track of your mileage.
31. Start pedaling SLOWLY!

Chapter 148: BAMF

My mother raised me to be a NICE boy! Using foul language was frowned upon as my mother's father, my grandfather, George Cemo, would NEVER use a cuss word nor would he EVER speak a bad word about anyone. Growing up, I held Grandfather Cemo in high esteem. Despite my grandfather dying when I was only one year old, I modeled my ways after his amazing example of KIND and HONEST living!

While most of my junior high school friends would revel in their newfound use of profanity, I would NOT! Oftentimes, I felt a bit out of place as my morals, even as a youngster were mostly honorable. The words I used meant something, even as a youngster and I would NOT sacrifice my character even for peer acceptance! In most cases, you wouldn't hear swear words coming from my mouth!

As I grew older, I was mostly known as a "goody-goody," but despite having an overall respectable behavior, I did have a mischievous nature. At times I could be found toilet-papering homes in Richland Township around Halloween usually with my comrade, toilet-papering extraordinaire, Vern Campigotto, and the gang. At other times during my senior year of high school, I was known to organize and profit from numerous teenage beer-drinking parties along with my "business partner," Eric Kocsis, but overall, I was a decent kid.

While considering this particular chapter, it was particularly DIFFICULT contemplating the chapter title as I did NOT want to use an expletive! But no matter how hard I thought and how many options I considered, I found it IMPOSSIBLE to convey the true essence of this vitally-important cross-country cycling chapter without using a cuss word as part of the acronym representing this chapter's name. With consideration to my inability to gracefully and respectfully name this chapter, I hereby ask my beloved and saint-like deceased grandfather, Grandpa Cemo, to forgive me as I owe it to my readers to hear the TRUTH about the Southern Tier and I cannot do it without using a few VERY SEVERE curse words!

All through this book I have WARNED you about the psychological, emotional, and physical DANGERS of attempting a SOLO and UNSUPPORTED bike ride across America. You were told about dozens of situations capable of easily ending your trip or worse. But despite my many warnings, there will still be some of you who cannot deny the cross-country cycling urge! Some of you might even decide to take on the Southern Tier alone and unsupported like me. For YOU, this chapter is dedicated!

In order to have even a remote chance of completing the daunting feat of a solo and unsupported bike ride across the country, you MUST have an underlying attitude BIGGER than any obstacle you may face as you will encounter heavy-weight impediments during your cross-country pursuit! How pretty you look or how soft you talk does not matter. Whether you are tall or short is of no consideration. Being overweight or underweight is not very important. Old or young has no bearing. Being experienced or inexperienced is of little value. What really matters is your underlying ATTITUDE!

When everything goes wrong and you are left with nowhere to turn, how tough are you? How low does the temperature have to drop to cause you to turn your bike around and travel back to the nearest airport or train station? How many flat tires in one day does it take for you to break? How much physical pedaling pain can you endure in your legs until you finally find yourself sitting alongside the road waiting for an Uber driver to pick you up?

At the heart and soul of whether you finish the Southern Tier or not is ONE crucial factor! Without it, you are destined to fail. If you are missing this ONE ingredient, you will NOT and CANNOT complete the Southern Tier. The ONLY way to endure the culture shock, the new life, the massive change of routine, the physical punishment, the mental torture, and the changing severe weather is to be a BAMF! To complete the Southern Tier, you must be a BAD-ASS MOTHER FUCKER (BAMF)!

If somewhere at your core you have a strong sense of survival prompting you to REMAIN on course even when your life is seemingly falling apart all around you, then you MIGHT have what it takes to complete the Southern Tier. If you don't have adequate FIGHT deep within, then the chances of you completing the esteemed passage is very LOW!

Being a Bad-Ass Mother Fucker (BAMF) has NOTHING to do with how you talk, walk, or carry yourself, but rather has everything to do with how you handle yourself when something major goes wrong! Anybody can LOOK the part, but only a few have the HOLDING POWER to struggle through and OUTLAST the excruciating pain. It is always easy to quit and often it is the most difficult task in the world to "hold on!" Those cyclists who somehow HOLD ON when there is "nothing left within you" as per the words of the famous British writer, Rudyard Kipling, are the ones whom I classify as a BAMF! If you are a BAMF, then you hold on because others quit and you don't want to be like the masses! A BAMF is their own person! Nobody can sway the stubborn thinking of a BAMF!

The following poem entitled "If" by Rudyard Kipling seems to depict the type of BAMF mindset you will NEED if you plan to pedal a bicycle alone, unsupported, and continuous across the southern boundary of the United States of America. The words in this CLASSIC poem SAVED me on the Southern Tier on more than one occasion! Read it SLOW!!! FEEL the author's powerful words of wisdom!

IF
by Rudyard Kipling

IF YOU CAN KEEP YOUR HEAD WHEN ALL ABOUT YOU
ARE LOSING THEIRS AND BLAMING IT ON YOU;
IF YOU CAN TRUST YOURSELF WHEN ALL MEN DOUBT YOU,
BUT MAKE ALLOWANCE FOR THEIR DOUBTING TOO;
IF YOU CAN WAIT AND NOT BE TIRED BY WAITING,
OR, BEING LIED ABOUT, DON'T DEAL IN LIES,
OR BEING HATED, DON'T GIVE WAY TO HATING,
AND YET DON'T LOOK TOO GOOD, NOR TALK TOO WISE;

IF YOU CAN DREAM – AND NOT MAKE DREAMS YOUR MASTER;
IF YOU CAN THINK – AND NOT MAKE THOUGHTS YOUR AIM;
IF YOU CAN MEET WITH TRIUMPH AND DISASTER
AND TREAT THOSE TWO IMPOSTERS JUST THE SAME;
IF YOU CAN BEAR TO HEAR THE TRUTH YOU SPOKEN
TWISTED BY KNAVES TO MAKE A TRAP FOR FOOLS,
OR WATCH THE THINGS YOU GAVE YOUR LIFE TO, BROKEN,
AND STOOP AND BUILD'EM UP WITH WORN-OUT TOOLS;

IF YOU CAN MAKE ONE HEAP OF ALL YOUR WINNINGS
AND RISK IT ALL ON ONE TURN OF PITCH-AND-TOSS,
AND LOSE, AND START AGAIN AT YOUR BEGINNINGS
AND NEVER BREATHE A WORD ABOUT YOUR LOSS;
IF YOU CAN FORCE YOUR HEART AND NERVE AND SINEW
TO SERVE YOUR TURN LONG AFTER THEY ARE GONE,
AND SO <u>HOLD ON WHEN THERE IS NOTHING IN YOU</u>
EXCEPT THE WILL WHICH SAYS TO THEM: "HOLD ON!"

IF YOU CAN TALK WITH CROWDS AND KEEP YOUR VIRTUE,
OR WALK WITH KINGS – NOR LOSE THE COMMON TOUCH;
IF NEITHER FOES NOR LOVING FRIENDS CAN HURT YOU;
IF ALL MEN COUNT WITH YOU, BUT NONE TOO MUCH;
IF YOU CAN FILL THE UNFORGIVING MINUTE
WITH SIXTY SECONDS WORTH OF DISTANCE RUN,
YOURS IS THE EARTH AND EVERYTHING THAT'S IN IT,
AND – WHICH IS MORE – YOU'LL BE A <u>MAN</u>, MY SON!

Think about it. Why are you riding your bike across America? Isn't it because you want to prove to yourself and maybe to the rest of the world that you are different! You are NOT like everyone else! Frequently in my own life, I am well-known for stating, "I am my own man!" Ask my wife and those who spend the most time around me and SOME will say I'm stupid, crazy, or extreme, but ALL of my friends and fellow adventurers would AGREE on one universal truth…… I am MY OWN MAN!

To be a BAMF, you MUST be your own MAN or your own WOMAN! When your bike breaks down at 4:00 a.m. in the middle of the Yuha Desert with coyotes howling all around you, you have no one to turn to but yourself! You are ALONE! The terrifying experience will either break you or make you stronger. You will either get MAD and somehow find a way to get the job done while OUTLASTING the severe challenges of the Southern Tier or you will QUIT and go back home like thousands have done before you!

Your basic attitude when all else is stripped from you will determine what you do NEXT! If you are a BAMF, you will grit your teeth and do the necessary work. If you are anything less than a BAMF, your cross-country bike escapade might be over!

When I got a flat tire in the middle of the night in the Yuha Desert in California, I panicked and immediately texted my father as he is my go-to person when I get myself in a bind. My text read, "Oh my God!!! Flat tire in desert!!! Complete darkness!!! Alone!!!" Within seconds, my dad replied with a text I will NEVER forget. "You can do it!" was dad's immortal words!

Dad was getting out of bed when he sent me the encouraging text as he woke up at about 7 a.m. eastern time as the time zone was 3 hours later at his home on the east coast. Dad's simple, but powerful text reply reminded me I was a BAMF as he would NOT have sent that text to me if he had not FULLY believed his own words. My father does NOT lie! Dad will tell the truth to anyone, even at times if the person doesn't want to hear the truth! Dad said I could do it and do it is what I did!!!!

With great respect to Grandpa Cemo, my father, and many others whom have helped me to foster my overall life attitude, I urge each of you to dig deep into your mental make-up and try to catch a glimpse of what might be inside. Do you have some white-hot fire deep within your core? Do you get MAD when the crap hits the fan or do you tremble and cower amidst adversity? Do you have what it takes to be a BAMF?

In my case, I'm not really sure if I was a BAMF or not on Day 1 at the Pittsburgh Airport amidst my terrifying panic attack, but I know for sure when my front bike tire connected with the cool waters of the Atlantic Ocean in sunny Florida upon the conclusion of my epic cross-country bicycle ride on Saturday November 10, 2020, I was a BAMF!!! Maybe I was a WUSSY when I started my epic bike ride, but the Southern Tier HARDENED me and by the glorious end 43 days later, I was a genuine Bad-Ass Mother Fucker!!!

When you arrive on the Southern Tier, you are marking your life! The choices you make in the next several days will label your attitude and set the course for the rest of your life. Are you a quitter? Are you a "talker" or a "doer?" Do your decisions really mean anything or could they change like a leaf in the wind? What you do in your first several days of your cross-country bike ride will set the tone for ALL of your days to follow as well as for the REST OF YOUR LIFE!

Choose wisely your precious attitude when the Southern Tier breaks you and your tears are dripping from your face. Many gallant cyclists preceding you also dripped salty tears to the streets of the Southern Tier and most of them quit, but some of them continued. Your cross-country bike endeavor is NOT going to be easy! You are signing up for HELL! Be ready! This is not a vacation! Are you a BAMF? Are you willing to BECOME a BAMF? Maybe you should hop on your bike and FIND OUT!? Welcome to the Southern Tier!

DAY 43: Jacksonville Beaches 13 miles away...... I might actually finish!!!

Chapter 149: Rest Days

More important than the miles you pedal each day is the REST you take periodically. My cross-country bicycle gaunt lasted exactly 43 days in which only 2.5 days were spent resting. In my case, my rest days were NOT scheduled. Instead, my days off happened merely by chance as one full rest day and three half rest days were necessary due to my particular circumstances involving travel, bike repairs, and severe weather.

My first "half day of rest" occurred on Day 1 BEFORE I even got started! Most people probably wouldn't consider waking up at 2:30 a.m., driving 2 hours to the airport, flying across the country, assembling your bicycle at the airport, and then pedaling 45 miles mostly uphill as a "half rest day," but in my case, I considered it a half-day of rest as I only rode my bike from about 2 p.m. to 8 p.m. on that memorable Day 1 of the Southern Tier.

My next rest day was a full rest day and the ONLY day I had ZERO miles. It was Day 5 when I discovered my gravel bike tires were INADEQUATE to my cross-country bike quest! The heat of California's Yuha Desert was too much for my unworthy gravel tires and my tire tubes could NOT withstand the increased temperature as they became pliable thus causing tears in my tire tubes which released all the air from my tires and left me stranded. For me, Day 5 consisted of renting a truck and driving 85 miles to the nearest bike repair shop in Lake Havasu, Arizona to buy good quality ROAD BIKE TIRES!

On Day 28, I reluctantly took another half day off only biking 42 miles as I got a vehicle ride from Jamie from Rising Phoenix Adventures in Bastrop, Texas about 35 miles to the nearest bike repair shop in Austin, Texas where I got a broken spoke fixed and some general maintenance including a shortening of one link from my bike chain.

On Day 37 I pedaled my bike with another broken spoke to Tri Hard Sports in Ocean Springs, Mississippi where ace mechanic, Jacob, repaired my spoke, checked over my entire bike, and replaced my worn-out road bike tires. Jacob did all of this work on a Sunday when his bike shop was officially CLOSED! Jacob was AMAZING!

By deducting my "resting" days from my 43-day total, it took me exactly 40.5 days of actual biking to cross the country. Looking back on my bike travels and considering what I would do differently if I was to do my trip over again, I would probably take a few more days off. Although I finished the Southern Tier in the best shape of my life, I did experience some severe health issues beginning about 2 months after my epic bike trip which are still affecting me even as I STRUGGLE to finish writing this book over three years later. Maybe I should have rested a bit more? I'm not really sure!? Maybe I over-exerted myself on the Southern Tier? Maybe I didn't? Maybe my current health problems have NOTHING to do with the Southern Tier?

In no way do I regret my cross-country biking adventure, but I do regret NOT taking a few more rest days. My bike trip lasted just over 6 weeks and I only took 2.5 days of rest. In reality, I only had 2 days of rest as it seems unfair to count Day 1 as a half-rest day when I didn't even officially get started yet! So, resting 2 days in 6 weeks is NOT quite enough. My official advice is to rest at least 1 day per week. Even God rested on the 7th day after creating the heaven and the earth! In my case, I should have rested at least 6 days, not 2 days! Maybe I over-stressed my body, mind, and spirit too much? I'll probably never know!

Resting is essential if you wish to be a LONG-TERM, premiere athlete. Your body MUST be given adequate time to recover. Only through recovery does your body remain healthy and strong. Without proper rest, you are DESTROYING yourself!

Scheduling rest is a great idea. It also seems reasonable to plan bike maintenance at certain convenient intervals while you are resting. Another idea is rest while visiting a friend or relative somewhere along your epic route. While on the Southern Tier, my wife and I tried to arrange a brief meet-up in Phoenix, Arizona, El Paso, Texas, Austin, Texas, or New Orleans, Louisiana, all of which have airports, but we couldn't quite coordinate all the details in time and we never did get to see each other during my epic trek, but at least I tried to schedule some additional rest.

One caveat I must mention while on the topic of rest is the danger of taking off more than one day of rest in a row. Resting too much is an easy way to DESTROY your current momentum and diminish your rising mental toughness. It is TOO EASY to quickly become accustomed to the luxury of rest. Many cross-country cyclists rested TOO LONG and destroyed their positive momentum which resulted in a DNF (Did Not Finish).

Resting more than one day in a row could put your newfound BAMF mindset at risk and you may find yourself getting weaker, thus putting the entire remainder of your cross-country travels at risk. In my best estimation, it only takes about 36 hours of inactivity to lose MOST of your positive momentum from your cross-country efforts. Do NOT take more than one day off at a time! If you find yourself in a very unique situation in which you are semi-forced to take more than one consecutive day off, then set a DEFINITE day and time to return back to your route or else your newly experienced complacency could EXTINGUISH your will to finish!

Staying HUNGRY is the best way to describe your most useful overall demeanor as you slowly progress across the country on your bicycle. You must WANT to remain biking as many days as reasonably possible, but you must also be wise enough to offer your body some respite from time to time. The amount of rest you choose might also be dependent upon your age as the older you get, the more important it seems to be to schedule the right amount of rest into your bike travels.

The amount of rest required for a 20-year-old is much different than the amount of rest required for a 60-year-old! Regardless, it is ALWAYS the best idea to carefully monitor EXACTLY how you are feeling throughout EVERY day and night of your bike journey. Be sensitive to your own body's guidance as to how much rest you actually need. Paying close attention to your body and mind will guide you to making healthy decisions involving the exact amount of essential down time for your particular circumstances.

If you have read this far, then you are probably a hard-driving, "get it done" achiever who regularly surpasses any obstacles in your path. You are probably the type of person who puts your mind on your goal and you get the job done. In short, you don't let anything get in your way! Unfortunately, it is YOUR hard-driving personality type which is at the HIGHEST risk of over-working and damaging your body.

High achievers in particular must be VERY careful to get adequate rest as their tendency is to over-due it. Sometimes your noble determination might cloud your body's request for a day off. Be wise in your approach to your life and to your Southern Tier efforts. Give adequate respect to the value of rest as proper time-outs will serve to prolong your high-activity level for many years to come!

DAY 43: Some of the Southern Tier roads can be VERY busy with vehicular traffic, but when you have a biking lane like this, life is good!

Chapter 150: Dry

Other than the toughest day of my bike travels when I encountered snow and hail, there were only two other half days consisting of minor rain. For the most part, I had IDEAL, sunny biking weather along my cross-country bicycle travels. The weather I experienced was probably similar to what most aspiring cyclists would hope for while riding the Southern Tier Bicycle Route. To this day, my father continues to be amazed at how LUCKY I was with regards to the overall favorable weather I experienced as I crossed the southern portion of the United States on my bicycle!

Despite my overall fortunate weather conditions, I was prepared for rain! My Arkel pannier bags were waterproof and I had quality rain bib pants and a quality rain jacket. Although my fabulous Arkel pannier bags were TRULY waterproof, I REFUSED to rely on them for total waterproofing. In addition to having great Arkel waterproof pannier bags, I kept my sleeping bag and precious camp clothes in a SEPARATE waterproof bag inside of my waterproof bike pannier bags. By doing so, I KNEW my essential sleeping gear and WARM camp clothing would be dry upon arrival at my daily destination! Arriving at my daily destination with wet camp clothes and a soggy sleeping bag could have been a devastating blow to my overnight experience and could have negatively affected my subsequent day of bike riding by disrupting my precious positive attitude or weakening my good overall health!

Arriving at your daily destination with a dry sleeping bag and dry clothes is a high priority, especially on a chilly day! Toughing it out through the rain on your bicycle is often necessary, but you should NEVER have to struggle through a night in your tent being wet and cold! Make certain your sleeping bag and camp clothes are DRY no matter what!!!!

It is also important to purchase a tent with a 100% waterproof rain cover! Your waterproof rain cover should come down to about three inches from touching the ground on all sides and it should be COMPLETELY waterproof, even in the worst of rain! My waterproof tent of choice on my bicycle excursion was a 2-person, Yosemite tent sold by Hyke and Byke. When I go hiking, I use a slightly lighter and somewhat smaller Big Agnes tent which is specifically made for backpacking.

Both my biking tent and my hiking tent have SUPREME waterproofing and each being a 2-person tent, they both offer a single person a bit of extra room to move around. When my wife and I go on a bike adventure, we also use the Hyke and Byke 2-person Yosemite tent, but once Tink and I situate our sleeping gear inside our marvelous tent, there is NO EXTRA ROOM for anything else. ALL of our other gear must be stored outside the main tent area in one of the two small, covered "vestibule" areas. In the future, we will likely invest in a 4-person tent to be used on biking adventures when Tink and I will be sharing tenting accommodations!

Storing your clothes and sleeping bag in a separate WATERPROOF bag inside of your waterproof bike pannier bag should keep your clothes and sleeping bag dry under ANY condition. Having completely dry clothing will greatly help you to recover from your long daily bike ride as you rest comfortably throughout the night. Your dry clothes and your dry sleeping bag will allow you to transition from the DEMANDS of a long day of biking into a comfortable recovery mode where you can recharge for your biking adventures on the following day! It is absolutely CRITICAL for you to keep your clothes and sleeping bag 100% DRY!

Oftentimes as my wife and I prepare for an adventure, my wife will ask me, "Is it going to rain?" Without fail, my automatic answer EVERY SINGLE TIME without referring to a published weather prediction is, "Yes, it's going to rain." Sometimes she argues with me and even pulls up a weather forecast "proving" to me it is not going to rain, but I still maintain my certainty of rain! Having a 100% rain mindset like mine is wise because it will DEFINITELY rain today somewhere! Don't let a specific weather forecast change the way you pack for a short overnight bike trip or a long, multi-day excursion. Always EXPECT rain! Being prepared for rain is important. Failing to prepare for rain could leave you MISERABLE, wreck your attitude, and quickly send you back home!

As a way to avoid being miserable, a worthy rain suit is ALWAYS a part of my cycling gear! While biking the Southern Tier, I wore a very-decent "construction rainsuit" manufactured by Pioneer. My rainsuit consisted of bib rain pants extending upward all the way to my chest with straps extending over my shoulders. Over top of my bibs, I wore a highly rated rain jacket, but neither my pants or jacket were "breathable" which caused me to sweat profusely, but they sure were BRIGHT as the pants and jacket were both reflective and they were loaded with neon yellow and neon orange colors.

Since the Southern Tier, I broke down and purchased a much more expensive Adventure Cycling recommended "Showers Pass" rain pants and rain jacket in which I LOVE!!!! Many cyclists also purchase GORE-TEX rain gear as it also considered among the BEST waterproofing material available. Although Gore-Tex is probably as close to being truly waterproof as any material, it is VERY EXPENSIVE! Some of you will not be able to afford it, but don't worry as there are other rain gear VERY CLOSE to the quality of Gore-Tex and much less expensive.

Do some research and make a smart purchase with regard to your rain gear, but don't forget to actually test your rain gear out in a hard rain prior to your cross-country escapade! There is A LOT of "waterproof" rain gear for sale that does NOT keep you dry in the pouring rain! If you wish to take the easy way, then buy the Showers Pass rain gear from Adventure Cycling as I have tested this gear through wicked rains and it keeps me 100% dry!

The Pioneer brand of rainsuit I wore on the Southern Tier was designed for street construction workers as to make sure they are seen by oncoming vehicles. Nonetheless, my rain gear worked well for me in the POURING rain when I tested it prior to my epic ride and I cannot say a bad word about it. When purchasing your rain gear, buy the brightest color you can. To this day, I don't understand why the STANDARD color for biking rain gear is not neon yellow or neon orange with tons of reflective material.

The other option you have is to wear a lightweight neon yellow reflective vest overtop of your rain jacket as to offer extra visibility for vehicles. You might even buy reflective strips from Adventure Cycling and stick them on your jacket, bike, helmet, pannier bags, etc. to make your bike more reflective on a dark, rainy day like I did! On my bike, I also bought push-on, bright-orange plastic reflective spoke covers to reflect additional light and make my bicycle even more visible in darker conditions. For me, safety is of UTMOST importance. My goal is to be as visible as possible. Anything you can reasonably add to your "rig" to increase your visibility is a GOOD idea!

Staying dry is a somewhat controversial topic as some cyclists make the argument that wearing a GOOD, truly waterproof rainsuit might be too hot and cause excessive sweating. Although this argument is legitimate, I'd much rather be sweaty and warm than cold and shivering! Take it from me, get a good rainsuit and use it! Most of the modern-day rainsuits are made to be much more "breathable" than rainsuits of the past and excessive sweating should not be too much of a problem anymore. Nowadays, there is rain gear made with zippers under your arms as to allow a cyclist to unzip and release much of the build-up of hot sweaty air as to prevent overheating.

My most recently purchased hiking rain gear was NOT Gore-Tex, but I did spend about $250 total buying both HIGHLY rated rain pants and a HIGHLY RATED rain jacket in which I have since put to the SEVERE test in hard pounding rains lasting for 6 hours!!! The name of my hiking rainsuit is "Ultra" and it is sold by Mountain Warehouse. It has a 20,000 waterproof rating which means the fabric can withstand 20,000 millimeters of water pressure without leaking! My research indicates that rain gear rated at 10,000 millimeters can withstand light to average rain for a short period of time. Rain gear rated at 15,000 millimeters can withstand moderate rain for a sustained amount of time. Rain gear rated 20,000 millimeters are SERIOUS shells for HEAVY, INTENSE rain over a prolonged rain lasting for hours! Although I don't really know exactly what all the technical waterproofing verbiage really means, it sure sounds impressive! Bottom line, I tested the Ultra gear and IT WORKS! The ONLY issue I had with my Ultra rain jacket was my two zippered pockets filled up with water during a wicked multi-hour rain. Although I did NOT get wet, it was very strange that I did have to empty my 2 pockets of about 5 ounces of water each after the wicked storm.

If I was to do it all over again, I'd probably get the most current CYCLOSOURCE Magazine from Adventure Cycling and buy ALL of my biking rain gear directly from their catalog. In my opinion Adventure Cycling is the BOMB! They KNOW what gear works for touring cyclists and they know what gear does not work! Numerous times I tried to outsmart Adventure Cycling by buying gear elsewhere as to save money and I regretted my poor decisions most of the time! If you want to be dry, do yourself a favor and follow Adventure Cycling's most recently recommended rain gear for cyclists!

There is no other bike organization that even comes close to the quality and expertise at Adventure Cycling. Even if you are CHEAP like me, buying your biking gear from the CYCLOSOURCE magazine will save you DAYS of time. So what if you end up paying slightly more for your waterproof cycling gear! At least you will know you are getting the proper QUALITY gear needed for a serious cross-country biking pursuit!

With all the mention I have made throughout this book with regard to Adventure Cycling Association, it seems proper to mention, I have NO AFFILIATION whatsoever to Adventure Cycling! In no way do I benefit when you buy something from them. Upon the publishing of this book, it is my hope Adventure Cycling will add EPIC FAIL to their product line, but at this point in time, I don't even know a single person from Adventure Cycling and I've not spoken to anyone at Adventure Cycling Association about selling my book.

In short, Adventure Cycling sells GREAT PRODUCTS, produces a GREAT MONTHY MAGAZINE, and promotes cycling like no other! Anyone reading this far into this book should be either a member of Adventure Cycling or make a DONATION to their iconic worldwide organization! My wife and I are so impressed with the Adventure Cycling organization and what they have done to promote healthy bike travel, design awesome bike routes, and make bike travel SAFER for us all, we have actually listed Adventure Cycling in our living trust so we can continue to make contributions to this wonderful cycling organization long after we are both dead!

DAY 43: This selfie was taken as I stopped at the FINAL traffic light within a quarter mile from my unlikely finish at Jacksonville Beach, Florida. My body was shaking so badly with adrenaline, I could hardly handle my cell phone! Notice, how my bike took over the ENTIRE lane of vehicular traffic.

Chapter 151: Aches and Pains

For much of my teenage and adult life, I have struggled with lower back pain. At times, the pain would be almost debilitating. During most of my bike rides prior to the Southern Tier, my lower back area gave me consistent, nagging problems. Initially, while riding the Southern Tier, the shabby condition of my lower back was no different from all of my previous biking trips, but as my cross-country trip progressed into the second and third weeks, my back seemed to MAGICALLY heal! No longer did my back feel tight or ache while riding and when I stopped riding and dismounted my bike, I was pain free for the first time in YEARS! The pain relief seemed MIRACULOUS!

In addition to back pain, the first week of my epic bike ride triggered some numbness in my hands, wrists, and forearms, even though I was wearing biking gloves and my bike handlebars were heavily padded. For some reason, the numbness would follow course directly to my funny bone at my elbow location. Although the discomfort wasn't as bad as my many previous bike rides without my homemade padded handlebars, the pain was still bothersome for the first week or so of the Southern Tier. Then, at the beginning of the third week, almost magically my pain and numbness in my hands and arms seemed to DISAPPEAR!

During past bike rides prior to the Southern Tier, significant neck pain has also haunted me. Depending on my exact riding position, it was easy for me to aggravate my neck muscles from maintaining a single riding position for too long. Being cautious of this tendency, I intentionally altered my cycling positions frequently on my cross-country ride as to prevent any particular area of my body from becoming stiff, especially my prone neck area! Stopping every 10 miles to take a brief walk back and forth along the roadside and to do a few basic stretches also helped greatly to "reset" my muscles, tendons, and ligaments. Keeping LOOSE was VERY important!!!

As I aged through my forties, I developed a rather strange, but severe health scenario involving my third and fourth toes on my left foot. For some unknown reason, toe 3 and toe 4 seemed to be crowding each other as to cause me INTENSE localized pain at sporadic times, sometimes serving up severe enough discomfort as to mandate the stopping of my bike at random places alongside the road.

With most biking shoes being known for having very TIGHT toe boxes, it is no wonder why my two suspect toes would be prone to excessive over-crowding. To relieve myself of my toe discomfort, I would stop alongside the road, take my shoes and socks off, and YANK my toes in all different directions frantically stretching them to the max trying to trigger quick relief of my toe agony. Applying some Bag Balm to my toes also seemed to help avoid excessive pain by giving my toes some lubricant to slide past each other without getting hung up in a painful posture.

Last year for Christmas, my dad bought me a few pairs of toe-spacing socks. Most nights while at home, I wear these cutting-edge socks overnight as to train my toes to remain further apart from each other. Wearing these colorful socks at night while I sleep seem to retrain the natural splay of my toes as to create slightly more space between toes 3 and 4, thus avoiding some of the intense pain. So far, dad's toe socks seem to be very helpful. Dad's sock gift was also very special to me as my mom usually does 100% of the Christmas shopping. The toe socks were one of the FEW gifts my father has ever actually personally bought for me!

Another plan I have for future bicycle rides is to try to buy WIDE biking shoes to give me more room in the toe box, a strategy I have effectively implied in my recent backpacking adventures with the purchase of WIDE hiking shoes. Hopefully, biking shoe manufacturers will read this book and begin to offer a greater selection of WIDE biking shoes!!!!

Another ailment of mine during my cross-country bike journey involved my knees. About halfway through my cross-country expedition, my bike seat came loose. After tightening my seat, I must have mistakenly moved my seat ever so slightly from its original position which quickly resulted in pain in my left knee. Fortunately, I made additional adjustments to my bike seat over the following days and I applied some compression padding to my knee which allowed me to recover from this rather serious injury and prevent additional injuries. Finding just the right positioning for your bike seat is VERY IMPORTANT. Once found, consistently tighten your seat bolts as to make it highly unlikely for your bicycle seat to ever shift into a detrimental position!

Saddle sores is another common injury among cyclists. Sitting on a skinny bike seat for 7 hours a day can have severe consequences quickly if you are not prepared! Saddle sores are so prevalent and devastating in the cycling community, I dedicated an entire previous chapter to it.

To avoid saddle sores, apply Bag Balm to any part of your skin contacting your bike seat. Also, remember to wear a TIGHT base biking bib short possibly with a second pair of biking shorts over top. At least start your trip with two pairs of biking shorts until such time you feel confident enough to experiment whether or not you could possibly get away with wearing only one pair of biking shorts. In my case, I stayed with a tight base bib bike short combined with a traditional snug bike short over top and I did not sway from this strategy all the way across the country as chaffing in the saddle area has been a HUGE past problem of mine!!!

Regardless of your particular nagging injuries, you can count on the Southern Tier or any other long-distance bike route to REVIVE all of your past injuries. The Southern Tier will re-introduce you to ALL of your past aches and pains and FORCE you to deal with each one of them! Make sure you consider each of your prior injuries before you leave on your very long pedaling adventure as any one injury could easily send you back home! Welcome to the Southern Tier!

Chapter 152: Plan B

Although I never had an appointment with a mental health professional during my rather normal childhood, there is a strong chance a psychologist would have diagnosed me as having Obsessive-Compulsive-Disorder (OCD). Touching a certain item a specific number of times, taking a certain number of steps as I approach a particular boundary line, and saying certain statements over and over all plagued me as a child, not to mention my incessant worrying about EVERYTHING! Struggling with mental issues and feeling the need to have things "perfect" was quite a disturbance to my healthy growth and development. As I grew older, I got stronger mentally and have intentionally worked VERY HARD on my ongoing "mental toughness." In many ways, I have achieved most of my healthy and commendable mental objectives, but some ongoing mental illness lingers on.

As an adult, I continue to suffer from and cause those around me to suffer from an overriding tendency of mine to OVERPREPARE for my adventures. On canoe camping adventures, while the other 4 or 5 canoes are already in the river waiting to begin, I'm still on shore double-checking everything and frantically going back through my list to make sure my wife and I are "fully prepared."

Some of the people close in my life regard me as having "control issues" or being a "control FREAK." If you ever met me, you would quickly recognize my mental deficiencies and my tendency to slow down any good-intentioned group with my obsessive planning and control problems. Not a single item can be out of place or else there will be an annoying ensuing discussion, just ask my wife!

It's probably a good thing I married a wife whom also suffers from OCD, often to the point of being NEUROTIC! Otherwise, a wife of lesser mental deficiencies might find me difficult to live with much like my former first-wife probably did. It is interesting to note, my "full-blooded" younger sister, Kelli, seems to be completely normal and well-functioning mentally despite growing up alongside me, but on occasion Kelli's husband has expressed some possible concerns.

With that mental deficiency disclosure out of the way, I maintain my position and I officially recommend having a Plan B while planning your epic bike travels! Someone like myself will have a Plan A, Plan B, Plan C, Plan D, and Plan E, but a regular, non-psycho cyclist like yourself will be fine having only a Plan A and a Plan B!

Before you take your first pedal stroke of your epic bike ride, while you are still at home, take individual phone photos of each page of your paper map. Even if you have the incredible Adventure Cycling Bicycle Route Navigator GPS phone application, you should also have a phone COPY of each of the DOZENS of individual paper maps of your particular route. Doing so will avoid a potential mental meltdown when you lose or accidentally destroy one or more of your paper maps. Taking phone photos of your paper maps BEFORE your epic ride will also give you the extra back-up paper map copy image you may need in the case of an unexpected loss.

Having disclosed my history of mental mishaps, you probably aren't surprised when I tell you that I also downloaded my phone photos of all 140 tiny paper maps of the Southern Tier to a thumb drive and gave it to my dad for reference throughout my bicycle journey along with 140 computer-printed pages of the Southern Tier maps.

Supplying my father with all these map pages allowed my dad to ASSIST me by advising me of what lies ahead and giving his insight on various daily options I had with regard to my route and planning. Had I not been so CHEAP, I would have bought TWO sets of paper maps from Adventure Cycling and given my father one full set instead of making the whole process cumbersome and time consuming by giving dad a large stack of photos of the maps and a thumb drive! If you are lucky enough to have a "map coordinator" on your cross-country cycling team back home, then break down and spend the extra money and buy your special helper a proper set of worthy paper maps!

DAY 43: I'm so close……. I can see the sparkling sands!!!

Chapter 153: Hamstrings

During the first few days of the Southern Tier, I found himself in a blazing hot desert confused as to how I could have possibly allowed myself to get suckered into this ridiculous pursuit of a cross-country bicycle crossing! Although I wasn't without any biking experience, having done 4 Ironman triathlons about 10 years previous, I wasn't even close to being an accomplished cyclist. My first week of cycling the Southern Tier seemed more like some type of cruel physical TORTURE than anything else. My entire body from my head to my toes was sore and tight!! As far as I was concerned, this bike ride was NOT fun at all and I only continued to pedal because I felt CALLED to this very strange pursuit. With one SLOW pedal stroke after another, I struggled to make it through each day.

It wasn't until the beginning of the third week of my bike travels as I was performing my daily pedaling chore when I actually noticed some fluidity in my pedal stroke. No longer did I feel like some THUG who never before pedaled a bicycle. For the first time possibly ever in my life, I felt like an accomplished CYCLIST! Never before did my legs ever feel so activated and engaged in the biking process. During my many prior bike rides, I could only feel my quads and calves working, but during week 3 of the Southern Tier, I sensed my HAMSTRINGS engaged in the cycling process and it FELT GOOD! There was no question, I was now riding as smoothly and EFFICIENTLY as I ever have!

To this day, I'm not quite sure what happened as to suddenly involve my hamstrings. Most likely, it was the mere expiration of a certain amount of time passage on my bike that activated a full range of different muscles, but as I experienced this unfamiliar phenomenon, I paid as close attention as possible to my positioning, seat height, seat angle, leg extension, shoe clip position, etc. as to be able to replicate the EXACT positioning in all of my future bike rides. Finally, as per my evolving physical condition, it felt like I was an official cyclist!

Perhaps the most significant indication of my newfound cycling reality was the fresh sensations in both of my hamstrings. As I began to bike with much less effort and better results, I could feel my hamstrings healthily engaged in a brand-new way. "Am I doing something different?" was my recurring question to myself. Something was different, but I wasn't sure what it was. Maybe it was as simple as the development of my hamstrings and other tiny supporting muscles resulting from the many hours on my bike or maybe the change was more psychological when I finally accepted my new life as a "pedal man?" Maybe my hamstrings finally loosened up when my mind finally loosened up?

Whatever happened, I might not ever know, but in all subsequent bike trips, I have focused on my hamstrings and I normally can feel them engage as I have enjoyed the many positive results. Being tight is definitely a bad idea. The looser you are, both MENTALLY and PHYSICALLY, the more efficient will be your ride. Engaging the proper muscles with the proper thoughts will also result in

SMOOTHER, FASTER, and more ENJOYABLE bike rides!

Pay attention as you ride. Try to use the BIG muscles above your knees on the front and back of your legs as you ride with smooth confidence across the country. When you feel your hamstrings finally engage in your labored pedaling process, then you will know you have tapped into the "secret muscle of the Southern Tier!"

DAY 43: My first glimpse of the Atlantic Ocean. Oh my God!!!!

DAY 43: Upon finishing, I was OVERWHELMED with emotion!!!! I could NOT speak!

Chapter 154: Tent Zipping

The thought of a rattlesnake surreptitiously crawling into my sleeping bag did cross my mind a time or two during my epic bicycle travels. The unpleasurable and crippling vision caused me to zip my tent QUICKLY as to keep all of the various unwanted creatures OUTSIDE of my contained area, especially snakes! Animals of all shapes and sizes are CRAFTY and SLY! It only takes a MOMENT for an unwanted guest to slip into your tent, or worse, into your sleeping bag!

Some of you might initially label me as overly cautious and possibly pathetic, but I uphold my notion to keep my tent FULLY ZIPPED immediately upon my entry or exit. When I go to bed, I want to know I am the ONLY one in my sleeping bag. Sleeping is crucial to sustaining a successful bike ride and I was not willing to sacrifice the quality of my sleep worrying about which creatures may or may not have entered my sacred tent space!

Even if I might be slightly exaggerating by making reference to a "rattlesnake in my sleeping bag," I don't feel like it is unreasonable to take an extra couple of seconds each time you access your tent to make certain your zippers are COMPLETELY shut! Spiders, mosquitoes, ants, and other bugs would love to lodge with you for the night. It was important to my continued sanity to ensure I had no additional roommates in my tent! Being confident I was the only one inside my tent and sleeping bag allowed me to sleep soundly through the night.

There are other cyclists whom zip their tent fully shut even when they "camp" inside as they feel secure knowing they are the ONLY one in their tent! As I zipped my tent shut on those many secluded Southern Tier nights, I felt a sense of finalization. The day was now over and it was time to enter a different and very important phase of my bike trip involving much-needed REST!

Most nights on the Southern Tier, I felt EXTREMELY tired! More than once I actually fell asleep talking to my wife on the phone in the early evening hours!!! I'd startle myself and wake up as I heard Tink saying "Z, Z, did you fall asleep on me again?" As I regained consciousness, I would apologize as I repeatedly proclaimed my DEEP fatigue! When I told my wife "I am Southern Tier TIRED," she knew exactly what I meant! Few times in my life can I ever remember being so consistently tired at such a DEEP level!

Looking back, it probably would have taken a rattlesnake in my sleeping bag to thwart me from a good night's sleep on many of those exhausting Southern Tier nights. Only extreme foolishness on my part would have disrupted my precious sleep time! Nonetheless, allow your body and mind the necessary time to RECOVER by keeping your tent zipped as doing so will serve your restoration needs. Zip your tent shut EVERY TIME! Why add unnecessary potential problems to one of the most DIFFICULT pursuits of your life?

Chapter 155: Personal Transformation

Often throughout this book, I've made mention to coming back home after my epic bike travels as a different person. The whole idea of personal transformation through long-distance cycling was so significant to me, I had to make a chapter all of its own! For me, "what it would make of me" was my primary reason for taking on the Southern Tier. Despite the Southern Tier being classified as an "advanced" bike route and I was NOT an advanced cyclist, I KNEW it was my calling. Although I was scared to death, the thrill of what the revered bike route would do to me personally was undeniable! There was no other option for me. I had to take on the Southern Tier and find out for myself!

Throughout my life, I've read hundreds of personal development books, attended dozens of personal-improvement seminars, and turned every vehicle I've ever owned into a "classroom on wheels" through the use of audio recordings in an attempt to LEARN more about life and to develop myself into a quality of person. For YEARS, I didn't even know if the radio in my vehicle worked as I ONLY listened to personal development audio programs while driving! As I was raising my beloved young children, Stacey, Curtis, and Anthony, they would often ask, "Daddy, do we have to listen to 'smart tapes' all the time?" Of course, my answer was "Yes!"

Despite my particular level of dedication to refine my personal growth, there was NOTHING in my former life that DEVELOPED me to the degree I experienced on the Southern Tier! Every book, seminar, and audio program prior to the Southern Tier were merely a prelude to my Southern Tier biking experience. My early adult educational resources got me to the place where I was strong enough to finally take on a HUGE challenge like the Southern Tier! And the Southern Tier proved to be personal development on STEROIDS!

While you are away on your pedal journey of self-discovery and personal mastery, you will sense yourself becoming different. While riding the Southern Tier, it is IMPOSSIBLE to remain the same! Something happens quietly and unobtrusively somewhere along the majestic route as you are spinning your pedals around in a tedious manner for many hours daily as your mind drifts back and forth in an unstable fashion. At some point amidst the monotony of pedaling, you intuitively realize you are DIFFERENT. There is a MAGICAL point in the ride when you finally pass the critical mile and noticeable change is triggered!

The Southern Tier as well as the many other rigorous long-distance epic bike routes are mysterious in nature. To the visible eye, the long-distance bike route is just a bunch of roads, but to the cyclist who faces the route ALONE, UNSUPPORTED, and CONTINUOUS, there is a SPECIAL POWER in the route. It's almost like you can tap into the experiences of the many other cyclists who came before you. Some prior cyclists have triumphed and CONQUERED the Southern Tier while most others have hit their limit early and tapped out before they really EXPERIENCED the magic of the epic ride. If asked under oath in front of a judge, "Is there really a SPIRIT of the

Southern Tier?" Without hesitation, my integrity would force me to reply a resounding "YES!"

After riding the Southern Tier from end to end, I would be a LIAR if I didn't admit to a very real present POWER on the iconic bicycle route. There is something distinct on the course that CANNOT be seen with our physical eyes! There exists a sacred power reserved ONLY for those rare cyclists whom can BARE the intensity of the shattering experience for just ONE MORE DAY. It's almost like the special TRANSFORMATION is saved only for those who can withstand enough SUFFERING to earn its prized delivery. Although I have attended over one thousand religious services in my lifetime and have been HUGELY impacted by many of them in very positive and healthy ways, I have NEVER experienced the sheer magnitude and intensity of SPIRITUAL TRANSFORMATION as I did while riding the Southern Tier ALONE!

Upon returning home after completing my Southern Tier quest, I was different. No, I didn't divorce my wife, abandon my kids, or sell my businesses, but I had entered a new DIMENSION of reality. My degree of poise was uplifted to a whole new level as I also had a much greater sense of humility, compassion, and respect for life. Suddenly, many of my previous worries, especially financial, seemed to be of much less magnitude as most of my previous problems naturally slipped away.

Prior to my epic bicycle adventure, I worried A LOT about MONEY, but at the conclusion of my bike travels, my monetary obsessions seemed to be significantly less without simultaneously losing any of my solid financial planning and basic economic care. Upon returning home, I was concerned MUCH LESS with what others thought or said about me as I felt like a new person was born into my body and soul. And perhaps most of all, the confidence I gained from riding the Southern Tier was off the charts! Achieving a MAJOR Southern Tier victory caused my mind to think, "What else am I capable of doing?"

If you are a teenager with great aspirations for an amazing future full of glorious achievements, then you might want to consider riding a section of the Southern Tier as soon as possible. Get out on the route and FEEL the early morning glory of the land. Experience the blazing heat of the road or the mystical expanse of the never-ending desert. Get a taste of this strange existence as I PROMISE you with ALL OF MY HEART, whatever you invest in the Southern Tier, WILL be MULTIPLIED back to you! Hold out just one more day and the Southern Tier will release a PRICELESS GIFT to you, a gift NOBODY can ever take back!

For anyone who is mentally broken, depressed, or even suicidal, before you give up on your life, consider taking a very long epic ride on your bicycle. If you consider your life to be over anyway, why not leave this world doing something really CRAZY like pedaling across the country!? Killing yourself physically dead is easy as anyone could quickly carry out the unthinkable task, but killing yourself mentally, emotionally, and spiritually while you are still ALIVE is mind-boggling and should be seriously considered by all of us! Witnessing yourself actually DYING to your past life as you pedal onward to your NEW LIFE is an exhilarating experience! You have NOTHING to lose and possibly something IMMENSE to gain! With absolute certainty, I GUARANTEE you there exists no therapy, medicine, or medical procedure in existence capable of providing the massive personal transformation benefits afforded by pedaling the Southern Tier Bicycle Route ALONE!

DAY 43: After regaining some semblance of composure, I convinced a stranger to take a photo of me as I posed for my official Southern Tier FINISHING photograph!

Chapter 156: Bears, Coons, and Coyotes

At regular intervals throughout the year, my wife and I like to take adventures into the wilderness. Our favorite adventures probably involve canoe camping, but we also enjoy a wide variety of other activities, most of which take place in the deep forests where wild life is abundant. On several occasions, we have been HONORED to experience many real-life animal encounters with snakes, eagles, fox, deer, raccoons, beavers, turtles, chipmunks, squirrels, coyotes, alligators, groundhogs, and even BEAR!

While traveling extensively throughout mountainous regions of the United States and other countries, it is possible you might have a bear encounter at camp or possibly while pedaling your bike. In most cases, you will only catch a glimpse as the beautiful, sleek creature quickly scampers away, but in any case, you must be prepared as a bear presents a real potential danger.

If you happen to come upon a bear, it is best to continue with your business and NOT stop to take a closer look. Although bear seem to be big and slow, they can run MUCH faster than you and I! If you are on foot when you encounter a bear, slowly begin to walk AWAY from the bear. Do not run as you may trigger the bear's natural primordial instinct to CHASE you, in which you will CERTAINLY lose! Slowly walking away while you grab hold of your 9-ounce can of commercial bear spray is your highest probability of avoiding an escalating event. Raising your arms up as high as possible as to make yourself appear BIG is also a good idea. You might even want to talk calmly and confidently as you slowly depart as to make it clear to the bear you are a human and you are NOT food! "I am a human. You are a bear. Go away and leave me alone." might be a good starting point for your conversation with the encountered bear!

Another favorite overall animal deterrence tactic of mine involves the use of LOUD NOISE. Making the loudest noise you can possibly make often startles any animal and causes them to run away. In my case, I usually have an extremely LOUD-SOUNDING whistle around my neck. Although I've never used it in any bear encounter, my plan is to blow fervently into the whistle under the right circumstances as to startle the bear and scare it away. Banging pots and pans together or making any other type of loud, piercing noise is also usually enough to avoid an unpleasant scenario or even dire consequences.

In most cases when I am out in the wild, I have a 9-ounce can of commercial bear spray with me. Most of those who accompany me on my travels into the wilderness tease me about my bear spray, but in more than one instance, I have been glad to have it! Although I have NEVER actually used my bear spray, commercial bear spray is considered the BEST way to detour a charging bear. Although I do NOT carry a gun on my wilderness adventures, I know others who wouldn't think about going into the woods without their pistol. To me, I'd be much more afraid if my wife and I carried a gun as the idea of a gun ACCIDENT scares me much more than a possible wild life encounter gone bad!

After having experienced 41 dog chases on the Southern Tier with several of the chases being VERY intense, I cannot even imagine the sheer TERROR of a bear chase! But don't worry, as long as you don't tease a bear, it is HIGHLY UNLIKELY a bear will pursue your bicycle! Most bear are not aggressive unless you give them reason to be. If you see a bear as you ride along, don't stop to take a photo. Just keep pedaling as not to draw unnecessary attention to yourself and your bicycle!

After spending LOTS of time in the woods, I've come to the conclusion that the most dangerous wild animal sighting you could ever see in the woods is a bear cub! Although bear cubs appear to be the most adorable little creatures you have even seen as they seem to invite you to come take a closer look, I strongly urge you to quickly walk away from the cub as you are only a FEW SECONDS away from a horribly unpleasant interacting with the MOST DANGEROUS wild animal in the forest, MAMA BEAR!!!

Without a doubt, Mama Bear is within 100 yards of her cubs and she definitely SEES you! Heed my advice and slowly, but steadily put as much space as possible between you and the bear cub(s). Trust me, Mama Bear is your worst NIGHTMARE! Mama bear, like most other dedicated mothers, will protect her babies AT ALL COSTS, even risking her own life to do so. Do NOT underestimate the ferocity of a Mama Bear! Witnessing a bear cub in the wild should be an INSTANTANEOUS sign to LEAVE the area PRONTO! Grab hold of your bear spray while you SLOWLY and diligently retreat from the immediate vicinity!

The Southern Tier Bicycle Route is NOT known for bears with the exception of the few dozen miles of the Black Mountains of New Mexico and possibly a few other very brief sparce areas, but the Northern Tier and the Transatlantic bike routes which are the other two primary cross-country bicycle routes across the United States as published by Adventure Cycling Association have a much more significant bear population along their respective bike routes.

While traveling through bear country, it is a VERY GOOD idea to use a 40-foot piece of paracord rope to hang your food pannier bag from a tree at night when you are sleeping outside in your tent. Make sure your pannier bag is hanging at least 12 feet high and 4 feet out from the trunk of the tree. You also want to make sure your food bag is hanging at least 4 feet down from the tree branch above. Situating your food with a strong piece of paracord rope according to these distances should guard your food against all of the animals of the forest.

As an act of FULL DISCLOSURE, I must admit, along my travels of the Southern Tier, most nights I did NOT hang my food from a tree as I did not feel as though it was necessary in most cases. Instead, I kept my food in my bike pannier bag and simply parked my bike away from my tent as the GOLDEN RULE of tent camping is NEVER STORE FOOD INSIDE YOUR TENT! Storing food inside or even close to your tent could cause you a TERRIBLE disturbance throughout the night in your sacred tent space. Although I did not hang my food in a tree during some of the Southern Tier nights, not once was my food disturbed by the animals of the night. Of course, during the nights I spent indoors at either a Warmshowers host or a cheap motel, I took my food inside with me.

As I was preparing for the Southern Tier, my wife and I spent numerous nights bike camping at FREE "hike and bike" campsites along the awesome 184.5-mile C&O Canal Towpath which spans from Cumberland, MD to Washington, DC. This iconic rails-to-trails bike route also directly connects to the outstanding 150-mile Greater Allegheny Passage which forms a continuous 334.5-mile "Rails to Trails" connection between Washington, DC and Pittsburgh, Pennsylvania. Any serious cyclist MUST add this incredible adventure to their bucket list!

One night while camping along the C&O Canal Towpath as the sun was setting, I heard a rumbling in the bushes. After some investigation with help from my trusty headlamp, I discovered a raccoon as his eyes showed up bright red when the beam of my light peered into his face. As a way to deter the curious, little animal, I gently tossed a small rock in his general direction as to scare him off, but the minor scare was hardly enough!

To our surprise, we were apparently in the raccoon's territory and he was NOT leaving! As my wife went to bed in our tent, I relaxed by the fire. Upon hearing another disturbance in the bushes, I shined my flashlight and spotted the bright red eyes of our raccoon friend again. After stirring up the bushes with a long stick, once again our new raccoon friend scampered away. With our food hung properly high in a tree far away from our tent, we figured the meddlesome raccoon would NOT be a problem through the night, but this was NOT the case!

Five minutes later while I was still sitting by the campfire, our overly-assertive raccoon buddy blatantly walked out of the tall grass, brazenly entered our campsite, jumped up on my wife's bike, and tried to open her pannier bags. All of this shameless activity occurred while I was sitting about 10 yards away from the little fellow at our campfire. This intrusive raccoon was obviously NOT afraid of people! He desperately wanted our food and he knew where to get it.

Despite not having one bit of food in our bike pannier bags, the menacing raccoon continued to delve into my wife's pannier bag. Yelling at the raccoon didn't even scare off our furry friend as he was DETERMINED to get some food. It wasn't until I grabbed a branch and actually CHARGED the raccoon that he finally scampered away into the woods. Considering this particular raccoon's high level of BOLDNESS, it was clear we were in for additional trouble during the course of the night!

Without much surprise, at about 1 a.m. in the morning, my wife and I were both awoken from our comfortable sleep inside our tent as we heard my wife's bike crash to the ground. As I hustled out of the tent and fumbled to turn on my headlamp, I saw the determined raccoon run off. To my amazement, the raccoon succeeded in opening my wife's pannier bag despite the pannier bag being fully folded and snapped shut! By the time I got out of the tent, our naughty animal guest had thrown about 10 different gear items from my wife's pannier bag to the ground as I later learned raccoons have thumbs and they can open a bike pannier bag, just like a human being! How Interesting!

In the morning, our cycling neighbors whom camped at the adjacent campsite asked us about the prying raccoon as their pannier bags were also ravaged likely by the exact same raccoon! In similar fashion, the raccoon also opened their pannier bags, but our neighbors must not have confronted the raccoon soon enough as the raccoon permanently discarded two important pieces of their gear items into the mighty Potomac River never to be seen again!

Another potential nuisance animal is a coyote. Coyotes are pack animals in which most adults weigh about 35 pounds or so. A coyote's size is comparable to a medium-sized dog. Coyotes also have four toes front and back with each toe having a very sharp claw. That's a grand total of 16 sharp "knives!" Even though a coyote is not a big animal, they also have 4 sharp canine teeth as part of their 42 total teeth. Considering the 16 sharp claws and 42 sharp teeth, a coyote is capable of inflicting serious harm to a human being, especially if the coyote joins forces with other coyotes from their pack. Fortunately, coyote attacks on humans are very rare, but it could happen.

During my bicycle tire malfunction in the middle of the night in the Yuha Dessert between Brawley, California and Blythe, California, I heard coyotes on both sides of the road howling at me in unison while I was struggling to change my flat bike tire in the dark. The intense coyote experience would rank as one of the most terrifying of my life! Although I did NOT have a direct, actual confrontation with the howling coyotes, the overpowering fear I experienced was ravaging!

In most cases, if you don't bother an animal, the animal won't bother you! Research indicates most snake bites result from people being stupid and purposely getting too close to the intriguing creature. Most dummies get bit while they are trying to catch the snake or play with it. Instead, enjoy your glimpse of any captivating animal from a distance and don't make it your mission to get too close or to disturb it. And definitely don't try to feed it! Being halfway intelligent and respectful of any fascinating animal is your best chance to avoid an unpleasant encounter. Meeting the local animals along your bike trip is an HONOR, but STAY ALERT and always carry your bear spray!

Chapter 157: Journal

For the past 15 years or so, I have kept a personal journal in which I make one or more entries EVERY DAY of my life. Usually in the early morning after my daily meditation, I make a few quick entries about what occurred on the previous day. Included as part of my journal entries is any interesting occurrence throughout the world, a brief listing of the highlights of my day, and anything of interest concerning my wife, our pets, and any other family members.

For the most part, my journal writing is private, but my wife does refer to it from time to time to clarify particular dates, recall specific order of events, or consider timelines. Although my journal overall is not very exciting, it does help me to gain greater clarity about my own life and the daily writing process helps me to access more lucidity about life in general. Being an ardent student of life, I am always looking for ways to go deeper and LEARN more about the mysteries of life, especially my own! It was probably my passionate internal drive to learn, grow, and discover which attracted me to a cross-country bicycle ride in the first place!

Despite having years of habitual daily journal writing, I found it EXTREMELY difficult to keep up with my journal writing while riding the Southern Tier. At times, I found myself two or three days behind in my writing. It seemed like the energy exerted on my actual bike travels itself consumed almost every last drop of oomph available for anything else! Thus, my writing suffered a bit, but being an EXTREMELY STUBBORN man, I FORCED myself to write a few journal entries for EVERY DAY of my trip, even if the entries were made 3 days late!

When I say "write" in my journal, I actually mean "talk into my phone." Most days, I found myself pacing back and forth alongside the road talking into my phone trying to use talk-text to make a semi-coherent set of journal entries for the previous day. For the most part, talk-texting worked well. In my previous life prior to the Southern Tier, I would actually write in my journal early each morning when my thoughts from the previous day remained active in my mind, but on the Southern Tier, I didn't feel like I had enough time in the morning for an additional activity, so my journal writing was postponed until I took my first or second 10-mile walking break during the day. Only with my strong sense of rugged determination mixed in with massive stubbornness did I manage to make my daily entries and keep track of my LIFE-CHANGING bicycle trip. Later in this book, you will have the opportunity to read the actual journal entries I made during my epic Southern Tier bike travels!

Journal writing is a great way to keep track of your life. It also allows you to look back and get a quick idea of EXACTLY what was going in your life during any given day or time frame of your life. Otherwise, relying solely on your memory is oftentimes INACCURATE as our memories fade with each passing day, but the words on your computer screen REMAIN for decades or more!

It is important to capture your thoughts and experiences while they are FRESH in your mind. Even waiting one extra day like I often did while riding the Southern Tier will make the process of journal writing much more difficult than it could be had you been DISCIPLINED enough to make journal writing a daily habit. The best idea is to get into a strong daily habit and DO IT every morning! Some days you will NOT feel like journal writing, but you should do it anyways. Do it because you said you would do it! Even making one or two simple entries perpetuates your positive writing and discovery habit. You can always add entries later, but at least make a few initial entries EVERY day!

Commit to one month of journal writing no matter what and evaluate your new writing habit after completing your 30-day discipline. As you write more and more, you will notice it takes less and less time to complete. After 30 days, you should be able to complete your daily writing task in less than five minutes and some days in less than one minute. Journal writing is also a great way to help make sure you use EVERY DAY of your life to work on yourself, spend time with your family, establish new goals, and glorify God through your positive actions. Journal writing keeps you pointed in the correct direction with your life. Years ago, I read a passage from personal development guru, Tony Robbins, whom was quoted as saying, "If your life is worth living, then your life is worth RECORDING!" I agree!

Remember, this is YOUR LIFE! Write down how you feel. List the dominant thoughts in your mind. Make notes about what is important to you and what you think is futile. STUDY your life by looking for patterns, clues, and enigmas. Gather all the information you can to help you determine your various "callings," discover the causes you wish to promote, and maybe even uncover the big mission of your life! Regardless of whether you consider yourself a writer or not, it does not matter. The mere act of typing a few notes daily on your computer screen will help you to make much more sense out of your life and doing so will put you in a much stronger place to make all of your FUTRE DECISIONS!

Don't be concerned about proper punctuation, good grammar, or anything else. Just get your words on the computer screen and save your work daily while always being sure to keep ALL of your computer work backed up to the cloud or some type of external storage device not located in the same building as your computer!

As you build your habit of daily writing, you will find it only takes about 5 minutes or less each day to complete. You don't even need to write in complete sentences and your spelling is hardly important at all. Just get a few lines on paper. Some days it will seem like a chore and other days you might feel semi-inspired. Commit yourself to making at least one rudimentary entry every day. Even if you only write, "This was the most boring day of my life." or "This was the WORST day of my life." you will propel your positive habit and enhance your overall character. Do more if you feel compelled to do so, but at least make one journal entry per day. Later in the book, you will see EXACTLY how I write my journal and you will notice it is nothing special!!! My journal is only a few quick notes each day, nothing more!

Although I believe EVERY DAY of life is an amazing day REGARDLESS of what specifically happens, your days pedaling your bicycle on the Southern Tier or any other major bike route, will be EXTRA precious days. You do NOT want to miss making a few notes about each day of your epic bicycle ride, especially how you are feeling, the people you meet, the miles you pedaled, and the abundant challenges in your way! Even if you never make another journal entry in your life, don't miss out on your life-changing thoughts and experiences while riding the Southern Tier!

Remembering the challenges you overcome on the Southern Tier might be the BREAKTHROUGH you need to build your future confidence. Don't neglect to take advantage of this rare opportunity to DISCOVER more about yourself. In a few short weeks along your epic bike ride, you may discover more about yourself than in ALL the previous years of your life!!!! A cross-country bike trip is an INCREDIBLE way to catch a glimpse of your SOUL! Don't miss it! Find out who you really are! Like me, you might be surprised! Welcome to the Southern Tier!

DAY 43: Mom sent me a screenshot of her LIFE 360 notification pertaining to my EXACT location as of my finish of the great Southern Tier Bicycle Route!

Chapter 158: Time

Have you ever forgotten what day it is? During my time spent on the Southern Tier, forgotten days happened FREQUENTLY! While pedaling a major bike route, there are NOT separate days, only one LONG, seemingly endless day or at least it feels that way as each day involves the same monotonous act of pedaling! After a few days on bike tour and definitely after a few weeks on tour, you won't even know what day it is unless you really think hard about it!

After a week of daily bike travels, all the days begin to feel the same. There is no more excitement for Friday evening happy hour and no more dread of the Sunday evening blues preluding your return to work on Monday. All days hold the same power as each day has the same goal consisting of spinning those pedals round and round! Your life has been diminished to the mere act of pedal spinning! Suddenly, no specific day is any more significant than another!

As you begin your cross-country quest, you might have a very strong sense of daily awareness and knowing exactly what you would NORMALLY be doing at home or at work on any given day, but as your bicycle adventure progresses and you slowly release your hold on your former life, you will begin to experience a new sense of time. Each day will be equally precious as there is but one day and it is TODAY! There is but one time and the time is NOW! Every day on the Southern Tier is TODAY! There is no favoritism. Every day is the SAME. There is no looking forward or preferring one day over another day. As it is written in the Bible, "Today is the day the Lord hath made, let us rejoice and be glad!"

On the Southern Tier, it was interesting to reflect on the days of the week. I remember when I thought, "Today is Saturday. This is my SECOND Saturday of my trip." Although I had no preference of days, recognizing the second Saturday of my trip was a special moment as I officially lasted a week on my epic ride!

Officially graduating into my SECOND WEEK of the Southern Tier was BIG!!! No longer was I just another "wannabe," I was now a "REAL CONTENDER!" Even though I was barely hanging on and every day was a risk of going back home, I remained on route. A week had passed and I remained pedaling. Despite all of my insecurities, I continued pedaling the Southern Tier! I was NOT back at home on my recliner chair nor was I sitting at my kitchen table eating lunch. It was the start of the second week of the hailed Southern Tier and I was pedaling my way through Arizona! Making it to my second week gave me a glimmer of hope and maybe even once I might have let myself fantasize about what it would be like to finish my EPIC bike journey at the glorious salt-waters of the Atlantic Ocean!

While riding the Southern Tier, Saturdays seemed to be sacred for me, probably because I started my epic mission on a Saturday and each successive Saturday represented a special PASSAGE of time. Each Saturday marked another week of sanctified time as with each passing week my trip felt more and more REAL. During those times when I left my reality and dreamed of what it would be like to finish the Southern Tier, tears would drip down my face as I envisioned myself arriving at the Atlantic Ocean on my bicycle! But those crazy thoughts would quickly be interrupted by my monotonous pedal strokes and my seemingly futile progress.

The Southern Tier is NOT about DAYS! The Southern Tier is about PEDAL STROKES! As long as your pedals are spinning, you are doing GREAT! Don't fall into the trap of days, miles per hour, or time passage. Days, time, and miles are NOTHING!!! All that matters is when you look down and you see your pedals rotating! If your pedals are spinning, then you are moving and as you are moving, you are inching closer and closer to the greatest discovery of your life!

DAY 44: After biking about 7 miles to the Amtrak station, I waited about 4 hours for my train to arrive to take me back home to my amazing wife and beloved cats!

Chapter 159: Curbs

As I have repeatedly mentioned throughout this seemingly endless book, the Southern Tier and all other major cross-country bike routes are loaded with MANY DANGERS inherent in the basic route! There isn't enough space in this lengthy book to cover all of them, but I have made a reasonable attempt to WARN you about many of the pitfalls and dangers! If I could impress only one bit of advice to you as you begin your cycling adventure of a lifetime, it would be to PAY ATTENTION! Be fully conscious and aware of your surroundings. Know where you are at all times and CONSTANTLY be on the lookout for DANGER! Danger is EVERYWHERE! Potential HARM is all around you. BE ALERT!

As I was pedaling my bicycle in El Paso, Texas during one of those semi-frequent times when my attention dropped for a few moments, my right pedal came down and contacted the 4-inch curb to my right. The impact of the connection almost catapulted me off of my bicycle and on to my face! As I awkwardly regained my balance without a crash, I was reminded about the importance of paying attention. For just a few moments, I let my attention wane and I almost paid dearly for it! During that moment of brief despair as my pedal contacted the unforgiving cement curb, I was reminded about the <u>never-ending</u> dangers surrounding me.

My lesson had to do with being humble at ALL times as I may have briefly let my newfound confidence outshine my more important sense of humility. In a quick instance of haphazard attention, I almost found myself on the GROUND impacting the hard asphalt road surface! Resist the temptation to think you are doing well and never fall to the ploy of thinking you are a great cyclist! Consistently remind yourself you are susceptible to the ABUNDANT potential harm and dangers ALL AROUND YOU! Even an innocent little cement curb can end your epic ride! Be on constant look-out for danger. Pay full attention all the time!

MANY cyclists have lost their lives pedaling on the public streets and you are NO DIFFERENT than many of those riders who perished. The only difference is you and I are here! We are LUCKY! Don't ever forget it! Cycling on major bike routes is dangerous! No, I'm NOT saying you shouldn't do it because life-threatening danger is all around us at every moment of every day no matter what you do or don't do, but you must have supreme RESPECT for the many dangers around you, especially while cycling. The more respect you have for the excessive danger in your close proximity, the less your chances of busting up your body and damaging your bicycle.

Every intersection you approach is a potential termination point. Every passing vehicle could mark your end. Any divot in the road could propel you to a painful demise. Even the next gust of wind could be enough to ruin your day! Pay attention at every moment. Be ready for EVERYTHING! Hopefully, this book is giving you an INTRODUCTION into some of the pitfalls awaiting you as you take on perhaps the greatest discovery ADVENTURE of your life!

When you approach the next intersection, EXPECT the car at the stop sign to pull out in front of you. Expect poor road conditions loaded with potholes. Expect glass shattered along the berm. Expect inclement weather. Expect busy roads with no berms. Expecting unfavorable conditions and being alert to recognize dangers BEFORE you get hurt will greatly increase your odds of SURVIVING an epic bike route! Welcome to the Southern Tier!

DAY 45: This is where Amtrak kept my bike and pannier bags during my rail travels.

Chapter 160: Intersections

Crossing in front of a stopped tractor trailer or large box truck at a traffic light on a four-lane road (2 lanes of traffic going each direction) is an easy way for a cyclist to lose their life. As you are approaching an intersection with a large truck in the left lane stopped at a traffic light waiting to make a left turn, it is DEADLY to think you can cross in front of the stopped truck and proceed BLINDLY out into the second lane of MOVING traffic on the other side of the truck! Even if the trucker waives you on, NEVER trust another person with YOUR life!!!!! While riding your bike on an epic route or pedaling around your neighborhood, take FULL RESPONSIBILITY for your own safety and NEVER obey the hand motions of a driver in a vehicle and never pull out into a lane of moving traffic unless you can see it is clear with your own two eyes!

While riding the remarkable, predominantly NON-ROAD Greater Allegheny Passage (GAP) bicycle trail from Cumberland, Maryland to Pittsburgh, Pennsylvania, my wife was almost killed at a busy intersection as we approached the conclusion of the amazing route at one of the few busy streets near downtown Pittsburgh. Instead of remaining calm and WAITING to cross the busy street until she was 100% SURE it was safe, my wife obeyed the driver of a large box truck who mistakenly waived her in front of him directly in the path of a car moving at a fast rate of speed in the next lane to his right. Fortunately, at the top of my lungs, I fiercely and desperately yelled "STOP" in time for my wife to recognize the oncoming car and to wait in front of the huge box truck before proceeding across the street!

After this semi-traumatic cycling experience, I would NEVER take another driver's word and pull out into moving traffic regardless of whether I was in a car or on a bicycle. If I cannot see what is ahead of me, I'm WAITING! And I don't care how long I have to wait. My life is worth waiting all day if I have to! Don't ever give your precious life to someone else to make decisions for you! Look for yourself and make sure the road is CLEAR before you proceed. Never believe a driver who waives you into a blind traffic crossing!

Remain calm and go slow. ALWAYS maintain your composure and never succumb to the pressures of your cycling buddy, another driver, or a good-hearted pedestrian when your life is in question. Let others blow their horn at you or call you names, but never be forced to act BLINDLY! Block traffic if you have to, but don't ever make hurried, hasty decisions amidst traffic. All bike maneuvers should be SLOW and DELIBERATE while you are negotiating through busy vehicular areas!!!

My wife could have been KILLED as she pulled out in front the stopped box truck and almost continued into the next lane over. Yes, the huge truck was stopped, but the vehicles in the next lane over were moving at FULL SPEED! Tink was lucky she was alert enough to make a last-second correction, obey my strong demand to STOP, and avoid a possible accident!

Intersections pose one of the greatest risks to a biker. Be ON GUARD as you approach any intersection as stopped vehicles and moving vehicles all represent a severe threat to your safety. Briefly sounding your horn bringing extra attention to yourself as you approach a busy intersection is also a very good idea, even if you have the green light and the traffic seems to be stable! A cyclist cannot afford to make a mistake at a busy intersection!

DAY 45: Here I am standing next to my dad at the Amtrak Station upon my safe return home to Johnstown, Pennsylvania.

DAY 45: From left to right: my mom, Mary Jo Hockensmith, me, my wife, Tina Rae Hockensmith, and my dad, Thomas Hockensmith

Chapter 161: Garmin InReach Mini

For all 3,000 miles pedaled on the Southern Tier, I relied ONLY on my cell phone for any type of emergency service. Fortunately, I did not need any formal emergency services while riding the Southern Tier, but it could have EASILY been a different story as there were two different times I came CLOSE to needing official emergency HELP! My first time of need occurred when my bike tires kept going flat while in the middle of California's Yuha Desert during the middle of the night. The second time was later the SAME DAY when I developed HEAT EXHAUSTION during the mid-afternoon of a 105-degree blazing hot, sunny desert day.

Nobody likes to anticipate the need for any type of emergency services, but you SHOULD be well-prepared in the unlikely case you might need ambulatory and/or some other type of rescue services while on your epic bicycle ride. About 85% of the Southern Tier seemed to have GOOD Verizon cell phone service for me, but there was about 15% of the cycling terrain where I did NOT have any cell phone service whatsoever! What if something would have happened to me while I was in those dead-zone areas? What would happen to me if my phone FROZE, OVER-HEATED, or decided to stop working? What if my phone battery died and it wouldn't take a charge? What if my charger broke and I couldn't charge my phone. What if my phone was lost, broken, or stolen? The "What-if's" are ENDLESS!!!

Since completing the Southern Tier, I have purchased a tiny, orange-colored Garmin inReach Mini. The Garmin inReach Mini is a GPS communication device. Instead of relying on a cell phone signal, the Garmin product communicates through the use of satellites located high in the sky orbiting around the Earth! Therefore, ANYWHERE on planet Earth, my Garmin inReach Mini can send a message to a loved one or send an SOS message to emergency rescue services. There is NOWHERE on the planet in which my Garmin inReach Mini is "out of service!" In the case of an emergency, all I have to do is open a plastic tab and press the SOS button and emergency personnel will be dispatched to my EXACT location as determined by my GPS coordinates embedded upon my Garmin inReach Mini.

Although I paid about $400 for this fine Garmin product, there is also a small $12 monthly fee or so for the most basic Garmin service plan as it is MANDATORY to have an active monthly plan or else your Garmin product will NOT work! Regardless of the specific acquisition cost or ongoing monthly fee, my Garmin inReach Mini is now an ESSENTIAL companion on ALL of my adventures! Even though I have NEVER used my Garmin GPS satellite device to summon emergency services, I relish in the peace of mind knowing I have a RELIABLE communication device with me and I could use it quickly and easily if the unlikely need ever arises! The newfound peace of mind alone makes the Garmin inReach Mini a "must have!"

Chapter 162 Life Bivy

Life Bivy is an emergency "sleeping bag." It is made from a mylar material and only weights about 4 ounces. Life Bivy folds down into a small drawstring pouch only about 4 inches by 3 inches in total size!

Life Bivy is like wrapping yourself in a piece of aluminum foil as the product is designed to REFLECT and TRAP your body heat inside the super-thin, 3-foot by 7-foot envelope. Originally, the Life Bivy was designed for emergency purposes to help keep you alive during cold, inclement weather, but the uses have expanded a bit since its initial product development. Once inside the Life Bivy, it will SHIELD you from the elements as rain, wind, and snow can quickly decrease your body temperature! In the case of an emergency, you will be glad you have a Life Bivy in your possession!

Although I have NOT used my Life Bivy for emergency purposes and I hope I NEVER do, I HAVE used my Life Bivy to line the outside of my sleeping bag as to create an additional layer of warmth on frigid cold nights. My Life Bivy easily wraps around the outside of my regular sleeping bag and keeps me slightly WARMER than I would be otherwise, but the last time I used this particular strategy, a large amount of condensation developed in between my sleeping bag and the Life Bivy resulting in a VERY wet sleeping bag which may have contradicted my original intentions!

Considering the hundreds of possible emergency scenarios you COULD possibly find yourself; it makes great sense to add 4 ounces to your bike weight and take a Life Bivy along with you even if you are doing your epic bike tour in the summer months. Cold weather is NEVER far away!! Don't ever forget it! Most emergencies seem to end with a pending threat of hypothermia! ALWAYS prepare for the COLD!!!! Welcome to the Southern Tier!

Chapter 163: Passing Vehicles

It can be a lot of fun passing slow and stopped vehicles while riding your bike, but it is also one of the most DANGEROUS cycling actions. While you are traveling in the bike lane or on the berm of the road, it is important to be HIGHLY ALERT as vehicles will SUDDENLY make right hand turns crossing over YOUR bike lane and/or berm WITHOUT even looking for a possible cyclist!!! As a cyclist, it is your job to EXPECT vehicles to pull out in front of you or cross over into your biking lane!

While cycling through congested vehicular areas, make sure you are going SLOWER than the vehicles on the roadway to your left. By maintaining a speed LESS THAN the cars to your left, you give yourself much more stopping time if a car suddenly turns across your biking lane.

As a cyclist, you want to retain as much CONTROL as possible. When you are traveling at a rate of speed FASTER than the cars to your left, you put yourself at GREAT RISK of a car suddenly turning into your biking lane, contacting your bike, and causing you severe bodily injury! A right-hand-turning vehicle can end your biking efforts before you even get a chance to apply your brakes, but by moving slower than the cars to your left, you allow each passing car plenty of time to see you, thus greatly reducing your chances of injury. Practicing DEFENSIVE cycling is basically what I am advising. Keeping the vehicles out in front of you while maintaining a STEADY speed will keep you the most VISIBLE to all the potentially dangerous cars to your left!

Cyclists traveling at high speeds during times of heavy auto congestion put themselves at HIGH RISK of accident as most vehicles are NOT thinking about or looking for cyclists, especially cyclists whom appear very quickly seemingly out of "nowhere." Yes, vehicle drivers need to be more AWARE of cyclists, but in the meantime, let's SLOW down our speed of bike travel while we are in vehicular traffic and proceed as safely as possible!

If you ever find yourself in a scenario in which you need to pass a car(s), it is a much better idea to pass the car(s) on the left instead of the right! Most vehicle drivers will look in their left side-view mirror before moving into the passing lane, but most drivers will NOT glance in their right side-view mirror before darting to make a right-hand turn! Drivers do NOT expect cyclists to be traveling to their right and therefore, drivers will usually NOT look to their right before making a right-hand turn. Go EXTRA SLOW when you are in traffic congestion of any kind as YOU will be the one paying the most-dear price for any and all hasty decisions made by the drivers on the road!

Chapter 164: Daily Destination Arrival To-Do Checklist
(What To Do Upon Arriving at Your Daily Destination)

After a long day of biking, you will eventually arrive at your daily destination. Use the following "TO-DO LIST" upon arrival at your daily destination:

1. In appreciation of your safe arrival to your daily destination, say a quick, informal prayer of thanks! My simple and quick prayer went something like this, "Thank you God for delivering me today safely to my destination for the night!" That's it!!! You traveled many dangerous miles today. If any one of those hundreds of vehicles on the road made contact with your bike, then you could have easily died, but instead, you made it safely to your destination. Give thanks to God!
2. Send a quick group text to your loved ones letting them know exactly where you are. If possible, attach a photo or two to your text message. You will be the HIGHLIGHT of their day!
3. Eat and drink something. Always eat before you are hungry and always drink before you are thirsty. Eating and drinking A LOT are FUNDAMENTAL to an epic bicycle adventure!
4. Secure your bike and belongings. Using your bike lock is a good idea. You might even consider looping your bike lock around a strap on your pannier bags and even possibly around your helmet strap in addition to your bike frame. Even if you park your bike in a "safe" location, locking your bike will help you to sleep better!
5. Get a shower! Get out of those sweaty bike clothes as soon as possible. Wash your saddle area like a surgeon washes his hands before surgery! Get a "shower" even if it means jumping into a lake, pouring water over your head with a Gatorade bottle, or using a "bathing wipe." Regardless of your specific scenario, find a way to get yourself CLEAN!
6. Wash your sweaty clothes! In most cases, I hand-washed my clothes during my shower or in any available sink. When you have access to an electronic washing machine, use it! Apply extra attention to the areas of your dirty clothes that contact your skin, especially the saddle area! Use plenty of soap! The best way to wash your clothes is by using a small 2 or 3-gallon garbage can or using your "stack" dry bag. Fill one of these small containers with warm water and soap and then use your hands to thoroughly wash your clothes. The small containers serve as a miniature washing machine and your HANDS are the agitators!
7. After thoroughly rinsing the soap out of your clothes, wring out your clothes as best as you can to get them as DRY as possible. Tightly fold and twist your clothes as to get every last drop of water out of them. There is a good chance your clothes WON'T dry AT ALL throughout the night! As dry as you get your cycling clothes after your shower is usually about how dry they will be early the next morning when you put them back on!
8. Hang up your wet/moist clothes somewhere as to give them the best chance to dry before morning. If there is any sun left in the sky, take advantage of

it! If you are in a motel, use the hair dryer or place your wet clothes near the room heater or air conditioning unit. Spread open your clothes as to give them maximal opportunity to dry. Putting on wet clothes in the early morning sucks, but it is often necessary and you should get used to it and accept it!
9. Apply "Chamois Buttr" (pronounced SHAMMY BUTTER) to your entire saddle area. This specialty cycling crème is expensive, but it is WORTH IT! You have to get some of this fantastic healing substance!
10. Wear comfortable, loose "camp clothes." Let your body BREATH as it starts to recover for tomorrow's ride! Make sure you have boxer underwear as to allow as much air to infiltrate your saddle area as possible!
11. Set up your tent if you will be sleeping outside. Keep your tent zipper closed!!!
12. Open your paper map and figure out how far you want to travel tomorrow. Choose a proposed destination target for tomorrow!
13. Send a text to one or more Warmshowers hosts in tomorrow's destination town. Before sending the text, read the biography of the potential host on the Warmshowers website to make sure the host seems to be a good fit for you. Double-check the grammar on your text before sending your message as not to appear as an illiterate idiot to your potential host!
14. Refill your water bottles for tomorrow. You are always preparing for the next biking day! Thinking one day in advance is wise.
15. Remove your pannier bags and check your bike for any broken spokes, loose seat nuts, crud build-up on your sprockets, low air-pressure in your tires, etc. LOVE your bike. Remember, you are now MARRIED to your bicycle!
16. Take a nap if you have time. This is a rare occurrence, but it did happen a few times on my cross-country venture!
17. Find a nice local restaurant to eat supper. Try to eat some hearty, home-cooked quality food. Make sure you eat some vegetables as most of your food consumption while "on the road" will be filled with lower-quality, fast-food, and convenience-store food.
18. Call your potential Warmshowers host if he/she has not yet returned your previous text, but never "blow up" their phone. If the host is unavailable or unwilling to accommodate you, then try the next host on your list. If you reached out to more than one Warmshowers hosts, then make sure to cancel your other requests as soon as you get confirmed accommodations. If you are more prepared and better at predicting your daily destinations than me, then you should reach out to Warmshowers hosts 2 days in advance as to give your potential host a bit more time, but I do not believe in planning more than one day in advance on an epic bike route.
19. If you don't have a Warmshowers host available for tomorrow's destination town, then investigate other possible overnight accommodation options like campgrounds, cheap motels, etc. Call and make sure the campground, etc. is still open for business or check to make sure it is not booked full. Sometimes, your Adventure Cycling map will have other AWESOME

possible overnight accommodations like hostels, FREE biker sleeping places, etc. listed on the map for you to consider. Motels were usually my last choice as I preferred to SAVE as much money as possible, but it is definitely ok to spend some nights in hotels from time to time. Adventure Cycling maps normally give you LOTS of overnight options as per the listings on their fabulous maps. Some of the Adventure Cycling options are very CREATIVE like sleeping in a local town park like I almost did in Hillsboro, New Mexico until some unknown local lady unexpectedly and graciously offered for me to sleep in an old, vintage camper she owned in the local RV campground about 200 yards down the road. When you travel with a full biking "rig," good things will happen to you too! People LOVE to be a part of your EPIC adventure!

20. Call your spouse or significant other!
21. Return business phone calls, texts, and emails.
22. Talk text your daily "Journal" entry into your cell phone and then save it as a "draft" in your email. When you get back home, you can copy and paste your journal entries to your personal computer journal file. Even if you don't journal the rest of your life, you will want to keep a daily journal during your special epic bike ride!
23. Do at least one daily Spanish lesson on the Duolingo phone app! Keep your mind sharp by applying some type of knowledge effort each day.
24. Brush your teeth.
25. Moments before going to bed, apply "Anti-Monkey Butt" powder to your entire saddle area. Let the powder work through the night. Keeping a dry and healthy saddle area is CRUCIAL!!!
26. Say a night-time prayer. "Almighty Lord, watch over me. May I experience a SOUND, RESTFUL, and SAFE night's sleep."
27. Go to bed early, but not too early! If possible, stay awake until at least 9 p.m. Going to bed too early might interfere with your regular bodily rhythms and cause you to sleep poorly.

Chapter 165: Airport Containers Checklist
(The 4 Containers Needed for Your Epic Bicycle Adventure)

Take the following 4 containers with you when you get dropped off at the airport to begin your epic bicycle adventure:
1. Bike box (This box must be checked-in with your airline.) Your airline will probably require this box to be under 50 pounds or else extra charges may apply.
    a. My box weighed 51 pounds, but I pushed up on the edge of the box while the clerk was weighing my bike box. Doing so relieved a slight bit of weight and the scale suddenly read 49.8 pounds. Yes, this tactic was dishonest and I am embarrassed to admit to such a pitiful ploy. Since then, I have discovered that MOST airlines will allow one extra pound if your box or luggage is slightly over the published weight limit.

2. Check-In Luggage Bag (This bag must be checked-in with your airline.) Your airline will probably also require this piece of baggage to be under 50 pounds or else extra charges will apply. Here's what you should pack into your check-in bag.
    a. Handlebar bike bag
    b. Front right pannier bike bag (bike tools, bike parts, etc.)
    c. Rear right pannier bike bag (sleeping stuff)
    d. Tower stack bike bag
        i. If your tower stack bike bag won't quite fit into your check-in luggage as was the case with me, then you can empty your tower stack bike bag and place your gear individually into your check-in luggage bag as to make everything fit. Your check-in luggage bag must be able to zip shut. Repacking your individual items back into your tower stack bag before you begin pedaling on Day 1 is easy.
    *** Bring an OLD check-in luggage bag as you will be disposing of your check-in bag at your destination airport after you remove your bike bags. You could mail the luggage container back home, but the hassle and costs are too high to make it a viable alternative. After your interior bags are removed, set your luggage bag by the garbage and the airline personnel will figure out what to do with it!

3. Carry-On Item (Rear left pannier bike bag)
    *** You will carry this bag with you on to your flight. As per your airline, this bag is considered your "carry-on" bag. All of your liquids, cremes, toiletries, loose batteries, etc. will be stored inside this bag so that these items can be easily scanned at airport security while in your presence. Don't bring any liquids exceeding 3 ounces or any other prohibited items like CO2, knives, guns, mace, etc. as these items will be confiscated by airport security and you will NEVER see them again.

4. Personal Item (Front left pannier bike bag)
   *** You will also carry this bag with you on to your flight. It is your "personal" bag.

   *** Most airlines allow you to have one "carry-on" item and one "personal" item to be carried by you on to your flight. If your airline does NOT allow these two items, then you will either have to pay EXTRA for these bags or you will have to make some other reasonable adaptation. Remember, you are on an ADVENTURE! Be ready to be creative when necessary!!! Prepare as best as you can in advance!

   *** If you are overweight on either your bike box or your check-in luggage, then you may try to transfer some of the weight into your personal item bag or your carry-on bag as there is generally no weight limit imposed by the airline concerning these two bags as long as these two bags are within the airline's published size limits.

Upon arrival at the airport, get a luggage cart or have a loved one come with you briefly to assist with your four containers as they are more than one person can possibly manage alone.

My pannier bags are made by Arkel, a Canadian company. I HIGHLY recommend them! Even if you are cheap like me, you will be SAVING money in the long-term by spending more money up front to buy the highly-acclaimed Arkel pannier bags as they are truly WORTHY of a cross-country bicycle ride! They also work very well as a "carry-on item" and as a "personal item" while flying to your starting destination.

All of your bags including your pannier bags, bike box, checked-in luggage bag, handlebar bag, tower stack, chair bag, etc. should be NEATLY labeled "Sean Hockensmith 814-241-4832" with a dark black or brilliant white permanent marker! Label everything to help ensure NONE of your PRECIOUS gear is lost!

Chapter 166: Bike Box Checklist
(What to Pack Inside Your Bike Box)

1. A "Bike Box" is a large cardboard box designed to pack your bicycle after you dissemble a few minor parts from your bicycle and take a few additional easy steps.
2. Most airlines will require your bike box to be under 50 pounds, but will give you up to 51 pounds without charging you extra. Check with your airline to find out EXACTLY how much your bike box can weigh without incurring extra fees!
3. NEATLY write "Sean Hockensmith – San Diego Airport FRAGILE 814-241-4832" on the outside of your bike box in big, thick, black ink.
4. Pedals must be removed as your bike box is too narrow for them to fit regularly. Store your pedals inside your bike box wrapped with packing wrap unless you are overweight as I was, in which case, I stored my pedals inside my front left pannier bag which was my "personal item" and therefore had no weight restrictions.
5. Your handlebar will have to be dissembled and turned sideways as to fit inside the bike box. Keep all of your cables attached and be very careful to screw all of the small bolts back into their proper holes as to avoid losing any critical hardware.
6. Remove your front wheel completely and store it alongside your bike inside the bike box. Otherwise, your bike would be too long to fit into the bike box. Place some additional cardboard around the wheel as to protect the wheel spokes.
7. Install a simple hard plastic cover over your rear sprocket. This will help to protect your bike. Your local bike shop will have one of these for you to use for FREE.
8. Insert a plastic front disc spacer on the front brake of your bike after removing your front wheel. Otherwise, you risk LOCKING your front brakes in a way which might be VERY difficult for you to UNLOCK. Ask your local bike shop for this free, tiny piece of plastic.
9. Attach 2 ROK straps to your rear bike rack. At the time of assembly, these awesome straps will secure your "stack" to your rear bike rack.
10. Place 3 empty water bottles into your 3 water bottle frames on your bike.
11. Your front and rear pannier bike bag hardware racks remain attached to your bike. They are NOT removed from your bike during shipping.
12. Keep your waterproof phone case and all mounting hardware attached to your handlebars.
13. Keep your headlight hardware mounted on your handlebars, but keep your actual headlight stored inside your front left pannier bag. Storing your headlight in this manner should avoid any potential damage as it is more likely for your headlight to be damaged in your bike box than packed safely inside your front left pannier bag, which is your "personal item" as far as your airline is concerned.

14. Remove your bike seat along with the long mounting metal tube and securely store your seat and seat tube inside your bike box.
15. Place your helmet with your awesome pre-attached bright-yellow brim hat inside your bike box.
16. After you DOUBLE and TRIPLE check all of your packings, duct tape your bike box shut at all the seams.
    a. Most likely, airport security will cut your duct tape to INSPECT your bike box, but there is nothing you can do about it. You should duct tape your bike box securely shut anyways as to give strong indication to the FRAGILE contents inside the box! Don't worry, airport security has lots of duct tape and they will re-tape your bike box after they conduct their private inspection of the contents of your bike box.

DAY 45: Here are the 4 containers I took with me on my airline flight across the country to San Diego, California to start my EPIC cross-country bicycle ride!

Chapter 167: Airport Clothing Checklist
(What You Should Wear to the Airport)

1. Boxer underwear
   a. Wear loose "boxer" underwear and let your saddle area BREATHE as long as possible. You will be wearing your tight bike shorts A LOT in upcoming days and weeks!
2. Socks
   a. Wear whatever socks you plan to wear when you start pedaling on Day 1 later today.
3. Adventure pants (lightweight and loose).
4. Short-sleeve, bright-colored, wicking biking shirt
   a. This is the shirt you plan to wear while riding your bike later today!
5. Sweatshirt
6. Croc shoes (easy on, easy off shoes)
   a. These are the shoes you will wear at camp each night.
   a. Buy "restaurant crocs" as they have a FULLY ENCLOSED front section of the highly-convenient shoe.
7. Identification wrist band
8. Pouch

*** All of the items listed above will also be listed in the various checklists to follow. Do not duplicate these items as extra ounces make pounds and pounds make pain!

*** About a half hour prior to landing in your destination city, take a nice whiz in the airplane's bathroom and then remove your adventure pants and your boxer underwear. Apply some amazing Bag Balm to the skin of your saddle area to prevent chaffing and to guard against the possible formation of saddle sores. Change into your tight bib biking shorts with a second pair of regular biking shorts over top of your bib biking shorts. Put on your biking shoes and get mentally ready to begin the ride of your life within 2 short hours!

Chapter 168: Pouch Checklist
(What to Pack Inside Your Pouch)

*** You should wear your pouch around your waist at all times. When you are about to begin your bike ride, you will place your pouch inside your front left pannier bag.

1. Phone
2. Paper Boarding Pass for your plane flight
    a. Having a second copy of your boarding pass on your phone is also a great idea!
3. Passport
    a. You will need a passport if you are traveling outside of your home country.
4. Wallet
    a. Driver's license
    b. Cash money (about $300 or so)
    c. Credit card
    d. AAA card
    e. Health insurance card
    f. Health Savings Account debit card (the card you use to pay for medical expenses)
    g. Debit card (the card you use to access more paper money if needed)
    h. MISSION STATEMENT (a small hand-printed reminder card stating WHY you are taking this "insane" bike ride!)
5. Reading glasses
6. 2 pens
7. To Do list (your regular everyday list of tasks you plan to do)
8. Whistle (there are MANY reasons you should have a whistle!)
    a. Attach a lanyard to your whistle so you can wear it around your neck, especially while you are at camp.
9. Medicine
    a. Keep at least one or two days of any regular, daily medicine in a tiny container.

Chapter 169: Front Left Pannier Bag Checklist
(What to Pack Inside Your Front Left Pannier Bag)

*** Pouch and Bike Hardware (bike tools, bike parts, etc.) belong in this bag.
*** While traveling to your starting destination, you will wear your pouch around your waist. Moments before you are ready to begin pedaling, you will store your pouch inside this bag.
*** This bag is also your "personal item" as per your airline. You will carry this bag with you on to your airplane flight.

1. Pouch
    a. Attach your pouch around your waist every time you lock your bike and enter a store or restaurant.
2. Spare Cash and Spare Credit Card (Store inside an envelope with a handwritten decoy word printed on the front.)
    a. Zip the decoy envelope inside a small inner compartment of your pannier bag.
3. Complete set of paper maps for your particular route (Store in a waterproof map case or Ziploc bag to keep dry)
    a. Zip the waterproof map case inside a small inner compartment of your pannier bag.
4. AAA state map for ALL the states on your bike route (put inside a waterproof map case or Ziploc bag)
    a. Zip the waterproof map case inside a small inner compartment of your pannier bag.
    b. You are a AAA member, right?
5. Bike Lock
    a. Get a rope-type lock with a combination lock. Do not use a lock requiring a separate key.
6. 3 Taillights
    a. One is for the back of your helmet. One is for the back of your rear pannier bag frame. One is a spare.
7. 2 Headlights
    a. One attaches to the base mount on your handlebars. The other headlight is a spare.
8. Air Pump
    a. Make sure it fits your Presta or Schrader tire tubes.
9. Spare Derailer Hanger
    a. Use as a replacement in case of a break.
10. 3 Spare Spokes
    a. Use to replace any broken spokes on your bicycle wheel.
11. 2 "Fiber Fix" kits
    a. Use if you get a broken spoke and you cannot replace the broken spoke with another actual spoke.
12. 2 Tire Boot Repair Patches
    a. Use if you wear off the rubber from your tire and you have not yet

arrived at a bike repair shop to buy two new ROAD tires.
13. 3 <u>Metal</u> Tire Irons (plastic tire irons are too flimsy and have a tendency to break)
    a. Use to help get your tire off of the rim in case of a flat tire.
14. 1 Bottle of 2-ounce White Lightning chain lubricant
    a. Keep your bike chain lubed regularly.
15. Duct tape (wrap it around your air pump)
    a. You will probably need a small piece of duct tape for something!
16. Chain Connector (put this small piece in a Ziploc bag as not to lose it)
    a. Use in case you break your bike chain and you need to re-attach it back together.
17. 3 Spare Tire Tubes (my size was 700-38)
    a. Know your tire tube size and have PROPERLY-SIZED spare tire tubes available.
18. Allen Wrenches
    a. Make sure you have a separate properly-sized Allen wrench that fits ALL the various Allen bolts on every part of your bicycle.
19. Several Tire Tube Patches
    a. Tire patches are used if you decide to REPAIR a flat tire tube instead of discarding the damaged tire tube and installing a brand-new tire tube.
20. Tire Tube Cement
    a. Tire tube cement is needed to adhere the tire tube patch to the damaged tire tube.
    b. The tire tube patches and the tire tube cement are usually sold in a set!

Prior to my epic ride, I bought a small bike repair kit from Adventure Cycling Association. The handy set came in its own small cloth container. It contained many of the items listed above. I LOVED IT!

DAY 45: My sister, Kelli, unexpectedly greeted me upon my arrival at the Amtrak station. Kelli is slightly prettier without her COVID-19 mask!

Chapter 170: Front Right Pannier Bag Checklist
(What to Pack Inside Your Front Right Pannier Bag)

*** Rain gear and extra biking clothing belong in this bag.
*** Store this bag inside your check-in luggage during your airplane flight.
*** Store these items listed below inside 2-3 separate, pliable, thin, water-resistant storage "dry bags" as to add another layer of waterproofing to your gear.

1. Rainsuit bottoms (MUST be worthy of use in SEVERE weather)
2. Reflective Velcro bands (Wrap around your ankles as to keep your rain pants out of your bike mechanicals)
3. Rainsuit top – medium-weight (MUST be worthy of use in SEVERE weather)
4. Rainsuit top – lightweight ((MUST be worthy of use in SEVERE weather)
5. Waterproof shoe covers (Cold and wet feet can be MISERABLE)
6. Helmet rain cover (Usually worn over your helmet, but could also possibly be worn under your brim helmet.)
7. Baklava (Full head/face lightweight polyester hat used in COLD weather during biking or at camp)
8. Winter mittens (Use on VERY COLD, dry biking days or at camp)
9. Full-finger regular bike gloves (Use on chilly, dry biking days)
10. Full-finger waterproof biking gloves (Use on chilly, rainy biking days)
11. Half-finger regular biking gloves (Use on warm biking days)
12. Bandana/head band (Use it to keep sweat out of your eyes)

For an EPIC Christmas gift following my UNLIKELY finish of the Southern Tier, my unrelenting, supportive sister, Kelli, and her loving family bought me this ONE-OF-KIND throw blanket to commemorate my Southern Tier adventure! The generous gift brought tears to my eyes. I look at the blanket EVERY DAY I am home!

Chapter 171: Rear Left Pannier Bag Checklist
(What to Pack Inside Your Rear Left Pannier Bag)

*** Easy-access items, clothing, and toiletry items belong in this bag.
*** This bag is also your "carry-on" bag as per your airline. You will carry this bag with you on your airplane flight.

Front outside compartment (easy-access location)
1. Toilet paper (inside a sturdy Ziploc storage bag)
2. Shovel (tiny one-ounce backpacking shovel to dig crapping holes)
3. Ear buds
4. Garmin inReach Mini (emergency GPS satellite SOS device)
5. Headlamp
6. Sunscreen (3-ounce or less bottle as per airline regulations)

Big main compartment of bag (clothes and toiletry items)
*** Your clothes should be stored in pliable, thin, <u>water-resistant</u> storage "dry bags" as to add another layer of waterproofing to your clothing. These are the SAME dry bags I use while hiking. Use 5 different dry bags (each being a different colors) to organize your bags logically as follows:

BAG #1 (SOCKS AND UNDERWEAR)
1. 1 pair of boxer underwear (for camp)
2. 1 pair of fast-drying wicking ankle socks
3. 1 pair of fast-drying wicking crew socks
4. 1 pair of thick wool socks (Always be ready for COLD!!!)

BAG #2 (SHORTS AND PANTS)
1. 1 pair of padded spandex biking bib shorts (with the straps that go over your shoulders)
2. 1 pair of regular padded spandex biking shorts
3. 1 full-leg, padded bike pants
    *** Bright yellow would be nice. Mine were blue!
4. 1 pair of lightweight gym shorts (for camp)
5. 1 pair of skin-tight, wicking spandex/wool leggings (for camp)
    *** My spandex pants are bright yellow and SKIN TIGHT.
    *** My wife thinks I look "TOO GOOD!"
6. 1 pair of loose adventure pants (for camp)

BAG #3 (TOPS)
1. 2 skin-tight quick-dry, long-sleeve, spandex/wool shirts
2. 1 short-sleeve, quick-dry, wicking, bright-colored biking shirt
    *** My shirt was bright yellow.
    *** Most biking shirts have a convenient rear pocket, but I wore a bright regular non-biking shirt.
3. 1 regular quick-dry loose-fitted, comfortable T-shirt (for camp)

4. 1 polyester/wool quick-dry, fleece sweatshirt (for camp)

BAG #4 (COLD, ETC.)
1. Winter hat (for camp)
2. Small hand towel (to dry your body after a shower)
3. ACE compression bandage (in case of an injury)

BAG #5 (TOILETRIES)
1. Toothpaste (under 3 ounces as per airline regulations)
2. Toothbrush
3. Bag Balm (for saddle area, etc.)
4. Anti Monkey-Butt powder (Apply to saddle area before bed.)
5. Chamois Butt'r crème (Apply to saddle area after shower.)
6. 3 spare AAA batteries (for your headlamp)
7. Deodorant (smelling good is important)
8. Bio-Freeze or Icy Hot (for body aches and pains)
9. Soap (one bar)
10. Knife (very small)
11. Nail clipper (small)
12. Band aids
13. Antibiotic ointment (in case you get a cut or a sore)
14. Naproxen, Ibuprofen, and/or Tylenol
15. Bathing wipes (in case there is no shower available)
    *** Buy individually-wrapped wipes or store the packet of opened wipes in a secure Ziploc bag as to remain moist.

Small Rear pocket
1. 3-4 Plastic bags (Walmart or Dollar General bags are fine.)
   a. Use for trash, short-term food storage, pooping container, etc.

My wife, Tink, is the most THOUGHTFUL person I ever met in my life!!!! This creative work of art she gave to me upon completion of the Southern Tier caused my knees to feel weak!!! WOW!!! The effort applied to create this LOVELY designation can only be matched by the size of my wife's kind heart! Someday, one of my great-grandchildren might have this plaque hanging in their home!

Chapter 172: Rear Right Pannier Bag Checklist
(What to Pack Inside Your Rear Right Pannier Bag)

*** Sleeping gear and food belong in this bag.
*** This bag will be stored inside your check-in luggage during your airplane flight.

Small front outside part of the bag (easy access location)
1. Extra drinks (Gatorade, Powerade, chocolate milk, etc.)
   a. You cannot bring liquids exceeding 3 ounces on to the airplane! Buy your drinks at a store shortly after you pedal out of the airport and start your epic bicycle ride.

Large main compartment of the bag
1. Sleeping bag (Get a zero-degree Fahrenheit rated bag and place it inside a separate waterproof dry bag!)
2. Sleeping pad (Therm-a-Rest air sleeping pads are the BEST)
3. Air pillow (Sea to Summit is the best)
   a. Try to fit this small item inside your sleeping pad bag.
4. Pillowcase (lightweight and comfortable material)
   a. Before going to bed at night, stuff unused clothes in your soft pillowcase and make a COMFORTABLE pillow!
5. Life Bivy (4-ounce waterproof emergency "sleeping bag shelter")
6. Food
   a. If needed, disperse some of your food into your other 3 pannier bags. Try to keep the overall weight of your bicycle as BALANCED as possible by keeping the weight of each of your front pannier bags and the weight of each of your rear pannier bags approximately the same!

Small Rear pocket
1. Sunglasses
   a. Store in a hard or semi-hard case as to prevent damage.

Chapter 173: Tower Stack Checklist
(What to Pack Inside Your Tower Stack Bag)

Your tower stack bag will be stored inside of your check-in luggage during your airplane flight. If this rather large bag (about 20-liter size) cannot fit inside of your check-in luggage bag as a single piece, then remove the items from your tower stack bag and store them individually inside of your check-in luggage bag.

A "tower stack" is the 20-liter, heavy-duty, 100% truly waterproof, brightly-colored, dry-bag. It is attached with ROK straps to the top of your rear rack. Your tower stack bag is located above your rear tire and directly behind your bike seat.

1. Tent (2 person Hyke and Byke Yosemite tent) (5.6 pounds)
   a. A "2-person" tent is really a 1-person tent in my opinion!
   b. Get a GOOD ground covering mat for your tent! Some tents have a GOOD factory ground covering mat as part of their tent package and others do not include a ground covering mat as part of the tent package. Hyke and Byke DOES include an excellent ground covering along with their tents. If your tent does not have a ground mat, then buy a piece of Tyvek at Lowes or on eBay and use it as your ground covering. A ground covering mat will PROLONG the life of your tent!
2. Fold-up camp chair (2.1 pounds)
   a. I used black electrical tape and I taped all 4 ends of my camp chair as to help ensure the ends won't become detached if they sink deep into the ground. I also taped all 4 ends of the metal framework pieces that connect to the fabric of the chair as to make the metal pieces a bit less sharp as to prevent any potential damage to my chair.
   b. I used extra pieces of small clothing fabric and gorilla glue to reinforce all 4 of the tiny pockets where the metal frame pieces connect to form the actual chair. Otherwise, over time, the metal framework pieces WILL eventually poke a hole through the original factory fabric and you will be left with an UNUSABLE chair!
3. Croc shoes (easy-on and easy-off shoes to be worn at camp)
   a. Buy "restaurant chef" croc shoes! This type of croc shoe has the FULL covered front as to provide a bit of waterproofing around your toes as you walk around camp in the likely damp grass.
   b. Buy croc shoes one size bigger than usual so your feet can still fit inside the shoes even when you wear heavy wool socks at camp during cold temperatures!

Chapter 174: Handlebar Bag Checklist
(What to Pack Inside Your Handlebar Bag)

*** This bag will be stored inside of your check-in luggage during your airplane flight.

1. Small 2-liter dry bag containing
   a. 2 Anker Power Banks (to keep your electronics charged!)
   b. USB charging cord that fits your phone
   c. USB charging cord that fits your GPS watch
   d. USB charging cord that fits your bike's headlight
   e. 2 USB charging cords that fit your battery bank (to recharge your battery banks)
   f. 1 electric, multi-port, USB, electric charging box with folding electrical prongs
      i. Use this device to plug into a regular electrical outlet power to re-charge your power banks!
1. Digital camera
   a. You will want to take photos of sunrises, sunsets, state welcome signs, famous landmarks, and most of all, the many AMAZING people you will encounter along the way.
   b. Your cell phone will be too hard to access while you are pedaling. Your digital camera will be much easier to access than your cell phone. Plus, your cell phone should already be in use as it should be set to your Bicycle Route Navigator GPS phone application map.

Chapter 175: Other Possible Items Checklist
(Additional Items You May Consider Bringing Along)

1. Bear spray (9-ounce commercial bottle)
   a. Bear spray will not be permitted on the airplane. Buy it at Walmart or another sporting goods store somewhere along your bike route.
2. First-aid kit
3. Jetboil or tiny stove
4. Fuel cannister for your Jetboil or tiny stove
   a. Fuel cannisters are NOT permitted on the airplane. Buy it at Walmart or another sporting goods store somewhere along your bike route.
5. Insect repellent (bugs could possibly be bad!)
   a. Insect repellent larger than 3 ounces will not be permitted on the airplane. If needed, buy it at Walmart or another sporting goods store somewhere along your bike route.
6. Etc…..

My hometown newspaper published this well-written and interesting article about my cross-country bicycle journey. The intriguing article was written by the talented Patrick Buchnowski from the Johnstown Tribune Democrat.

Chapter 176: Questions and Answers
(Sean's Answers to Specific Questions)

1. What one word would you use to describe the Southern Tier?
    a. Fulfilling
2. Who was the most interesting person you met on the Southern Tier?
    a. Myself
3. What did you learn on the Southern Tier?
    a. Self-reliance
4. What was your hardest day on the Southern Tier?
    a. Day 18. The day from HELL (Sierra Blanca, Texas to Van Horn, Texas)
5. What was your fondest memory of the Southern Tier?
    a. The glorious finish at Jacksonville Beach
6. What did you fear the most on the Southern Tier?
    a. The desert in the middle of the night
7. Who did you miss the most on the Southern Tier?
    a. My wife, Tink
8. What was the biggest mistake you made on the Southern Tier?
    a. Thinking I could do it alone and unsupported
9. What is your advice for an aspiring cross-country cyclist?
    a. Read this book carefully before you buy your airline ticket!
10. Who made the biggest difference in your cross-country travels?
    a. God
11. Where was your favorite place to stay on the Southern Tier?
    a. The Beehive in Marathon, Texas on Day 20
12. What was the highest number of miles you pedaled on the Southern Tier during one day?
    a. 108 miles on 2 different days in Louisiana
13. Why didn't you go home after you quit on Day 2?
    a. The logistics were too complicated and it annoyed me to think about it. Plus, I felt I DESERVED to be punished for being so stupid!
14. Why did you name the book EPIC FAIL?
    a. I QUIT on Day 2, but I refused to go back home.
15. Would you ever attempt another cross-country bicycle journey?
    a. Yes!!!
16. What was the scariest animal you saw on the Southern Tier?
    a. Coyote
17. Did you ride your bike in the dark at all on the Southern Tier?
    a. Yes. I rode in the dark for about 60 hours.

18. What did you regret about your Southern Tier bicycle tour?
    a. Not doing it earlier in life.
19. What would you do different if you could it all over again?
    a. I would start with road tires, not gravel tires.
20. What injuries did you sustain on the Southern Tier?
    a. Knee injuries
21. What was your easiest day of biking on the Southern Tier?
    a. My last day, Day 43
22. What words made the biggest difference in your completing the Southern Tier?
    a. Dad text me, "You can do it!"
    b. Brother-In-Law, Steve, text me, "Out of ALL the people I know, YOU are the ONE person who might actually be capable of finishing a solo, cross-country bicycle ride!"
23. Where did you pee on the Southern Tier?
    a. On the side of the road
24. Why did you pick the Southern Tier as your cross-country bicycle route?
    a. It was the shortest cross-country route and it was warm.
25. Why didn't you sign up for a group ride instead of a solo adventure?
    a. I'm a loner!
26. Who scared you the most on the Southern Tier?
    a. Warmshowers host, Gene, on Day 40.
27. Who was the nicest person you met on the Southern Tier?
    a. Jamie from Rising Phoenix River Adventures in Bastrop, Texas
28. Did you think you would finish the Southern Tier?
    a. No!!!!
29. Did your bike break down at all on the Southern Tier?
    a. Yes. 7 times.
30. Why wouldn't you come back home after you realized the solo cross-country bike adventure was too much for you?
    a. I decided I would rather DIE somewhere along the desolate roads of the famed route, if necessary.
31. Did anybody help you on the Southern Tier?
    a. Yes. Many!
32. How cold did it get on the Southern Tier?
    a. 26 degrees Fahrenheit with a 5-degree wind chill
33. How hot did it get on the Southern Tier?
    a. 105 degrees Fahrenheit
34. What did you eat on the Southern Tier?
    a. Anything and EVERYTHING!!!

35. Did you eat a lot on the Southern Tier?
    a. YES!!!!
36. Did you get in any trouble on the Southern Tier?
    a. YES! I almost went to jail in Louisiana.
37. What was your favorite part of your daily bike rides?
    a. Riding in the early morning DARKNESS!
38. Where did you poop?
    a. At gas stations, restaurants, in a bag in my tent, or alongside the road!
39. What kept you going instead of going back home?
    a. I was too STUBBORN to go back home.
40. Prior to your epic bike trip, did anybody believe you could actually pedal a bicycle across the country?
    a. My wife, Tink, and my daughter, Stacey
41. Did you cry while riding the Southern Tier?
    a. Yes. Many times!
42. What activity is most responsible for your eventual finish of the Southern Tier?
    a. Prayer!!!!
43. Were you qualified to ride the Southern Tier alone and unsupported?
    a. NO!!!!
44. What do you regret about your Southern Tier adventure?
    a. Not doing it earlier in my life!
45. Was the Southern Tier what you expected?
    a. NO!!!!!!!!
46. Why did you ride the Southern Tier in the first place?
    a. For what it would make of me as a person.
47. Did you get sick on the Southern Tier?
    a. Yes. I almost DIED from heat exhaustion on Day 4.
48. What did you look forward to while you were pedaling?
    a. My 10-mile walking breaks
49. What do you remember most about the Southern Tier?
    a. The desert!!!
50. What songs capture the essence of the Southern Tier?
    a. "Wanted Dead or Alive" & "Blaze of Glory" by Jon Bon Jovi
51. What surprised you about the Southern Tier?
    a. There is sacred spiritual power ALIVE along the route
52. Did you ever get mad on the Southern Tier?
    a. Yes, when I got lost!
53. When did you realize that you were actually going to finish the Southern Tier?
    a. 10 miles from Jacksonville Beach!

54. What did it feel like when you contacted the Atlantic Ocean and completed the grueling Southern Tier Bicycle Route?
    a. The greatest feeling of my life. I was OVERWHELMED!
55. Do you believe in angels?
    a. YES!!!!
56. Did the Southern Tier change you?
    a. YES!!!!!!!
57. Did you think you were going to die on the Southern Tier?
    a. YES!!
58. What were the people like you met on the Southern Tier?
    a. Kind
59. What organization played the biggest role in your completion of the Southern Tier?
    a. Adventure Cycling Association
60. What did you do when you got back home from the Southern Tier?
    a. Back to work, like usual
61. Why did it take so long for you to complete this book?
    a. I experienced 3 debilitating, life-threatening health issues.
62. Was the Southern Tier worth it?
    a. Yes!!!!
63. What type of bike did you use to cross the country?
    a. Motobecane Gravel X-Pro from Bikes Direct
64. Are you a professional athlete?
    a. No!
65. Did you ever doubt yourself while on the Southern Tier?
    a. Yes. Every day!
66. Why did you write EPIC FAIL?
    a. I was called to write it. I did NOT want to write it!!
67. Who supported you back home while you were away on the Southern Tier?
    a. My wife, Tink. My mom and dad. My sister, Kelli.
68. Why is this book so long?
    a. I thought it was going to be short! I was WRONG!
69. Did you suffer on the Southern Tier?
    a. YES!!!

Chapter 177: Sean's Daily Destination Listings
(Listing of Sean Hockensmith's Daily Destinations along the Southern Tier)

Below is a quick summary listing of my beginning daily locations and my ending daily destinations for each day of my 43-day bike adventure across the Southern Tier Bicycle Route. Also included is the APPROXIMATE mileage traveled on my bike each day. The mileage may NOT be EXACT, but it is close!

DAY 1: San Diego, California to Alpine, California (45 miles)
*** As I began my epic journey, I traveled 10 miles in the WRONG direction through San Diego as I ASSUMED the famed Southern Tier bike route started in Mission Beach instead of Ocean Beach!!!! I'm SO STUPID!!!!!!
*** I only rode a half-day today as I began pedaling at 1:45 p.m. and I ceased pedaling AFTER dark around 8 p.m.
*** I wild camped in my tent under a gazebo behind Town Hall.

Day 2: Alpine, California to Ocotillo, California (60 miles)
*** I stayed in my tent on a cement sidewalk at the Red Feather Market and Café in the PURE WILDERNESS of the DESOLATE Yuha Desert.

Day 3: Ocotillo, California to Brawley, California (60 miles)
*** I stayed at The Desert Inn.

Day 4: Brawley, California to Blythe, California (94 miles. 86 miles by bike and 8 miles by a stranger's truck)
*** I suffered from heat exhaustion 8 miles outside of Blythe, California. A stranger named Rudy saved my life!
*** I stayed at Travelodge Motel.

Day 5: Blythe, California (0 miles) I rented a truck and drove 85 miles one-way to get my bike fixed at the nearest bike repair shop in Lake Havasu, Arizona
*** I stayed a second night at the same Travelodge Motel.

Day 6: Blythe, California to Salome, Arizona (86 miles, 8 miles westbound back to the exact place of my DEMISE 2 days ago and then 8 miles eastbound back to Blythe, California. Finally, 70 miles eastbound to Salome, Arizona.)
*** I stayed at Sheffler's Motel.

Day 7: Salome, Arizona to Surprise, Arizona (88 miles)
*** I stayed at a Warmshowers house.

Day 8: Surprise, Arizona to Mesa, Arizona (49 miles)
*** I stayed at a Warmshowers house.

Day 9: Mesa, Arizona to Tonto Basin, Arizona (80 miles)
    *** I stayed at the Tonto Basin Inn.

Day 10: Tonto Basin, Arizona to Globe, Arizona (57 miles)
    *** I stayed in my tent in the far corner of the parking lot at Apache Grand Casino.

Day 11: Globe, Arizona to Stafford, Arizona (71 miles)
    *** I stayed at a Warmshowers house.

Day 12: Stafford, Arizona to Duncan, Arizona (41 miles)
    *** I stayed in my tent in a gorgeous courtyard at a Warmshowers house outside the Simpson Hotel.

Day 13: Duncan, Arizona to Silver City, New Mexico (79 miles)
    *** I stayed at a Warmshowers house.

Day 14: Silver City, New Mexico to Hillsboro, New Mexico (59 miles)
    *** I stayed for FREE in a tiny 1947 camper trailer. I planned to stay for FREE in the tiny Hillsboro Town Park in my tent, but as I was setting up my camp, Kristin drove by and offered me to stay in an old camper trailer about a block away at her small RV campground. Why not!?

Day 15: Hillsboro, New Mexico to Las Cruces, New Mexico (85 miles)
    *** I stayed at a Warmshowers house.

Day 16: Las Cruces, New Mexico to Fabens, Texas (80 miles)
    *** I stayed at Fabens Inn.

Day 17: Fabens, Texas to Sierra Blanca, Texas (66 miles)
    *** I stayed at Americana Inn.

Day 18: Sierra Blanca, Texas to Van Horn Texas (34 miles) (The HARDEST biking day of my life!)
    *** I stayed at Motel 6. Thank you, mom! You booked the third to last room at this motel for me on this FRIGID, windy day!

Day 19: Van Horn, Texas to Marfa, Texas (76 miles)
    *** I stayed at a Warmshowers house.

Day 20: Marfa, Texas to Marathon, Texas (58 miles)
    *** I stayed for FREE in a very small, mostly-stone/cement shed called "The Beehive" at the La Loma Del Chivo Hostel.

Day 21: Marathon, Texas to Sanderson, Texas (57 miles)
    *** I stayed in my tent at Canyons RV Park.

Day 22: Sanderson, Texas to Comstock, Texas (88 miles)
*** I stayed at Comstock Motel.

Day 23: Comstock, Texas to Brackettville, Texas (69 miles)
*** I stayed in my tent at the Fort Clark Army Campground.

Day 24: Brackettville, Texas to Leakey (pronounced Lay-key), Texas (71 miles)
*** I stayed at the Leakey Inn.

Day 25: Leakey, Texas to Kerrville, Texas (75 miles)
*** I stayed inside a motorhome in the driveway of a Warmshowers house

Day 26: Kerrville, Texas to Johnson City, Texas (57 miles)
*** I stayed at Hill Country Inn.

Day 27: Johnson City, Texas to Bastrop, Texas (88 miles)
*** I stayed at the Bastrop Inn.

Day 28: Bastrop, Texas to La Grange, Texas (42 miles)
*** This was a "half day" of biking as I began biking around 2 p.m. after getting some repairs to my bike.
*** Huge thanks to Jamie, owner of Rising Phoenix River Adventures in Bastrop, Texas, whom drove me 30 miles to Austin, Texas to get my bike repaired!!!
*** I stayed at Cottonwood Inn Motel.

Day 29: La Grange, Texas to Navasota, Texas (67 miles)
*** I stayed in my tent in the grass yard behind the Navasota Fire Company.
*** The firefighters were VERY nice! I got a hot shower in their beautiful facility. The cordial crew also permitted me to wash my laundry in their REAL washing machines and dryers while staying on their property. This was one of the few days I did my laundry in actual commercial machines instead of cleaning my clothes BY HAND in the shower!

Day 30: Navasota, Texas to Shepherd, Texas (79 miles)
***I stayed in "The Love Shack," an incredible cabin for a very reasonable cyclist rate of ONLY $20 per night at the Shepherd Sanctuary Campground.
*** My delightful hosts at the one-of-a-kind campground cooked a DELICIOUS supper for me for FREE!!!

Day 31: Shepherd, Texas to Kirbyville, Texas (89 miles)
*** I wild camped in my tent at a vacant lot close to the United Methodist Church. The United Methodist Church was NOT currently hosting cross-country cyclists due to COVID-19 concerns.

*** Nobody bothered me, but 2 angelic, elderly, church women whom were determined to remain anonymous, DELIVERED me a HUGE hearty supper for FREE from the local grocery store!

Day 32: Kirbyville, Texas to Oberlin, Louisiana (83 miles)
*** I stayed in my tent on the front porch of the Allen Parish Tourist Commission.
*** Once again, I was AMAZED at the true-to-name SOUTHERN HOSPITALITY of Adagria and her FINE group of women administrators working at this ultra-respectful county seat! Adagria also brought me FREE food and a bottle of sugar cane as a gift. How nice!!!

Day 33: Oberlin, Louisiana to Simmesport, Louisiana (108 miles)
*** I stayed in my tent behind Rabalais Seafood Restaurant.
*** Owners Ray, Debbie, and Calvin insisted I fill my belly with their WONDERFUL restaurant food for FREE!

Day 34: Simmesport, Louisiana to Easlyville, Louisiana (108 miles)
*** I stayed in my tent at Hyde Park Campground.

Day 35: Easlyville, Louisiana to Poplarville, Mississippi (87 miles)
*** I stayed in a beautiful single-family house in the middle of town. My parents paid a discounted cyclist rate of only $75 for me to rent this amazing house for one night. I would NOT have paid for this particular LUXURY accommodation on my own! Thanks mom and dad!

Day 36: Poplarville, Mississippi to Vancleave, Mississippi (76 miles)
*** I stayed in my tent at Camp Journey End Campground.

Day 37: Vancleave, Mississippi to Bayou La Batre, Alabama (48 miles)
*** I only rode a half day today. The morning was dedicated to bike repairs by Jacob from Tri Hard Bikes in Ocean Springs, Mississippi. Jacob was the most IMPRESSIVE 18-year-old <u>MAN</u> I have ever met!
*** I stayed at the Bayou La Batre Inn and Suites.

Day 38: Bayou La Batre, Alabama to Pensacola, Florida (87 miles)
*** I semi-wild camped in the grassy area next to the ominous woods behind the Pensacola Fire Department #3 on Summit Road as full permission was QUESTIONABLE, but nobody bothered me!

Day 39: Pensacola, Florida to Defuniak Springs, Florida (86 miles)
*** I stayed at the Sundown Inn.

Day 40: Defuniak Springs, Florida to Chattahoochee, Florida (82 miles)
*** I stayed at a Warmshowers house. My host, Gene, was very UNCONVENTIONAL and slightly scary, but Gene proved to be nothing

less than cordial, kind, and welcoming with me!

Day 41: Chattahoochee, Florida to Monticello, Florida (72 miles)
*** I stayed at the Brahman Motel also known as the Monticello Inn. There weren't too many cockroaches in my room.

Day 42: Monticello, Florida to Lake City, Florida (80 miles)
*** I stayed at the Getaway Inn.

Day 43: Lake City, Florida to Jacksonville, Florida (98 miles. 82 miles to my GLORIOUS FINISH at the Atlantic Ocean at Jacksonville Beach and then 16 more miles until I finally found an available hotel.)
*** I stayed at the Scottish Inns.

DAY 43: Upon completion of the arduous Southern Tier Bike Route, I'm surprised I didn't drop my cell phone into the ocean as I was SUCCUMB by the overriding emotion of ELATION! Finally, I was the CHAMPION I had always dreamed of!

Chapter 177: Sean's Journal

Below are my PERSONAL journal entries comprising all 45 days of my EPIC solo, unsupported, non-stop Southern Tier bicycle journey from the shore of the Pacific Ocean in San Diego, California all the way 3,000 miles across the southern portion of the United States of America to the sparkling waters of the Atlantic Ocean in Jacksonville, Florida. 43 days involved my bike travel and the last 2 days involved my Amtrak railroad train travel back home.

Saturday October 10, 2020
DAY 1: San Diego, California to Alpine, California (45 miles).
- Tink and I wake up at 3:15 a.m. Mom and dad pick us up in their truck at 3:45 a.m. Today is the first day of my epic Southern Tier bike journey.
- It was a VERY emotional farewell at the Pittsburgh International Airport when I parted ways and waved goodbye to Tink, mom, and dad.
- I had the MOST SEVERE panic attack EVER while sitting at the airport waiting for my plane. Pacing back and forth seemed to be the only thing I could do to calm myself! This bike trip might be too much for me!?
- I flew American Airlines from Pittsburgh to Dallas and then Dallas to San Diego. My plane arrived in San Diego at noon and I had my bicycle assembled by 1:30 p.m. My bike assembly was a HUGE achievement for me as I am NOT known for being "handy."
- I made the mistake of riding my bike to Mission Beach when the actual starting point for the Southern Tier Bike Route was at Ocean Beach. I was upset over wasting 10 miles pedaling around the BEAUTIFUL city of San Diego. How could I be so foolish? How am I going to cross the country on a bicycle when I get lost finding the starting point?
- I LOST my composure today. Rough day! Bad start! I'm in trouble already!
- I almost got KILLED riding my bike CARELESSLY in heavy traffic in San Diego frantically searching for the starting point of the Southern Tier! I was a MESS!!!!
- A very nice, 50-plus-year-old man used my camera and took some excellent photos of me with my rear bike tire contacting the mighty Pacific Ocean as I began my epic bicycle journey. Maybe someday, these photos might prove to be EXTREMELY valuable!?
- I bought 2 Gatorades at a convenience store.
- I stopped at Burger King and bought 16 chicken nuggets for supper.
- I rode 45 minutes in the dark. My front and back bike lights work great!
- Around 8 p.m., I got VERY TIRED (not just physically!) so I pulled into the Town Hall in Alpine, California and spoke with one of the departing vendors whom was packing up her stuff. The cordial and creative lady mentioned about me possibly staying overnight in a Gazebo out back. Why not? Wild camping on the first night was a PERFECT start for my bike adventure! So, I slept on CONCRETE under a gazebo in my tent WITHOUT any prior permission whatsoever!!! I am crazy!

- No water tonight for my shower, just "man wipes!" Wow, this is absurd!!!
- My legs are sore!!! The climb out of San Diego was much TOUGHER than I expected! Now, I understand why so many other cyclists quit the Southern Tier on their FIRST DAY!
- I am physically depleted. I am mentally and emotionally depleted. I am also worn-out from a lack of sleep. I'm also feeling troublesome effects of what seems to be CULTURE SHOCK. This biking adventure is a HUGE stretch outside of my comfort zone. Maybe I should have signed up for a group cross-country bike tour instead.?
- Today felt like a DREAM. Did it really happen? I'm feeling VERY weird!!!! I guess I'm experiencing culture shock.?
- I'll feel better tomorrow. I just need some sleep. I'm still ok. Tomorrow is another day.
- I did NOT contact our son, Sean Thomas, whom is currently living in San Diego as I did not want to impose on him as it seems like he is currently doing well making a good life for himself. Plus, I wanted to tell as few people as possible about my trip! I'm so glad Sean Thomas seems to be doing well!!!
- I miss my wife ALREADY!

Sunday October 11, 2020
Day 2: Alpine, California to Ocotillo, California (60 miles)

- I woke up at 5 a.m. this morning and was on the road biking by 5:45 a.m. I had a restful night sleep and nobody bothered me as I slept under a gazebo on a cement slab behind the township building in Alpine, CA without any prior permission. This was my FIRST time ever wild camping! What a suitable start to the Southern Tier!
- For the first hour of this day, I rode in the dark. I was so scared!!!!! For the first 10 miles or so my pedals seemed to spin around AUTOMATICALLY as I was powering my bike with my ANXIETY! I am DEFINITELY having CULTURE SHOCK! I am really UNSTABLE!
- My bike ride was tremendously difficult for the first 20 miles uphill to Pine Valley. The rest of the ride had some hills and then a huge 7-mile downhill with a 6% grade on Interstate 8 to Ocotillo in the muggy Yuha Desert. My top speed of 40 miles per hour was way TOO FAST as I travelled along the break-down lane of Interstate 8!!!
- At Pine Valley, I went to Majors Diner and had a $17 "Hungry Man" breakfast. I forced myself to eat everything on my plate even though I was NOT hungry.
- There is NO WAY I'm going to finish this cross-country bike ride!!!!! I QUIT!!!! I'm just going to try to finish out this day and consider coming home early tomorrow!
- At about 1:30 p.m., I arrived at my overnight accommodation at the Red Feather Market where I ordered a double cheeseburger and French fries for supper shortly before the store's seemingly early mid-afternoon closing. I camped along the right side of the building on a cement slab.

- After supper, I walked over to my bike and noticed my front tire was completely flat. Why is my tire flat? It doesn't make sense!? I was surprised and nervous! Is there something wrong with my bike? I was REALLY worried!
- After about an hour or so, I finally got the new tube properly fitted on the tire and reinstalled. I'm super thankful the flat tire occurred at camp and NOT on the lonely Southern Tier roads! It pays to pray!
- I was so tired. I tried to do my daily Duolingo Spanish lesson, but I couldn't do it! I was asleep as soon as I closed my eyes!
- Mom and dad had Tink over for supper tonight. What a nice gesture!

Monday October 12, 2020
Day 3: Ocotillo, California to Brawley, California (60 miles)
- Although feeling VERY discouraged, I decide to ride ONE MORE DAY!
- I woke up at 5 a.m. By 5:45 a.m., I was on the road pedaling. Why does it take me SO LONG to get started in the morning?
- Today's 60-mile ride was mostly flat.
- I stopped in Calexico, California to eat 2 delicious Sausage Egg McMuffins from McDonald's. The McDonald's dining room was closed due to coronavirus concerns, so I ate outside on the sidewalk while speaking on the phone with Tink and returning some business calls.
- At about noon, I arrived in Brawley, but I rode around Brawley for 45 minutes in WICKED HOT temperatures exceeding 100 degrees Fahrenheit wasting unnecessary energy looking for the Desert Inn. I didn't realize West Main Street was further down along Main Street. Why am I so senseless? Why didn't I use Google Maps?
- I walked a quarter mile much too far to Domino's Pizza and got a large cheese pizza for supper.
- I walked across the street to Rite Aid and purchased some bandages for what appears to be possible saddle sores as there are two pinkish marks on my butt where my butt contacts the saddle. I'm worried BIG TIME! Saddle soars can end my bike trip! Several other times in my life, butt sores ended my various overnight bicycle rides!
- Tink is having a hard time figuring how to make time for all of her new business responsibilities since I'm away, but she always finds a way to get the job done. She is an amazing woman!
- How am I going to handle this sudden EXTREME HEAT? Should I try to ride my bike through the night while its cooler?
- I skipped Duolingo again tonight as I could not keep my eyes open. I have NEVER felt so severely TIRED in all my life! I was in bed by 9:30 p.m.

Tuesday October 13, 2020
Day 4: Brawley, California to Blythe, California (94 miles. 86 miles by bike and 8 miles by a stranger's truck!)
- At 3 a.m. I woke up by my alarm and I was on my bike riding without a shirt at 3:25 a.m. Wow, it's hot even in the middle of the night! Although

the early morning hours were hot, it was much cooler than the wicked hot afternoon temperatures!!!
- I was riding strong until the 30-mile point when I noticed my back tire was getting low on air. I stopped and put some air in it, but five miles later it was low again and I knew I had to change the tire as I heard some hissing from the tire. Changing my tire in the middle of the night in the desert was one of my greatest fears! NOBODY was around to help me. I was a MESS!
- I texted my dad, "Oh my God! Flat tire! Nobody in sight! Absolute darkness!" Dad replies, "You can do it!"
- As I was changing my tire tube with the help of my valuable headlamp, I suddenly heard the unmistakably sounds of coyotes howling all around me. It sounded as if they were on BOTH sides of the road, getting closer and closer to me with each passing second. Were they preparing an AMBUSH? Are the coyotes surrounding me? Am I their next meal? In that moment, I got so freaked out, POOP starting coming out of my butt as I frantically yanked my biking shorts down on the side of the road in a desperate attempt to prevent CRAPPING MY PANTS! At this point, my mental equilibrium was GONE! I LOST all of my composure!!!!
- At Mile 48, I got another flat tire while riding on Route 78 in the middle of the desert. This time it came after I was aggressively pedaling up a hill with the back end of my bike swaying a bit.
- While I was stopped for lunch at the convenience store in Palo Verde, California, I got my 3rd flat tire of the day! At this point, I realized these flat tires are NOT traditional flats, but instead there must be a problem with the actual tire sidewalls caving in and puncturing the inner tube.
- My 4th flat tire occurred 12 miles outside of Blythe California when I stopped to ask for directions at some small office complex building as I was pitifully LOST in the desert! After installing my LAST tire tube, I borrowed a bucket of water from one of the office workers and I located all of the holes in the 4 previous flat tires and then I fixed them all with a patch over each hole.
- As I was eight miles away from my pre-arranged Warmshowers host at the B&B Bait Shop in Blythe, California, I got VERY TIRED and WEAK. Luckily, I pulled off the road at some commercial pest-spraying shop as it was 105 degrees and I feared I was close to COLLAPSING from heat exhaustion. Rudy, the owner of the shop, brought me inside to the air conditioning while he packed ice around my neck and wrists. Once I regained some semblance of stability, the nice gentleman put my bike and bags into the back of his truck and drove me into the small city of Blythe, California to the Travelodge Motel where I stayed the night.
- Throughout this evening, I kept in close contact with Tink, mom, and dad as they were all very worried about my condition after my apparent bout with heat exhaustion!
- During this particular night, I did some "soul searching." The continuance of this bike ride looks very bleak!
- What am I going to do with this bicycle? It is NOT in rideable condition. I'm in trouble......

My brother-in-law, Steve, sends me a text. "Out of ALL the people I know, YOU are the ONE person who might actually be capable of finishing a solo, cross-country bicycle ride!"
- I thought a lot about Steve's motivational words…
- I ordered two McChicken sandwiches at McDonald's and some fries, but I could only eat the one McChicken because the other one was much too spicy for me.
- I went to bed at 8 p.m. California time. I was STUPID tired!!!!!

Wednesday October 14, 2020
Day 5: Blythe, California (0 miles)
- I woke up at 4 a.m. California time and returned texts, emails and phone calls.
- At about 8 a.m., I started searching for a bicycle shop willing to repair my bike TODAY. After numerous calls, I finally found a bike shop called "Cycle Therapy" in Lake Havasu, Arizona whom was willing to do the work on my bike. Cycle Therapy was 85 miles away, but I found a truck rental at U-Haul just around the corner from my motel. After paying the $120 daily rental fee for the truck, I drove to Lake Havasu, Arizona and spent several hours waiting for my bike to be repaired.
- Brett and Ryan from Cycle Therapy in Lake Havasu did a great job replacing my old inappropriate, weak gravel tires with strong, proper road tires with a liner and an appropriate inner tube with the right length of nozzle. They also fixed my derailleur as it was rubbing on the frame.
- The landscape of Arizona is GORGEOUS!!!!! WOW!!!!!
- Tink and I spent LOTS of time on the phone today taking care of business matters. We both agreed we should have spent MUCH MORE time prior to my departure training her to take over my specific office responsibilities as she was obviously only accustomed to doing her own specific office duties.
- I bought a large Domino's Pizza with pepperoni, mushroom, and ham on it. I ate until I was STUFFED as I sense I am losing TOO MUCH weight!
- I returned the rental truck to U-Haul and I road my bike back to the motel.
- For the past 3 days I have not done my Duolingo Spanish lesson. I feel like a FAILURE!
- To bed at 10 p.m.

Thursday October 15, 2020
Day 6: Blythe, California to Salome, Arizona (86 miles)
- At 3:10 a.m. I woke up to avoid riding my bike in the intense 100-PLUS-DEGREE heat of the afternoon.
- No flat tires today and no bicycle problems. What a relief! I am so appreciative of the fine bike mechanics at Cycle Therapy. My bike is now "road worthy!"
- I stayed at the Sheffield Motel at the top of an amazing mountain pass. I arrived around noon and I even took an hour nap after I got a shower. Of course, I did my laundry by hand while in the shower.

- The extremely HELPFUL motel owner/manager, Marjorie, gave me a ride 2 miles or so down the road to the wonderful and ONLY local restaurant where I ate some down-home roast, vegetables, and mashed potatoes for supper. The service was super-fast! The hearty food was just what my body needed!!!! After eating at the fine restaurant, I got a ride 2 miles back to my hotel from 3 older male strangers who planned to hunt quail the next day in Salome. What an adventure!!!
- This day was HUGE for my confidence level as only 24 hours prior I was considering plane flights back home. I still cannot believe I tried to do a cross-country bike trip with gravel bike tires! At times, I think I could win an award for STUPIDITY!!!!!

Friday October 16, 2020
Day 7: Salome, Arizona to Surprise, Arizona (88 miles)
- Our son, Maxmillion, turned 23 years old today! Early in the morning, I called and got Max's voicemail. I sang him a happy birthday message. I also followed up with a text. I wish I could have seen Max in person today!!!
- I started riding my bike at 3:30 a.m. as to avoid as much of the 102-degree afternoon heat as possible.
- Around mid-afternoon, I arrived at the beautiful, upscale, suburban home of my Warmshowers host, Pat Scocuzza. Pat was waiting for me in his driveway. Pat has done extensive bike touring and he gave me several excellent bits of cycling advice during my stay!
- Pat cooked himself and I STEAK, broccoli, and asparagus on his grill! It was delicious!!!!! How thoughtful!
- I helped Pat move his old couch outside the home into the garage and we brought the new couch in to his living room. I was happy to be a small help to Pat!
- Pat was a GREAT Warmshowers host!

Saturday October 17, 2020
Day 8: Surprise, Arizona to Mesa, Arizona (49 miles)
- Today is Tink and I's 7th wedding anniversary! I am so blessed to have such a wonderful wife! We have such a powerful, passionate relationship. We truly LOVE each other. Our relationship is by far the most valuable asset we possess in our lives!
- I woke up at 5 a.m. and quietly gathered my stuff. I was on the road by 5:30 a.m. I didn't even make enough noise to wake up my Warmshowers host, Pat.
- Most of this day was spent riding my bicycle through lots of excellent bike trails throughout the City of Phoenix, Tempe, and Scottsdale. My bike riding day was completed with about 10 miles of road-riding as I finally arrived at the excellent suburban home of Warmshowers host, Layne Gneiting, his wife, and two sons in Mesa, Arizona.

- Layne met me in his driveway and immediately took a selfie photo of him and I as we instantly KNEW we were kindred souls!
- Layne is a professor at Arizona State University in Phoenix and he has led numerous bike tours overseas in other countries. Little did I know, I was staying with an international bike touring expert!
- Layne may have saved my entire cross-country bike trip by SOLVING my ongoing dilemma of recurring saddle sores. Layne drove me to Paragon Cycling in Mesa, Arizona only moments before closing and he advised me to buy a TIGHT-FITTING bib bike short as he figured my previous bike shorts were too LOOSE thus causing a rather MODERATE skin irritation on the head of my penis!
- The $100 I spent on the new bib biking shorts at Paragon Cycling was the BEST $100 I ever spent in my life! I love the bib biking shorts and I hope they keep my saddle area HEALTHY!!!
- At Layne's house, I also lost 11 pounds by means of a "SHAKEDOWN!" Layne invested 2 hours with me and helped me to lighten my load by 11 pounds. He promised to mail my excess weight back home to me. Layne assured me I NEEDED the weight loss as I will be encountering HUGE mountains as I travel eastbound tomorrow!!!
- I ate a superb home-cooked supper with the amazing Gneiting family and their three IMPRESSIVE visiting 19-year-old Mormon missionary students. What an UNFORGETTABLE family experience!!!
- NEVER will I forget kneeling down and PRAYING with the Gneiting family in their living room before going to bed. The prayer time was so POWERFUL!!!!! It felt like Jesus Christ was present in the room! Although I am not a member of the Mormon religion, I LOVE the Mormon religion! The spiritual experience impacted my SOUL!!!

Sunday October 18, 2020
Day 9: Mesa, Arizona to Tonto Basin, Arizona (80 miles)
- My alarm was set for 4:45 a.m., but I got up a few minutes before my alarm sounded. This was the fourth day in a row I woke up BEFORE my alarm went off. Very quietly, I gathered my stuff as not to disturb the sleeping Gneiting family.
- I ate a bowl of granola cereal and a banana and I was on the road pedaling at 5:30 a.m.
- It took me about 10 miles to get out of the city of Mesa and then I began traveling Route 87 upward through the mountains. This was a TOUGH day of climbing on this very HOT day! Today involved a VERY CHALLENGING biking route!
- At Jake's Corner in Payson, Arizona, I stopped at a cowboy biker sports bar appropriately named, Jake's Corner Bar. At the biker bar I ate a chicken quesadilla, house salad, and bean lunch.
- As I entered the stylish country bar, a tough-looking woman dressed in leather motorcycle chaps approached me in disbelief and shook her head at me as she VERY STERNLY stated, "Do you know it's 103 degrees this

afternoon? I can BARELY stand the heat on my motorcycle. You have no business being out here on these roads today on a bicycle. You are going to kill yourself!" This hardcore motorcycle lady along with the remainder of the rough and tough motorcycle crowd ACCEPTED me as part of their gang! As far as the motorcycle posse was concerned, I was as TOUGH as any one of their bikers!
- I pedaled 10 more miles to Punkin Center Lodge, but the price was a little high at $82 per night so I went three miles down the road to the Tonto Basin Inn where I stayed for $65 a night.
- The local restaurant in the very small town of Tonto closed at 7 p.m. this evening instead of 8 p.m. as advertised, so I rode my bike an extra half mile westbound to Dollar General and bought some frozen lasagna and Combos for supper.
- Tink and I spoke on the phone for a long time as we handled lots of business matters back home. Tink is starting to get more familiar with her HEAVILY increased business responsibilities.

Monday October 19, 2020
Day 10: Tonto Basin, Arizona to Globe, Arizona (57 miles)
- I woke up at 4:15 a.m. and I was pedaling eastbound by 5 a.m.
- The early-morning sunrises are BREATHTAKING!!!!
- At about 35 miles, I came to the bottom of a mountain pass. It took me 6.1 miles to get to the summit of the mountain pass. WOW, what a climb!
- While on the mountain pass, I met my "long-lost brother," Matthew Wentzell, who was riding a Surly mountain-bike with 3-inch tires. He and his friend, Michael, travelled all the way from the Canadian border throughout the United States 2,000 miles southbound on their mountain bikes through WICKED HARD mountain trails. They plan to finish their adventure at the Mexican border on Friday.
- For lunch today, I stopped at Little Caesars and bought a whole pizza for myself. I sat out back of Little Caesars by the employee entrance in my fold-up camp chair and ate the pizza in the SHADE. While eating the pizza, I handled some business matters on my cell phone.
- Today was ONLY 90 degrees. It felt so refreshing to FINALLY get out of the 100-plus-degree temperatures from all last week!!! 90 degrees actually felt cool to me today! It is AMAZING how the human body can adapt to our environment!
- I took a short nap in my tent upon arrival at my remote camp location in the far corner of the Apache Grand Casino parking lot.
- For supper, I ate leftover pizza and ramen noodles.
- I walked to the convenience store at the gas station on the Apache Indian property and bought a green drink and refilled my water bottles.
- Tink and I spent lots of time on the phone talking about business matters and trying to arrange for her to meet up with me in El Paso, Texas for a brief two-day visit next Sunday. We really miss each other!!!!
- Our 22-year-old son, Curtis, called me this morning as he ran out of gas in his car in downtown Johnstown, PA. Curtis wanted me to deliver some

gas to him, but I told him I was "out of town." Curtis does not know I have been out of town for 10 days on a cross-country bicycle trip.
- Tink finally made it to Planet Fitness today to exercise. This was her first time exercising since I've been away as she has been OVERWHELMED trying to do her own regular office jobs, my office jobs, and of course, all of her regular household duties.

Tuesday October 20, 2020
Day 11: Globe, Arizona to Stafford, Arizona (71 miles)
- Before my alarm sounded, I woke up a few minutes before 4 a.m. on this 54-degree early morning in my semi-chilly tent.
- It took me 45 minutes to pack up camp and get my bike ready. I was pedaling at 4:45 a.m.
- Today was mostly a level ride with some hills.
- For my second breakfast of the day, I stopped at Mt. Apache Marketplace in Bylas, Arizona and bought some chocolate milk, peanut butter, and some other random groceries. The more calories, the better!
- I biked pretty strong today and I mostly felt pretty good. My bike seems to be operating very well after replacing my gravel tires with proper road tires.
- For the first time this trip, I listened to some music from my Spotify phone app with my wireless ear buds. The music was so refreshing. It was just what I needed!
- Shortly after noon, I arrived at the Safford, Arizona home of Warmshowers host, Jay. Jay permitted me to stay in his extra bedroom. Jay was a nice host!
- I walked over to Burger King to get lunch. It actually felt GOOD to walk instead of pedaling my bike!
- I took a brief 45-minute nap in the afternoon.
- Jay cooked me some awesome salmon and carrots for supper and then I walked over to Little Caesars and got a whole pizza as my evening "snack."
- Tink and I spoke on the phone for a long time today getting business matters in order.
- Tink and I realized we are NOT going to be meeting in El Paso as we had originally hoped as the logistics for the trip didn't seem to be reasonable. Crap! I miss my wife!

Wednesday October 21, 2020
Day 12: Stafford, Arizona to Duncan, Arizona (41 miles)
- I woke up at 5 a.m. and I was on the road biking at about 5:50 a.m.
- The first 15 miles of my bike ride went well, but then I got a rather fierce headwind for about 2 hours. The harsh headwind slowed me down to an 8 mile per hour pace. Then, seemingly out of nowhere, the wind changed its direction and provided me with an unsuspecting tailwind for the rest of my ride into Duncan, Arizona.
- My gracious Warmshowers host, Deborah Clayton, owner of the renovated and classic Simpson Hotel, permitted me to use their inside bathroom to get

a warm shower and then I set up my tent in the BEAUTIFUL, outside courtyard camping area.
- I took a much-needed nap in my tent this afternoon! I LOVE naps!!!!
- For supper, I walked over to Hilda's Diner in Duncan, Arizona which was offering a special on tacos. Eating here was symbolic as my grandma's first name was Hilda. As a teenager, I OFTEN stopped over Grandma Hilda's house to eat lunch with her.

Thursday October 22, 2020
Day 13: Duncan, Arizona to Silver City, New Mexico (79 miles)
- I rode VERY strong today. I've been taking very good care of myself, especially with regard to eating and sleeping which seems to be translating into more efficient cycling!
- I stopped at the excellent, authentic Mexican restaurant, Los Victors in Silver City, New Mexico, for a delicious lunch!
- The Dave and Carol Konopnicki family hosted me via the Warmshowers program in their lovely home atop Silver City, New Mexico. Dave is a super-smart, kind, and responsible man who owns various McDonalds restaurants.
- I enjoyed playing fetch with the Konopnicki dog!
- The Konopnicki family was so gracious to me! Carol cooked an AMAZING meal for me, allowed me to use the family's washer and dryer, and gave me my own bedroom with my own bathroom and desk! The Konopnicki family displayed the highest graciousness to me! This was the first time during my trip I washed my clothes in an actual washing machine and dried my clothes in an actual dryer!
- As far as the Konopnicki family was concerned, I was their PRIZED guest! They wanted their children to KNOW me as it was VERY IMPORTANT to Dave and Carol for their children to speak with me and interact with me as they considered me a ROLE MODEL! I was honored!
- Dave warned me about the SUPREME cycling difficulties of New Mexico's Black Mountains which await me tomorrow!!!

Friday October 23, 2020
Day 14: Silver City, New Mexico to Hillsboro, New Mexico (59 miles)
- I woke up at 5 a.m. and I QUIETLY ate breakfast at the kitchen table. As I was in the garage getting ready to leave, Carol came in to say goodbye and took a picture of me with my bike. Dave and Carol were amazing hosts!
- By 6 a.m., I was out on my bike traveling eastbound toward Hillsboro. It was a 14-mile climb up the Black Mountain Range to Emory's Pass which had an elevation of exactly 8,228 feet. The climb took me about 3 and a half hours to complete! The switchbacks near the summit of the mountain were incredible! What a beautiful transcending experience to pedal every foot of the ascent! Yes, I stopped numerous times to rest briefly, but I did NOT walk my bike at all!

- The 20-mile downhill on the other side of the mountain was REFRESHING as I came into Hillsboro at 2:50 p.m., only ten minutes before The General Store and Café, the ONLY restaurant in town, closed for the day. Quickly, I bought $20 worth of food as to try to refuel my body for my next biking day tomorrow.
- As I was setting up my tent at the free campsite in the tiny Hillsboro Town Park as per my Adventure Cycling map, a WONDERFUL lady named Kristin from the local RV campground convinced me to camp for FREE in her vacant 1947 vintage camper trailer. Kristin was so nice! She LOVES bikers as she realizes how tough it is to summit Emory's Pass! Kristen was aware of the many difficulties involved in a cross-country bicycle adventure!
- Kristin also let me use her landline phone as there was no cell service at the campground.
- The shower was NOT deluxe in any way, but it was running water and I got clean. Getting a cool shower is a good idea once in a while anyway!
- Upon the advice of Kristin, I walked across the street and up to the top of the cemetery about five blocks away to get cell phone service!
- Tink felt high levels of stress today as her worker did NOT show up as scheduled for the paintball party this afternoon. Tink is also feeling heavy-duty pressures and demands with regard to our rental home business.
- I called and yelled at my 25-year-old daughter Stacey as she also works in our rental home business. I feel like Stacey is NOT doing her job well!
- As I laid on the comfy mattress in the very old camper trailer, I fell asleep around 8:40 p.m. and slept well!

Saturday October 24, 2020
Day 15: Hillsboro, New Mexico to Las Cruces, New Mexico (85 miles)
- I woke up at 5 a.m. and I was pedaling by 6 a.m.
- I really LIKE riding in the dark in the early mornings! It's scary and ominous, but there is a SACRED power amidst the quiet and still ambiance of the early morning! It is REALLY special!
- For the first 8 miles of my bike travels today, I did NOT see a vehicle!
- This morning was very chilly. The temperature was only 48 degrees Fahrenheit. As I began biking today, I wore my baklava headpiece, crew socks, full-length biking spandex pants over top of my bib biking shorts, long sleeve spandex shirt, short-sleeved biking shirt, light wind breaker jacket, and full-length biking gloves.
- Most of today's ride was flat with some occasional hills.
- I've been taking biking breaks about every 10 miles to walk a little bit and to eat a little snack. The walking seems to REALLY HELP to keep my body feeling loose! Breaking up the monotonous bike ride into 10-mile intervals is a GOOD IDEA!
- For lunch, I stopped in the really cool town of Hatch, New Mexico at the Santa Fe Cafe and had a chicken burrito. When I resumed pedaling, I got mixed up and I biked about 1 mile in the wrong direction before figuring

out my blunder and turning around. Making senseless navigational errors ENRAGES me! The trip is already 3,000 miles. Do I really have to get LOST and add extra unnecessary miles to my plight????
- I've been drinking about every two miles, but I have been whizzing TOO MUCH! By the time I take my ten-mile stop, I am almost whizzing my pants as urine is squirting like a sprinkler out of my penis as I quickly pull down my shorts and stretch my bib pants down below my waist. Maybe I'm drinking too much water?
- At about 3:30 p.m., I arrived in Las Cruces, New Mexico and met Dan Phillips, Warmshowers host extraordinaire! In February 2020, Dan moved to his new Las Cruces house. Dan has led several bicycle tours for Adventure Cycling. Dan has also completed the Trans American Bicycle Route across the country. It took him 90 days to complete the iconic cross-country route. Dan is a FINE MAN!
- Prior to my arrival at his home, Warmshowers host, Dan Phillips, emailed me asking EXACTLY what I wanted to eat. I gave him a few ideas of my favorite foods and drinks including CHOCOLATE MILK. Dan went to the grocery store and bought EVERYTHING on my list! When I arrived at Dan's home, I felt like ROYALTY!!! Dan knows how hard a bike tour can be. It was Dan's sincere pleasure to provide me with proper nourishment and care. What a great guy!
- I also enjoyed meeting Dan's two dogs, Fred and Ethel, whom are part Basset Hounds.
- New Mexico is known for harvesting cotton, green peppers, and pecans. Hatch, New Mexico is also the green chili pepper CAPITAL of the WORLD!
- I was so tired! I went to bed at 9:10 p.m. mountain time and I didn't even do my Duolingo! I ate way too much ICE CREAM before going to bed and the excessive sugar caused me to wake up SEVEN TIMES throughout the night to pee. How annoying!!!! Usually, I only wake up once or twice per night to whiz!
- My mischievous and overly cursory adult son, Curtis, called asking for food as he claims he "ran out" at his house. I told him to stop over our house and Tink would hook him up, but I'm not sure if he ever did. Curtis still does NOT know I am out of town on an epic biking adventure.
- At 11:15 p.m. eastern time, Tink got a terrible phone call. Tink's BEST FRIEND, Deb Trotz, passed away. Tink was VERY upset and cried. My being away made the tragic situation even worse!

Sunday October 25, 2020
Day 16: Las Cruces, New Mexico to Fabens, Texas (80 miles)
- I woke up at 5 a.m. from Dan's house in Las Cruces New Mexico and I was on my bike pedaling before 6 a.m. I rode about 12 miles before the sun broke through the sky with its majestic brilliance.
- I finally entered Texas today! I have now pedaled my bicycle through the entire states of California, Arizona, and New Mexico. WOW!!!!!!!!! This is hard to believe!!!

- It was another chilly morning. I was dressed in my cold-weather biking gear. I'm HAPPY to be dressed in cold weather gear as the prior 100-plus-degree temperatures were relentless!
- Shortly after entering Texas, four dogs simultaneously chased me as I pedaled my bike down a VERY remote section of Route 152. My pre-ride research indicated EAST TEXAS was known for dog chases on the Southern Tier route, but I was NOT prepared for a LEVEL 9 dog chase in WEST TEXAS as my FIRST dog-chase of my epic bicycle trip. I survived and the four dogs survived, but I was AFFECTED deeply. I completely underestimated the intensity of the dog-chases. My first dog-chase was much more severe than I ever imagined. My heart was still beating fast 30 minutes after the TERRIFYING chase. I'll never forget my first-ever dog- chase!!!
- Today's ride was mostly level, but any terrain would seem like it was level after pedaling through the challenging mountains of Arizona and New Mexico!
- My legs are getting MUCH STRONGER!!! I've NEVER felt my legs so strong! Did my legs turn into iron?
- I stopped for breakfast at the McDonald's in El Paso. In my typical fashion, I bought the MOST CALORIES for the cheapest price. I eat about anything. I'm NOT picky at all! I ate outside as the dining room was closed due to COVID-19 issues.
- It was VERY difficult following my paper map directions through the big city of El Paso, Texas, but I did it! It was a relief to get back on Country Road 76 which didn't require a whole lot of thinking about directions and turning.
- It felt so much better today with the front part of my bike seat moved down slightly as to make my seat more level.
- At about 3 p.m. I arrived in Fabens Texas where I stopped and ate lunch at McDonald's and then purchased Powerade, a banana, and an apple at the San Eli Supermarket across the street before checking into my room at the Fabens Inn which was located very close to the massive I-10 interstate.
- I got a shower and then prepared for my next big day of biking.
- I walked ONE MILE to get a pizza at Little Caesars for supper. This walk was TOO LONG for someone who just biked 80 miles! I talked to my mom and dad on the phone during this LENGTHY walk.

Monday October 26, 2020
Day 17: Fabens, Texas to Sierra Blanca, Texas (66 miles)
- I woke up at 4:15 a.m. and I was pedaling by 4:45 a.m. This half hour transition has been my fastest morning transition so far.
- The wind was SUPER-STRONG all day switching between a crosswind and a headwind. Biking was VERY DIFFICULT today. Today was probably my hardest biking day so far! With the strong headwinds, it felt like I was pedaling uphill ALL DAY!
- For lunch, I ate leftover pizza from a bag. While eating along the side of the road, I had to stay close to my bike because the wind was so strong it

could have easily blown my bike over. I CANNOT let my bike fall to the ground!!!
- My original plan was to bike to Van Horn today, but by lunch I realized my plan was NOT happening! The winds were too TOUGH!!!! Plus, it is starting to get REALLY COLD! What a difficult day of cycling!
- I ate supper at an amazing local Mexican restaurant located only a few hundred feet away from my motel.

Tuesday October 27, 2020
Day 18: (The day of HELL!) Sierra Blanca, Texas to Van Horn Texas (34 miles)
- My ex-wife, Gina, notified me that our son, Anthony, whom is currently in jail, was diagnosed with COVID-19! I hope he is OK!!! I LOVE Anthony dearly, but I do NOT provide any type of financial support for any of our children while they are in jail! I know Anthony will eventually do something GREAT with his life, but for now I am very WORRIED about him!
- I look outside and notice SNOW ON THE GROUND!!!! What the heck? The Southern Tier is NOT supposed to be snowy, especially in October! After taking a quick glance at my phone, I noticed the weather in Sierra Blanca, Texas was now 26 degrees with an expected daily high of only 29 degrees! Oh no, what do I do?
- As I'm contemplating my decision, my father suddenly calls me and warns me NOT to ride today! "It is way too dangerous." cautions my dad.
- After speaking with my dad on the phone, the manager of the motel passes by my room and unexpectedly advises me to "stay another night." Finally, my wife, Tink, calls me and BEGS me to stay at the motel as not to expose myself to the SEVERE inclement weather conditions.
- Last night I was hoping to GO BIG today and possible surpass 100 miles biking all the way to Marfa, Texas, but as per the current weather conditions, clearly, I was NOT pedaling to Marfa today!
- Instead of taking a ZERO DAY with regard to my total daily mileage, I decided to take a "nice and easy" bike ride only 34 miles over to Van Horn, Texas.
- Immediately upon walking outside of my motel, I noticed considerable wind force. Within the first one mile of my bike ride, I got a hint as to how tough the cycling was going to be today.
- A 30-mile per hour HEADWIND battered against me for the first 4 hours of my ride! It took heavy-duty effort to maintain a paltry speed of 5.5 miles per hour with the severe, non-stop winds! Combined with the 26-degree temperature, my "nice and easy" bike ride quickly became TORTURE!
- At mile 18 of the day, my jaw was semi-frozen as I called my mom minutes before my phone battery FROZE and shut-off. Through mumbled words from my frigid lips, I asked mom to book me a room in Van Horn at any motel <u>regardless of the price!!!</u>
- Despite the sub-freezing temperatures, I was sweating profusely under all the layers of clothes as I pumped out my pedal cadence. If I had gotten a flat tire or was forced to stop pedaling, I could have FROZE TO DEATH!

- At mile 22, I was stopped by a United States Border Patrol agent in a white SUV vehicle. The federal agent asked, "What the HECK are you doing out here in this severe weather?" Through my tight, frozen jaw, I slurred "Riding to Florida!" He offered me some unfrozen water and then drove away. I was too proud to accept any other help from him! Sometimes I wonder if I'd rather die on the street instead of asking for or accepting help from others?
- Finally, after four hours of pure abuse, I OUTLASTED the fierce winds! Wow!!!! For the last 10 miles to Van Horn, Texas, I pedaled on the break-down lane of big-time Interstate 10 as the headwind majorly decreased to about 15 miles per hour and my speed increased to what seemed to be at the time, a rather speedy 9 miles per hour pace.
- When I arrived at Motel 6 in Van Horn, Texas, I put my head down on the front check-in desk. The cordial front desk worker lady said, "You must be Sean?" With a slight nod of my head, I confirmed the congenial clerk's empathetic statement.
- On this frosty day, I sweated through all five layers of my clothing. It was great to get a nice hot shower and wash my clothes.
- This was the HARDEST day of biking in my entire life! The cold combined with the strong winds produced a wind chill of approximately 5 degrees Fahrenheit!!! I will NEVER forget the self-inflicted TORTURE on this FRIGID day!
- For supper, I walked over to McDonalds.
- After supper, I bought some food at Dollar General while I spoke to my sister, Kelli, on my recently UNFROZEN phone. We talked for about half an hour or so getting caught up on her family's life and especially her recovery from her recent shoulder surgery in which she seems to be doing very well. Kelli helped to keep me focused on ONE DAY AT A TIME. Kelli sensed I was on the brink of OVERLOAD and I was near the BREAKING POINT! Kelli kept me grounded and tried her best to PURSUADE me to pedal ONE MORE DAY. Kelli is a BOSS!!!!
- In EVERY way, this wretched day DESTROYED me!!!!!

Wednesday October 28, 2020
Day 19: Van Horn, Texas to Marfa, Texas (76 miles)
- In atypical fashion, I began pedaling today at 8:45 a.m. as to allow the outside FREEZING temperatures to rise a bit as to minimize the risk of a possible crash on the icy roads. Despite waiting an extra almost four hours to depart from my toasty warm hotel room, the temperature in Van Horn, Texas was still only 29 degrees Fahrenheit when I started pedaling.
- Once again, the headwinds held me back for the first 23 miles, but it was minimal compared to yesterday's FIERCE headwinds!
- On the 24th mile, the winds changed direction a bit and I encountered more of a crosswind which prompted an emotional celebration on my part! The
biking was still hard, but the required effort was not BRUTAL like yesterday!

- On mile 50, the winds suddenly changed again and I actually had a biker's dream, a TAILWIND!!!! It was amazing as I averaged 16 miles per hour for the last 25 miles of my bike travel on this glorious day!!
- I ate lunch at the Subway restaurant at the small gasoline store in Marfa, Texas.
- Today, I stopped every 7.5 miles and celebrated as each 7.5-mile stop represented another 10% of my anticipated 75-mile ride completed. Each stop, I would walk a little bit and get a little bite to eat and drink. I was still DEPLETED from the agony of yesterday's ultra-human investment of INHUMANE biking exertion!!!
- Today's terrain was mostly desolate desert all the way from Van Horn, Texas to Marfa, Texas. The desert and I are now ONE!!!!!! I LOVE the desert! No, I must correct the previous statement...... I AM THE DESERT!!!
- I stayed in a very comfortable and ultra-modern detached guest house at the home of Warmshowers host, David Lanman, and his beautiful and talented Asian wife. The very generous hosts made me a DELICIOUS, big plate of stir fry for supper. Warmshowers hosts are AMAZING as David and his wife was nothing less than TOP NOTCH!
- This morning, I found out my long-term dear friend, Doris Huffman, died on Saturday. Being unable to attend her funeral, I called and spoke on the phone with Doris' son, Larry Huffman, a great, long-term friend of mine. In my physical absence, I offered Larry and his family my deepest sympathy for their loss. I have many fond memories of Mrs. Huffman as our families spent lots of time together at scholastic wrestling tournaments during my childhood! Being away from home is TOUGH!
- My sister, Kell, stopped over to visit with my wife, Tink. Kelli's surprise visit was exactly what Tink needed! Tink will never forget this LOVING ACT from my compassionate sister!

Thursday October 29, 2020
Day 20: Marfa, Texas to Marathon, Texas (58 miles)
- I woke up at 6:30 a.m. in the wonderful, ultra-modern Lanman guest house in Marfa, Texas. The Lanman's made me some delightful green tomato pie served with delicious, ice-cold almond milk for breakfast.
- Today was a much later departure than most days. It was 7:30 a.m. and the sun was beginning to rise when I finally began pedaling. This is now two days in a row in which I began pedaling after sunrise. Am I LOSING my mental toughness? Am I still TOUGH?
- I battled hard crosswinds for most of my ride until mile 35 when the wind turned around and I got an unexpected tailwind for about 14 miles. Winds make a HUGE difference while biking, especially out here in the desert!
- For lunch today, I stopped at McDonald's in Alpine, Texas. I filled my belly for only four dollars.
- Every day I feel ELATED when I actually arrive at my destination! These daily bicycle rides are so LONG!
- Shortly after my arrival at the La Loma Del Chivo Hostel, the owner, Ingrid, arrived and showed me where I could take a shower and asked me where I

would like to stay. La Loma Del Chivo is a "hippie community" with many different, little, unique cabin homes and one big, stylish hostel. I chose to stay in "The Beehive" as it was made for only one person and I generally prefer to stay alone when possible. The Beehive was the size of a SMALL shed! Ingrid was very friendly and made sure I had clean bedding. Since I was a cross-country biker, she did NOT charge me to stay there!
- I got a semi-warm shower and washed my sweaty biking clothes in the bath tub like normal.
- I rode my bike about a mile into the small town of Marathon, Texas and bought a few groceries at the trendy French Co. Grocer.
- For supper, I ate at The Brick Vault, a fabulous desert restaurant, where I devoured brisket meat, pulled pork, potato salad, beans, bread, and ice water. Outside next to my bicycle is where I enjoyed this delicious meal as it was imperative for me to make sure my bike was safe and secure. The various food was exceptionally GOOD and the overall atmosphere was soothing!

Friday October 30, 2020
Day 21: Marathon, Texas to Sanderson, Texas (57 miles)
- I woke up at 6:30 a.m. after another good night's sleep.
- Throughout the night, I peed in my Gatorade "whiz bottle" three times instead of walking outside of The Beehive into the chilly desert air to take a whiz. I LOVE peeing in a WHIZ bottle!!!
- It was very enjoyable and peaceful sleeping in the 42 square foot "Beehive." Nobody bothered me at all. Although I had a 100% positive experience, I did have a very minor reservation about sleeping in The Beehive as the structure was made of stone and cement and in addition to the one wooden entrance door, it only had one small window which was NOT big enough for me to get out in the case of any type of emergency.
- Upon waking at 6:30 a.m., I spent about a half hour working on my itinerary as to figure out a way to meet up with my wife next week somewhere along my bike route.
- After eating breakfast and packing my belongings. I was on the road biking by a VERY LATE 8 a.m., but I knew today was a relatively short biking mileage day with less than 60 miles to complete before arriving in my expected daily destination of Sanderson, Texas.
- Upon arriving in lovely Sanderson, Texas around 1 p.m. or so, I ate a chicken, mashed potato, and coleslaw lunch while sitting outside at a local Mom and Pop's restaurant known as "The Ranch House" which was down the street from my campground at Canyons RV Park.
- Management was not present at Canyons RV Park, so I did a quick, self-check-in and paid $10 cash into an envelope for my tent site.
- For supper, I ate an enchilada meal from the small, local gas station in Sanderson, Texas. There are NOT many stores in Sanderson, Texas!!!
- The weather today was a high of only 69 degrees. It felt GREAT to get back into some mild conditions. My bike travels up to this point has been UNSEASONABLY HOT!

- I averaged about 12.3 miles per hour today pedaling throughout the desert on Highway 90. The wind was a mild crosswind today. My bike ride was very enjoyable! On certain pleasant days like today, I'm starting to really accept this new bike life!
- There were NO SERVICES between Marathon, Texas and Sanderson, Texas. No water! No food! No stores! NOTHING! What beautiful DESOLATION!!! I get chills just thinking about it! This section of my bike ride was nothing less than AMAZING!!!!!
- The phone service is POOR at my campground in Sanderson, Texas. All I can do is text with my Verizon cell phone. For some reason, I cannot get enough of a signal to make a call. It feels like I'm at the end of Earth!

Saturday October 31, 2020
Day 22: Sanderson, Texas to Comstock, Texas (88 miles)
- I woke up at 6 a.m. and I was pedaling by 6:45 a.m.
- After pedaling a mile or so, I stopped at the Sanderson VFW Post and ordered an $8 breakfast to help support the VFW cause. Last night, I found out about this special fundraising breakfast from some random person passing through my campground. Attending the breakfast benefit was a great way to FILL MY BELLY and support a worthy cause! I DEVOURED all kinds of food and my stomach was JAM-PACKED!!!
- A few years ago, one of the volunteers at the VFW breakfast pedaled his bicycle all the way from Massachusetts to Sanderson, Texas! Ever since accomplishing the mighty cycling feat, this humble man has made his home in desolate Sanderson, Texas! This generous VFW guy also supplied me with my "second breakfast" of the day as I graciously agreed to stuff my rear right pannier bag with a pancake, two pieces of toast, a sausage, and some fruit. Two hours later, I ate my second breakfast!!!
- There are VERY FEW SERVICES, possibly NONE depending on the time of day and the time of year, between Sanderson, Texas and Comstock, Texas.
- Today was another day of strong biking, but I did stop every 10 miles to eat and I took a big drink of 3 or more ounces every 3 miles.
- Today's weather began as very cold, but as the day continued, I took off more and more layers of clothes in correlation with the consistently rising temperatures. By the end of the day, I was riding my bike without a shirt as the high daily temperature reached a comfortable and warm 78 degrees. I LOVE riding shirtless!
- I stayed at the Comstock Motel. The front-desk manager gave me a deal for $50 cash. The motel worker, Shawn, also let me use his personal cell phone to call Tink as my cell phone did not have any reception AT ALL in Comstock, Texas! I am in the MIDDLE OF NOWHERE!!!!
- I ate supper across the street at the convenience store where I purchased a made-to-order Hunt Brothers pizza.
- My family was worried about me most of this day as the cell service in this part of the desert in West Texas was NON-EXISTENT!

- I pedaled 88 miles today and I averaged 11.9 miles an hour.
- My legs feel pretty strong and most of my body feels healthy.
- For the first time, my mom now believes I have a chance of finishing this incredulous cross-country bike ride as she mentioned greeting me along with dad and Tink at the Atlantic Ocean in St Augustine, Florida upon completion of my bike travels! I was so excited to hear about the gracious support, but I remain unable to imagine actually finishing this exasperating bike journey. I'm not even sure if I'm at the halfway point yet? I don't really care where I'm at, I just PEDAL!!!
- Today, Tink and I decided we are NOT going to meet up in Austin, Texas as I had originally hoped as the logistics were too complicated.
- I got a big problem! My parents now believe I will finish the Southern Tier, but I continue to have HUGE doubts about doing so as I am barely hanging on, clinging to ONE DAY AT A TIME. It is VERY difficult for me to discuss any matters with my family involving decisions more than ONE DAY away!!!!

Sunday November 1, 2020
Day 23: Comstock, Texas to Brackettville, Texas (69 miles)
*** I stayed in my tent at the Fort Clark Army Campground.
- Early this morning the clocks "fell back" an hour. Before going to bed last night, I thought I turned my watch clock back an hour, but for some reason I tried to get on the road at 7 a.m. today, but it ended up being 8 a.m. according to my Garmin watch. Obviously, I messed up the "fall back" feature as the sun had already risen in the sky by the time I began pedaling.
- At mile 30 of the day, I stopped in Del Rio, Texas at Walmart. After parking and locking my bike against an immovable object amidst hundreds of Walmart shoppers, I went inside and I ate a large breakfast at McDonalds while HOPING my bike would be ok.
- After breakfast, I purchased a can of pepper spray as per my dad's advice. There is a rumor of MANY upcoming DOG CHASES in East Texas and Louisiana!!!
- As I was entering Brackettville on the outside of town, my heart started beating REALLY FAST, but after I took a drink of water, ate a fig newton, and rested for a few minutes, it seemed to go away rather quickly. After about 5 minutes, the situation had subsided. This was the first time my heart had an "SVT" (supraventricular tachycardia) this entire trip. I've been having these SVT's on and off for about 25 years and each episode is very SCARY! These harrowing episodes seem to occur monthly and can be SEVERE at times.
- After traveling 69 miles from Comstock, Texas to Brackettville, Texas, I stayed at the Fort Clark Army historical site in Brackettville, Texas. I camped directly in front of the main check-in office in my tent and I used the inside day room as my office area. It was GREAT having a makeshift office with an electric plug to recharge my electronics and to have some privacy to handle my business communications. Manager, Curtis, only charged me seven dollars as my entire camping fee! Everyone seems to

LOVE cross-country cyclists!!!!
- Manager Curtis happily agreed for me to take his photo. I wish I had taken more photos of the many other intriguing people I have met so far!
- My biking strategy involving walking and eating every 10 miles and drinking every 3 miles seems to be working WELL for me!
- I averaged about 12 miles an hour today. I feel pretty good overall.
- My entire saddle area seems to be doing well with no markings, bruises, or sores. It's hard to believe this is actually Day 23 and I'm still going!
- After my shower and the completion of my other daily tasks, I rode my bike a VERY LONG 1.5 miles out to Route 90 in Brackettville, Texas to the Pizza Outpost, home of awesome New York Style Pizza, where I greatly enjoyed an amazing, oversized piece of lasagna and zesty Italian bread for supper. I pedaled back "home" in the dark to Fort Clark Army Campground. I LOVE riding my bike in the dark!

Monday November 2, 2020
Day 24: Brackettville, Texas to Leakey (pronounced Lay-key), Texas (71 miles)

- I set my alarm and woke up at 5:30 a.m. After changing my clothes, packing my tent, and taking a crap, I was leaving the wonderful town of Brackettville, Texas by 6:30 a.m. I was slightly annoyed as I expected to start my ride prior to the sunrise, but sunrise occurred at 6 a.m. which was 30 minutes prior to my start.
- I did not enter the Texas Hill Country until 50 miles later when I turned onto Route 337 just beyond Camp Wood, Texas. Texas Hill Country is known for lots of BIG HILLS! I was VERY excited to ride through this POPULAR and highly-acclaimed cycling terrain!
- Upon entering Camp Wood, Texas I ate lunch at King's Texas Smokehouse Restaurant which is located DIRECTLY on the Southern Tier Route. King's Texas Smokehouse made me an amazing TEXAS cheeseburger and French Fries. This restaurant has some SERIOUS COWBOY STYLE! If passing through Camp Wood, Texas, make sure you stop here to eat!!! I really felt the HEART AND SOUL of Texas while eating lunch at this fine southern establishment!
- On today's ride, there was one really big mile and a half hill with switchbacks near the top. I rode all the way up this massive hill. I'm THE BOMB! This hill had amazing views and the downhill was exhilarating even though I held up two cars and three motorcycles behind me on my descent of this thrilling, narrow downhill road!
- As I entered Leakey Texas, I stopped at the post office and spent $15 mailing home another 5 pounds of unnecessary stuff. The total weight of all of my pannier bags are now about 65 pounds. I feel good about my remaining supplies. Prior to today, I remained over-packed!
- I rode 71 miles today to the Leakey Inn in Leakey, Texas where I was given the special biker's rate of $49 per night. My fine room was Cypress number three.

- Toes 3 and 4 on my left foot hurt me very badly today! Those two toes crowd each other and periodically cause me INTENSE pain! I had to stop pedaling and take my shoes and socks off numerous times today alongside the road to pull, massage, and STRETCH my throbbing toes as to relieve the high-level pain. I also applied some Bag Balm to my toes which seemed to help slightly.
- I walked over to Family Dollar and bought a Hungry Man chicken meal for supper with some chocolate milk and some cinnamon rolls for dessert.
- I added air to my bike tires and I tightened my water bottle holder. Regular bicycle maintenance is important!
- At the hotel and for most of my biking day, there was NO cell phone coverage for my Verizon cell phone. The nice lady at the check-in desk let me use her personal phone two different times to make phone calls.
- Tink called and arranged for a Warmshowers host for me for tomorrow night in Kerrville, Texas.
- As the new CEO of our rental home business, Tink has been waking up at 5:45 a.m. daily to keep our rental real estate business thriving. On my end, I'm still handling a large volume of phone calls, texts, and emails throughout the day with many of the phone calls handled while I'm actually pedaling my bicycle, but Tink is taking care of the vast load of the day-to-day work in the office and she is doing a fine job of it!

Tuesday November 3, 2020
Day 25: Leakey, Texas to Kerrville, Texas (75 miles)
- I woke up at 5 a.m. at the Leakey Inn in Leakey, Texas and I was pedaling by 5:45 a.m. I rode about an hour in the dark. I LOVE riding in the dark!
- Today, I averaged 11.5 miles per hour with lots of SIGNIFICANT ups and downs in elevation as I ventured through Texas Hill Country! What a beautiful scenic route! All of my body parts are still feeling good!
- As I experience the new hilly terrain, I can sense I am FINALLY transitioning out of the desert! The desert and I are truly ONE!!!
- In Kerrville, Texas, I stayed with Warmshowers host, Michael Stanard. Michael and his lovely wife own a beautiful ranch estate. Michael allowed me to stay in his deluxe motorhome in which he graciously parked in front of his garage. Michael even hooked up the electricity for me to use.
- I ordered Domino's Pizza for supper, but it took the driver 90 minutes to deliver my pizza. Today was election day and I guess lots of people were ordering pizza as they sat in front of their TV watching to see who is elected president of the United States. Donald Trump or Joe Biden are the two favorites to win.
- Little did I know, my Warmshowers host, Michael Stanard, is a WORLD-CLASS runner! About a week ago, Michael finished a particular 100-mile race in which he had previously FAILED to finish 9 previous times! This was Michael's fourth 100-mile race finish in his life. AMAZING!!!
- Michael and I sat in his motorhome sharing stories with each other as we ate chocolate chip cookies. Michael and I were clearly made from the SAME MOLD!!!!!

- I also enjoyed throwing the ball for Michael's friendly, but rambunctious, 2-year-old female dog, Yulu, as she chased the ball and retrieved it EVERY time without fail.
- This evening, I finally broke down and spent $55.00 and ordered the Adventure Cycling Bicycle Route Navigator phone app of the Southern Tier. The Southern Tier phone app easily loaded on to my phone app and I'm eager to use my new phone app tomorrow as I pedal along the famed route. Tomorrow, I will know if the money invested in Bicycle Route Navigator was money well spent or not.
- Our son, Curtis, keeps stopping over the house asking Tink where I'm at. Curtis is getting frustrated as he has not seen me in three and a half weeks. Curtis does not know where I'm at or what I'm doing, but he will figure it out soon enough as he is very smart. We would tell Curtis about my whereabouts, but we are afraid if we do, he might get an idea to do something STUPID!

Wednesday November 4, 2020
Day 26: Kerrville, Texas to Johnson City, Texas (57 miles)
- I woke up at 5 a.m. and I was pedaling my bike at 5:45 a.m.
- I averaged 11.5 miles per hour today. I continue to break every 10 miles to eat and walk.
- Toes 3 and 4 did NOT hurt today as I continued to apply Bag Balm, wear two pairs of socks on that foot, and STRETCH my toes frequently! FREQUENTLY stretching my toes and feet are the key to my toe pain RELIEF!!!!
- For some unknown reason, my RIGHT KNEE hurt me most of the day. Maybe I started the day pedaling TOO HARD or maybe I didn't loosen up my body parts quite enough before applying heavy-duty pedal force?
- For lunch, I ate last night's cold pizza while standing on the side of the road. I've transformed myself into a SAVAGE!
- For supper, I ate a burger and fries at Dairy Queen across the street from my hotel.
- This bike ride has been difficult in many ways. For several days, Tink and I have been criticizing each other and arguing much more than usual, but today we worked everything out. We decided that we are NOT going to criticize each other anymore for the REST OF OUR LIVES!

Thursday November 5, 2020
Day 27: Johnson City, Texas to Bastrop, Texas (88 miles)
- I woke up at 5 a.m. and I was pedaling my bike by 5:30 a.m.
- This morning was much warmer than most of the recent previous mornings as it was 55 degrees at 5:30 a.m.
- I did not wear my baklava headpiece nor did I wear my windbreaker. I also wore my half gloves instead of my full finger gloves.
- Today, I rode my bike through the big city of Austin, Texas. My recently purchased Adventure Cycling Bicycle Route Navigator phone app is

working GREAT! It was especially helpful as I navigated through the big city of Austin making MANY turns! I could ZOOM in and out of the GPS map as necessary depending on the detail I needed. I LOVE the Bicycle Route Navigator mobile phone application!
- Early this morning, I very carefully eased into my daily ride hoping not to aggravate the outside part of my right knee as I did yesterday. For the first 45 miles, my right knee felt pretty good, but then around mile 46, my left knee suddenly began hurting. By the 60-mile point, BOTH of my knees were hurting A LOT!
- At the 80-mile point, the pain was SEVERE in BOTH knees and I stopped. While thinking about what could have caused my pain in both knees, I suddenly remembered my bike seat coming loose yesterday requiring me to put it back in place and re-tighten it. Maybe my bike seat is out of position? Maybe my bike seat is too high, too low, too far to the front, or too far to the back? Immediately, I took a CAREFUL look at my seat and I changed the position of the seat as to be a tad closer to the front toward my handlebars and tilted slightly more upward. Could the MINOR misalignment of my seat really result in serious knee injuries? For now, the change seemed to help and I managed to LIMP through the rest of my 88-mile ride to Bastrop, Texas where I stayed at the Bastrop Inn.
- While I was checking my bike over and tightening up Allen bolts, especially with regard to my bike seat position, I noticed I had a broken spoke! My Adventure Cycling map indicated a bike repair shop in Bastrop, Texas only about three miles from my motel. I'll go there in the morning to get the spoke fixed!

Friday November 6, 2020
Day 28: Bastrop, Texas to La Grange, Texas (42 miles)
- I woke up at 6 a.m. and I walked over to Walmart and bought ACE bandages and compression knee pads to wear biking with hope as to lessen the pain and provide the needed support to my ailing knees! Will Bastrop, Texas be my breaking point? Do I have another day of biking left inside of me? Can my knees rebound from this MAJOR SETBACK?
- At 7:30 a.m., I left the hotel at Bastrop Inn in Bastrop Texas and I rode my bicycle 2 miles over to Rising Phoenix River Adventures whom is listed on the Adventure Cycling maps as a bicycle repair shop. After waiting over an hour in their company driveway until 9 a.m. when they were scheduled to open, I found out they are no longer a bike repair shop. They are a kayak outfitter business!
- Instead of abandoning me, the gracious owner of Rising Phoenix, Jamie, gave me a ride 35 miles to Austin, Texas to Pedal Pushers to get my broken bike spoke fixed. At Pedal Pushers, I watched the repair while the talented bike technician fixed my spoke and also shortened my chain, rotated my rear tire to the front, and tightened my gear cables. All the repairs cost me $100.
- Two hours or so later, Jamie picked me up at Pedal Pushers and gave me a ride back to Bastrop, Texas where I began pedaling at 2:30 p.m. and

continued my bike journey eastbound. Jamie was an ANGEL!!!! She wanted NOTHING other than to HELP me! What a GREAT person! There are STILL good people in our country!!! I promised Jamie, in the future, I would return the generous favor to someone else in need as to keep her KINDNESS alive and thriving!
- I was ANNOYED as I was charged $5 to ride my bike through Bastrop State Park. Shouldn't a cyclist be admitted for FREE?
- After making my way through some back streets and riding my bike 45 minutes in the DARK, eventually I arrived at La Grange, Texas at my motel for the night.
- My left knee hurt A LOT today even though I wore an ACE bandage and a compression knee pad on it, but it SEEMS to be improving slightly! My right knee felt MUCH BETTER than yesterday even though I did not wear anything on it today! Maybe moving my bike seat forward a bit is helping both of my knees? Tomorrow should give me the answer!
- My first stop in La Grange, Texas was at Walmart where I bought tighter compression fittings for my left knee for tomorrow's ride. I'm trying to hang in there and correct my knee issues instead of "tapping out." I'm scared! The pain is almost enough to end this trip. God, please help me!
- After Walmart, I rode my bicycle over to McDonald's and I bought two regular McChicken sandwiches as a carry-out. I took my food back to the Cottonwood Inn in La Grange, Texas where I stayed the night in room 238.

Saturday November 7, 2020
Day 29: La Grange, Texas to Navasota, Texas (67 miles)
- Today, I found out that Joe Biden won the presidential election in the United States of America by defeating incumbent president, Donald Trump. I have great respect for the USA and their presidential election, but I cannot understand how Biden defeated Trump! After riding my bike through 4 states in the last 4 weeks, I got a VERY STRONG feeling that Donald Trump was the HEAVY FAVORITE to win! Could foul play be involved? I did not vote, so I cannot complain!
- I woke up at 5:15 a.m. and I began pedaling my bike at 6 a.m.
- My left knee was wrapped in an ace bandage with a knee sleeve with four rigid supports pulled over top of the ace bandage. I also wore a copper knee sleeve on my right knee. During the ride my right knee did not hurt much at all, but my left knee produced pain with EVERY pedal stroke. I'm not sure if my left knee is getting better or not. At least, the compression helps to support the knee and minimize the pain. I have also begun taking ibuprofen every 6 hours for my swollen knee and for some pain relief! How much more pain can I endure?
- I stopped every 10 miles like usual and I ate while I paced back and forth. Every 3 miles I forced myself to drink as to stay properly hydrated as well.
- It was a beautiful, sunny day with a high of 81 degrees Fahrenheit. The wind was light at 7 miles per hour, but it was another easterly wind which meant another HEADWIND for me! Most of this bike trip has been HEADWINDS, just like my research indicated would be the case!

- I ate lunch at Burger King in Navasota, Texas.
- I also ate supper at Burger King at Navasota which required a 2-mile bike ride one way with my bum knee from my camping spot at the Navasota Fire Department.
- The Navasota Fire Department was extremely gracious allowing me to use their shower and laundry facilities. I LOVE using a washing machine as my hands finally got a break today from the physically-demanding task of hand-washing my dirty biking clothes!
- The fire chief at the Navasota Fire Department yelled at me for walking around the station with my shirt off! Instantly, I corrected the situation and offered my apologies. It was very important to me to follow the rules and show respect to the nice group of firefighters whom allowed me to stay overnight at their awesome modern facility! Thanks guys!
- Even though I am very tired tonight, I managed to do one Duolingo Spanish lesson.
- To bed at 9 p.m. sharp! I don't like to go to bed TOO EARLY, but 9 p.m. was the latest I could keep my eyes open. All this biking is VERY tiring!!!

Sunday November 8, 2020
Day 30: Navasota, Texas to Shepherd, Texas (79 miles)
- I woke up at 5 a.m. and I was pedaling by 5:45 a.m.
- Initially, both of my knees felt pretty good until about 30 miles into the ride when my left knee started aching and it only got worse until about 65 miles into my ride at which point it became numb and no longer bothered me until I arrived at my destination for the night, Shepherd Sanctuary Campground. Upon dismounting my bike, I was visibly limping! My left knee is BADLY injured even though I keep fine tuning the positioning of my bike seat in an attempt to help alleviate pain from my left knee. At times, it feels like I'm making progress and at other times, it seems to be a futile effort! I don't know if I can continue?
- As I pedaled through Coldspring, Texas, I took a wrong turn and I got lost for about two and a half miles which cost me a total of 5 miles of wasted pedaling. Part of the lost terrain included a BIG uphill climb that took significant effort to summit! I'm glad my mother wasn't around because the words that came out of my mouth when I realized I was lost were horrendously vulgar and unrefined! Upon getting lost, I turned into PSYCHO BIKER!!! Wasting PRECIOUS mileage with a BUSTED KNEE really irritated me! My poor choice of vocabulary words revealed a deep level of immaturity on my part!
- I promised myself to pay closer attention to my route guidance on my phone as every mile I wasted made the possible completion of my epic excursion two miles less likely!
- I ate lunch at the gas station in Shepherd, Texas named TD's Market. I ate a wonderful pizza with loads of toppings. While sitting inside at one of the picnic tables, I drank 2 pints of chocolate milk. Chocolate milk is my SECRET WEAPON!
- The owner of Shepherd Sanctuary Campground was a WONDERFUL lady

named Peach. I'm SO GLAD I chose to spend the night here!!!! The expansive campground is an entire community of little, tasteful "shacks." I got the special "bike across America" overnight rate of only $20 and I stayed in the adorable "Love Shack."
- Peach and her friends at Shepherd Sanctuary Campground cooked me an awesome cheeseburger on the grill and then gave me some special hydration drink along with a can of 7-Up which tasted awesome. Peach and her crew played music and hung out with me like it was a party. They were so WELCOMING of me as they truly supported my mission to ride the Southern Tier! What a memorable experience!!!

Monday November 9, 2020
Day 31: Shepherd, Texas to Kirbyville, Texas (89 miles)
- I left my nice, little "Love Shack" cabin in Shepherd, Texas at 5:30 a.m. after waking up at 4:45 a.m.
- Today was a MIRACLE!!!! SUDDENLY, both of my knees felt good for the ENTIRE 89-mile ride to Kirbyville, Texas on this overcast, slightly rainy day. In addition to the many prayers made on behalf of me and my ailing knees, my best guess as to my sudden knee HEALING might have something to do with my bike seat finally getting adjusted back into the PERFECT position like it was for the first 1,500 miles of my bike trip prior to me having any knee problems! Several times over the past few days, I have made slight adjustments to my seat as to find the PERFECT position. The compression fittings on my knees also helped a lot. Starting out every day SLOWER and EASIER was also helpful to my recovery! Prayer was probably the MAJOR contributor to my healing!
- Most of this bike ride today was level as I hardly stood up at to pedal my bike as I pedaled in the sitting position almost all day.
- I ate last night's leftover pizza for lunch. Regularly, I eat leftover, cold pizza directly out of a Walmart bag from inside my bike pannier bag.
- During my travels today, I was chased by 6 different dogs bringing my current dog chase total to 17. Two of the chases were borderline severe while the other 4 dog chases were alarming, but did not pose much of a threat to me! During one of the two serious dog chases, a crazed, mid-sized dog actually got in front of my bike and tried to stop my bike. In a moment of panic, I decided to keep riding and I almost ran the dog over! This particular dog WANTED to eat me! I HATE dog chases!
- Surprisingly, upon my arrival in Kirbyville, Texas, I was informed by the secretary of the United Methodist Church about the church no longer hosting cyclists because of the current COVID-19 pandemic! I was alarmed as I counted on this church for my overnight accommodations as they were listed as an available host as per my Adventure Cycling map.
- With no other overnight plan in place, I decided to WILD CAMP in a vacant lot adjacent to the church. The empty lot was out in the OPEN in the MIDDLE OF TOWN! So, without permission, I set up camp in the MIDDLE of town!!!! It was my assumption I would receive a visit from a local police officer, but to my dismay, nobody bothered me!

- While I was setting up my tent in this UNAUTHORIZED camping location, two nicely-dressed elder ladies from the adjacent church visited me and asked me what I would like to eat for supper. 30 minutes later, my two new church-lady friends, whom refused to share their names with me, brough me enough food to feed TWO hungry Southern Tier cyclists!!! The ladies were so SWEET as they only wanted to HELP ME, especially since their church declined my request to spend the night inside their capable facility.

Tuesday November 10, 2020
Day 32: Kirbyville, Texas to Oberlin, Louisiana (83 miles)
- I woke up at 4:45 a.m. in my tent in the middle of an open, grassy WILD CAMPING area in a suburban neighborhood of Kirbyville Texas.
- As I was changing my clothes, nature prompted a familiar and IMMEDIATE urge in my stomach area. Without any bathroom or time to pedal my bike anywhere to find an available bathroom, I was forced to relieve my rectal urge INSIDE MY TENT!!!! Quickly, I grabbed one of my spare Dollar General bags and I placed the bag on the floor of my tent as I squatted down and CRAPPED into the bag! After using some toilet paper and meticulously cleaning my tail, I completed the inconvenient, but urgent deed, and casually walked over to the local dumpster and NEATLY deposited my special, tied-up bag of human dung inside the convenient dumpster! I have turned into an animal. I'm not even human anymore!
- The humidity was so dense it caused the entire rain flap of my tent to be soaked. Unwillingly to wait the necessary time for my tent to dry naturally, I packed it away completely wet knowing it would dry quickly later in the day after re-opening it.
- This was the first day I did not wear compression on my right knee and my right knee actually felt mostly good for the entire ride. I wore an ACE bandage and a compression knee pad on my left knee, but the compression pad CUT my skin in two places on the back side of my knee despite my wearing Bag Balm on my skin prior to applying the compression fittings. I will have to be much more careful tomorrow! The breaking of skin in key bodily areas has ended many cyclist's dreams!
- I left my unofficial campsite at 5:45 a.m. without a single question from the dozens of neighbors in view of my tent. Not even the local law enforcement paid me a visit! Everything was fine!
- The terrain was mostly level today as I averaged about 13 miles per hour which was about 2 miles per hour faster than most of my other biking days.
- At Mile 19 this morning, I crossed the Sabina River and entered Louisiana. Not too many cyclists have pedaled a bicycle 1,000 miles across the entire enormous state of Texas! I am now two-thirds of the way across the country! Am I DREAMING? Is this really happening? Although I've made good progress, I do NOT expect to finish!
- Upon entering one of the small towns in Louisiana, a young black man clearly and deliberately stood up and gave me a STANDING OVATION as I pedaled past him! As I passed by, we made a special bonding eye contact with each other. I will never forget this special young man! Deep in my

heart, I KNEW he was MY BROTHER! My brother recognized I was riding the Southern Tier and he KNEW how many miles I had tallied to this point and he wanted to let me know how much he RESPECTED my efforts! This young man touched my soul as he gave me a SECOND WIND like no other!
- I had five more dog chases today bringing my total dog chase number to 21.
- My back was sore today, but not too bad. This is only the second day of this bike trip in which my back hurt. Overall, my back has never felt better!
- Upon arrival at the Allen Parish Tourist Commission in Oberlin, Louisiana, the director, Adagria Haddock, bought me a tasty hamburger meal from Sonic's Restaurant! I LOVE southern hospitality! Adagria and her two staff ladies were DELIGHTFUL! They even gave me some fresh homemade southern sugar cane syrup which I took with me to eat over the course of the next few days! Their kindness made me feel right at home!
- For supper, I walked down the street to the Time Loop gas station and bought a Hunt Brothers Pizza. I ate half the pizza for supper and I will eat the other half tomorrow for lunch. I could LIVE on pizza! CORRECTION….. I DO LIVE on pizza!

Wednesday November 11, 2020
Day 33: Oberlin, Louisiana to Simmesport, Louisiana (108 miles)
- I woke up at 4:45 a.m. in Oberlin, Louisiana at the Allen Parrish Tourist Commission. I packed my tent and all of my supplies and I was on the road biking by 5:30 a.m.
- I was chased by 7 dogs today. One of today's dog chases involved a GERMAN SHEPHERD which got the hairs on my forearms to stand straight up! It was terrifying!
- Although the German Shepherd dog chase was CHILLING, I made a HUGE discovery! Within the first few seconds of being engaged in the fierce dog chase, I firmly and loudly YELLED "YOU SIT!" and the dog STOPPED!!!!!! With the continued use of my newly discovered "You sit!" technique, I found many of the chasing dogs OBEYED my command and STOPPED IN THEIR TRACKS……… at least for a few seconds, thus giving me enough distance to clear the dog's pursuit!
- While biking through Chiswick State Park, in typical "Sean Hockensmith fashion," I DISREGARDED a GIANT, flashing neon sign clearly reading "DO NOT ENTER." A couple miles later, a harsh and stern Louisianna ranger pulled me over and threatened to take me to jail for blatantly disobeying a FEDERAL roadway sign! He informed me of a severe COVID-19 outbreak which caused the road to close. Despite my best "bike across America" sob story, the ranger was NOT the least bit interested in my pitiful anecdotal tale. Happily, I turned around and extended my daily trip by 20 miles as I took a RIDICULOUS detour all the way out and around the gigantic Chiswick State Park!
- While pedaling my bike, Constable Terry Geibig calls me and informs me of a warrant issued for my son, Curtis. Could Curtis be going back to jail?

- When will he learn to stay out of trouble?
- Louisiana roads seem to be VERY ROUGH!!! A few of them were rougher than some of the mountain bike trails I've ridden in previous adventures. I was worried about a possible flat tire or other probable damage to my bike, but fortunately, my bike seems to be in good shape as I continue to monitor my seat, chain, tires, spokes, etc. for any possible indications of problems.
- Several roads did NOT have any shoulder and I was forced to ride in the car lane which made me a bit tighter with traffic than I would ideally prefer! Louisiana roads seem to lack extra berm space in general.
- Overall, I'm feeling FULLY healthy now. I believe my left knee has recovered 100% and is back to normal. Thank God!
- One word to describe this afternoon's biking was "TAILWIND!" A tailwind is a beautiful thing on a bicycle!!! Thanks to an unexpected tailwind, I tallied my FIRST day with over 100 miles traveled!
- Tonight, I stayed at the Rabalais Seafood Restaurant. Owner Ray, wife Debra, and their son Clay gave me the option of sleeping inside after the restaurant closed, but instead, I decided to erect my tent outside in the back of the property so I could get to bed early like I have been doing throughout much of my bicycle travels.
- Ray, his wife, and their son Clay cooked me rabbit, rice, vegetables, and a roll for supper. They were a very generous and accommodating Warmshowers hosts!
- To my surprise, another long-distance biker named Max showed up at the restaurant. Max was 22 years old and lives in Maryland. He pedaled his bike from Maryland and is heading to San Antonio, Texas to meet up with family. Max also stayed outside the restaurant next to me in his own tent.
- I was too cheap to pay $8.00 for a shower at the local truck stop down the street. Instead, I used wipes to clean myself. Even without using running water, I did a VERY GOOD JOB cleaning myself!
- It is so humid in Louisiana. My sweaty clothes do NOT dry overnight!!!
- Tink continues to work 10 to 12-hour days with our rental home business. She is holding the business together VERY WELL, but I'm still VERY CONCERNED about her health! Tink is such a DEDICATED, HARD-WORKING woman! She is doing a GREAT job handling the bulk of our company responsibilities while I'm away!

Thursday November 12, 2020
Day 34: Simmesport, Louisiana to Easleyville, Louisiana (108 miles)
- I woke up at 4:45 a.m. and was pedaling my bike by 5:40 a.m. Why does it take me so long to get ready in the mornings?
- My tent was drenched with dew from the high humidity overnight. My sopping wet tent was haphazardly folded and stuffed into the storage bag as I knew it would dry out quickly later tonight when I set it up.
- My biking clothes were wet and sweaty from yesterday. They did NOT dry at all through the night! It was VERY uncomfortable, but I wore them anyways as I had no other reasonable alternative.

- It was a chilly 50 degrees as I started my daily bike ride. Wearing my light windbreaker felt great for the first 10 miles or so until I got too warm. I'd rather begin my bike ride warm and take off clothes as needed than to start my ride cold and try to get warm!
- Within the first mile of today's journey, I crossed over the Great Atchafalaya River.
- At the 45-mile point of today's trip, I crossed the mighty Mississippi River which was a HUGE landmark feature and symbolized a MASSIVE accomplishment on my part!
- I ate lunch at Subway in Jackson, Louisiana.
- I ate supper at the Hatfield Country Store inside the gas station in Greensburg, Louisiana. I got one of the meat lovers Hunt Brothers Pizzas for $10.99 and a 32-ounce cold chocolate milk. I also bought two bananas, some oatmeal cookies, and 2 cold Powerades. I ate the pizza at a table inside the gas station while I talked on the phone.
- Even though I was only expecting to cover 92 miles according to last night's plan, I biked 108 miles today thanks to an unsuspecting tailwind.
- Today was a beautiful, clear day with a high of about 80 degrees Fahrenheit. In typical fashion, I rode without a shirt for about 3 hours in the afternoon. I LOVE riding shirtless!
- I rode the last 3 miles in the dark as I finally arrived in Easleyville, Louisiana at the Hyde Park Campground. Even though it is a bit scary, I LOVE riding my bike in the dark!
- Initially, I thought the rudimentary camp shower had no hot water, but I was wrong. As it turned out, the shower faucet knobs were REVERSED! The hot-water knob on the left was actually supplying cold water and the cold-water knob on the right was actually supplying hot water. It only took me running the left knob for five minutes or so to realize it was NOT producing any hot water! Why am I so dumb? Eventually, it felt SO GOOD to get a HOT shower tonight despite the shower facility being a bit tricky.
- All by myself in the back of the park, I slept in my tent on a concrete slab under a large pavilion. I was warned about a possible encounter through the night with wild pigs, but I was so tired it didn't bother me much. As far as I know, the pigs did not visit me. Before going to sleep, I placed my pannier bag containing my food on top of the picnic table as I was told the pigs CANNOT climb or jump, but I was warned about the pigs having SHARP teeth and strong, hard footings.
- It was a pleasant surprise to discover the pavilion had electric, but I had to use duct tape to hold my electrical charging cube in the very loose electrical socket. There is always a need for duct tape!

Friday November 13, 2020
Day 35: Easlyville, Louisiana to Poplarville, Mississippi (87 miles)
- I woke up at 5 a.m. and I was pedaling by 5:45 a.m.
- It was a very chilly morning as I put on my wet clothes from yesterday. At least, my clothes were CLEAN!
- I ate breakfast at McDonald's in Bogalusa, Louisiana.

- Alongside the road, I ate yesterday's leftover pizza for lunch.
- I ate the remainder of my leftover pizza for supper. I do NOT waste food!!!
- Mom and dad paid the discounted "cross-country cyclist" rate of $79.50 for me to stay overnight at the lush, Bed-and-Breakfast, single-family house in Poplarville, Mississippi.
- It seems like EVERYONE likes to help a cross-country cyclist!
- By adding five more dog-chases to my tally, I am now up to a total of 38 dog-chases so far this expedition. I'm getting used to the dog-chases!! My "You sit!" technique is AMAZING!!!!
- My parents and wife are planning to travel from Johnstown, Pennsylvania to meet me in St Augustine, Florida upon the possible conclusion of my bike ride. Although I am excited to see them, I cannot and will not allow myself to focus on the finish. As far as I am concerned, I am taking daily rides and I really have no idea about anything beyond TOMORROW! Finishing is much too far away to consider! I really don't think I have what it takes to finish anyways!

Saturday November 14, 2020
Day 36: Poplarville, Mississippi to Vancleave, Mississippi (76 miles)
- I woke up at 5 a.m. and was biking by 5:40 a.m.
- I only had two dogs chases today. My total number of dog chases is now at 40.
- At my rest stop at 51 miles, I noticed I had a broken spoke on my back wheel. After investing over an hour trying to fix the broken spoke with a product known as "Fiber Spoke," I realized I couldn't thread the fiber spoke through the tiny hole because the rear cassette/sprocket was blocking it. Instead, I taped the broken spoke to the neighboring spoke as to prevent any collateral damage and I proceeded to ride my bike with 31 spokes instead of 32 spokes all the way to Camp Journey End Campground, 25 miles away without any additional maintenance issues.
- After taking a shower and talking with Tink, I looked up some bike shops on Google. To my surprise, the first bike shop I called, Tri Hard Sports in Ocean Springs Mississippi (9 miles away), was in the process of closing for the day, but I did manage to speak with mechanic, Jacob. After hearing my cross-country story, Jacob agreed to open the bike shop for me at 9 a.m. tomorrow (Sunday) morning to fix my spoke and to inspect my bike for any other recommended maintenance.
- Today's weather was another pretty day with lots of sunshine and a high temperature of 80 degrees. I pedaled the last 2 hours of this day without a shirt.
- Next door to my camp was a VERY UNIQUE restaurant named "The Shed: Barbeque and Blues Joint." It was an amazing, outdoor, festival-like, casual restaurant with incredibly tasty PORK and great music! The whole experience felt more like an EVENT than a meal! The unique southern venue provided MUCH MORE than just a scrumptious pork sandwich!!!!
- After supper, I walked to the gas station across the street and bought some chocolate milk! Chocolate milk really does something SPECIAL for me!!!

- I went to bed VERY EARLY at about 8:15 p.m. as I was "Southern Tier tired," emotionally and physically!

Sunday November 15, 2020
Day 37: Vancleave, Mississippi to Bayou La Batre, Alabama (48 miles)

- Intentionally, I woke up 6 a.m. which was later than normal as I knew I had a scheduled meeting with the bike mechanic, Jacob, at 9 a.m. at Tri Hard Sports in Ocean Springs, Mississippi. This was probably my LONGEST night's sleep of my entire trip with a total sleep time approaching 10 hours! Usually, I will NOT sleep over 8 hours!!!! Most days, I prefer to sleep 7 hours at night and take a one-hour nap after lunch.
- My tent rain cover was SOAKED again from the heavy humidity overnight.
- This was an UNUSUAL morning as I spent over an hour responding to texts, phone calls, and emails before I began biking as I did not want to arrive too early for my 9 a.m. meeting with Jacob, the bike mechanic.
- At promptly 9 a.m., bike mechanic extraordinaire, Jacob, arrived in true fashion on his own bicycle to Tri Hard Sports where he fixed my bike with supreme PROFESSIONAL quality! Jacob was a slender, young man about 21 years old whom reminded me of our very good-looking son, Maxmillion. Jacob was an ANGEL in jeans!
- Jacob did an AMAZING, conscientious job fixing my spoke, replacing both of my road tires, and checking over everything on my bike. By 10:45 a.m. my bike was "ROAD WORTHY" again! He only charged me $68, but I tipped him $40 because Jacob was WORTH IT! Jacob did me a HUGE favor as his bike shop was NOT even scheduled to be open on Sundays!
- I ate lunch outside of Burger King in Ocean Springs, Mississippi as COVID-19 continues to be VERY PROMINENT and the restaurant's dining room was closed.
- Upon arriving at the "Welcome to Alabama" road sign, I pulled over and took a phone selfie photo with the welcome sign in back. While doing so, a nice, older couple pulled their vehicle off to the side of the road and offered to assist me with my special photos. How nice! It seems like everyone wants to help me! A cross-country cyclist can easily get a lot of assistance!!!
- It is hard to believe I have pedaled my bike through 6 states so far and I have traveled over 2,000 miles on pure LEG POWER!
- After eating supper in the dining room inside of McDonald's, I bought some chocolate milk, 3 burritos, and some brownies from Dollar General for my "second supper" which I planned to eat later in the evening.
- I had another peaceful night's sleep. It seems like the Southern Tier Bike Route would be a perfect SOLUTION for anyone with sleeping problems! After pedaling 70 miles a day, sleeping is NOT a problem!!!!
- Our 25-year-old daughter, Stacey, called today and informed me she is PREGNANT! Stacey is NOT married and her boyfriend, Bryce, walked out of the house when she told him she was with child. I'm NOT excited about the news as Stacey is not in a solid relationship nor is she

financially stable yet. I'm concerned for her! One thing I know for sure is……. Tink and I are NOT raising any grandchildren!!!!!
- Our 21-year-old son, Anthony, remains in jail. Today, he got put into "The Hole" (solitary confinement) for fighting. I'm concerned for him! We LOVE Anthony dearly and we hope he figures out how to be a PRODUCTIVE and RESPECTFUL member of our community as he has so many wonderful qualities to offer! He is so smart, athletic, and talented! Regardless of Anthony's current challenges, I firmly believe this will be Anthony's year to turn his life around!

Monday November 16, 2020
Day 38: Bayou La Batre, Alabama to Pensacola, Florida (87 miles)
- I woke up at 5 a.m. and I was on the road pedaling my bike at 5:45 a.m.
- The winds were FIERCE on the Gordon Persons Bridge from mainland to Dauphin Island, Alabama! Numerous times, my bike was ALMOST blown over by the force of the heavy winds. I crouched down on my bicycle as low as I could get as I nervously awaited the next heavy gust of wind as I gazed out over the guardrail into the 100-foot drop into the waters of Mobile Bay! I held on to my bicycle handlebars for dear life!!!
- At 7:10 a.m., I celebrated as I finally arrived at the Mobile Bay Ferry at Dauphin Island, Alabama. After patiently waiting until 8 a.m. to see if the ferry would operate due to the violent winds, I paid $5.00 and pushed my bike aboard the ferry for a ride across the bay to Fort Morgan, Alabama. There were four vehicles, two workers, a captain, and me and my bike on the ferry. The winds were wicked as the waves kept splashing up on deck! Fortunately, I put my bike into the little covered area to keep it safe and secure.
- I stopped at Burger King in the Gulf Shores, Alabama vicinity and ate lunch.
- As I approached the "Welcome to Florida" sign, I was emotionally MOVED! At no other point in my bike travels so far have I been flooded with such raw positive emotion! My entire body had tingles as tears streamed from the outside corners of my eyes. The Florida welcome sign was a MAJOR milestone in my journey! Florida is a special place for me as it was the long-term home of my beloved grandfather, Jesse Hockensmith, my father's father. Florida was also the location of my college as I attended the University of Tampa for two full years before dropping out. I also worked as a food vendor selling gourmet coffees at many of the large Florida fairs for many years including the Florida State Fair, the South Florida Fair, and the Florida Strawberry Festival. It was really dear to me as I contemplated pedaling my bicycle from the Pacific Ocean to the western tip of the state of Florida! As I sat staring at the welcome sign at the beginning of my 8th state, I briefly wandered if I might possibly finish this INCREDIBLE bicycle journey!?
- In Pensacola, I ordered two medium "pick-up" pizzas from Domino's Pizza for supper. I ate one whole pizza! There is NOTHING like an APPETITE of a hungry cyclist! My daily food consumption consists of the same number of calories as would feed 2 and a half "regular" adults! The second

pizza will be my lunch for tomorrow.
- I couldn't find any convenient Warmshowers hosts or camping in Pensacola, so I called the local fire department and ended up staying in a tent behind the fire department near the border of the woods on Summit Road at Pensacola Fire Department number three. I did NOT have official permission to camp there, but someone involved in the fire company seemed to think it MIGHT be ok for me to stay there overnight. I kept a LOW PROFILE like usual and nobody bothered me.

Tuesday November 17, 2020
Day 39: Pensacola, Florida to Defuniak Springs, Florida (86 miles)
- It was mildly chilly through the night with a low of 49 degrees. This was the first night I got chilly as my "zero degree" synthetic down mummy sleeping bag seemed to lose much of its loft! I'm pretty sure it's not really the fault of the sleeping bag as I believe I've been improperly caring for my sleeping bag prior to my Southern Tier adventure. Instead of loosely hanging my sleeping bag in long-term storage when I'm not on an adventure, I kept my synthetic down sleeping bag tightly shoved into its compression bag for extended periods of time which damaged its insulation properties. I'll have to care for my next down sleeping bag much more carefully by hanging it loosely from our garage ceiling when it's not in use!
- I woke up at 5 a.m. and I was pedaling by 5:50 a.m. My clothes were still sweaty wet from yesterday as they didn't dry AT ALL overnight! This was one of the FEW times I began pedaling in DIRTY and WET biking clothes!
- As I was pedaling through Crestview, Florida, I picked up three unopened bottles of Diet Pepsi which were lying in the middle of the road on Route 90. Apparently, the soda bottles recently fell out of a vehicle. Since the intact soda bottles were NOT opened, I perceived the occurrence as a "gift from God" and I drank ALL of them! The opportune soda tasted especially good with my leftover Domino's Pizza!
- Route 90 is a very nice biking road with a very generous berm!
- My left knee is hurting a little bit today and I'm not sure why.?
- I stayed at the Sundown Inn in Defuniak Springs, Florida which was conveniently located across the street from Walmart which was only 1 mile from the Southern Tier Bike Route.
- With great disappointment, mom, dad, and Tink informed me they will NOT be meeting me at the finish in St Augustine, Florida due to COVID-19 concerns! The disappointing news was a big blow to me as I was MAJORLY looking forward to seeing my parents and my wife as I possibly finish this arduous 3,000-mile bicycle journey! Although it was discouraging to find out my family was not meeting me at the anticipated finish, the realization was not devastating as I remain very uncertain as to whether or not I can actually finish this grueling Southern Tier Bicycle Route!

Wednesday November 18, 2020
Day 40: DeFuniak Springs, Florida to Chattahoochee, Florida (82 miles)
- I woke up at 5 a.m. and was pedaling by 5:40 a.m.
- It was a VERY chilly ride in the morning as my feet didn't completely thaw out until mile 40! I rode the whole day wearing my long bike pants and my long tight thermal shirt. I'm not really sure why I felt so cold today! It seems like some days my body can withstand cold better than other days.
- I stayed on Route 90 ALL day! Route 90 is an AWESOME biking road!
- On the sidewalk outside of the Marianna, Florida McDonald's is where I ate my lunch today. The dining room was closed due to COVID-19 concerns.
- I ate four small Walmart pies today during my bike ride. I LOVE these little pies! Like usual, my strategy is to eat as many calories as possible for the least cost!
- Upon arrival at my Warmshowers house in Chattahoochee, Florida, I noticed the house was REALLY rundown as my host, Gene Floyd, recently purchased the home from a tax sale auction and he was in the process of renovating it. Gene lives in a country area and raises chickens and rabbits as part of his food consumption throughout the year. It was hard for me to imagine killing those cute animals for food, but I understand we all have to eat! Although Gene was a great host, I felt slightly uncomfortable talking to him about butchering animals and even more uncomfortable when he showed me one of his ASSAULT RIFLES from his gun collection! Despite my contrary feelings about animals and guns, Gene was a GREAT GUY and I enjoyed my stay at his house! He was a GREAT host!
- Gene made some yummy pork, rice, and collard greens in the crock pot for supper. In typical fashion, I ate plenty! It was slightly confusing to me as to why Gene cooked "pork" when his stated plan to me was to eat chickens and rabbits. It is quite possible I was eating rabbit, but it didn't matter much to me anyways.
- Gene had a young friend, Patrick, who also stayed at his house as Patrick was helping Gene renovate the newly-purchased house. Patrick slept on the couch. I had the spare bedroom all to myself.
- Upon speaking with my "route coordinator" (my dad) and considering the possibility of taking an Amtrak train home, I decided to aim for a possible finish to my epic bike ride in Jacksonville, Florida instead of St. Augustine, Florida, even though St. Augustine is the <u>official</u> Southern Tier finish destination as published by Adventure Cycling Association. Jacksonville seemed to me like the more convenient finish as the Amtrak train station was only about 25 miles away from my projected finish at Jacksonville Beach.
- In anticipation of a POSSIBLE finish, my mother bought me an Amtrak train ticket home. The purchase of this ticket felt REALLY weird as I continue to have MAJOR doubts as to whether or not I will actually finish! Anyways, it was a SUPER-NICE gesture on behalf of my mom buying me the Amtrak ticket home! It was also surprising Amtrak continued operating as COVID-19 concerns are NOW at an all-time high!

Thursday November 19, 2020
Day 41: Chattahoochee, Florida to Monticello, Florida (72 miles)
- I woke up at 5:15 a.m. and I was pedaling by 5:45 a.m. on this very chilly 45-degree morning. Finally, I now have an effective and efficient rhythm for my morning bike preparation routine!
- For breakfast, I stopped at McDonald's in Quincy Florida where some 30-year-old, ADHD-type man unexpectedly interviewed me as he was fascinated by my bike journey from San Diego, California to his small town of Quincy, Florida. It was an honor to be held in such high esteem! It felt like I was a FAMOUS person!
- For lunch, I stopped at Olive Garden in Tallahassee and had a nice lasagna and salad meal. It was kind of weird eating all by myself, but I quickly got over it! This was the most extravagant lunch I've had so far, but I felt like I NEEDED it! I made sure my bike was locked up really good as I placed it in the most secure location very close to the entrance of the exquisite restaurant!!!
- The roads were pretty busy while riding through Tallahassee, but I followed the Adventure Cycling phone app map and made it through smoothly with only two disapproving honks from disgruntled drivers.
- One of the disapproving honks resulted in quite a scene in downtown Tallahassee in which I INTENTIONALLY caused a traffic jam angering numerous weekday Tallahassee drivers!
- After getting my shower and doing my laundry, I tried riding my bicycle 1.5 miles to Burger King, but on the first little hill, only a quarter mile from my motel, my legs said, "No!" and I was FORCED to stop at the gas station and settle for another Hunt Brothers Pizza meal with chocolate milk for supper.
- At 8:45 p.m., I go to bed. I'm "Southern Tier TIRED!"
- COVID-19 cases are VERY HIGH in the United States. Today, Pennsylvania had 7,000 new COVID-19 cases. The United School District in western Pennsylvania was SHUT DOWN today and my 14-year-old nephew, Zachary, and my 16-year-old niece, Jordyn, were quarantined as they were both in close proximity to a classmate recently diagnosed with COVID-19. This COVID-19 virus is REALLY scary!!!! There is a rumor the state of Pennsylvania could be CLOSED soon and I might not be able to re-enter my state and get back home!

Friday November 20, 2020
Day 42: Monticello, Florida to Lake City, Florida (80 miles)
- I woke up at 5 a.m. and I was pedaling by 5:35 a.m. It seems like I'm getting a little bit faster with my morning duties, but the process will never be much faster than 30 minutes as there are so many tedious things to do to ensure a good daily bike ride!
- My legs felt great and my knees felt great. No problems at all today! I'm not sure why my left knee felt a bit of pain yesterday.?
- At 5:30 a.m., I got a phone call from a very special person in my life, but this person would not stop arguing with me and I was forced to hang up

- and BLOCK the number! Nobody was preventing my pedals from spinning around on this day!
- All of today's miles were pedaled on the LOVELY, cyclist-friendly Florida Route 90.
- For lunch, I ate leftover pizza out of a Walmart bag from last night. I feel like a SAVAGE! I AM a savage!!
- For supper, I walked three quarters of a mile over to Cracker Barrel and I ate a wonderful, home-cooked meatloaf, mashed potato, macaroni and cheese, and cornbread meal. Yummy! The hearty dinner was necessary for my ongoing good health. Foremost in my mind is avoiding any possible COVID-19 implications!
- On the way back to my motel, I walked past some homeless people living under a bridge. As I glanced at their desperate conditions, I realized I was NO different! We were ONE and the SAME!
- Tonight, I was startled as I realized I am only 82 miles from my destination of Jacksonville Beach! Am I dreaming? Is this really happening? Could I possibly finish?
- Tomorrow is day 43. Tomorrow might be my final day of this amazing bike adventure! Tomorrow is a possible finish!!!! I still have doubts!

Saturday November 21, 2020
Day 43: Lake City, Florida to Jacksonville, Florida (98 miles)
- I woke up at 5 a.m. and I was pedaling my bike by 5:30 a.m. The early morning riding in the dark no longer scares me at all. I LOVE riding in the dark!!! Darkness is just darkness. It poses no special danger to me! The early morning darkness feels RIGHT to me!
- I felt COMPLETELY healthy today! There were no problems at all with my body! I NEVER felt better in my entire life!
- For lunch, I stopped in Jacksonville at Subway and ate a wonderful 12-inch-long oven roasted chicken sub.
- I was so excited to conclude this incredible journey, I could hardly contain myself. I'm pretty sure I could have pedaled 200 miles today if necessary!
- There are GOOD REASONS why Adventure Cycling routes their maps as they do. By abandoning the Adventure Cycling map and making my own finish route in Jacksonville instead of St. Augustine, I found myself on some rather busy roads which were NOT ideal for biking, but I managed. One such road was a very short stint on the MAMMOTH Interstate 95 in which I'm quite sure I was NOT permitted to use!!!!
- As I pedaled through the extremely LONG city of Jacksonville, Florida, I stopped 10 miles from my Atlantic Ocean destination and sent the following text to my loved ones on a group text thread: "Pedaling through Jacksonville. Taking Route 90 all the way to the beach. Possible finish in 45 minutes!"
- To my SURPRISE, I pedaled a half mile or so on the breakdown lane of the massive Interstate 95 roadway as I was UNAWARE Route 90 eastbound and Interstate 95 briefly shared the same roadway!!! I'm pretty SURE bikes are NOT permitted on Interstate 95, but at that point, NOTHING was going

to stop me! It was Route 90 all the way to the beach FINALE!
- For the last ten miles before arriving at Jacksonville Beach as I neared the conclusion of my 3,000-mile odyssey, a group of angels surrounded me on my bicycle giving me an escort, like none other, to the glorious sands covering the shore of the Atlantic Ocean. For the last ten miles to my magnificent finish, I did NOT expend any energy whatsoever propelling the pedals of my bicycle as I was as HIGH as a human being could possibly be! My ENTIRE body was in CONSTANT tingles as I approached the completion of the great Southern Tier Bicycle Route! The unlikely attainment of my cross-country biking dream had come true!
- As I waited at the final traffic light less than 1/8th of a mile from the sands of the Atlantic Ocean, off in the distance I could see the waters of the Atlantic. Tears were streaming down my cheeks as the final traffic light of my splendid cycling odyssey turned green. I was NOW the CHAMPION I had always dreamed of!
- Upon contacting the sparkling sand with my front tire, I was OVERTAKEN with emotion as I put my head down on my handlebars and WEPT! I DID IT!!!!! I COMPLETED THE SOUTHERN TIER!!!!!!
- Upon contacting my bicycle tires on the sands in the Atlantic Ocean, I openly knelt down in the cold water and gave thanks to God for protecting me and delivering me to the completion of this LIFE-CHANGING bicycle journey. It was extremely hard for me to process the fact I had actually made it! MISSION COMPLETE!!!!!
- While standing in the salty water, I convinced some passing stranger to take several photos of me and my trusty bicycle as the cool ocean water trickled over the edge of my bike tires.
- As I searched for a motel in the vicinity of the Amtrak station, I stopped at Walmart and bought 6 small, 4-ounce pies of various flavors. I also bought Gatorade, cereal, Danishes, and chocolate milk! It's party time!!!!
- I'm VERY EXCITED to return to my family as this is my 43rd day away from home. I GREATLY miss my dear wife, our 5 adult children, my parents, my sister, our 3 cats, and my many other wonderful family members and friends. I even miss my JOB!!!

Sunday November 22, 2020
Day 44: Jacksonville, Florida to the Amtrak Train Station (7 miles)
- I woke up at 5:30 a.m. and instead of working diligently to prepare myself for a long bike ride, I meditated like the "old days." After meditating, I completed a few Spanish lessons on Duolingo, returned phone calls, handled texts, and processed emails. Afterward, I took a nap before I checked out of my hotel room at 11:30 a.m.
- It was so weird not biking anywhere early this morning!
- As I pedaled the paltry 7.4 miles to the Amtrak Station, I stopped and ate lunch at Subway.
- Google Maps provided me with GOOD and ACCURATE directions to the Amtrak Train Station.

- Jacksonville was an enjoyable city to tour on my bicycle!
- I arrived at the Amtrak Station about 4 hours before my 5 p.m. train departure to Philadelphia, Pennsylvania. I set up my fold-up camp chair and made a semi-office station outside of the Amtrak entrance doors as I conducted my business like usual. I hate WASTING time!
- Checking-in my bike and bags was EASY as an Amtrak employee had me walk my bike and bags to a special part of the train where my bike and gear were safely and securely stored for the long, pending train ride.
- The train ride overnight to Philadelphia was awesome! I slept pretty well except for some minor leg and hip discomfort which prompted me to change positions about once an hour as I sprawled out over my seat and into the empty seat next to me. Train travel is the way to go!

Monday November 23, 2020
Day 45: Amtrak Train from Philadelphia, Pennsylvania to Johnstown, Pennsylvania (0 biking miles)
- Riding the train allowed me to catch up on LOTS of work. As long as I have my cell phone with me, I can work from ANYWHERE in the world!!!
- For breakfast, I bought a plate of sausage, bacon, eggs, etc. all mixed together. I also ate a tasty Walmart pie and a semi-crushed Danish pastry from my bike bag.
- After eating too much food for breakfast, I reminded myself the Southern Tier is over. No longer do I need to eat such HUGE amounts of food! Unfortunately, habits are hard to break!
- At 9:30 a.m., my train arrived in Philadelphia, but I was overly involved in a phone conversation with boss-lady, Yvette Penrod, from the Johnstown Housing Authority Section 8 office and I ALMOST missed my stop as I did NOT realize how BRIEF the train stop would be! Due to my lack of necessary preparation and anticipation of the train stop, I felt some MAJOR stress as I HUSTLED to grab my stuff and frantically claim my bike and gear moments before the train departed from the station!!! This was VERY POOR planning on my part! There was no good reason I wasn't READY to depart from my train. My lack of preparation was very disappointing to me! Maybe I'm now an accomplished cross-country cyclist, but I remain as STUPID as ever!!!!
- There was a 3-hour Amtrak layover in Philadelphia, Pennsylvania. After the layover, I rode the connecting train to my hometown in Johnstown, Pennsylvania. There was an hour delay as the train was supposed to arrive in Johnstown, Pennsylvania at 6 p.m., but it didn't get to the train station until 7 p.m. Apparently, train delays are common!
- To my surprise, my wife, Tink, met me at the bottom of the ramp as I was bringing my bike out of the Amtrak station. My sister, Kelli, was also at the train station taking video clips and photos of my arrival. My parents were also in attendance! What a nice welcoming reception!!!!! I did NOT expect anyone but my wife to come to the train station! How nice!!!!
- Amidst the mini-celebration, my bike almost tipped over and crashed as I frantically SAVED it from falling to the ground. My bicycle did NOT fall

- to the ground AT ALL during my ENTIRE Southern Tier trip!
- For the first time in 45 days, I DROVE a motorized vehicle back to our Richland Township home! It was so STRANGE driving a gas-powered vehicle and not pedaling my bicycle!!!
- Upon my wife's neurotic request, I stripped naked outside on the back porch in the FREEZING cold as Tink wanted to make sure I did not bring any bugs into our home! Although I was quite certain I didn't have any bugs on me or in my stuff, I complied to my wife's reasonable request like a good boy. Immediately, all of my clothes went into the washing machine and they were washed with hot soapy water!
- Tink made me an amazing meatloaf, mashed potatoes, peas, and bread supper! Mom also sent over a big piece of homemade apple pie for me! I have to stop eating so much! I'm not on the Southern Tier anymore!
- Tink gave me a tour of our home with the many improvements she made while I was away. In my absence, Tink purchased a new kitchen table and chairs, bought a new foyer seat, painted several rooms, renewed several elegant motivational posters of mine, and made many other positive décor changes. Tink is a VERY talented decorator and organizer!!! Our cozy home looks better than ever!
- The Southern Tier is officially over, but the Southern Tier will forever be ALIVE within my SOUL!

ABOUT THE AUTHOR

Sean Hockensmith was 48 years old when he pedaled his bicycle 3,000 miles across the United States of America from the glorious shores of the Pacific Ocean in San Diego, California at Ocean Beach to the sparkling sands of the Atlantic Ocean in Jacksonville, Florida at Jacksonville Beach. Sean pedaled an average of 70 miles per day along Adventure Cycling Association's EPIC bike route known as "The Southern Tier." With a VERY LOW statistical probability of success, Sean defied the odds and finished his classic 43-day cross-country biking journey.

ALONE, UNSUPPORTED, and CONTINUOUS, Sean struggled through over 100 potentially trip-ending obstacles on the way to the unlikely completion of the esteemed cross-country bicycle route. Prior to his improbable cross-country cycling feat, Sean had NEVER taken a bike tour lasting longer than 3 days and 2 nights! Many of Sean's previous bike rides ended in painful FAILURE!

On Day 2 of the Southern Tier, Sean couldn't take any more of the pain and he actually QUIT! His quest to complete the Southern Tier was an EPIC FAILURE! Although the Southern Tier DEFEATED him, Sean Hockensmith was unwilling to abandon the revered bike route and go back home. Instead, he stubbornly remained on the brutal route ALONE facing countless daily obstacles. Each day, Sean struggled and found a way to take "one more ride!"

Thanks to Sean's severe STUBBORNESS, some angelic words of encouragement, and the GRACE OF GOD through the POWER OF PRAYER, Sean Hockensmith completed the arduous Southern Tier Bicycle Route! Although Sean's motivation to ride the cross-country route was purely for what the experience would make of him as a person and the positive example he would provide for others, Sean could NOT deny the overwhelming CALLING to write EPIC FAIL which includes over one hundred reasons why aspiring cross-country cyclists FAIL and how to avoid doing so!

Two months after his unlikely completion of the Southern Tier, Sean Hockensmith contracted a life-threatening case of COVID-19 combined with a serious heart ailment which caused a SIGNIFICANT DELAY in the writing of EPIC FAIL. It took Sean over a year to recover as his body was badly damaged. Shortly after his suspected recovery, Sean suffered a major stroke damaging the right frontal lobe of his brain and crippling his neurological system, thus further delaying the publication of EPIC FAIL for another year. While in the process of taking back his life for a second time, Sean Hockensmith had a seizure resulting in a devastating concussion which marked his third near-death event and left him INCAPACITATED for many additional months. The publication of EPIC FAIL appeared to be extremely unlikely.

Thanks in large part to the life-changing character formed on the Southern Tier, Sean struggled daily writing EPIC FAIL. He worked only as long as his damaged brain would allow as he was only capable of writing for very short daily intervals. In similar fashion to the completion of his triumphant Southern Tier bicycle journey, Sean laboriously wrote one difficult page at a time. In spite of significant mental impairments, nasty residual neurological stroke symptoms, and ongoing disabling coronavirus effects, Sean eventually completed EPIC FAIL, the signature of his life!

seanhockensmith@verizon.net
814-241-4832

BOOK SALES

EPIC FAIL: The Southern Tier by Sean Hockensmith: $29.99 ($31.79 with sales tax)

Smashing the Wall of Fear by Sean Hockensmith: $19.99 ($21.19 with sales tax)

A Teenager's Guide to Smashing the Wall of Fear by Sean Hockensmith: $9.95 ($10.55 with sales tax)

Shipping: Add $4 for the first book and $2 for each additional book.

Place your order in one of the following ways:
1. Call or text Tina at 814-418-5496.
2. Email Tina at tinaraehock@gmail.com
3. CASH APP: $IronCapitalLLC
4. Mail your check or money order to:
   Iron Capital, LLC
   PO Box 5472
   Johnstown, PA 15904

*** Contact us about discounted pricing for bulk book purchases.